International Conference on Education Innovation and Modern Management (EIMM 2022)

SHS Web of Conferences Volume 166 (2023)

Sanya, China
22 - 23 December 2022

Editors:

Anum Shafiq
Wei Chooi Yi

ISBN: 978-1-7138-7345-7

Printed from e-media with permission by:

Curran Associates, Inc.
57 Morehouse Lane
Red Hook, NY 12571

Some format issues inherent in the e-media version may also appear in this print version.

No changes have been made to the content of these proceedings. There may be changes to pagination and minor adjustments for aesthetics.

Printed with permission by Curran Associates, Inc. (2023)

For additional information, please contact EDP Sciences – Web of Conferences at the address below.

EDP Sciences – Web of Conferences
17, Avenue du Hoggar
Parc d'Activité de Courtabœuf
BP 112
F-91944 Les Ulis Cedex A
France

Phone: +33 (0) 1 69 18 75 75
Fax: +33 (0) 1 69 28 84 91

contact-edps@webofconferences.org

Additional copies of this publication are available from:

Curran Associates, Inc.
57 Morehouse Lane
Red Hook, NY 12571 USA
Phone: 845-758-0400
Fax: 845-758-2633
Email: curran@proceedings.com
Web: www.proceedings.com

TABLE OF CONTENTS

edp sciences

Web of Conferences

Statement of Peer review

In submitting conference proceedings to *Web of Conferences*, the editors of the proceedings certify to the Publisher that

1. They adhere to its **Policy on Publishing Integrity** in order to safeguard good scientific practice in publishing.
2. All articles have been subjected to peer review administered by the proceedings editors.
3. Reviews have been conducted by expert referees, who have been requested to provide unbiased and constructive comments aimed, whenever possible, at improving the work.
4. Proceedings editors have taken all reasonable steps to ensure the quality of the materials they publish and their decision to accept or reject a paper for publication has been based only on the merits of the work and the relevance to the journal.

Title, date and place of the conference

2022 International Conference on Education Innovation and Modern Management

Sanya, China on December 22-23, 2022

Proceedings editor(s):

Anum Shafiq, Nanjing University of Information Science and Technology, China

Date and editor's signature

2022 International Conference on Education Innovation and Modern Management

December 22-23, 2022 in Sanya, China

https://www.eimm2022.com/

Committee

German "duale ausbildung" vocational education and its enlightenment to China's vocational education

Min Wu*, and *Ping* Liu

Ningbo Polytechnic, Ningbo, Zhejiang, China

Abstract. Taking the key factors for the success of German "duale ausbildung" vocational education as the starting point, this paper introduces in detail five aspects: the leading role of the government, the main role of enterprises, the degree of social recognition, the team of dual qualified teachers, and the assessment and evaluation system. This paper analyzes the problems faced by vocational education in China, such as low social recognition, weak cooperation between schools and enterprises, inadequate talent training in schools to meet social needs, and insufficient attention from the government, and draws on the successful factors of dual vocational education in Germany to propose four inspirations for the reform of vocational education in China, including: improving laws and regulations, improving the security mechanism, improving the attractiveness of vocational education, strengthening the construction of "dual teachers" team Improve the social applicability of vocational education.

1 Introduction

With the development of vocational education and the transformation and upgrading of national industries, new requirements for talents are put forward, and the contradiction between talent training and social needs is particularly prominent[1]. The German vocational education and training system has always been a model for all countries to learn from[2] . The "dual ausbildung" vocational education and training model is the pillar and key of German vocational education[3]. The dual ausbildung is a school running system supported by national legislation and co built by schools and enterprises, which highlights the cultivation of practical ability, gives consideration to the study of theoretical knowledge, and aims to cultivate high-quality skilled talents[4].Through in-depth analysis of the characteristics of German vocational education and the current situation of vocational education in China, this paper draws on the German "dual ausbildung" vocational education model to provide effective reference for the reform and development of vocational education in China [5].

* Corresponding author: 53760012@qq.com

2 Key factors of "duale ausbildung" vocational education

The characteristics of the duale ausbildung are as follows: First, a sound legal guarantee system. The federal government has issued the Federal Vocational Education Law and the Enterprise Training Regulations, which make unified provisions on enterprise training. Enterprises sign vocational education and training contracts with students and schools. Second,Social recognition is high, and students actively choose vocational education. Third,Vocational education takes enterprises as the main body, and enterprises are deeply involved in teaching and curriculum. Fourth, We have teachers with reasonable structure, clear responsibilities and qualified qualifications. Fifth,Complete assessment and evaluation system.

1. The government plays a leading role .The government plays a leading role in the success of Germany's "dual ausbildung". First, The German government provides financial support for public vocational schools. Second, The German government unifies the vocational education standards of enterprises and schools through the Federal Vocational Education Law, the Handicraft Regulations, the State School Law and other laws and regulations. Under the unified legal framework, schools, enterprises and students jointly implement the vocational education standards[6]. Third,The government attracts enterprises to actively participate in vocational education through incentive policies, such as tax reduction, subsidies, incentive programs, etc., to encourage enterprises, especially small and medium-sized enterprises, to actively participate in vocational education and training.Fourth,The government provides a consultation and cooperation platform for enterprises, schools and industry associations to form a mechanism of multi-party cooperation.

2. The main role of the enterprise. In Germany's "dual ausbildung" education system, enterprises play a leading role. First, The students of the school are recruited independently by the enterprise according to the job needs, and the students are recruited to sign training contracts with the enterprise. Therefore, vocational education students have dual identities, both as employees of the enterprise and as students of the school. Second, The specialties and courses set up by the school shall be set by the enterprise under the supervision of the guild according to the regional economy. Third,The "dual ausbildung" vocational education funds in Germany are mainly invested by enterprises, which account for about 70% of the vocational education costs, while the government only accounts for about 30%. Fourth,The enterprise provides vocational education students with training and practical posts. The "dual ausbildung" vocational education students use the form of work study alternation. One third of the time they spend in school learning theoretical knowledge and public quality, and two thirds of the time they spend in the enterprise doing practical learning. The enterprise teachers are responsible for training the content of practical learning. The practical assessment of students is decided by the enterprise according to the requirements of laws and guilds.

3. High social recognition.Another reason for the success of Germany's "dual ausbildung" vocational education model lies in the respect and recognition given by the state to skilled workers. [19] Germany's "dual ausbildung" vocational colleges are favored by young people. In the German education system, about 55.7% of young people choose to participate in vocational education. The first reason is the high employment rate. The employment rate of graduates of the "dual ausbildung" vocational education is as high as 95%, the unemployment rate is only 7%. The second is high salary. German vocational education students do not need to pay tuition fees. On the contrary, for students who have signed training contracts with enterprises, enterprises need to pay students an average monthly living allowance of 795 Euros, to provide living security for students. Third, the national qualification framework recognizes that higher vocational education has the same

academic level as higher education, [24] vocational colleges have the opportunity to further their studies after graduation, and it is allowed to convert vocational knowledge and skills obtained outside of colleges and universities into credits, but not more than 50%.

4. "Double qualified" teachers.The teaching staff of Germany's "dual ausbildung" vocational education includes vocational school teachers and enterprise vocational educators. The two teams perform their respective duties in the training of vocational and technical personnel, and cooperate with each other. The two teams together form a complete "double qualified" teaching team, forming the "double qualified" quality of individual teachers and the "double qualified" structure of the team.

5. Complete assessment and evaluation system.German "dual ausbildung" vocational education has a complete set of assessment and evaluation system. The assessment covers a wide range of areas, is difficult and closely follows the economic development. The assessment is divided into three parts: school assessment, enterprise assessment and vocational skills assessment. Vocational schools are responsible for assessing students' basic theoretical knowledge, enterprises are responsible for assessing students' corporate training and training achievements, and two vocational skills assessments of relevant majors are conducted during the whole vocational education study period. If the assessment is qualified, the vocational qualification certificate of the Federation of Industry and Commerce (IHK) will be issued. Students can only graduate after obtaining academic certificates and vocational qualification certificates.

3 Problems in vocational education in China

Compared with the German "dual ausbildung" vocational education model, the development of vocational education in China still faces a series of problems.

1. Low social recognition. The social recognition of vocational education in China is not high, which is mainly reflected in: First, influenced by traditional ideological education, the society generally has a prejudice against vocational education, believing that only poor students can go to vocational colleges. In terms of schools, the evaluation of a middle school (junior high school, senior high school) is based on the number of students entering the general high school and the undergraduate rate. In terms of parents, many parents have the idea that vocational schools are inferior. Some parents of junior high school students would rather spend expensive tuition to send their children to international schools or private high schools than let their children go to vocational high schools. Second, the social status of vocational college graduates is not high. At present, there is a "diploma only" phenomenon in China. Some highly paid enterprises, government agencies, institutions and other institutions have a high threshold for employment. They only recruit people with ordinary higher education qualifications. The working environment of vocational college graduates is poor, their wages are low, and there is limited space for career improvement affected by their qualifications. Third, the society also has a prejudice against the teaching staff engaged in vocational education, believing that vocational colleges are lower than ordinary colleges and universities, so vocational colleges often cannot recruit talents with high skills, high quality and high scientific research ability to engage in teaching and research.

2. The school enterprise cooperation is not deep enough.At this stage, the main way of cooperation between enterprises and vocational colleges is to provide students in vocational colleges with post placement internships, followed by enterprise technicians serving as part-time teachers in vocational colleges, and again, enterprises entrust vocational colleges to train employees. It can be seen that the reason why enterprises are willing to cooperate is that they can recruit appropriate employees and train employees through cooperation, and they are unwilling to have more in-depth cooperation. The first reason is that there is no

incentive policy and cooperation mechanism, the investment and return of enterprises are not proportional, and the interests of enterprises are not guaranteed. Second, the students' loyalty to the enterprise is not high. Now, the students are unwilling to engage in front-line work, can't bear hardships, and the resignation rate is high. Therefore, the enterprise is worried about the loss of trained talents, and is unwilling to spend much effort to train students. Third, the overall scientific research ability of vocational colleges is not strong, and there are few projects that can cooperate with enterprises to tackle key problems. In addition, due to the heavy teaching workload of teachers in vocational colleges and the lack of incentive policies for scientific research, teachers' enthusiasm to participate in enterprise research projects is not high.

3. The school's talent cultivation cannot meet the social needs.The school's talent cultivation cannot meet the social needs. The author found that the students trained by the school are out of touch with the needs of the enterprise and need to be retrained by the enterprise. The reasons are as follows: First, the traditional curriculum system is used in the course setting, the talent training program formulated by the school has no standards to follow, and whether the talent training program meets the regional economic development cannot be judged. Second, in terms of the teaching staff, the vocational education teachers in China are mainly school teachers. From school graduation to vocational school employment, teachers often lack enterprise work experience, so the professional and technical abilities of teachers themselves are not strong. On the other hand, vocational schools will hire technical personnel from enterprises to teach as external teachers. However, because enterprise personnel have not received special training, they are often skilled, but do not know how to speak. In addition, the school has not built a cooperation platform for on-the-job teachers and external teachers. School teachers and external teachers of enterprises often do not communicate with each other, do not divide labor, do not cooperate, and only complete their own teaching tasks. Therefore, they cannot learn from each other. Third, in terms of student assessment, the current vocational education examination lays particular emphasis on theoretical knowledge, while the vocational skills assessment is little or no, and the examination content is assessed according to the experience of teachers and the overall receptivity of student groups. Different teachers or students of the same course often have different contents, and there is no standard scale to measure whether students meet professional requirements.

4. The government pays insufficient attention.The fundamental reason why the society does not recognize vocational education and the school enterprise cooperation is not deep enough is that the government does not pay enough attention to vocational education. On the one hand, the government has no overall planning for vocational education, and the implementation of vocational education lacks reference standards, resulting in the development of vocational education not keeping up with the economic development. On the other hand, although the country has issued a series of policies on vocational education, they are not fully implemented, and there is no strong mechanism to ensure the implementation of policies. Third, few local government staff know about vocational education and do not know about vocational education, so it is difficult to make correct decisions.

4 The enlightenment of "Dual System" on China's vocational education reform

1. Improve laws and regulations and safeguard mechanism.Relevant departments of the national government should issue detailed laws and regulations to clarify the responsibilities and rights of enterprises, industries and schools in vocational education. Relevant incentive policies have been introduced, and a multi-party cooperation platform

has been created to encourage enterprises to devote themselves to education, give play to the main role of enterprises in vocational education, and stimulate enterprises and schools to deepen the integration of industry and education. Organize enterprises, guilds, education and other departments to jointly draft and formulate vocational education teaching framework standards and enterprise training rules, define the training objectives, teaching and training contents, assessment and evaluation standards of each specialty, and incorporate them into legislation to ensure that school teaching and enterprise training are implemented in accordance with the standards. Give play to the supervision role of industry associations and other third parties, develop a third-party assessment and evaluation system, and actively carry out the separation system of teaching and examination. Create a collaborative development and cooperation model of education and economy featuring "government, universities, industries, enterprises and capital".

2. Improve the attractiveness of vocational education. Governments at all levels should innovate the talent evaluation mechanism, improve the social status of highly skilled talents, break the tradition of academic credentials, and promote vocational college graduates to enjoy the same treatment as ordinary college graduates in terms of settlement, employment, participation in recruitment of institutions, professional title evaluation, rank promotion, etc. Enterprises should improve the treatment of technical and skilled talents, and the salary treatment and promotion opportunities should be inclined to front-line highly skilled talents. At the same time, the government, society and education departments should vousigorly promote the spirit of craftsmanship, and start the enlightenment of professional quality and skills from the education of children and primary and secondary schools, so as to make the most glorious concept of loving science and technology, loving skills and working deeply rooted in the hearts of the people.

3. Strengthen the construction of "double division" team.As the saying goes, "A good teacher makes a good student". The ability of teachers directly determines the quality of students. To cultivate highly skilled talents, teachers should first be highly skilled talents. Therefore, to improve the selection criteria of vocational teachers, vocational teachers should not only have a high degree, but also have relevant professional enterprise work experience. Therefore, it is necessary to break the existing educational background oriented mechanism of teacher recruitment, and allow enterprises' technical experts and skilled masters to apply for vocational teacher posts. At the same time, it is also necessary to introduce incentive policies to encourage teachers to constantly improve their personal technical ability and scientific and technological breakthrough ability, break the paper only title promotion evaluation system, and adopt flexible title evaluation mechanism. For example, teachers with outstanding skills can be specially employed as industry professors. As vocational education enterprise training teachers are indispensable, the government departments should issue corresponding policies to give enterprises and enterprise training teachers participating in vocational education training corresponding welfare treatment and preferential policies. At the same time, government functional departments should also formulate corresponding regulations on the qualification of enterprise training teachers. Only those who meet the vocational training qualification can engage in enterprise training when they have obtained the vocational teaching qualification, so as to ensure the teaching quality of enterprise training.

4. Improve the social applicability of vocational education.First, reconstruct the curriculum system based on the professional work process. Courses shall be set according to the requirements of enterprise posts, work tasks and professional abilities, and curriculum standards shall be formulated and improved according to the requirements of professional posts (groups). New processes, new technologies and new specifications shall be included in the curriculum standards and teaching contents. Secondly, documentary evidence accommodation. The examination contents and evaluation standards of vocational

qualification certificates will be incorporated into the curriculum design, and practical skills and professional quality training will be strengthened to highlight the characteristics of vocational education with students as the main body and high skill training as the core. Finally, guide students with employment as the guidance, cultivate students' professional identity and healthy career outlook, pay attention to the cultivation of students' sustainable academic ability and social adaptability, pay attention to students' psychological health, and enable students to adapt to the identity change from learning to employment.

This work was supported by the Zhejiang Higher education in the 13th Five-Year Plan Foundation of China [Grant No. JG20190726], Zhejiang Education planning project Foundation of China [Grant No. 2021SCG106], Ningbo Education Science Planning Project [Grant No. 2022YZD019].

References

1. Song Zhengfu. Germany's "dual system" education from the perspective of school enterprise cooperation and its reference to China's higher vocational education ,China's Higher Education, 61-62(2018)
2. Li Mengqing, Yu Jing. Operation Logic, Mechanism and Enlightenment of German "Dual System" Universities, Education and Profession, 17, 26-33(2021)
3. Hu Yue, Tu Yingqing. Characteristics and enlightenment of German "dual system" vocational education ,Vocational Education Forum, 14,90-92(2017)
4. Wang Yajing The Organizational Dimension of German Dual System in China -- Taking the Organizational Evolution of New Star Vocational Schools as an Example (1984 - 2002) . Education Academic Monthly, 3,34-42(2021)
5. Zhou Chunyan, Zhen Ren, Shi Huili Research on German "dual system" school enterprise cooperation system from the perspective of new institutionalism in organizational sociology ,Vocational and Technical Education, 19, 67-72(2019)
6. Zhou Yanbing. Analysis and Reference of Germany's "Dual System" Model from the Perspective of Integration of Industry and Education ,Education and Occupation,12,65-70(2020)

Research on the construction of "Internet of Things + X" compound characteristic course cluster in vocational normal education

Xingzhi Lin, and *Xiang* Pan[*]

School of Computer and Information Engineering, Guangxi Vocational Normal University, Nanning, China

Keywords. Vocational normal education, Internet of Things + X, Compound characteristic course cluster.

Abstract. The construction of "Internet of Things+X" compound characteristic course cluster is an important link in the development of new engineering subjects in vocational normal education. This paper analyzes the mechanism of the "Internet of Things+X" composite course cluster, and puts forward the construction idea of "Internet of Things+X" compound characteristic course cluster, including the condensation of the characteristics of the course cluster based on specific industries, the integration of the four chains of "training objectives - course content - professional ability - teacher training ability", and the introduction of composite characteristic course resources. Then it puts forward some suggestions on the construction of compound characteristic course cluster in vocational normal colleges.

1 Introducton

The "Internet of Things + X" is the embodiment of the new model of "Internet+" in education, as the Internet of Things (IoT) provides technical support for the transformation and development of vocational normal education. The development of vocational normal education based on the Internet of Things inserts IoT knowledge system and cross-border thinking in the traditional curriculum, and relies on the integration of industry and education and collaborative education to converge enterprise resources, multi-channel vocational education and normal education, thus forming the "Internet of Things + X" compound characteristic course cluster.

[*] Corresponding author: panxiang_px@126.com

2 Function mechanism of "Internet of Things + x" compound characteristic course cluster

The "Internet of Things + X" compound curriculum meets the development needs of vocational education in the Internet of Things era. Vocational colleges and universities should combine the needs of social productivity with their own development status to build a characteristic "Internet of Things + X" compound disciplines, cultivate skilled professionals, and solve the lack of technical personnel in the Internet of Things industry. The "Internet of Things + X" compound curriculum differs from traditional vocational education. It innovates the content, approach, mode and evaluation of teaching. The content changes from single to compound features, showing diversification. The approach is more intelligent, and the mode shifts from classroom teaching to distance teaching, online and offline teaching, hybrid teaching, being more diversified [1]. Accordingly, the learning space and teacher-student relationship have also changed, with the space shifting from monism to pluralism and the teacher-student relationship shifting from mutual antagonism to equal interactive subjects. Therefore, the teaching form of vocational education under the Internet of Things background must be a composite posture. Through the construction of "Internet of Things + X" compound characteristic course cluster, the transformation of vocational education can be achieved. First is the transformation of the curriculum concept, with the meaning of curriculum changing from "point" to "space"; second is the transformation of student learning mode from the traditional classroom lectures to intelligent adaptive learning; and third is the transformation of teacher teaching, where the role of teachers has been logically displaced to "teacher with dual qualifications" in digital era.

3 Structure of "Internet of Things + X" compound characteristic course cluster

The "Internet of Things + X" Compound course cluster is based on the core algorithms, hardware and systems of the Internet of Things, and injects sensing data collection, learning emotion recognition and knowledge network transfer into the course system of computer, electronics technology, Internet of Things, intelligent architecture, software engineering, logistics management and technology, etc., forming a new intelligent technology permeated course system. This will make the new curriculum system develop in the direction of universality, transferability and permeability, and form a group of courses that will act as a chain reaction in its entire specialty, in the various knowledge of the entire discipline, and in the theoretical and practical systems constructed. A series of courses and knowledge are associated to develop across borders to achieve new innovations, new practices and new products, pushing vocational normal education to a new realm of teaching with innovative capabilities.

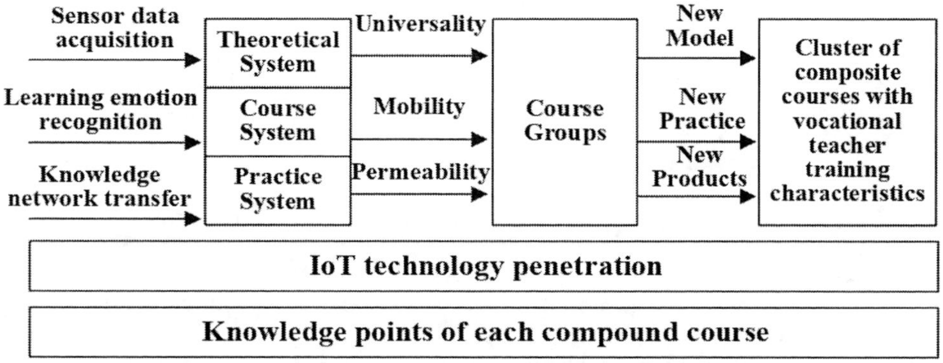

Fig. 1. Structure of "Internet of Things + X" compound characteristic course cluster.

4 Construction of "Internet of Things + X" compound characteristic course cluster

4.1 The condensation of the characteristics of the course cluster based on specific industries

Taking Guangxi Vocational Normal University as an example, the industrial base of the university to carry out industry-education integration is the transportation industry and logistics industry, and the more specific and deeper science-education integration fields are intelligent production network-connected vehicles and intelligent water transportation logistics. Focusing on those two industry sectors, combined with the university's applied electronics education, Internet of Things engineering, information management and information systems and other majors, the "Internet of Things + X" course cluster features are condensed. Starting from the selection and setting of courses in the cluster, we analyze the basic knowledge, core technologies and vocational skills required by the above industries, introduce industry-related intelligent equipment and project cases, and build corresponding practical training scenarios such as "Intelligent Networked Vehicle Simulation Laboratory" for learning. The condensation of the characteristics of the course cluster based on specific industries brings vocational education a broader development space in the context of the Internet of Things.

4.2 The integration of the four chains of "Training Objectives - Course Content - Professional Ability - Teacher Training Ability"

The chain of training objectives is a logical chain composed of different training goals in the compound course cluster, including goal types, levels, capable positions, talent types and technical skill requirements in talent training [2]. In the chain of training objectives, the upstream nodes are the basis for the realization of the downstream nodes. In order to realize the chain nodes, the corresponding course content chain should be constructed. The course content chain nodes should correspond to the nodes of the chain of training objectives, and the logical relationships between the nodes correspond to each other. The professional ability chain is extracted from the chain of training objectives and is the occupational competence that must be achieved after the completion of the course content chain nodes, including basic occupational competence and key competence. The chain of teacher training ability is a series of competencies for teacher training, including theoretical competencies of vocational education, psychological education competencies, traditional teaching methods application competencies, information technology education competencies, and "Internet of Things +" intelligent education competencies [3]. The four chains of "training objectives - course content - professional ability - teacher training ability" are inseparable. They are the essence of "Internet of Things + X" compound characteristic course cluster.

4.3 The introduction of composite characteristic course resources

The construction of "Internet of Things + X" characteristic course teaching resources library will introduce composite characteristic course resources, and realize the sharing of teaching resources for vocational normal education. The focus of the composite characteristic course resources is "composite" and "characteristic". First of all, the course resources should be built with specific industry application cases. For instance, the curriculum resources involved in the new energy intelligent networked vehicle industry can be divided into several categories: automotive electronics, intelligent hardware, communication software, intelligent control and integration technology, etc. Each category corresponds to a specific application on the car, while the split items correspond to different knowledge of several courses, reflecting the composite nature of the resource [4]. The introduced resources can be divided into knowledge/skill level resources, course level resources and cluster level resources according to the hierarchical relationship. The first-level granular resources include text and images, instructional courseware, micro-lessons, animations, videos and virtual simulations. The second level includes course content, teaching tasks, cases, teaching materials and exercise tests. The third level is the integrated practical training that can be carried out only after completing the course cluster learning. When introducing resources, we should pay attention to the reconfiguration, integration and development of coupling logic among resources, and maintain the unity of individuation and demonstration.

5 Suggestions for the construction of "Internet of Things + X" compound characteristic course cluster in vocational normal education

Figures and tables, as originals of good quality and well contrasted, are to be in their final form, ready for reproduction, pasted in the appropriate place in the text. Try to ensure that the size of the text in your figures is approximately the same size as the main text (10 point). Try to ensure that lines are no thinner than 0.25 point.

5.1 Standard construction of "Internet of Things + X" compound course in vocational normal education

We should strengthen the standardization of the certificate system of "Internet of Things + X" compound course in vocational normal education. Vocational qualification certificates are evidence of competence obtained by students after passing theoretical and practical examinations in the process of professional teaching. It is a necessary condition for a profession in the future career. The standardized development and management of vocational education competency level certificates facilitates the optimization of students' vocational skills qualifications, so that they have competency levels that correspond to their occupational positions in terms of skill levels and qualifications.

5.2 The establishment of compound vocational normal teacher groups

We should incorporate the construction of compound vocational normal teacher groups into the overall planning of the university, so as to take advantage of the system to guarantee the continuous enhancement of the teaching force. We should establish an applicable incentive mechanism, a technical rating system, and a recognized qualification system, and introduces a third-party certification and evaluation system. We can recruit part-time teachers from enterprises and society, such artisan teachers can inject fresh blood into the faculty because they have professional and technical as well as managerial work experience [5].

5.3 The construction of teaching quality assurance and accreditation system in "Internet in the Things + X" compound characteristic course

To promote the improvement of the teaching quality assurance and accreditation system in the "Internet of Things + X" compound course, the first is to highlight the main position, which requires teachers and students to be clear about the role requirements and responsibilities. The second is to strengthen the internal systematic nature of the system by integrating the implementation units, supervision units, management units and evaluation units in education and teaching at all levels, enhancing the interconnection and support among them, and forming the action force to coordinate and control the key points and elements of the system, so as to ensure the benign operation of the system. The third is to pay attention to the talent training target of vocational education in the context of Internet of Things, and make appropriate adjustment to the talent training target of "Internet of Things + X" compound majors according to the teachers' resources, career development, job market and the planning layout in the Internet of Things industry.

We should establish sound operation organization of teaching quality assurance and accreditation system in the "Internet of Things + X" compound course. According to the needs of education teaching quality assessment, relevant system operation agencies should be set up, including monitoring agencies, scoring agencies and guarantee agencies, with each agency operating independently and dividing work among themselves to complete the assessment together.

We should adapt the structure of the elements of the teaching quality assurance and accreditation system in the "Internet of Things + X" compound course. We should establish the training goal of composite and applied talents and make it become the consensus of students, teachers, education and teaching administrators. We can improve the code of conduct for student learning, teacher teaching, and administrator education and teaching management. We can also take the means of taking a temporary post, dispatching, and introducing teachers to achieve the improvement of the business capacity of teachers, supervisors, administrators, and evaluators [6].

Finally, we should expand the scope of monitoring and management of the teaching quality assurance and accreditation system in the "Internet of Things + X" compound course. At the student level, the "intelligent technical skills" indicator should be added, and students will be assessed on the extent to which they have achieved various vocational skills from the moment they enter the university. At the teacher level, the indicators of "teacher development" and "teacher structure" should be added to improve and guarantee the level of teachers in terms of their composition. At the school level, a three-level progressive teaching quality monitoring system by semester, academic year and graduate should be established.

6 Conclusion

The construction of "Internet of Things + X" compound characteristic course cluster in vocational education is an important element in the cultivation of composite application-oriented talents in vocational education in the era of artificial intelligence. The development mode of artificial intelligence + vocational education can solve the educational and teaching drawbacks of traditional vocational education and make vocational education develop to the high-end form of intelligent teaching.

This work was supported by New Engineering Research and Practice Project of the Ministry of Education under Grant No. E-JSJRJ20201332, Guangxi Higher Education Undergraduate Teaching Reform Project under Grant No. 2019JGZ172, Humanities and Social Sciences Research Project of the Ministry of Education under Grant No. 20YJA880028, Guangxi High Level Innovation Team and Outstanding Scholar Program of University under Grant No. GuiJiaoShiFan〔2019〕52-6.

References

1. M. Sean, Leahy, H. Charlotte, W. Francis, The digital frontier: Envisioning future technologies impact on the classroom. Futures. J. 113(2019)
2. Z. Olaf, I. Victoria. Marín, B. Melissa, G. Franziska, Systematic review of research on artificial intelligence applications in higher education – where are the educators? International Journal of Educational Technology in Higher Education. J. 16(2019)
3. Subagyo et al, The Development of Curriculum School Model Based on the Internet of Things. International Journal of Engineering & Technology. J. 96(2018)
4. Y. W. Huang, J. Wang, Quality Evaluation Model of Education in Remote Learning and IoT Based on College Students' Quality Cultivation. Wireless Communications and Mobile Computing. J. 15(2022)
5. Y. H. Chen, Evaluation of teaching effect of internet of things education platform based on long-term and short-term memory network. International Journal of Continuing Engineering Education and Life Long Learning. J. 31(2021)
6. F. Borges, Adriano, C. Fortuna, Magali et al, Analysis of professional implication as a tool of permanent education in health. Revista latino-americana de enfermagem. J. 27(2019)

A study of China-ASEAN "University-Enterprise" new engineering collaborative education with multiple subjects

Xiang Pan, and *Xingzhi* Lin[*]

School of Computer and Information Engineering, Guangxi Vocational Normal University, Nanning, China

Abstract. The integration of industry and education has become an important way for universities to cultivate new engineering talents. The cooperation to create "university-enterprise" alliances can improve the collaborative education mechanism of multiple subjects by building a bridge of communication for the new engineering, which is an important means of integration of industry and education. This study of "university-enterprise" new engineering collaborative education with multiple subjects analyzes the collaborative education mode and its implementation path for China-ASEAN new engineering cooperative education of multiple subjects from the perspective of discipline professional construction and industrial transformation and upgrading, discipline professional group and industrial agglomeration development, and the effect of the ability of multiple subjects.

1 Introduction

In the context of the rapid development of big data and economic globalization, artificial intelligence has become an important driver of economic development in various countries, and the application of artificial intelligence has brought about new changes in industry and technology, profoundly changing the way people work, live, and learn. According to the current situation of China-ASEAN AI development, the cooperation on practical AI education, scientific research, and other aspects can effectively promote the development of China-ASEAN AI and education cooperation and broaden the new cooperation in frontier science and technology. Building a China-ASEAN collaborative education platform for the integration of industry and education between universities and enterprises with multiple subjects can form a double-creative talent training system that adapts discipline and professional construction to industrial transformation and upgrading, to promote the development of discipline and professional clusters and industrial clustering, bring into play the native effect of the ability of multiple subjects, and make the discipline and professional system closely matches the industrial chain and innovation chain for the cultivation of double-creative talents.

[*] Corresponding author: lxz4562509@qq.com

2 Problems of China-ASEAN "University-Enterprise" new engineering collaborative education with multiple subjects

2.1 Existing problems

Firstly, the cooperation mechanism and framework are not sound enough. Although China-ASEAN has signed numerous inter-university cooperation agreements and regional education cooperation frameworks on education cooperation, the overall coordination and planning of the above joint training programs as well as the characteristics of cross-border cooperation in education are not obvious. Secondly, the funding support for China-ASEAN education cooperation is insufficient and the development of policy funds in ASEAN countries is uneven. Thirdly, the quality of China-ASEAN international cooperation in education is poor, as joint education is mainly offered by Thailand, Laos, Cambodia, and China's less well-known institutions at a low level. Fourthly, the communication between China and ASEAN is mostly in the traditional way such as forums, meetings, and visits, with a single form of personnel exchange and cooperation.

2.2 Solutions and development trends

Based on the differences in the education systems of China and ASEAN member countries, the existing "China-ASEAN", "Davos Forum", "Boao Forum for Asia", "Shanghai Cooperation Organization", "Xiamen International Ocean Week" and other organizational platforms can be used. With the help of these trade agreement organizations, we can promote international education cooperation and enrich the content of education exchange and cooperation. In the future, China-ASEAN education cooperation will be oriented towards and closely focused on the "One Belt, One Road" strategy. It is an inevitable trend to strengthen the construction of new engineering science between China and ASEAN countries along the route, build the brand of Silk Road New Engineering University Alliance, and cultivate international talents in new engineering science [1]. Under the background of the booming new economy led by artificial intelligence, it is meaningful to cultivate and export new engineering talents in China-ASEAN "university-enterprise" education cooperation with multiple subjects.

3 Structure of China-ASEAN "University-Enterprise" new engineering collaborative education with multiple subjects

The China-ASEAN "university-enterprise" new engineering collaborative education with multiple subjects will be carried out based on the establishment of the alliance of engineering colleges and universities for the construction of new engineering, with the construction of new engineering talent cultivation system as the core, and relying on strong disciplines to deepen new engineering innovation education, the integration of arts and science, and humanities exchanges. The structure is shown in the figure below.

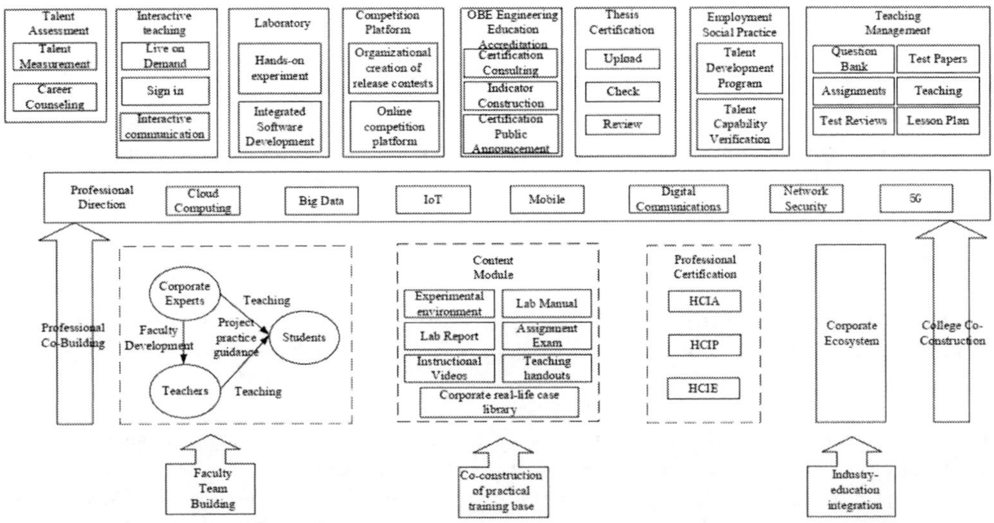

Fig. 1. Structure of China-ASEAN "University-Enterprise" New Engineering Collaborative Education with Multiple Subjects.

Market-oriented, by the school-enterprise cooperation, engineering, and certificate training model, to train cloud computing composite innovative high-quality high-skilled personnel. Meet the professional teaching, skills training, teaching and research, and training needs of cloud computing platform operation and development certification courses. The organization form of a "university-enterprise" new engineering university alliance with multiple subjects is confirmed, and the cultivation system of internationalized talents in new engineering is formulated from the aspects of curriculum, assessment, and quality standard. We will focus on building a new international talent cultivation model with integrated and interdisciplinary collaboration among higher education institutions, research institutes, and new industries.

4 Mode of China-ASEAN "University-Enterprise" new engineering collaborative education with multiple subjects

4.1 Facing Internationalization-oriented discipline construction and industrial transformation and upgrading

We will make up for the shortcomings with the power of industry to develop advantageous disciplines, and integrate industrial production, management, and services into professional courses. The construction of academic disciplines will be always closely focused on international social and economic development, playing the role of "power source" to accelerate industrial transformation and upgrading [2].

An ecosystem of new engineering university alliance with interconnection and interdependence of China-ASEAN "university-enterprise" multiple subjects will be created, and a new engineering talent cultivation system that adapts discipline and professional construction to industrial transformation and upgrading will be formed. We will also develop an action plan for the integration of industry and education to establish models for different disciplines and industry needs and promote the development of clusters of disciplines and industries. Then, we will break through the boundaries of disciplines, majors, and courses according to the needs of industrial development, and build an innovative system of industry linkage, diversified schooling, and virtual supply chain industry-education integration. We will construct a collaborative education platform across majors, schools, and regions through cooperation among schools, campuses, and enterprises. We will promote two-way docking between education supply and industrial demand according to the relationship between discipline structure and industrial structure suitability. Finally, in the construction of the ecological environment for the integration of industry and education, we will strengthen the function of technology and talent gathering, industrial traction ability, and establish different models for various disciplines, specialties, and industrial demand.

4.2 The development mode of discipline professional group and industry clustering under the support condition of "University-Enterprise" multiple subjects

The development mode of academic specialties and industrial clusters is based on the overall circle of China-ASEAN "university-enterprise" multiple subjects. According to the internal and external correlation and development trend of the cluster, we will match the advantageous discipline groups and industrial clusters to form a "discipline-industry" education alliance, to eliminate the drawbacks of single, crude, and transient cooperation. Then, the discipline and industry can integrate, support, and develop as a whole. Industry development needs to guide the adjustment and optimization of discipline clusters in the region, and the iterative renewal of academic specialty clusters builds a solid scientific and technological foundation for regional industrial clusters. Therefore, the linkage, integration , and division of advantageous discipline clusters and industrial clusters will not only enhance students' knowledge and technical ability but also increase the industrial-added value of enterprises [3].

The linkage mechanism of academic specialties and industrial clustering should insist on the integration of "industry-university-enterprise" subjects. We should promote industrial clustering enterprises and make universities associate with enterprises so that the subjective initiative of multiple subjects can work to carry out education and teaching practice, scientific and technological research, and product development on the collaborative education platform. The cooperation between China and ASEAN universities, enterprises, and research institutions will build high-level international training bases with radiation leading roles. This will promote the development of academic disciplines and internationalized industry clusters, and bring into play the native effect of the ability of multiple subjects so that the cultivation of new engineering innovation talents is closely connected with the industrial chain, and the innovation and entrepreneurial ability and level of talents can be improved[4]. Industry, universities, and enterprises influence and promote each other to promote the win-win development of disciplinary specialization and industry agglomeration.

4.3 The mode of the native effect of ability of multiple subjects of "University-Enterprise" collaborative education to dock with innovation chain

The ability-based effect of university enterprise is a talent training method that takes the industry and market demand as the starting point and aims to master the professional knowledge, practical ability, and innovation ability of the job. Oriented to the competence-based approach, the development of the China-ASEAN collaborative education model with multiple subjects for the construction of new engineering disciplines is the cross-organic integration of "theory, practice, and innovation ability", in which innovative concept and innovative ability play a decisive role in the cultivation of new engineering talents. Education alliance will form an organic integration that connects universities, students, industries, companies, and employees. By determining the training objectives of different industries for each job ability demand, the theoretical courses, practical courses, scientific research, and innovation and results from incubation can be set up and optimized into a reasonable curriculum system, so that the various abilities of university students and enterprise employees in scientific research, practice and innovation will be greatly improved [5].

Technological innovation and knowledge innovation can be used to promote the organic combination of each innovation involved in the "university-enterprise" multiple subjects, to promote the achievement of technology and knowledge and the optimization of the innovation system.

5 Implementation path of China-ASEAN "University-Enterprise" new engineering collaborative education with multiple subjects

Joint college mode among colleges and universities. By actively exploring the new form of cooperation and exchange between China-ASEAN colleges and universities with multiple subjects, we can realize cross-border, cross-university, and cross-professional cooperation and sharing of educational resources, and develop the internationalized talent cultivation mode of new engineering disciplines. On the one hand, we can explore international joint training mechanisms such as "1+3", "2+2", "4+1", "3+2" programs, etc. to rapidly enhance the internationalization of the education of new engineering talents in the process of joint training. On the other hand, we can encourage China-ASEAN universities, research institutions, and multiple entities of enterprises along the route to cooperate, conduct joint research on specific topics, and carry out overseas internships and short-term practices for students.

Joint training mode among majors. First of all, we should clarify the professional talent training programs. According to the requirements of the idea of new engineering construction, the joint interdisciplinary training should realize the deep integration of emerging industries and engineering science, Chinese culture, and ASEAN culture in synergy and coexistence, so that the training program of new engineering talents has distinctive characteristics. Secondly, we should formulate sound planning of the professional curriculum system. We can develop a curriculum system that strengthens the foundation of mathematics and science, logical thinking, and project research ability, and focuses on the characteristics of cultivating new technology applications and transformation ability of new engineering talents. Finally, we should construct a curriculum guarantee system. We can take full advantage of the discipline's leading domestic faculty and the large-scale introduction of international high-level faculty to ensure the smooth implementation of the construction of the curriculum system.

Inter-disciplinary scientific research cooperation mode. Through the vigorous development of inter-disciplinary scientific research cooperation among China-ASEAN universities, we can study various ways for scientific research cooperation to serve the cultivation of talents, drive the exchange of talents with scientific research cooperation, and drive the teaching cooperation with scientific research cooperation [6]. We can also utilize the competitive advantage of cross-disciplinary knowledge creation to realize the establishment and development of multi-level synergistic relationships between multiple disciplines and their members, to achieve a synergistic effect of resource integration.

6 Conclusion

Under the new historical opportunity brought by the "One Belt, One Road" strategy, higher education is an integral part of humanistic exchanges in the construction of interconnection. To innovate new contents and forms of China-ASEAN cooperation of multiple subjects, we should improve the quality assurance system of international student education, establish an education quality monitoring mechanism, and enhance the quality of international student education service internally. Internationally, we can create a high-quality education system open to the outside world, explore and innovate new paths for China-ASEAN cooperation, promote China-ASEAN university cooperation, and realize the common construction, sharing, and win-win situation of education resources. Moreover, we can utilize the multilateral dialogue framework to promote regional integration and institutionalize quality assurance in higher education.

This work was supported by New Engineering Research and Practice Project of the Ministry of Education under Grant No. E-JSJRJ20201332, Guangxi Higher Education Undergraduate Teaching Reform Project under Grant No. 2019JGZ172, Humanities and Social Sciences Research Project of the Ministry of Education under Grant No. 20YJA880028, Guangxi High Level Innovation Team and Outstanding Scholar Program of University under Grant No. GuiJiaoShiFan〔2019〕52-6.

References

1. X. Ding, X. N. Guo. Research on the paradigm of collaborative education between industry and education in applied colleges and universities in the context of new engineering construction. Modern Vocational Education. J. **12**, 88-90 (2022)
2. F. L. Qin, H. P. Cheng, W. Y. Yan, C. D. Li, X. L. Wang, X. Liu. Research on the multi-faceted collaborative training model of artificial intelligence professionals. Journal of Chengdu Institute of Technology. J. **4**, 108-111(2021)
3. X. Lan, G. E. Xia, Q. Yang. Study on the operation mechanism of China-ASEAN higher education cooperation in the context of "One Belt and One Road". "One Belt and One Road" and China-ASEAN Cooperation Development Research. J. 52-64(2021)
4. X. P. Li, J. B. Fan, J. R. Li et al, The construction and practice of "five-in-one" new engineering excellence talent cultivation system for food majors in local universities. Chinese Journal of Food. J. **11**, 417-425(2021)
5. Q. F. Zhang, M. F. Yang. Problems of China-ASEAN vocational education cooperation in the context of "One Belt and One Road" and strategies to promote it. Education and Career. J. **7**, 12-18(2021)
6. G. Li, L. S. Sun, J. Yan, Y. G. Zheng, C. Q. Yang. Research and practice of a new system of internationalization of engineering education for "one belt and one road". Mechanics and Practice. J. **4**, 470-474(2020)

Research on platform-based transformation of traditional engineering consulting enterprises based on the dynamic embedding of value chain - Taking Glodon as an example

Si Wu*, and *Wenjia* Zhang

School of Economics and Management, Beijing Jiaotong University, Beijing, China 100044

Abstract. Nowadays, the information revolution with digital technology as the core is taking place in the engineering consulting industry. Traditional engineering consulting enterprises should follow the trend and change with the trend, give full play to their long-accumulated knowledge and skills, and realize platform-based and digital transformation. Combining the existing literature research, this paper proposes the platform-based transformation of Chinese traditional engineering consulting enterprises based on dynamic embedding of value chain, and verify it with the platform transformation practice of Glodon Company. Taking environmental perception ability as the basis, relationship and structure debugging as the guarantee, and innovative learning as the driving force, engineering consulting enterprises adopt contingency and active embedding behavior to integrate resources along the value chain, and build a digital intelligence platform at the same time to support the strategic reconstruction of enterprises, form a platform ecology with themselves as the core and multiple subjects participating, complete the value chain leap, and adopt a digital governance system of cooperative governance of multiple subjects in order to maintain the healthy development of the platform ecology.

1 Introduction

Chinese traditional engineering consulting enterprises have taken shape after more than 20 years of development, and many industry benchmark enterprises have emerged. However, nowadays, in the background of national future investment structure differentiation and more obvious homogeneous competition in engineering consulting industry, it is increasingly difficult for enterprises to undertake business, and the requirements for brand, scale, qualification and staffing of enterprises are getting higher and higher. At the same time, its pursuit of professional development has also brought about synergistic contradictions such as business fragmentation, stage fragmentation and process fragmentation, which makes it difficult to adapt to the owner's complex demand for

* Corresponding author: wusiiii@126.com

comprehensive, cross-stage and integrated projects. The transformation of engineering consulting enterprises is imminent.

Some researchers have studied from the perspective of the internal capabilities of enterprises and the value chain in which they are located, and advocate that the capability upgrade of enterprises can be achieved through value chain embedding. However, the information technology represented by "cloud, big data, IoT, AI" are widely combined with the field of engineering and construction nowadays, which is reconstructing business infrastructure. The time and space limitations of the enterprise management are broken through, and the development of the enterprise management network without borders is achieved. The combination of information technology and traditional industries has created a new business model - the platform model.

To meet the challenges in the era of network economy, traditional engineering consulting industry must embrace digital transformation and deeply integrate with digital technology for development. On the basis of dynamic embedding theory of value chain, this paper will conduct research on the platform-based transformation path of traditional engineering consulting enterprises with a view to providing reference for their future development.

2 Literature review

2.1 Theory of the dynamic embedding of value chain

Professor Porter (1985) mentioned in his book "Competitive Strategy of Enterprises" that value chain is a variety of activities that are strategically composed by enterprises. If enterprises want to acquire their competitive advantages, they need to carry out the value chain strategic movements that are better than those of their rivals[1]. However, not only value chains exist within an enterprise, but also its value chains are interconnected with those of other economic entities, The value chains of all enterprises are linked together, to form a value system consisting of many value chains[2]. Subsequently, some scholars began to apply the embeddedness theory to the value chain theory, arguing that Chinese traditional enterprises can improve their comprehensive capabilities by embedding in GVC[3]. Further research shows that double embedding in GVC/NVC can promote traditional enterprises to grow faster and then complete the upgrade of the value chain[4].

The value chain embedding capability is a static capability, which refers to The ability of a enterprise to build relationships with value chain partners or to take up a position in the value chain and use that position to obtain resources in a static market environment[5]. When the market environment evolves from static competition to dynamic competition, it is not enough to depend only on the static value chain embedding capability, but only to enhance the GVC/NVC dual dynamic embedding capability[4]. Traditional enterprises can obtain information, knowledge and resources[6] from GVC/NVC dual dynamic embedding, and realize enterprise transformation and upgrading through environment perception, value chain relationship and structure debugging, innovative learning and strategic reconstruction[5]. And when it comes to strategic reconstruction, this paper believes that building a digital intelligence platform to empower the digital transformation of industry is the only way to seek long-term development in the complex and changing environment.

2.2 Theory of the platform

Previous researches have defined platforms from different viewpoints, and the current widely accepted definition considers that a platform brings together users in a bilateral or multilateral network by providing products and services through a set of access points or interfaces[7], bringing together producers and consumers, and providing infrastructure and rules as the basis for complementary products and services[8]. Platforms use system resources to coordinate and facilitate transactions between demand and supply sides, creating network effects among multilateral users of the platform and creating value through interactions between groups of platform participants[9]. The core enterprises that develop the platform are called platform companies, which are critical in the formation and development of the platform and its ecosystem[10]. The platform ecosystem includes not only platform enterprise, providers, demanders, public sector, other subjects and the relationships among them, but also a variety of connections and differences among platforms[11]. Faced with the challenges of subject plurality, environment dynamics and system complexity, it is also necessary to build an ecological governance model based on platform plurality and diversified competition and cooperation. Platform governance means to set up platform rules to regulate and manage the activities of platform participant groups, so as to realize the safe development of platform ecosystem and the expansion of participant groups[9].

Although the research on the platform-based development of enterprises has made great progress, the scope of industries and enterprises involved in the existing research is still relatively limited, for example, the research on the platform-based transformation and development of engineering consulting enterprises is relatively lacking. Therefore, this paper will conduct an in-depth study on the platform-based transformation path of traditional engineering consulting industry based on the theory of dynamic embedding of value chain.

3 The transformation path of traditional consulting enterprise platform based on dynamic embedding of value chain

3.1 Dynamic embedding of value chain

Modern enterprises are no longer a highly structured closed system as considered by traditional industrial organization theory, and their survival and development cannot only rely on the adjustment of internal structure[12], but also should respond to complex dynamic environmental changes through transformation and upgrading[13]. However, it is far from enough to focus the starting point and acting point of transformation and upgrading on the cultivation of internal business capability, which will limit the long-term development of enterprises. Therefore, traditional engineering consulting enterprises must perceive environmental changes in time, continuously reconfigure and develop enterprise resources, and carry out transformation and upgrading at the right time in order to truly form sustainable competitive advantages.

In a complex and dynamic environment, the environment may has already changed before the transformation of the enterprise is fully implemented[14] and the strategic direction of the enterprise should change from pursuing the internal resource capability as the basis of enterprise development to the reconstruction of resource capacity for the purpose of adapting to environmental change. Therefore, the transformation and upgrading of enterprises is no longer a static cultivation of resources and capabilities, but a continuous dynamic adjustment process, which requires enterprises to have the dynamic embedding ability of value chain, and "environmental perception - Debugging of relationships and structures along the value chain - innovative learning - strategic reconstruction" is the effective path for traditional engineering consulting enterprises to carry out transformation and upgrading based on the theory of dynamic embedding of value chain[15].

1) Environment perception. Traditional engineering consulting enterprises occupy a certain position in the value chain by virtue of their business capabilities and are influenced by the variable, interlocking and complex environment in the value chain. The dynamic embedding of value chain requires enterprises to have insight into external environmental changes, timely identify uncertainties in the value chain, strengthen their own risk resilience, and at the same time accumulate internal resources and capabilities, actively seek opportunities and change the value chain environment. 2) Debugging of relationships and structures along the value chain. Traditional engineering consulting enterprises can actively acquire information flow, policies, science and technology resources among partners in the value chain, such as suppliers, bidders, tender evaluators and contractors, through relationship embedding and structure embedding[16] .They need to enhance the strength of independent innovation and use the resources in the value chain to build their own core competitive advantages. 3) Innovative learning. In the process of embedding, enterprises will face the problem that the resources in the value chain are more and more difficult to obtain[17] , so they need to conduct innovative learning, explore and integrate the obtained resources creatively to optimize the internal structure of enterprises and realize independent innovation[18] . 4) Strategic reconstruction. On the basis of "environmental perception - Debugging of relationships and structures along the value chain - innovative learning", the structure and use of resources, internal strategies and organizational structure are adjusted so that the value chain resources obtained by the company can be better matched with the objectives.

In the process of dynamic embedding of the value chain, the digital intelligence platform can have powerful ability of resource integration by virtue of network effect, "Cloud, Big Data, IoT, AI, 5G" and other technologies, connect and coordinate multilateral groups by virtue of bilateral or multilateral effect, and break the information silos. Therefore, enterprises can build a digital intelligence platform to promote the upgrading and reconstruction of core business scenarios of engineering consulting industry, and use the digital intelligence platform to promote the platform-based transformation of enterprises[19], which is an effective approach for engineering consulting enterprises to actively respond to the opportunities and challenges of the complex and dynamic environment.

3.2 The path of platform-based transformation of engineering consulting enterprises

3.2.1 Construction of Digital Intelligence Platform for Engineering Consulting

The digital intelligence platform is going to generate a new driving force for the transformation and upgrading of engineering consulting enterprises. Traditional engineering consulting enterprises can firstly operate their enterprises through digital technology[20], and at the same time use the PAAS platform provided by platform service providers to carry out rapid secondary development, so as to build a digital intelligence platform in line with their own enterprise characteristics, precipitate advanced industrial capabilities and realize the digitalization of each business link. Secondly, enterprises can use the digital intelligence platform to run through the whole process of traditional engineering consulting projects, upgrade all elements of the industry, connect all participants of engineering consulting projects, and provide virtual consulting services or twin consulting services that combine reality with virtuality, systematically realize the optimal allocation of resources in the whole industrial value chain, maximize efficiency, empower all parties in the industrial value chain with technology, and provide core competitive capabilities for engineering consulting enterprises.

The digital intelligence platform provides a digital base for the transformation of engineering consulting enterprises, and it is the digital infrastructure for building the enterprise platform ecology. Through platform building and dynamic embedding of value chain, more and more traditional consulting enterprises can realize digital upgrading and ecological integration of value chain, resulting in efficient linkage brought by the penetration of value chain and industry chain, finally developing a new model, new driving force and new ecology of traditional consulting industry.

3.2.2 Platform ecology of engineering consulting enterprises

Based on the digital intelligence platform, engineering consulting enterprises can attract and connect huge multilateral user groups through network effect[21] and multilateral effect, and each group can develop synergistically and mutually benefit from each other, thus forming a solid platform ecosystem, and the enterprise becomes a platform enterprise and is in a leading position in the formation and development of the platform ecosystem [22].

Based on the Internet framework, the platform ecology of engineering consulting enterprises, driven by digital technology, is jointly constituted by multiple subjects in its value chain and their stakeholders. The participating subjects are multiple in nature, including suppliers, bidders, bid evaluators, contractors, platform service providers, etc. Each participating subject has relevance to other subjects due to interconnection, and the intensity of relevance is different, so multiple subjects will form a multi-layer multilateral and compound network relationship in the actual operation of the participating platform. A schematic diagram of the platform ecology with the digital intelligence platform as the endpoint is shown below:

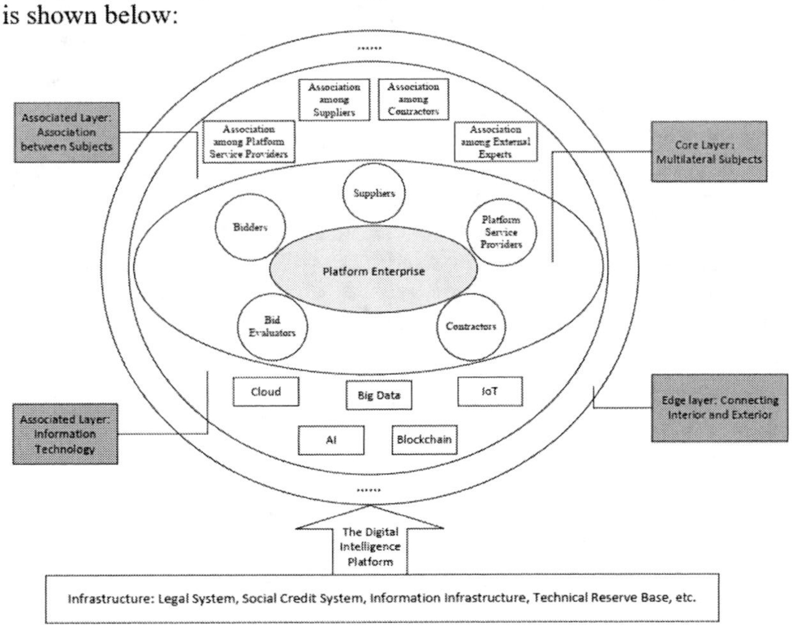

Fig. 1. Schematic diagram of the platform ecology of engineering consulting enterprises.

1) The development of platform ecology is built on certain infrastructure, including institution, society, technology etc., which constitute the infrastructure layer of platform ecology development together, and the platform enterprise builds engineering consulting digital intelligence platform by fully integrating the infrastructure. The infrastructure layer includes the regulatory system, social credit system, information infrastructure, technical reserve foundation, etc.

2) The inner composition of the platform. The digital intelligence platform is managed and operated by engineering consulting enterprises, providing a connection channel for both supply and demand sides and promoting their transactions, creating revenue with services, maintaining existence and stimulating development with revenue. Platform enterprises set their development goals, fully utilize the sharing advantages of "vertical to the end and horizontal to the edge" to build a platform development model, establish a new organizational structure, and design based on digital technology to better serve the platform value goals and execution, collecting data in the front office, storing and processing data in the back office.

3) The platform ecology contains the participation of multiple subjects.Engineering consulting enterprises connect multiple subjects through the platform, forming bilateral or multilateral relationships,and also generating platform spillover effect in the process of operation, the layered pushing away of spillover effect forms a differential order network relationship. With its bilateral or multilateral market attributes and association advantages, the engineering consulting digital intelligence platform attracts suppliers, platform service providers, bid evaluators, bidders, contractors and others actors to take part in the platform.At the same time, the connection service provided by the engineering consulting digital intelligence platform for both supply and demand sides runs in the Internet framework, which has network relevance and reaches transactions based on the relevance and sociality of supply and demand among various groups, thus deriving association layer subjects, such as association among suppliers, association among contractors, association among platform service providers and association among external experts. It's also associated with information and communication technologies represented by cloud, big data, IoT, AI, blockchain, etc., so as to achieve the data sharing and information interoperability, comprehensively promote the construction of platform ecology of engineering consulting enterprises. Finally, the associated layer subjects further expand the new associated secondary layer with the innovation of the whole process engineering consulting service mode, forming a sustainable platform ecology.

To sum up, the platform ecology of engineering consulting enterprises not only includes the platform operator (engineering consulting enterprises), bilateral or multilateral customer groups and their transaction relationships, but also includes the mutual influence and interaction among various elements. The platform operator needs to manage the internal and external associations of groups with different attributes and forms in a hierarchical and graded manner to ensure the effective operation of the digital intelligence platform.

3.2.3 Platform ecological governance for engineering consulting enterprises

The ecology of engineering consulting enterprise platform is characterized by openness, multiple participating subjects, dynamic change of environment, complex evolution of system, etc. The applicability of traditional unidimensional governance mode is reduced, and the collaborative governance of multiple subjects led by platform enterprise is needed[23] . In the context of the information age, the modern information technique represented by "Cloud, Big Data, AI, 5G, IoT, Blockchain" can be applied to the governance process, forming a new model with shared goals, participation of multiple actors, clear rights and responsibilities, and building a platform-based ecological governance system of diversified competition and cooperation. At the same time, to make the platform multiple subjects play their proper role in the common governance, the systematic configuration of rights, responsibilities and benefits is needed. The structure of rights and responsibilities of each subject is the driving force and guarantee of the common governance. A reasonable structure of rights, responsibilities and benefits means that this structure can balance various incentive and constraint relationships in the common governance.

Platform enterprises lead the governance. In the common governance system of engineering consulting enterprise platform ecology, platform enterprises are the core players and play a leading role, leads bilateral or multilateral participating subjects and various participants of the subsystem to act in accordance with the law, takes the lead in implementing the concept of co-creation value[24], expresses the self-restraint mechanism of co-creation value clearly, plays a leading and demonstration role, improves the platform governance mechanism continuously, stimulates and restrains the governance activities of multilateral subjects. Platform enterprises can govern the ecological chaos of the platform through private supervision, such as deducting deposits, adjusting the price structure, strengthening the reputation mechanism and improving the payment mechanism[25]. Meanwhile, platform enterprises can comprehensively apply big data technology in the governance process, establish the cooperation architecture system of governance subjects through effective design, build a digital governance platform in line with the characteristics of their own enterprises, realize the digitalization of all links and the ubiquitous connection of all elements, so that the isolation between the participating subjects in the traditional governance mode is broken. And it accelerates the construction of governance system and completes the digital transformation of vertical governance subjects. Based on the digitalization of the vertical governance chain, the digital upgrade of other subjects such as business centers and branches is conducive to multi-level and multi-body collaborative governance, this results in a new pattern, new power and new ecology of the governance system.

Multilateral subjects collaborate to govern. Multilateral subjects mainly include suppliers, bidders, bid evaluators, contractors, platform service providers and other stakeholders, which can enhance their own governance roles within the rules of the platform. Multilateral subjects pursue profit maximization, so they have the right and responsibility to monitor the factors affecting the ecology of the platform and maintain the healthy development of the platform. Its governance can also be combined with information technology, so as to digitally upgrade itself to enter the digital governance process of the platform enterprise, jointly promote the construction of the ecosystem of the governance platform, expand the governance network through virtual operation, realize the development of the network "power" without boundaries[26], and generate efficient linkage effects.

In a diversified and digital platform ecological governance system led by platform enterprises, multilateral groups within the platform ecology can not only conduct transactions or other activities on common rules, but also contribute their respective strengths to create a common platform ecosystem; not only make transaction activities orderly, but also jointly create a platform ecosystem of continuous co-learning, co-creation of value and common governance.

4 Practical examples: the practical experience of Glodon

Founded in 1998, Glodon started with the DOS version of "Software Series in Project Cost", established a foothold in the construction industry, and built an efficient research, operating, marketing and service system around the whole life cycle of engineering projects.

Its digital costing business has gradually matured to the forefront of the domestic digital costing field, including engineering costing, engineering calculation, engineering information, and e-government business lines.

In 2015, the construction industry is facing many problems, such as difficult management coordination, high procurement costs, shortage of funds, serious arrears, financing difficulties, high factor costs, etc. This has led to the increasingly prominent conflicts in the informationization of construction enterprises. In terms of software integration, most domestic enterprises have established scattered, single-point consideration of information systems based on the business itself, such as financial management systems, human resources systems, etc. It is difficult to provide a complete system to achieve interoperability between various businesses and levels. At the same time, with the increasing degree of digitization, not only software integration capabilities, but also the problem of hardware integration capabilities is becoming more serious.

Recognizing the problems faced by construction enterprises in informatization, Glodon was actively seeking opportunities with the massive customer and data resources it accumulated over the years. In 2015, it officially announced its comprehensive transformation into the "Internet Platform Service Provider of Construction Industry", which takes professional applications in the field of construction engineering as the core foundation support and consider industrial big data, industrial credit and industrial finance as value-added services, so as to create a platform ecology and promote the modernisation of the construction industry.

The transformation strategy of Glodon is expressed by "two aggregations, two enclosures and one construction", which points to the market with great potential. The "two aggregations" is to gather the quantity and people. The aggregation of quantity means to aggregate the bulk purchase between buyers and suppliers so as to reduce the cost. "The aggregation of quantity" is the gathering of all participants involved in the construction site. "Two enclosures" is short for "the enclosure of lands" and "the enclosure of buildings", meaning that Glodon will try to occupy the operation and maintenance market of construction sites and buildings. The "one construction" means building a BIM-based component library. Through the relationship embedding and structure embedding of the value chain, Glodon debugs the relationship and structure of the value chain, takes the initiative to acquire, accumulate and integrate the resources of the partners in the value chain, so as to realize the transformation strategy.

The simple absorption and internalization of the acquired resources is no longer sustainable, enterprises should create and utilize them further. Glodon serves the industry actively and integrates into the industry continuously. It uses BIm, Cloud, Big Data, AI, 5G, IoT, Blockchain, etc. to carry out innovative learning in the whole life cycle management of project production activities, such as design, production, procurement, construction, operation and maintenance. It also expands information technologies to all links upstream and downstream of the whole industrial value chain, which can cross the limits of space and time, improve the ability of resource acquisition and allocation, and create incremental value for customers and enterprises themselves.

For better connection with external resources, Glodon has built a digital intelligence platform to support its strategic reconstruction, achieving the transformation from a traditional engineering consulting enterprise to a platform-based enterprise. The "one construction" in the transformation strategy of Glodon refers to building a BIM-based component library to establish core advantages, obtain big data, and then carry out related credit services with engineering projects as the core. Glodon firmly grasps the key points of "design, schedule, measurement and collaboration" in engineering projects to build the enterprise platform ecology, and plays the role of platform in consulting services, solutions and ecological cooperation to integrate ecological resources. After years of practice and accumulation, it has formed sustainable enterprise core competitiveness, including digital design capability represented by BIM deepening design, schedule control capability represented by network planning, engineering calculation capability represented by bidding calculation and construction calculation, and collaborative management capability represented by Project Intelligence and intelligent scheduling, becoming the leader of digital transformation in the industry.

In the process of enterprise transformation, Chinese local engineering consulting enterprises, represented by Glodon, can follow the path of "environment perception - relationship and structure debugging among the value chain - innovative learning - strategic reconstruction" based on the theory of dynamic embedding in the value chain. They can combine information technology with enterprise transformation. Through the integration of "construction gene" and "digital gene", the integration of "construction ecology" and "digital ecology", a new paradigm of "ecological win-win and integrated development" and a new industrial ecology of resource sharing, symbiotic development, multi-win can be established. They also need to accomplish the platformization of horizontal business , break through the whole process of value chain and support partners to ensure that they can carry out the whole process engineering consulting business on the platform. As a result, an ecosystem of mutual empowerment and integration in the construction industry is formed.

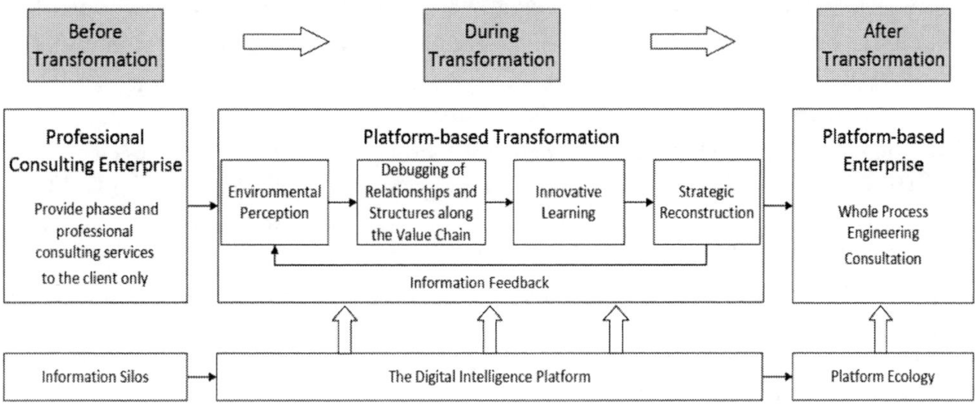

Fig. 2. The path diagram of platform-based transformation.

5 Conclusion

As a form of service that can adapt to the cross-stage, integrated and comprehensive needs of the client, whole-process engineering consulting has become an important development trend for high-quality development in the engineering consulting industry. To adapt to the development of whole-process engineering consulting, cope with complex environmental changes and explore new opportunities, this paper proposes a platform-based transformation path based on the dynamic embedding of the value chain. And the theoretical path of this paper is verified by Glodon's successful platform transformation. The transformation of enterprises in complex and dynamic environments is no longer a simple "static" mode of re-embedding in the value chain, but a continuous dynamic evolution process. To cope with the highly uncertain market environment and ensure the timeliness and long-term of enterprise transformation, traditional engineering consulting enterprises should firstly perceive the changes in the environment quickly and coordinate relationships with partners along the value chain actively. Secondly, they can take the initiative to integrate and utilize external resources through repositioning in the value chain. Next, they use information technology to learn innovatively from external and their own resources. Finally the engineering consulting enterprises should reshape enterprise strategy and organizational structure by building a digital intelligence platform, which can form a symbiotic and mutualistic platform ecology of multilateral groups. This will break the limit of time and space, improve the ability of resource allocation, increase the management span and shorten the management radius. Meanwhile, the platform ecology should be jointly governed by multilateral groups, so as to implement the value co-creation of multiple subjects, the platform-based transformation of traditional engineering consulting enterprises and high-quality development of industry. It is hoped that this study can enrich the theoretical research on the platform-based transformation of traditional engineering consulting enterprises and maintain the sustainable development of engineering consulting industry.

References

1. M. Porter, *Competitive advantage* (New York: Free Press, 1985).
2. X. Zhang. International Economics and Trade Research, **03**, 34-37(1997).
3. J. Wang, Journal of Zhejiang University (2006).
4. X. Wang,F. Hu, Science and Technology Management Research, **08**, 228-233(2013).
5. J. Yu, B. Sun, F. Hu, Fujian Tribune(The Humanities&Social Sciences Monthly), **09**, 97-107(2020).
6. W. Li, Modern Management Science,**04**, 54-56(2015) .
7. K. Rong, Y. Lin, Y. Shi, et al, International Journal of Technology Management, **01**, 62(2013).
8. T. R. Eisenmann, , G. Parker, and M. van Alstyne. Social Science Electronic Publishing, **10**, 84(2006).
9. E.G. Anderson, G.G. Parker, B. Tan, Social Science Electronic Publishing, **01**, 25(2014).
10. A. Gawer, M.A. Cusumano. Mit Sloan Management Review, **02**, 49(2008).
11. G. Jiang, Frontiers, **Z1**, 32-39(2021).
12. G. Ray, J.B. Barney, W.A. Muhanna, Strategic Management Journal, **01**, 25(2004).
13. C.K. Prahalad, G. Hamel, Strategic Management Journal, 15(1994).
14. R. Cao, Y. Cang, Academic Exchange, **04**, 115-126+192(2019).
15. D.J. Teece, Strategic Management Journal, **13**, 1319-1350(2007):.
16. M. Granovetter, American Journal of Sociology, **03**, 481-510(1985).
17. H. Zhong, X. Liu, Science & Technology Progress and Policy, **07**, 74-81(2018).
18. Y. Wang, H. Cai, Construction Economy, **07**, 31-34(2021).
19. R. Fan, Social Sciences in China, **12**, 131-152+202(2021).
20. Z. Wu, L. Yu, Informatization of China Construction, **06**, 32-35(2022).
21. A. Afuah, Strategic Management Journal, **03**, 257-273(2013).
22. P. Li, H. Hu. Science & Technology Progress and Policy, **10**, 1-5(2016).
23. Y. Zheng, Journal of Public Governance Research, **05**, 92-98(2021).
24. Q. Zhong, X. Yang, Z. Wu, System Engineering - Theory&Practice, **02**, 421-430(2021).
25. Y. Wang, H. Feng. The Economist, **11**, 73-80(2017).

26. H. Yang, P. Ning, Social Science Journal, **05**, 135-144(2021).

Research on the impact of leadership empowerment behavior on task performance - Based on the moderation of employee maturity

Shengnan Wang[1]*, and *Zhengyang* Sun[2]

[1]School of Economics and Management, Beijing Jiaotong University, Beijing, China
[2]School of Computer and Information Technology, Beijing Jiaotong University, Beijing, China

Keywords: Leadership empowerment behavior, Task performance, Employee maturity.

Abstract. This paper explores the impact of leadership empowerment behavior on employee task performance and the moderation of employee maturity in it, based on conservation of resources theory. By analyzing 308 valid questionnaires through polynomial regression analysis, the research shows that (1) leadership empowerment behavior has a positive impact on task performance; (2) employee maturity moderates the relationship between leadership empowerment behavior and task performance. This research constructs the influence path of leadership empowerment behavior on employee task performance, reveals the moderation of employee maturity, and provides insights into the leadership behavior practices of Chinese enterprise managements.

1 Introduction

At present, China is in a crucial period of economic transformation, and for enterprises, the external environment is becoming more and more complex, various uncertainties are intertwined, and the competition among enterprises is becoming more and more intense. In order to gain a foothold in the complex external environment, enterprises need to continuously create new value and performance, and the important subject of creating value for enterprises is employees. Therefore, the urgent problem that enterprises need to solve is what kind of measures can be taken to improve employee task performance. Among the successful cases in China and abroad, the successful implementation of highly empowered enterprises such as Haidilao, Wall-Mart, and KFC has attracted widespread attention. Gradually, leadership empowerment behavior began to be adopted and applied by the majority of managements. By delegating authority to employees to participate in the management activities of the enterprise, instead of just allowing employees to mechanically complete the tasks they have been given, the enterprise truly let employees feel respected and valued as owners[1]. Currently, leadership empowerment behavior is regarded as an effective means to improve employee task performance. How to implement delegation scientifically not only has an important impact on improving employee task performance, but also has a great research value for the future long-term development of enterprises.

* Corresponding author: 13840249665@163.com

2 Literature review

Leadership empowerment behavior has a positive impact on employees' initiative in enterprise management. Leadership empowerment behavior(LEB) is the behavior that leaders delegate authority to lower management or employees[2], so that subordinates have more autonomy to complete tasks, which can help leaders spare more time for management and decision making, and also can mobilize subordinates' motivation and improve organization management efficiency[3].Current domestic and international research on the outcome variables of leadership empowerment behavior can be roughly classified into the following categories: the effects of leadership empowerment behavior on employee attitudes such as organization commitment[4], work satisfaction[5], and work burnout[6], the effects on employee performance, and the effects on the organization[7]. In recent years, the effect of leadership empowerment behavior on task performance has received extensive attention from scholars in China and abroad.Numerous studies have verified that leadership empowerment behavior has a significant positive impact on employee task performance [8,9,10]. However, existing researches have shown that the relationship between leadership empowerment behavior and task performance is not completely linear [11], that is, leadership empowerment behavior is a "double-edged sword" for individuals. On the one hand, leadership empowerment behavior can improve task performance by enhancing self-efficacy, sense of meaningfulness, and sense of competence. On the other hand, excessive leadership empowerment behavior can cause unnecessary pressure to subordinate employees, which can negatively affect their task performance [12]. Therefore, it is an important theoretical issue that needs to be addressed under which circumstances leadership empowerment behavior affects task performance.

In addition, the individual characteristic of employee is an important factor influencing the relationship between leadership empowerment behavior and task performance [13]. Corporate senior managements should delegate more work authority to mature employees and let them participate in enterprise management as much as possible, so that they can give full play to their work autonomy in their daily work[14], which in turn has a positive impact on employee task performance [15].Thus, in terms of individual characteristics, employee maturity may play an important role in the relationship between leadership empowerment behavior and task performance. However, no consistent conclusion has been reached as to how this influence works. Based on this, this research investigates the moderation of employee maturity in the relationship between leadership empowerment behavior and employee task performance from the perspective of individual employee characteristics.

3 Theoretical model and research hypothesis

3.1 Theoretical model

Using a sample of local Chinese corporate employees, this research examines the relationship between leadership empowerment behavior and task performance on the one hand, and constructs a model to examine the moderation of employee maturity between leadership empowerment behavior and task performance on the other. Based on this, the theoretical model of this research is shown in Figure 1.

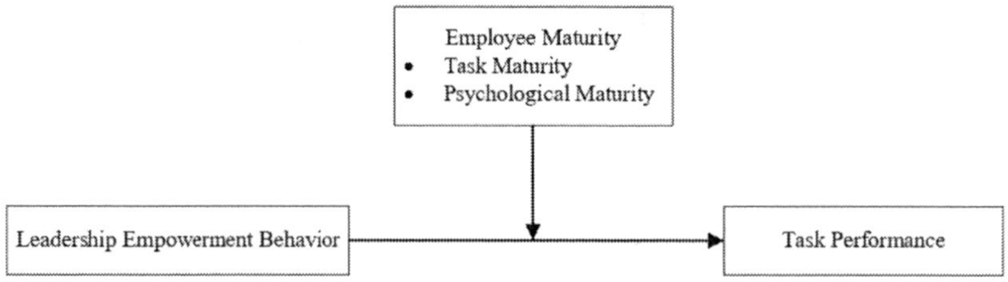

Fig. 1. The theoretical model.

3.2 Research hypothesis

According to conservation of resources theory [[16], leadership empowerment behavior has an empowering impact on employees when work resources provided by leaders are exactly what the employees need. On the one hand, employees acquire work resources by means of leadership empowerment behavior and apply them to their work to improve their original work performance. On the other hand, leadership empowerment behavior make employees feel emotionally energized and motivated to keep learning, thus promoting improved task performance.Based on the above discussion, this paper proposes the following hypothesis:

H1: Leadership empowerment behavior has a positive impact on task performance.

Employee maturity is usually defined as the ability and willingness of employees in enterprises to perform a given task, including both task maturity (ability) and psychological maturity (willingness) [17]. Task maturity mainly includes skill proficiency, work experience and knowledge of work requirements. Psychological maturity mainly includes whether the employee work attitude is positive, the degree of responsibility and the degree of confidence in the work.

Employees with higher task maturity tend to have outstanding personal ability, stronger independence in work, and want to work according to their own ideas and plans[14]. For such employees, more autonomy given by leaders is beneficial to their divergent thinking and access to work resources to carry out their work better. Conversely, employees with lower levels of task maturity are relatively less skilled and less familiar with the workflow. At this point the leadership empowerment behavior for such employees is not conducive to the completion of their tasks.Based on the above discussion, this paper proposes the following hypothesis:

H2a: Employee task maturity positively moderates the relationship between leadership empowerment behavior and task performance, which means that when employees have a high level of task maturity, leadership empowerment behavior help improve employee task performance.

Employees with high psychological maturity tend to have responsibility and self-confidence in their work. By empowering and encouraging, these employees can acquire positive emotions (such as motivation, responsibility and work recognition) and social resources (help from colleagues). In this case, employees are more motivated to spend the emotions and social resources on their work in order to achieve greater task performance [18]. Employees with low psychological maturity often show no confidence in accomplishing their work in the face of leadership empowerment and high expectations, fear criticism from leaders, and are more likely to develop negative emotions such as frustration and loss. In this situation, employees are often accompanied by greater work pressure and are more inclined to accomplish the tasks assigned by their leader with as few of their own resources as possible while retaining existing resources and avoiding the loss of more resources[19]. Under the dual influence of work requirements and work pressure, the task performance of employees with low psychological maturity will decrease.Based on the above discussion, this paper proposes the following hypothesis:

H2b: Employee psychological maturity positively moderates the relationship between leadership empowerment behavior and task performance, which means that when employee psychological maturity is a high level, leadership empowerment behavior contributes to improve employee task performance.

4 Data collection and measurement

4.1 Data collection

This research conducted questionnaire survey in Beijing and surrounding areas from August to September 2022. Four hundred questionnaires were collected mainly through online. Three criteria for the questionnaire to be judged as invalid: (1) five or more questions were not selected; (2) five or more consecutive questions with the same selection; (3) screening questions that did not pass or had an obvious regular arrangement. The total number of valid questionnaires after eliminating invalid questionnaires was 308, and the questionnaire efficiency rate was 77%.

4.2 Variable measurement

(1) Leadership Empowerment Behavior(LEB). This research draws on the Leader Empowering Behavior Questionnaire developed by Konczak, Stelly & Trusty (2000), with 14 selected items[20]. The scale has been validated by many scholars and has high reliability and validity.

(2) Employee maturity(EM). This research draws on a scale developed by Rongbing Zhu (2013) on employee maturity with 6 items[21]. The scale includes two dimensions, employee task maturity(ETM) and employee psychological maturity(EPM), and higher scores indicate higher employee maturity.

(3) Task performance(TP). This research draws on the task performance questionnaire developed by Van & Motowidlo (1996), with 14 selected items [22].

(4) Control variables. Seven common demographic characteristics, namely gender, age, education, management level, working years, nature of enterprise, and duration of working with direct leader (supervisor), were selected as control variables in this research.

4.3 Reliability and validity analysis

4.3.1 Reliability analysis

As can be seen from Table 1, the Cronbach's α coefficient values of this questionnaire for leadership empowerment behavior, employee maturity, and task performance are 0.858, 0.864, and 0.780, respectively, which are all greater than 0.7. Thus the scale has high reliability and empirical analysis can be performed afterwards.

Table 1. Scale reliability (N=308).

Variables	Number of items	Cronbach's α
LEB	14	0.858
EM	6	0.864
TP	5	0.780

Note: Based on the results of the reliability analysis of SPSS25.0.

4.3.2 Validity analysis

The fit indexes are shown in Table 2. All values of $\chi 2$/df are less than 3, RMSEA are less than 0.08, NFI, RFI, IFI, CFI and TLI are greater than 0.9, indicating the structure of the test is reasonable.

Table 2. The fit indexes of the questionnaire (N=308).

Variables	*df*	χ^2	χ^2/df	RMSEA	NFI	RFI	IFI	CFI	TLI
LEB	67	165.93	2.48	0.07	0.91	0.98	0.95	0.95	0.93
EM	8	23.35	2.93	0.08	0.97	0.95	0.98	0.98	0.96
TP	5	10.12	2.02	0.06	0.97	0.95	0.99	0.99	0.97

Note: Based on the results of confirmatory factor analysis of AMOS 25.0.

5 Data analysis and hypothesis verification

5.1 Common method bias test and multicollinearity test

5.1.1 Common method bias test

In this research, the data were tested for common method bias using Harman's single factor test, and five factors with characteristic roots greater than one were extracted from the 25 items of the scale using unrotated exploratory factor analysis. Because the maximum factor variance explained was 36.79% (less than 50%), the common method bias in this research was within acceptable limits.

5.1.2 Multicollinearity test for the moderation of employee task maturity

As shown in Table 3, the coefficient of variance inflation for each variable is greater than 1 and less than 3. The tolerance of each variable is smaller than 1, indicating that the analysis of the moderation of employee task maturity is not affected by multicollinearity.

Table 3. Results of multicollinearity test for the moderation of task maturity (N=308).

Explanatory variables	DV: task performance	
	TOL	VIF
Gender	0.920	1.087
Age	0.527	1.898
Edu	0.918	1.089
Management level	0.806	1.24
Working years	0.386	2.588
Enterprise nature	0.899	1.113
Duration of working with direct leader (supervisor)	0.509	1.966
LEB	0.655	1.528
ETM	0.581	1.723
LEB×ETM	0.767	1.304

Note: Based on the results of regression analysis according to SPSS 25.0.

5.1.3 Multicollinearity test for the moderation of employee psychological maturity

As shown in Table 4, the coefficient of variance inflation for each variable is greater than 1 and less than 3. The tolerance of each variable is smaller than 1, indicating that the analysis of the moderation of employee psychological maturity is not affected by multicollinearity.

Table 4. Results of multicollinearity test for the moderation of psychological maturity (N=308).

Explanatory variables	DV: task performance	
	TOL	VIF
Gender	0.921	1.086
Age	0.527	1.898
Edu	0.931	1.075
Management level	0.809	1.237
Working years	0.387	2.581
Enterprise nature	0.922	1.084
Duration of working with direct leader (supervisor)	0.515	1.944
LEB	0.542	1.844
EPM	0.477	2.098
LEB×EPM	0.668	1.497

Note: Based on the results of regression analysis according to SPSS 25.0.

5.2 Descriptive statistics and correlation analysis

The correlation analysis is shown in Table 5 and all correlation coefficients are significant at the 0.01 level. Among them, leadership empowerment behavior was significantly correlated with task performance (r=0.536, p<0.01), employee task maturity with task performance (r=0.632, p<0.01), and employee psychological maturity with task performance (r=0.656, p<0.01).

Table 5. Results of descriptive statistics and correlation analysis of unobserved variables (N=308).

	M	SD	1	2	3	4	5	6	7	8	9	10	11
1.Gender	1.48	.50	1										
2.Age	2.16	.70	-.109*	1									
3.Edu	2.86	.61	-.050	-.061	1								
4.Management level	2.92	.84	.192**	-.275**	-.168**	1							
5.Working years	2.77	.93	-.074	.673**	-.035	-.287**	1						
6.Enterprise nature	2.15	.93	.114*	.078	.027	.087	.135*	1					
Duration of working with direct leader	3.73	.97	.045	.478**	.027	-.259**	.636**	-.019	1				
8.LEB	4.02	.60	-.026	.010	.158**	-.156**	-.021	-.128*	.215**	(.86)			
9.ETM	4.11	.70	-.053	.153**	.189**	-.204**	.148**	-.191**	.308**	.534**	(.81)		
10.EPM	4.37	.61	-.032	.079	.160**	-.165**	.078	-.074	.235**	.646**	.676**	(.80)	
11.TP	4.29	.49	.047	.145*	.126*	-.191**	.105	-.047	.240**	.536**	.632**	.656**	(.78)

Node: *p<0.05, **p<0.01; Based on the results of correlation analysis of SPSS 25.0.

5.3 Hypothesis verification

5.3.1 Verification on the relationship between leadership empowerment behavior and task performance

In the previous section, this research has analyzed the correlation between leadership empowerment behavior and task performance, and the results have shown a strong correlation.On the basis of this, this research establishes regression equation M1 after controlling for demographic characteristics variables, and then determine the role of leadership empowerment behavior on task performance. The results of the analysis are shown in Table 6, which shows that leadership empowerment behavior has a significant positive impact on task performance (β=0.505, p<0.01) and hypothesis 1 is verified.

5.3.2 Verification on the moderation of employee task maturity

To determine the moderation of employee task maturity, this research puts control variables and leadership empowerment behavior in the regression equation of model 1, employee task maturity in the regression equation of model 2, and adds a new product term of the two in the regression equation of model 3 to regress the dependent variable task performance.

Table 6. Verification on the moderation of employee task maturity (N=308).

Explanatory variables	DV: Task performance		
	M1	M2	M3
CV			
Gender	0.085	0.089*	0.084
Age	0.107	0.077	0.068
Education level	0.041	-0.015	-0.017
Management level	-0.08	-0.064	-0.046
Working years	-0.013	-0.032	-0.045
Enterprise nature	0.009	0.076	0.079
Duration of working with direct leader (supervisor)	0.063	-0.005	0.005
IV			
LEB	0.505**	0.280**	0.309**
Moderator Variable			
ETM		0.487**	0.540**
LEB×ETM			0.153**
R^2	0.324	0.475	0.493
ΔR^2	0.324	0.151	0.018
F	17.904**	29.977**	28.902**
ΔF	17.904**	85.889**	10.568**

Note: *p<0.05, **p<0.01.

The analysis of Table 6 suggests that employee task maturity has a significant explanatory ability on task performance (M2, β=0.487, p<0.01). Meanwhile, the coefficient of the regression equation incorporating the interaction term of employee task maturity and leadership empowerment behavior is significant (M3, β=0.153, p<0.01), which indicates that the higher the employee task maturity, the stronger the positive impact of leadership empowerment behavior on task performance, i.e., employee task maturity positively moderates the relationship between leadership empowerment behavior and task performance. Additionally, the ΔR^2 value of M3 is 0.018 and the ΔF value is 10.568 and is significant at the 0.01 level, which indicates that the expansion of the interaction term in M3 significantly increases the explanatory ability of task performance by 1.8%, which means that this interaction term has a important explanatory role on task performance. The above results validate hypothesis 2a.

5.3.3 Verification on the moderation of employee psychological maturity

To determine the moderation of employee psychological maturity, this research puts control variables and leadership empowerment behavior in the regression equation of model 4, employee psychological maturity in the regression equation of model 5, and adds a new product term of the two in the regression equation of model 6 to regress the dependent variable task performance.

Table 7. Verification on the moderation of employee psychological maturity (N=308).

Explanatory variables	DV: Task performance		
	M4	M5	M6
CV			
Gender	0.085	0.088*	0.083
Age	0.107	0.100	0.081
Education level	0.041	0.011	0.011
Management level	-0.08	-0.067	-0.042
Working years	-0.013	-0.03	-0.039
Enterprise nature	0.009	0.007	-0.001
Duration of working with direct leader (supervisor)	0.063	0.029	0.045
IV			
LEB	0.505**	0.188**	0.218**
Moderator Variable			
EPM		0.512**	0.627**
LEB×EPM			0.242**
R^2	0.324	0.473	0.512
ΔR^2	0.324	0.149	0.039
F	17.904**	29.706**	31.146**
ΔF	17.904**	84.243**	23.721**

Note: *p<0.05, **p<0.01.

The analysis of Table 7 suggests that employee psychological maturity has a significant explanatory ability on task performance (M5, β=0.512, $p<0.01$). Meanwhile, the coefficient of the regression equation incorporating the interaction term of employee psychological maturity and leadership empowerment behavior is significant (M6, β=0.242, $p<0.01$), which indicates that the higher the employee psychological maturity, the stronger the positive impact of leadership empowerment behavior on task performance, i.e., employee psychological maturity positively moderates the relationship between leadership empowerment behavior and task performance. Additionally, the ΔR^2 value of M6 is 0.039 and the ΔF value is 23.721 and is significant at the 0.01 level, which indicates that the expansion of the interaction term in M6 significantly increases the explanatory ability of task performance by 3.9%, which means that this interaction term has a important explanatory role on task performance. The above results validate hypothesis 2b.

5.4 Research findings

Based on the results of the research described above, the research hypothesis verification of this paper is summarized as shown in Table 8.

Table 8. Summary of hypothesis verification findings.

Research hypothesis	Verification results
H1: Leadership empowerment behavior has a positive impact on task performance.	Valid
H2a: Employee task maturity positively moderates the relationship between leadership empowerment behavior and task performance.	Valid
H2b: Employee psychological maturity positively moderates the relationship between leadership empowerment behavior and task performance.	Valid

6 Conclusion

This research constructs a moderation model based on conservation of resources theory to investigate the effect of leadership empowerment behavior on employee task performance. The results indicate that leadership empowerment behavior can positively impact task performance. Employee maturity positively moderates the relationship between leadership empowerment behavior and task performance, and both employee task maturity and psychological maturity positively moderate the relationship between leadership empowerment behavior and task performance.

According to the above conclusions, this paper mainly provides two insights for enterprise managements: (1) Enterprise managements should delegate their authority properly. On the one hand, the managements guide employees to participate in the daily management of the enterprise, and encourage them to propose different opinions. On the other hand, the senior managements should strive to consider the suggestions of each employee in making decisions about them, adopt and apply the feasible suggestions proposed by the employees in practice. Enterprise managements should delegate the appropriate degree of authority according to the different maturity of employees at different stages in their careers. For example, for employees with higher maturity level, managements can delegate more authority, which can inspire them to engage in enterprise management with subjective initiative. Conversely, for employees with lower maturity, the leadership empowerment behavior is not conducive to employee task performance, so it is required to appropriately reduce delegation and increase guidance and instruction.

References

1. Y.H. Zhang, H. Wang, L. Guo, S.M. Liu, Economic Science, 118-128(2016).
2. D. J. Leach, T. D. Wall, & P. R. Jackson, Journal of Occupational and Organizational Psychology, **76**, 27-52(2003).
3. P. Hao, W. He, L. R. Long, Journal of Leadership & Organizational Studies, **25**, 85-100(2018).
4. R. C. Liden, S. J. Wayne, R. T. Sparrowe, Journal of applied psychology, **85**, 407(2000).
5. G. M. Spreitzer, M. A. Kizilos, S. W. Nason, Journal of management, **23**, 679-704(1997).

6. C.P. Li, X.X. Li, K. Shi, X.F. Chen, Journal of Psychology, 99-106(2006).
7. X.D. Chen, M.M. Yin, Leadership Science, 38-41(2021).
8. J. R. Van Scotter, S. J. Motowidlo, Journal of applied psychology, **81**, 525(1996).
9. J. A. Conger & R. N. Kanungo, Academy of Management Review, **13**, 471-482(1988).
10. L. Xu, Journal of Hubei College of Economics (Humanities and Social Sciences Edition), **11**, 45-46(2014).
11. K. Yin, L. Xing, J. Wang, Psychological Science, **41**, 680-686(2018).
12. M. Cheong, S. M. Spain, F. J. Yammarino, et al., The Leadership Quarterly, **27**, 602-616(2016).
13. H.B. Luo, Mall Modernization, 248(2008).
14. C.H. Cai, Journal of Economic Research, 171-173(2014).
15. N.N. Guo, Human Resource Management, 37-38(2014).
16. S. E. Hobfoll, American Psychologist, **44**, 513-524(1989).
17. Y. Liu, *Management Psychology* (2nd ed.) . Chengdu: Sichuan University Press, 2008.
18. J. E. Bono, T. M. Glomb, W. Shen, E. Kim & A. J. Koch, Academy of Management Journal, **56**, 1601-1627(2013).
19. T. Ståhl, C. Van Laar & N. Ellemers, Journal of Personality and Social Psychology, **102**, 1239-1251(2012).
20. L. J. Konczak, D. J. Stelly & M. L. Trusty, Educational and Psychological Measurement, **60**, 302-308(2000).
21. R.B. Zhu, Guangxi University, 2013.
22. S. J. R. Van & S. J. Motowidlo, Journal of Applied Psychology, **81**, 525-531(1996).

Study on system construction of integrating moral education into college English teaching

Chunye Yang[1,*], and *Defeng* Xu[2]

[1]School of Foreign Languages, Wuhan Business University, Wuhan, Hubei Province, 430056, China
[2]College of Civil Engineering, Hubei Urban Construction Vocational and Technological College, Wuhan, Hubei Province, 430205, China

Abstract. College English, as a general education curriculum with huge amounts of audiences, is the main filed to put moral education into practice. This paper, aiming to provide theoretical framework and practice guidance, focuses mainly on system construction of integrating moral education into college English. The paper, firstly illustrates the chronological development of moral education in China, followed by the literature review at home and abroad. Lastly, a hypothesis of top-level design from a macroscopic perspective and a teaching model from a microcosmic perspective are proposed, which form an integration with open access to adjusting according to practical situations of different universities, leading to diversification and specialization of the system of moral education in the "New Art" Era.

1 Introduction

The concept of "moral education of Chinese characteristics" was initially proposed in 2014. In 2016, it was strengthened that all the courses should go hand-in-hand with the political ones so as to better coordinate with each other and put political and ideological education in colleges. In 2019, it was proposed that moral education should go through all higher education all the time[1].

College English is a core course in higher education, and it should be "an elementary course to cultivate students[2]". With a large number of audiences as the students, *College English* plays a vital role in higher education. Besides, *College English* mainly introduces western cultures, thus it is of great significance to integrate moral education and foster virtue through education[3].

2 Literature review

2.1 Domestic researches on moral education

Domestic researches on moral education mainly covers the following aspects: (1) methodologies for practice and construction of moral education[1, 6-11] (2) analysis of

* Corresponding author: 1058227292@qq.com

requirements for moral education elements[12] (3)teaching materials of moral education[13-14] (4)construction of the curriculum system[15] (5) telling China's stories in foreign languages[16-18] (6) teachers' teaching ability for ideological & political theories teaching[19-20] (7) connotation of moral education[2, 21-22]. All in all, moral education in college English has been heated discussed in recent years from a vast perspective with a qualitative method. However, there still lacks a systematic research on course construction and development of the teaching materials.

2.2 Foreign researches on moral education

Domestic translation of "moral education" mainly includes: (1) moral education[2] (2)morality cultivation[7] (3) ideological and political education[8,19][23-24] (4) political and virtuous awareness[21][22] (5) value education. While in foreign studies, "moral education" mainly refers to "moral education" "character education" "virtue education". And "moral education" is almost equivalent to "character education"[25].

Researches on moral education starts in an early time with different methods, such as empirical study, theoretical study, and comparative study. Pamela Bolotin Josephand sara Efron[25]studied seven worlds of moral education: character education, cultural heritage, caring community, peach education, social action, just community, ethical inquiry. In their thesis, analysis of moral element in Book of Virtues was also presented, which said that moral elements mainly refers to: self-discipline, compassion, responsibility, friendship, work, courage, perseverance, honesty, loyalty and faith[25]. Jan W. Steutel[26] clarified core norms in moral education from the perspective of virtue approach: (1) traits of character as aims of moral education (2) traits of character are the only aims of moral education (3) moral education founded in an ethics of virtue. Jaap Schuitema et al.[27] gave a comprehensive literature review to moral education from 1995 to 2003. Nel Noddings[28] from Stanford University analyzed moral education in the global world with care theory. Marvin W. Berkowitz, Fritz Oser[29] wondered if moral education was part of philosophical psychology in the postconventional level of moral education. Le Page et al.[30] compared teachers' views on morality and moral education in Turkey and the United States. In short, with vast research perspectives and methodologies, foreign studies on moral education could provide theoretical guidance, patterns, norm clarification and system construction for domestic researches.

3 Measurements for system construction of integrating moral education into college English teaching

3.1 Top-level design from a macroscopic perspective

It is a complicated task to construct objective, comprehensive and scientific moral education system. "To better put moral education into practice, it is urgent to give top-level designs[4]". This research offers some measurements from both macro- and micro-perspective. The former covers re-design of the teaching objectives, updating of the teaching philosophy, design of the teaching systems, revision of the teaching materials, optimizing teaching staff, guidance for teaching practice, and design for teaching assessments (see Fig. 1).

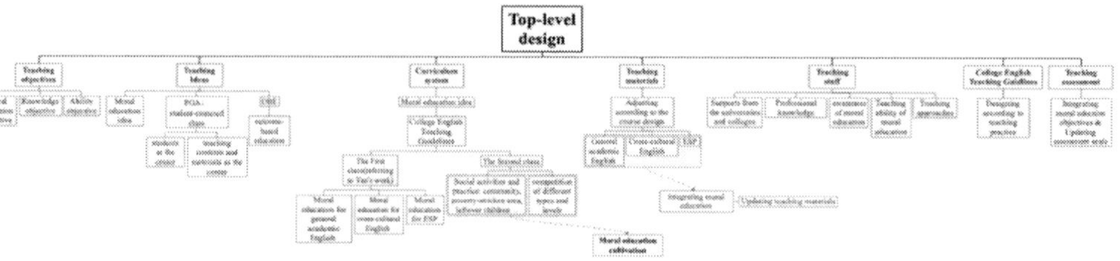

Fig. 1. Macroscopical perspective: top-level design of moral-education.

It is a primary and radical question to answer what to cultivate, how to cultivate and for whom should universities cultivate. Cultivating students is the essential task for higher education and implementing moral education in college English is a important way to complete this task. The aims of college English include both knowledge transmission and virtue cultivation: patriotism, responsibility, critical thinking, spirit of utter devotion, etc. With the guidance of moral education, the primary task for college English teaching is to update teaching objectives, including the moral education objective, knowledge objective, and ability objective, which conclusively forms a three-dimensional system and help to implement moral education in college English teaching by the staff, for the students and through all the time.

Setting up the teaching objectives and moral education teaching ideas, moral education systems for college English should be constructed. Universities and colleges are the main field to implement moral education to cultivate students. Teaching ideas such as POA (product-oriented-approach), OBE (outcome-based education) and moral education teaching ideas can coordinate in teaching practice, thus helping to improve students' professional ability and cultivate their virtues.

Yan Wenqing[31] classified the first class into three categories: general academic English, cross-cultural English, and ESP (see Fig. 1) to meet the demand of students in different learning levels. College English Teaching Guidelines provided guidance for college English teaching, which gives theoretical supports for constructing diversified yet specialized college English curriculum systems[15]; the second class includes social practice and competitions. Pamela Bolotin Joseph and Sara Efron pointed out that teachers should encourage students "to generate ideas, negotiate subject matter, and find learning resources outside of the school setting[25]." "The caring community emphasizes the ethic of care — nurturing, closeness, emotional attachment, and respectful, mutually supportive relationships[25]". As for the second class, more social practice should be encouraged. Students could join in the communities to visit the old, do the laundry or go to the remote poverty places to help the leftover children, etc. besides, students should also be encouraged to participate in English competitions so as to test and improve themselves.

"Teaching materials are important carriers of teaching contents, foundation of teaching practice and guarantee of realizing teaching objectives[3]". To integrate moral education in college English teaching, updating the teaching materials is another action that should be taken. Moral education materials and elements should be included in the novel teaching materials with cultural connotative meanings.

Teaching ability of the teachers will help put moral education into practice as well as improve teaching efficiency of moral education[19] and to set up moral education platform in universities is the foundation, through which teachers could transmit knowledge to students while improving professional abilities, cultivating moral education awareness, perfecting teaching skills and enriching current teaching modes.

"Objective assessments form teachers and peers are indispensable in foreign language teaching[2]." The outcome of moral education in college English teaching need systematic, objective and comprehensive assessments from a multi-dimension. With the guidance of teaching objectives, an assessment scale suitable for college English needs proposing to give process assessment and summative assessment. Moreover, students' assessments, peer assessments, and self-assessments form a tri-dimensional assessment system.

3.2 Teaching model from a microcosmic perspective

Teaching practice from the microcosmic perspective includes three phrases: pre-class, in class and after class (see Fig. 2).

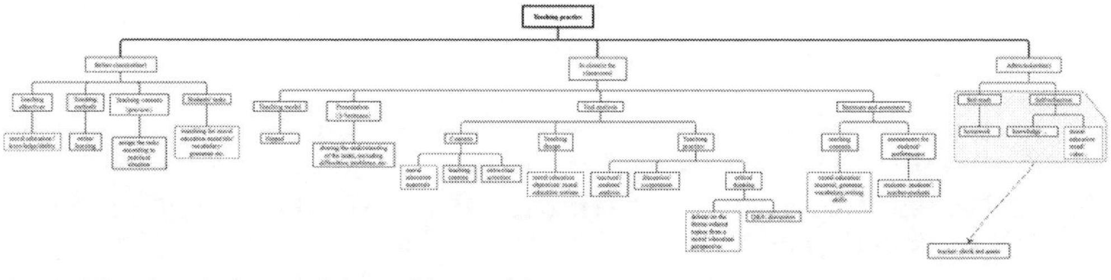

Fig. 2. Microcosmic perspective: teaching practice.

Before the class, online tasks are assigned according to moral teaching objectives, including (1) knowledge tasks: words, long and difficult sentences, paragraph dividing, summary, rhetorical devices etc., through previewing, students have a rough understanding of the teaching contents; (2) moral education tasks: searching for moral education elements. These tasks help students get familiar with the teaching materials and laying the foundation for the following discussion, critical debating in class.

In class, with flipped class, students need to do a presentation (3-5minutes/person) on the understanding of the pre-class tasks, such as the key and difficult points of the teaching materials. Teachers will give comments on the presentation and explain the key and difficult points in class. Text analysis with moral education objectives, discussion and critical thinking are included in the teaching process, and assessments from peers and teachers will help to have a comprehensive and objective process evaluation on the teaching effects.

In the after-class period, students will mainly have a self-disciplinary study to complete both the online and offline assignments. They need to give a comprehensive reflection on their studies: previewing achievements, feeling in the class, impacts of moral education on cultivating them, knowledge achievements, abilities improvements and self-assessments, etc. As for the teachers, they need to assess students performance and reflect the whole teaching process so that they can perfect the teaching contents and teaching methods.

System construction of integrating moral education in college English from both top-level design and teaching practice provide theoretical and practical references for teachers since this system combines universities, teachers and students, thus forming a circle to implement moral education in the whole teaching process.

4 Conclusion

Cultivating students is the radical task of higher education. "What to cultivate, how to cultivate and for whom should universities cultivate" in fact, have a direct influence on students' virtues and professional abilities. With the coordination of the courses in universities and colleges, it won't be a long time before cultivating students with patriotism, social responsibilities, senses of national pride. College English, with plenty students as the audiences, is the "main field" to implement moral education. Meanwhile, to deepen the implementation of moral education in higher education, it is time to construct systemic and scientific curriculum system, combining top-level design from the macro-perspective and teaching practice from the micro-perspective, and involving teachers and students into moral education.

This work was financially supported by the research project "Methodologies and Teaching Practice of Moral Education in College English" from the Program of Education and Planning in Wuhan, Project Number: 2021C167.

References

1. Chen Xuezhen. Teaching Practice of Moral Education in College English from the Perspective of Optimization Theory [J]. China University Teaching, 2019(10):4.
2. Wen Qiufang. A Framework of Integrating Moral Education into College Foreign Language Teaching[J]. Foreign Languages in China. 2021:47-52.
3. Xu Jinfeng. Exploring the Practice and Research of Integrating Ideological and Political Elements into College English Teaching [J]. Journal of University of Shanghai for Science and Technology, 2021:303-308.
4. Mei Qiang. From spots to all aspects——Exploring and Teaching Practice of Moral Education in Two Types of Courses in Higher Education [J]. China University Teaching, 2018(9):4.
5. Cui Ga. Exploring and Teaching Practice of Moral Education [J]. Leading Journal of Ideological and Theoretical Education, 2019(7):3.
6. Yang Jing. Practical Research of Ideological and Political Education in College English Courses [J]. Technology Enhanced Foreign Languages, 2020(4): 6.
7. Liu Zhengguang. Resetting the Educational Philosophy and Restructuring Learning Content to Implement Morality Cultivation in Foreign Language Course Instruction [J]. Journal of Foreign Languages, 2020(21):1.
8. Zhang Jinyuan, Wang Na. Construction of Foreign Language Courses with Ideological-Political Elements: Components, Principles and Methods [J]. Foreign Languages in China, 2020, 17(5):7.
9. Meng Lan. Research on Methods of Moral Education in College English with Blended Learning [J]. Social Scientist, 2020(12):6.
10. Ye Jun, Pan Hua. Research on the Realization of College English Moral Education from the perspective of "Four-Sphere Confidence" [J]. The Party Building and Ideological Education in Schools, 2020(20):3.
11. Mao Herong, Yang Yongping. Value and Pathways of Moral Education in College English [J]. The Party Building and Ideological Education in Schools, 2021(16):3.
12. Liu Jing. An Analysis of EFL Learners' Needs for "Curriculum-Based Political and Virtuous Awareness" Elements in College English in the Context of Liberal Education [J]. Foreign Language Teaching and Research, 2021: 24-29.
13. Huang Guowen. An Analysis of English Teaching Materials from the Ideological-Political Perspective [J]. Foreign Languages in China, 2020, 17(5):9.
14. Xiao Qiong, Huang Guowen. Integration of ideological-political elements in the writing of foreign language teaching materials: With New Era Mingde College English as an example (p.400) [J]. Foreign Language and Literature Studies, 2021: 400-412.

15. Xiang Mingyou. Promoting System Construction of Moral Education in College English——Comments and interpretation of College English Teaching Guidelines [J]. Foreign Language World, 2020(4):7.
16. Yang Hua. Exploring on Moral Education Practice in Foreign Language Teaching——Take "telling China's stories in foreign languages" as an Example [J]. Foreign Language World, 2021(2):8.
17. Chang Haichao. Telling China's Stories Well in College English Courses: Current Situations, Pathways, and Methods [J]. College English Teaching and Research, 2021:96-100.
18. Sun Shuguang. Integrating moral education into a practical course "Telling China's Stories in English" [J]. Foreign Language Education in China, 2021:26-33.
19. Zhang Yufeng, Meng Xiaoping. A Study of College English Teachers' Teaching Ability for Ideological & Political Theories Teaching in All Courses (IPTTIAC)[J]. Theory and Practice of Education, 2021, 41(21):3.
20. Pan Haiying, Yuan Yue. Practical Exploration of Ideological and Political Education in College Foreign Language Courses: Problems and Solutions [J]. Shandong Foreign Language Teaching, 2021: 53-62.
21. Shi Jian. The Connotation Construction of Curriculum-Based Political and Virtuous Awareness under the Concept of "Morality-Strengthening Education" [J]. Technology Enhanced Foreign Languages, 2021:43-45.
22. Cai Jigang. A Study of Ideological and Political Education and Mora l Education in College English [J]. Foreign Languages Research, 2021, 38(3):7.
23. Jiang Zhibin. Cultivating "Multilingual+" Foreign Language Talents: The Connotation, Path and Effect under the Background of All-Course-Based Ideological and Political Education [J]. Technology Enhanced Foreign Languages, 2020(4):5.
24. Xu Jinfeng. Research on ideological-political construction of the English curriculum in Higher Education [J]. Foreign Language World, 2021:18-24.
25. Efron J. S. Seven Worlds of Moral Education[J]. Phi Delta Kappan, 2005, 86(7):525-533.
26. Steutel J W. The virtue approach to moral education: Some conceptual clarifications[J]. Journal of Philosophy of Education, 1997, 31(3): 395-407.
27. Schuitema J, Dam G, Veugelers W. Teaching strategies for moral education: A review[J]. Journal of curriculum studies, 2008, 40(1): 69-89.
28. Noddings N. Moral education in an age of globalization[J]. Educational philosophy and theory, 2010, 42(4): 390-396.
29. Berkowitz M W, Oser F. Moral education: Theory and application[M]. Routledge, 2013.
30. Le Page P, Akar H, Temli Y, et al. Comparing teachers' views on morality and moral education, a comparative study in Turkey and the United States[J]. Teaching and teacher education, 2011, 27(2): 366-375.
31. Yan Wenqing. College English Teaching Guidelines For Moral Education [M]. East China Normal University Press, 2021.

The effects of abusive supervision on cyberloafing behavior

Ye Liu[1,*], and *Wenbing* Wu[2]

[1]Beijing Jiaotong University,School of Economics and Management,100044 No.3 sahngyuan cun ,China
[2]Beijing Jiaotong University,School of Economics and Management,100044 No.3 sahngyuan cun ,China

Abstract. With the development of the Internet, cyberloafing becomes the workplace problem for many organizations. It will negatively influence organisations' productivity and performance. In this study, we examined the direct and indirect relationship (via meaningful work) between abusive supervision and cyberloafing, based on the theory of social cognition and social exchange. Data collected from 183 participants were analysed using hierarchical regression. The results showed that abusive supervision has a significant positive impact on cyberloafing, both directly and indirectly. We suggest that organizations should reduce abusive supervision by leaders and take measures to cultivate employees ' sense of work meaning.
Keywords : abusive supervision, cyberloafing, meaningful work

1 Introduction

According to the report released by the China Internet Network Information Center, as of June 2022, the number of Internet users in China has reached 1.051 billion. The Internet can meet people' s various needs, such as online shopping, communication and online education. Gradually it becomes an indispensable part of daily life. In the era of knowledge economy, Internet technology has flourished and has become an important force to promote China 's economic development. In particular, due to the impact of the epidemic, network office plays an important role in supporting the fight against the COVID-19, resuming work and production and stabilizing employment. It has brought great convenience to enterprises, made information exchange between colleagues more convenient, and improved work efficiency. However, working online also makes employees vulnerable to the temptation of network information, engaging in behaviors unrelated to the task, such as viewing news push and browsing short videos. Scholars refer to the spontaneous use of the company's network by employees to engage in non-work-related private Internet surfing during work as cyberloafing [1]. To achieve personal interests and purposes, employees can engage in cyberloafing while pretending to be working hard, which are hidden, universal and harmful.

This kind of counterproductive behavior may have some positive effects on employees, Wang Shuanglong pointed out that moderate cyberloafing can alleviate employees' job burnout and reduce negative emotions. Other studies have also shown that the supplement

* Corresponding author: 1730812890@qq.com

of personal resources such as self-esteem and self-control ability can be achieved through cyberloafing, which may bring better mental health. However, cyberloafing is viewed as more destructive for the organization in most studies, in which have confirmed that cyberloafing will bring hidden dangers to the information security of the organization [2]; reduce employees' job performance and satisfaction[1] and increase psychological pressure[3]. In addition, some cyberloafing, such as distributing inappropriate remarks and spreading indecent videos, may also make enterprises subject to legal punishment.

Therefore, it is important to study the antecedents of cyberloafing, which can help managers take targeted measures to reduce that. Previous studies have investigated the antecedents through different theoretical perspectives. Wagner based on the self-depletion theory[4], Askew based on the theory of planned behavior[5] and Sheikh.based on the big five personality model[6] found the effects of sleep deprivation, cyberloafing attitude and individual personality characteristics on cyberloafing.

However, some scholars point out that the research on the antecedents of the cyberloafing behavior is still in its infancy stage and needs to be further explored. Therefore, this study aims to explore the influence mechanism of abusive supervision on cyberloafing, from the perspective of social cognitive and social exchange theory. Abusive supervision refers to subordinates perceptions of the extent to which their supervisors engage in the sustained display of hostile verbal and non-verbal behaviors, excluding physical contact[7]. Although some scholars have revealed the relationship between the abusive supervision and cyberloafing, the research on the mediating mechanism is still far from enough. Previous studies have focused on personality characteristics and emotional factors to reveal the indirect relationship. For example, Lim confirmed that abusive supervision is more likely to lead to cyberloafing under the intermediary role of emotional exhaustion when employees ' organizational commitment is low[8]. Research found that the environment will affect cognitive judgment of employees and then affect their behavioral choices. From the cognitive perspective[9], this study introduces the indirect effect of meaningful work, and combines social cognitive theory(SCT) and social exchange theory(SET). We believe that the abusive supervision will cause the reduction of employees' perception of the meaning of work, and block the intrinsic motivation of active work. Therefore employees will take the non-productive behavior of cyberloafing to reduce their efforts to work driven by the psychology of revenge. On this basis, this study proposed that the relationship between abusive supervision and cyberloafing is mediated by meaningful work.

In summary, this study constructed a research model with the meaningful work as mediator, and explored the direct and indirect effect of abusive supervision on cyberloafing from the theoretical viewpoint of SCT and SET. The research model is presented in Fig. 1.

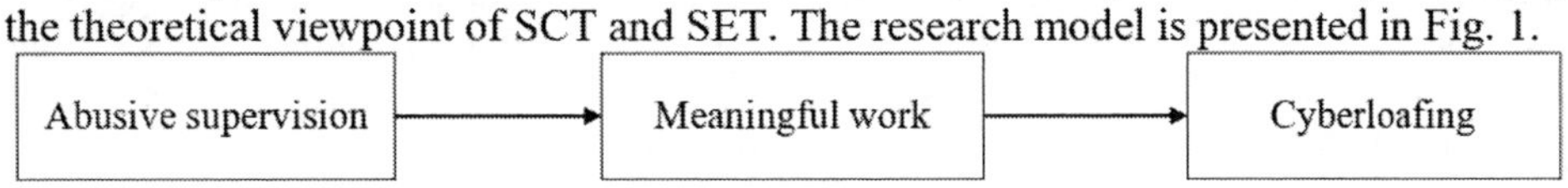

Fig. 1. Research model.

2 Hypothesis development

2.1 Abusive supervision and cyberloafing

Abusive supervision refers to the persistent verbal or nonverbal hostile behaviors that subordinates perceive from their leaders, excluding physical contact. Ignoring subordinates and breaking promises are the most typical behaviors. Many scholars have shown that abusive supervision can cause psychological stress and invite resistance from employees, such as counterproductive behaviors[10] and aggressive behaviors. SET argues that the relationship among colleagues is maintained through a fair exchange of resources based on the principle of reciprocity[11]. The benefits employees perceive they receive from the organization will directly affect their contribution to the organization. Thus, when the organization or supervisor provides the resources that employees need, they will feel obligated to work hard and adopt positive attitudes to repay the organization. On the contrary, when employees are treated unfairly, they tend to achieve psychological balance through retaliatory behaviors, such as generating work slackness and cyberloafing. Cyberloafing is defined as a set of non-work related online activities for personal reasons, particularly through the company's Internet. This study suggested that abusive supervision can lead to work deviant behaviors such as cyberloafing. Abusive supervisiors treat employees improperly, ignoring, denying their abilities or even embarrassing them in front of the public. All of those represented a continuous emotional and psychological hostile treatment, which is highly likely to cause anxiety among employees[12], and reduce organizational commitment. SCT and SET offer a possible explanation to link abusive supervision to cyberloafing. Abusive supervision conveys a hostile information to the subordinates. Reasonably, they will act out of negative reciprocity to retaliate against the supervisor by resorting to confrontational behavior. Nevertheless, influenced by Chinese tradition, employees will not confront them directly to avoid being fired.It is possible for them to adopt behaviors that are not easily perceived to express dissatisfaction[13], such as cyberloafing. Hence, we proposed the following hypothesis.

H1: There is a positive relationship between abusive supervision and cyberloafing.

2.2 The mediating role of meaningful work

Meaningful work is the feeling of individuals' perception of the value and importance of the work they engage in[14], which plays an important role in the formation of intraindividual motivation for work. Social relationship networks formed in work situations can transmit both instrumental and affective resources, which play a pivotal role in influencing employees' interpretation and perception of meaningful work. Due to the requirement to regularly transmit information related to work tasks, a close network of friends is formed between supervisors and employees. Consequently, leaders interact more with their subordinates, having a greater impact on employees' meaningful work. According to SCT, leadership styles will have an impact on subordinates' cognition. This paper believes that abusive leadership will affect subordinates' perception of meaningful work through the following aspects: firstly, abusive leaders will treat subordinates in ridicule, ignorance or even abuse way, lowering employees' self-esteem and ulteriorly hindering the source of meaningful work. Secondly, abusive leaders cannot provide guidance and suggestions about work. Moreover, employees will not be given timely and effective feedback. They will feel that they are losing the support of superiors, that their experience or opinions are unaccepted or even not important at all. They can not be inspired when performing difficult tasks. Gradually, they perceived isolated and their basic psychological demands are not satisfied. All of those seriously affected the perception of the importance of their work. Finally, abusive supervisors may not assign important tasks to their subordinates because they thought they were incompetent. Lacking of authorization, employees had no opportunity to express potential and realize self-development needs, thus reducing the possibility of developing meaningful work. We formulated the following hypothesis.

H2: Abusive supervision is negatively and significantly related to the meaningful work.

Studies have shown that meaningful work has a positive impact on job satisfaction, and prosocial organizational behaviors[15]. Meanwhile, meaningful work plays an important role in inhibiting counterproductive behaviors[16] such as absenteeism, late arrival, early departure and dimission. According to SCT, employees' cognitive factors affect their behaviors. So they tend to believe that the work they do is extremely important for those employees who have high meaningful work. They have a high passion for their work tasks and will seize the opportunity to use their talents to work hard. We believe these employees will not spend much time on cyberloafing[17]. On the contrary, for those employees who have low meaningful work, they do not perceive the value brought by their work.To make up for the lack of emotion, they may resort to counterproductive behaviors that disengage from the organization, such as cyberloafing. So we proposed the following hypothesis.

H3: There is a negative relationship between meaningwork and cyberloafing.

On top of that, this paper further proposed that meaningful work mediates the relationship between them. SCT suggests that leadership style, as a situational factor, can influence employees' perceptions and further change their behaviors. Abusive supervision hampers undermines employees' self-confidence, self-esteem and interest in work. Furthermore, employees with low meaningful work will be reluctant to put more effort into work and take actions to compensate for the lack of cognitive and emotional resources by cyberloafing. So we argued that abusive supervision can reduce meaningful work and thus cut down the occurrence of cybeloafing. Hence, we proposed the following hypothesis.

H4: Meaningful work mediates the relationship between abusive supervision and cyberloafing.

3 Methodology

3.1 Research sample

Data were collected using questionnaire survey. We collected 206 questionnaires by snowballing, like forwarding them through the WeChat group. The invalid questionnaires with short response time and obvious patterns of answers were eliminated. A total of 183 usable data were retained for analysis, with a valid recovery rate of 88.8%.

3.2 Measurement tools

All measures used in this survey were adopted from the established scales, with both good reliability and validity.All items were measured on a five-point Likert scale with employees choosing from "1 - strongly disagree" to "5 - strongly agree".

Abusive supervision. We measured abusive supervision using thirteen items adapted from Tepper. For example: “My supervisor puts me down in front of others ”. The Cronbach’s alpha reliability of the scale in this study was 0.971.

Meaningful work. A nine-items scale was adapted from Steger. For example: “I understand how my work contributes to my life’ s meaning ”. The Cronbach’s alpha reliability of the scale in this study was 0.963.

Cyberloafing. A six-items scale was adapted from Blau to measure cyberloafing. And we refer to the scale adapted to the Chinese situation, which was deleted and tested on the basis of Zhou Enxi 's scale. For example: “ during working hours, I will shop online for personal goods”. The Cronbach’s alpha reliability of the scale in this study was 0.902.

4 Data analysis

In this study, confirmatory factor analysis were conducted with Amos 24.0. And SPSS 25.0 was used to conduct descriptive statistical analysis, correlation analysis, validity and reliability test, common method variance test and research hypothesis test.

4.1 Confirmatory factor analysis

Amos 24 was used to perform confirmatory factor analysis on each variable. The results are shown in table 1. The results showed that revealed that the hypothesized three-factor model has the best fitting degree, which is significantly better than all other models. It revealed that the discriminant validity of the three constructs is satisfying and therefore the variables can be used for the next regression analysis.

Table 1. Confirmatory factor analysis.

model	X^2	df	X^2/df	RMSEA	CFI	TLI
Three-Factor Model	713.49	337	2.117	0.078	0.935	0.927
Two-Factor Model 1	1076.209	341	3.156	0.109	0.872	0.859
Two-Factor Model 2	1483.099	343	4.324	0.135	0.802	0.782
One-Factor Model	1724.884	344	5.014	0.149	0.76	0.737

Note(s):Three-Factor Model: AS,MW,CY; Two-Factor Model 1: AS,MW+CY; Two-Factor Model2:AS+MW,CY; One-Factor Model:AS+MW+CY. + indicates fusion.

4.2 Common method variance

Each employee participating in the study was asked to answer all variables in the same report, which may have common method variance. We used Harman test for principal component analysis. The results showed that the variance explained by the first factor was 33.77%, indicating that there was no serious common method bias problem in this study.

4.3 Descriptive statistics and correlation analysis

In the valid sample, males accounted for 38.8%, others are females. In terms of age group, 18% were below 25, 26.2% were 26-35, 21.3% were 36-45, 30.6% were 46-55, 3.8% were over 55. Those below high school accounted for 5.5%, those in technical secondary school accounted for 14.2%. About 68.3% of them were undergraduate. And graduate and above made up 12%. Working years statistics showed that 11.5% were working for less than one year, 8.2% for 1-3 years, 9.3% for 4-5 years, 13.1% for 6-10 years, 13.1% for 11-20 years, and 44.8% for more than 20 years. The means, standard deviations, and correlation coefficients of each variable are presented in Table 2. The results showed that there was a positive correlation between abusive supervision and cyberloafing ($r=0.609$, $p<0.001$), a negative correlation with meaningful work ($r=-0.619$, $p<0.001$), and a negative correlation between meaningful work and cyberloafing ($r=-0.596$, $p<0.001$).

Table 2. Descriptive statistics and correlation analysis of variables.

variable	M	SD	1	2	3	4	5	6	7
gender	1.610	0.489	1.000						
age	2.760	1.180	-0.125						
edu	3.860	0.720	0.124	-0.396**					
years	4.430	1.792	-0.124	0.844**	-0.319**				
AS	1.627	0.830	-0.061	0.017	-0.063	-0.164*	(0.847)		
MW	4.148	0.820	0.025	0.107	0.049	0.223**	-0.619**	(0.85)	
CY	2.028	0.853	-0.070	-0.053	-0.014	-0.147*	0.609**	-0.590**	(0.789)

Note(s):**p<0.01,*p<0.05, Values on the diagonal represent the square root of the average variance

4.4 Validity and reliability tests

Table 3 shows the results of the reliability and validity tests. The standardized loadings of the items are above 0.6. The average variance extracted values are all greater than 0.5, indicating that each variable has good convergent validity. The square root of AVE is greater than the correlation coefficient of each variable, indicating that the discriminate validity of each variable is good. Furthermore, the composite reliability were above 0.7 and the Cronbach's α was above 0.9, which indicated that each scale has good reliability.

Table 3. Reliability and validity of the main variables.

Variable	Standardized load range	CR	AVE	the square root of AVE	Cronbach's α
AS	0.738-0.911	0.97	0.717	0.847	0.971
MW	0.763-0.932	0.959	0.722	0.850	0.963
CY	0.636-0.94	0.907	0.623	0.789	0.902

4.5 Hypothesis testing

This paper used SPSS25 to test the research hypotheses using hierarchical regression analysis. Table 4 presents the regression relations of variables. As can be seen from Table 4, Model 4 shows that there is a significant positive relationship between abusive supervision and cyberloafing (β=0.629, p<0.001) after controlling for the demographic variables of gender, age, education, and years of work.Thus H 1 was supported.

As shown in Model 2, after controlling for demographic variables, abusive supervision significantly affected employees' meaningful work (β=-0.595, p<0.001), and H 2 was supported. A negative indirect effect of 0.358(β=-0.358, p<0.001) from abusive supervision to cyberloafing was found with meaningful work as mediator in Model 6. The results presented that the effect of abusive supervision on cyberloafing decreased from 0.629 (p<0.001) to 0.415 (p<0.001) The three conditions for the mediating effect to be established were satisfied, suggesting that meaningful work plays a mediating role, and H 4 was supported. Furthermore, as shown in model 5, there was a negative effect between meaningful work and cyberloafing(β=-0.602, p<0.001), and therefore H 3 was supported.

Table 4. Hierarchical regression results of abusive supervision on cyberloafing.

variable	MW		CY			
	1	2	3	4	5	6
gender	0.068	0	-0.145	-0.072	-0.103	-0.072
age	-0.163	0.052	0.165	-0.061	0.067	-0.043
edu	0.11	0.077	-0.033	0.002	0.033	0.03
years	0.209**	0.038	-0.171**	0.009	-0.045	0.023
AS		-0.595***		0.629***		0.415***
MW					-0.602***	-0.358***
R^2	0.082	0.403	0.047	0.377	0.354	0.448
ΔR^2	——	0.32	——	0.33	0.307	0.071
F	3.995	23.878	2.198	21.406	19.383	23.762

Note(s): ***p<0.001, **p<0.01, * p<0. 05

5 Discussions

This study aims to explore the mediating effect of meaningful work between abusive supervision and cyberloafing through SCT and SET. The implementation of abusive supervision will reduce meaningful work by destroying self-esteem and interest in work, thus reducing their efforts to work and triggering cyberloafing.

This study revealed the direct and indirect relationship between abusive supervision and cyberloafing and enriches the literature on the influence of leadership style on meaningful work. Different from most previous studies, this paper introduced the cognitive factor of meaningful work as a mediator to enrich the research on the mediating mechanism of the relationship between them based on the social cognitive theory.

We put forward the following proposals. First, managers should reduce abusive supervision in the management process, give subordinates enough respect and support and build a strong relationship between them. Secondly, the organization should also take various effective measures, such as creating a good team atmosphere, to cultivate the meaningful work. Finally, the organization should censors the management style of candidates in the promotion process to minimize the number of abusive leaders at the top.

This study still has some limitations. First, data was collected by forwarding, so the sample distribution was not uniform, which had a certain impact on the universality of the conclusions. If a larger range of random sampling can be carried out, the results will be more convincing. Second, all the variables in this study are self-reported by employees. Although the results showed that there is no serious common method variance, it still cannot be completely ruled out. Third, this study only explores the mediating effect of abusive supervision on cyberloafing. In future research, we can explore the moderating effect on this process, such as individual personality traits or values.

References

1. V.K.G. Lim, D.J.Q. Chen. BIT, **31**, 343-353 (2012).
2. G.D. Moody, M. Siponen, Inform Manage, **50**, 322-335 (2013).
3. S. Sonnentag, L. Reinecke, J. Mata,et al. Organ Behav, **39**, 369-383 (2018).
4. D.T. Wagner, C.M. Barnes, V.K.G. Lim, D.L. Ferris. JAP, **97**, 1068-1076 (2012).
5. K. Askew, J.E. Buckner, M.U. Taing, A. Ilie, J.A. Bauer, & M.D. Coovert, CHB, **36**, 510-519 (2014).
6. A. Sheikh,A. Aghaz,and M. Mohammadi, Behav Inform Technol, **38** , 1-12 (2019).
7. Tepper, B. J. AMJ, **43**, 178-190 (2000).
8. Lim P K, Koay K Y, Chong W Y., Internet Res (2020).
9. Steger, M.F., Littmanovadia, H., Miller, M., Menger, L., & Rothmann, S.JCA, **21**, 348-361 (2013).
10. Y.M. Low, M. Sambasivan, J.A. Ho, Asia Pac.J. Hum. Resour, **59**, 250-278 (2021).
11. R.Cropanzano, and M. S. Mitchell. JOM, **31**, 874-900 (2005).
12. Li Zhicheng, Wang Zhen, Zhu Zhenbing, Zhan Xiaojun.. JOM, **15**, 358-365 (2018).
13. Yu Ao-Chen, Fan Ming-Lei, Zhao Ran. B&M, (2021).
14. M.F. Steger, B.J. Dik, R.D. Duffy. JCA, **20**, 322-337 (2012).
15. R. Yeoman, JBE, **125**, 235-251 (2014).
16. J.R. Hackman, and G. R. Oldham.Organ Behav Hum Perform, **16**, 250-279 (1976).
17. H. Jia, R. Jia, S. Karau. Leadersh Org Stud, **20**, 358-365 (2013).

The effects of organizational trust climate on creative deviance behavior

Yiran Zhang[1,*], *and Wenbing* Wu[1]

[1]Beijing Jiaotong University, 100044 No.3 Shangyuancun, Beijing, China

Abstract. Based on resource conservation theory, this study investigates the influence mechanism between organizational trust climate and creative deviance behavior, and constructs a model with psychological security as a mediating variable. Through questionnaire research and empirical analysis of 186 employees, the study shows that organizational trust climate positively influences employee creative deviance behavior; psychological security plays a mediating role between organizational trust climate and creative deviance behavior. The study enriches the exploration of the antecedents of creative deviance behavior and verifies the role of organizational trust climate in promoting creative deviance behavior for the first time, which provides certain insights for enterprise management practice.

1 Introduction

In the face of a complex and fast-changing global economic environment, innovation has become one of the most important tools for companies to enhance their core competitiveness and stand in the fierce market competition. However, due to the existence of internal regulations and limited resources, not all innovative ideas proposed by employees can be successfully supported and put into practice by the organization and leaders[1]. In this case, some employees may ignore the veto of their superiors or the organization and secretly continue to implement their innovative ideas through informal means. This practice which has been defined as "Creative Deviance" has received a great deal of academic attention.

The study adopts explicit definition of creative deviance of Mainemelis as "the behavior of employees who persist in innovating against management's orders to stop developing new ideas"[2]. Despite the differences in definitions, scholars generally agree that employees engage in deviant innovation behavior with the ultimate goal of achieving organizational benefits. Studies have shown that organizational factors have a significant impact on the generation of creative deviance behavior[3]. Organizational management processes, innovative, fair, and friendly organizational climate all contribute to the generation of creative deviance behavior among employees[4]. Trust is an indispensable factor for organizational operation, but at present, there is a lack of empirical research on the role of trust atmosphere in China. Also, there is a lack of research that deeply explores the influence mechanism of organizational trust atmosphere on creative deviance behavior. This paper

*Corresponding author: zyr0815@126.com

aims to analyze the influence process of organizational trust climate on creative deviance behavior from the perspective of organizational factors and individual factors acting together. Based on the foundation of previous studies, this study takes the first attempt to analyze the influence mechanism and process of organizational trust climate on employees' creative deviance behavior and introduces psychological security as a mediating variable. This study has two main contributions: Firstly, it explores the influence of organizational trust climate on creative deviance behavior and expands the research on the antecedents of creative deviance behavior. Secondly, it proposes a path to stimulate employees' creative deviance behavior based on psychological security as a mediating variable, which has a certain reference value for corporate practice and employee management.

2 Theory and hypotheses

2.1 Organizational trust climate on creative deviance behavior

The creative deviance behavior has been a hot topic in the field of organizational behavior in recent years. In this study, the creative deviance behavior is more reflective of violation, so the definition of Mainemelis is used which refers to an employee's violation of a managerial order to stop pursuing a new idea. At present, scholars have conducted some research on the antecedent factors and mechanisms of creative deviance. It has been found that three levels of factors, individual, leader, and organization, all have an impact on employees' creative deviance behavior. In terms of the organizational level, which is the focus of this study, established research indicates that structural tensions in organizations is possible to contribute to creative deviance, mainly because of the limited and scarce organizational resources that can hardly support all innovation and thus may motivate employees to conduct creative deviance[2]. From the perspective of the psychological contract, the fair, friendly and innovative atmosphere in the organization will promote the generation of creative deviance behaviors among employees[5]. However, The research on organizational trust climate on creative deviance is still in a vacant state. Although the positive promotion effect of team trust climate on constructive deviance behavior is corroborated through the mediation of positive emotion, creative deviance behavior is essentially an innovative behavior, with innovation as the purpose and deviance as the means, which is still different from the extensive and unfocused nature of constructive deviance behavior[6]. Therefore, this study aims to fill this vacancy and explores the mechanism of how organizational trust climate affects creative deviance behavior.

The concept of organizational trust climate as a sub-dimension of organizational climate was first proposed by Costigan et al., which refers to the cognitive or subjective evaluation of employees' work activities and those behaviors that may be valued and expected in a certain environment[7]. It mainly focuses on portraying a trust evaluation of members within the organization for the overall organizational environment. According to resource conservation theory, individuals with more resources are less susceptible to attacks of resource loss and are more capable of acquiring resources[8]. The organizational trust climate, as a social resource valuable to employees, can generate an increment of own resources and thus promote positive work behaviors[9]. Even though creative deviance behavior may bring the risk of resource loss due to the violation of organizational norms, organizational trust provides employees with a rich enough resource increment, so employees do not need to worry too much about the negative results it brings. Instead, investing their resources into creative deviance behavior may bring greater benefits to the organization. On the other hand, it has been shown that employees' work attitudes and behavioral styles are influenced by organizational trust. Under the basis of trust, it increases the possibility of resource exchange between the two parties, and employees' innovative behaviors are relying on resource sharing[10]. Accordingly, this paper proposes the following hypothesis:

H1: Organizational trust climate is positively associated with creative deviance behavior.

2.2 Organizational trust climate on psychological security

Psychological security is a perception that employees feel safe in their work relationships when they believe that their image, role, and status will be fairly evaluated when they are truly presenting themselves at work[11]. The study focuses on the emotions and behaviors of individual employees and therefore uses the individual-level definition of psychological security, which means employees will have a strong sense of psychological security in the organization when they can demonstrate their true selves without worrying about the negative impact on their image and status in the organization[12]. According to Weiss & Cropanzano, the characteristics of the work environment can trigger certain emotional reactions, which in turn affect the individual's attitude or behavior, forming an "event-emotion-attitude behavior" response chain[13]. As a feature of the organizational environment, organizational trust shows good interpersonal trust with leaders, colleagues, and the organization. This interpersonal trust can make employees feel supported and encouraged, thus giving them a sense of psychological security. According to Kahn, a clear and predictable environment is conducive to the formation of individual psychological security, and a trusting organizational relationship enhances the predictability of the organizational environment and improves employees' psychological security[12]. It has been found that trust and support from the organizational side can enhance employees' perception of organizational safety[14-16]. In summary, this paper proposes the following hypotheses.

H2: Organizational trust climate is positively associated with psychological security.

2.3 The mediating role of psychological security

Psychological security is a psychological state that influences internal motivation of individuals and shapes their behavior. When employees experience more psychological security, they take higher work engagement[12]. Creative deviance behavior, as a kind of work behavior that benefits organizational interests, also tends to occur under a high sense of psychological security. Moreover, individuals who are psychologically insecure value their existing resources and are sensitive to further expenditures of their psychological resources, resulting in less possibility of engaging in bottom-up innovative behaviors beside their roles[4]. In contrast, when psychological security is high, employees are equipped with richer psychological resources. On the one hand, they believe that it is safe to perform such challenging behaviors in the organization, thus putting the creative deviance behaviors into practice[17]. On the other hand, they will actively evaluate their own resource interactions with the organization and tend to increase the investment of their resources, thus promoting creative deviance behaviors as a method of investment, aimed at enhancing the overall benefits of the organization[18-19].

According to previous study, individuals will adjust their attitudes and behaviors based on the safety of the environment, thus responding to and preventing the uncertain events[20]. When the organizational trust atmosphere is strong, employees can feel support from the organization. Under this circumstance, they can feel a stronger sense of psychological security, and will show less resistance to creative deviance behavior with high uncertainty. They are less susceptible to resource loss after accumulating solid psychological resources, so they will make risky investments in an effort to create resource surpluses to maintain and protect these resource utilization opportunities[4]. Even if the behavior goes against the leadership or organizational norms, employees believe that they are willing to proactively defend the interests of the company. When employees engage in creative deviance behaviors that create tangible benefits for the organization, the stock of employee resources increases. Even when creative deviance fails to achieve the desired goal, the strong psychological security due to high organizational trust can reduce the threat of employee resource depletion[21]. In summary, this paper proposes the following hypotheses:

H3: Psychological security mediates the relationship between organizational trust climate and creative deviance behavior

In summary, the research model of this study is shown in Figure 1.

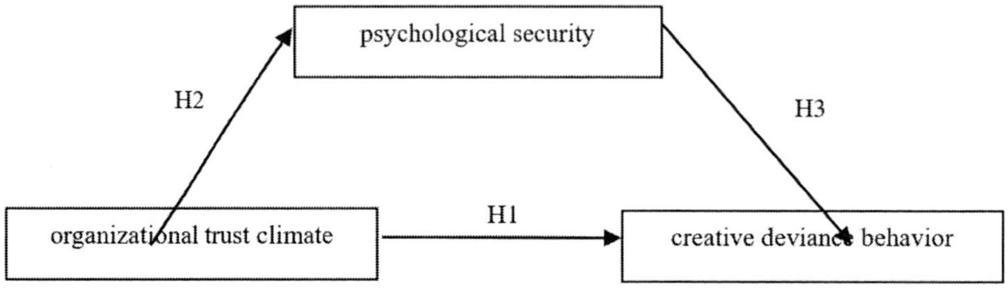

Fig. 1. research model.

3 Methods

3.1 Sample

In this study, the questionnaire was used to conduct the study, and the respondents came from different enterprises in Beijing, Liaoning, Shandong, and Guangdong provinces. A total of 205 questionnaires were distributed to the respondents. After eliminating 19 invalid questionnaires, 186 valid questionnaires were finally collected, with a valid return rate of 90.73%.

3.2 Measures

All items in our questionnaires were rated on a 5-point scale ranging from 1 (strongly disagree strongly) to 5 (strongly agree).

Creative Deviance: Creative deviance behavior is measured by the Chinese scale of Lin et al, consisting of nine items[19]. The scale was developed based on Chinese local contexts, in line with the actual situation of employees in Chinese companies, and is widely used by domestic scholars in their research. It has shown acceptable levels of reliability (α =0.948).

Psychological Security: Psychological Security is measured by the scale developed by Detert & Burris, consisting of three items, such as 'mistakes are tolerated or accepted by the organization[22]. It has shown acceptable levels of reliability (α =0.904).

Organizational trust climate: Organizational trust climate is measured by Liu Shuang's scale, which was modified based on Kuhnert's organizational trust scale[23]. She divided the organizational trust climate into three dimensions measured as trust in the organization, trust in the leader, and trust in colleagues, with a total of 13 question items. It has shown acceptable levels of reliability (α =0.970).

4 Results

4.1 Validation factor analysis

In this study, validated factor analysis was performed by AMOS21.0 and the results are shown in Table 1. The three-factor model fits well ($\chi2/df$=2.663, CFI=0.909, TLI=0.898, RMSEA=0.095), indicating that the measurement model has high convergent validity. Regarding the discriminant validity, it was found that the three-factor model fitted best and the square root of the mean-variance extracted from each latent variable was greater than the correlation coefficient of the variable with other variables, indicating that the measurement tool used in this study had good discriminant validity.

Table 1 Validation factor analysis.

Model	x^2	df	x^2/df	RMSEA	CFI	TLI
3-factor	836.144	314	2.663	0.095	0.909	0.898
2-factor	1327.374	320	4.148	0.13	0.824	0.807
1-factor	2415.024	322	7.5	0.187	0.635	0.602

Note(s): Three-Factor Model: OT, PS, CD; Two-Factor Model: OT, PS+CD; One-Factor Model: OT+PS+CD. + indicates fusion.

4.2 Common method deviation check

The variables used in this study were self-reported by employees. Each employee who participated in the questionnaire study was asked to answer questions measuring all variables in the same questionnaire, which may have the problem of common method bias. Therefore, this study used Harman's one-way test for principal component analysis. The results of the analysis show that the variance explained by the first factor was 35.024%, which is below the critical value of 40%, indicating that there is no serious common method bias problem in this study.

4.3 Descriptive statistics and bivariate correlations

In the valid sample, 38.8% were male, 61.2% were female. 18% were 25 years old or younger, 26.2% were 26-35 years old, 21.3% were 36-45 years old, 30.6% were 46-55 years old, and 3.8% were 55 years old or older. In terms of education level, 1.1% were below junior high school level, 4.4% were high school, junior college or vocational high school, 14.2% were college 14.2%, undergraduate 68.3%, postgraduate and above 12%. In terms of working years, 11.5% worked for less than one year, 8.2% for 1-3 years, 9.3% for 4-5 years, 13.1% for 6-10 years, 13.1% for 11-20 years, and 44.8% for more than 20 years. The means, standard deviations and correlation coefficients of each variable are shown in Table 2. The results showed that there was a positive correlation between organizational trust climate and creative deviance behavior ($r=0.667$, $p<0.001$), a positive correlation with psychological security ($r=0.618$, $p<0.001$), and a positive correlation between psychological security and creative deviance behavior ($r=0.588$, $p<0.001$).

Table 2. Descriptive statistics and bivariate correlations.

variable	M	SD	1	2	3	4	5	6	7
sex	1.59	0.493	1.000						
age	2.88	1.123	-0.058	1.000					

edu	3.83	0.699	0.093	-0.377*	1.000				
work years	4.62	1.641	-0.040	0.814*	-0.274	1.000			
OT	4.430	0.450	0.018	0.032	0.078	0.017	1.000		
CD	4.285	0.369	-0.004	0.089	-0.039	0.075	0.667*	1.000	
PS	3.725	0.971	0.014	0.024	-0.014	0.014	0.618*	0.588*	1.000

Note(s): **p<0.01, * p<0. 05

4.4 Hypotheses testing

This paper used SPSS 25.0 to test the research hypotheses using cascade regression analysis of main and mediating effects, and the results of the study are shown in Table 4. Hypothesis 1 proposes a direct relationship between organizational trust climate and employees' creative deviance behavior. As shown in the model 4, after controlling for the demographic variables of gender, age, education, and years of experience, there was a positive association between organizational trust climate and creative deviance behavior (β=0.499, $p<0.001$), and hypothesis 1 was supported. In model 2, after controlling demographic variables, organizational trust climate significantly and positively affects employee psychological security (β=0.625, $p<0.001$), and hypothesis 2 is supported. Model 5 added the mediating variable psychological security to model 4, and the results show that the effect of organizational trust climate on creative deviance behavior decreased from 0.673 ($p<0.001$) to 0.499 ($p<0.001$), which means psychological security plays a partial mediating role in the relationship between organizational trust climate and creative deviance behavior, and hypothesis 3 was supported.

Table 3. Results of regression analyses.

Variables	PS=psychological security		CD = Creative Deviance		
	Model 1	**Model 2**	**Model 3**	**Model 4**	**Model 5**
Control variables					
sex	0.033	0.017	0.002	-0.005	-0.007
age	0.028	-0.028	0.026	0.003	0.006
edu	-0.010	-0.101	-0.004	-0.041	-0.030
years	-0.008	0.006	0.002	0.008	0.007
Independent variable					
OT		0.625***		0.673***	0.499***
Mediating variable					
PS					0.279
R^2	0.001	0.387	0.008	0.455	0.503
ΔR^2	-0.021	0.370	-0.014	0.440	0.486
F	0.042	22.718***	0.365	30.112***	30.199***
ΔF		113.32***		147.92***	17.136***

Note(s): ***p<0.001, **p<0.01, * p<0. 05

5 Discussion

This study constructs a model between organizational trust climate and employee creative deviance behavior with the mediating effect of psychological security. By distributing questionnaires to employees in enterprises and empirically analyzing, the study obtains the following conclusions: (1) Organizational trust climate positively affects employees' creative deviance behavior. (2) Organizational trust climate positively affects employee psychological security. (3) Psychological security plays a partial mediating role between organizational trust climate and employees' creative deviance behavior. In terms of the contributions of the study, on the one hand, this study expands the research on the antecedents of creative deviance behavior, and for the first time, it takes organizational trust climate as an antecedent variable affecting creative deviance behavior, constructing an action mechanism with psychological security as a mediating variable and verifying the positive influence of organizational trust climate on creative deviance behavior through empirical support. On the other hand, at the level of management practice, managers should pay attention to creating an internal trust atmosphere and focus on enhancing employees' psychological security from multiple perspectives, so as to stimulate more constructively creative deviance behaviors and thus improve the overall organizational benefits.

In terms of the limitations of the study, firstly, this paper explores the role played by psychological security as a mediating variable and suggests a solution idea to the generation of creative deviance behaviors, but there may be other mediating effects or chain mediators in this mechanism. Multiple potential mediating variables should be further explored to reveal the inner mechanism connecting the relationship. Second, moderating variables are not included in this model, so the boundary conditions of the mechanism can be further explored in the future.

References

1. Liu, X., Baranchenko, Y., An, F., Lin, Z., & Ma, J., Leadership. Org. Dev. J, 42(2), **219-232** (2020).
2. C. Mainemelis, Acad. Manage. Rev, 35, **558–578** (2010).
3. P. Criscuolo, A. Salter, T. Wal, & A. L. J. Organ. Sci, 25(5), **1287-1305** (2014).
4. W. Shijian, D. Mengzhen, Z. Zhongbao, Sci. Tech. Prog. Policy, 37(17):**142-151** (2020).
5. D. P. McCauley, K. W. Kuhnert, Public. Admin, 16(2): **265-283**(1992).
6. Cui et al., Collected Essays on Finance and Economics, 11:**83-92**(2020).
7. R. D. Costigan, S. S. Iiter, J. J. Berman, J. Manage. Issues, 10(3) : **303—317**(1998).
8. S. E. Hobfoll, Appl. Psychol, 50(3), **337-421**(2001)..
9. L. Shuang, Science Research Management, 40(03):**188-196**(2019).
10. S. Tingting, Nanjing Tech University(2017).
11. Y. Guang & Z. Yi, Human Resources Development of China, 38(06):**97-109**(2021).
12. W A. Kahn, Acad. Manage. J, 33(4): **692-724**(1990).
13. H. M. Weiss, & R. Cropanzano, Research in organizational behavior: An annual series of analytical essays and critical reviews,Vol. 18, pp. **1–74**(1996)..
14. S. D. Salamon, & S. L. Robinson, J. Appl. Psychol, 93(3), **593–601** (2008).
15. X. Liu, Y. Baranchenko, F. An, Z. Lin, & J. Ma, Leadership. Org. Dev, 42(2), **219-232**(2020).
16. J. K. Rempel, J. G. Holmes, & P. Z. Mark, J. Pers. Soc. Psychol, 49(1): **95-112**(1985).
17. H S. Hogdins, E. Liebeskind, J. Exp. Soc. Psychol, 39(4): **297-316**(2003).
18. Jia & Liu, J. Manage. Sci, 34(02): **69-80**(2021).
19. B. Lin, C. Mainemelis, & R. Kark, Leadership. Quart, 27(4), **537-556**(2016).
20. K. Van den Bos, J. Van Ameijde, H. Van Gorp, Basic. Appl. Soc. Psych, 28: **333–**

341(2006)
21. A. V. Appu, &S. K. Sia, Int. J. Hum. Resour. Man, 17(3-4), **205-219**(2017).
22. J. R. Detert, & E. R. Burris, Acad. Manage. J, 50(4), **869-884** (2017).
23. K W.A. Kuhnert, Public. Admin. Quart, 16(2): **265-284**(1992).

Research on the emergence mechanism of shared leadership: The mediating role of self-efficacy

Yiqing Jiang*

School of Economics and Management, Beijing Jiaotong University, Beijing, China 100044

Abstract. Current academic research on shared leadership has focused on the impact of shared leadership, with relatively little research on its causes and operational mechanisms. To fill this gap, this paper identifies, analyzes, and tests the emergent mechanisms of shared leadership. Firstly, by defining the concept, I constructed a theoretical model of the study based on theories such as social exchange. Secondly, I used SPSS 25.0 and AMOS 24.0 software to analyze the 227 valid questionnaires collected. The results show that team member exchange has a significant positive impact on the emergence of shared leadership, and self-efficacy plays a positive mediating role.

1 Introduction

Much of the research on leadership has focused on individual leadership, with less research on team members participating together and sharing leadership behaviors [1]. However, with the increased complexity, variability, and unpredictability of the environment faced by organizations, it is no longer realistic for a single leader to successfully perform the leadership functions required by the team [2]. At the same time, with the advent of the era of knowledge integration and innovation, the complexity and responsibility of team tasks have increased, organizational structures have flattened, and virtualized, self-managed teams have become important work units, which makes the traditional top-down, strictly controlled leadership approach unable to meet the management needs of teams with specialized expertise and self-management capabilities [3]. Accordingly, it is crucial to explore the antecedents of shared leadership in the context of organizational environment variability and increased task complexity [4]. In contrast, most of the current research on shared leadership has focused on the impact it brings, including studies on team performance [1,5-7], and employee behavior [8-10]. There are relatively few studies, especially empirical ones, on the causes and operational mechanisms of shared leadership [11-13]. Therefore, in this paper, i will identify, analyze, and test the emergent mechanisms of shared leadership based on an empirical research approach to dissect the mediating mechanisms of the impact of team member exchange on the emergence of shared leadership.

* Corresponding author: yqjiang98@163.com

Shared leadership focuses on the operation of interpersonal influence among team members, including the ability to participate in constructive horizontal influence, give and receive feedback. Its purpose is to better achieve team goals through mutual leadership among team members. Team member exchange is a horizontal exchange relationship within an organization, representing the quality of relationships between individuals in the team and other members of the team, representing individual perceptions of team member information and resource sharing, mutual assistance [14], and the degree of recognition of team member roles. Therefore, the emergence of shared leadership is inseparable from the exchange of team members. In addition, according to social exchange theory, high-quality team member exchange brings psychological support such as trust and help among team members [15] and recognition of peers' abilities and roles [16], which can enhance employees' self-efficacy.

In summary, this paper intends to explore in depth the mechanisms underlying the emergence of shared leadership from the perspective of social exchange theory, in conjunction with the effects of team member exchange on self-efficacy. It will enrich the existing research on shared leadership and provide a theoretical basis and practical guidance for the implementation of shared leadership as a more flexible and effective model in enterprises.

2 Theory and hypothesis

2.1 Shared leadership and team member exchange

Since the 1990s, scholars at home and abroad have carried out research on shared leadership, but the definition of shared leadership has not been agreed [17]. Their definition of shared leadership is mainly divided into macro and micro levels. First, the macro level focuses shared leadership on the team as a whole, describing shared leadership as a process. Carson et al. (2007) [18] defined shared leadership as a spontaneous team attribute in which leadership functions are assigned to team members rather than focusing on a designated leader. Secondly, at the micro level, shared leadership is described as a relational phenomenon, involving the interaction and leadership of team members in their efforts towards team goals [19]. Leadership functions are voluntarily shared among members of the team [11]. Therefore, this paper argues that shared leadership is a dynamic and interactive process among team members. Leadership responsibilities are widely distributed among team members rather than concentrated in the hands of a leader. The goal is that team members lead each other and achieve team or organizational goals. It has the characteristics of responsibility sharing, equality, multi-center, collaboration, and dynamics.

In order to describe the relationship quality between individuals and other members of the team, Seers (1989) proposed the concept of Team Member Exchange (TMX) based on role theory and social exchange theory [20]. It is defined as individual members' perceptions of the overall exchange relationship between themselves and other team members. It is used to measure the reciprocal relationship formed in the process of team member exchange, that is, the willingness of individual members to assist colleagues, share opinions and feedback, and accept opinions, obtain help and recognition from colleagues [20]. Team member exchange differs from vertical leader-member exchange in that it is a horizontal exchange relationship within the organization that represents the quality of the relationship between individuals in the team and other members within the team, and represents the individual's perceived sharing of information and resources and mutual help among team members [14]. Furthermore, team member exchange can be used as both a group-level variable and an individual-level variable, depending entirely on the individual's research perspective [21]. Team member exchange in this paper is an individual-level variable.

The impact of team member exchange on shared leadership. First of all, according to the view of social exchange theory, high-quality team member exchange makes employees feel good interaction in the team [15]. Good interaction will make team members more willing to show feedback behavior that is beneficial to the team to express their attention to high-quality relationships in the team. They are willing to contribute their strength to achieve team goals [22]. Therefore, when there are situations that are beneficial to team development or that may affect team interests, employees are more willing to share ideas with others and actively participate in team decisions, making it easier for shared leadership to occur in team work. Secondly, team member exchange can reflect the degree of recognition of the ability and role of team members [23], and team members' recognition of each other's ability is also a necessary condition for individuals to try to accept peer influence [4]. Based on the above discussion, hypothesis 1 is proposed :

H1 : Team member exchange will positively affect the emergence of shared leadership.

2.2 The mediating role of self-efficacy

Team member exchange measures the quality of relationships between individuals in the team [24]. A high-quality team member exchange promotes collaboration, support, and trust among team members [15, 20], and generates a sense of obligation and reward, which is conducive to enhancing emotional support among members [25], which in turn will make individuals more confident in their work and dare to challenge it even when it is difficult. Secondly, high-quality team member exchange will enable individuals to gain the affirmation and trust of other team members in their work [26], which will also enhance individual leadership self-efficacy. Finally, information processing theory holds that the relevant information obtained by individuals from the organizational environment affects their perception of self-ability. Therefore, a series of behavioral, cognitive and social rewards generated by high-quality team member exchange are likely to lead to greater self-efficacy. Liao et al. (2010) confirmed the positive effect of high-quality team member exchange on self-efficacy [27]. Xue (2020) also confirmed that high-quality team member exchanges would enhance employees' recognition of their own abilities through reciprocal exchanges [28].

Self-efficacy refers to an individual's belief in his or her ability to achieve expected results in life (such as achieving goals and changing events that have an impact on life), and is one of the important determinants of human behavior [29]. Therefore, high self-efficacy will make team members confident that they have the necessary skills to participate in the common leadership work, and actively participate in decision-making, support, and encourage other team members. At the same time, self-efficacy is based on specific situations or relatively specific behaviors in situations, and individuals may have high self-efficacy for some tasks and low self-efficacy for others [4]. Therefore, according to the imitation and learning behaviors of team members, in a team with high-quality exchange, when individuals perform leadership behaviors and gain recognition from other members by assuming leadership roles, they will also stimulate the self-efficacy of other team members, take the initiative to assume corresponding responsibilities in the part they are good at, and show leadership behaviors. This dynamic and mutually influencing process promotes the emergence of shared leadership.

In short, high-quality team member exchange will make team members trust and support each other, and recognize the role and work effect of team members, so that individuals have confidence in their own ability, are willing to and believe that they are competent for the leadership role, actively participate in decision-making at work, and put forward suggestions that are conducive to the realization of team goals. Based on the above discussion, the following hypotheses are proposed:

H2: Team member exchange has a positive impact on self-efficacy.

H3: Self-efficacy has a positive impact on the emergence of shared leadership.

H4: Self-efficacy plays a mediating role in team member exchange and the emergence of shared leadership.

Combined with the above analysis, this study constructs a theoretical model as shown in Figure 1.

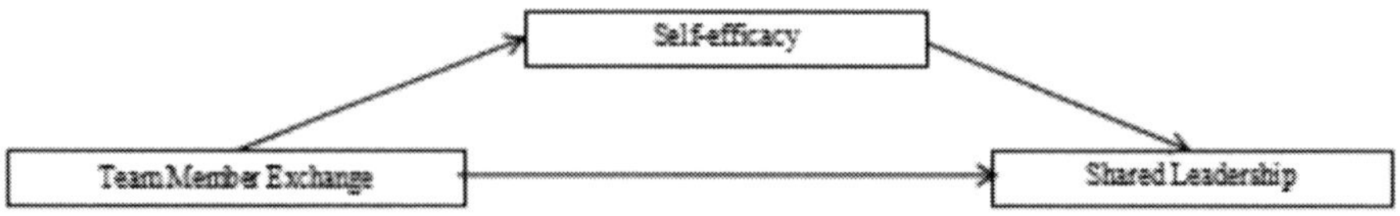

Fig. 1. Theoretical model.

3 Method

3.1 Sample

An online questionnaire survey was used to collect data from enterprises in Beijing from September to October 2022. A total of 260 questionnaires were collected, and 227 valid samples were obtained after eliminating invalid questionnaires with incomplete and regular answers. The effective recovery rate was 87.31 %. In order to ensure the generalization of the research conclusions, the samples selected in this study cover many industries, such as the IT industry, manufacturing industry, energy, and finance.

Of the valid samples, 48.5 % were male and 51.5 % were female ; 25 years old and below accounted for 14.1 %, 26-35 years old accounted for 51.1 %, 36-45 years old accounted for 31.7 %, over 45 years old accounted for 3.1 %. The education level of secondary school and below accounted for 3.1 %, college accounted for 10.1 %, undergraduate accounted for 34.4 %, master and above accounted for 52.4 % ; among the working years, less than 1 year accounted for 8.8 %, 1-3 years accounted for 11.9 %, 4-5 years accounted for 10.1 %, 6-10 years accounted for 23.3 %, and more than 10 years accounted for 45.8 %. Team size, 1-5 people accounted for 16.7 %, 6-10 people accounted for 18.5 %, 11-20 people accounted for 20.7 %, more than 20 people accounted for 44.1 %. Overall, the respondents are mainly 26-35 years old, highly educated, high work experience. These people pay more attention to work autonomy and have a certain understanding of the behavior of shared leadership. Therefore, the obtained data fit the research content and purpose of this paper.

3.2 Variable measurement

The main variables of this study include shared leadership, team member exchange and self-efficacy. All scales used the Likert-5 point scoring method, and the scores from 1 to 5 were " very disagree " to " very agree ". As the content of this study are individual level, therefore, the use of employee self-assessment.

Shared Leadership (SL) uses the shared leadership scale developed by Muethel et al. (2012) [30], with a total of 7 items. Combined with the statistical results of this paper, " I will seek other members for their own work performance information " was deleted, and the final Cronbach 's α coefficient was 0.859.

Team member exchange (TMX) adopts the team member exchange scale developed by Seers et al. (1995) [15], with a total of 10 items. Combined with the statistical results of this paper, " I often recommend better working methods to other members of the team " was deleted, and the final Cronbach 's α coefficient was 0.884.

Self-efficacy (SE) was developed by Chen et al. (2001) [31], a total of 8 items. Combined with the statistical results of this paper, " I can perform well even if I encounter difficulties " was deleted, and the final Cronbach 's α coefficient was 0.875.

Control variables. First, basic demographic variables may have some effect on the results. Second, previous studies have found that team size and work experience have an impact on shared leadership [32]. Therefore, the control variables of this paper are gender, age, education level, working years and team size.

4 Data analysis and results

4.1 Common method bias and discriminant validity test

This paper adopts the method of employee self-evaluation, so there may be common method bias. To ensure reliability, Harman single factor test was performed using SPSS 25.0. The analysis results show that the variance interpretation of the first factor is 20.432 %, which is lower than the empirical judgment standard value of 40%, indicating that the common method deviation problem is not serious.

Secondly, through AMOS24.0, the confirmatory factor analysis of shared leadership, team member exchange and self-efficacy was carried out to test the discriminant validity of each variable. The results are shown in table 1. The fitting indexes of the three-factor model were the best and all in the acceptable range, indicating that there was a good discriminant validity between the variables in this study.

Table 1. Confirmatory factor analysis.

Models	**$\chi 2$**	**df**	**$\chi 2$/df**	**RMSEA**	**CFI**	**TLI**
three-factor model(TMX, SE, SL)	422.466	204	2.071	0.069	0.914	0.903
two-factor model(SE+SL, TMX)	516.484	207	2.495	0.081	0.879	0.865
two-factor model(SE+TMX, SL)	561.52	207	2.713	0.087	0.861	0.845
one-factor model(SL+SE+TMX)	669.923	209	3.025	0.099	0.819	0.800

Note : + means that two variables are combined into one variable , TMX : Team Member Exchange , SE : Self-efficacy , SL : Shared Leadership.

4.2 Descriptive statistics and correlation analysis

The mean, standard deviation and correlation coefficient of each variable are shown in Table 2. Team member exchange is significantly positively correlated with shared leadership ($r = 0.702$, $p < 0.01$) and self-efficacy ($r = 0.688$, $p < 0.01$). Self-efficacy was positively correlated with shared leadership ($r = 0.72$, $p < 0.01$). Therefore, H1, H2 and H3 are preliminarily verified.

Table 2. Descriptive statistics and correlation analysis.

Variable	M	SD	SEX	AGE	EDU	YEAR	SCALE	TMX	SE	SL
SEX	1.52	0.501	1							
AGE	2.24	0.726	-0.022	1						
EDU	3.36	0.788	-0.014	0.143*	1					
YEAR	3.85	1.347	0.007	0.791**	0.212**	1				
SCALE	2.92	1.138	-0.044	0.103	-0.205**	0.044	1			
TMX	3.8223	0.69352	-0.023	-0.042	-0.075	-0.044	0.118	1		
SE	3.9742	0.65034	-0.004	0.001	0.07	0.041	0.132*	0.688**	1	
SL	3.9398	0.70662	-0.077	0.004	0.079	0.033	0.089	0.702**	0.72**	1

Note: Significance (bilateral): ** $p < 0.01$, * $p < 0.05$. M : mean , SD : Standard Deviation , TMX : Team Member Exchange , SE : Self-efficacy , SL : Shared Leadership.

4.3 Hypothesis testing

The SPSS25.0 software was used to test the hypotheses by hierarchical regression. The results are shown in Table 3. H1 demonstrated that team member exchange has a significant positive impact on the emergence of shared leadership ($\beta = 0.721 > 0$, $p < 0.001$), according to M4. Secondly, step-by-step regression analysis is performed on the variables, and the mediating effect is tested by observing the changes in the regression results of the independent variables after adding the mediating variables. H2 demonstrated that team member exchange has a significant positive impact on self-efficacy ($\beta = 0.646 > 0$, $p < 0.001$), according to M2. M6 On the basis of M4, after adding the mediating variable self-efficacy, the impact of team member exchange on shared leadership decreases from 0.721 to 0.418, and self-efficacy has a significant positive impact on the emergence of shared leadership($\beta = 0.469 > 0$, $p < 0.001$). To sum up, the three conditions for the mediating effect are met, so H4 is proved. In order to further detect the mediating effect, bootstrapping was used to set the sample size to 5000, and the confidence interval was 95 %. The test results are shown in Table 4. The indirect effect of team member exchange on shared leadership is [0.1852, 0.4336] at the 95 % confidence interval, which does not include 0, indicating that the mediating effect of self-efficacy is significant and H4 is supported again.

Table 3. Regression analysis of mediating effect.

Variable	SE		SL			
	M1	M2	M3	M4	M5	M6
SEX	0.002	0.019	-0.102	-0.083	-0.104	-0.092
AGE	-0.095	-0.068	-0.076	-0.046	-0.002	-0.014
EDU	0.080	0.105*	0.087	0.115*	0.025	0.066
YEAR	0.047	0.049	0.036	0.038	0.000	0.015
SCALE	0.091*	0.046	0.069	0.019	-0.002	-0.002
TMX		0.646***		0.721***		0.418***
SE					0.780***	0.469***
R^2	0.032	0.498	0.025	0.517	0.525	0.610

ΔR^2	——	0.466	——	0.492	0.499	0.093
F	1.447	36.335	1.139	39.227	40.446	49.002

Note: Significance (bilateral): *** $p < 0.001$, * $p < 0.05$, TMX : Team Member Exchange , SE : Self-efficacy , SL : Shared Leadership.

Table 4. Bootstrap mediating effect test.

Response relationship	Models	Effect	Boot SE	Boot LLC	Boot ULC
Direct effect	X→Y	0.4185***	0.0784	0.2528	0.5589
Indirect effect	X→M→Y	0.3029***	0.0643	0.1852	0.4336

Note: Significance (bilateral): *** $p < 0.001$, X : Team Member Exchange , Y:Shared Leadership , M : Self-efficacy , Boot SE : standard error , Boot LLCI : Lower limit of 95 % confidence interval , Boot ULCI : 95 % confidence interval upper limit.

5 Discussion

Based on the process performance of shared leadership, this paper confirms that team member exchange has a positive impact on the emergence of shared leadership and self-efficacy plays a positive mediating role in the impact of team member exchange on the emergence of shared leadership.

5.1 Theoretical implications

First of all, although the current academic research on shared leadership is gradually carried out, there are relatively few studies on the antecedents, formation and development of shared leadership, especially empirical tests. Based on social exchange theory, this paper incorporates team member exchange, self-efficacy and shared leadership into the research framework and confirms the framework. Secondly, most of the current research on the emergence of shared leadership is based on individual personality traits [11,32]. This paper studies leadership from the perspective of interpersonal perception, which provides a new perspective for the emergence of shared leadership. Finally, the data analysis results show that there is a certain correlation between self-efficacy and team size. In the future research on self-efficacy, team size can be used as a moderating variable for further research.

5.2 Practical significance

The research in this paper provides ideas for the transformation of enterprises from traditional vertical leadership mode to shared leadership mode and sustainable and healthy operation. First, team member exchange will positively influence the emergence of shared leadership. Therefore, formal leadership should create a friendly atmosphere for the team, encourage and support team members to form common goals and commitments, and promote information exchange, feedback and member reciprocity among team members. Second, the mediating role of self-efficacy. Leaders should pay attention to the cultivation of employees' sense of self-efficacy, and give timely recognition for the work achievements and roles of members. Third, give full play to the role of leaders as coaches, and establish a sound training and development system for shared leadership development. For example, how to train team members to be responsible and constructive leaders ; train basic leadership skills such as setting goals, reporting team status, etc.

5.3 Research limitations and future prospects

Although this study has certain theoretical and practical significance, there are still some shortcomings to be improved. First of all, from the data point of view, the data of this paper comes from the self-assessment of employees. Although it has been verified that the homology bias problem is not serious, it will also have an impact on the accuracy and external validity of the causal relationship inference in this paper. Therefore, future research can be supplemented by situational experiments and other methods. Secondly, from the research level, this paper focuses on the individual level. Future research can combine the two levels of individual and team to conduct cross-level research to further explore the impact of individuals on groups, and then the impact on the emergence of shared leadership. Finally, from the model point of view, this paper is a mediation model. In the future, collectivism or power distance in the Chinese context can be introduced into the model as a moderating variable to further clarify the research boundary.

References

1. X. Liu, Z. Liu, Soft Science, **33**, 114-118 + 140 (2019).
2. X. Sun et al. Front Psychol, **7**, 1964 (2016).
3. F. Chai, B. Cheng, Enterprise Economy, 28-32 (2015).
4. M. Bligh, C. Pearce, J. Kohles, J Manage Psychol, **21**, 296-318 (2006).
5. X. Cao, S. Wang, N. Yao, Finance and Accounting Monthly, 147-154 (2022).
6. L. Wang, X. Niu, G. Shi, Science & Technology Progress and Policy, **34**, 141-146 (2017).
7. L. D'Innocenzo, J. Mathieu, J Manage, **42**, 1964-1991 (2016).
8. H. Wang, Q. Peng, The Theory and Practice of Finance and Economics, **41**,138-144 (2020).
9. P. Hao, L. Long, Journal of Industrial Engineering and Engineering Management, **34**, 11-20 (2020).
10. P. Yuan, X. Dong, H. Zhai, Q. Feng, Soft Science, **32**, 87-91 (2018).
11. H. Liu, S. Gao, L. Xu, Finance and Accounting Monthly, 121-127 (2021).
12. S. Gao, H. Liu, Y. Zhang, L. Xu, Modernization of Management, **37**, 113-116 (2017).
13. P.Hao, L. Long, Management Review, **29**, 87-101 (2017).
14. F. Steven , V. Linn, K. Dishan, J Appl Psychol, **100**, 583-595 (2015).
15. A. Seers, Group Organ Manage, **20**, 18-38 (1995).
16. H. Tse, Group Organ Manage, **33**, 194-215 (2008).
17. C. Chiu, B. Owens, P. Tesluk, J Appl Psychol, **101**, 1705-1720 (2016).
18. J. Carson, P. Tesluk, J. Marrone, Acad Manage J, **50**, 1217-1234 (2007).
19. A. Mehra, B. Smith, A. Dixon, B. Robertson, Leadership Quart, **17**, 232-245 (2006).
20. A. Seers, Organ Behav Hum Dec, **43**, 118-135 (1989).
21. K. Yin, J. Sun, K. Zhang, L. Chen, Management Review, **30**, 132-141 (2018).
22. Y. Zhu, Y. Jin, Y. Ye, Science Research Management, **37**, 114-121 (2016).
23. K. Dishan, V. Linn, J Appl Psychol, **92**, 1286-1298 (2007).
24. H. Jin, P. Diao, C. Yang, Journal of Jiangsu University(Social Science Edition), **24**, 103-113 (2022).

25. U. Baek, H. Olya, S. Lee, Serv Ind J, **38**, 584-606 (2018).
26. W. Zou, J. Liu, Advances in Psychological Science, **19**, 1193-1204 (2011).
27. H. Liao, D. Liu, R. LOI. Acad Manage J, **53**, 1090-1109 (2010).
28. H. Xue, Enterprise Economy, 77-83 (2020).
29. Z. Wan, *Psychological advantage affects life satisfaction : the role of self-efficacy and coping style* (2022).
30. M. Muethel, S. Gehrlein, M. Hoegl, Hum Resour Manage-Us, **51**, 525-548 (2012).
31. G. Chen, Organ Res Methods, **4**, 62-83 (2001).
32. J. Hoch, J. Dulebohn, Hum Resour Manage R, **27**,678-693 (2016).

SHS Web of Conferences **166**, 01010 (2023) https://doi.org/10.1051/shsconf/202316601010
EIMM 2022

On the creative teaching in primary school music classroom

Mengyuan Xue, and *Yingying* Xian*

School of Music, Bohai University, Jinzhou, China

Abstract. Music creative teaching has a positive influence on developing students 'consciousness of music creation, students' creative thinking and cultivating innovative practice ability. This paper focuses on the connotation and significance of primary school music creation teaching, analyzes the factors affecting the creation of teaching in primary school classroom, and puts forward suggestions for teaching implementation. It aims to develop students' creative potential and enhance their creativity, hoping to provide a new perspective for relevant research fields and contribute to the cultivation of innovative talents in the new era of the 21st century.

1 Connotation and meaning of creative teaching

1.1 Connotation of creative teaching

Creative teaching refers to the teaching that cultivates students' creativity and develops creativity in the process of imparting knowledge and developing intelligence. Music creation teaching belongs to the category of creative teaching, which is a teaching practice activity that takes cultivating students' creative ability and innovative spirit as the main purpose, and permeates in all fields and links of music teaching.

China Compulsory Education Art Curriculum Standard (2022 edition) clearly stipulates the specific learning content of "creation", which mainly includes three aspects: sound and music exploration, improvisation and music compilation.

1.2 Meaning of creative teaching

Music is a unique and creative subject. Creative teaching in the music classroom is conducive to the development of students' creative thinking, stimulating students' association and imagination ability, and also has a positive impact on cultivating students' observation ability, thinking ability and performance ability.

China's 14th Five-Year Plan and the 2035 Vision Outline have laid out a series of national strategies for strengthening the country. In general, it is necessary to train a large number of top scientific and technological talents and high-quality innovative talents to achieve the goal of strengthening the country. The training of innovative talents should start

*Corresponding author: xianyingying1980@126.com

from the children, and attach importance to the cultivation of scientific spirit, innovative ability and critical thinking. Therefore, music creative teaching is the need of cultivating all-round development talents and the need of national construction and development.

2 Factors that affect the creative teaching in the primary school classroom

2.1 School culture construction and the introduction of teaching resources

Campus culture has the creativity and charisma, which can stimulate the subject consciousness of all teachers, students and staff, mobilize their enthusiasm, initiative and creativity, and promote the common development of individuals and the school. Whether the school attaches great importance to the cultivation of students' creative ability, and whether it often organizes activities conducive to stimulating students' creative thinking ability, all determine the development of primary school music creative teaching. In addition, the teaching resources of schools are also important factors affecting the teaching of music creation. If the school does not pay attention to the introduction of advanced teaching equipment and does not introduce the instruments essential for creative teaching, it is difficult for music creative teaching to go on smoothly.

2.2 Old teaching methods of teachers

Relevant investigations and studies show that, many primary school music teachers 'teaching awareness of music creation has been greatly improved. Most teachers believe that it is very important to cultivate creativity and improve students' creative thinking for the development of students. However, in the actual music classroom teaching, there are still some teachers who think that music creative teaching is a time-consuming and slow work, resulting in teachers will not invest a lot of energy in creating teaching. In addition, due to the deep-rooted traditional teaching concept, most of the domestic primary school music classroom teaching method is single, still using the traditional teaching method. Music classroom atmosphere is relatively stiff, the old teaching method is not conducive to the development of students' creative thinking.

3 The implementation strategy of creative teaching in Primary school music classroom

3.1 Create a relaxed classroom atmosphere to stimulate students' interest in creation

A relaxed, democratic and equal classroom atmosphere is very important for students' learning, especially in the teaching of music creation. In the process of music teaching, teachers should try to create a relaxed and happy classroom atmosphere for students, enable students to learn through fun and play. For example, when taking students to explore the "voice in life", teachers use the common paper around them, through rubbing, tearing the paper and other different actions to make the paper make a different sound. Then asked: " What other way or action can make the paper produce more different sounds? Please have a try!"Through the intuitive display, make the students realize the diversity of voices. With a strong curiosity, the students were actively thinking and trying, to show and share their learning results, so as to gain satisfaction and a sense of achievement.

3.2 Respect the students as the main body of creation to give full play to the students' subjective initiative

Teachers are the organizers and implementers of educational activities, and they are the instructors and leaders of learners' learning, the students are the main body of classroom teaching. In music teaching, teachers should change "teaching" into "guidance", fully respect and trust students, and try not to interfere with students' creative process as much as possible, so that students truly become the master of learning. For example, in the teaching section of "lyrics creation", students are invited to create simple lyrics in groups, tell a simple story, and emphasize that the lyrics should rhyme. Teachers don't have to interfere too much to the group that discuss smoothly; and for the group that didn't go well, teachers should simply inspire and guide, such as let the students recall the little things in daily life or impressive campus life, guide students to learn to observe and think..While recording the good life around, exercise thinking ability and cultivate good living habits and learning habits.

3.3 Attach importance to the cultivation of music knowledge and skills to lay the foundation of music creation

Having a certain basic music knowledge and skills is a necessary prerequisite for music creation. Without basic musical ability, music creation is difficult to continue. Although music creative teaching in primary school is a simple compilation of music , it does not mean that students adapt it freely without logic, the results of the display must conform to the most basic law of music. This requires students to master the basic music knowledge, such as rhythm, melody, speed and other basic elements of music, as well as the ability to read music, sing and play small classroom instruments. In the choice of musical instruments, different instruments can be selected according to students' age and musical ability. For example, students in the low school can choose more simple percussion instruments, such as triangle iron, wooden fish, sand hammer and so on. Students in the middle and high school can add simple instruments such as clarinet and melodica.

3.4 Protect students' interest in creation to cultivate different thinking

Creative teaching emphasizes paying attention to students' creative process and creative experience. Teachers should pay more attention to students' learning process, do not hesitate to encourage and praise students, cultivate their self-confidence, and motivate them to progress. Respect students' personality, guide students to think from multiple aspects, directions and levels, dare to boldly raise questions and challenges, break through the habitual thinking pattern, enhance the divergence and agility of thinking. For example, through divergent questions, " What else can be done to express the grandeur of the music?". Some students start from the rhythm, some students start from the musical instruments, their answers are different, the images and emotions that the students feel are also very different. It is the ambiguity and polysemy of the musical image itself that leaves more imagination space for students, which is conducive to cultivating students' thinking of seeking differences, understanding the diversity of things, expanding their musical horizons.

3.5 Flexibly use teaching methods to improve students' creative enthusiasm

There are often differences between the actual teaching and the teachers' preset teaching, teachers should flexibly regulate teaching methods according to students' age, personality, musical ability and other situations in the classroom, so that the classroom is always kept on the normal track. The in-depth reform needs to change the single and rigid teaching mode in the traditional classroom, and it should absorb the essence of various teaching modes, be scientifically compatible, optimize the combination, and teach intelligently. For example, use pictorial graphics to show students the characteristics of melody and feel the emotions of music; use modern information technology to visualize abstract music theory into intuitive pictures and sounds, making it easier for students to understand; organize students to work together and create independently according to a certain theme; integrate the concepts of project learning, thematic learning or interdisciplinary learning to stimulate students 'divergent thinking and promote students' comprehensive literacy.

3.6 Strengthen practical activities to cultivate creative practice ability

The theory of "learning from doing" proposed by American educator John Dewey emphasizes that students should not simply "learn from listening", but suggest that students should cultivate their interest in "doing". Music is a practical discipline, and music practice is an indispensable way to cultivate students' innovative ability. Teachers should guide students to carry out small creation, small production, small exploration, and then mobilize students' enthusiasm, cultivate students' innovative ability, develop intelligence, and promote the development of students' comprehensive ability. For example, students stimulate the diversity of their thinking by participating in instrumental performance and learning, promote the coordinated development of eye, mouth, hand and foot organs; in the creation and presentation of learning tasks, using a wide variety of sound materials and musical instruments, make simple rhythm and melody; according to a certain theme, choosing the appropriate form of presentation, cooperate with their peers to create and perform simple music stories and short musicals,etc.

The paper is the result which is a Doctoral Start Program study of Bohai University on *Aesthetic analysis of different pursuit of timbre in Chinese and Western's vocal music*

Reference

1. L.Cao, *Music subjects in pedagogy* (Capital Normal University Press, Beijing, 2000)
2. N.Peng, Research on teaching practice of "Creative Field" in primary school music class, Guizhou Normal University (2018)
3. K.X.Zhou, Problems and countermeasures of primary school music improvisation teaching research, Hunan Normal University (2020)
4. Ministry of Education, RC, *Art curriculum standards for compulsory education* (Beijing Normal University Press, Beijing, 2022)
5. X.F.Gao, Research on creativity cultivation of middle students in primary school music education, Hubei Normal University (2021)

Feasibility plan for ideological and political construction of engineering courses-Take the course "Motor and Electrical Control Technology" as an example

Ping Liu*, and *Min* Wu

Ningbo Polytechnic, Ningbo Zhejiang 315800, China

Abstract. Our country's higher education is based on "literacy" and "cultivating people" as the core. How to silently integrate ideological and political elements into the teaching process of engineering professional courses is a problem that requires thinking and long-term construction. In order to cultivate high-skilled and high-quality talents with both talents and virtues, it is urgent to build an ideological and political program suitable for engineering courses. On the basis of analyzing the national boundary attributes of engineering majors, this paper integrates ideological and political elements into engineering majors, and constructs an ideological and political teaching system for engineering majors. On the basis of knowledge imparting, ability training, and spiritual shaping in the design of professional courses, six ideological and political goals of courses are cultivated, and the ideological and political curriculum construction framework of professional courses is constructed by combining three teaching modules, and three ideological and political strategies are integrated into three courses. Taking the course of "Motor and Electrical Control Technology" as an example, this paper discusses the feasibility of the ideological and political construction plan for engineering majors.

1 Introduction

In May 2020, the Ministry of Education's "Guidelines for the Ideological and Political Construction of Courses in Colleges and Universities" showed that the Marxist-Leninist standpoint, viewpoint, and scientific spirit should be organically combined with method education in the teaching process of engineering majors, in order to improve students' awareness, analysis and analysis. ,Ability to solve problems. To cultivate students' spirit of being a great country craftsman, pay attention to the education and training of students' engineering ethics, and then stimulate the patriotic feelings and mission of young students to serve the country through science and technology. As an engineering major, mechatronics technology major has strong practicality and professionalism, and puts forward higher requirements for students' logical thinking ability, innovation and creativity ability and ability to solve practical engineering problems. In the process of practice, on the

* Corresponding author: 52599570@qq.com

basis of understanding our country's national conditions and people's conditions, we can cultivate students' spirit of not being afraid of difficulties, courage to explore, innovation and creativity, and teamwork spirit. The organic integration of professional curriculum education and ideological and political elements not only improves students' professional knowledge, but also improves students' moral and ideological literacy.

Engineering majors include many aspects of the national economy and people's livelihood. How to organically integrate professional courses into ideological and political elements to achieve the effect of subtle and silent education is a problem that needs to be considered and long-term construction[1]. As an engineering major based on basic disciplines such as mathematics, physics, and chemistry, it is a technical discipline developed by accumulating a large amount of practical experience in production[2], For the purpose of training employees who solve practical problems, most professional teachers and classmates believe that engineering majors are science and technology without borders that are separated from ideological attributes. But in real life, the emergence, development and application of every science and technology are inseparable from the advocacy and requirements of the state, so science and technology also have the attributes of ideology with national boundaries. There are three aspects of national border attributes.

1.1 The origin of science and technology

The research and development of science and technology is closely related to the needs of the country. The purpose of the development of science and technology in our country is to serve the interests of the broad masses of the people, so as to realize the sustainable development of the country. It is to serve the people, enhance our country's competitiveness, become an industry leader and standard setter, enhance our country's competitiveness and influence in the field of electromechanical science and technology, and then establish our country's international image.

1.2 The property of science and technology

From the shortage of chips in the past two years, it is proved that core technology cannot be bought or obtained. Only by mastering the core technology, can we achieve real autonomy and controllability, and realize the power of science and technology.

1.3 Serviceability of science and technology

Due to the different development stages and national conditions of different countries in the world, the development of science and technology is also very different. The development of science and technology in our country is to seek happiness for the people and development for the country.

Therefore, engineering professional courses contain a large number of ideological and political elements, and more ideological and political education content is needed in teaching. It is necessary to cultivate red and professional talents, and combine the knowledge teaching, practical ability and innovation ability of professional courses with thinking and thinking. The spiritual shaping of Zhengcheng and the organic combination of patriotic education have transitioned from "ideological and political courses" to a new model of "course ideological and political". According to the law of ideological change and psychological characteristics of young students, combined with the discipline law of engineering majors, we will carry out value guidance for students in a targeted manner, so that they can integrate family and national feelings into their study, life and work.

The "course ideology and politics" of engineering majors is an innovation of education and teaching concept, a rational return of educational value, not a simple teaching method or teaching method[3]. And the function of shaping value, they should take the responsibility of "cultivating morality and cultivating people". The original intention of professional curriculum design is to impart knowledge and let students understand the interpretation of knowledge. The basic task of teachers is to educate people. Therefore, as a teacher, not only should we impart professional knowledge to students, but also need to master more professional ability, so that students can shape their moral norms, political views and ideological concepts on the basis of subtly cultivating students' professional ability.

The major of mechatronics technology is an important subject in the high-tech field in today's world. The degree of development of mechatronics technology in a sense represents the level of scientific and technological development of a country, so its teaching and research occupy a very important role in our country. Location. As the core course of mechatronics technology major, "Electrical and Electrical Control Technology" plays an important role in teaching and cultivating high-quality professionals. It has very important reference significance and reference value for many engineering professional courses to integrate ideological and political elements of courses.Taking "Motor and Electrical Control Technology" as an example, on the basis of knowledge imparting, ability training, and spiritual shaping in the design of professional courses, six ideological and political goals of courses are cultivated, and three teaching modules are combined to construct the ideological and political course construction of core professional courses. Based on the framework, three curriculum ideological and policy strategies are given to provide methods and ideas for the curriculum ideological and political construction of engineering majors.

2 The ideological and political goals of the six courses

"Lide morality and cultivate people" is the foundation of curriculum ideology and politics, "idea practice" is the core of curriculum ideology and politics, and "full education" is the guarantee of curriculum ideology and politics. Ideological and political elements are integrated into engineering professional courses, which play a role in teaching and educating people. According to the characteristics of the "Motor and Electrical Control Technology" course, combined with General Secretary Xi's point in October 2019 that "six efforts" should be followed in cultivating young people in the new era [4], the ideological and political courses of engineering courses in my country are in the content of In terms of design, efforts should be made in six aspects to train young students.

2.1 Work hard to cultivate students' firm ideals and beliefs

In the course of engineering curriculum design, combined with China's national conditions, using the characteristics of mechanical and electrical courses, through the comparison of the historical evolution, current status and future prospects of the development of mechatronics technology, through the "national standards" of electrical technology and "China's intelligent manufacturing" "Enhancing students' "four confidences" in socialism with Chinese characteristics. To cultivate students' ability to control my country's science and technology development strategies, and to establish firm beliefs and ideals to realize the great rejuvenation of the Chinese nation.

2.2 Efforts are made to cultivate students' patriotism

In the process of engineering curriculum design, it is necessary to rely on the major of mechatronics technology, compare with the international advanced technology vertically and horizontally, look for advantages, make up for deficiencies, and identify directions in the comparison, and guide young students to establish a correct view of the country, The national outlook and the historical outlook take family and country feelings as the driving force for self-improvement and unremitting struggle, organically combine one's own future and destiny with the development of the country, and achieve the purpose of enhancing students' "four consciousnesses".

2.3 Efforts are made to train students to strengthen moral cultivation

In the process of engineering curriculum design, on the basis of ensuring the improvement of students' professional technical skills and knowledge and cultural literacy, we should pay attention to the guidance of socialist core values and a correct outlook on life. The explanation and analysis of the hot and current affairs, let the students experience the great love, great virtue and great feelings of the role model, and cultivate the newcomers of the era with moral character, self-cultivation, responsibility and responsibility.

2.4 Make great efforts in cultivating students to increase their knowledge

In the process of engineering curriculum design, it is necessary to stimulate students' desire for knowledge and professional love, so as to increase students' knowledge, temper students' thinking, and lay a solid foundation for students' sustainable development and lifelong learning. With the popularization and prosperity of the Internet, it is more convenient and efficient for students to obtain information, which helps students accumulate knowledge, improve the system, broaden their horizons, and become talents in the new era with family and country feelings.

2.5 Work hard to guide students to cultivate the spirit of struggle

In the course of engineering course design, we will continue to excavate examples in the field of mechatronics that reflect the great struggle spirit of the Chinese nation, organically combine professional exploration, national prosperity, national rejuvenation with personal development and destiny, and integrate the struggle spirit into daily learning and practical activities. In order to achieve personal ideals and the great rejuvenation of the Chinese nation, students are trained to persevere and strive hard for the national spirit.

2.6 Make efforts to cultivate students' comprehensive quality

In the course design process, theory and practice are combined, focusing on project-based teaching to integrate theory into real projects. Cultivate students' ability and comprehensive quality to solve real engineering practice problems, so that students' innovative and creative thinking, comprehensive quality and civilization quality can be cultivated and improved, and become a new youth of the era with teamwork spirit and creative vitality.

The above six curriculum ideological and political goals point out the design direction for the curriculum ideological and political courses of professional courses. The above six elements are integrated into the teaching process of engineering majors to construct the ideological and political system of the course "Electrical and Electrical Control Technology".

3 Three teaching modules

As the core course of mechatronics technology major, the course "Motor and Electrical Control Technology" is highly professional and puts forward higher requirements for students' professional theoretical study and practical operation skills. It is particularly important to integrate political elements into professional courses. The "Motor and Electrical Control Technology" course is divided into three modules: basic theoretical reserve, single-phase skills training, and comprehensive skills application. Each module has distinct characteristics, and its integration into ideology and politics has different characteristics.

3.1 The basic theoretical reserve module

The basic theoretical reserve module is mainly based on the background of the curriculum and discipline, and the ideological and political elements of the curriculum are easier to integrate than the skills training link. The basic theoretical reserve mainly expounds the origin and development of the motor, the history and current situation of the development of the motor in China, and the study of the history and current situation of the motor. While students increase their knowledge and knowledge, they can stimulate students' patriotism and patriotism through the comparison between China and foreign countries, ancient and modern comparisons. Strong national self-esteem and pride.

Through the explanation of the invention process of the motor, the main purpose is to guide students to discover and solve problems. Combined with the explanation of hot current affairs and the country's development strategy (such as the application of electric motors on my country's high-speed rail), it plays a role in enhancing cultural self-confidence and cultivating patriotic feelings. According to the uniqueness of each professional knowledge, it sets off different philosophies of life. While accurately imparting professional knowledge, it allows students to experience the way of being a human being, so as to increase professional knowledge and knowledge, and at the same time enhance students' comprehensive quality and improve moral cultivation. In the course of explaining the theoretical reserve module, strengthen classroom interaction, fully arouse the enthusiasm of students, let students search for examples of scientists related to electrical machinery through the Internet in groups, and share the scientific research spirit of scientists in the classroom to improve students' knowledge Acquiring and screening ability helps young students discover the hidden social phenomenon behind professional knowledge, and strengthens students' ideological and political cultivation and morality. In the special report, students exercise their expressive ability and improve the comprehensive quality of young students.

3.2 The single-phase skill training module

The basic theoretical reserve module presents theoretical knowledge in the form of skill training, intuitively allows students to understand the application of basic theories, and deepens their knowledge and understanding of professional theoretical knowledge through hands-on operation. Exercise the practical ability of young students. In the process of skill training, each student is required to complete the corresponding practical operations, temper their strong will and character, and experience their psychological quality of not being afraid of failure; rank and assign scores to students' completion status, and cultivate the enterprising spirit of striving for the first; Let the students who completed first help those who have not completed, which has the effect of "giving roses and leaving fragrance in the hands", and cultivates the spirit of mutual help among students. To verify theoretical knowledge in practical projects, let students learn to see the essence through phenomena, condense the philosophy contained in professional knowledge, improve students' perception ability, and improve their comprehensive quality.

3.3 The comprehensive skills application module

In the comprehensive skills application module, the theoretical knowledge is integrated into the comprehensive project, and the ideological and political elements are integrated into the comprehensive project, so that students can find and discover the sense of superiority and pride of socialism with Chinese characteristics, and strengthen the young students' respect for the country. cultural self-confidence and ideal self-confidence, cultivate patriotic feelings, and cultivate their spirit of fighting for the Chinese nation. In the process of project implementation, it is used for self-exploration, strengthening teamwork, actively discovering and solving problems, stimulating creativity and innovation, and improving the professional quality and comprehensive quality of young students. The ideological and political elements of the course are organically combined with the teaching of engineering majors. That is, the ideological and political curriculum of "Motor and Electrical Control Technology" is realized, which makes imparting knowledge, improving ability and shaping spirit organically compatible.

In the course design process of "Motor and Electrical Control Technology", knowledge imparting, ability training, and spiritual shaping are both mutually reinforcing and closely linked. In recent years, among the students who are teaching, through questionnaires, face-to-face communication, sampling statistics, etc., the feedback of the teaching effect is obtained, showing that the training mode of knowledge imparting, ability training, and spiritual shaping (Figure 1) can be achieved through limited offline training. The combined effect of study time and unlimited online study time is excellent. In the training time, let t1 be the time for knowledge imparting, t2 is the time for ability training, t3 is the time for spiritual shaping, and the total time t1+t2+t3=1, that is, the training time of the three is 1, but the training time is 1. Effects According to various forms of feedback to students, the results show that the comprehensive efficiency of educating people can reach 145%.

Fig. 1. The cultivation of knowledge imparting ability and the cultivation mode of shaping spirit.

4 Professional courses are integrated into the curriculum thinking strategy

Different teaching modules have different ideological and political goals, and different methods of integrating ideological and political courses. Combined with the course of

"Motor and Electrical Control Technology", the ideological and political construction plan of the course is as follows:

4.1 National conditions of science and technology strategy

Combining my country's national conditions with the development of electromechanical scientific and technological achievements, let students understand that scientists are based on nationality, and science and technology have national boundaries. For example, according to the characteristics of my country's vast area of energy distribution and unbalanced economic development, the problem of east-west development solved by west-to-east power transmission not only makes full use of the regional advantages of abundant water resources and large altitude difference in western my country, but the electricity cannot be digested locally. It also solves the problems of economic development in the eastern region, large demand for electric power and insufficient power supply, and realizes the optimization of resources and complements the surplus and deficiency. Combined with the characteristics of my country's national conditions, electrical scientific research workers must take the road of scientific research with Chinese characteristics, rather than blindly follow the direction of international research hotspots. Through the analysis of national conditions of science and technology, let students understand the great innovative spirit of the Chinese nation, and realize that in order to realize the people's yearning for a better life, my country's scientific research workers need to continue to innovate, forge ahead, and transform science and technology into productive forces for the benefit of the people.

4.2 Track current affairs strategy

Through professional hot news, combine cutting-edge technology with patriotism. The combination of social hot current affairs and professional knowledge can not only cultivate students' patriotism and social responsibility, but also help stimulate their enthusiasm for professional learning and interest in scientific research. For example, in February 2020, Leishenshan Hospital and Huoshenshan Hospital moved two 10KV lines with a total of 45 base poles, installed 24 box-type transformers, and four 10kV ring networks within five days. In early 2022, during the COVID-19 outbreak in Xi'an, Xi'an State Grid completed three 800KVA box-type transformers, 1 630-kVA box-type transformer, and 1 box-type transformer within 38 hours. The installation of the ring network cabinet, the laying of six high-voltage cables and the production of cable terminals are all work. The amazing speed bought time for epidemic prevention and control, made students feel the great spiritual power of the Chinese nation, once again reflected the power of "China Speed" and "Made in China", and reflected the Chinese people's sense of responsibility and mission, encouraging students As the future technicians and scientific researchers in our country, we must use the time in school and arm our minds with professional knowledge, and then we will be able to seek happiness for the people in the socialist construction of our country .

4.3 Scientific spiritual strategy

From the devotion of scientists and the far-reaching influence on social development, the determination of young students to devote themselves to scientific research is inspired. In the process of explaining, the famous scientists in the industry are introduced. The majors of these scientists are the same as those of the students, which makes the students more friendly and draws strength from these scientists. Such as: Zhong Zhaolin, a famous electrical scientist known as the father of Chinese electrical machinery, developed China's first AC motor and generator. In 1927, upholding his patriotism, he gave up the favorable treatment of the Westinghouse Electric Company in the United States and resolutely returned to China. Adhering to the teaching concept of "good practice, bad empty talk" in the teaching process, it is suggested that education should be combined with productive labor, and the development of industry should be guided by the development of science and education. In 1954, the state moved Jiaotong University to Xi'an, and Professor Zhong "led to move westward to teach Xi'an Jiaotong University". In the early days of the establishment of Xi'an Jiaotong University, he was hands-on, faced with difficulties, overcame many difficulties, and established the first electrical machinery manufacturing laboratory in New China. Through Professor Zhong's deeds, he guides young students to closely combine personal development with national development, organically combine theory and practice, love their jobs and work hard, concentrate their efforts for the prosperity of the country and the prosperity of the motherland, and seek personal development.

5 Conclusion

Knowledge imparting, ability training, and spirit shaping are the basis of professional curriculum design, and curriculum ideology and politics are integrated into professional curriculum design. Focus on the teaching of professional knowledge in the course of teaching, let students feel the scientific and rigorous scientific attitude and the patriotic sentiment of rejuvenating the country through science and technology, and combine the theory of professional knowledge with the practice of ideological and political construction of the curriculum. Integrate the basic theories and values of ideology and politics into the learning of engineering professional courses, influence students' behavior and thinking in a silent way, and impart knowledge, cultivate ability, and shape spirit in professional curriculum design. Organic integration, three strategies of explaining national conditions, technology, tracking current affairs and scientific spirit are integrated into it, and ideological and political education is subtly integrated while teaching professional courses, so that close to the major gives students a sense of intimacy and makes students easy to accept. Taking Lide and cultivating people as the fundamental task of education, organically running ideological and political theories into the whole process of teaching professional courses, realizing the education pattern of all staff, whole process, all-round and whole courses, and forming a synergistic effect.

This work was supported by the Ningbo Education Science Planning Project [Grant No. 2022YZD019].

References

1. Sun Qiuye, Huang Yujia, Gao Jiawen. The Curriculum Ideology and Politics Construction Plan of Engineering Professional Course -- Taking the Course of Power System Analysis as an Example[J] Chinese Journal of Electrical Engineering, 41 (02): 475-486(2021)
2. Zhu Guiping, Lin Jin, Sun Hongbin, et al. Reform and Practice of the Undergraduate Teaching System of Electrical Engineering for the Energy Internet [J]. Chinese Journal of Electrical Engineering, 40 (13): 4063-4071(2020)

3. ZHU Guangqin. A probe into the educational elements and mechanism of "ideology-oriented courses" on the basis of morality cultivation[J] . Journal of Nanjing University of Science and Technology: Social Sciences Edition, 32(6): 84-87(2019)
4. Xu Qinghua. Cultivating new people of the times requires efforts to enhance their comprehensive quality [J]. Beijing Education (Moral Education), (4): 74-77(2019)

"New Singing of Ancient Poems" in music education of primary and secondary schools

Nan Li, and *Yingying* Xian*

School of Music, Bohai University, Jinzhou, China

Abstract. "The new singing of ancient poetry" refers to a musical innovation form that takes the ancient poetry culture as the source of lyrics and rearranges the melody with modern music style and lasting appeal. It makes ancient poetry discourse from the perspective of music and breaks the barriers to understanding the ancient poetry culture. In recent years, Chinese ancient poetry has attracted more and more people's attention and love because of its unique value of recreation in music, and has become an important source of poetry and music. Through the discussion of the form of "new singing of ancient poetry", this paper hopes to arouse some music educators in primary and secondary schools to pay attention to how to guide students to learn the music culture of ancient poetry, so that the traditional culture of ancient poetry can play its charm in music education of primary and secondary schools.

1 The meaning of "New Singing of Ancient Poems" in music education

1.1 Meaning of "New Singing of Ancient Poems

"New singing of ancient poetry" refers to a musical innovation form that takes the ancient poetry culture as the source of lyrics and rearranges the melody with modern music style and lasting appeal. The so-called "new" is more reflected in bringing modern art into traditional culture, building a fierce collision between modern music culture and ancient traditional culture based on the emotional trend of lyrics, making traditional culture closer to modern people's emotional understanding, so as to modernize the tradition. As the name implies, "new singing of ancient poetry" is a way to make ancient poetry discourse from the perspective of music, so that modern people can more easily understand the poet's feelings, close to the poet's life, and break the barriers to modern people's understanding of ancient poetry culture. "New Singing of Ancient Poetry" focuses on using modern music to stimulate modern people's love for traditional ancient poetry culture, so as to achieve the effective combination and collision of traditional culture and modern music.

*Corresponding author: xianyingying1980@126.com

1.2 The meaning of "New Singing of Ancient Poems" in music education

The culture of ancient poetry is the crystallization of the wisdom of the Chinese people, and is a concentrated reflection of the psychological characteristics and way of thinking of the Chinese nation. With the deepening of curriculum reform in China, attaching importance to the traditional culture of ancient poetry has become an indispensable part of music education in primary and secondary schools. However, due to the simple language and profound artistic conception of ancient poetry culture, in the past music teaching classes in primary and secondary schools, learners lacked interest in their learning, and it was difficult to understand the cultural flavor expressed therein. Therefore, the teaching of the integration of ancient poetry culture and music has become a concern of music educators. With the development of the times, taking the form of "new singing of ancient poems" as a new attempt has become a teaching method for music educators to study the music teaching of ancient poems. "New Singing of Ancient Poems" adorns the ancient poetry culture with modern music style, making the ancient poetry music more musical and interesting in the process of interpretation, so as to mobilize students to take the initiative to learn the cultural knowledge of ancient poetry and understand the cultural charm and polarity of ancient poetry culture, which not only meets the requirements of ancient poetry culture teaching, but also promotes the excellent traditional culture of the Chinese nation.

2 The value significance of ancient poetry culture in primary and secondary school music education

2.1 Cultivate the learning interest of the learning subject

Ancient poetry is a long history and culture in China, is one of the main forms of literature, with high literary and artistic value. The ancient poetry music culture is an important part of the primary and secondary education in China, but the traditional poetry music teaching is still just to help students understand music, music and simple understanding of songs. The teaching method is too conservative, which easily gives students the illusion that the ancient poetry culture is too boring and tasteless, causing students to be tired of learning, unwilling to take the initiative to learn the ancient poetry culture and feel the connotation of the ancient poetry culture. It can be seen from this that as a new teaching method, "New Singing of Ancient Poems" teaches students ancient poetry culture from a new perspective of modern music, enables students to learn ancient poetry culture under the rhythm of modern music that they understand themselves, enables students to feel the beauty and charm contained in ancient poetry through hearing, and gives students a new hearing experience, which is one of the effective ways to stimulate students' active learning interest.

2.2 Improve the comprehensive quality of the learning subject

Ancient poetry culture is the essence of Chinese excellent traditional culture and the treasure of Chinese art. As far as the spreading time and influence are concerned, ancient poetry culture itself has great advantages. In the Han Dynasty, there had been Yuefu poetry that integrated music and ancient poetry culture. In modern China, school songs also appeared. Both of them were based on the ancient poetry culture as the source of lyrics, and combined with the music style at that time to fill in songs and sing songs. It can be seen from this that there is a retroactive existence of "ancient poetry and new singing" as a teaching method. This method has been proved to be feasible by time, and this teaching method enables students not only to learn ancient poetry culture and modern music style, but also to trace back to history, experience the artistic charm of ancient poetry music culture in each period, so as to improve their comprehensive quality.

2.3 Inherit the excellent culture of the Chinese nation

With the deepening of curriculum reform in China, attaching importance to the traditional culture of ancient poetry has become an indispensable part of music education in primary and secondary schools. In the music education of primary and secondary schools, taking the "new singing of ancient poems" as a teaching form, and transforming the ancient poetry culture into the form of modern music for singing, can not only enrich the cultural connotation of students, but also show the charm of China's excellent traditional culture to students, thus effectively inheriting the excellent culture of the Chinese nation. China's music curriculum standards clearly put forward the value of music curriculum, which is to provide students with beautiful experience, cultivate emotions, inspire wisdom, develop the possibility of creation, and inherit the excellent traditional culture of the Chinese nation. China is a civilized country with 5000 years of cultural heritage, and ancient poetry culture is an indispensable part of Chinese cultural heritage. In the music education of primary and secondary schools, it is necessary to strengthen the learning of ancient poetry culture in the form of "ancient poetry and new singing", so that students can experience the charm of Chinese poetry culture with a new sense of hearing, which can not only strengthen the effective interaction between music and literature, but also achieve the goal of cultivating students' feelings and providing students with a sense of beauty in a unique and not simple teaching method, and can effectively inherit the excellent traditional culture of China.

3 Application of "New Singing of Ancient Poems" in music education of primary and secondary schools

Ancient poetry culture is an important part of music education in primary and secondary schools. It is also an important breakthrough for music educators in primary and secondary schools to find new ways of improvement to adapt to the teaching methods that primary and secondary school students are willing to actively accept. "New Singing of Ancient Poems" makes ancient poems discourse from the perspective of modern music, breaks the barriers of students' understanding of ancient poetry culture, and effectively promotes the education of ancient poetry music culture.

3.1 A case of promoting the aesthetic value of students by "Singing Ancient Poems New"

"Dwelling in the Mountains at Autumn Night" is a poem by Wang Wei, a poet of the Tang Dynasty. It is a traditional chapter of Chinese culture that focuses on primary and secondary school compulsory education. The whole poem expresses the poet's love for the beautiful life of the mountain village with a beautiful picture of the mountain village in the evening when the autumn rain is sunny. The scene of Living in the Mountain at Autumn Evening is clearly expressed, and the students have a clear understanding of its artistic conception. It is a typical work of the teaching form of "ancient poetry and new singing". In the music teaching of primary and secondary schools, the poem "Dwelling in the Mountains at Autumn Evening" is introduced into the music education of primary and secondary schools in the form of "ancient poetry and new singing", so that students can express their yearning for the beautiful scenery of natural villages on the basis of modern music they know, and the known drives the unknown, thus enriching the unknown. It can be inferred that the "new singing of ancient poetry" is an effective way for music educators in primary and secondary schools to give students the artistic conception and emotion of ancient poetry culture, and it is also one of the effective ways for music educators in primary and secondary schools to improve students' aesthetic feelings.

3.2 A case of promoting the aesthetic value of students by "Singing Ancient Poems New"

The Song of the Chiles is a poem that most Chinese people are familiar with. It is a traditional chapter of Chinese culture that is the focus of primary and secondary school compulsory education. Although the number is short, the scenes are clearly expressed and the contrast is clear. It completely outlines the vast, rich and desirable scenery of the northern grassland. It is a classic work of ancient folk songs. In the music teaching of primary and secondary schools, in the form of "new singing of ancient poems", the use of modern music style can add exaggeration to the picture sense of "Chiles", which can effectively enable students to experience the vast grassland, more deeply understand the emotions expressed by poets, and stimulate students' interest in ancient poetry culture in the perspective of cultivating students' aesthetic outlook, so as to achieve effective teaching of ancient poetry music culture. It can be inferred that the "new singing of ancient poetry" plays an important role in the infiltration of ancient poetry culture into music education in primary and secondary schools. For music educators in primary and secondary schools, cultivating students' aesthetic ability in the form of "new singing of ancient poems" is one of the effective ways to improve students' aesthetic value.

In the music education of primary and secondary schools, the performance of "Dwelling in the Mountains at Autumn Dusk" and "Chile Song" tends to cultivate students' aesthetic ability, so that students can experience and feel the beauty in the real world, so as to stimulate students to love the ancient poetry music culture and experience the artistic charm of ancient poetry music culture in each period, so as to improve students' comprehensive quality and promote the orderly development of music education in primary and secondary schools. "New singing of ancient poetry" is a new teaching form, which makes ancient poetry discourse from the perspective of music and breaks the barriers to cultural understanding of ancient poetry. Ancient poetry is the essence of Chinese traditional culture, the crystallization of the wisdom of the Chinese people for more than 5000 years, and has profound cultural heritage. In recent years, Chinese ancient poetry has attracted more and more people's attention and love because of its unique value of recreation in music, and has become an important source of poetry and music. Through the discussion in the form of "new singing of ancient poetry", this paper hopes to arouse some music educators in primary and secondary schools to discuss how to attract students' enthusiasm for the music culture of ancient poetry, so that they can better and more comprehensively understand China and Chinese culture, achieve the ultimate goal of inheriting traditional music culture, and make the traditional culture of ancient poetry play its unique charm in the inheritance of modern music culture, It also makes the music culture of ancient poetry get more extensive attention and understanding in the music education of primary and secondary schools.

The paper is the research result of the key point scientific research project *Research on the timbre of Chinese vocal music art* which is funded by Bohai University.

References

1. Chen Dandan. The Importance of Ancient Poetry and New Singing in College Vocal Music Teaching [J]. Art Education, 2016 (12): 90-91
2. Gong Min. On the Significance of "New Singing of Ancient Poems" in Music Teaching in Primary Schools [J]. Times Education, 2015 (16): 255-255
3. Hu Bo. The Influence of Chinese Classical Poetry on Popular Songs [J]. Success (Education), 2013 (07): 297
4. Li Fangyi. On the Characteristics and Singing of Chinese Ancient Poems and Artistic Songs [J]. Yuefu Xinsheng, 2010, (3)
5. Liu Li. Singing Low, Singing High and Singing Deeply -- On the "New Singing of Ancient Poems" in Music Teaching [J] China Out of School Education (Mid term), 2015 (12): 161-161

Research on the development strategy and talent training of vocational Chinese language

Yan Zhang*

College of Chinese Language and Culture, Jinan University, 510610 Guangzhou, China

Abstract. There are some problems in the development of vocational Chinese, such as the unsystematic teaching materials, the unreasonable curriculum, the simple cultivation mode and insufficient professional teachers. Therefore, it puts forward strategies such as creation of special courses, optimization of training objectives and establishment of "Double Tutor" system. In terms of personnel training, we should clarify the career orientation and update the training concept. We recommend establishing a flexible joint training and exchange student system and advocating School-enterprise cooperation.

1 Introduction

Vocational Chinese refers to variations of general Chinese in the workplace, such as tour guide Chinese, business Chinese, medical Chinese etc.

The language talent training plan includes not only how to accelerate the training of talents who are proficient in the languages of countries along the Belt and Road routes, but also how to accelerate the training of talents who are proficient in Chinese for countries along the routes (Jianming Lu,2016). This paper focuses on cultivating Chinese talents from countries along the road

2 Problems in the development of vocational Chinese

With economic globalization, industrial integration, and the implementation of the "One Belt and One Road" policy, vocational Chinese is currently in the stage of vigorous development. But in the process of development, there are still some problems.

2.1 Unsystematic construction of teaching materials

Since the 1980s, when foreign students came to China to study Chinese in colleges and universities, there have been no less than 150 textbooks on medical Chinese, business Chinese, science and technology Chinese, etc. However, at present, the specialized Chinese textbooks published are mainly business Chinese, scientific Chinese and medical Chinese,

* Corresponding author:zyahsf@163.com

among which there are more than 80 business Chinese textbooks, while other professional Chinese textbooks are insufficient (Kehua Yu , Lili Xu, 2019).

With the deepening of cooperation between countries and the development of tourism and trade, the current vocational Chinese teaching materials cannot meet the needs of learners. Even if some textbooks exist sporadically, their quality varies. There is no certain vocabulary level grammar outline and other standard reference, lack of science.

2.2 Unreasonable curriculum

The curriculum mainly focuses on the cultivation of basic language ability, following the mode of "language knowledge plus language skills plus cultural knowledge". The major features are not obvious, and there is no connection with occupation, ignoring the career development goals of students. Practice courses are superficial. Theory and practice are disjointed, which is not conducive to the development of students' comprehensive ability.

2.3 Simple cultivation mode

The focus of talent training is toward general Chinese talents, and the training mode is simple and stylized. Ignoring the development of vocational skills and students' individual needs and ignoring the characteristics of the fields and market demand too. The cooperation with enterprises is limited to a certain language practice and visit, lack of effective and substantive vocational skills training, lack of in-depth research and investigation.

2.4 Insufficient professional teaching staffs

At present, most of the professional Chinese teachers are Chinese teachers majoring in linguistics, who lack professional knowledge and practical experience, so they are not competent to teach complex vocational knowledge. Quan Li (2011) pointed out that the compound knowledge structure of "Chinese knowledge and teaching skills plus relevant professional knowledge and teaching skills" is a reasonable structure of knowledge and ability for specially used Chinese teachers.

Therefore, it is necessary to build a professional and innovative team of teachers, broaden their horizons, and strengthen the training of teaching methods, teaching concepts and practical skills.

3 Strategies for vocational Chinese language development

3.1 Integrate science and technology elements to create special courses

According to students' interests and market demand, we need to develop specialized courses with "career" as the core and language assistance technology. Encouraging students to experience the front line of the work and developing language practice are recommended. We had better establish a "language service" channel to connect students with the market. Besides, we should take advantage of the school, combined with regional characteristics, to enrich the curriculum system.

In recent years, the "technical content" of Chinese digital resources is getting higher and higher, and the intelligent products are more and more abundant. Speech recognition technology, speech synthesis technology, character recognition, handwriting recognition, virtual simulation experiments, etc., have been integrated into the international Chinese education industry. Vocational Chinese can make full use of modern media technology to expand the teaching scene and increase the sense of reality and experience of learning.

3.2 Optimize cultivation objectives

With the market demand as the guidance, cultivate new compound talents, formulate reasonable talent training program. Making full use of regional and professional advantages of each school is advised. Carrying out multi-field, multi-level and multi-specialty characteristic training and creating a unique talent training mode are all good choices. We need to highlight the double characteristics of "Chinese plus career", precise training and shaping high-quality talents.

3.3 Establish and improve the system of "Double Tutors"

The "Double Tutor" refers to the professional teachers of the school and the technical and managerial personnel of various departments of the enterprise (Xindan Hu, Yanjun Wang, 2020). From theory to practice, from knowledge to application, comprehensively guide students to improve their language and professional skills. The coordination and cooperation of the two tutors can learn from each other and improve themselves to a certain extent, which is conducive to the improvement of teaching quality.

"Double Tutors" can also refer to tutors in China and tutors in the country of origin. When the "2 plus 2" co-training is implemented, students have 2 years in China and another 2 years to complete the internship in their home country. Dual tutors can provide targeted guidance according to students' learning needs at different stages and appropriate teaching resources according to students' development characteristics.

4 Reform and innovation of talent training

4.1 Clarify the career orientation and update the training concept

We must broaden the horizon and break away from the traditional concept of knowledge talent training. Establishing a new training concept centered on students' career development and oriented by market demand is our aim. On the basis of listening, speaking, reading, writing and translation skills, We also need to strengthen students' multilingual ability and cultivate high-quality talents with" one specialized and multiple abilities".

4.2 Establish a flexible system of joint training and exchange students

To meet the requirements of vocational Chinese learning in overseas markets, new teaching and training modes, such as "2 plus 2" and "1 plus 3", should be established. Students in China will complete 1 to 2 years of language learning in China, and the remaining 2 to 3 years is left for internship in their native country to complete professional course learning, teaching practice and graduation thesis writing. Chinese teachers will be arranged to local teaching sites regularly to give lectures and guidance.

4.3 Build School-enterprise cooperation

Actively cooperate with enterprises in overseas markets and Chinese enterprises' associations abroad to implement order training, two-way selection and targeted employment. For example, we can cooperate with overseas institutions to recruit students and cooperate with overseas enterprises such as Huawei and Gree, Chinese enterprises' associations and chambers of commerce, etc. And conducting in-depth cooperation in curriculum setting teaching practice and employment are considered too.

5 Conclusions

We should positively face all kinds of problems in the development of vocational Chinese, develop appropriate strategies, and guide the development of vocational Chinese concretely from macro to micro level. At the same time, we should strengthen the reform and innovation of personnel training mechanism, take the market as the guide to promote diversified and specialized personnel training mode.

References

1. Jianming Lu, The Belt and Road Initiative need language to pave the way and build Bridges. R. Cul. Sof. Pow. **1**, 33(2016).
2. Kehua Yu, Lili Xu, The textbook construction of Chinese for special purpose under the background of the "Belt and Road" initiative. T. & R. **6**, 62(2019).
3. Quan Li, Teaching Chinese for specific purpose and its textbook compilation. Appl. Lan. **3**, 116(2011).
4. Xindan Hu, Yanjun Wang, On the mode of overseas concurrent reading system: A case study of Master of Chinese international education in Jinan University. O. C. Edu.**1**, 55(2020).

Design of ideological and political teaching case of analytical chemistry based on EDTA Titrator

Jinfen Niu*, *Leilei* Lu , *XiaojiaoYu*, *Ningning* Zhao, and *Zheng* Chang

School of Science, Xi'an university of technology,710048 Xi'an, China

Abstract. Under the background of ideological and political education in the curriculum, according to the requirements of talent training in applied universities, the authors take the analytical chemistry curriculum as the implementation carrier of ideological and political education. Taking case teaching as an innovative means, a teaching case with EDTA as coordination titrant was designed. Based on the explanation of the principle that metal ions and coordination atoms coordinate to form stable compounds in Lewis acid-base theory, the ideological and political education was effectively combined with the teaching point of analytical chemistry knowledge, and the reason why EDTA had wide adaptability was proposed. From the perspective of ideological and political education, the teaching designs carried out with values education as the main line. The curriculum not only imparted professional knowledge, but also guided students' values. A reasonable teaching design can realize the educational goal of the same frequency resonance between professional courses and ideological and political education.

1 Introduction

Analytical Chemistry is an important basic course for chemistry, chemical engineering, materials, applied chemistry, biology, food, medicine and other related majors[1-2]. It has a complete knowledge framework and strong knowledge intersection with many disciplines. It is a comprehensive discipline based on multiple disciplines and contains rich philosophical ideas and values. The teaching objective of this course is to cultivate students' craftsmanship spirit of striving for perfection, shape engineering ethics, stimulate students' learning interest and patriotic enthusiasm, require students to control the analysis and operation process strictly from the perspective of "quantity", be able to reasonably handle the analysis results obtained, scientifically design analysis plans and write reports. Analytical chemistry has a wide range of applications, closely related to life science, environmental science and material science, and has developed rapidly, such as food safety, environmental protection, new material development, etc., which are closely related to people's lives. In theory teaching, the course not only pays attention to basic theory teaching, but also includes the latest theoretical frontier of analytical chemistry, and timely

* Corresponding author: niujinfen@xaut.edu.cn

integrates ideological and political teaching elements. The whole course adopts the task driven teaching method and integrates various teaching methods such as case method and discussion method, and provides students with rich extracurricular resources for independent learning[3-4]. In this paper, EDTA titrant is selected to design a case of ideological and political education, so as to achieve the ultimate goal of "establishing morality and cultivating people".

2 Case introduction

Coordination titration is an important part of the teaching content of analytical chemistry. In this case, the teaching content of coordination characteristics and coordination balance between EDTA and metal ions is selected[5]. This case introduces the principle that metal ions coordinate with coordination atoms to form stable compounds in Lewis acid and base theory, and proposes how to select a coordination agent that has extensive adaptability to different metal ions, stimulate students' interest in learning through their independent thinking, then introduces the structure of EDTA as a coordination agent, and introduces the reason why it has extensive coordination ability as a coordination agent; Finally, let the students think about how to choose appropriate experimental conditions to improve the selectivity of titration. Because EDTA can cooperate with almost all metal ions, in the teaching process, gradually guide students to independently find side reactions in various equilibrium reactions, and answer how to define primary and secondary reactions. Finally, how to improve the selectivity of coordination titration through reasonable design of experimental conditions is proposed, which is used as a question for students to think and discuss in groups after class.

In this case, the course mainly integrates the following ideological and political contents: 1. From the experience of Louis, a physical chemist, engaged in scientific research, students feel the outstanding quality of great scientists' unremitting scientific research; 2. Cultivate the students' spirit of exploration to discuss problems step by step by building a step-by-step in-depth solution to the problem of stabilizing metal ion coordination compounds; 3. Fully tap the philosophical dialectical relationship in titration, and cultivate students' scientific spirit of dialectically handling problems; 4. Complete the thinking questions after class through group cooperation.

3 Ideas and objectives

In this case, how to select a universal titrant leads to the reason for selecting EDTA as a coordination titrant. Through the introduction of Lewis theory and the life of chemist Lewis, this paper introduces the use of Lewis theory, and students themselves explain why they chose EDTA as the metal ion titrant. Through the characteristics of coordination between EDTA and metal ions and coordination balance, the dialectical materialism contained in this course is deeply extracted. During teaching, we should consciously and designedly integrate the elements and functions of moral education into the teaching process, practice and explore the ideological and political curriculum, so that all kinds of courses and ideological and political theory courses can go in the same direction and form a synergistic effect. The teaching objectives of course are as showed in Fig.1.

 https://doi.org/10.1051/shsconf/202316601014

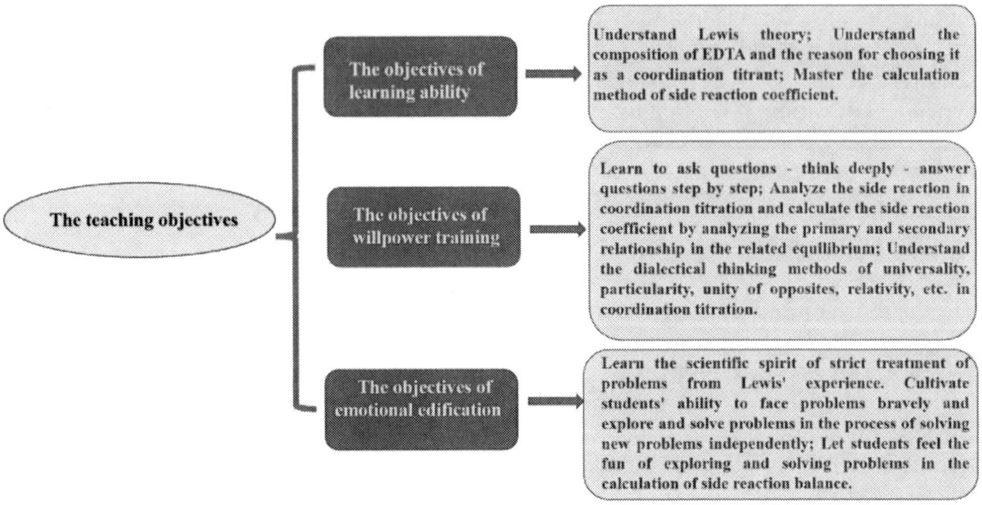

Fig. 1. The objectives of the course.

4 Instructional design

This case selects the lecture contents about the characteristics of coordination between EDTA and metal ions and coordination balance, and deeply explores the ideological and political elements in this case. The main teaching contents are as follows:

First of all, in the form of small videos played in the classroom, we shared the life of Don Lewis, a physical chemist, who had been engaged in scientific research from the age of 70 until his retirement, so that students could feel the excellent quality of perseverance of great scientists. Secondly, by gradually introducing the principle of metal ions and coordination atoms to coordinate to form stable compounds according to Lewis acid-base theory, students will be trained to explore the problem step by step. Thirdly, by fully tapping the philosophical dialectical relationship in coordination titration, we hope to cultivate students' scientific spirit of dialectically looking at problems. Finally, through the way of group cooperation to complete the thinking questions after class, fully stimulate students' independent learning ability, and cultivate students' spirit of unity and cooperation. The specific teaching design was showed in Table1.

5 Features and innovation

The construction of "Ideological and Political Course" can not only achieve the teaching objectives of this course, but also play an important role in cultivating students' dialectical thinking ability, cultivating and practicing the socialist "four self-confidence" and core values, and establishing a sense of social responsibility. After the course, most students feel that they have gained a lot and have more confidence in their major. Many students still communicate with teachers through QQ, WeChat, SMS and other contact methods. When they encounter other problems, they will also consult teachers at any time. This shows that the integration of dialectical thinking and ideological and political elements in classroom teaching can better stimulate students' exploratory thinking, master correct epistemology and methodology, and coordinate the relationship between teachers and students.

Table 1. The specific teaching design of the case.

Main topic	Teaching contents	Objectives	Teaching methods and means
Lewis acid-base theory	Personality of Lewis	Excellent quality of perseverance	Watch video
Selection of coordination titration	Principles for the formation of stable complex compounds	Advocate the spirit of exploration and science	Q1. How to select a titrant with wide adaptability?
Characteristics of coordination between EDTA and metal ions	Strong coordination ability, strong stability,and universality,	Reveal the dialectical relationship of philosophy: universal and special; opposition and unity.	Q1: Why does EDTA have strong coordination ability? Q2: How to select and design titration conditions for coordination titration of different metal ions with EDTA?
Coordination equilibrium	Dynamic Equilibrium and Side Reaction of Coordination Reaction	Reveal the dialectical relationship of philosophy: absolute and relative; Two sides of things	Q1: How do the formation and dissociation of coordination compounds proceed? Q2: How to define the main reaction and side reaction?
experimental design	In the mixed solution where $Bi^{3+}$and Pb^{2+}coexist, how to improve the selectivity of coordination titration through reasonable experimental conditions design.	Improve students' autonomous learning ability and solidarity spirit	Solve problems through project cooperation

6 Conclusion

At present, the introduction of ideological and political elements into the ideological and political education of analytical chemistry is only a preliminary exploration. In fact, the teaching content system itself and its development process contain many ideological and political elements. To achieve a good ideological and political education effect, it is important to tap the connotation of the current knowledge system, and "timely updating of teaching content and enriching teaching methods" is also a very important aspect. In the teaching of coordination titration, it is the in-depth promotion and expansion of relevant knowledge on the basis of the original teaching content system. It inspires students to master titration and understand titration methods in a dialectical way. In the future, we still need to constantly explore the ideological and political elements from the teaching content, so as to finally achieve the goal of professional course teaching and ideological and political education to go hand in hand, promote each other, and achieve the ultimate goal of "building morality and cultivating people".

The ultimate goal of higher education is to train students to be all-round development, ability oriented, subject knowledge and dialectical thinking. Therefore, teachers should not only impart professional knowledge to students, but also impart their correct thinking methods, scientific research methods and correct cognitive approaches to scientific development. As the main body of classroom teaching, teachers should not only have a solid foundation of professional knowledge, but also have a certain foundation of dialectics. They should infiltrate dialectical materialism, materialistic dialectics, and dialectical materialistic epistemology into the classroom teaching content without trace, so that they can come at their fingertips, be flexible, open and close freely, and make professional education resonate with ideological and political education, so as to give full play to the teaching and educational function of analytical chemistry, cultivate students to be professional talents with dialectical thinking and scientific exploration spirit.

We thanks to the financially support from the research Project of Education and Teaching Reform Project of Xi'an University of Technology (Item Number: xjy2102 , xjy2103 , xqj2119 , 251032205 and 252042029).

References

1. C. Xu, Y. Wang, H. Wu, Y. Shen, Z. Dai, J. Li, Y.Xiao, D. Li, D.Li, H. Zhang,Univ. Chem. **37**,10 (2022)
2. H. Liu,N. Shao, J. Ouyan, N.Na, Chin.J.Chem. Edu. **43**,16 (2022)
3. W. Song , R. Fan, L. Yu,Univ. Chem. **38**,1-7 (2023)
4. Y. Liao , Chi. Edu.Tech. Equ. **538**,16 (2022)
5. L. Lu,Q. Shuai, J. Li, H.Qiu, Y. Peng, Univ. Chem. **35**,5 (2020)

The evolution of a symbiotic ecosystem of Chinese e-commerce retail logistics in the post-COVID-19 epidemic era

Dan Zhao[1,*], and *Elena Aleksandrovna* Smirnova[2]

[1]Shaoyang University, School of Economics and Management, 422000 Shaoyang, China
[2]St. Petersburg State University of Economics, Department of Logistics and Supply Chain Management, 191023 St. Petersburg, Russia

Abstract. Since February 2020, the COVID-19 pandemic has spread across the world, greatly affecting the global economic situation and peoples lifestyles. Mass consumption has shifted from offline to online, suggesting a permanent trend and making e-commerce one of the few industries to go against the global trend of economic downturn. With a continuous increase in online consumption, the supporting logistics ecosystem has also evolved. By analyzing and comparing the development status of e-commerce logistics industries before and after the initial impact of COVID-19, this paper finds that after the initial impact of COVID-19, China's e-commerce logistics ecosystems are more stable, and an e-commerce logistics ecosystem in China, consisting of a guiding layer, a backbone layer, a filling layer, a basic layer and a bearing layer, has taken shape, providing strong support for the continued development of e-commerce in China.

The COVID-19 global pandemic forced countries around the world to control the epidemic by establishing a variety of quarantine policies, and implementing quarantine policies that have affected the normal functioning of national economies to varying degrees. Despite the efforts of governments to weaken the negative impact of quarantine policies on economic development, statistics and forecasts given by the World Bank and the World Monetary Organization show that all national economies will experience varying degrees of slowdown or even recession in the coming years [1,2] . At the same time, consumers changed their spending habits under quarantine policies and increased online shopping, resulting in e-commerce rising against the trend of overall economic downturn [3-6]. To adapt to the rapid development of e-commerce, e-commerce logistics system – an important support industry for e-commerce – has evolved, with logistics enterprises and players influencing and constraining each other in a relatively stable and dynamic equilibrium over the past few years. Compared to the logistics ecosystem commonly defined as consisting of logistics enterprises together with other related industries, the logistics ecosystem in this paper consists only of the participants within the e-commerce logistics industry [7]. The division of labor among the components in an evolved e-commerce logistics ecosystem is clearer, as

* Corresponding author:240301451@qq.com

the objectives are more explicit. And a symbiotic logistics ecosystem adapted to the new economic realm of e-commerce is better developed. A study of the evolution of the e-commerce logistics ecosystem can effectively help logistics enterprises to clarify their position in the ecosystem, help e-commerce practitioners to choose logistics modes better suited to themselves, and effectively help solve problems arising in e-commerce activities.

1 The impact of COVID-19 on the world economy

1.1 The impact of COVID-19 on GDP of major economies

In February 2020, the global economy was hit hard by the COVID-19 pandemic. According to the World Bank's data, in 2020, the GDP of major economies will be adjusted by -3.4% in the United States, -6.4% in the euro zone, -2.7% in Russia and -4.6% in Japan. While it is the only major economy in the world to achieve positive economic growth, China's real GDP growth rate of 2.2%[1] is also well below the previously projected target of 7% growth.

Table 1. GDP Growth by Major Economies, 2020-2023 (%)

	The World Bank				IMF			
	2020	2021e	2022f	2023f	2020	2021	2022f	2023f
China	2.2	8.1	4.3	5.2	2.2	8.1	3.3	4.6
United States	-3.4	5.7	2.5	2.4	-3.4	5.7	2.3	1
Eurozone	-6.4	5.4	2.5	1.9	-6.3	5.4	2.6	1.2
Russia	-2.7	4.7	-8.9	-2	-2.7	4.7	-6	-3.5
Japan	-4.6	1.7	1.7	1.3	-4.5	1.7	1.7	1.7

*e=estimate; f=forecast. Data source: The World Bank, IMF

Table 1 shows that after the overall negative growth in 2020, all major economies returned positive growth in 2021. However, the impact of the international situation has shown that the World Bank and IMF's growth prediction over the next two years have dropped significantly. The IMF is negative about the economic situation in 2022 and 2023, and the July 2022 expected growth rate has been adjusted from 3.6% down to 3.2%, 3.6% in 2023 down to 2.9%. This is the third time the IMF has lowered expectations, indicating that the global economy has not yet recovered from the impact of COVID-19.

1.2 The impact of COVID-19 on the world of e-commerce retailing

Unlike most traditional industries whose growth was hampered by the COVID-19 pandemic, e-commerce, due to its own particularities, has maintained a steady and sustained growth momentum in total and in share of all commerce at a time of global economic downturn. The total amount of the global online retail market will increase from $US3.5 trillion in 2019 to about $US5.7 trillion in 2022[8]. According to a report released by the United Nations Conference on Trade and Development (UNCTAD) [3], the share of online retailing as a part of retailing increases from 16% to 19% in 2020, with South Korea reporting the highest proportional share of 25.9%. In addition, according to government data from Australia, Canada, China, South Korea, Singapore, the United Kingdom, the

United States and other leading economies, online retail sales will grow from about $US2 trillion in 2019 to $US2.5 trillion in 2020 and about $2.9 trillion in 2021.

Table 2. Online retail sales in selected economies of UNCTAD from 2018 to 2020.

	Total retail sales (billions of dollars)			Online retail sales (billions of dollars)			Online share (%)		
	2018	2019	2020	2018	2019	2020	2018	2019	2020
China	5755	5957	5681	1060.4	1233.6	1414.3	18.4	20.7	24.9
United States	5269	5452	5638	519.6	598.0	791.7	9.9	11.0	14.0
United Kingdom	565	564	560	84.0	89.0	130.6	14.9	15.8	23.3
Korea	423	406	403	76.8	84.3	104.4	18.2	20.8	25.9
Canada	467	462	452	13.9	16.5	28.1	3.0	3.6	6.2
Australia	239	229	242	13.5	14.4	22.9	5.9	6.3	9.4
Singapore	34	32	27	1.6	1.9	3.2	4.7	5.9	11.7

Data source: IMF

Table 3. Changes of total retail sales and online retail sales in selected countries before and after the epidemic.

	Total retail sales increased year-on-year from the previous year (%)		Year-over-year growth in online retail sales over the previous year (%)		Online share increased compared to the previous year (%)		Online share growth rate
	2019	2020	2019	2020	2019	2020	
China	3.51	-4.63	16.33	14.65	2.3	4.2	1.8
United States	3.47	3.41	15.09	32.39	1.1	3	2.7
United Kingdom	-0.18	-0.71	5.95	46.74	0.9	7.5	8.3
Korea	-4.02	-0.74	9.77	23.84	2.6	5.1	2.0
Canada	-1.07	-2.16	18.71	70.30	0.6	2.6	4.3
Australia	-4.18	5.68	6.67	59.03	0.4	3.1	7.8
Singapore	-5.88	-15.63	18.75	68.42	1.2	5.8	4.8

Table 3 shows that among the countries selected by UNCTAD, with the exception of China the year-on-year growth rate of online retail sales is greater than 20%, with Canada, Singapore and Australia all growing by more than 50% year-on-year, and the United Kingdom also exceeding 40% (The year-on-year growth rate of online retail sales in China is below 20% due to the large base of online retail sales). Online retail sales in major countries are expanding rapidly as a percentage of total retail sales, with UK online retail sales in 2020 growing 8.3 times faster than the previous year, the highest among the selected countries. The rate of growth values for the other countries in this study are: 1.8 times for China, 2.7 times for the United States, 2 times for South Korea, 4.3 times for Canada, 7.8 times for Australia, and 4.8 times for Singapore. China, one of the most mature country in the online retail market, has reached a bottleneck in growth and has opened a new generation of online retail models, namely live streaming e-commerce and online community retail, which for technical reasons are difficult to account for. For this reason we suggest that that the actual online retail sales in China exceeds that shown in the statistical data.

1.3 Impact of COVID-19 on consumption habits

Accenture reports that COVID-19 has driven many users who were not yet fully digital to move from offline to online and to adopt new interaction habits; a change that is not expected to be reversed [9]. As COVID-19 continues to undergo mutations and new outbreaks continue around the world, delaying the end of the pandemic, it is expected that consumer habits will continue to be affected for a time to come. Thus, it is expected that e-commerce volumes will maintain a high growth rate into the future.

2 The impact of COVID-19 on China's logistics

With continued development of e-commerce, logistics, as a supporting industry, has also undergone a period of rapid development. China, as one of the first countries to recover from the COVID-19 economic downturn, has gained a head start in the development of retail e-commerce logistics in the post-COVID-19 era, and the direction of further development is focused on three aspects: automation, intelligence and digitalization.

2.1 Logistics automation

The advantages of logistics automation can be clearly seen in the early outbreak of COIVD-19 in February 2020, which erupted during the Chinese New Year when a large number of migrant workers returned home, causing a shortage in human resources and preventing the initial logistics models in the city from functioning properly. The lack of human resources was filled by a range of automated equipment, including warehousing machines, drones, and unmanned vehicles.

Warehouse machines solve the problem of warehouse sorting by using automated equipment such as automatic matrices and automatic sorters to dramatically improve the efficiency of warehouse sorting. Data show that JD's "Asia No.1" sorting center in Zhengzhou can handle more than one million orders per day on average, and the sorting efficiency is five times higher than traditional operations [10]. At the same time, the time needed to erect a robotic warehouse is about 1/4 of that of an unautomated warehouse, and makes subsequent maintenance and expansion more flexible.

Drones and unmanned vehicles solve the problem of logistics delivery. Currently, retail logistics systems around the world are facing a problem in the ‘last mile’. With the continuous development of e-commerce logistics, greater demand is placed on the requirements for logistics and delivery services. The point-to-point process has not met the needs of consumers, as home delivery has become a basic service and consumers demand greater choice in time and mode of delivery service. This task is difficult to accomplish using only human resources, as many consumers choose delivery times that fall outside of normal working hours. During the pandemic SF Express's drones, JD's unmanned delivery vehicles and other technical products offered effective solutions to this ‘last mile’ problem[11].

The continuous development of driverless car technologies can also help to complete the process of cargo transportation. Although this technology is not currently widely used, technology companies such as Nuro, Trunk.tech, Google Waymo, AutoX and other technology companies continue to develop L4 level driverless logistics vehicles that have been put to use in specific areas. It is foreseeable that the popularization of 5G technology and the maturity of related technology will bring large-scale use in the future.

2.2 Logistics intelligence

Logistics intelligence includes artificial intelligence logistics tools and systems. In order to control the spread of COVID-19, measures taken by governments such as the quarantine of personnel or localized lockdowns mean that the logistics system face more complex requirements and therefore need to be able to make rapid and accurate adjustments and optimizations. These rely on the use of IoT application architecture in express scenarios, 5G+Cloud warehouse, transportation, and distribution integration, 5G+IoT supported smart park solution architecture, and other technologies.

The application architecture of the Internet of Things in an express delivery scenario refers to the integration of wireless networks and the Internet, the targeted analysis and processing of object data, the use of information by artificial intelligence technologies such as cloud computing, the implementation of intelligent control, and real-time and accurate transmission of object information to users.

5G + Cloud warehouse transportation and distribution integration predominately solves two aspects about logistics warehousing. One is through the combination of 5G technology and big data analysis derived from logistics network traffic distribution and looking for the best location to establish a warehouse, planning the scale of the warehouse, and supporting further establishment of warehouse facilities. The second aspect comes via the monitoring platforms used to ascertain order volume, cargo volume, warehouse storage volume, warehouse heat maps and other abnormal data, cargo code identification, behavior detection, intelligent security, and vehicle management. These are needed to complete the management of the inventory system, equipment management system, task system, attendance system, and to manage the warehouse operation.

The use of 5G+IoT-supported smart park solution architecture establishes a smart logistics park by connecting the terminals in the logistics park. The platform integrates and coordinates to complete the operation, security, access, management, investment, and other applications of the logistics park, ultimately achieving a completely open, intelligent, integrated and connected logistics park.

2.3 Logistics Digitalization

The digitalization of logistics includes three dimensions: the digital supply chain, the digital collaboration platform, and the digital infrastructure service platform.

2.3.1 Digital supply chain

Under the support of blockchain, an immutable, transparent, and reliable product record is generated at every point in the supply chain in real time to support the operation of the supply chain of enterprises. Whereas in traditional chain supply models a supply problem upstream will affect the shipment of downstream manufacturer, resulting in a market shortage. Digital supply chains provide real-time and online services in all scenarios. By integrating data from various sources, they can conduct real-time acquisitions and provide analysis to better support forward-looking decisions of enterprises, thus bringing additional benefits. Data shows that an 'always on' supply chain can increase sales by 1-4%, reduce production costs by 5-10%, and reduce inventory by 20-30% compared with the traditional supply chain.

2.3.2 Digital collaboration platform

SaaS-based management systems improve collaboration between supply chain and logistics, complete manufacturing, distribution, and retail synergy in achieving end-to-end integration. This mainly includes the collaboration between a supply chain and an industrial internet platform, and the collaboration between a supply chain and a distribution/retail platform. The scope of business use is mainly in planning, warehouse management and collaboration, transportation management and collaboration, and intelligent scheduling.

2.3.3. Digital infrastructure services platform

Digital infrastructure service platforms are platform enterprises that provide related services or hardware, equipment, and other infrastructure for logistics operations, and make logistics operations more digital and standardized using the Internet of Things and other technologies.

The development of automation, intelligence and digitalization is an inevitable trend for the logistics industry to match consumer demand and technological development. However, this development process relies on a large amount of resources and technical reserves to support it, which raises concerns for larger logistics enterprises. Small, medium, and micro logistics enterprises, most without the ability to research and develop their own systems, can only wait for these technologies to become popular before considering using them. When the associated costs are reduced to an acceptable range such firms will look toward their own positioning beyond the market occupied by the leading logistics enterprises.

3 The evolution of logistics system under new e-commerce

3.1 Traditional e-commerce retail logistics before the evolution

China's e-commerce retail industry has become a large and mature industry since its emergence in the late 1990s, and having undergone more than 20 years of development its national online retail sales reached 13.09 trillion yuan in 2021. According to the '14th Five-Year' E-commerce Development Plan issued by the Ministry of Commerce, the Central Internet Information Office and the Development and Reform Commission, the national online retail sales will reach 17 trillion yuan in 2025. This shows that development momentum will remain strong in the coming years. China's mature e-commerce industry has driven the development of the e-commerce logistics industry, and express delivery, as a major component of e-commerce logistics, accumulating 108.3 billion pieces with a revenue of 1,033.23 billion yuan in 2021. This is expected to reach 150 billion pieces with revenue of 1.8 trillion yuan in 2025 [12]. All major e-commerce retail platforms except JD.com use third-party logistics. The traditional e-commerce logistics market share is occupied by large logistics enterprises, and small and medium-sized logistics enterprises struggle to survive.

3.2 Live streaming e-commerce logistics triggered a new form of logistics

COVID-19 led to new ways of working, living and learning and has given rise to new industries such as the home economy and the no-touch economy. As a result of the epidemic, live e-commerce has undergone explosive development. Data shows that the live e-commerce market has been growing rapidly since 2019, with an average annual scale of over a trillion. [13] It has now become a mature part of the e-commerce retail segment, with about 473 million users, and a market value of over 3.4 trillion. The scale of live e-commerce transactions is expected to account for about 1/4 of online retail sales in 2022.

Table 4. 2019-2022 live streaming e-commerce statistics in China.

	Market size (billion yuan)	Growth rate (%)	User size (billion people)	Growth rate (%)	Penetration rate (%)	Penetration growth (%)
2019	4437.5	227.7	2.5	13.63	4.3	168.74
2020	12850	136.61	3.72	48.8	8.6	100
2021	23615.1	83.77	4.3	15.59	17.97	108.95
2022e	34879	47.69	4.73	10	24.1	34.11

Data source: 100ec.cn

As each live platform increases its support for streaming, a series of policies for merchants to be stationed on the platform to carry out live-streaming have been introduced to help offline merchants open their online marketing mode by implementing policies such as lowering technical service fees, optimizing the merchant stationing process, helping merchants to harvest initial traffic, training for online streamers to enhance their professionalism, subsidizing some goods, and reducing or waiving commissions. Opening the door of live marketing for offline individual businesses from the perspective of cost, entry process, staff training, subsidies, and so forth suggests China's e-commerce shows great vitality.

Originally, the rise of the e-commerce had a huge impact on offline physical stores, and isolation policies enacted during the epidemic have deepened their plight. With policy support, many offline physical stores began to shift their sales to the O2O model. The main customer group for this type of live streaming e-commerce comes from within the city or region where the retailed is located, and does not need the logistics service of large-scale transportation. These then derive a new O2O logistics ecosystem that requires a daily delivery of no more than 100 orders, and a delivery distance of no more than 10 km per order, with delivery generally done by the store owner themselves or other individual staff. With the development of live streaming e-commerce, more individuals such as taxi drivers, delivery drivers and other professionals are involved in this system in a personal capacity, and there are documented cases of commuters earning commissions on the way to work during their daily commute. This kind of logistics system can be regarded as a form of 'crowdsourcing'. That is, with no fixed staff the models rely mainly on otherwise idle social resources to complete the delivery. This form of logistics emerged so that the lower rung of the logistics ecosystem can develop further, providing a more robust logistics ecosystem and a useful solution to the problem of the 'last mile' of logistics. For this new ecology, Ali Group, JD.com, Meituan and other Internet companies have launched their own crowdsourcing platform, further integrating otherwise idle social resources, providing an intermediary service offering further supervision, guaranteeing provision of service, and further promoting and improving the development of this model.

3.3 Online community retail logistics trigger new logistics forms

Online community retail is similar to live streaming e-commerce. Traditional community retail is concerned with offline purchases and constituent parts such as supermarkets, grocery stores and convenience stores in the community, and consumer groups have shown a certain consumer 'stickiness'. With the development of mobile internet and instant delivery, traditional community convenience stores and other retailers cannot meet the needs of consumers, and people's consumption habits are gradually changing from in-store consumption to a combination of home consumption and in-store consumption. New online community retail models such as front-end warehouse and warehouse-store integration are beginning to emerge.

With the emergence of the online community retail model, consumers are increasingly accustomed to the consumption model of placing orders online and having them delivered to their homes within 2 hours, and this change in consumer habits has in turn driven the development of this model. The 3-5 km instant delivery range has expanded the coverage of retail store fronts/warehouses and provided consumers with more choices. This aligns with current consumption trends of diverse and frequent consumption and fragmented scenarios. The group buying model of community retail has also made a significant contribution to reducing the movement of people during epidemic control, while safeguarding the lives of residents.

The traditional community retail supply chain is a linear structure in which brands develop products and transfer them through distributors to downstream retailers and customers. Online community retailing places more emphasis on user demand-centric supply chain services, which are characterized by just-in-time delivery (delivery close to the customer, providing fast and on-time delivery services), low inventory sales, and inventory transparency.

Traditional B2C e-merchants cover a comprehensive range of categories and require a nationwide supply chain and consumer network to support the number of orders. The supply chain of community retail e-commerce has strong localization attributes. Community retail usually takes the fresh produce category as the entry point, having obvious high-frequency and just-need characteristics. In the long-distance transportation process, the loss of fresh produce is serious, combined with the need for immediate delivery once it reaches the retail end of the community. The supply chain cost is significantly higher than traditional e-commerce logistics. Therefore, community retail usually needs to establish cooperation with the local supply chain, and fresh produce is sold from local sources as far as possible to ensure the control of logistics costs while completing efficient end delivery.

On December 22, 2020, the State Administration for Market Regulation, together with the Ministry of Commerce, organized Ali Group, Tencent, JD.com, Meituan, pinduoduo, and Didi to participate in the administrative guidance meeting to regulate the order of community group purchasing. These six internet platform companies are required to strictly regulate community group purchase business practices and comply with the 'nine shall not' ruling, significantly compressing the profits and advantages of large the internet platforms and guiding the online community retail industry back to the route dominated by small supermarkets and convenience stores. This allows for small and micro logistics enterprises and individual logistics personnel to participate in the developments, promoting the continued evolution of the logistics ecology and creating a favorable environment for the formation of a symbiotic logistics ecosystem.

4. The evolution of China's e-commerce logistics ecology in the post-epidemic era

With the development of new logistics models such as live e-commerce logistics and online community retail logistics, the logistics ecology traditionally controlled by CR8 has changed significantly, and the number of enterprises and practitioners involved in logistics has similarly increased. New e-commerce logistics models have emerged, and the original e-commerce logistics ecosystem consisting of large and medium-sized enterprises has evolved into a symbiotic logistics ecosystem consisting of large enterprises, small, medium, and micro enterprises, and ordinary individuals. According to the characteristics of the roles assumed by each member of the symbiotic logistics ecosystem, and with reference to the composition of a natural forest ecosystems [14], the current e-commerce logistics market can be divided into a guiding layer, a backbone layer, a filling layer, a basic layer and a bearing layer.

4.1 Guiding layer

The guiding layer's role is like the forest canopy layer in a forest ecosystem, and consists of of large e-commerce logistics companies such as China Post, SF and Jingdong, which occupy most of the market share and gain the most profits while simultaneously bearing most of the market risks and policy impacts. They have the most resources and technology research and development capabilities within the ecosystem, and hold most of the technology patents that can drive the development of the industry. This partly determines the scale that the whole ecosystem can reach.

4.2 Backbone layer

The positioning of the backbone layer is similar to that of the understory layer in a forest ecosystem and consists of large and medium-sized e-commerce logistics enterprises such as ZTO Express, STO.Express, Yunda Express, and J&T Express. Its essence is like that of the logistics enterprises constituting the bootstrap layer, and most of them are listed companies. However, the influence, innovation capacity and R&D investment are not as strong as those located in the bootstrap layer, and the market risks and policy shocks they need to bear are much smaller. This part of the ecosystem has the highest share of the overall market and is the main stabilizing force of the whole ecosystem. It also has certain R&D capabilities and can make the layer leap to the upper layer under specific conditions (e.g., developing unique leading technologies).

4.3 Filling layer

This layer includes all logistics enterprises that only operate in a small region (e.g., a single province or city), and can be likened to the shrub layer in a forest ecosystem. It can only survive through the market share left over by the guiding layer and the backbone layer. With little regard for the risks brought about by the market and policy changes, and no ability to develop new technologies themselves, it is difficult to achieve a layer leap. At the same time, because it is difficult to compete with the upper two layers for survival resources, it may be easy for an enterprise to be eliminated by the competition. However, upon being eliminated, similar types of enterprises will soon appear to take over any vacated position.

4.4 Basic layer

This tier is comprised of individuals such as crowdsourced personnel involved in logistics. This layer in the ecosystem does not need to consider market risk and policy impact at all and can achieve layer change by attaching to the above layer (e.g., joining a parent company), but after the change no longer exists in the form of a separate individual, instead becoming part of the larger enterprise. Crowdsourcing in e-commerce logistics has long existed, Meituan, hungry and other take-out platforms are particularly active in the evolution of e-commerce logistics system, and more individuals for ‘no extra time spent’, ‘by the way’ and other reasons participate in e-commerce logistics activities. This is in line with the concept of the ‘sharing economy’. The basic layer, as the bottom layer of the ecosystem, occupies little market share but retains great significance. On the one hand, the labor force is idle due to lower income or company closures caused by the epidemic, and activating these individuals to participate in e-commerce logistics activities can solve income and employment problems. On the other hand, more participants involved in e-commerce logistics brings greater possibilities for the above-mentioned layers. More participants engaged in the processes of e-commerce logistics brings greater possibility for the logistics enterprises mentioned above to supplement labor.

4.5 Bearing layer

The bearing layer in this ecosystem refers to the e-commerce market. The e-commerce market is the foundation of the whole e-commerce logistics industry, and the e-commerce logistics industry cannot exist separately from the e-commerce market. Like soil in a forest ecosystem, the fertility of the bearing layer determines the development scale of the whole ecosystem, and the development scale of the e-commerce market determines the development scale of the e-commerce logistics ecosystem. The layers above also feed the bearing layer, making the environment of the e-commerce market more solid, forming a virtuous cycle.

As consumer habits develop and mature it will become more difficult for logistics companies in the ecosystem to move up the hierarchy. Considering the characteristics of internet companies, we cannot rule out the possibility of downward acquisitions by companies in the guiding and backbone layers, or the evolution of monopolistic companies by merging with each other in the backbone layers, which will lead to further evolution of the ecosystem.

5 Conclusion

E-commerce in the post-COVID-19 era has become an important part of the domestic cycle, and the role played by e-commerce logistics in e-commerce is self-evident. The better promote the development of e-commerce, e-commerce logistics will have to strengthen its adaptability to help e-commerce and give full play to the advantages of its interactive convenience. At the same time, the new e-commerce model has seen the emergence of a new e-commerce logistics ecology, making the positioning of the constituent enterprises in the ecosystem clearer, the direction of development clearer, the ecosystem more stable, and the ability to address perceived risk between the various components more robust. Stable development of the e-commerce logistics ecosystem provides a solid foundation for promoting deeper reform and innovation of e-commerce and is of great significance to the common and sustainable development of both.

References

1. World Bank, Global Economic Prospects,(2022)
2. International Monetary Fund (IMF), World Economic Outlook, (2022)
3. United Nations Conference on Trade and Development (UNCTAD), Estimates Of Global e-Commerce 2020 And Preliminary Assessment Of Covide-19 Impact On Online Retail 2020, (2021)

4. Datainsinght. Internet Commerce in Russia 2021,(2022)
5. Department of E-Commerce, Ministry of Commerce of China, China E-Commerce Report 2021, (2022)
6. United Nations Conference on Trade and Development (UNCTAD), Recovering from COVID-19 in an increasingly digital economy: Implications for sustainable development, (2022)
7. S.E.Barykin, E.A.Smirnova , D Chzhao, I.V.Kapustina, S.M.Sergeev, Y.Y.Mikhalchevsky, A.V.Gubenko, G.A.Kostin, E De La Poza Plaza, L.Saychenko, N.Moiseev, Digital Echelons and Interfaces within Value Chains: End-to-End Marketing and Logistics Integration. *Sustainability* **13**, 13929. https://doi.org/10.3390/su132413929,(2021)
8. Intelligence Research, 2022-2028 China E-Commerce Logistics Industry Market Competition Pattern and Future Development Trend Report, (2022)
9. Accenture, Deconstructing the Five New States of the Human Mind to Fuel Customer Experience Innovation, (2020)
10. R. Shen , Place an order in the morning and receive it in the afternoon, Zhengzhou Asia No. 1. is here! China Storage & Transportation (12): 56-57, (2020)
11. D. Zhao, Analysis of China's logistics system under COVID-19 epidemic. *Proceedings of St. Petersburg State University of Economics* **3(123)**, 180-184, (2020)
12. China National Post Office, China National Development and Reform Commission, Ministry of Transport of China, 14th Five Year" Postal Industry Development Plan,(2021)
13. 100ec.cn, 2022 (first half) China Live E-Commerce Market Data Report, (2022)
14. Y.X. Jiang,Q.S. Guo , J. Ma, Classification of forest communities in China and their community science characteristics. *Science Press*, (2018)

Distribution rules of conflict events and management countermeasures of large-scale construction engineering projects

Yi Wang[1], *Yiru* Hou[2], and *Xueliang* Hou[3,*]

[1]Economy and Management Department, North China Electric Power University, 102206 Beijing, China
[2]School of Construction Management Technology, Purdue University, 47907 West Lafayette, IN, USA
[3]School of Economy and Management, North China Electric Power University, 102206 Beijing, China

Abstract. The processes of large-scale construction projects implementation are often affected with various internal and external factors, which result in various conflict events in different stages of the project, and bring different degrees of harm to the construction project. In order to understand and master the distribution rules of various conflict events in different stages in large-scale construction projects, a massive investigation was carried out on 96 large-scale engineering construction units in China, and 325 effective research samples were obtained. Based on this investigation results, the mathematical analysis and summary of the conflict events of large construction engineering projects have been made by multiple statistical analyses, which reveal the distribution law and the primary and secondary relationship of various conflict events in each stage of engineering projects. Combined with the research results, the management countermeasures and suggestions of conflict events are put forward, which provide valuable references for the project managers to effectively manage the conflict events and improve the management level of engineering projects.

1 Introduction

In recent years, in order to promote the stable development of China national economy, and reduce such disadvantages results from covid-19 and the world economic recession, trillions of investments have been used for many large-scale constructions, such as Xiong an district, Guangzhou big bay area, Beijing-Shanghai high-speed railway, UHV engineering, Winter Olympic venues, and other projects. The consequences of these construction projects have proved by the real effects that the projects not only greatly promoted the development of China's related industries, but also played a huge role in ensuring employment and promoting people's livelihood in China, and brought significant economic and social benefits to China's economic development. However, large-scale

* Corresponding author: hou-xl@163.com

construction projects are very complex systematic engineering, and are often influenced or interrupted by various factors from inside and outside the engineering system in the process of construction [1]. Therefore, many kinds of conflicts and contradictions often happened among partners, and such phenomena as low quality, progress delay, cost over-expenditure, safety accidents, contract disputations, and legal conflicts often appeared in the construction [2-3]. Relevant research results have shown that once relevant conflicts occur in the construction project, it may cause certain economic losses to the construction enterprises, lead to the complete failure of the project, and sometimes even bring a certain degree of negative impact to the stability and social development in local areas [4-5]. Just because of this, the question has become one of the important practical problems for construction enterprises and government management departments on how to fully understand and correctly grasp the producing, developing and distribution rules of large-scale construction project conflict events in order to help project managers make the scientific and correct decision.

2 Investigation and statistics of conflict incidents

In order to understand the conflict events in large-scale construction projects, and reveal the objective situation and distribution of conflict events systematically, an extensive investigation has been carried at the support of China national social science fund project and ninety-six large-scale construction enterprises in twenty-seven provinces. After researchers completed the questionnaire edition on the bases of determining survey parameters such as survey object, survey content, survey methods, and survey sample demands, 438 questionnaires were issued in the survey. Finally, 376 questionnaires were recovered. Through the identification, 325 valid questionnaires were obtained, and the questionnaire recovery rate was 85.84%. Based on the actual recovered sample, the response rate of the questionnaire was 86.43%. Therefore, this survey sample size can fully meet the quantity required for large sample studies [6].

2.1 Sample statistics

Captions should be typed in 9-point Times. They should be centred above the tables and flush left beneath the figures. According to the theory of engineering project management knowledge system[7], it is known that the project is divided into four stages of decision-making, preparation, construction and completion based on the actual needs of the project construction and management. In order to find the distribution of conflict events and their main characteristics clearly and accurately in each stage of large-scale construction projects, the four stages that appear all kinds of conflict events in construction projects have been determined in advance before investigation. So, the respondents can be more concise, objective and accurately reflect the conflict problems of each stage of the project. According to the analysis of 325 valid samples, the investigators reported 726 items of conflict events. Through the consolidation analysis of 726 conflict events, it is known that there are 76 representative conflict events in 19 categories in large construction projects, that is, 9 in the decision-making stage, 12 in the preparation stage, 42 in the construction stage, and 13 in the end stage. The category of conflict events in each stage and their cumulative reflection frequency in the survey are shown in Table 1.

Table 1. Statistic of conflict events in each stage.

Stage	Category of conflict	Frequency	Total
Decision-making	Project scheme decision-making	15	71
	Project feasible study	24	

	Project investment estimation	19	
	Report submission and approval	13	
Preparation	Engineering survey and design	59	155
	Project bidding	39	
	Land expropriation and resident migration	26	
	Construction procedures transaction	31	
Construction	Safety management	64	401
	Contract disputes	28	
	Engineering quality	46	
	Environmental problem	48	
	Construction schedule	53	
	Personnel coordination	45	
	Resource allocation	67	
	Technical problems	50	
Ending	Expense settlement	34	99
	Residual problem handling	45	
	Project confirmation and handover	20	

2.2 Mathematical distributional characteristics of the conflict events

In the multivariate statistical theory, the mean and median can effectively depict the position characteristics of the study subsample, and the extreme difference, variance and standard deviation can effectively represent the dispersion characteristics of the study subsample [8]. Therefore, to further find and know the distribution characteristics of conflict events in large-scale construction projects, the mathematical distribution characteristics of conflict events have been analyzed through the mathematical analysis of various conflict events in various stages of large-scale construction projects based on the scientific theory of multiple statistics.

(1) Mean and median values

In the multivariate statistical theory, the mathematical model for obtaining the average of the study sample is $\mu = 1/n(\sum \mu_i)$, where, n is the calculated number of samples, μ_i is the i th sample number value. Because the number of samples is even, the corresponding value of the median is 401. Based to the data in Table 1:

$$\mu = \frac{1}{n}\sum_{i=1}^{n}\mu_i = \frac{1}{4}(71+155+401+99) = 181.5$$

(2)Extremum, variance and standard deviation

Similarly, according to the multivariate statistical theory, the maximum value $Max(\mu_i)$ is 401, the minimum value $Min(\mu_i)$ is 71 in the four studied subsample values, so, the extremum, variance and standard deviation can be known as follows.

$$R = Max(\mu_i) - Min(\mu_i) = 330$$

$$\sigma^2 = \frac{1}{n}\sum_{i=1}^{n}(\mu_i - \mu)^2 = \frac{1}{4}\left[(71-181.5)^2 + (155-181.5)^2 + (401-181.5)^2 + (99-181.5)^2\right] = 67899$$

$$\sqrt{\sigma^2} = 260.57$$

Based on the above analysis of data, it can be found that the conflict events in large-scale construction projects generally possess partial normal distribution characteristics. From the project decision stage to the preparatory stage, the amount will increase significantly, and the number of conflict events will reach a peak at the project construction stage. According to the rule, project managers just could realize that all kinds of preparations should be done in advance when the project gradually enters the preparation stage from the decision-making stage. So that, in the process of engineering management, they can have sufficient project resources and working time to effectively deal with various conflict events that appeared in the preparation stage and construction stage, avoid burying potential troubles, and provide more advantageous conditions for the smooth implementation of the construction project.

3 The primary and secondary relationship of conflict events

It can be seen from Table 1 that there are different numbers of conflict categories in different stages, which have also different frequencies. Obviously, those conflict events that occur more frequently and have a great impact on the project will undoubtedly consume more resources of the project and need managers to invest more energy in processing and controlling. Therefore, from the perspective of engineering project management, a comprehensive and systematic analysis of the impact on the frequency and consequences of conflict events has a higher scientific significance and value.

For this problem, it can be known based on the multi-factor integration theory of system science that the frequency f_i and consequences q_i of conflict events have a high positive correlation with the degree r_i that project managers need to pay attention to the conflict events [9]. If let f_i as the level value of the conflict event, let q_i as the weight value of the conflict event, the level weight summary value r_i reflecting the importance of the conflict event is product value of the two parameters.

Just based on such consideration in the research, the investigators were required that not only described the conflict events in each stage, but also gave the corresponding qualitative analysis results of every conflict event according to five degrees of the consequences caused by conflict events, that is, very serious, serious, general, small and negligible. In this way, the consequences qualitative degree of conflict events can be quantified through the conversion of membership grade in fuzzy mathematics. Here, let 0.9, 0.7, 0.5, 0.3, and 0.1 respectively delegate very serious, serious, general, small, and negligible. Thus, the weight value of each conflict consequences severity can be learned, and the level weight summary value reflecting the importance of every conflict event in each stage can also be obtained furtherly. According to this analysis method, the comprehensive values of various conflict events in large construction projects can be shown in table 2 together with the data of Table 1 and the survey result.

Table 2. The comprehensive values of various conflict events.

stage	Category of conflict	f_i	q_i	r_i
Decision-making	Project scheme decision-making	15	0.81	12.1
	Project feasible study	24	0.76	18.2
	Project investment estimation	19	0.75	14.3
	Report submission and approval	13	0.81	10.5
Preparation	Engineering survey and design	59	0.75	44.5
	Project bidding	39	0.73	28.3
	Land expropriation and resident migration	26	0.77	20.0
	Construction procedures transaction	31	0.76	23.7
Construction	Safety management	64	0.77	49.2
	Contract disputes	28	0.76	21.4
	Engineering quality	46	0.74	34.0
	Environmental problem	48	0.72	34.4
	Construction schedule	53	0.72	38.3
	Personnel coordination	45	0.72	32.5
	Resource allocation	67	0.75	50.1

	Technical problems	50	0.74	37.0
Ending	Expense settlement	34	0.75	25.5
	Residual problem handling	45	0.76	34.2
	Project confirmation and handover	20	0.75	15.0

According to the analysis results in Table 2, the conflict events in each stage of large construction projects have the following characteristics.

(1) In the decision-making stage, the main conflict events focus on the disputes of project feasibility study among participators, and the lowest one is such problem as the report submission and approval.

(2) In the preparation stage, the problems of the conflict events are mainly concentrated in the conflicts and contradictions among participators in the drawing review and technical explanation due to the poor engineering survey and design, the secondary problems are mainly such conflict events as project bidding, construction procedures transaction and land expropriation and resident migration.

(3) In the construction stage, the main occurring conflicts from the top to low are respectively the resource allocation, safety, construction schedule, technology, environment, quality, personnel management and contract disputes. It can be seen that the prominent conflict event in the project construction stage is the project resources and interest allocation closely related to all participants.

(4) In the completion stage, the conflict events mainly turn to the residual problem handling and the cost settlement, which has a high degree of consistency with the actual problems appearing in the construction project.

4 Related countermeasures and suggestions

It can be seen based on the above empirical data and theoretical analysis results that a variety of conflict events closely related to various works in their stages appear at different stages in large-scale construction projects. These conflict events may not only occur in their stage but also continue to the next stage if the conflict problem has not been solved in the previous stage. For example, if some problems exist in engineering design in the preparation stage and the problem is not solved thoroughly, then, the problem will appear again in the construction stage. Meanwhile, the problem would make relative participators debate each other, and bring a series of adverse effects to engineering quality, schedule, cost, safety, and so on. Therefore, combined with the main characteristics and distribution rules of various conflicts in each stage of the large-scale construction project, the following relevant countermeasures and suggestions are given as follows to improve the construction project management level.

(1) At the decision-making stage of the construction project, project managers and decision-makers should carry out the platitudinous survey and feasibility study of the proposed project; determine the effective construction plan and scheme through deep discussion and analysis with relative participators. Thus, some advantageous conditions could be formed for avoiding and reducing the occurrence of conflict events in the later stages.

(2) In the preparation stage of the project, the project managers and decision-makers should actively organize the project participating parties, and let them carefully read and understand the project's detailed construction plan. On the base of this, clarify the functions and responsibilities of all parties. These actions can avoid more conflicts and contradictions among the relevant parties in the late construction stage.

(3) In the construction stage, whether the various project resources can be provided in time is not only related to whether the parties can complete their respective tasks in time but also

their enterprise's economic benefits, so, resource conflict becomes the main problem in the construction project. Therefore, the project managers and decision-makers should establish the information management system of project resources in advance, and understand and grasp the requirements of resource allocation in the process of construction comprehensively and accurately, ensuring all participators enable to get the necessary resources support and guarantee.

(4) In the completion stage of the construction project, all parties expect to quickly complete the project handover and cost settlement, and obtain their profit To this, the project managers should make the overall arrangement, and treat different conflict events together with their different situations in face of project confirmation and handover, residual problem handling and expense settlement. Thus, the end work of the project can be completed smoothly, and the conflicts among all participators can be minimum.

The research has been supported by the national social science foundation, No. 21BGL123, and ninety-six large-scale construction enterprises, the authors especially thank them for this work.

References

1. Shan Tengfei, Hou Xueliang. Conflicting and influencing factors in the construction stage of construction projects. Journal of Engineering Management. 36,102-106(2022)
2. Liu Cong, Wu Guangdong, Duan Kai Feng. Research on Conflict Management Strategies of Construction Engineering Projects Based on CAS Theory. Journal of Engineering Management, 31, 102-107(2017)
3. Wang Conghan,Zhang Shuibo. Trust Repair in The Aftermath of Conflict Occurrence in Construction Subcontracting: An Intergroup Contact Perspective.Construction Management and Economics, 40,102-106(2022).
4. Hou xl. Research on Randomcity of Conflict Events in Construction Engineering Project. ICCREM 2015: 377-380.
5. Adeyemi Ben, Suan Jamen. An Exploratory Factor Analysis for Conflict Resolution Methods among Civil Construction Profession. Buildings, 12,136-141(2022)
6. Ma zhuangguo. *Management Statistics*. Beijing, Science Press (2002).
7. Hou Xueliang, Guo Yu, Wang Yi. Ergodic relationship of management objects at each stage of large-scale construction projects. Journal of Systems Science, 29,113-117(2021)
8. Wang Rongxin. mathematical statistics. Shaanxi,Xi'an Jiaotong University Press(2002)
9. Wu Mengqiang, He Danfeng Yi. Research on the Coordination Mechanism of Government Investment Project Based on Contradiction. Construction Economy,42,83-87(2021)

A useful method for postgraduate of chemical engineering in understanding the public opinions of public events related to their major: A case study of health communication and public opinions of COVID-19 on Twitter in Germany

Ningning Zhao[1], *Xiaojiao* Yu[1], *Zhicheng* Zhang[2,*], *Zhong* Yu[1], *Binghua* Yao[1], *Jinfen* Niu[1], *Nailiang* Liu[1], and *Junpeng* Li[1]

[1]Xi'an University of Technology, School of Science, 710054 Xi'an, Shaanxi, China
[2]Xi'an International Studies University, School of Journalism and Communication, 710028 Xi'an, Shaanxi, China

Abstract. In order to adapt to the latest development of higher education in the era of big data, improve the sensitivity for postgraduate of chemical engineering in the public opinions of public events related to their major, this study took "the pandemic of COVID-19 on Twitter in Germany" as an example and investigated the health communication and public opinions on COVID-19 based on the Python scripts and Twitter streaming application programming interface using statistical analysis and chi square feature selection. The provided method is helpful to improve the insight, prediction, scientific literacy and innovation ability of postgraduate of chemical engineering.

1 Introduction

With the development of information technology and the continuous improvement of information construction, significant changes have taken place in the technical and social environment. Employees in various fields are facing huge challenges, which also puts forward higher requirements for cultivation of high-level talents in colleges and universities as well as the higher education development. The postgraduate stage is one of the main stages to focus on cultivating research capabilities such as problem analysis and problem solving. Improving their scientific literacy and introducing the new research ideas and methods bred in the era of big data into the postgraduate education system, which are conducive to expanding the vision of the postgraduate, and stimulate them to adopt new research ideas and methods to solve scientific and practical problems in their chosen fields, and promote the improvement of the innovation ability of postgraduate students.

* Corresponding author: zhangzhicheng@xisu.edu.cn

At present, the world is in a critical period of the COVID-19. The social public opinions brought by the COVID-19 will have an important impact on the insight, prediction and research innovation ability of the postgraduate students of chemical engineering, especially the postgraduates in biochemical engineering. The postgraduate students of chemical engineering should be able to obtain the source of big data related to their major, have a comprehensive vision of big data, be able to fully understand the public opinions brought about by the COVID-19 through reasonable methods, analyse and use big data to solve key problems and problems in the practice, promote scientific research innovation and development of science and technology.

World Health Organization (WHO) announced a Public Health Emergency of International Concern (PHEIC) on January 30, 2020 [1]. China National Health Commission confirmed that the virus was human-to-human transmissible [2]. WHO announced "COVID-19" as the name of this new disease on 11 February 2020. ICTV announced "severe acute respiratory syndrome coronavirus 2 (SARS-CoV-2)" as the name of the new virus on 11 February 2020 [3]. Social distancing was widely used by governments aiming to reduce physical contact between people. In this case, more and more social interactions move online, the conversation around COVID 19 has continued to expand, with increasing users turning to social media. Twitter has become central to allow us to stay connected during the crises.

Twitter data provides us with a very good opportunity to analyse the perception and reaction to a public disease outbreak among the same linguistic and cultural group of populations.

In this study, 1.5 million Twitter posts including tweets, retweets and replies were obtained employing Python scripts and Twitter streaming application programming interface. On which basis, the health communication on COVID-19 has been demonstrated and public opinions to the pandemic of COVID-19 on Twitter in Germany has been investigated using statistical analysis and chi square feature selection.

2 Methodologies and results

We obtained all the Twitter data via Python programming scripts from January 20, 2020. For this study, we ran Python scripts to access all the samples of tweets in German using the topics including coronavirus, COVID-19, SARS-CoV-2, Wuhan coronavirus and nCoV. The time frame was January 20 to August 2(Coordinated Universal Time).

We calculated the basic descriptive statistics including the number of posts, the number of posts per user, retweets, hashtags and embedded URL links. We estimated the Pearson's correlation between the proportion of tweets with hashtags and the proportion of tweets with embedded URL links.

We retrieved COVID-19 related Twitter data in five key topics: coronavirus ($N = 948525$), COVID-19 ($N = 665590$), SARS-Cov-2($N = 60974$), Wuhan coronavirus ($N = 1143$) and nCoV($N = 2476$). More than 200 thousand unique users joined health communication of Covid-19 during that period of time on Twitter. The mean number of posts per user ranged from 1.81 to 5.75. However, the distribution for the number of posts per user is 1.0 for all 5 corpora. Across the five corpora, as the proportion of tweets with hashtags increased, the proportion of tweets with URLs increased ($r = 0.986$, $p < 0.005$). More than 60 percent of tweets are embedded with URLs in total.

Then we analysed retweets to test participation in each corpus. We ranked the number of retweets for each tweet and extracted all user names. The number of retweets indicates the influence of its tweets. Thus, we identified the most influential twitter participants in the COVID-19 discussion. We chose the top 30 users ranking the top of the retweet list from each corpus, and categorized them into the following categories of users:

Media: Twitter profiles of media, reporter, anchor and journalists.

Political: Twitter profiles of government agencies, political groups or parties and politicians.

Medical: Twitter profiles of hospitals, health care organizations and the medical practitioners.

Others: Twitter profiles that do not belong to the three categories referred to above.

We found that the categories of the top 30 users differed between the corpora. In coronavirus and nCoV and SARS-CoV-2 corpora, the number of media users are 11(36.67%), 12(40%) and 8(26.67%) separately. While in COVID-19, nCoV and SARS-CoV-2 corpora, seven (23.33%) 11 (36.67%) and ten (33.33%) were medical users respectively. Political users take up 16.67 percent (5 political users) and 20 percent (6 political users) in Coronavirus and COVID-19 corpora.

Keywords selected will be able to present the public opinion and trend of discussion. We ran Python scripts to calculate the weeks when the most tweets were published. The week number in this study will follow ISO-8601 standard. After preliminary analysis, we found that the largest number of tweets came in the 12th week (N = 207858). Then we ran chi-square feature selection algorithm to select the keywords in the 12th week when the public were more willing to share their ideas online [4].

We performed a chi-square feature selection analysis to pick the keywords that are most unique to a specific corpus and on a specific date. Chi-square feature selection is very helpful in machine learning by testing the relationship between the features [5]. Chi-square test measures how expected count E and observed count Q deviates each other, testing the independence of the two variables, following the equation as below:

$$x_c^2 = \sum \frac{(Q_i - E_i)^2}{E_i} \quad (1)$$

In the equation, c is the degree of freedom, Q is the observed value, E is the expected value.

The algorithm vectorizes the corpus into a sparse matrix, calculating the scores of each word in the bag-of-words model [6]. The null hypothesis of chi-square test is that each word in the bag-of-word model is independent and there is no relationship. A high score of chi-square value tells that the hypothesis of independence is incorrect, indicating the particularity of the word to a specific corpus. We picked the keywords with the highest scores of chi-square values, ranking on top of the list calculated. German words were translated into English through Google translation service. Table 1 showed the top 20 most unique words in each corpus. The higher it ranks, the more unique it is.

Table 1. Top 20 keywords for each corpus, selected by chi-square feature selection.

	Coronavirus	COVID-19	nCoV	SARS-CoV-2	Wuhancoronavirus
1	Trumpfail	Bum	SOS	June	Condemn
2	Market	Cacao	Cannabidiol[1]	Stock[2]	Friend
3	Heidekreis[3]	Sicker	IFSG[4]	Stupid	Trump
4	Pollination	Kiss	Sick	EAU5	Mask
5	Radical	Sending prayer	Made[6]	BAföG[7]	Blackout
6	VDGN[8]	Cold	Dead	Wonnemar9	CCP[10]
7	Member	Eat	Zombie	Good luck	Pandemic
8	Foreign	Explanation	South America[11]	DGB[12]	People
9	Senator	Disruption	Sars	Borkheide[13]	WHO[14]

10	CVP[15]	Quarantine area	CoV	MAYDAY[16]	China
11	ASB[17]	Pollination	Virus	AStA	November
12	Velo[18]	Senator	Coronavirus	Diakonia[19]	Tenant
13	Najaf[20]	SOS	Gene sequencing	LOINC[21]	Lie down
14	Mühlenkreiskliniken[22]	Foreign	Inspect	Weight loss	Local
15	China	AStA[23]	Relaxed	Billion[24]	Pneumonia
16	Elbow	Goodbye	Genom	Extra time	Make
17	Vitamin	Pray	Genomic	Muslim	Mainstream
18	Disinfectant bottle	Shetland[25]	Wordag[26]	Save[27]	Market
19	Amberg[28]	Manufacture	Concern	Daily	Over
20	Delta[29]	Tripsdrill[30]	Lean back	Bruck[31]	Media

Notes: 1. Cannabidiol oil might benefit patients infected with COVID-19; 2. Stock toilet paper; 3. The name of a place in Germany; 4. German Infection Protection Act; 5. European Association of Urology; 6. The virus appeared originally; 7. Abbreviation of Bundesausbildungsförderungsgesetz, Germany's Federal Training Assistance Act; 8. German land usage organization; 9. A recreation center in Germany closed temporarily during pandemic; 10. China communist party; 11. Governments tightened the measure to prevent pandemic in south America; 12. German trade union confederation; 13. The name of place in Germany; 14. World health organization; 15. The Christian Democratic People's Party of Switzerland; 16. A pop music band; 17. Charity emergency rescue organization; 18. Pro-cyclist organization; 19. A public service organization of the protestants; 20. An Iraqi city which is locked down because of COVID-19; 21. Logical Observation Identifiers Names and Codes,a medical research organization; 22. Medical organization; 23. University student union; 24. Billion dollars; 25. A place of UK where suffered serious covid-19 pandemic; 26. A German doctor; 27. To save people's life; 28. A German city; 29. An airliner; 30. The oldest park in Germany; 31. A German city.

The words 'SOS', 'China' and 'Market' appeared in different corpora. Most of the words are specific to this outbreak (i.e., 'Coronavirus', 'Virus','Gene Sequencing'), we found that this pandemic had potential influences on various aspects of society. AStA referred to a student union. Tripsdrill is a famous and popular park in Germany and DGB referred to German Trade Union Confederation. A pop star group with the name of MAYDAY posted tweets cancelled their concerts because of the pandemic. Some medical organizations were involved to confront with COVID-19, including 'EAU' (European association of urology), 'WHO' (world health organization), 'LOINC' (logical observation identifiers names and codes, a medical research organization) and 'Mühlenkreiskliniken' (a medical organization group). We also find keywords 'stock' which indicates people are stocking toilet paper. 'Elbow', 'Disinfectant bottle', 'Cold' and 'Sick' keywords appeared in some educational tweets that helps the public about COVID-19.

3 Discussion and conclusion

First, our findings suggest that the online reactions to the COVID-19 outbreak in Germany differed between various topics. More than 200 thousand German users joined Twitter public communication on COVID-19 in total. Coronavirus and COVID-19 topics received more participants than others. Twitter community is a specific platform for social topics. An understanding of social media culture of a specific topic will contribute to the success of social media communication. Second, media and medical Twitter users play significant roles among Twitter communication about COVID-19 in Germany, who are more willing to join social media communication and receive broad public trust. Beyond that, Twitter communication brings a large number of users in various areas or background. Twitter users are more willing to spread educational information on social media in Germany.

Third, keywords selection found that COVID-19 has numerous influences in various aspects of society and life. Numerous negative keywords were selected. Medical, political, educational and international centers and organizations are involved. Twitter plays an important role in educating the public with millions of tweets and information. Fourth, sources of retweets data identify that professional Twitter users (medical, political and media users) received more trust and their tweets received more retweets by Twitter users.

To conclude, we observed dramatic differences in COVID-19 related Twitter communication between various topics. COVID-19 pandemic requires profound public health policies among countries and states. The results will help nation public health agencies in Germany and across the globe understand their own communities' Twitter communication cultures.

The research method of this paper can be extended to the big data analysis and research in the chemical industry, which helps chemical graduate students to have basic big data literacy and good scientific literacy, and solve key problems and problems in the industry by analysing and using big data, so as to promote scientific research innovation and promote scientific research development.

This work was supported by Research Project on Postgraduate Education and Teaching Reform of Xi'an University of Technology (No. 252042029), the Education and Teaching Reform Research Project of Xi'an University of Technology (Nos. xqj2119, xjy2103, xjy2102, and 251032205), Scientific Research Project of Education Department of Shaanxi Province (Project title: Big data and social media communication; No. 19JK0711), and Scientific Research Project of Xi'an International Studies University (Project title: Big data and social media communication; No. 19XWB09).

The authors declare that they have no known competing financial interests or personal relationships that could have appeared to influence the work reported in this paper.

References

1. WHO. Statement. https://www.who.int/news-room/detail/30-01-2020-statement-on-the-second-meeting-of-the-international-health-regulations-(2005)-emergency-committee-regarding-the-outbreak-of-novel-coronavirus-(2019-ncov), (2020)
2. WHO. WHO Timeline - COVID-19. https://www.who.int/news-room/detail/27-04-2020-who-timeline---covid-19, (2020)
3. WHO. Naming the coronavirus disease (COVID-19) and the virus that causes it. https://www.who.int/emergencies/diseases/novel-coronavirus-2019/technical-guidance/naming-the-coronavirus-disease-(covid-2019)-and-the-virus-that-causes-it, (2020)
4. Y. Yang, J.O. Pedersen. A comparative study on feature selection in text categorization. In: Proceedings of the international conference on machine learning, **412** (1997)
5. Scikit-learn. SelectKBest. https://scikit-learn.org/stable/modules/generated/sklearn.feature_selection.SelectKBest.html, (2020)
6. Scikit-learn. CountVectorizer. https://scikit-learn.org/stable/modules/generated/sklearn.feature_extraction.text.CountVectorizer.html, (2020)

Construction and exploration of practical education system of applied chemistry under the background of new engineering

Xiaojiao Yu [1,*], *Yuchen* Wei[2], *Ningning* Zhao[1], *Zongbin* Liu[1], *Jinfen* Niu[1], *Zhong* Yu[1], *Nailiang* Liu[1], *Guangjun* Liu[1], and *Jian* Zhang[1]

[1] Department of Applied Chemistry, Xi'an University of Technology, Xi'an 710048, China
[2] School of Materials Science and Engineering, Xi'an University of Technology, Xi'an 710048, China

Abstract. Chemistry is an experimental science. Practical teaching is a significant link in the cultivation of students majoring in chemistry to foster students' practical, professional application, and innovation abilities. Based on the investigation and analysis of the problems existing in the cultivation of the practical ability of applied chemistry major, take specific measures, such as constructing the practical teaching system of applied chemistry major, explored a better practical teaching system for students of applied chemistry major; applied to the reform and innovation of training mode of students majoring in applied chemistry and achieved good results.

1 Introduction

Since February 2017, the Ministry of Education has actively promoted the construction of new projects, and has successively formulated the "Fudan Consensus", "Tianda Action" and "Beijing Guidelines" to adapt to a new scientific and technological revolution and industrial change, and support a series of national strategies such as scientific and technological innovation-driven development and "Made in China 2025". The "Notice on Carrying out Research and Practice of New Engineering" and the "Notice on Promoting Research and Practice Projects of New Engineering" were announced to explore the Chinese model and experience of engineering education to assist build higher education in a powerful country. It is also announced in the "Notice on Carrying out Research and Practice of New Engineering" and the "Notice on Promoting Research and Practice Projects of New Engineering" that the Chinese model and experience in engineering education should be explored with all efforts to assist to establish higher education of a strong country. To break through key technologies, build first-mover advantage and occupy the strategic commanding position in the approaching global innovation system. There is an urgent need for emerging engineering talents with scientific knowledge structure, comprehensive practical ability, strong sense of innovation, broad international vision, positive teamwork spirit and communication ability [1]. The new engineering major is a transformation and upgrading of traditional engineering majors such as chemical engineering, civil engineering,

* Corresponding author: yxjw@xaut.edu.cn

materials, electrical appliances and machinery in an intelligent and controllable way. Different from conventional engineering fields, the development of emerging industries needs high-quality interdisciplinary talents with strong engineering practice ability and strong innovation consciousness and capability [2].

2 Existing situation of practical teaching system

The major of Applied Chemistry at Xi 'an University of Technology aims to cultivate talents with high-quality for the society based in northwest China and facing the whole country. Therefore, the training of innovation awareness and burgeon practical ability of undergraduates has always been the focus of our attention. After revising the talent training program for many times, the experiment content has been integrated and optimized, the proportion of comprehensive experiments has been increased, and the organization and implementation of professional skills competitions have been increased, which has aroused the enthusiasm and initiative of students to participate in scientific research practice and innovation activities to a large extent. However, with the popularity of emerging industries and the upgrading of traditional industries, the current engineering practice education system and platform, such as practice teaching, can no longer meet the requirements of the development of "new engineering" in terms of teaching objectives, system design, practice content, teaching methods, teaching quality evaluation and comprehensive practice platform. The existing problems are mainly reflected in the following aspects.

The teaching objectives of various practical teaching in the current training programs cannot accurately connect with the needs of emerging industries and a new economy, which is not conducive to the cultivation of students' engineering literacy and innovative thinking.

The current practical teaching system has strengthened the cultivation of students' engineering practical ability, but there are deficiencies in the cultivation of students' interdisciplinary ability, innovative consciousness and comprehensive ability.

The number of design experiments, school practical teaching funds and the relevant equipment matching with new technologies and new industries in the professional basic experiment, which is insufficient. Thus, the practical teaching content is slightly traditional and outdated, and relatively lagging behind compared with the development of the industry.

The practical teaching method and method are single, which cannot fully mobilize the enthusiasm and participation of students. It is not conducive to the improvement of students' practical operation and problem-solving abilities. Besides, This does not conform to the training goal of cultivating high-quality "new engineering" talents.

The promotion of students' engineering practice ability and the formation of innovation consciousness cannot be separated from the construction of perfect construction of practical teaching base inside and outside the school and the scientific management, assessment and evaluation mechanism. However, the current situation of practical teaching is worrying. For enterprises, economic benefits are the first demand. Their normal production order and economic benefits will be disrupted and affected for students' internship. Thus, universities and practice base cooperation level is relatively low. Moreover, student practice gave priority to visit and view are not conducive to the practical and innovative capability of students. In addition, the lack of practical ability of practical teaching teachers in colleges and universities also leads to the absence of guidance, assessment and evaluation of students 'practical links. And this also limits the cultivation of students' practical ability and innovative consciousness to a certain extent.

Based on the above analysis, it is urgent and important work to meet the needs of cultivating new engineering talents and emerging industries and new economy by exploring the engineering practice education system and the construction of platform for new engineering, which also has important theoretical research and practical significance.

3 Goal and building of practical teaching system

3.1 Reform the traditional practical teaching system and build a multi-level practical teaching system to meet the needs of professional development

With new engineering education put forward the practice ability training goal as the guidance, to integrate and design applied chemical professional practice ability training system, build to adapt to the development of new engineering "thick basic experiment, wide caliber of technical experiment, teaching and research combination of professional experiment and personalized innovation experiment" practice teaching system. The main purpose of the solid basic experiment is to cultivate the practical ability of applied chemistry students related to basic subjects, organically integrate basic disciplines with engineering technology, so that students can have solid professional basic practical skills, and lay a foundation for the subsequent study of professional courses. The broad caliber technical basic experiment is to strengthen students' professional engineering background and cultivate engineering awareness and engineering literacy through the cultivation of professional practical ability. It mainly includes the basic experiment of the applied chemistry major, the specialty direction characteristic experiment, and the applied chemistry comprehensive experiment courses. The professional experiment combining teaching and scientific research aims to sublimate students from textbook knowledge to practical application through the real scientific research and practice environment. Personalized innovation experiment is composed of various practical links, such as quality development practice, applied chemical innovation experiment, graduation thesis, national college student chemical skills competition, college student chemical experiment competition and other professional competitions, and innovation and entrepreneurship training projects approval. By building a new practice teaching system and earnestly implement it in the practice process of practice, strengthen the students 'cognitive ability, improve students' ability to analyze and solve problems, cultivate students 'innovation consciousness, and in the comprehensive practice activities to cultivate students' interdisciplinary learning ability, communication and coordination ability and teamwork ability, so as to realize the engineering practice ability and humanistic accomplishment.

3.2 Reform the traditional practical teaching content, and compile the practical teaching syllabus and practical teaching materials with professional characteristics and advantages

With the development of science and technology, new testing instruments, testing technologies and methods are constantly emerging, representing the future development direction of science and technology. And the current advanced science and technology and testing methods are constantly introduced into students 'practice teaching, expand students' knowledge and horizon, improve their practical ability and innovation ability. Through transformation, update will be relatively backward practice teaching platform, establish advanced, with high technical level, represents the development direction of practice teaching platform and practice teaching content, the practice teaching can coordinate with the progress of science and technology, can adapt to the development of the current society, can meet the needs of the enterprise, improve students' practical ability.

3.3 Reform experimental teaching method, and build a virtual practice teaching platform system and online and offline sharing practice platform

Virtual experiment teaching is a modern teaching method, which is a supplement to physical experiments and which is a popular experimental teaching method in the world [3, 4]. By connecting the network with the virtual experiment centre, the remote teaching experiment combining virtual and real can be realized, and it is established to overcome the teaching experiment which is difficult to be implemented due to the restrictions of investment, environment, equipment, consumption, safety and operation difficulty under normal circumstances. It integrates real equipment, virtual technology, simulation technology and remote technology. It can realize the plasticity, diversity, comprehensiveness and openness of practical teaching. According to the teaching requirements, students can not only carry out their own field experiments on the relevant experimental platform, but also improve the number of students, experimental technology level and experimental effect, and enhance the autonomy and openness of the experiment. Through a variety of teaching means, broaden students' vision and improve students' interest in learning.

3.4 Deepen school-enterprise cooperation and build a platform for school-enterprise cooperation

Actively carry out the construction of the school-enterprise cooperation platform, based on the construction and planning of the professional practice and training base, including the existing engineering practice education system and practice platform, increase the construction of school-enterprise cooperation platform, make full use of enterprise conditions, and carry out all-round practical training. The practical problems encountered in enterprises are provided to the major in the form of horizontal projects or graduation papers, so that students can practice in enterprises in a wide range of high-class hours. So that professional and enterprises can achieve collaborative education and collaborative innovation. Create real or simulated professional atmosphere from the aspects of production training environment, production training project design, enterprise culture atmosphere, enterprise management mode and so on, simulate the production process, and build a number of comprehensive training rooms and production practice workshops. It provides opportunities and conditions for students to participate in production, learning and research activities through the joint construction of high-level, sharing and open practice teaching platforms between the school and enterprise.

3.5 Build a team of high-level practical teaching teachers

The construction of a high-level practical teaching platform and teaching staff is the basis of achieving teaching objectives [5]. Through the joint construction of a high-level, sharing and open practice teaching platform between the school and the university and enterprise, establish a "school-enterprise joint" instructing teacher team, build a stable "combination of professional and professional" high-level practical teaching teacher team, truly establish a "double-qualified" teaching team, achieve the improvement of software and hardware conditions, improve the overall teaching and research level of regional teachers, and guarantee resources of teaching materials and teachers.

https://doi.org/10.1051/shsconf/202316601018

4 Implementation effect

In recent years, through continuous reform, the experimental teaching demonstration center has completed more than 100 open experimental projects and more than 2000 people in open experiments every year. The opening of various forms of laboratory has effectively improved the practical ability of students majoring in applied chemistry. A large number of "national and provincial college student innovation and entrepreneurship plan" projects, internet plus, challenge cup and discipline competition award-winning works have been cultivated. All kinds of internships, professional practice and comprehensive practice education platforms are conducive to the expansion of students' professional quality. Taking chemical experiment and chemical design competition as an example, the entries and awards in recent three years are shown in Figure 1. As can be seen from Figure 1, the number of participants in the competition and the number of winners has increased year by year, and there will be a great increase in 2022.The construction and promotion of the extra-curricular practice system have greatly improved the practical education level of our school and achieved good results.

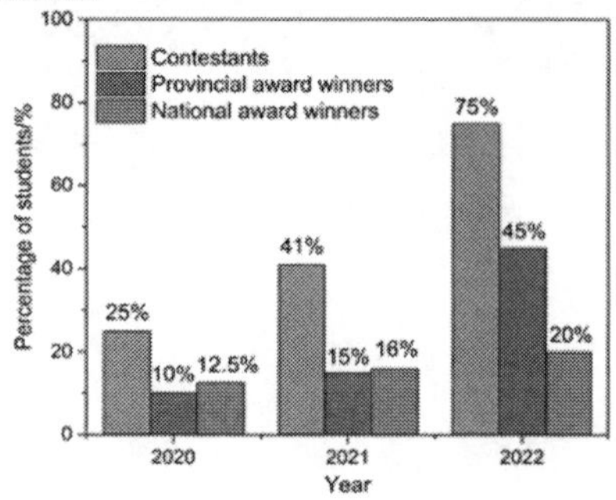

Fig. 1. Percentage of participants and winners in recent three years.

5 Conclusion

In recent years, aiming at the traditional practical teaching mode, we have actively carried out the construction of an innovative practical teaching platform, focused on promoting the reform of experimental course teaching content and method, strengthened the construction of comprehensive, designed and open experimental projects, and focused on strengthening the construction of practice base with the mode of school-enterprise cooperation education and school-enterprise professional construction as the starting point. Through continuous exploration and practice, the practical teaching system of "solid basic experiment, wide aperture technical basic experiment, professional experiment combined with teaching and research, personalized innovative experiment" has been formed. The implementation results are remarkable, and can provide useful reference for the practical teaching of applied chemistry major.

This work was financially supported by the Education and Teaching Reform Research Project of Xi'an University of Technology (Nos: xjy2103, xjy2102), the Research Project on Postgraduate Education and Teaching Reform of Xi'an University of Technology (Nos. 252042033, 252042029), the Education and Teaching Reform Research Project of Xi'an University of Technology (Nos. xqj2119, 251032205).

References

1. W.P. Chen, Y.X. Lin, Z.Y. Ren, D. Shen, Comput. Appl. Eng. Educ. **29**, 1(2021).
2. X.Y. Kong, W.Q. Lu, Q. Guo, Y.H. Zhu, F. Zhang, B. Li, Int. J. Eng. Educ. **36**, 6(2020).
3. F. Wang, Y. Hu, C. Liu, Modern Chem. Res. **8**(2021).
4. L. Bai, L. Wu, P. Gu, J. HUBEI Correspond. Uni., **30**,18(2017).
5. J. Zhou, M. Han, Edu. Teaching Forum, 44(2017).

Exploration on the cultivation of innovative talents in the course of chemistry teaching

Nailiang Liu[1,*], *Shasha* Li[2], *Junpeng* Li[1], *Ningning* Zhao[1], and *Zhong* Yu[1]

[1]Department of Applied Chemistry, School of Science, Xi'an University of Technology, 710048 Xi'an, Shaanxi, China
[2]Faculty of Printing, Packaging Engineering and Digital Media Technology, Xi'an University of Technology, 710048 Xi'an, Shaanxi, China

Keywords: Teaching reform, Chemistry courses, Innovation ability, Engineering colleges.

Abstract. Cultivating innovative talents to meet the needs of professional development is an urgent mission of higher education institutions under the situation of "Double First-Class" construction. As one of the foundations of science and technology major, chemistry courses play an essential role in promoting an innovative spirit, cultivating creative consciousness, and improving creative ability. This paper discussed the optimization of the curriculum system, the construction of the teaching mode, and the transformation of the cultivation mode of chemistry courses in engineering majors from the aspects of curriculum design, theoretical teaching, experimental teaching, and out-of-class training. Through cultivating innovation consciousness in theory and experimental teaching, and improving innovation ability in extra-curricular practical education, we hope to bring a positive effect on the reform of the cultivation mode of innovation ability in the teaching process of chemistry courses in engineering colleges and universities.

1 Introduction

It is the most important goal of contemporary higher education institutions to stimulate the innovative ideas of talents, cultivate their innovative consciousness, improve their innovative ability and create innovative talents who can adapt to the development of modern society in the process of teaching and educating people [1]. The thinking and methods of chemistry for the understanding and exploration of the world cannot be replaced by other disciplines, and the learning of chemical knowledge plays an important role in the cultivation of innovative talents [2]. Chemistry is the science of chemical disciplines that are based on the study of principles, laws and methods of the chemical behaviours of objective material systems. It covers the study from macroscopic to microscopic, the laws of the relationship between structure and properties, the mechanism of chemical processes and

* Corresponding author: liul-2001@163.com

their control, and is the theoretical basis for chemistry and the study of material change at the molecular level, and is the core basic course for chemistry, chemical, biological, materials, mechanical, energy, environmental and other majors in higher education [3], which plays a vital role in the cultivation of innovative talents.

2 Integrating innovative ideas in the course design

The chemistry courses of Xi'an University of Technology are set up for all majors in the university, which are conducive to enhancing students' understanding and knowledge of chemistry, and are compulsory for majors in energy, materials, environment, pharmaceuticals and chemistry. The purpose of the course is to enable students to understand and master the basic knowledge and skills of chemistry, and to cultivate their scientific thinking methods and analytical and problem-solving abilities. In the process of learning the course to improve students' scientific literacy, enhance their ability to innovate and entrepreneurship, so that they can better adapt to the development of society while stimulating students to appreciate the knowledge of chemistry, and love the emotions of the chemical profession. The course design uses a combination of forms to enrich classroom content, stimulate learning interest, and enable students to develop in a harmonious and unified manner.

2.1 Knowledge and skills

Understand chemistry in daily life and the essential principles of chemical knowledge; understand the process and methods of experimental design and master the necessary experimental skills through consolidation of experimental teaching; understand the basic knowledge of chemistry and its related disciplines and be able to analyse and solve problems in chemistry; understand the frontier scientific and technological developments in the development of chemistry and have enthusiasm for the learning of chemical knowledge.

2.2 Processes and methods

Through the whole process of chemistry theory and experimental teaching, learn to use the method of scientific investigation, and form the spirit of teamwork in practical activities; form the awareness of explaining and solving chemical phenomena and chemical problems encountered in life with scientific attitudes and methods, learn to collect data, analyse data, and develop good habits of problem identification and problem-solving.

2.3 Emotional attitude and values

Students are interested in exploring the effects of chemistry on environmental changes, understanding the role of chemistry and the chemical industry in promoting social development, and developing an interest in studying chemistry; developing a love of life, cherishing life, dedication, and dedication to work, viewing the relationship between chemistry and the environment, chemistry and human society correctly, and pursuing the ultimate goal of chemistry in the service of mankind.

The construction of chemistry courses combines the professional curriculum, the layout of the knowledge system and the characteristics and advantages of related majors, highlighting the basic theoretical knowledge, applied technology and the policy of comprehensive ability cultivation. It promotes the cultivation of students' innovative ability, perfects the comprehensive knowledge system and improves the comprehensive professional quality. At the same time, the construction and implementation of these courses are of great significance in giving play to professional characteristics, optimizing professional layout, building and enhancing professional advantages, cultivating innovative talents, and promoting professional construction and the healthy and sustainable development of talent training.

3 Establishing the spirit of innovation in theoretical teaching

Teaching content is the key and core of the curriculum, and it is the basic guarantee and concrete embodiment of the goal of cultivating innovative talents [4]. Chemistry courses contain conceptual, theoretical, systematic and logical contents, which involve many formulas in the learning process, harsh application conditions, relatively abstract and difficult to learn. The theoretical teaching process in chemistry class courses is aimed at imparting basic knowledge, cultivating chemical quality, and improving innovative ability. The curriculum is designed to reorganize the lecture system of chemistry courses, focus on summarizing experience, improving teaching methods and optimizing the teaching process. We introduce the history of science and modern scientific and technological achievements and frontier developments appropriately to broaden students' horizons, stimulate their enthusiasm and interest in learning, and improve their autonomy. In each teaching session, a systematic knowledge framework is constructed and teaching objectives are clearly defined. In the process of theoretical teaching, students are motivated to learn, guided to think differently based on theoretical learning, and to learn independently by applying the same knowledge to the learning content.

3.1 Linking teaching content with daily life

Although chemistry courses are very theoretical, systematic and logical, they still have very concrete manifestations in all aspects of daily life, which can link some difficult to understand abstract concepts to phenomena in daily life, deepen students' understanding of the concepts and increase their interest in learning.

3.2 Linking teaching content with scientific research topics

Theoretical teaching process interspersed with the relevant scientific research content in the department, these can see and hear the content, not only can expand the students' knowledge, but also enrich the classroom teaching, but also help to improve the students' interest in learning, and participate in scientific research activities enthusiasm. By linking the teaching content with relevant research topics, students can ask the relevant teachers for more in-depth information, which will more effectively promote students' enthusiasm for learning and research, and help improve the teaching effect.

3.3 Linking teaching content with industrial development

Taking the cultivation of engineering innovative talents as the starting point, we pay attention to the accumulation of relevant knowledge of engineering technology background, the exercise of creative thinking, and the cultivation of self-learning ability. Introducing the actual production of enterprises into the teaching of chemistry courses not only enriches the teaching content, but also enhances students' knowledge of industrial production and helps link theory and practice. By linking the teaching content to the actual production process, students improve their understanding of the theoretical basics, understand the relationship between theory and practice, and expand their knowledge of chemistry.

4 Cultivate the sense of innovation in experimental teaching

The driving force of scientific development comes from experiments, and the new phenomena, new methods and new theories discovered by experiments promote the progress of science and gradually revolutionize mankind's understanding of the objective world. Experiments in chemistry courses are used to study the chemical properties of substances and the relationship between these properties and chemical reactions through experiments, from which regular understanding is formed and students master the relevant theories, experimental methods and experimental techniques in chemistry. Through experimental teaching, students can verify and consolidate theories and concepts, deepen their knowledge of theoretical fundamentals, improve their ability to understand, analyse and solve problems, promote teamwork, and strengthen the cultivation of students' creative consciousness and innovative ability.

To stimulate students' enthusiasm for learning chemistry courses, students should be given more autonomy and flexibility in experimental settings, and experimental teaching should be reformed by adhering to the concept of student-oriented "subjective education" [5]. In the reform of experimental teaching of chemistry courses, the experimental content can be reformed to take into account both consolidation of the basics and expansion of the content, and adopt a three-stage teaching mode consisting of basic experiments, application experiments and comprehensive experiments. Condense the basic experiments to cultivate students' basic operation skills in chemistry experiments and strengthen their basic training; expand the comprehensive experiments so that students have more choices and exercises to improve their application ability to apply basic knowledge of chemistry to analyse and solve problems; set up open experiments, which require students to complete the whole process of experiments independently and cultivate students' ability of comprehensive application of chemical knowledge and innovative design ability.

5 Improving innovative ability in extra-curricular practice

In the teaching process of engineering chemistry courses to cultivate innovative talents to meet the needs of social development, in addition to building an innovative talent cultivation system, it is also necessary to gradually enhance talents' innovative consciousness, cultivate innovative thinking and improve innovative ability in innovative practice. Therefore, while reforming in-class teaching, students should also be vigorously guided to participate in extra-curricular practice. The learning and penetration of innovative quality are carried out in the in-class teaching, and the cultivation and improvement of innovative ability are carried out in the concrete practice. Students gradually acquire innovative abilities through systematic scientific and standardized training in concrete practice. And they can get in touch with the frontier knowledge in the professional field and understand the advanced new ideas, technologies and methods. It helps to broaden knowledge, improve knowledge structure, stimulate innovative ideas and cultivate innovative consciousness. In the process of extra-curricular practice, we should follow the objective rules from simple to complex, from known to unknown, and exercise from information collection, scheme design, experiment optimization, data recording, result analysis, paper writing, product improvement and other aspects, accumulate practical experience and improve innovation ability in the process of continuous trial and error and improvement, thinking and enhancement.

6 Conclusion

The cultivation of innovative talents is an important task given to higher education by society under the situation of double-class construction. As an important part of higher education, higher education institutions should take the establishment of innovative spirit, cultivation of innovative consciousness and improvement of innovative ability as the main purpose of talent cultivation in educational reform. Chemistry courses are important basic courses for chemistry, chemical engineering, biology, materials and other majors in engineering colleges and universities, which are of great significance for the cultivation of innovative talents. Through reforming the teaching mode of curriculum design, theoretical teaching, experimental teaching and extra-curricular teaching, recognizing and cultivating innovative consciousness in theoretical teaching and experimental teaching, and practicing and improving innovative ability in extra-curricular teaching, the strategy of cultivating innovative talents in engineering colleges is constantly improved.

Education and Teaching Reform Research Project of Xi'an University of Technology (xjy2152)

References

1. K. Wang. Tu. Chem. Eng. (China). **50**, 10 (2022)
2. X. Feng. Chin. J. Chem. Educ. **40**, 2 (2019)
3. Y. Su, C. Zheng. Univ. Chem. **35**, 6 (2020)
4. Y. Shen. Y. Wang, J. Li, J. Chang, F. Zhang. Univ. Chem. **33**, 9 (2018)
5. X. Wang. X. Wang, X. Wang, F. Tian, X. Tian, B. Chen. Univ. Chem. **34**, 11 (2019)

Exploration and practice of BOPPPS model in teaching reform of engineering chemistry for materials specialty

Ningning Zhao[1,*], *Yuchen* Wei[2], *Zhong* Yu[1], *Binghua* Yao[1], *Jinfen* Niu[1], *Nailiang* Liu[1], *Junpeng* Li[1], and *Xiaojiao* Yu[1]

[1]Xi'an University of Technology, School of Science, 710054 Xi'an, Shaanxi, China
[2]Xi'an University of Technology, School of Materials Science and Engineering, 710048 Xi'an, Shaanxi, China

Abstract. Engineering chemistry is the basis of materials science. Students majoring in materials specialty should learn engineering chemistry well and closely link it with materials science. However, it is difficult to achieve the expected teaching effect in the actual teaching process. By analysing the problems existing in the traditional teaching process of engineering chemistry, this study proposes a teaching strategy based on the BOPPPS teaching mode, such as the introduction of the flipped classroom and the classroom Interaction to enhance the interests of students in learning and their self-efficacy, so as to enrich their specialized knowledge and develop their creative thinking and abilities.

1 Introduction

Engineering Chemistry is a required professional basic course for students majoring in materials such as material physics, material chemistry, material science and engineering, material forming and control engineering. The purpose of setting up the course of Engineering Chemistry in the materials specialty is not only to let students be familiar with various materials, such as nano materials, polymer materials, ceramic materials, metal materials, surfactants, etc., but also to make students understand the thermodynamics, kinetics, heat and mass transfer processes involved in the reaction process of materials, be able to regulate the conditions required for reaction, grasp the degree of reaction progress, clarify the reaction mechanism, and establish the reaction models. This course contains many concepts in the theory of chemical reaction, as well as the complicated mathematical formulas, which is widely regarded as one of the difficult subjects to teach, learn and test in university courses. In the teaching process, it is found that students are easily bored with learning, especially in learning with concepts and formula derivation. According to these problems in the learning process and in combination with the characteristics of the Engineering Chemistry course, teachers need to carry out targeted teaching process design and adopt various forms of teaching methods to achieve the all-round interactive teaching

* Corresponding author: zhaonn@xaut.edu.cn

of teachers and students, so as to provide effective guarantee for the achievement of the curriculum objectives.

BOPPPS teaching model [1,2] is just to achieve the teaching objectives as the core, and ensure the success of the classroom through six elements: bridge-in, objective/outcome, pre-assessment, participatory learning, post-assessment and summary [3]. This teaching model is highly practical and operable to provide a theoretical system in guiding all aspects of classroom teaching for teachers, and make the arrangement of classroom teaching more orderly and reasonable.

2 Traditional teaching model in the course of Engineering Chemistry

The Engineering Chemistry course offered by the materials specialty takes 32 hours to complete, and the corresponding classroom teaching is mainly multi-media based combining with blackboard writing. This course covers thermodynamics, dynamics foundation, electrochemistry, material chemistry, environmental chemistry, energy chemistry, interface chemistry and other chapters, with many complicated knowledge points. The traditional teaching model mainly depends on the detailed explanation of teacher. Students can recognize and understand basic concepts, formulas and theorems through blackboard writing, animation, video and other auxiliary means. Students could be more familiar with key and difficult knowledge through the practical examples, and exercise and strengthen their application skills of relevant knowledge through some exercises after class. However, during the practical teaching process, there are many problems. Most students can't do pre class preview and review after class, which leads to poor effect of classroom questioning, and they lack continuity in understanding and mastery of the subsequent knowledge points. Some students have poor enthusiasm for classroom participation, and sometimes they play with mobile phones, read extracurricular books, doze off, etc. The phenomenon of copying homework is relatively serious, which leads to that the teachers cannot make accurate judgments on the real study situation of students. Considering the above situation, teachers should first start with the design of classroom teaching, take a more reasonable teaching model to replace the traditional teaching method, in order to fully mobilize the learning enthusiasm and subjective initiative of students. In addition, teachers should pay attention to enhance the cooperative spirit and consciousness of students during the classroom teaching, so that the students can learn more knowledge in the limited classroom teaching hours, and have inspiration for their future study and work.

3 Application of BOPPPS model in the course of Engineering Chemistry

3.1 Characteristics of BOPPPS teaching model

The BOPPPS teaching model, originated in the Instructional Skill Workshop (ISW) in British Columbia (Canada, in the 1970s) [4,5], is famous for the effective teaching design, the student-centered concept, and the ideal learning effect [6].

Based on the BOPPPS teaching model, the purpose of "Bridge-in" is to attract students' attention, establish their learning motivation, and stimulate their enthusiasm for learning by introducing the specific problems, relevant examples, video animations, experimental phenomena, etc. Then, teachers should set the specific, observable and evaluable classroom goals, in order to know the students' mastery of the knowledge points after class. Before class, it is necessary to know what the students have mastered about the course and whether they have wrong ideas or opinions about the relevant content, and then teachers need focus on the course content and adjust the breadth, depth, difficulty and rhythm of the course accordingly. In order to obtain the students' feedback during the pre-assessment process, strategies such as asking open/closed questions, brainstorming, and quizzes can be used, so that teachers should make appropriate adjustments in the course of classroom design and teaching. "Participatory learning" is the core segment of BOPPPS teaching model and the main part of the classroom teaching process. The purpose of in-depth learning can be achieved through the participatory learning in many ways, such as the interaction between students and teachers/students, the fully participation of the students, peer learning, and teachers' guidance, etc. Post-assessment is a stage to understand the students' learning achievements and check whether the present learning goals are achieved. At this stage, short answer questions and multiple-choice questions can be used to test students' understanding of knowledge; students' comprehensive analysis ability of practical problems can be evaluated through teaching cases in order to test students' flexible application skills of learned knowledge. Finally, teachers need to summarize the main points of the lesson, and expand the contents of the course. In the summary stage, the after-class discussion, homework, and the solutions to students' problems and doubts are also essential.

It should be pointed out that BOPPPS is not an isolated model and does not require teachers to teach according to a fixed model. Its significance lies in standardizing the curriculum design and classroom teaching process. It points out that the key link of classroom teaching is participatory learning.

3.2 Implementation of BOPPPS in the course of Engineering Chemistry

Based on the characteristics of the current Engineering Chemistry course, the problems in the traditional teaching process and the basic situation of students, the following measures are mainly taken in the classroom implementation process:

First, BOPPPS teaching model is introduced. During the preparation of multimedia courseware, the setting-up of questions, examples controversial points is to arouse students' interest. Put forward specific measurable learning objectives before each lesson, and test students' learning effects in the following stages. Set up a pre-test to understand the students' prior knowledge of the content of the lesson. Guide students to participate fully in the Engineering Chemistry classroom through improving the teaching methods. Set the post-test stage to grasp the students' mastery of the course content. Finally, summarize and expand the teaching content. The BOPPPS teaching model makes the classroom teaching more orderly and fully mobilize the students' subjective initiative.

The second is to take a variety of forms of participation and mutual learning. The common ways of "Participatory learning" includes group discussion on relevant issues or cases, questionnaire survey, some course relevant topics/events given, reflections on micro-lecture video or other associated short teaching video, online test, etc. All above ways could make students fully participate in classroom teaching, cultivate their teamwork ability and enterprising consciousness, encourage students to actively think about and solve problems, and exercise their language organization and expression ability.

Third, in order to improve the teaching effect, a teaching method of the flipped classroom [7] combining with the BOPPPS teaching model is used. The BOPPPS teaching model can greatly improve the students' participation in the classroom, and the phenomenon of students' attention wandering, nodding off, and playing with mobile phones in the class is significantly reduced. However, some problems are still encountered in the practical implementation process. Most of the students cannot perform the pre-class preparation and review after class, and they do not consult the related textbook or reference materials on their own initiative for the knowledge points they do not understand. As a result, students cannot establish a complete knowledge framework, and the cohesion between the front and back knowledge points is poor. In the group discussion, due to the insufficient preparation of students, they are short of in-depth thinking and exploring. The online learning model of flipped classroom can greatly improve students' extracurricular learning effect, enable students to understand what they have learned before class, put forward questions, and think about and consult materials in advance, which can significantly improve the teaching effect and efficiency of participatory learning in BOPPPS model. Students can integrate, digest and absorb the knowledge they have learned in time after class, which can enhance the depth of learning and deepen the level of knowledge internalization.

4 Conclusion

In view of the problems in the traditional teaching of Engineering Chemistry, this study proposes a teaching strategy that focuses on BOPPPS teaching model and appropriately combines flipped classroom teaching. For teachers, it can arouse students' interest in learning and clarify teaching objectives. It also could adjust the teaching form according to the study situation of the students, and fully mobilize the enthusiasm of students through participatory mutual learning. Through the post-assessment, students can be reasonably tutored and reviewed after class. The use of flipped classroom can ensure the smooth implementation of the teaching plan and help to improve the effect of the classroom teaching. For students, it can improve their subjective initiative, exercise their independent learning ability, and obtain the self-satisfaction and achievement during the learning process, and ultimately improve the learning effect.

This work was supported by Research Project on Postgraduate Education and Teaching Reform of Xi'an University of Technology (No. 252042029), the Education and Teaching Reform Research Project of Xi'an University of Technology (Nos. xqj2119, xjy2103, xjy2102, and 251032205).

References

1. Y. Yang, J. You, J. Wu, C. Hu, L. Shao, J. Dent. Educ. **83**, 5 (2019)
2. X.Y. Liu, C. Lu, H. Zhu, X. Wang, S. Jia, Y. Zhang, H.X. Wen, Y.F. Wang, BMC Med. Educ. **22**, 1 (2022)
3. W.L. Shih, C.Y. Tsai, Asia-Pacific Edu. Res. **29** (2020)
4. P. Pattison, D. Russell D, Instructional skills workshop handbook. Vancouver, Canada: UBC Centre for Teaching and Academic Growth; 2006.
5. L. Chen, X.J. Tang, X.K. Chen, N. Ke, Q. Liu, BMC Med. Educ. **22**, 437 (2022)
6. H.Cui, *IES* **12**, 12 (2019)
7. X.M Ma, X.W. Ma, L. Li, X.Y. Luo, H. Zhang, Y.Q. Liu, Adv. Physiol. Educ. **45** (2021)

Design of smart learning environment monitoring system based on multi-mode

Ling Zhou, *Yuting* Wu, *Siwei* Qiu, and *Jianjun* Wang*

School of Electronic Information, Hunan First Normal University, 410205 Changsha, China

Abstract. The traditional smart campus pays attention to improving the management efficiency and neglects to improve the learning effect. This paper studies that the physical factors of smart learning environment affect students' learning effect, and designs a monitoring system of smart learning environment. The sensor is used to sense the temperature, humidity and air quality of the learning environment. The microcontroller system processes the sensing information of the sensor, and the server analyzes the data and generates the physical environment report and equipment control information to build a multi-mode multi-user smart learning environment monitoring system.

1 Introduction

On the basis of the Internet of Things, cloud computing and ubiquitous network technology, the smart learning environment adds new capabilities such as real-time situational awareness and automatic analysis to intelligent education, including online virtual environment and offline physical environment. It is an important part of the smart campus. At present, the mainstream smart campus management system manufacturers include Microsoft, Lenovo, Tencent, etc., which mainly solve the problem of how to improve management efficiency through smart means, but ignore that the main purpose of smart campus is to achieve smart education and promote learning effects.

Smart learning environment is an integrated online learning space that serves students. It provides learning resources, collaboration tools, learning evaluation tools, etc., supports students to carry out richer learning activities inside and outside the curriculum, provides students with personalized and intelligent learning services, and promotes a new talent training model [1]. Based on ThingSpeak IoT open source platform [2], this paper designs a smart learning environment physical condition monitoring system, which collects various physical factors of learners' environment through various sensors, such as (light, temperature, humidity, air quality, noise), improves learners' learning efficiency by monitoring and improving the learning environment, and provides different students with personalized learning services, It is a functional supplement to the current mainstream smart campus products.

* Corresponding author: wjj5351@163.com

2 Physical factors of smart learning environment

Smart learning environment is the "basic guarantee" for smart learning. Smart learning environment is a set of conditions that support learners to carry out constructive learning, including physical environment, technical environment, resource environment and emotional environment [3].

The tidy, beautiful, elegant and spacious smart learning environment makes people feel comfortable, full of vitality and vitality, improves the level of brain activation, and can reduce or eliminate fatigue; However, if the natural environment is untidy, dirty and narrow, it will make people feel depressed, irritable, dull and unhappy, affect the interest and efficiency of students' learning activities, and also affect their physical and mental health [4]. To create a good natural environment for college students is to create a good learning and living environment. The classroom is the main place for students to study. The lighting, ventilation, temperature, etc. of the classroom directly affect the learning efficiency [5]. The lighting in the classroom should be sufficient and uniform to reduce students' fatigue, improve students' attention, and reduce tension and anxiety. The indoor temperature and humidity should be moderate, such as too high or too low temperature, too wet or too dry humidity, which makes people feel uncomfortable, emotional instability, or upset, or depressed. Air quality and noise level also affect people's mentality and mood [6].

2.1. Temperature

Research shows that staying indoors with high temperature for a long time will not only affect people's study and rest, but also easily lead to irritability and irritability, as well as adverse effects on cardiovascular system, nervous system, digestive system and other systems [7]. However, the efficiency of brain use can be improved by 20%~35% when working and learning in a suitable environment. The overheated or too cold classroom environment will affect the work and learning efficiency to a certain extent [8].

2.2. Humidity

It has been found that high humidity environment is not conducive to lowering the body temperature through heat conduction, which is likely to cause physiological dysfunction, affect the heat balance of the human body, increase the body temperature, and make the emotion sensitive, unstable and impulsive. In a high humidity environment, due to low air pressure, people will feel depressed, excited or listless, inattentive, upset, and also prone to increase blood pressure and heart rate. High temperature and humidity are not conducive to people's mental health, and even suffer from mental diseases [9]. The humidity that the human body feels comfortable is: the relative humidity is lower than 70%.

2.3. Air pollution

Air pollution does not seem to cause physical pain like natural disasters, crowding or noise, but its impact on psychology and behavior is also quite serious. The most obvious signs of air pollution are the dust, smoke, haze we can see and the odor we can smell. However, air pollution is not always detected by us. Sealed residential or teaching buildings have more pollution than outdoor buildings. Long term air pollution will lead to air pollution syndrome, with headache, fatigue, insomnia, depression, irritability, eye inflammation, gastroenteritis and other symptoms [9]. Under the background of low CO2 concentration, it has the highest accuracy, the shortest reaction time and the highest learning efficiency.

3 Smart learning environment monitoring system

The smart learning environment monitoring system considers the impact of the main physical environment factors (temperature, humidity, CO2 concentration) of the intelligent learning space on learners. Based on ThingSpeak Internet of Things open source platform, data fusion technology and intelligent learning algorithm, it designs a learning emotion evaluation system for the smart learning environment based on multimodal physical factors, which is capable of automatically collecting the physical environment data of the intelligent learning space The function of integrating analysis data and intelligent judgment of environmental comfort can affect learners' learning mood and improve learners' learning efficiency by adjusting environmental comfort.

3.1. Thingspeak

Data processing and sharing at the computer end, combined with the latest Internet of Things technology Thingspeak, allows customers to conduct online testing and process data. Sensor data can be transferred to ThingSpeak from Arduino, Raspberry Pie, BeagleBone Black and other hardware. ThingSpeak can use MATLAB to analyze and visualize the data, and use MATLAB to perform relevant processing to reduce the difficulty of compilation, while helping to achieve more technologies. Thingspeak enables the edge node to communicate with the data aggregator through line connection. The data aggregator establishes a connection with the PC and communicates with each other, thus realizing data transmission, analysis and communication, and realizing an interactive system from "things" to "networks" and from "networks" to "people".

3.2. Description of smart learning environment monitoring system

The smart learning environment monitoring system consists of three parts: sensor, microcontroller and server. Its system structure is shown in Figure 1.

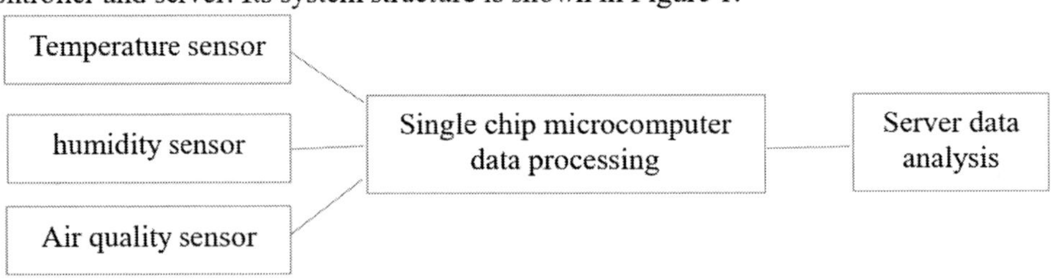

Fig. 1. Smart learning environment monitoring system.

The smart learning environment monitoring system is developed based on Thingspeak platform. The sensor collects data and transmits it to the microcontroller for processing, and then stores it in the server for data analysis. The microcontroller with high cost performance ratio is used to drive the micro sensors of various parameters, collect the temperature, humidity, oxygen content, light and other physical parameters of the learning environment, digitize and send them to the corresponding server through the network interface in the microcontroller. The server runs the corresponding application program to get the comfort evaluation report of the learning environment according to the algorithm of the relationship between specific human feelings and various environments.

3.2.1 Sensors

①Temperature and humidity sensor

DHT11 digital temperature and humidity sensor is a temperature and humidity composite sensor with calibrated digital signal output. As shown in Figure 2 [10].

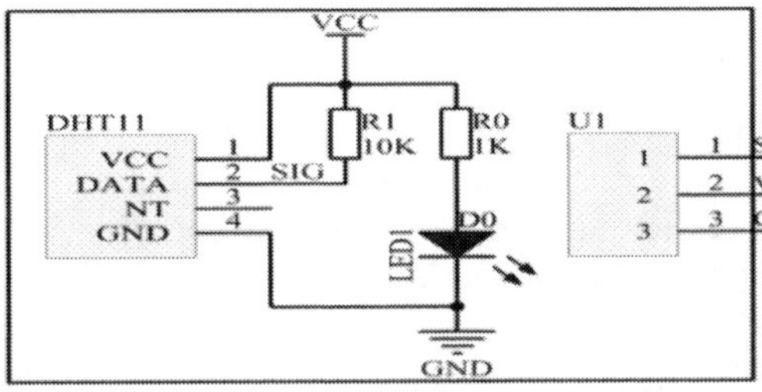

Fig. 2. Working principle diagram of DHT11 digital temperature and humidity sensor.

DHT11 digital temperature and humidity sensor applies special digital module acquisition technology and temperature and humidity sensing technology to ensure high reliability and excellent long-term stability of the product. The sensor consists of a capacitive humidity sensor and a NTC temperature sensor, which are connected to a high-performance 8-bit microcontroller.

②Air quality sensor

The gas sensing material used in MQ135 air quality sensor is tin dioxide (SnO_2) with low conductivity in clean air. When there is polluted gas in the environment where the sensor is located, the conductivity of the sensor increases with the increase of the concentration of the polluted gas in the air. The change of conductivity can be converted into the output signal corresponding to the gas concentration by using a simple circuit.

3.2.2 Single chip microcomputer

Using a cost-effective microcontroller to drive the micro sensors of various parameters, you can collect the temperature, humidity, oxygen content, light and other physical parameters of the learning environment, digitize them, upload them to the server through the network interface of the microcontroller, and get a learner's comfort evaluation report through the algorithm processing of the relationship between human perception and various environments. Users can easily view the user's learning environment comfort report through the app or related websites. At the same time, users can control various devices through their mobile phones to make themselves always in their own learning environment, or submit personalized customization through the app to control the microcontroller to fine tune various controllable environmental factors, so that the physical learning environment can reach the best state.

3.2.3 Server

The server side program uses the thread pool model to handle multi-user and highly concurrent access to the server, and provides standard interfaces for corresponding App access and computer side access.

The server receives the physical environment parameter data (temperature, humidity, noise, CO_2 concentration, etc.) sent by the microcontroller, analyzes the data, and generates the physical environment status report according to the human comfort and the dynamic season model of each parameter.

3.3 Working mechanism of smart learning environment monitoring system

3.3.1 Sensor sensing data

The sensor has rich digital I/O ports, analog I/O ports, and supports serial communication. Through a variety of sensors to perceive the environment to perceive the physical environment (temperature, humidity, noise, CO2 concentration, etc.) information, and send the sensing information to the microcontroller.

3.3.2 Single chip processor processing data

The mcu receives the sensing information of the sensor, and processes the sensing information with data. using the added network module, ip packets are used to transmit the data to the server. The server transmits the results of data analysis to the microcontroller, and the microcontroller controls the background servo system to change the physical environment parameters.

3.3.3 Server analysis data

The server side uses the thread pool model to deal with multi-user and highly concurrent access to the server, and provides standard interfaces for corresponding App access and computer access. After the server receives the environment message sent by the SCM, it starts the corresponding application to analyze the physical parameters (temperature, humidity, noise, CO2 concentration, etc.) in the environment message, and generates the physical environment report and equipment control information according to the human comfort and the dynamic season model of each parameter. The SCM or App makes various micro controls on the equipment according to the received equipment control information.

4 Conclusion

The main purpose of smart learning environment is to improve learners' learning efficiency. The physical conditions of smart learning environment are important factors that affect learners' learning effect. In this paper, a multi-mode multi-user intelligent learning environment monitoring system is designed, which uses sensors to sense the temperature, humidity and air quality of the learning environment. The microcontroller system processes the sensor's perception information, and the server analyzes the data and generates the physical environment report and device control information, which realizes the adaptive adjustment of the physical conditions of the smart learning environment and has a positive impact on the learning effect of learners.

This paper is supported by the General Program of Hunan Provincial Philosophy and Social Science Foundation, "Research on the Innovation Model of the Integration of "Production and Teaching Evaluation" of New Engineering Subjects in Local Colleges and Universities" (21YBA229).

Reference

1. Z. Zhong, S.C. Zhong, Y.W. Tang. Research on the construction of intelligent learning model supported by artificial intelligence. E-education research, Vol 42, No. 12, 71-78+85(2021).
2. IoT Analytics - ThingSpeak internet of things. https://thingspeak.com/.
3. W. Zhou, J. Du, Y. Wang, etc. Computing framework for learning environment for smart education. Research on modern distance education, Vol 34, No. 05, 91-100(2022).
4. R.H. Huang, J.F. Yang, Y.B. Hu. From digital learning environment to smart learning environment: changes and trends of learning environment. Open education research, Vol 18, No. 01, 75-84(2012).
5. W.Y. Guo, X.Y. Feng, M.J. Cai. Influencing factors of learners' learning effect in smart learning environment. Modern educational technology, Vol 30, No.12, 69-75(2020).
6. Z. Liu, C.L. Fang, S. Liu, etc. A review of learners' emotion perception in physical learning spaces. Journal of distance education, Vol 37, No. 02, 33-44(2019).
7. G.L. Yu, T.T. Chen, F.Q. Zhao. Effects of temperature and temperature change on mental health. Advances in psychological science, Vol 28, No. 08, 1282-1292(2020).
8. L. Zhong, Y.H. Hu, C. Zhang, etc. Discussion on the influence of high humidity environment on human physiology and psychology. Southwest china defense medicine, Vol 21, No. 10, 1114-1116(2011).
9. J. Jiang, D.J. Wang, Y.F. Liu, etc. Experimental study on the effect of indoor carbon dioxide concentration on learning efficiency. Building science, Vol 36, No. 06, 81-87(2020).
10. https://chinacqzgp.blog.csdn.net/article/details/108445714

Research on randomcity of conflict events in construction engineering projects

Xiaohong Liu[1], *Yiru* Hou[2], *Yi* Wang[3], and *Xueliang* Hou [1,*]

[1]School of Economy and Management, North China Electric Power University, 102206 Beijing, China
[2]School of Construction Management Technology, Purdue University, 47907 West Lafayette, USA
[3]Economy and Management Department, North China Electric Power University, 071003 Baoding, China

Abstract. The conflict events that occurred in construction engineering projects (CEP) often bring about many adverse effects on project implementation and show a character of randomcity. To find out the occurring rule of conflict events, all sorts and occurring frequencies of conflict events in CEP are analyzed based on the investigation. The representing rule of conflict events in every stage has been revealed in a new concept referred to as the representation degree by the method of quantitative analysis combined with qualitative analysis. Then, according to the basic principle of the analytic hierarchy process, every stage's judgment matrixes of conflict events are set up. Latent roots of these matrixes have revealed the influence order of cumulative results of conflict events at each stage. The harvest has obvious theoretical and practical value for forecasting conflict events, mastering the whole project situation, avoiding and reducing conflict events, and improving project management ability.

1 Introduction

The conflict events in construction engineering projects show different forms in different stages [1-2], these conflict events seem randomcity and contingency on their surface, but this randomcity might have some inherent rules. At present, an authoritative viewpoint in conflict events management is Harold Kerzner's research harvest based on the universal application of project management. The research shows seven factors that result in conflict in the project, which are project priority, management program, technical view, resource of manpower, cost, schedule, and personality[3]. For this, the most important view in the research is that the seven factors appear at the same time in different stages of the project, although have different occurring frequencies. However, this view might not fit construction project management, and their countermeasures to solve conflicts could not be effective in construction conflict management. Therefore, it is necessary to learn and master the random rule of conflict events in CEP to manage and control conflicts in large-scale construction projects..

* Corresponding author: hou-xl@163.com

2 Investigation and statistics of conflict events

In order to understand the conflict events in large-scale construction projects, and reveal the objective situation and distribution rule of conflict events, an extensive investigation has been carried at the support of China national social science fund project and ninety-six large-scale construction enterprises in twenty-seven provinces. After researchers completed the questionnaire edition on the bases of determining survey parameters such as survey object, survey content, survey methods, and survey sample demands[4], 438 questionnaires were issued. Finally, 376 questionnaires were recovered. Through the identification, 325 valid questionnaires were obtained, and the questionnaire recovery rate was 85.84%. Based on the actual recovered sample, the response rate of the questionnaire was 86.43%.

In this survey, in order to find the occurring characteristics of conflicts in different project stage, the occurring frequency degree of conflicts is set up in advance, that is, little, less, normal, much and more. Thus, according to the analysis of 325 valid samples, the investigators reported 726 items of conflict events. Through the consolidation analysis of 726 conflict events, it is known that there are 76 representative conflict events in 19 categories in large construction projects, the category and occurring frequency degree of conflict events in each stage and their cumulative reflection number in the survey are shown in Table 1.

Table 1. Statistic of conflict events in each stage.

Stage	Category of conflict	Frequency					Number
		Little	Less	Normal	Much	More	
Decision-making	Project scheme decision-making				●		15
	Project feasible study			●			24
	Project investment estimation		●				19
	Report submission and approval				●		13
Preparation	Engineering survey and design					●	59
	Project bidding				●		39
	Land expropriation and migration			●			26
	Construction procedures transaction			●			31
Construction	Safety management		●				64
	Contract disputes		●				28
	Engineering quality			●			46
	Environmental problem			●			48
	Construction schedule				●		53
	Personnel coordination				●		45
	Resource allocation					●	67
	Technical problems		●				50
Ending	Expense settlement			●			34
	Residual problem handling					●	45
	Project confirmation and handover				●		20

3 The occurring rule of conflict events in every stage

It can be seen from Table 1 that there are different numbers of conflict categories in different stages, which have also different occurring frequencies. In order to reveal the occurring rule of conflict events in every stage, a new concept referred to as the representation degree φ that quantitatively expresses the occurring intensity of conflict events is introduced here. It means that these conflicts in very high frequency would have obvious occurrence. If using representation degree to describe the intensity of obvious occurrence, then, the greater the degree of representation is, the more attention is needed in construction management. Based on the ideal, let $\varphi_i = \varpi_i \times n_i$, where, n_i is the i th cumulative value of response number to each conflict event from informants, ϖ_i is its corresponding weight value based on qualitative frequency in table 1. For quantitative analysis, the qualitative frequency is divided into five kinds, which are 1, 2, 3, 4, 5, and respectively mapping with little, less, normal, much, and more in the investigation. After dealing with unitary theory[5], all corresponding weight value and their representation degree of conflict events can be obtained in table 2.

Table 2. The representation degree of conflict events.

stage	Category of conflict		n_i	ϖ_i	φ_i	Order of degree
Decision-making	D1	Project scheme decision-making	15	0.81	12.1	D2>D3>D1>D4
	D2	Project feasible study	24	0.76	18.2	
	D3	Project investment estimation	19	0.75	14.3	
	D4	Report submission and approval	13	0.81	10.5	
Preparation	P1	Engineering survey and design	59	0.75	44.5	P1>P2>P4>P3
	P2	Project bidding	39	0.73	28.3	
	P3	Land expropriation and resident migration	26	0.77	20.0	
	P4	Construction procedures transaction	31	0.76	23.7	
Construction	C1	Safety management	64	0.77	49.2	C7>C1>C5>C8 >C4>C3>C6>C2
	C2	Contract disputes	28	0.76	21.4	
	C3	Engineering quality	46	0.74	34.0	
	C4	Environmental problem	48	0.72	34.4	
	C5	Construction schedule	53	0.72	38.3	
	C6	Personnel coordination	45	0.72	32.5	
	C7	Resource allocation	67	0.75	50.1	
	C8	Technical problems	50	0.74	37.0	
Ending	E1	Expense settlement	34	0.75	25.5	E2>E1>E3
	E2	Residual problem handling	45	0.76	34.2	
	E3	Project confirmation and handover	20	0.75	15.0	

4 Conflict event's latent roots and their consistency test

Construction engineering project is made of four stages and cumulative results of conflict events in every stage must bring about different effects on construction. If every stage is regarded as a subsystem, then, the effect of the subsystem on whole could be made sure by a judgment matrix set up by elements in the subsystem[6]. According to the analytic hierarchy process (AHP), the matrix's latent root would comprehensively reflect this subsystem characteristic[7]. So, cumulative results of conflict events in one stage can also be analyzed in the judgment matrix set up by conflict events of the subsystem.

For instance, take the construction stage as an example, using the calculation procedure of AHP theory, the judgment matrix M_c of conflict events in the construction stage can be set up based on the comparative result between any two representation degrees of conflict event, and the matrix maximum latent root can be obtained as follows. Because of the universality of the analytic hierarchy process, the calculation procedure of AHP and the meaning of symbols don't introduce again.

$$M_C = \begin{vmatrix} 1.000 & 0.435 & 0.691 & 0.699 & 0.778 & 0.661 & 1.018 & 0.752 \\ 2.299 & 1.000 & 1.589 & 1.607 & 1.790 & 1.519 & 2.341 & 1.729 \\ 1.447 & 0.629 & 1.000 & 1.012 & 1.126 & 0.956 & 1.474 & 1.088 \\ 1.430 & 0.622 & 0.988 & 1.000 & 1.113 & 0.945 & 1.456 & 1.076 \\ 1.285 & 0.559 & 0.888 & 0.898 & 1.000 & 0.849 & 1.308 & 0.966 \\ 1.514 & 0.658 & 1.046 & 1.058 & 1.178 & 1.000 & 1.542 & 1.138 \\ 0.982 & 0.427 & 0.679 & 0.687 & 0.764 & 0.649 & 1.000 & 0.739 \\ 1.330 & 0.578 & 0.919 & 0.930 & 1.035 & 0.878 & 1.354 & 1.000 \end{vmatrix} \qquad \omega = \begin{vmatrix} 0.089 \\ 0.204 \\ 0.128 \\ 0.127 \\ 0.114 \\ 0.134 \\ 0.087 \\ 0.118 \end{vmatrix}$$

$$M_C \times \omega = \begin{vmatrix} 1.000 & 0.435 & 0.691 & 0.699 & 0.778 & 0.661 & 1.018 & 0.752 \\ 2.299 & 1.000 & 1.589 & 1.607 & 1.790 & 1.519 & 2.341 & 1.729 \\ 1.447 & 0.629 & 1.000 & 1.012 & 1.126 & 0.956 & 1.474 & 1.088 \\ 1.430 & 0.622 & 0.988 & 1.000 & 1.113 & 0.945 & 1.456 & 1.076 \\ 1.285 & 0.559 & 0.888 & 0.898 & 1.000 & 0.849 & 1.308 & 0.966 \\ 1.514 & 0.658 & 1.046 & 1.058 & 1.178 & 1.000 & 1.542 & 1.138 \\ 0.982 & 0.427 & 0.679 & 0.687 & 0.764 & 0.649 & 1.000 & 0.739 \\ 1.330 & 0.578 & 0.919 & 0.930 & 1.035 & 0.878 & 1.354 & 1.000 \end{vmatrix} \begin{vmatrix} 0.089 \\ 0.204 \\ 0.128 \\ 0.127 \\ 0.114 \\ 0.134 \\ 0.087 \\ 0.118 \end{vmatrix} = \begin{vmatrix} 0.709 \\ 1.630 \\ 1.026 \\ 1.014 \\ 0.911 \\ 1.073 \\ 0.696 \\ 0.943 \end{vmatrix}$$

Based on this, the matrix maximum latent root $\lambda_{C\max}$ can be calculated furtherly, that is 8.126, this matrix's index CI of consistency test is 0.018. When the rank number of the matrix is 8, the standard index RI of the consistency test is 1.41 by relative table[8], then, the ratio of 0.018 and 1.41 is 0.0127. Because the ratio is much less than the specified value of 0.1, so, according to multivariate statistics[9], the result fits the rule.

In the same way, another three stages of matrixes and maximum latent roots can be obtained too, and every maximum latent root is also satisfactory in the consistency test. Where, the matrix maximum latent root of decision-making, preparation, and ending stage are as follows respectively.

$$\lambda_{D\max} = 5.021 \quad \lambda_{P\max} = 7.722 \quad \lambda_{E\max} = 4.130$$

5 Conclusions and suggestions

According to the analysis results in Table 2, the conflict events in each stage of large construction projects have the following characteristics and occurring rules.

(1) In the decision-making stage, the main conflict events focus on the disputes of project feasibility study among participators, and the lowest one is the such problem as the report submission and approval. The order of representation degree from D1 to D4 shows in table 2.

(2) In the preparation stage, the problems of the conflict events are mainly concentrated in the conflicts and contradictions among participators in the drawing review and technical explanation due to the poor engineering survey and design, the secondary problems are mainly such conflict events as project bidding, construction procedures transaction and land expropriation and resident migration. Thus, the order of representation degree from P1 to P4 can be made.

(3) In the construction stage, the main occurring conflicts from the top to low are respectively resource allocation, safety, construction schedule, technology, environment, quality, personnel management, and contract disputes. It can be seen that the prominent conflict event in the project construction stage is the project resources and interest allocation closely related to all participants.

(4) In the completion stage, the conflict events mainly turn to the residual problem handling and the cost settlement, which has a high degree of consistency with the actual problems appearing in the construction project. The order of representation degree from E1 to E3 can be shown in table 2.

Meanwhile, seeing from the whole project view, according to the latent root of every stage, the influence order on the whole construction project can be obtained as follow.

$$\lambda_{C\max} > \lambda_{P\max} > \lambda_{D\max} > \lambda_{E\max}$$

This means that a great number of conflict events would appear in the construction stage, and lots of resources would be consumed. If these conflict events in this stage could not be resolved effectively, the construction project might be affected seriously. Therefore, it is necessary to strengthen conflict management in the construction stage. At the same time, due to the smaller difference of latent root between the preparation stage and construction stage, the effect of preparation stages is not ignored either. The smaller difference tells construction managers that whether the project would be developed smoothly in the construction stage is connected tightly with the state of each work in the preparation stage. So, making every task perfect by all means in advance is a necessary condition for avoiding and cutting down conflict events in the later stage.

The research has been supported by the national social science foundation, No. 21BGL123, and ninety-six large-scale construction enterprises, the authors especially thank them for this work.

References

1. Shan Tengfei, Hou Xueliang. Conflicting and influencing factors in the construction stage of construction projects. Journal of Engineering Management. 36,102-106(2022)
2. Hou Xueliang, Guo Yu, Wang Yi. Ergodic relationship of management objects at each stage of large-scale construction projects. Journal of Systems Science, 29,113-117(2021)
3. Wu Mengqiang, He Danfeng Yi. Research on the Coordination Mechanism of Government Investment Project Based on Contradiction. Construction Economy,42,83-87(2021)
4. Wang Shu, Zhu Yunqiang,etc. A novel rapid web investigation method for ecological agriculture patterns in China. Science of The Total Environment. 842, 156653(2022)
5. Huffman Zach. A Unitary Theory of Strict Deference. Fordham Law Review,88,2651-2691(2020)
6. Adeyemi Ben, Suan Jamen. An Exploratory Factor Analysis for Conflict Resolution Methods among Civil Construction Profession. Buildings, 12,136-141(2022)
7. Wang Rongxin. *Mathematical statistics*. Shaanxi,Xi'an Jiaotong University Press(2002)
8. Ma zhuangguo. *Management Statistics*. Beijing, Science Press (2002)
9. Fang Kaitai. *Practical statistics*. Shaanxi, Tongji University Press (2019)

Exploration and practice of practical teaching of automobile inspection and maintenance major in higher vocational education under the background of "Three Education" reform

Chunhong Zhu[1,*], *Jiantong* Song[2], *Yiwei* Fu[1], and *Meili* Sui[1]

[1]Department of Automotive Technical Services Beijing Polytechnic, 100176, Beijing, China
[2]Department of New Energy Vehicle Technology Beijing Polytechnic, 100176, Beijing, China

Abstract. The "three education" reform was explicitly proposed in the National Vocational Education Reform Implementation Plan in January 2019, that is, the reform of teachers, teaching materials and teaching methods, which runs through the whole process of talent training, directly related to the fundamental issue of "who, how and for whom to train people", and is the top priority of the development of higher vocational education in the new era. The biggest difference between higher vocational colleges and undergraduate colleges is to cultivate high-end skilled talents. The cultivation of skilled talents cannot be separated from practical teaching. Taking the automobile inspection and maintenance specialty in higher vocational colleges as an example, this paper analyzes the role and importance of each practical teaching link in cultivating students' skills and other qualities.

1 Introduction

The talent training goal of vocational colleges is to cultivate compound talents who can meet the needs of society. The purpose of implementing the "three education" reform in higher vocational colleges is to cultivate high-quality technical and technical talents who combine morality and technology, knowledge and practice. The cultivation of skilled talents can not be separated from practical teaching. Therefore, it is of great significance to explore how to pass the practical teaching in the teaching process under the background of the "three education" reform in vocational colleges. It is an important guarantee to cultivate students' safety awareness, standardization awareness, time awareness, responsibility awareness, craftsmanship spirit, labor spirit, model labor spirit, exploration spirit, and innovation spirit in the goal of talent cultivation.

Since 2006, the automobile inspection and maintenance specialty of our school has cooperated with Mercedes Benz in schools and enterprises. It has successively cooperated with BMW, Citroen, Jaguar Land Rover, Ford and other car brand dealers or manufacturers in schools and enterprises, and sent teachers to Germany, France, Britain or specialized training classes organized by enterprises for training in teaching methods, practical skills,

* Corresponding author: zhuchunhong2009@126.com

theoretical knowledge, assessment methods, etc. After training, teachers have introduced the advanced teaching methods of foreign vocational education, enterprise training staff and the latest technology of enterprises into the classroom. At present, the practical teaching of the automobile inspection and maintenance specialty of our school mainly includes the following forms: integrated teaching of theory and practice, centralized practice of the specialty inside and outside the school, post placement practice, graduation thesis. Through these forms of practical teaching and training, Students can quickly become qualified maintenance technicians and technical backbones after graduation.

2 Integrated teaching of theory and practice

At present, the professional courses of automobile inspection and maintenance in our school adopt the integrated teaching method of theory and practice. This method is to transfer the course teaching from the ordinary classroom to the training room. There are theoretical teaching areas and practice stations in the training room. During the course, teachers use teachers to teach and organize students to learn theoretical knowledge or practice in different forms in groups After students finish learning in groups or operations, they can share the results of group or independent learning and other teaching methods through lectures, posters, PPT and other different ways. Theoretical learning and practical learning account for about 50% each. Through a variety of learning methods, we can mobilize the enthusiasm of students to learn, and turn "I want to learn" into "I want to learn". In terms of learning materials, in addition to traditional textbooks, teachers will also use self compiled handouts and enterprise maintenance materials corresponding to practical models as learning materials, prepare work orders for students, and record the work process and test results. Through this way of learning, students can learn how to use basic tools; It can cultivate students' awareness of safety and standardization; Ability to retrieve, read and understand maintenance data; Cultivate teamwork and communication skills in the process of group work and learning; In the process of teachers or students' explanation, the students who listen to the lecture can learn to listen carefully. At the same time, after listening, they can also supplement or comment on the students' explanation, so as to exercise the students' ability to think independently; For the students who explain, exercise their language expression ability.

3 Centralized practice in the school

The centralized practical training in the school is generally arranged after a part of theoretical courses are completed, and usually 1-2 weeks are arranged in each semester. In the process of integrated learning of theory and practice, because of the limited class hours, students have no opportunity to do some operations every time, and some operations with certain difficulties have no time to practice repeatedly. Through concentrated practice in the school, they can carry out comprehensive project training after learning several courses, under the guidance of the old teachers of practical training, and integrate the knowledge learned from several courses as a whole practical training project, Through repeated practice, improve students' practical skills. In the centralized practice class, teachers will also have about 20% of theoretical knowledge to explain in order to cooperate with the practice teaching, so that students can better master the practical knowledge. The combination of centralized practice meeting and 1+X evidence collection not only tests the learning achievements of centralized practice, but also enables students to obtain skill certificates. In the process of concentrated practice, students can personally experience what is craftsmanship spirit, labor spirit, inquiry spirit, etc.

4 Concentrated practice of enterprises outside school

The centralized practice of enterprises outside the school is generally based on the students' completion of the integrated theory and practice courses such as Automobile Maintenance, Automobile Power System Fault Diagnosis and Detection, or 1-2 times of centralized practice in the school, and according to the talent training program, students are arranged to go to the automobile 4S store for 2-3 consecutive weeks of practice. Generally, according to the size and reception capacity of 4S stores, each store arranges 3-6 students for internship. During the internship, each student will have a master from the 4S store for one-to-one guidance. The internship positions are mainly mechanic. Sometimes, according to the wishes of students or the specific conditions of 4S stores, students are arranged to work as service reception, parts warehouse administrator, warranty officer, dispatcher and other positions. Generally, during an internship, in order to enable students to deeply learn the work content of a certain post, they will not change their posts during an internship. During students' internship, teachers should do a good job in management and guide students to practice how to communicate with teachers, how to learn from teachers, and what aspects to focus on. Students write a summary of the practice every day after the practice and send it to the teacher. The teacher makes a timely evaluation according to the summary of the students. If necessary, the teacher guides students how to solve various problems encountered in the practice through telephone, WeChat, etc. The teacher will also communicate with the teacher of the enterprise about the students' performance during the internship, and give timely guidance and correction to the students' improper practices during the internship. Through enterprise practice, because students are doing practical work, they have made rapid progress under the one-to-one guidance of a master. Some students have been able to independently carry out maintenance for customers on various models of vehicles and solve some actual fault cases after the internship. Students are very welcome to participate in this kind of practice. In the process of enterprise practice, students' safety awareness, standardization awareness, time awareness and responsibility awareness have been better tempered and improved than centralized training in schools.

5 Post practice

After two and a half years, after completing all the courses of the school, the last semester, after being recommended by the school, the students and the enterprise make a two-way choice through interviews, go to the professional counterpart enterprises to directly participate in the production process, comprehensively use the knowledge and skills learned in this major, complete certain production tasks, further obtain perceptual knowledge, master operating skills, and learn enterprise management, It is a practical teaching form to develop a correct attitude towards work. In the process of internship, students, as a regular employee of the enterprise, participate in the production of the enterprise, and are under the dual management of the school and the enterprise. The enterprise pays salaries, provides labor security, and enjoys the benefits provided by the enterprise according to the standards of interns. By the end of the internship period, students can successfully pass the enterprise assessment, and they are willing to stay in the enterprise to continue working. The enterprise can sign a formal employment agreement or labor contract with students. Some students can be promoted to regular employees after obtaining their graduation certificates, and do not need to go through the probation period again. Students feel that employment is guaranteed, and enterprises also welcome such a recruitment mode, because during the internship, students and enterprises have a very deep understanding of each other.

If during the internship period, students are not suitable for some management modes of the enterprise, or are incompetent or dissatisfied with the job content of the job, or the enterprise is dissatisfied with the students' performance and work ability, students can return to school and wait for new enterprise recruitment opportunities. The school understands the reasons through both students and enterprises, and provides corresponding guidance for students're employment. Avoid being returned by the enterprise for many students' personal reasons, which will affect the final employment of students.

6 Graduation design (Thesis)

Graduation design (thesis) is a comprehensive assessment for students. In the process of doing graduation design or writing graduation thesis, students should have a certain theoretical basis and practical skills. For students majoring in automobile inspection and maintenance, the graduation design is generally to design or improve the tools and equipment for automobile inspection and maintenance. The graduation thesis is to write a solution to a system fault of automobile. It is required to describe the fault phenomenon, explain the working principle and composition of the system and the role of each component, analyze the possible causes of the fault, and finally find the fault point and solve the problem through troubleshooting from easy to difficult. Whether it is the graduation design or the writing of graduation thesis, in the process of completing this practice link, the students have been trained to comprehensively use the professional knowledge they have learned, the computer application ability, the ability to summarize, and the students' spirit of inquiry and innovation. In the defense link, students' language expression ability, speech ability and communication ability can be trained.

7 Conclusion

In a word, under the background of the "three education" reform, as a school, we should make overall arrangements for a more reasonable stage of practical teaching and prepare for the corresponding training conditions; As a teacher, we should carefully organize and arrange each practical course, so that students can learn real knowledge and skills in the classroom, so that every student majoring in automobile inspection and maintenance can truly master professional skills through certain practical learning at different stages of the learning period. At the same time, for the long-term development of students, students should ensure that they learn not only professional knowledge and skills, but also learning learning methods, so that they can learn new knowledge and skills in the future; Learn how to communicate and get along with others better in a team; Learn how to work as a team. Many tasks cannot be completed by one person alone. You must learn how to work as a team to better complete the work; Cultivate safety awareness, standardization awareness, time awareness, and responsibility awareness to complete the corresponding work safely and effectively; Only by cultivating the spirit of craftsman, labor and model worker can we complete the work with quality and quantity guaranteed and make due contributions to the society and the country; Only by cultivating the spirit of inquiry and innovation can we be competent for more challenges in the future of continuous technological development. As a vocational college, we cultivate more high-end skilled talents, so that each talent can make corresponding contributions, which can converge into the development and progress of the country and society, and make our country lead the world in automotive and all related technology fields.

Reference

1. Jiang Lixia, Jiang Libo, Yang Hua. Exploration on the development of loose leaf teaching materials in higher vocational education based on the reform of "three education" [J].. Forestry Teaching, 64-67 **9** (2022)
2. Zhou Bin, Research on the Reform Path of "Three Education" for Accounting Major under the Background of Artificial Intelligence [J], Economist 164-165 **9** (2022)
3. Zhong Ming. Exploration of the "Three Education" Reform of the New Engineering Major under the "1+X" Certificate System: Taking the Industrial Robot Major of Suzhou Vocational University as an Example [J]. 84-86, 92 **17** (2022)

The research on the cultivation of college students' innovation ability based on academic competition

Yuchen Wei[1,*], *Ningning* Zhao[2], and *Liling* Ge[1]

[1] School of Materials Science and Engineering, Xi'an University of Technology, Xi'an 710048, China
[2] Department of Applied Chemistry, Xi'an University of Technology, Xi'an 710048, China

Abstract. The innovation ability of college students is become more and more important in the world. But most students are lack of the ability. At the same time, the traditional teaching program colleges provided can't give students enough exercise of this kind of ability. In this way, faculty should improve the teaching program to help students build their innovation ability. Their are many roads to achieve this goal but the most useful way is the academic competition. The competition is a comprehensiveness program and students not only can improve their ability, but also have a higher level to thinking. It will have great help to students in their future research and self-employed career.

1 Introduction

On October 12,2021, The General Office of the State Council issued *The Guiding Opinions on Further Supporting the Innovation and Entrepreneurship of College Students* (hereinafter referred to as the Opinions). The Opinions pointed out: "college students are the new force for mass entrepreneurship and innovation, and it is of great significance to support college students' innovation and entrepreneurship. The XiJinping new era of socialism with Chinese characteristics will be used as a guide, fully implement the party's education policy, the implementation of education fundamental task, based on the new stage of development, carry out new development concept, build a new development pattern, adhere to the innovation leading entrepreneurship, entrepreneurship, create more employment opportunities, improve the quality of human resources, realize college students more fully higher quality employment."

General Secretary Xi Jinping also delivered an important speech at the 2021 Central Talents Work Conference, proposing to "accelerate the building of a world's important talent center and innovation highland"[1]. As an important talent resource of the country, whether college students can develop enough innovative consciousness and innovative thinking in the university stage will not only play an important role in their own future development, but also is closely related to the national strategies such as "strengthening

* Corresponding author: yweiaa@xaut.edu.cn

China through talents", "rejuvenating the country through science and education" and "rural revitalization"[2].

2 The necessity of cultivating college students' innovation ability

2.1 The inevitable requirement of quality education

Strengthening the innovation ability cultivation of college students is conducive to improving college students' innovation and entrepreneurship ability and comprehensive quality. The university should investigate ability of students, the corresponding comprehensive quality and ability training program should formulated based on the characteristics of the college students' personal ability and their future development needs. Through diversified innovation and entrepreneurship education, we can improve students' innovation ability and consciousness, improve their professional ability and accomplishment in practice, and finally improve the comprehensive ability and quality of college students in an all-round way[3].

2.2 The changing career prospects

Current employment prospects become more and more complex, under this background to do innovative entrepreneurship education, not only can enhance the students' comprehensive quality ability, at the same time can strengthen their innovation consciousness and improve their entrepreneurial skills. It also can help fully promote college students' comprehensive ability, for their learning stage and the growth after graduation lay important foundation. Through the school's innovation and entrepreneurship ability cultivation, college students can choose the direction they are best at to carry out the corresponding entrepreneurial activities on the basis of following the actual development status of the society, and give full play to their own value in the innovation and entrepreneurship activities, and effectively alleviate the severe social employment pressure.

3 The problems existing in the current innovation ability cultivation

3.1 Students' innovation consciousness is insufficient

As young people, college students have wide field of vision and flexible thinking, for new knowledge new form has a good acceptance ability, adaptability and participation of the Internet is high. But in the innovation entrepreneurship consciousness is weak, in a state of passive acceptance, cannot actively use the knowledge innovation entrepreneurship, also not combine innovative entrepreneurial knowledge and their own employment together. Although some students have the idea of innovation and entrepreneurship, they are lack of relevant knowledge reserve. In this way, they cannot actively participate in relevant activities.

3.2 Students' comprehensive quality is unbalanced

Nowadays, with the rapid development of the world, the social requirements for students' comprehensive quality are also becoming higher and higher, and the traditional training methods have gradually been unable to meet the needs of innovative and comprehensive talents. Especially according to the existing university training system, students in the university mainly focus on professional knowledge, but the university course time is limited. And different teachers are responsible for different professional courses, lead to the weak link between the specialized courses, knowledge fragmentation phenomenon is more serious. It is difficult to get into a system of knowledge system. In this way, there are not only certain obstacles in practical application, but also negative effects in scientific research. Needless to say, it is difficult to learn from the school when students are about to conduct innovation and entrepreneurship activities.

4 The method of training innovation ability

4.1 Build up the relevant knowledge system

In practice, it is found that cultivating students to build a perfect knowledge system can not only improve students' learning efficiency, but also strengthen students' innovation ability and provide help for innovation and entrepreneurship. This requires faculty to keep up with the development trend of internationalization and informatization, and to carry out continuous innovation in teaching methods. Especially at the faculty level, as a direct maker of the student training plan, faculty should keep up with the trend of world and improve the cultivation of students' innovation ability from the system.

First of all, the faculty should establish knowledge system in the overall training program. In terms of the top-level structure, it makes the knowledge acquired by students more clear, the structure more complete, and helps students to establish a macro understanding from a higher perspective of market demand, academic research, and professional development.

Secondly, we should open innovative education and teaching courses, systematically and scientifically cultivate students' innovative consciousness and innovative thinking. At the same time, actively explore and excavate innovative educational elements in other courses[4]. The development of professional technology and scientific and technological innovation are often inseparable. In professional courses, students can be encouraged to think more, ask more, and communicate more in the professional content, so as to exercise students' analytical ability and critical ability, increase students' innovative thinking, and guide students to view problems and society from the perspective of innovation. The college should also organize the teachers of different professional courses to increase the communication, and strengthen the connection between different professional courses, so that students can better integrate and sort out their knowledge system through such a communication.

In addition to professional courses, teaching can also be integrated with the second classroom. Through the latest achievements of subject development, teachers can not only stimulate students' desire to explore new knowledge, new technology and new development. Also can cultivate students' sense of autonomy. It also require students to actively participate in academic research, not only can better understand the way of academic research, lay the foundation for future study. At the same time, participate in these research can arouse the enthusiasm of students, promote students to achieve mastery of professional knowledge, cultivate students' innovative thinking, inspire students advocating science, the pursuit of truth of noble emotion, improve the students' comprehensive quality.

Finally, the faculty should provide more practical opportunities for students, as the test and final practice of students' innovation and entrepreneurship training, so that students can combine theory with practice, and modify their knowledge system through the feedback of practice. This requires the faculty to pay more attention to the discipline competition, increase the participation of the discipline competition, publicity degree, and build more platforms for students to participate in the discipline competition. Teachers can integrate their own research projects with students' teaching, help students practice and explore in the learning process, and feedback themselves.

4.2 Cultivate the spirit and consciousness of innovation

As the most important source for students to obtain policy information, the faculty should actively cultivate students' awareness of innovation through various forms. For example, through theoretical study, social practice, offline salon and other forms, students can discuss their professional development prospects from their own perspective, and establish their own learning goals and career planning. At the same time, the faculty should guide students to establish a correct world outlook, life outlook and scientific research concept in the training plan. And encourage students to establish an active self-awareness. Faculty also need adjust the professional curriculum structure, help students change mentality, and providing scientific research, academic exchange platform, visit the practice experience to change students' subjective consciousness, passive to active. Then faculty should stimulate the students' innovation consciousness, let the students feel the sense of innovation and a sense of achievement in advance, cultivate the students' innovation ability. In particular, various discipline competitions can enable students to better combine what they have learned with innovation and entrepreneurship, and establish their own perfect knowledge system. Thus with the students' professional learning to achieve a complementary effect, and finally can let the students to achieve better results.

4.3 Publicize relevant policy information

With the development of social economy and the continuous change of employment situation, the country has attached more importance to innovation and entrepreneurship, and many relevant policies have been introduced. However, due to the identity characteristics of college students. As a result, college students are often faced with such problems in the specific process of innovation and entrepreneurship, and the final good results are very few.

The faculty should give full play to its own advantages, connect with all aspects, and play a good role of communication bridge. Every year, the government have a series of preferential policies for innovation and entrepreneurship, such as preferential taxes, guaranteed loans, settlement procedures and so on. Universities will also carry out relevant special lectures, industry forums, ability competitions and other professional activities. Faculty to timely comb integration, will be related to this major students policy and activities information to students, help students comb the key points, analysis of the situation, guide students to take an active part in innovation activities, summarizes the experience of predecessors rational entrepreneurship, guide entrepreneurship with innovation, entrepreneurship to promote employment opportunities, make innovation entrepreneurship education not only stay in form, but really implement into action. The discipline competition is the integration of the relevant policy information. By participating in the discipline competition, students will consciously and actively deepen the relevant policy information into their personal internal and guiding theories. At the same time, they will combine theory with practice, and learn and use it effectively in the competition.

4.4 Provide a platform for innovation and practice

College students' academic science and technology activities is the second classroom activity system of organic composition, generally include science and technology project training, social research, academic technology competition, academic science lectures, science exhibition propaganda, and other forms of content. The academic science and technology competition in the core position, is the main carrier of students' innovation practice ability exercise. The academic science and technology competition of college students generally refers to a series of activities that "on the basis of closely combining students with classroom teaching, stimulate the motivation of combining theory with practice and independent exploration by means of competition, and cultivate students' interest in learning and enhance their self-learning confidence through the process of discovering and solving problems". In recent years, as the "Internet +" college students' innovation entrepreneurship competition , "challenge cup" and "create youth" series of competition such as high level of college students' innovation entrepreneurship competition, college students' academic technology competition in university discipline development, comprehensive strength and improve students' quality ability training lead and supporting role increasingly prominent. Therefore, make full use of science creative competition platform carrier, help students' comprehensive quality training, speed up the innovation entrepreneurship education system construction, cultivate innovative talents that meet the demand of world has become an important subject of colleges and universities and research.

The faculty should building a practice platform, which can not only provide students with a better practical vision, but also can use the influence of the environment on college students' innovation and entrepreneurship, guide students' development direction, standardize students' behavior, and stimulate students' innovative consciousness. At the same time, it can cultivate a good sense of cooperation and team spirit, which is crucial for the growing and developing college students. In addition, good community activities can also provide important help to students in the process of innovation and entrepreneurship, especially playing an important role in learning to recognize, learning to do things, learning to survive, and learning to serve. Faculty should encourage students to join more social organizations that they are interested in, share their experience. So that every idea that can burst out. Finally, academic exchange is also an important part of innovation practice. Communication makes progress. By organizing students to conduct research and exchange with excellent innovation and entrepreneurship groups, more practical guidance methods can be obtained. The combination of experience and practice can achieve twice the result with half the effort.

5 The implementation effect of innovation ability training

In the past three years, under the negative influence of the decrease in the number of discipline competitions and the shortening of the holiday training time. The overall quality of students has been continuously increased by continuously deepening the cultivation of students' innovation ability and professional quality. The specific situation is shown in Figure 1. Especially in 2022, when the number of the national first prize and the second prize of the college has increased significantly. Freshmen have made zero breakthrough in national competitions such as Advanced Mapping Technology and Product Information Modeling Innovation Competition.

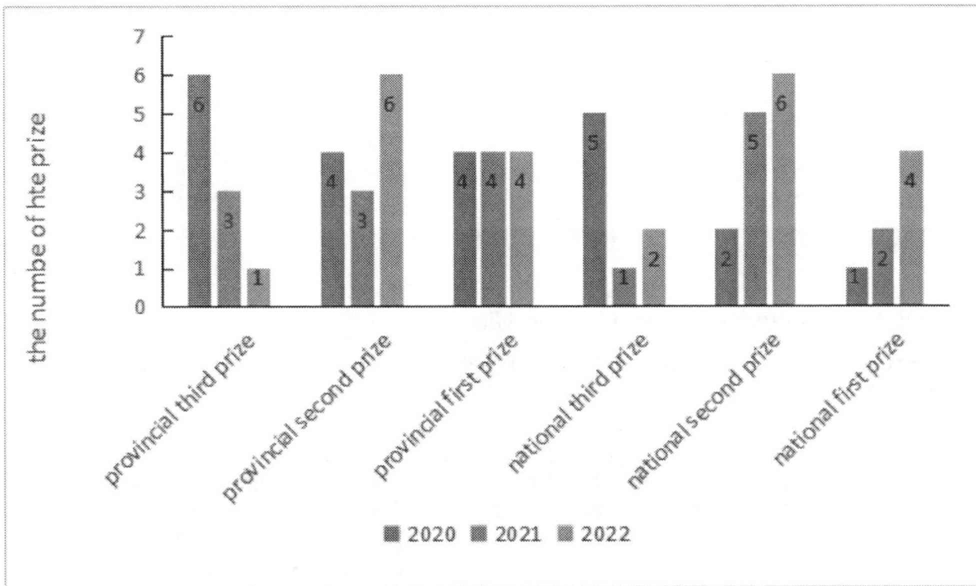

Fig. 1. Changes in the number of winners above provincial level from 2020 to 2022.

6 Conclusion

Today, under the influence of the epidemic, both the normal teaching planning of schools and the work of students have been seriously affected. However, today, how to cultivate new talents with innovative ability for the country has further become the key to university education. With its comprehensive, practical and innovative characteristics, the discipline competition provides a brand-new training idea for faculty under the current environment. The faculty should pay more attention to discipline competition, encourage students to participate in discipline competition through all-round system construction, practice what they have learned in the competition, give full play to their personal potential, strengthen innovation consciousness, improve innovation ability, and lay a good foundation for future scientific research and learning and personal career development.

This work was financially supported by the Education and Teaching Reform Research Project of Xi'an University of Technology (Nos: xjy2103, xjy2102), the Research Project on Postgraduate Education and Teaching Reform of Xi'an University of Technology (Nos. 252042033, 252042029), the Education and Teaching Reform Research Project of Xi'an University of Technology (Nos. xqj2119, 251032205).

References

1. Y.G.Wu, Management Observation, **1**(2019)
2. X.H. Yang, Higher Educ. Res. in China, **1** (2015).
3. J.X. Wang, Z.W. Zhu, M.G. Liou, Higher Building Educ. **27**, 4 (2018).
4. K.K. He, J.F. Lin, W.L. Zhang, Beijing: Higher Educ. Press, 2006

An optimization scheme of partial total homomorphic encryption

Guangqiao Luo, *Haijun* Zhao*, and *Huayue* Chen

School of Computer Science, China West Normal University, Nanchong 637002, China

Abstract. In order to further improve the effectiveness of homomorphic cryptography, we optimize Lauter et al. 's partial homomorphic cryptography scheme, and propose a new RLWE-based total homomorphic cryptography (FHE) scheme, which combines a series of existing techniques with the Chinese residual theory, and merges several "plaintext slots" into a ciphertext for homomorphic computation. The extended key transformation technology and modulo transformation technology are used to reduce the noise of ciphertext and enable it to carry out the next homomorphic operation. Compared with the original scheme, the security and effectiveness of the scheme were studied on the premise of ensuring CPA security, and the results showed that the performance of the scheme was improved by N times.

1 Introduction

With the rapid development of cloud computing, reliable and affordable access to large-scale shared computing resources is possible. However, such shared access poses huge privacy and security challenges. Therefore, new technologies are needed to guarantee the confidentiality of sensitive user data encryption, known as Full Homomorphic Encryption (FHE) [1,2], which enables cloud operators to perform extremely complex calculations of encrypted user data without decrypting it. This calculation based on homomorphic encryption is encrypted and can only be decrypted by the data owner. This excellent performance makes it widely used in cloud security [3], cloud computing [4], encrypted databases, and cipher retrieval among others. At present, the research on homomorphic cryptography has become one of the most active topics in cryptography theory.

Rivest et al [5] first proposed the concept related to FHE in 1978; it took nearly 30 years until 2009 when Gentry et al proposed a new FHE scheme based on the ideal lattice technique [6,7] to achieve a breakthrough.In 2010, Gentry et al [8] made the first attempt to implement the Gentry scheme, which can extend the homomorphism of single-bit messages to multi-bit In 2011, Smart et al [9] used the Chinese Remainder Theorem (CRT) to achieve encryption of multi-bit plaintexts, and in 2011, Brakerski et al in the literature [10] used key transformation techniques and simulation transformation techniques to achieve a hierarchical fully homomorphic cryptosystem without using homomorphic decryption

* Corresponding author: zhaohai_jun@163.com

techniques. In 2012, Gentry et al [11] gave an in-depth discussion of this technique, which led to a significant improvement in the performance of the overall homomorphic encryption.

The scheme in this paper is based on the SWHE scheme of Kristin Lauter et al. [12], in the original scheme, only one plaintext can be encrypted at a time, and the corresponding plaintext size is added to the public key and private key, and the encryption session is time-consuming. In this paper, according to the Chinese residual theorem, the packing of plaintexts is achieved by combining the SMID technique of literature [9]; based on this, a new optimization scheme for partial homomorphic encryption is introduced by using the extended key transformation technique and the mode transformation technique. By introducing new security parameters and a smaller computationally intensive ciphertext generation algorithm, this scheme is made easier to implement in hardware. This scheme is more intuitive and has a clearer structure; compared with the SWHE scheme, it can encrypt multiple plaintexts at the same time, which considerably improves its encryption efficiency.

2 Relevant knowledge

2.1 Basic notations

If A denotes an algorithm, then $x \leftarrow A$ implies that x is computed by algorithm A. If A denotes a set, then $x \leftarrow A$ implies that x is chosen randomly from the set A. For any integer q, denote $Z_q = [-q/2, q/2]$, and for an integer x, let $[x]_q$ denote $x(\mathrm{mod}\ q) \in Zq$. Denote a multidimensional vector in bold and lowercase letters, such as vector $\boldsymbol{y}$, where y_i denotes the ith component of vector $\boldsymbol{y}$. Undefined elements are polynomials of x, denoted by lowercase letters, such as $f(x)$.

2.2 Cyclotomic polynomial

Definition 1 (Cyclotomic polynomial) [13]: m is defined to be a positive integer not divisible by p, where p is an eigenvalue of the cyclotomic domain K. ζ_m is an m-th original unit root on K, then the polynomial $\Phi_m(x) = \prod_{i=1,\gcd(i,m)=1}^{m} (x - \zeta^i)$ is called an m-th cyclotomic polynomial on K. The m-th subcircular domain is expanded by adding the original unit root to the rational number field Q, $K = \mathbb{Q}(\zeta_m)$.

The cyclotomic polynomial over a finite field has the following lemma:

Lemma 1 [13] (Cyclotomic polynomials over a finite field): Let F_p be a finite field, m a positive integer, and $(m,p)=1$, then the partition polynomial $\Phi_m(x)$ over F_p $[x]$ can be decomposed into the product of φ(m) different d times integrable polynomials $n_i(x)$, $\Phi_m(x) = \prod_{i=0}^{l-1} f_i(x)$; d is the smallest integer that satisfies $p^d \equiv 1(\mathrm{mod}\, m)$, $l = \varphi(m)/d$.

Proof: Let ζ_m be any m-th principal unit root on F_p and $\zeta_m \in F_{p^k}$ when and only when $\zeta_m^{p^k} = \zeta_m$. When $k = d$, we have $\zeta_m \in F_p$, because, by the minimality of d, the true subdomain $\zeta_m \notin F_{p^k}$, so the minimal polynomial ζ_m over F_p is an integrable polynomial of d times. It also follows from the fact that ζ_m is an arbitrary principal unit root that every integrable polynomial of $\Phi_m(x)$ is of d times, and the number of partition polynomials $\Phi_m(x)$

is φ(m), so it can be decomposed into the product of $l=\varphi(m)/d$ different d times integrable polynomials $n_i(x)$.

2.3 Chinese remainder theorem

Definition 2 [14] (Chinese Remainder Theorem): Let $n_1,\ldots,n_l$ be $l>=2$ two mutually prime integers greater than 1. Let $N=n_1,n_2\ldots n_i$ then the system of congruent equations.

$$\begin{cases} g(x)\equiv r_1(x)\bmod n_1(x)\\ g(x)\equiv r_2(x)\bmod n_2(x)\\ \vdots\\ g(x)\equiv r_i(x)\bmod n_i(x)\end{cases} \tag{1}$$

There is a unique solution $x\equiv\sum_{i=0}^{l-1}a_ib_iN_i(\bmod N)$, where $N_i=N/n$ and $b_i\equiv 1/N_i(\bmod \mathrm{n}_i)$, where $i=1,2,\ldots,l$.

From the above definition, the Chinese Remainder Theorem over the number field is extended to polynomial rings as follows.

Let $n_1(x),\cdots,n_l(x)$ be $l\geq 2$ polynomials that are both approximately and such that $n(x)=n_1(x)\cdot n_1(x)\cdots n_l(x)$, then for any polynomial $r_1(x),\cdots,r_i(x)$, $\exists g(x)\in R[x]$ such that there is a system of congruent equations.

$$\begin{cases} g_1(x)\equiv r_2(x)\bmod n_2(x)\\ g_2(x)\equiv r_3(x)\bmod n_3(x)\\ \vdots\\ g_{i-1}(x)\equiv r_i(x)\bmod n_i(x)\end{cases} \tag{2}$$

There is a unique solution $g(x)=\sum_{i=0}^{l}r_i(x)h_i(x)m_i(x)(\bmod n(x))$, where $m_i(x)=n(x)/n_i(x)$, $h_i(x)=1/m_i(x)(\bmod n_i(x))$

The work in this paper is based on the algebraic structure $R_p=R/pR=\mathbb{Z}_p[x]/\Phi_m(x)$. $\Phi_m(x)$ is a partitioned circle polynomial of number φ(m), φ(x) is the Euler function. The elements in R_p are polynomials with coefficients in the interval [-p/2,p/2), whose operations are addition and multiplication under modulo $\Phi_m(x)$ and p on $\mathbb{Z}_p$. The polynomial $\Phi_m(x)$ can be decomposed into l different factors $n_i(x)$ under mod p with each number d, satisfying $p^d\equiv 1(\bmod m)$,and with $l\bullet d\equiv$φ(m),and $\Phi_m(x)=n_1(x)\cdot n_2(x)\cdots n_i(x)(\bmod q)$,combining the Chinese residue theorem with the following isomorphism.

$$R_p=\mathbb{Z}_p[x]/\Phi_m(x)=\mathbb{Z}_p[x]/n_1(x)\cdot n_2(x)\cdots n_i(x)\cong\mathbb{F}_{p^d}\times\cdots\times\mathbb{F}_{p^d}=\mathbb{L}_0\times\cdots\times\mathbb{L}_i \tag{3}$$

That is, R_p is isomorphic to the direct product of l and L_i. The elements of R_p are mapped to the elements of l in $\mathbb{F}_{p^d}\cong\mathbb{Z}_p[x]/n_i(x)$. Let L_i be a "slot" point, the elements of R_p are related to the l slots. This is done as follows.

We can define the mapping of $\mathbb{F}^l_{p^d}$ to $\mathbb{Z}_p[x]/n_i(x)$ as:

$$\phi:\begin{cases}\mathbb{F}^l_{p^d}\to\mathbb{Z}_p[x]/n_0(x)\times\cdots\times\mathbb{Z}_p[x]/n_i(x)\\ (n_0,\ldots,n_i)\mapsto(\psi_0(n_0),\ldots,\phi_i(n_i))\end{cases} \tag{4}$$

Define the mapping of $\mathbb{F}^l_{p^d}$ to R_p on the ciphertext domain as:

$$\gamma:\begin{cases}\mathbb{Z}_p[x]/n1(x)\times\cdots\times\mathbb{Z}_p[x]/n_i(x)\to R_p\\ (h_0,\ldots,h_i)\mapsto\sum_{i=0}^{l}h_iH_i(x)N_i(x)\end{cases} \tag{5}$$

where $N_i(x)=\Phi_m(x)/n_i(x)$, $H_i(x)=1/N_i(x)\left(\bmod n_i(x)\right)$.

2.4 Discrete gaussian distribution

Definition 3 [15] The error distribution χ is a discrete Gaussian distribution $D_{\mathbf{z}^n}$ for $\sigma > 0$, whose probability density function is $\forall \mathbf{e}\in\mathbb{Z}^n$, $P\left(\mathbf{e}\leftarrow D_{\mathbf{z}^n,\sigma}\right)=\frac{e^{-\pi\|\|\|^2/\sigma^2}}{\sum_{\vec{e}\in\mathbf{Z}^n} e^{-\pi\|\in\|^2/\sigma^2}}$, and a sample $\boldsymbol{e}$ drawn from the distribution χ corresponds to a polynomial. For a Gaussian distribution with standard deviation $e(x)\in R$, a randomly drawn vector $\boldsymbol{x}$ is bounded $B=\|\mathbf{x}\|_\infty=\sigma\sqrt{n}$.

2.5 Learning with errors over rings

Definition 4 (RLWE problem [12]): for a security parameter λ, let $f(x)=x^d+1$, where $d=d(\lambda)$ is a power of 2 and a positive integer $q=q(\lambda)>=2$. Let $R=\mathbb{Z}[x]/(f(x))$ be a polynomial ring over Z and $R_q=R/qR$ and let $x=x(\lambda)$be a discrete Gaussian distribution over the ring R. Take the random uniform distribution on $a_i\leftarrow R_q, s\leftarrow R_q$ and pick the noise $e_i\leftarrow\chi$, such that $b_i=a_i\cdot s+e_i$ where $i=1,\ldots,m$. *Decision-RLWE* problem: $\left(a_i,b_i=a_i\cdot s+e_i\right)\in R_q^2$ with random uniform hooks picked by $(a_i,b_i)\in\mathbb{R}_q^2$ is computationally indistinguishable; *Search-RLWEn, q, x* problem: The values of a_i,b_i are known and for $\left(a_i,b_i=a_i\cdot s+e_i\right)\in R_q^2$, solve for s.

3 Optimization scheme for partial homomorphic encryption

In this paper, based on the SWHE scheme [12], we construct a homomorphic encryption scheme supporting batch processing to encapsulate multiple plaintexts by using the Chinese residual theorem (CRT), and the scheme in this paper is constructed by combining two techniques of key conversion and mode conversion, which can reduce the ciphertext expansion rate and improve the encryption efficiency.

3.1 Program structure

Let the safety parameter of the scheme be λ and the number of circuit layers be L. Let $R=\mathbb{Z}[x]/\Phi_m(x)$, where $\Phi_m(x)=\prod_{i=0}^{l-1} f_i(x)$ is a partitioned circular polynomial and the number of is d, where $\phi(m)=n=dl=n(\lambda,L)$. Let the scheme have a total of L+1 prime modes, $q_0<q_1<\ldots<q_L$, correspondingly the circuit polynomial ring at the *i-th* level is $R_{q_i}=\mathbb{Z}[x]_{q_i}/\Phi_m(x)$, and the discrete Gaussian distribution of the circuit at each level is $X(\lambda,L)$. Choose a prime number t satisfying $t<q$, $\mathbb{F}_{p^d}^l$ is an explicit vector space, the mapping CRT_p is an isomorphic mapping from $\mathbb{F}_{p^d}^l$ to R_p, and CRT^{-1}_p is the inverse mapping from R_p to $\mathbb{F}_{p^d}^l$.

1) Batch key generation algorithm: randomly select $L+1$ ring elements $S_i \leftarrow X$, randomly and uniformly select the ring elements $a_i \leftarrow R_{qi}$, and error noise $\boldsymbol{e} \leftarrow X$, and $b_i = -a_i \cdot s_i + te$, where $i=0,1,\ldots,L$. Let $\boldsymbol{a}=(a_0,a_1,\ldots,a_L)$, $\boldsymbol{b}=(b_0,b_1,\ldots,b_L)$, set the public key pk= $(\mathbf{b},\mathbf{a})$, private key key $sk=\mathbf{s}=(s_0,s_1,\ldots,s_L)$.

2) Batch encryption algorithm: input public key pk and plaintext $(m_{i,0},\ldots,m_{i,l-1}) \in F^l_{pd}$, where $i=0,1,\ldots,L$. The encryption process is as follows.

Step1: Randomly select u and e_i, where $i=0,1,\ldots,L$,both of which have the number of elements L. To encrypt the message m $\in R_p$.

Step2: Let $M=(m_{i,0},\ldots,m_{i,l-1})$; use the Chinese residual theorem to calculate the plaintex $C_i \leftarrow CRT_p(c_{i,0},\ldots,c_{i,l-1}) \in R_p, i=0,1,\ldots,l-1$

Step3: Output the ciphertext $\boldsymbol{ct}=(\boldsymbol{c_0},\boldsymbol{c_1})=(\boldsymbol{m}+\boldsymbol{b} \cdot u+t \cdot \boldsymbol{e_1},\boldsymbol{a} \cdot u+t \cdot \boldsymbol{e_2}) \in R_q^{2L}$.

3) Batch decryption algorithm: The specific decryption process is as follows:

Step1: Calculation $M=(m,\ldots,m_{l-1})=(\mathbf{c}_0+\mathbf{c}_1 \odot \mathbf{s})(\bmod p \bmod t) \in R_P^L$;

step2: Output $(c_{i,0},\ldots,c_{i,l-1}) \leftarrow CRT_p^{-1}(C_i) \in \mathbb{F}^l_{p^d}$, where $i = 0, 1\ldots, l\text{-}1$.

4) Batch (expanded) key conversion algorithm:

After multiplying the above homomorphic operations, the elements of the original ciphertext expand from 2 (L + 1) in two dimensions to 3 (L + 1) in three dimensions, and the corresponding key also expands from (1, s) in two dimensions to (1, s, s^2) in three dimensions, which decreases the decryption efficiency. Therefore, this section proposes an extended key transformation technique based on the key transformation technique of Brakerski et al. [10] combined with the batch homomorphic encryption scheme in this paper to reduce the ciphertext dimensionality.

Set $\left(c_{0,i} \cdot c'_{0,i}, c_{0,i} \cdot c'_{1,i} + c_{1,i} \cdot c'_{0,i}, c_{1,i} \cdot c'_{1,i}\right) \leftarrow (c_{0,i}, c_{1,i}, c_{2,i})$ .Let $(c_0,c_1,c_2) \leftarrow \{(c_{0,i},c_{1,i},c_{2,i})\}_{i=0}^{L}$, $sk'=(1,\mathbf{s},\mathbf{s}\bullet\mathbf{s})$.*KeySwitch*(sk_1, $sk_2(c_0,c_1,c_2)$)) be the extended key conversion algorithm, which converts the ciphertext to: $\mathbf{ct}_{mlt}=(\mathbf{c}_0,\mathbf{c}_1,\mathbf{c}_2) \rightarrow \mathbf{ct}'_{mlt}=(\mathbf{c}'_0,\mathbf{c}'_1)$ and the corresponding private key to $sk''=(1,s')$, and the algorithm is as follows.

Input: sk', sk'', $\boldsymbol{ct}=(c_0,c_1,c_2)$

Output $\boldsymbol{ct}' = (c'_0,c'_1)$.

Step1:Calculation: i From 0 to L

(1) $c_{i,2} = \sum_{x=0}^{\kappa_i} t^{x_i} \cdot c_{i,2}^{k_i} \bmod q, \kappa_i = 0,\ldots,\lceil \log_t^{q_i} \rceil - 1, c_{i,2}^{k_i} \in R_t$

(2) $sk'' = \left[\left(\left[-\left(a_{\kappa_i,i}s'_i + te\right) + t^{x_i}s_i^2\right]_q, a_{\kappa_i,i}\right) : \kappa_i \in [0\ldots\lceil \log_t^{q_i} \rceil - 1]\right]$

(3) $c'_{i,0} = \left[c_{i,0} + \sum_{\kappa_i=0}^{\lceil \log_t^{q_i} \rceil - 1} sk''[\kappa_i][0] \cdot c_{i,2}^{\kappa_i}\right]_q, c'_{i,1} = \left[c_{i,1} + \sum_{\kappa_i=0}^{\lceil \log_t^{q_i} \rceil - 1} sk''[\kappa_i][1] \cdot c_{i,2}^{\kappa_i}\right]_q$

(4) $C'_0 = \left(c'_{0,0}, c'_{1,0}, \cdots, c'_{L,0}\right), C'_1 = \left(c'_{0,1}, c'_{1,1}, \cdots, c'_{L,1}\right)$

End

(5) $\boldsymbol{ct}' = (c'_0,c'_1)$

Step2:Return ct' ;

Then the new ciphertext is (c_0', c_1'), and its corresponding private key is (1, s').

5) Mode conversion algorithms

After performing a ciphertext multiplication, the ciphertext is first degraded using the KeySwitch algorithm to move to the next layer of the circuit. After that, the ciphertext noise is again reduced by the mode-conversion algorithm. The algorithm is as follows:

Input: *Scale(ct, q_i, q_{i-1}, t)*

Output $\mathbf{ct}'$.

Step1: $\mathbf{ct}' = [(q_i - 1/q_i).\mathbf{ct}]$;

Step2: $\mathbf{ct}' \equiv \mathbf{ct}$ (mod t);

Step3:Return $\mathbf{ct}'$

6) Batch homomorphic algorithm:

Addition: Step1: Let $\mathbf{ct} = (\mathbf{c}_0, \mathbf{c}_1), \mathbf{ct}' = (C_0', C_0')$ be two ciphertexts and in the same circuit layer, homomorphic addition operation that is added by bit: $\mathbf{ct}_{\mathbf{add}} = (c_0 + c_0', c_1 + c_1') \in R_q^{2L}$;

Step2: If not in the same circuit layer, the two pairs are made to be in the same circuit layer by calling algorithm $\text{Scale}(\mathbf{ct}', q_i, q_i, t)$ several times.

Multiplication: Step1: If the corresponding multiplication operation is not in the same circuit layer, the mode-conversion algorithm is called to convert to the same layer. Calculate $(\mathbf{c}_0 + \mathbf{c}_1 \cdot \mathbf{v}) \cdot (\mathbf{c}_0' + \mathbf{c}_1' \cdot \mathbf{v})$, where $\boldsymbol{v} = (v_0, v_1, \ldots, v_L)$ is the L+1-dimensional variable ring vector, and consider it as a quadratic polynomial vector about $\boldsymbol{v}$. Take its coefficients as the ciphertext $\boldsymbol{ct}_{mult}$ of the output of the ciphertext multiplication operation.

Step2: Call the algorithm $\text{KeySwitch}(\text{sk}', \text{sk}'', (\boldsymbol{c}_0, \boldsymbol{c}_1, \boldsymbol{c}_2))$ to get $\mathbf{ct}' = (\mathbf{c}_0, \mathbf{c}_1)$.

Step3: Call the algorithm $\text{Scale}_{(\mathbf{ct}', q_i, q_{i-1}, t)}$ to get the ciphertext under mode q_{i-1}.

The above multiplication operation is explained as follows:

Let $\mathbf{c}_0 = (c_{0,0}, c_{0,1}, \ldots, c_{0,L}), \mathbf{c}_1 = (c_{1,0}, c_{1,1}, \ldots, c_{1,L})$, and similarly have $\mathbf{c}_0' = (c_{0,0}', c_{0,1}', \ldots, c_{0,L}')$, $c_1' = (c_{1,0}', c_{1,1}', \ldots, c_{1,L}')$, then we have $(\mathbf{c}_0 + \mathbf{c}_1 \cdot \mathbf{v}) \cdot (\mathbf{c}_0' + \mathbf{c}_1' \cdot \mathbf{v}) = \mathbf{c}_0 \cdot \mathbf{c}_0' + (\mathbf{c}_0 \cdot \mathbf{c}_1' + \mathbf{c}_1 \cdot \mathbf{c}_0') \cdot \mathbf{v} + \mathbf{c}_1 \cdot \mathbf{c}_1' \cdot \mathbf{v} \cdot \mathbf{v}$

$$= (c_{0,0} \cdot c_{0,0}', \ldots, c_{0,L} \cdot c_{0,L}') + ((c_{0,0} \cdot c_{1,0}' + c_{1,0} \cdot c_{0,0}') \cdot v_0, \ldots, (c_{0,L} \cdot c_{1,L}' + c_{1,0} \cdot c_{0,0}') \cdot v_L) + (c_{1,0} \cdot c_{1,0}' \cdot v_0^2, \ldots, c_{1,L} \cdot c_{1,L}' \cdot v_L^2)$$

$$= ((c_{0,0} \cdot c_{0,0}' + (c_{0,0} \cdot c_{1,0}' + c_{1,0} \cdot c_{0,0}') \cdot v_0 + c_{1,0} \cdot c_{1,0}' \cdot v_0^2), \ldots, (c_{0,L} \cdot c_{0,L}' + (c_{0,L} \cdot c_{1,L}' + c_{1,0} \cdot c_{0,0}') \cdot v_L + c_{1,L} \cdot c_{1,L}' \cdot v_L^2))$$

Considering it as a quadratic polynomial vector with respect to vi, the ciphertext output from the ciphertext multiplication operation is $\mathbf{ct}_{mlt} = \left\{ (c_{0,i} \cdot c_{0,i}', c_{0,i} \cdot c_{1,i}' + c_{1,i} \cdot c_{0,i}', c_{1,i} \cdot c_{1,i}')_{i \in [0,L]} \right\}$.

3.2 Correctness of the program

The correctness of the decryption of the above scheme is verified below, which is known from the encryption algorithm: $\mathbf{ct} = (\mathbf{c}_0, \mathbf{c}_1) = ((\mathbf{m} + \mathbf{b}u + \mathrm{t}\boldsymbol{e}_1), (\mathbf{a}u + t\boldsymbol{e}_2))$

From the above equation and the batch encryption algorithm, it follows that:

$\boldsymbol{M} = (m_0,\ldots,m_{l-1}) = (\mathbf{c}_0 + \mathbf{c}_1 \odot \mathbf{s})(\bmod\, p \bmod t)$
$= (m_0 + b_0 u + t\boldsymbol{e}_1,\ldots,m_{l-1} + b_L u + t\boldsymbol{e}_1) + (a_0 u + t\boldsymbol{e}_2,\ldots,a_L u + t\boldsymbol{e}_2) \odot (s_0,\ldots,s_L)$
$= (m_0 + t(eu + \boldsymbol{e}_1 + \boldsymbol{e}_2 s_0),\cdots,m_L + t(eu + \boldsymbol{e}_1 + \boldsymbol{e}_2 s_L))$
$= (m_0, m_1,\ldots,m_{l-1}) = \boldsymbol{M}$

If $\left\| t(eu + \boldsymbol{e}_1 + \boldsymbol{e}_2 s_i) \right\|_{i\in[0,L]} < p/2$, then the correct decryption can be performed, and then the initial plaintext can be found by the Chinese residue theorem $(m_{i,0},\ldots,m_{i,l-1}) \leftarrow CRT_p^{-1}(m_i) \in \mathbb{F}_{p^d}^l$.

3.3 Homomorphism of the scheme

Let **ct** and **ct**$'$ are the ciphertexts of the above homomorphic encryption scheme, and both encrypt plaintexts $\boldsymbol{m}$ and $\boldsymbol{m}'$, respectively, corresponding to private keys $\boldsymbol{s}$ and $\boldsymbol{M} = (m_0,\ldots,m_L) = (\mathbf{c}_0 + \mathbf{c}_1 \bullet \mathbf{s})(\bmod\, p \bmod t) \in R_P^{L+1}$. First discuss the additive homomorphism: let $\mathbf{ct}_{\text{add}} = \mathbf{ct} + \mathbf{ct}' = (c_0 + c_0', c_1 + c_1')$, then decryption of it has:

$$(c_0 + c_0', (c_1 + c_1') \bullet s) = (c_0 + c_0', c_1 \bullet s + c_1' \bullet s) = (c_0, c_1 \bullet s) + (c_0', c_1' \bullet s)(\bmod\, p \bmod t) = \mathbf{m} + \mathbf{m}'$$

Since the noise is sufficiently less than p/2, the above equation can be decrypted correctly, so the scheme satisfies additive homomorphism.

We verify the multiplicative homomorphism as follows:

Let $\mathbf{ct}_{mul} = \left\{ \left(c_{0,i}\cdot c_{0,i}', c_{0,i}\cdot c_{1,i}' + c_{1,i}\cdot c_{0,i}', c_{1,i}\cdot c_{1,i}'\right)_{i\in[0,L]} \right\}$, Decrypting it using private key $\boldsymbol{s}$ has:

$$\mathbf{ct}_{\text{mul}} \bullet (1, \mathbf{s}, \mathbf{s}\bullet\mathbf{s}) = \left\{ \left(c_{0,i}\cdot c_{0,i}', c_{0,i}\cdot c_{1,i}' + c_{1,i}\cdot c_{0,i}', c_{1,i}\cdot c_{1,i}'\right)_{i\in[,L]} \right\} \bullet (1, \mathbf{s}, \mathbf{s}\bullet\mathbf{s})$$
$$= \left(\left(c_{0,0}\cdot c_{0,0}' + \left(c_{0,0}\cdot c_{1,0}' + c_{1,0}\cdot c_{0,0}'\right)\cdot s_0 + c_{1,0}\cdot c_{1,0}'\cdot s_0^2\right),\ldots,\left(c_{0,1}\cdot c_{0,L}' + \left(c_{0,L}\cdot c_{1,L}' + c_{1,0}\cdot c_{0,0}'\right)\cdot s_L + c_{1,L}\cdot c_{1,L}'\cdot s_L^2\right) \right)$$
$$= (\mathbf{c}_0 + \mathbf{c}_1 \bullet \mathbf{s}) \bullet (\mathbf{c}_0' + \mathbf{c}_1' \bullet \mathbf{s})(\bmod\, p \bmod t) = \mathbf{m} \bullet \mathbf{m}'$$

It is easy to obtain that the noise of the two is still less than p/2 after multiplication, so the scheme satisfies multiplicative homomorphism.

3.4 Proof of safety of the program

The security of the scheme in this paper is based on the RLWE problem, which is widely used in fully homomorphic cryptography because its public key scheme will be more efficient. The security of the RLWE problem depends on three main parameters: the modulus q, the number n of polynomials $\Phi_m(x)$, and the standard deviation σ of the discrete Gaussian distribution.

Definition 9 (IND-CPA secure) Let a public key encryption scheme ε, in bounded polynomial time, if there exists a minimal function negl(λ) such that the advantage of adversary A :

$$\text{Adv}_{CPA}[A] \triangleq \left| \Pr[A(pk, \text{HE.Enc}(0) = 1) - \Pr[A(pk, \text{HE.Enc}(1) = 1)] \right| = \text{neg}(\lambda) \tag{6}$$

Then the encryption scheme ε is IND-CPA secure.

Lemma 2 [16] Let $pk \leftarrow$ *Batch-Keygen*(*params*), pk is consistently indistinguishable on $R_p^{(L+1)/2}$ under the *RLWEn,qi,x* assumption.

Theorem 1 The scheme is CPA-safe under the DRLWEn,q_i,x problem.

Proof Let A be an IND-CPA adversary to the FHE scheme, and $Adv_H[A]$ denote the attack advantage in a series of *Hybird* as follows:

Hybird$_{L+1}$: The *Hybird* is an IND-CPA attack game of A against Batch. FHE, the adversary gets *pk,evk* generated by Batch. Keygen algorithm and encrypts 0 and 1 using Batch. Enc algorithm, the advantage of A in H_{L+1} is:

$$\mathrm{Adv}_{H_{L+1}}[\mathcal{A}] = |\Pr[\mathcal{A}(pk, \mathrm{HE.Enc}(0)) = 1] - \Pr[\mathcal{A}(pk, \mathrm{HE.}Enc(1)) = 1]| = \mathrm{neg}(\lambda) \quad (7)$$

Hybird H_L: This *Hybird* differs from the former in that its arithmetic public key is taken from a uniform distribution, setting up the existence of an adversary B_L that solves the DRLWEn,q_i,x problem in time t + poly(λ), and with the advantage that

$$\mathrm{DRLWE}_{n,q_L,\chi}\,\mathrm{Adv}[\mathcal{B}_L] \geq 1/2 |\,\mathrm{Adv}_{HL+1}[\mathcal{A}] - \mathrm{Adv}_{HL}[\mathcal{A}]| \quad (8)$$

Following the H_{L+1} to H_L approach acts until in H_1 , the arithmetic public key is replaced one by one by the way it is generated in the scheme to a consistent uniformly chosen element on $RqL\times$. *Hybird* H_0: In the H_0 public key of b_i is uniformly selected in R_{qi}. Under the assumption DRLWEn,q_i,x, H_1 and H_0 are computationally indistinguishable, then the adversary $\mathcal{B}_0$,who solves the problem in time t + poly(λ), has the advantage of

$$\mathrm{DRLWE}_{n,q_L,\chi}\,\mathrm{Adv}[\mathcal{B}_0] \geq 1/2 |\,\mathrm{Adv}_{HL+1}[\mathcal{A}] - \mathrm{Adv}_{HL}[\mathcal{A}]| \quad (9)$$

Adversary $\mathcal{B}_0$ performs L+1 random sampling b_i from the RLWE prophecy machine as the public key (***b***, ***a***). If the sample is taken from the distribution $A_{s,x}$, then b_i is generated by the H_1 generation method; if the sample is taken from the uniform distribution, then b_i is generated by the H_0 generation method.

Hybird H_{rand}:This *Hybird* is different from H_0 in the ciphertext generation method, taken from a consistent uniform distribution $R_{qi}\times$ R_{qi}.Since b_i is also taken from a uniform distribution, the ciphertext c0, c1) is indistinguishable from the uniform distribution on $R_{qi}\times$, therefore we have

$$|\,\mathrm{Adv}_{H_{end}}[\mathcal{A}] - \mathrm{Adv}_{H_0}[\mathcal{A}]| \leq \mathrm{neg}(\lambda) \quad (10)$$

Since in ***H***$_{rand}$, both the public key and the ciphertext are randomly and uniformly selected, independent of each other and the plaintext information, $\mathrm{Adv}_{H_{end}}[\mathcal{A}] = 0$. In summary, it is proved that the Batch.FHE scheme is IND-CPA secure.

4 Optimization scheme for partial homomorphic encryption

In this paper, we analyze the difficulty of the method according to the steps of Fan [17]. Let the security parameter: λ , the distinguishing advantage:ε, the modulus:q, the number of ring polynomials R:n, and the standard deviation of the discrete Gaussian distribution $\chi = D_{z^n,\sigma}$: σ.

Definition 10 [18] The Hermite Gen factor $\boldsymbol{\delta}$ .Let an n-dimensional lattice be L and one of the lattice bases be B. If $\| b_1 \| = \delta^n \cdot \det(L)^{1/n}$, where b_i is the shortest vector in the lattice base B, then $\boldsymbol{\delta}$ is said to be the Hermite Gen factor.

Theorem 2[18] Given $\boldsymbol{\delta}$, the time required to reduce a lattice group with Hermite factor $\boldsymbol{\delta}^n$ depends mainly on $\boldsymbol{\delta}$.

Lindner,Peiker[19] used the optimized attack strategy to obtain a lattice base with Hermitgen factor $\boldsymbol{\delta}^n$. Given an Hermitgen factor $\boldsymbol{\delta}$, the length of the shortest vector is $\alpha \cdot q/\sigma \leq 2^{2\sqrt{n\log q/\log\delta}}$, where $\alpha = \sqrt{\ln(1/\varepsilon)/\pi}$, and the time taken is about $\log T = 1.8/\lg\delta - 110$. If λ is the security parameter, let distinguish advantage $\boldsymbol{\varepsilon}$=2^{-64}, take the security parameter λ =128, attack time T=2^{128}, can calculate α≈3.758,δ≈1.0052, can be computed by substituting $\alpha \cdot q/\sigma \leq 2^{2\sqrt{n\log q/\log\sigma}}$ to obtain $1.910 + \log q - \log\sigma \leq 0.173\sqrt{n\log q}$, and the value of q,σ can be obtained by determining n. For example, if n=1024, log$q$=38,. The specific parameter settings are shown in Table 1.

Table 1. Parameter settings.

Parameter Name	Values					
n	128	256	512	1024	2048	4096
log$q$	19	19	20	38	74	120
σ	12.37	6.58	13.41	55.07	9.79	11.58

The scheme uses mode-conversion technique to downscale the ciphertext, and the riginal scheme is used as the basis for noise optimization of the product ciphertext; because the homomorphic scheme for single-bit encryption takes longer time, this paper uses the Chinese residual theorem to pack the plaintext, which increases the size of the ciphertext, public and private keys compared with the FV [17] scheme, but the amount of data processed in each batch is N times of the FV method. The efficiency of this scheme is significantly improved. Compared with the SWHE[12] scheme, the public and private key sizes are increased by λ times and the number of plaintexts per processing is $N\lambda$ times of the previous one, which improves the efficiency of encrypted transmission on the cloud.

Table 2. Comparison of programs.

Scheme	encrypted plaintext	ciphertext size	public key size	private key size
SWHE Scheme	$O(1)$	$O(\lambda \log_t qB)$	$O(\delta_R)$	$O(B)$
FV Scheme	$O(1)$	$O(\lambda\lceil \log t\rceil^2)$	$O(\lambda\lceil \log q\rceil)$	$O(\lceil \log 2\rceil)$
Our Scheme	$O(N\lambda)$	$O(\lambda \log_t^{qB})$	$O(\lambda\delta_R)$	$O(\lambda B)$

5 Conclusion

At present, full homomorphic encryption has extremely promising applications in huge data and cloud computing environments. In this paper, based on the literature [12], we propose an optimization method for partial homomorphic encryption schemes. The method adopts the Chinese residual theorem (CRT) to pack multiple "plaintext slots" into one ciphertext, and the paper also provides the results of homomorphic operations on compressed ciphertexts, and adopts two noise reduction techniques, so that the scheme can achieve multiple homomorphic operations; therefore, compared with the original scheme, the efficiency of the encryption scheme is significantly compared with the original scheme.

This research was funded by: the Natural Science Foundation of Sichuan Province under Grant 2022NSFSC0536

References

1. M. G. Kaosar, R. Paulet, X. Yi. FHE. B. Ass. R. M, **76** (2012)
2. H. Yan, J. Li, J. Han, A. Nov.E.Rem. D. Poss. Check. Pro. Cl. Stor, **12** (2016)
3. W. Wang, Y. Hu, L. Chen, Exp. Feas.FHE , **64**, 3 (2013)
4. J. H. Cheon, J. Kim, Hyb. Sch. PK. E. SHE, **10**, 5 (2015)
5. R. L. Rivest, L. Adleman, M. L. Dertouzos, DB. Pri. H, **4**, 11 (1978)
6. C. Gentry, FHE. Sche, (2009)
7. C. Gentry, FHE. Use. Ide. Lat, (2009)
8. C. Gentry, S. Halevi, Imp. G. FHE. Sche, (2011)
9. N. P. Smart, F. Vercauteren, FH. SIMD O. Des. C. Cry, **71**, 1 (2014)
10. Z. Brakerski, V. Vaikuntanathan, Effi. FHE. LWE, **43**, 2 (2014)
11. C. Gentry, S. Halevi, N. P. Smart, FHE. Pol. Overh, (2012)
12. M. Naehrig, K. Lauter, V. Vaikuntanathan, C. FHE. Prac, (2011)
13. M. Li, B. Hu, New FHE. Sch. B. T, (2018)
14. J. H. Cheon, J. Kim, M. S. Lee, CRT-based. FHE. Int, (2015)
15. C. Gentry, S. Halevi, N. P. Smart, HE. AES Cir, (2012)
16. Z. Brakerski, C. Gentry, V. Vaikuntanathan, Lev. FHE. Boot, **6**, 3 (2014)
17. J. Fan, F. Vercauteren, SW. Prac. FHE fully homomorphic encryption, (2012)
18. R. Lindner, C. Peikert, B. K. S. LWE. E, (2011)
19. Sofia, Bulgaria, Int. Conf. The. and Appl. Cry. Tec, (2015)

Teaching reform and practice based on OBE concept: Taking the course of Python programming and practice as an example

Cuihong Gu,*, *Xinghua* Zheng , and *Guangyan* Li

Shandong Union College, Licheng District, Jinan City, Shandong Province, China

Abstract. Python Programming and Practice is a professional course for computer related majors. Through teaching practice, and based on OBE (Outcome-based Education) concept of course reform, we have revised the course syllabus, reformulated the teaching plan, standardized the classroom teaching, adopted online and offline mixed teaching model to teach the basic knowledge online, and to teach with project case method in offline classroom teaching. The course is completely transformed into outcome-based teaching, which improves the depth and breadth of the course teaching, and improves the students' practical ability.

1 Introduction

OBE concept, also known as "output oriented education" or "results oriented education", mainly focuses on students' ability to achieve after the course [1].OBE is a core concept of engineering education certification, so it is particularly urgent to carry out education reform research under the guidance of OBE concept[2].

OBE is to clearly focus on and organize all links in the education system, develop different teaching plans according to different requirements around a goal, and provide different learning opportunities, so that all students can obtain the ability to be competent for work at the end of the learning process. OBE especially emphasizes what students have learned rather than what teachers have taught, which has changed from traditional teacher centered to student centered.OBE emphasizes the output rather than the input of the teaching process, the research-based teaching mode rather than the indoctrination teaching mode, and the personalized teaching rather than the "carriage" teaching. Personalized teaching requires teachers to accurately grasp each student's learning trajectory, and timely grasp each person's goal, foundation and process.

Taking the course "Python Programming and Practice" as an example, this paper introduces OBE education concept, sets course objectives, sets the course into different modules, and explores how to improve the teaching quality of the course by adopting the hybrid teaching method of online and offline.

* Corresponding author: 2192704698@qq.com

2 Classroom teaching reform based on OBE concept

Classroom is the main form of teaching implementation. Classroom teaching is the basis to enable students to achieve graduation requirements and training objectives. In order to meet the requirements of results oriented education, at least the following four changes should be achieved:

2.1 Change from indoctrination classroom to dialogue classroom

The traditional classroom is a "spoon fed" indoctrination classroom. Knowledge dominates the classroom. The dialogue classroom should achieve the dialogue of knowledge, thinking and mind. The dialogue of knowledge needs to transform one-way indoctrination into multi-directional communication, so that knowledge can be transferred, exchanged and interacted between teachers and students.

The class of "Python Programming and Practice" belongs to the dialogue class. In the class, students are willing to answer questions, snap answers, share and display, and even be able to teach some knowledge points. They can make documents of cutting-edge technologies to share with teachers and students[3].

2.2 Change from closed classroom to open classroom

The traditional classroom is closed, that is, the fixed teaching content is completed in a fixed place and a fixed time. In this mode, teaching activities revolve around teachers, classrooms and textbooks. Open classroom is to break through the three centers and realize the openness in time, space and content.

This course belongs to an open classroom. There are independent learning time and joint learning time in terms of time. Teachers will assign pre homework and post homework during independent learning time. In terms of space, classes are held in classrooms and computer rooms, and you can go to libraries and computer rooms in your spare time. In terms of content, instead of sticking to one textbook and several reference books, we will provide students with massive network resources, and the classroom can be open to the society and other professional students.

2.3 Change from knowledge class to ability class

The traditional classroom is dominated by knowledge. What we talk about is knowledge, what we learn is knowledge, and what we test is knowledge. In the class of this course, case teaching and project teaching are usually used. When students cooperate in groups, everyone has a clear job division, and they work together to complete each project; In their spare time, students formed many studios and undertook many practical projects.

2.4 Change from emphasis on learning and light on thinking to combination of learning and thinking

To a great extent, the traditional classroom has neglected the role of thinking in understanding and creating the world. In our classroom, students constantly think, rather than mechanically memorize, they constantly create, and gain a lot of fun, confidence and sense of gain.

3 Teaching design based on OBE concept

3.1 Course teaching objectives

The most important part of the course teaching is to define the teaching objectives of the course in the syllabus. This course introduces engineering education ideas, fully considers the actual needs of the market for professional talents, and determines the course teaching objectives from the aspects of knowledge, ability or skills, quality objectives, etc. See Table 1 for details.

Table 1. Course teaching objectives.

Knowledge objectives	M1. Be able to correctly understand the basic syntax of Python language, the installation and use of development environment, process control, object-oriented programming ideas, skillfully use lists, dictionaries, sets, tuples, and functions for coding, and be able to use Python for graphical user interface programming, web crawler, database operation, and other types of files M2. Can use Python to crawl data legally
Competency and skill objectives	M3. Master the basic tools required for program development, including development environment and documentation tools, understand the concept and significance of program correctness, and be able to debug and test programs M4. Be able to use Python language for algorithm analysis and design, software development and implementation of simple engineering problems, be familiar with project design process, methods and the application of theoretical knowledge learned in design, and design projects with specific industry knowledgeM5 . Self learning Python Web development framework
Literacy goals	M6. Through group experiments, cultivate students' interpersonal skills, communication skills, ability to receive and feedback information, and form a sense of teamwork M7. Develop good programming habits and write programs that conform to specifications

3.2 Content of courses

The course adopts the offline and online hybrid teaching method. Each teaching link is set up in the learning output based education mode. For the part of basic knowledge, the course is taught in the online mode. For the part that is difficult to understand, the offline case exercise and project training are used. The main teaching contents of the course are shown in Table 2.

Table 2. Course content.

No	Teaching unit content	Course Objectives
1	Getting Started with Python, Number Types and Strings	M1, M3, M4, M7
2	Program control structure	M1, M4
3	Lists and tuples	M1, M4
4	Dictionary and Set	M1, M4
5	function	M1, M4
6	Classes and Objects	M1, M4
7	Modules, Errors, and Exceptions	M1, M3, M4
8	Graphical User Interface Programming	M1, M4
9	Graphical User Interface Programming	M1, M4, M5, M7
10	Web crawler, data analysis and visualization	M1, M2, M4, M6, M7

3.3 Online and offline hybrid teaching mode

The teaching is divided into three parts. The online knowledge points are explained. In class, the teaching is conducted through experiments, cases and projects. After class, the students' learning is tested through tests and experiments.

3.3.1 Online knowledge point explanation

Teachers upload materials to the teaching support platform in advance, including: (1) syllabus, teaching calendar, courseware PPT, teaching plan, e-book, video and other teaching resources. (2) Upload software or software installation guidance documents. (3) Teachers prepare interactive materials to consolidate classroom knowledge points and improve the interactive effect of classroom teaching. If the courseware is used, test interaction can be interspersed in the courseware, and multiple choice questions, judgment questions, and subjective questions can be used interchangeably. On the one hand, it is to catch the students' attention and prevent them from burnout and inertia; On the other hand, it is also an indispensable part of formative evaluation. If it is an experimental course without courseware, you can issue quick answers to urge students to follow the pace of teachers and actively complete programming experiments[4]. (4) A course question bank has been prepared to generate test papers for the convenience of testing at the end of each course. After each course is completed, an online test will be conducted immediately, which can improve students' attention in class and urge them to actively participate in classroom teaching. (5) Upload the course assignments, and students can try to complete the assignments after self-study to test the learning effect. (6) Upload the recorded video of knowledge points of the course, put it on the teaching platform, and explain the knowledge points for students to preview before class. The course video should not be too large to facilitate students' learning and searching.

Through the study of this course, students also became interested in the recording of teaching videos, because each team work requires students to record and display videos, and students also participate in the recording process of teaching videos. In the future, under each video, you can link the videos recorded by each class of students. I believe that the video quality will be higher and higher, and students' interest in learning will be greatly improved.

3.3.2 Classroom teaching

The use of hybrid teaching cannot follow the traditional teaching methods and methods, especially the course "Python Programming and Practice". Because of its strong practicality and application, students need to practice and practice more to master it. The traditional teacher led teaching methods cannot achieve good teaching results. On the other hand, online and offline hybrid teaching is more appropriate, that is, to guide students to conduct online learning first, and then teachers can guide students to experiment through a large number of cases or projects in class to achieve the teaching objectives.

3.3.3 Self study after class

After class, teachers will arrange online tests and experiments, and students will test their mastery of basic knowledge and practice ability by completing tests and experiment reports.

3.4 Course assessment

If the course adopts online and offline hybrid teaching mode based on OBE concept, the course evaluation also needs to be reformed to stimulate students. Therefore, establishing a scientific and systematic learning evaluation mechanism has become the focus of teachers' attention. See Table 3 for details of the course evaluation. The specific proportion can be divided by teachers according to the course content.

Table 3. Course process assessment form.

Achievement items	Distribution	Evaluation method	Itemized distribution	Explain
Peacetime performance	70%	Practical evaluation	Attendance 10% (online)	1 point will be deducted for each absence from class, and 1 point will be deducted for each three times of being late. Deduct 10 points at most
			Classroom performance 10% (offline)	1 point will be added if the question is answered correctly, and 10 points will be added at most
		Practical evaluation	Experiment 40% (online+offline)	Full score: 40, 4 experiments in total
			Test 40% (online)	Full score: 40, 8 tests in total
Final exam	30%	Final big assignment	30% (online+offline)	30 points for project source code, 30 points for project paper, 10 points for project video, 30 points for defense and mutual evaluation

3.5 Concluding

According to the characteristics of Python language, this paper puts forward the teaching mode of "Python programming and practice" course, which adopts OBE teaching philosophy, online and offline mixed teaching mode, online is the teaching of basic knowledge, and offline project case teaching, which not only improves students' interest, makes them better master the basic programming methods and skills, but also improves students' ability to learn independently, solve problems and participate in projects.

2021 School level Teaching Reform Research Project, Entry name: Research and Practice on Python Curriculum Teaching Reform of "Three Sources Interconnection, Thought and College Integration", Item No: 2021XJ09

References

1. X.T. Wen, L.J. Xu, Y. Chen., Software, 7, 292-296 (2020)
2. Z.Y. Li, University teaching in China, 1, 8-14 (2017)
3. M.L. Liu, J.H. Li, C.B. Guan, Computer Engineering and Science, 12, 203-206 (2019)
4. R.L. Yang, Journal of Higher Education, 3, 135-137 (2019)

Research on the problems and paths of higher vocational school-enterprise cooperation education in the new era

Guangyan Li*, and *Cuihong* Gu

Shandong Xiehe University, 250100, JiNan, Shandong, China

Abstract. School-enterprise cooperation education plays a huge role in serving the people's livelihood, optimizing the talent supply structure, and promoting the transformation of type education. Facing the new challenges brought by the sharp increase in enrollment, the diversification of student source structure, the shortage of educational resources and the reform of teaching methods under the background of enrollment expansion, higher vocational colleges need to establish quality development based on the innovation of talent training mode, the sharing of educational and teaching resources and the quality of teaching management. Under the guidance of these objectives, we should emphasize the people-oriented values, the concept of ability first and the concept of quality first, so as to optimize the practice ecology of school-enterprise cooperation education, promote the connotation development of higher vocational education and the sustainable development of social economy.

1 Introduction

In 2019, the Government Work Report made the policy of expanding the enrollment of 1 million higher vocational students independent of the education sector, as a national strategic measure of "multi pronged stabilization and employment expansion", raised the development of vocational education from the education level to the national strategic height, and endowed vocational education with higher responsibilities and missions in serving the construction of a modern economy, stabilizing employment, and ensuring the people's livelihood[1,2]. Following the successful completion of this task, the 2020 Government Work Report again proposed the goal of expanding the enrollment of higher vocational colleges by 2 million people. This measure is a recognition of the responsibility mission of higher vocational education from the national strategic level[3], and also an important development opportunity to promote the deep integration of industry and education and the cooperative education between schools and enterprises[4,5].

How to actively adapt to changes and achieve quality based enrollment expansion is an important task that vocational colleges need to solve urgently.

* Corresponding author: 1327256889@qq.com

2 The target of school-enterprise cooperative education under the background of higher vocational enrollment expansion

In the face of the important strategic deployment of million enrollment expansion, we must clarify the goal of school-enterprise cooperation in educating people, and give full play to the important role of school-enterprise cooperation in cultivating high-quality technical talents and promoting the reform and development of higher vocational education.Table 1 shows the target.

Table 1. The target orientation of school-enterprise cooperative education.

Section	Target aim
1.Talent training system	Reconstruct the talent training system with diversified systems, hierarchical classification and prominent characteristics
2.Resource supply	Greatly improve interaction with enterprises
3.Quality of talent training	Teaching management is to ensure the quality of talent training

2.1 Reconstruct the talent training system

The diversity and complexity of the student source structure under the background of million enrollment expansion, which is based on the characteristic development goal created jointly by the talent training model, directly challenges the traditional, unified pace, offline based, full-time "learning+practice" training model of higher vocational colleges[6,7]. In the case that the current talent training model focusing on school students is difficult to couple with the actual demand of social students after enrollment expansion, promoting the collaborative innovation of talent training mode of higher vocational education, and reconstructing a talent training system with diversified systems, hierarchical classification and prominent characteristics has become the primary goal of the reform of the school-enterprise cooperative education mode.

2.2 Improve the interaction between schools and enterprises

Based on the scale development goal of high-quality education resource sharing, the million enrollment expansion makes higher vocational colleges face huge pressure in terms of per student cost, teachers, teaching equipment, training conditions, logistics services, etc[8]. The self-sufficiency of higher vocational colleges' resources is far from meeting the needs of diversified talent training, which also determines that the degree of external dependence of higher vocational colleges, especially the degree of interaction with enterprises, has been greatly improved.

2.3 Improve the level of teaching management

The quality of higher vocational education is ultimately reflected in the quality of technical personnel training[9,10]. Teaching management is an important means to ensure the quality of personnel training.

3 There are the reform paths of school-enterprise cooperation education, under the background of higher vocational enrollment expansion, in the new era

The expansion of enrollment has brought about problems such as diversification of student source structure, diversification of learning needs, and complexity of teaching management. In order to highlight the era value of school-enterprise cooperative education in the context of enrollment expansion, and achieve the development goal of school-enterprise cooperative education, it is necessary to establish rational value thinking, optimize the education structure, improve the system design, and promote the steady improvement of talent training quality and teaching management level.Table 2 shows the reform paths.

Table 2. The reform path of school enterprise-cooperation education.

Solutions	Specific indicators
1.people oriented	Systematic thinking
	Service thinking
	Rule of law thinking
2.Competence center, employment orient-ation	Optimize professional structure
	Optimize the structure of teachers
	Strengthen individual multiple structure
3.Innovate flexible educational manage-ment mode	Implement flexible school system
	Improve the double tutor system

3.1 "People-oriented" education

The change of thinking under the guidance of people-oriented values "people-oriented" is the essence of socialist core values. It attaches importance to the value of human life, meets the reasonable needs of people, and pursues the freedom, equality and all-round development of people. The strategic action of million enrollment expansion in higher vocational education is an important embodiment of the implementation of the core values of "people-oriented". School-enterprise cooperation should always adhere to the value concept and value pursuit of "people-oriented", establish scientific and rational system thinking, development thinking and rule of law thinking, avoid the blindness of enrollment expansion in higher vocational colleges and the tendency of excessive utilitarianism in higher vocational education, and provide all-round and whole process services to achieve the development of the comprehensive quality and employability of different groups of students.

3.2 "Ability based" education

Ability oriented structure optimization under the guidance of the concept of focusing on education is the main goal of technical and skilled personnel training in higher vocational colleges at home and abroad. TAFE (Technical And Further Education) has built a higher vocational education system with diverse levels, flexible school system and strong teachers with the purpose of "ability center and employment orientation", The double requirements of the German University of Applied Science and Technology in terms of academic qualifications and practical experience also reflect its ability based education concept, so as to promote the effective connection between talent training in higher vocational colleges and the employment market. Under the background of enrollment expansion, the reform of the talent training mode of school-enterprise cooperation should adhere to the education concept of "ability based", base on the cultivation of students' professional ability and comprehensive quality, optimize the structure of teachers and majors, and realize the dynamic adjustment of talent demand and talent supply.

3.3 Flexible educational management mode

System design under the guidance of quality based management concept.The school-enterprise cooperation education model under the background of million enrollment expansion has brought about changes in thinking and structure, but also impacted the traditional education management model. In addition to focusing on the effectiveness of education and teaching activities under the guidance of people-oriented values and ability oriented education concept, It is also crucial to innovate the flexible educational management mode under the guidance of scientific quality management concept.

4 Conclusions

School-enterprise cooperation education is the demand and inevitable choice of the times to serve the national employment and livelihood, optimize the supply of technical talents, and promote the deepening reform of higher vocational education under the background of million enrollment expansion.

Under the guidance of scientific and rational values, education outlook and management outlook, the in-depth cooperation between schools and enterprises in talent training mode, education resources, teaching management and other aspects needs to build a school-enterprise cooperation education ecology through systematic thinking, service thinking, rule of law thinking and other thinking changes, and promote the effective connection between talent training and market demand through the optimization of professional structure, teacher structure, individual conduct, knowledge, skills and other multiple structures, Through the optimization design of flexible school system, double tutor system and quality evaluation system, we will promote the improvement of talent training quality management level, improve the school-enterprise cooperation education mode with Chinese characteristics on the basis of the overall planning of the government, the in-depth cooperation between higher vocational colleges and enterprises, and develop higher vocational education with appropriate scale, distinctive characteristics and stable quality.

The Fourteenth Five Year Plan for National Business Scientific Education 2022 Annual Projcet: "the Exploration of the School-Enterprise Deep Cooperation Paths for the Talents Training of Higher Vocational Education of New Business Studies in the Digital Economy Era"(SKJYKT-220635).

References

1. ZHAO H Q,CHEN X H. Research on the Multiple Collaborative Education Model of Application-oriented Undergraduate Colleges under the Integration of Production and Education——Taking the Digital Media Technology Major of Shanxi Datong University as an Example [J] .Educational Theory and Practice, (2018),**38** : 6-8.
2. LU X Y, ZHANG Z C, LAN T, et al. Exploration of ways to improve the effective-ness of collaborative education of agricultural majors in local universities [J]. Higher Education Journal, (2018) **16**: 67-70.
3. WANG Y J. Research on Multi-subject Cooperative Education Mechanism in Higher Vocational Colleges [D]. Nanchang University, (2018).

4. LIU C C,WANG L. Discussion on collaborative education of social work majors in local colleges and universities——Taking HZ College as an example [J]. Higher Education Journal, (2018)**08**: 73-76.
5. LIU B. Research on the Evaluation of Graduate Education Quality Based on Collaborative Education [D]. Harbin Engineering University, (2018).
6. Bin Liu,Yalun Qin. Research on the Present Situation and Development Countermeasures of School-Enterprise Cooperation in Vocational Education[C].MEICI 2019.(2019):483-489.
7. Yin Jing. Discussion on the Measures of Constructing Long-Term Mechanism of Deepening School-Enterprise Cooperation in Vocational Education[C].Proceedings of 2022 the 6th International Conference on Scientific and Technological Innovation and Educational Development.,(2022):964-966.
8. Miao Shang,Jiale Zhang,Jingjing Kang. Influence of School-Enterprise Cooperation on Quality of Higher Vocational Mechanical and Electrical Talents Training[C].SSER 2019.(2019):639-642.
9. Bingli Huang,and Yan Li.Thinking and Practice of School-Enterprise Cooperation in Higher Vocational Colleges under the Background of Integration of Industry and Education.HSSD 2019. ,(2019), 74-78.
10. Yashen Xie. Exploration on the School-enterprise Cooperation Mode of International Trade Professionals in Higher Vocational Education[C].EREMS 2018.(2018):827-831.

Innovation and practice of production-education integration in private higher education under the background of new engineering

Mengxia Wang*

School of Computer science, Shandong Xiehe University, Jinan 250107, China

Abstract. The integration of production and education plays an important role in the cultivation of talents in higher engineering education. By reading literature, this paper studies the current situation of the development of production-education fusion of private higher education under the background of new engineering, analyzes its achievements and problems in the aspect of production-education fusion of private higher education. Based on the requirements of new engineering and private education, this paper puts forward the construction of a model fitting the actual situation of our country. From the education goal, training content,

1 The introduction

With the development of the new round of Industrial Revolution, the process of higher education popularization and marketization is accelerating. It has become a common understanding to bring into full play the joint efforts of various parties and to educate people in coordination. However, the integration of education and industry in the process of development, but also encountered a lot of problems. For civilian-run applied undergraduate colleges and universities, the students can not meet the requirements of employers. It may lower the reputation of our school, but also do harm to the stability of the students. At the same time, because of the lack of an effective standard of evaluation. It is difficult to measure the results of the integration of industry and education. So that universities, enterprises to participate in the coordination of the enthusiasm is not high. Most of it stays on the surface. The integration of industry and education, education, is a two-way interactive process. In this process, a third party is needed to organize the development and implementation of collaborative education activities, and this role is currently lacking in the country. The new engineering curriculum was proposed on the basis of the national development strategy. Therefore, the government should give full play to its Macroeconomic regulation and control role in the process of integration of industry and education, so as to promote the collaborative education of people towards the desired direction. Under such background, it is of great significance for private colleges and enterprises to study the integration of industry and education.

*Corresponding author: 115436806@qq.com

At present, there are generally the following problems in the model of production-education integration in private higher education in colleges and universities:

(1)The mechanism of production-education integration and collaborative education is not deep enough. At present, most colleges and universities in China have practical training courses, which are usually in cooperation with relevant new business enterprises or training companies, so as to strengthen the cultivation of students' practical operation ability. However, due to the disunity of the cooperation mechanism, fewer class hours and limited funds, the collaborative education mechanism is not deep enough.

(2)The link between production and education is weak. In many colleges and universities, the collaborative education between production and education only stays at the simple level of cooperation, and there is no deep integration of talent training programs and personalized teaching methods.

(3)Traditional evaluation methods and non-standard evaluation standards. The quality of collaborative education between production and education ultimately needs a talent evaluation system and evaluation criteria. However, at present, all colleges and universities are under development. The policy continuity is not maintained, resulting in a single evaluation method or evaluation system is backward.

2. The significance of implementing the new engineering strategy

The Ministry of Education requires universities to innovate the training mode of higher education under the background of the development of the scale of higher education training. In order to cope with the new round of scientific and technological revolution and industrial transformation, and to promote China's transformation from a major country in engineering education to a powerful one in engineering education, the Ministry of Education proposed to promote the construction of new engineering. The Fudan Consensus, Da Da Action and Beijing Guidelines have been formulated successively, exploring and forming the Chinese model and experience, leading the global engineering education and helping the construction of a powerful country in higher education. The new engineering major uses intelligent manufacturing, cloud computing, artificial intelligence and robotics to upgrade and transform the traditional engineering major. Compared with the traditional engineering talents, the emerging industries and the new economy in the future need high-quality composite new engineering talents with strong practical ability, innovation ability and international competitiveness . How to innovate, how to really reflect innovation in the concrete training practice? It is a problem worth thinking and researching put forward by the Ministry of Education for colleges and universities: take the new concept of engineering as the guide to gather more consensus; Under the traction of demand, diversified exploration; Strengthen exchanges and cooperation on the platform of project clusters; To integrate internal and external resources as a way to increase the project support.

3 Construction path of production-education integration education model for private higher education oriented to new engineering

Through the analysis of the current situation of the integration of industry and education in domestic private higher education oriented to new engineering, the opportunities and challenges facing the integration of industry and education are clarified. Meanwhile, based on the domestic situation, Shandong Union College is selected as the main research object to analyze its effectiveness and shortcomings in the development of the integration of industry and education, and focus on some difficulties commonly existing in domestic colleges and universities. Then, it looks outside the region and summarizes the experience of the integration of industry and education in foreign countries.

(1) Research on the talent training program and collaborative education path of the integration of industry and education

The goal of personnel training is the foundation of all educational reform. As the base of personnel training, colleges and universities are responsible for the important task of cultivating advanced and elite talents for the country. Therefore, all the major construction, subject reform and personnel training of colleges and universities are formulated around the goal of personnel training.

We should build the practice teaching system jointly by schools and enterprises, jointly build laboratories and practice bases, and improve the quality of personnel training. Taking Shandong Union College as an example, the software engineering major has established many laboratories and student practice bases jointly with Bosai Technology Co. , Ltd. . In the course design and practice teaching, invite enterprise project manager or senior accountant to participate in the whole process, effectively improve the application and guidance of course design and project practice. In addition, the software engineering profession also works closely with many companies, through the multi-party joint construction laboratory, the practice base and the characteristic class, enhances the talented person raise the quality effectively.

(2) Determine education objectives based on multiple stakeholders

The goal of talent training is the logical starting point of all educational reforms. The political function of education determines that the goal of talent training must fully reflect the national will. The development of engineering education promotes the transformation of economic structure and upgrading of industry. In turn, it affects the improvement of national comprehensive strength. Education policy requires education to serve socialist construction. Train socialist builders and successors. Under the new situation, it is more clear that education must serve the party and the country, red and professional engineering innovative talents. First of all, red specifically means that engineering students should not only have a correct political direction, but also have a correct world outlook, outlook on life and values. Support the leadership of the Party, and have a wealth of professional knowledge and technology. Secondly, engineering innovative talents are scientific and technological talents with engineering innovation ability cultivated for the realization of national strategies such as "Made in China 2025" and innovation-driven development strategy. These talents can provide the support of human and intellectual resources for national development and construction.

(3) The specialty reflects the industry, and the curriculum reflects the interdisciplinary

Specialty setting determines the future employment direction of engineering students. In the context of new engineering construction, specialty adjustment and layout is an important issue. In the course of construction of"New engineering", industry demand has become an important basis for the construction of engineering specialty structure. The relationship between educational development and economic development, in essence, has always been mutual coordination and mutual promotion of the interactive relationship. A new round of industrial transformation and upgrading has given birth to a large number of new industries, such as bioengineering, Big Data, internet of things, etc. . Shandong Union College also promptly set up a Smart City College, with its outstanding characteristics of the industry advantages, for the new engineering construction to help. At the same time, in the course of the integration of curriculum resources, we can establish a dynamic adjustment mechanism of curriculum, through the assessment of students and feedback of employers, timely eliminate outdated curriculum, improve the quality of curriculum. In a word, the curriculum should match the standard of engineer, so that engineering students can grow into a qualified engineer from the curriculum.

(4) Make full use of rich educational resources online and offline to promote project-based and case teaching

The choice of teaching method is also very important. With the development of information technology in education, online education is developing on a large scale. MOOC, SPOC and flip classroom have reshaped people's cognition of teaching methods, and improved the teaching effect and the interaction between teachers and students. For some wide-span and difficult courses, "Online + offline" teaching can deepen students' learning experience and improve learning quality through more abundant and convenient forms. The Peking Union Medical College has stepped up efforts to build an information-based education platform. Such as the use of a learning curve. Love the classroom and other network platform interactive teaching system, to reverse the classroom, online learning and online discussion and answer questions organic combination. Greatly improve the efficiency of teaching, through the online form of assessment, but also to let the teacher understand the knowledge of each student to make timely adjustments to teaching activities.

(5) Improve the campus and off-campus practice teaching system, break through the development barriers of industry, university and research

The practicality and comprehensiveness of higher engineering education require universities to always put engineering practice teaching in an important position, fully combine the internal and external practice teaching systems, and break through the development barriers of industry-university-research. The integration of production and education can effectively combine the teaching activities with the production process, and students can apply and transform the knowledge in the learning process, thus improving the engineering practice and innovation ability. It should be realized that engineering practice education at or above the undergraduate level is different from the simple hands-on operation in higher vocational colleges. It is a combination of theoretical knowledge and practical production. Practical education that can produce a number of innovative results is the combination of production-oriented and research-oriented. In view of the lack of relevance of practice teaching inside and outside the school, both schools and enterprises can design from the formulation of practice teaching program. Make full use of school-enterprise collaborative platforms such as school-enterprise joint laboratory and engineering practice education Center, combine basic experiment and comprehensive experiment with enterprise production practice, and combine innovative competition with engineering project design, as a powerful supplement to classroom teaching.

(6) Improve the teaching management system to ensure the integration of production and education in in-depth teaching activities

The smooth development of the integration of industry and education, system guarantee is the premise. Xidian University, as a university of science and technology with distinct discipline characteristics, should improve its teaching management system and ensure that enterprises play a greater role in teaching activities if it wants to integrate production and education. In addition to a certain proportion of enterprise training practices in the training program of the pilot class of the excellent Engineer education and training program, it should also be expanded to other classes. Increase the teaching time of enterprise training, increase the proportion of credits of enterprise courses in the study allocation ratio, so as to give full play to the education function of the integration of industry and education. In the examination and evaluation of students, student self-evaluation, enterprise evaluation and teacher evaluation are combined. Based on the present, facing the future, with the development of students' ability as the focus, comprehensive evaluation of students' learning and technical performance. The teaching quality monitoring system can be modeled after the United States and Japan, and a feedback information system can be established to record students' learning at each stage and feed back to universities and enterprises, such as students' comprehensive practice performance, professional quality, innovation consciousness, etc., so as to pay attention to students' overall physical and mental development.

4 Summary

The integration of industry and education is a basic school-running mode of our higher education and vocational education, and deepening the integration of industry and education is an important way to effectively improve the quality of national personnel training. Although the integration of industry and education in our country has achieved certain results, there are still a series of problems in the practice of deepening the integration of industry and education. Starting from the concept of integration of new engineering, non-governmental higher education and industry and education, this paper selects Shandong Xiehe University as the research object, analyzes its achievements and problems in the aspect of integration of industry and education and educates people, and makes an analysis of the reasons, carry out the integration of industry and education, school-enterprise cooperation experience and summarized. Finally, the paper puts forward the construction path of integration of production and education in the new engineering background. Put forward the government, industry, enterprise, university“Four-in-one” cooperative education mechanism strategy, school-enterprise deep cooperation is the basic premise of deepening the integration of industry and education, the close linkage of administration, administration, school and enterprise is the fundamental way to deepen the integration of industry and education.

China Association for Private Education 2022 Annual Planning Project: Research on the Model of Integrated Education of Production and Education in Private Higher Education under the Background of New Engineering (CANFZG22331)

References

1. Li Peigen. Why Engineering Becomes New [J]. Higher Engineering Education Research,2017(4):1-4,15.
2. Lu Guodong. Five Breakthroughs and Preliminary Exploration of "New Engineering" Construction [J]. China University Teaching,2017(5):38-41.
3. Zhang Lijuan, Ge Yunwang, Wang Xinwu. Research and Practice of Deepening the Integration of Production and Education in Undergraduate Talent Training [J]. Experimental Technology and Management,20,37(7):169-172. (in Chinese)
4. Huang Wenyan. Construction of "Eight Common" Mechanism oriented deep integration of Industry and education Collaborative Education Model of School-Enterprise Co-construction Industry College -- A Case study of Hezhou University [J]. Journal of Hezhou University,20,36(2):152-155,164.

Teaching reform and practice of object-oriented programming course

Yanhua Chen*

Shandong Xiehe University, 250100, JiNan, Shandong, China

Abstract. This article aims at the deficiencies in the teaching of object-oriented programming courses in our school, guided by the OBE teaching concept, and aimed at cultivating applied talents. On the one hand, carry out teaching reform and practice, and carry out the design of the ideological and political education system of the course,so as to fully mobilize the initiative and enthusiasm of students,stimulate students' innovative ability, effectively cultivate students' innovative thinking ability and unity and cooperation ability, and then improve students' ability to solve problems.To provide guarantee for improving the quality of personnel training.

1 Introduction

For the problems existing in the traditional Java teaching, based on the requirements of the current first-class discipline construction, information-based teaching, course ideological and political introduction, this paper carries out teaching reform and practice on the teaching content, teaching mode, practical teaching methods, course evaluation system and other aspects, and carries out the design of the course ideological and political education system, so as to fully mobilize students' initiative and enthusiasm, stimulate students' innovation ability, effectively cultivate students' innovative thinking ability and cooperation ability, thus improving students' ability to solve problems, and providing guarantee for improving the quality of talent training.

2 Shortcomings in traditional course teaching

The course of Object-oriented Programming takes Java language as the development language. There are many basic principles of programming in the course content. The traditional teaching mode leads to the boring daily learning of many students, who lack good engineering literacy. The main problems are as follows:

(1)The teaching content is outdated and limited to the teaching of simple theories. The original teaching content focuses on the teaching of basic concepts and principles, and focuses on the teaching of theoretical knowledge and grammar. The teaching is centered on the teacher and teaching content, and ignores the principal position of students, resulting in low interest of students in learning[1].

* Corresponding author: 290528163@qq.com

(2)The teaching mode is single. The teacher, as an actor, imparts knowledge to the students in the classroom through the introduction of new lessons, the explanation of knowledge, classroom exercises, homework and other teaching methods. The students just accept the knowledge passively. The students feel that the course is boring, and they are afraid of difficulties, which cannot mobilize the students' enthusiasm for learning.

(3)Practice teaching lacks systematicness. The experiments are mainly designed experiments and verification experiments, and there are a few comprehensive experiments. The practice content ignores the connection and practice with other software courses, which makes students unable to integrate the knowledge and is not conducive to the cultivation of students' ability to solve practical problems by integrating what they have learned.

(4)The assessment method is single and the assessment content is unreasonable. The assessment method of the course is mainly written examination, which focuses on the knowledge assessment of basic concepts and attempts, fails to reflect the ability of analysis and the ability of design and practice, and focuses on the evaluation of result rather than the combination of result and process[2].

(5)The ideological and political design of the course is weak. The course design emphasizes the study of professional knowledge, which is relatively weak in ideological and political education. Teachers hardly involve ideological and political education in the teaching process.

3 The implementation path of teaching reform of object-oriented programming course

Based on the OBE teaching concept, the implementation path takes cultivating students' software development ability as the main line, takes students as the center, and takes ability output as the guide, integrating into ideological and political elements such as love feelings for home and country, cultural literacy, scientific and technological innovation, and craftsman spirit. Based on Xuexitong and flipped classroom, it comprehensively uses inquiry-based teaching method, case teaching method and PBL teaching method to implement project-based teaching, strengthens teacher-student interaction and student-student interaction, so as to construct a learning community between teachers and students.

3.1 To reconstruct the teaching content and integrate the ideological and political education into the course

The post requirements of application software system development is investigated, and the teaching content is reconstructed based on the actual posts and tasks of enterprises. The content of the course is optimized to break through the chapter system of the current textbook, and it is divided into five modules: Java language foundation, object-oriented, collection, GUI, and file flow, driven by real project cases. The basic module of Java language is designed with the case of "simple calculator". The "student management system" is used throughout the course, and the knowledge points in each chapter are comprehensively applied.

It takes the "programmer craftsman spirit" as the core, strengthens the explicit ideology and politics of "persistence, preciseness, integrity, cooperation and excellence", refines the implicit ideology and politics of "value origin", integrates the love feelings for home and country, moral cultivation, cultural literacy, innovation and entrepreneurship into the course content, and optimizes the content supply. The course objectives are designed from four dimensions to realize the organic integration of knowledge, ability and quality values.

3.2 To innovate diversified teaching models

Guided by the work process, it realizes the integrated teaching mode of "introduction, teaching, learning, doing and evaluation" and combination of online and offline. It takes course learning as the main line, combines online and offline teaching, and focus on both theoretical teaching and practical teaching to build a learning community between teachers and students[3].

3.2.1 Teaching resources

The online course resources are constructed by using the Chaoxing Xuexitong network platform, which mainly includes three modules, namely, course chapter system and task list, course expansion learning resources and test question resource library.

Course chapter system and task list: each chapter releases the course learning task list, clarifying the learning objectives, learning contents, learning methods, homework and tests; recording micro lesson videos or selecting online high-quality resource course videos as the task points in the course, so as to facilitate students' pre-class learning.

Course expansion learning resources: it establishes complete course expansion learning resources, including enterprise recruitment written tests, interview questions, enterprise project cases, online learning resources recommendation, JDK instruction documents and other materials, so as to facilitate students to carry out expansion learning.

Course test question resource library: it sets stage tests according to chapter contents to conduct chapter tests, so as to timely understand the learning effect of students.

3.2.2 Teaching implementation

The teaching implementation is student-centered and teacher-led, realizing online and offline mixed mode teaching. Students complete the task points through online independent learning, teachers lecture the key and difficult points in class, teachers and students interact with each other, and the differences and individual needs of students can be solved.

(1) Online independent teaching

Teachers release videos, courseware, task lists, tests and other contents on the Xuexitong, and students complete each task point and test by learning independently. Teachers monitor the students' learning progress at any time through the statistical function of the completion of the task points on the Xuexitong teaching platform, discuss and answers questions online, and requires students to complete learning and classroom tests within the specified time, and test the students' learning effect through classroom tests and homework after class.

(2) Offline flipped classroom teaching

The flipped classroom teaching offline adopts a trilogy of "pre-class (knowledge teaching), in-class (knowledge internalization) and after-class (skill externalization)".

Pre-class: Knowledge is learnt through online resources. Teachers upload teaching PPT courseware, MOOC videos and various learning materials to the Chaoxing platform, assign topics for discussion, and enable students to learn independently. Teachers guide students to process information to achieve "learning" and effectively cultivate students' abilities to discover key information, summarize and apply knowledge.

In-class: Teachers carry out teaching by offline flipped classroom and students internalize knowledge by it. The teachers set up classroom tests to test the effect of pre-class preview and feedback students' pre-class preview. In the discussion of knowledge points, students are randomly selected to complete the explanation of relevant knowledge points, and a class discussion is conducted to express students' different understandings of knowledge. Teachers also participate in the discussion to guide, sort out and judge. Teachers are mentors rather than lecturers, and gradually cultivate students' abilities of problem-solving, teamwork and communication.

After-class: class knowledge review and summary, project-type tasks, and phased mind mapping. Teachers test the learning effect of students by assigning after-class practical homework, introducing project case design, encouraging students to participate in discipline competitions and other channels, which is the externalization stage of knowledge and skills.

3.3 Hierarchical practice teaching

According to the students' own characteristics and their mastery of the course, the hierarchical practice teaching method is adopted. The in-class practice teaching includes basic experiments, small projects, comprehensive projects and course design, so that students can master the knowledge points related to Java and have the ability to apply basic knowledge points to solve practical problems. The after-class practice is based on the second classroom. Students are encouraged to actively apply for college students' innovation and entrepreneurship training projects, actively organize teams to participate in various software development and Internet + competitions at all levels, so as to apply what they have learned to practice, promote learning through competition, and improve students' project development ability. Through hierarchical practice teaching, students' innovative consciousness and subjective initiative are cultivated, and their ability to solve practical problems and professional quality are improved.

3.4 Development strategy of integration of production and education

Based on the teaching effectiveness, the assessment and evaluation methods are reformed to solve the problem of single traditional assessment form. Centering on the effectiveness of course teaching, scientific and diversified assessment is carried out. Adhering to the design principles of process evaluation and diversification, the online assessment module is added, which effectively monitors the whole process of online and offline. The assessment is divided into two parts: online assessment (30%) and offline assessment (70%). The online assessment is mainly a process evaluation, mainly including access, video viewing, task points, number of discussions, homework, etc. The offline assessment includes a process evaluation and a final evaluation. The process evaluation includes class participation, reading report, project assessment and innovation assessment. The final evaluation is a unified final examination. The online assessment and offline assessment are organically combined to effectively monitor the whole learning process and achieve the process, effectiveness, expansion and innovation. The evaluation subject is diversified, including teacher evaluation, student self- evaluation and student evaluation evaluation.

4 Effectiveness of teaching reform

According to the needs of professional posts, we have reconstructed the teaching content, focused on students, promoted the online and offline mixed teaching mode, guided and instructed students to actively participate in skill competitions, promoted the ability cultivation of innovation and entrepreneurship, and realized the learning community of teachers and students. The following reform achievements have been achieved.

(1) The course content is consistent with the social needs. The course knowledge system is reconstructed according to the actual work posts and tasks of the enterprise, which breaks the silence of the classroom by using the Xuexitong, and integrates the ideological and political education of the course into the teaching content, so as to improve the quality of talent training.

(2) The assessment forms are diversified. The adding of online assessment module effectively monitors the whole process of online learning and offline learning, so as to achieve process, effectiveness, expansion and innovation.

(3) The class atmosphere is active. The "online and offline mixed teaching" is realized by using information means such as Chaoxing Xuexitong platform, which breaks the silence in class. Through online preview, students can take questions to the class, which makes them answer questions more actively, stimulate their interest in learning, improve their independent learning ability, and enhance their innovation awareness, so as to improve the teaching quality.

(4) The acquisition rate of skill certificates has been improved. The participation and acquisition rate of students in subject competitions and obtaining professional skill certificates (soft test, computer level test, etc.) have been improved.

5 Conclusion

In this paper, the OBE teaching concept and the ideological and political elements of the course are applied to the teaching reform of the object-oriented programming course. And the teaching content, teaching mode, practical teaching methods, and course evaluation system are optimized and improved based on the output of results. The teaching is student-centered, result- oriented, and the teaching resources are continuously improved to achieve the unity of skills and knowledge, methods and processes. It enhances the ability of students to analyze and solve complex problems. Based on the Chaoxing Xuexitong platform, the online and offline mixed mode teaching is carried out to achieve the deep integration of information technology and teaching process, achieve student participatory teaching, promote students' active thinking, achieve "teach them to fish", and cultivate students' ability of teamwork and communication. The teaching reform measures have been applied in the software engineering major of Shandong Xiehe University and achieved good teaching results.

Shandong Xiehe university 2020 university-level first-class course: Object Oriented Programming Design

References

1. LI Y B. Exploration of Ideological and Political Education in Advanced Language Programming Course Teaching [J].Western Quality Education, 2020,6 (2):37-39.
2. LIU A H, CHEN J. Research and Practice on Discussion based Teaching of Database Courses Based on OBE Concept [J] Computer Education, 2018 (9): 112-115.
3. LIU J L. Mixed teaching mode of Java programming[J].Accessory computer, 2020 (9): 182-183

Exploration and practice in the course of "Website Design and Production" form the ideological and political perspective

Lu Zhang*

Shandong Xiehe University, Jinan, Shandong, Research direction: Network Engineering, China

Abstract. Website Design and Production is the core course of the curriculum system for e-commerce majors. It is an integrated course of theory and practice of systematic design and development of an e-commerce website by comprehensively using HTML5+CSS3 program design, website art foundation, database and other e-commerce professional knowledge and skills. Guided by the goal of curriculum moral education, stay The knowledge points of website design and production are imperceptibly integrated into the ideological and political elements of the curriculum, and moral education runs through the whole process of teaching. At the important knowledge points, students are guided to brainstorm, imagine application scenarios, and apply what they have learned. At the same time, they pay attention to the current affairs of the country, understand the historical development and future development trend of the subject, link the content of the course with the national development, design teaching cases, and carry out Guided by the values, we can achieve the goal of making virtue, cultivating people, moistening things silently.

1 Introduction

In December 2016, In his speech at the National Conference on Ideological and political work in Colleges and universities, General Secretary Xi pointed out: "the ideological and political work in Colleges and universities is related to the fundamental problem of what kind of people colleges and universities cultivate, how to cultivate people and for whom to cultivate people. We should adhere to the establishment of morality and cultivate people as the central link, run the ideological and political work through the whole process of education and teaching, realize the whole process and all-round education, and strive to create a new situation in the development of China's higher education."

On May 6, 2019, the Ministry of education, the central political and Legal Commission, the Ministry of science and technology and other 13 departments officially jointly launched the "six excellence and one top-notch" plan 2.0 to comprehensively promote the construction of new engineering, new medicine, new agriculture and new liberal arts, and improve the ability of colleges and universities to serve economic and social development.

* Corresponding author: 493691953@qq.com

The implementation of the plan provides a rare historical opportunity for the construction of the "four new". In May, 2020, the Ministry of Education issued a notice on the guiding outline of Ideological and political construction of courses in Colleges and universities, pointing out that ideological and political construction of courses is a strategic measure to implement the fundamental task of Building Morality and cultivating people, and an important task to comprehensively improve the quality of talent training. Business education, which plays an important role in higher education, how to deal with the reform, solidly promote the "San quan" Education mode, implement the fundamental task of Building Morality and cultivating talents, and cultivate new business talents suitable for the development of the times has become an urgent problem that must be faced.

2 Significance

Contemporary college students grew up in the era of the rapid development of the Internet in China. Due to the lack of correct values guidance, they often lack the ability to identify materialism, money worship and improper words and deeds in the network, and are prone to form wrong values and outlooks on life; On the other hand, due to the pressure of employment and workplace competition, college students tend to pay more attention to the study of professional knowledge and vocational skills, and are easy to ignore the importance of learning outlook on life and values, resulting in the lack of social responsibility and poor sense of unity and cooperation among some college students.

Curriculum ideological and political education can effectively make up for the problem of emphasizing teaching and neglecting education in the current professional course teaching. The essence of curriculum ideological and political education is to establish morality and cultivate people. Teachers are required to organically integrate socialist core values such as socialist democracy and legal system, feelings of family and country, and the spirit of great country craftsman into the teaching of professional knowledge and professional skills, so as to form a synergistic effect with conventional ideological and political education. Compared with the conventional ideological and political courses, the course Ideological and political education plays an invisible role in educating people. By dispersing and Integrating Ideological and political elements into the teaching of professional knowledge and skills, we can achieve the purpose of ideological education that moistens things silently, which is easier to be accepted and recognized by higher vocational students, so as to achieve the goal of whole process and all-round education.

3 Course introduction of "Website Design and Production"

"Website design and production" is an elective course for e-commerce majors, which mainly introduces the basics of website design, primary applications, page layout, website testing and publishing, comprehensive applications, etc. Following the teaching concept of taking teachers as the guide and students as the center, through "case description", "case analysis" and specific "operation steps" in teaching, actively guide students to "learn by doing", "learn by doing" and "teach by learning", organically combine the learning of basic knowledge of "website design and production" with the practice of operation skills, and cultivate students' practical application ability from specific skill operation. Help students consolidate their knowledge and operate skillfully through knowledge expansion, and add web design materials for extracurricular display of traditional Chinese culture to cultivate students' patriotism. Through the study of this course, we will lay a solid foundation for students in web design and production, build a complete professional knowledge system of e-commerce, and cultivate high-level knowledge-based and skilled professionals who are "patriotic, dedicated, honest and friendly" for enterprises and society.

4 Exploration of curriculum ideology and politics in "Website Design and Production"

(1) Excavate the ideological and political education elements contained in the course of website design and production, and integrate the ideological and political elements into the knowledge points of the course. In order to achieve the teaching goal of "web design and production", this course takes classroom teaching as the carrier of knowledge and skills teaching and ideological and political education, excavates the elements of Ideological and political education in the process of knowledge and skills teaching, and explores and designs the explicit and implicit combination of Ideological and political education and knowledge and skills teaching in the links of basic knowledge, scheme design, application practice, etc.

(2) According to the ideological and political integration point of the course "web design and production", optimize the teaching design and strengthen the teaching management. According to the integration point of curriculum ideology and politics, optimize the curriculum of web design and production, improve the teaching design, and strengthen the teaching management.

(3) Strengthen process evaluation and improve course assessment methods. The effect of talent training is the primary criterion for the evaluation of Ideological and political construction of the curriculum. Scientific evaluation should be based on majors and courses, highlight the examination of students' development process, and apply the examination results to teachers' teaching reflection and improvement. In the course assessment, we should strengthen the process evaluation, and master the students' Ideological and political learning through discussion, testing, classroom answering and other forms. In addition, teachers can ask students to write their learning experiences as midterm assignments. In the final examination paper, teachers can add comprehensive questions to comprehensively test students' learning effect.

5 Ideological and political technology route of "Website Design and Production"

In each link of the teaching of Website Design and Production, fully tap the ideological and political elements, and organically combine the value shaping, knowledge teaching and ability training. In terms of professional content, we should excavate the ideological and political elements existing in knowledge points and optimize the ideological and political supply; In terms of teaching methods, micro classes, classroom discussions and other ways are used to introduce ideological and political elements. By setting tasks related to traditional culture, core values, meritorious figures and hot current events, students can think, increase group discussions and ideas sharing, fully mobilize the enthusiasm of students to participate in the classroom, and increase the interest of ideological and political elements; In the classroom practice link, guide students to combine the classroom content with the previous knowledge, solve the actual problems encountered and constantly optimize, and cultivate the craftsmanship spirit of excellence; The after-school homework integrating the ideological and political education of the course is designed, focusing on the basic theoretical knowledge of the course, grasping the pulse of the times, condensing the theme of professional ideological and political education, and cultivating students' patriotism and professional quality while consolidating and expanding their knowledge.

 https://doi.org/10.1051/shsconf/202316601030

The overall ideological and political construction technical route of Website Design and Production is shown in Fig 1.

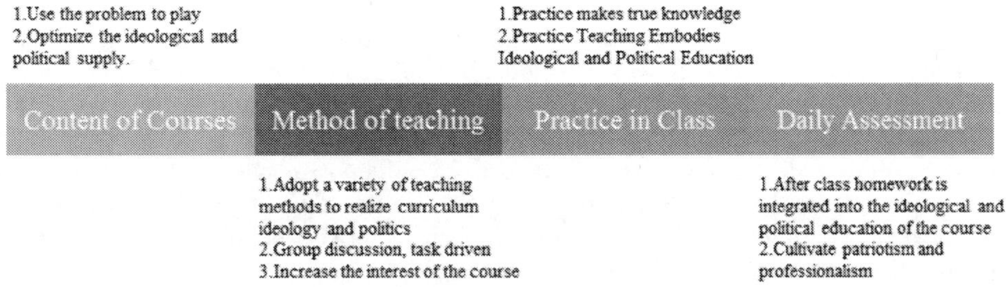

Fig. 1. Technical Route of Overall Ideological and Political Construction of "Website Design and Production".

6 Ideological and political integration point of "Website Design and Production"

The key is to integrate the ideological and political elements into the process of website design and production curriculum reform, excavate the coincidence point between curriculum teaching knowledge and ideological and political elements, and design appropriate teaching programs and curriculum resources. In the process of teaching and implementing the ideological and political course, we should pay attention to the publicity of national spirit and the correct guidance of ideals, beliefs and value orientation, cultivate the craftsmanship spirit of excellence and innovation, and exercise the students' realistic, pragmatic, rigorous and meticulous work style to meet the requirements of training information engineering talents in the new era of socialism with Chinese characteristics.

(1) Cultivate students' national spirit of self-reliance, enterprising and innovation.

In the teaching module of website operation principle, the main teaching content is to let students understand the operation process of B/S architecture and be able to use browsers to analyze page elements. In the course of classroom teaching, students are guided to adhere to the national spirit of self-reliance, enterprising and innovation by introducing the development history of browsers and the difficulties faced by domestic browsers, and reflecting on the Red Core browser event.

(2) Cultivating Scientific Aesthetic Outlook and Socialist Core Values

In the website analysis and design module, students can understand the mainstream tools used to design websites, learn to analyze website functions, and use tools to design website prototypes. In the process of knowledge explanation, prototype analysis is carried out for some red theme websites, and tasks are arranged to guide students to design their own red website prototype, focusing on the overall structure design of the website and the color matching of the website, in order to cultivate students' scientific aesthetics; In the process of website analysis and design, red stories are introduced to cultivate students' socialist core values.

(3) Cultivate students' pragmatic, rigorous and meticulous work style

In the HTML5 page design and production module, students should master the use of common HTML tags and be able to use HTML5 to edit website pages. In this module, students are required to make web pages by hand. Students often make page errors due to punctuation in Chinese and English, and some students make page errors due to improper use of tag attributes. Therefore, in the process of making web pages, students are required to be careful, try to avoid all kinds of page errors, and cultivate students' pragmatic, rigorous and meticulous work style.

(4) Guide students to be themselves bravely and show their personal charm

In the basic knowledge module of CSS style, you can compare the different characteristics of internal style sheets, inline style sheets, and linked style sheets horizontally and use objects to describe the truth of being a person and doing things. Aiming at the knowledge point of irreplaceable uniqueness of the internal style sheet, teach students that as long as they are brave enough to be themselves and maintain their unique personality, they will not be easily replaced by others; In view of the distinctive characteristics of simple writing method and high priority of in line style sheets, we will teach students to be thoughtful, courageous and characteristic people, boldly show their personality characteristics and fully show their personal charm.

7 Sumary

To sum up, in view of the current important measures of ideological and political education of professional courses in colleges and universities, this paper takes Website Design and Production as a case to explore the technical route and point of ideological and political integration of professional courses, explore and design ideological and political elements, and integrate the ideas of independent learning and lifelong learning into basic knowledge. The concept of standardization, preciseness and perfection is integrated into the scheme design, and the belief of patriotism and encouragement and innovation is integrated into the application practice, so as to achieve the ideological and political education of professional courses that moisten things silently.

The "14th Five-Year Plan" for National Business Education and Research in 2022, The exploration and practice of curriculum ideology and politics in the course of "Website Design and Production" under the background of New Business.(Subject No.: SKJYKT-220701)

References

1. Shi Hua, Wu Jie. Teaching Exploration of HTML5 Application Development Based on Curriculum Ideological and Political Promotion [J]. Industry and Technology Forum, 2021 (20) 24, 94-95.
2. Zhang Chengjiang. Research on Ideological and Political Practice of "Web Design and Production" Course [J]. Industrial and Information Education, 2021.08:55-57

Research on talent cultivation of software engineering under the background of integration of industry and education

Cuiyuan Jiang*

Shandong Xiehe University, Jinan, Shandong, Research direction: Software development, China

Abstract. With the rapid development of information technology, The Internet, Cloud Computing, Big Data Etc. Various emerging scientific and technological means and thinking modes are quietly and profoundly changing the thinking, production and learning methods of human society. At present, the education industry generally regards the integration of production and education as the path of vocational education development and personnel training, This paper discusses the current situation of the integration of industry and education, Analyze the problems in the process of the integration of industry and education, The talent cultivation scheme of software engineering under the background of integration of industry and education is proposed.

1 Introduction

In 2017, Enterprises will be encouraged to participate in the operation of vocational schools and universities in the form of sole proprietorships or joint ventures, and grant more intern vacancies to students to strengthen cooperation with educational institutes, according to a notice released by the State Council. It is an urgent requirement to implement the structural reform of the supply side of human resources[1]. Accompanied by a series of related policy announcement and implementation, The integration of production and education has gradually changed from the single to the diversified and the superficial integration to the overall integration.

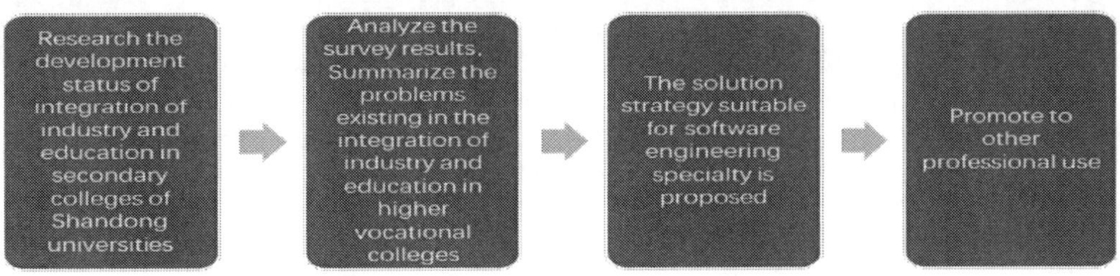

Fig. 1. Research methods.

* Corresponding author: 568169316@qq.com

As shown in Figure 1, through the above research methods, this paper obtains a set of talent training program suitable for software engineering major.

2 Development status of integration of production and education in higher vocational colleges

2.1 The policy guarantee mechanism is not sound

In recent years, the government has promulgated policy documents related to the integration of industry and education, Although governments at all levels have taken into account the implementation of industry-education integration policies when formulating policies, However, in the process of implementation of industry-education integration, there are still unclear responsibilities of government departments and industry enterprises, imperfect security system and working mechanism, and lack of policy guarantee in the process of implementation. For software engineering majors, At present, there is no clear policy to define the rights and obligations of both schools and enterprises, There is also no regulatory body to monitor and evaluate cooperation between the two. This will lead to less interest in the participation of both schools and enterprises, and the quality of the integration of production and education is difficult to measure, which is not conducive to the improvement of the quality of talent training.

2.2 School-enterprise cooperation is superficial, and the enthusiasm of enterprises is not high

In the process of implementing the integration of industry and education, it is a basic requirement for enterprises to participate in the course construction process of schools, It mainly includes specialty construction, curriculum construction, teaching staff construction and teaching evaluation, etc. However, the enthusiasm of enterprises is not high enough and remains on the surface. The reason for this is that enterprises usually start from their own interests and think that too much participation in the integration of industry and education can not bring profits to the enterprise. Enterprises believe that participating in the process of industry-education integration and collaborative education is mostly to provide a training base for schools and perform the function of training students. The attitude that the integration of industry and education can improve the quality of employees, improve production efficiency and help enterprises to innovate is not optimistic. Some higher vocational colleges cannot provide services such as staff training and technical research and development support for enterprises. In addition, The preferential policies provided by the government to enterprises participating in the integration of industry and education are weak and not fully implemented, which results in the weak attraction degree of school-enterprise cooperation to enterprises, In addition, industry organizations and associations have a low sense of presence in the process of industry-education integration, Supervision and guidance are not in place, as a result, enterprises did not get the expected benefits in the process of participation, and the enthusiasm fades away, lose the motivation to continue to participate in collaborative school running.

2.3 The construction of teaching staff needs to be improved

Vocational colleges and universities pay more attention to teaching and research, in the final analysis, because teaching and research results are important indicators of education system, from the education administration department to the university, then to the secondary college to grassroots teachers, this indicator is exerting enormous influence. For a long time, vocational education and general higher education follow the same evaluation mechanism. compared to quantifiable results of teaching and research, the evaluation of practical ability became dispensable, according to the survey, many vocational colleges have the phenomenon of “attaching importance to academic work and neglecting practice”. Many vocational colleges have followed the applied college talent introduction model, these colleges and universities are heavily recruiting new master's and doctoral graduates, these fresh graduates often have a high academic record and a solid theoretical foundation, but they have not worked in enterprises and lack practical experience. They are often entrusted with heavy responsibilities and do scientific research vigorously, which leads to lack of practical training opportunities for them. The reason for this is that schools emphasize theory over practice.

2.4 The curriculum structure is different from the industry demand, needs to be adjusted

The core of the talents training of the integration of production and education in higher vocational colleges is to cultivate talents who can adapt to the production of the industry and enterprises, therefore, in terms of specialty setting, higher vocational colleges should be closely connected with the needs of related industries and enterprises to build the curriculum system. At the same time, the current situation and future development trend of each specialty should be analyzed scientifically, scientific design of the industry-education integration of the course system, through the research industry enterprise talent demand characteristics and the professional graduates employment destination information, take this as the benchmark, overall planning, adjustment of the professional enrollment, curriculum, faculty, theoretical courses and practical courses proportion. From the perspective of curriculum provision, the curriculum provision of higher vocational colleges should be forward-looking, and actively docking with the industrial structure and future planning of the region. However, when vocational colleges offer courses, they often place more emphasis on theory than practice. Once the proportion of class hours can not be arranged, the first choice will be to reduce the practice class. The time for concentrated practical training is more limited, which is usually arranged in the third semester after the normal teaching. The content of practical training is mainly based on the cases in textbooks, which cannot be closely related to the cutting-edge knowledge and new technology of The Times.

3 The development strategy of integration of industry and education in software engineering major of higher vocational colleges

3.1 Strengthen the promotion of the policy system of production-education integration

At present, the government has issued a series of policy documents related to the integration of industry and education, providing strong support for the training of talents in the integration of industry and education in terms of policy guarantee. To a certain extent, it has played a role in guiding and promoting the school-enterprise cooperation for the integration of industry and education, and is also an indispensable link in the training system of talents for the integration of industry and education. In the specific implementation process, local education authorities should adhere to local conditions, combined with local industrial development, detailed analysis of the policy, the implementation of responsibilities and rights. Schools should stand in the perspective of "country, region and university", and actively strive to build a cooperation framework among the government, industry, enterprises and schools, and form an ecological chain of integration of industry and education with the linkage of "government, industry, enterprise and school". The government should restrict the responsibility of enterprises in vocational education from the legal level. On the one hand, it should determine the rights and responsibilities of the responsible subjects in the form of legislation, and strengthen the rigid conditions for the responsible subjects to perform their duties. On the other hand, it is necessary to cultivate the consciousness of responsibility subject of industry enterprises through policy guidance and policy incentive, so that enterprises can generate continuous motivation to undertake the responsibility of vocational education.

3.2 Deepen school-enterprise cooperation

Enterprises need to improve their awareness of social responsibility, clarify their obligations and responsibilities in talent training, and establish a better social service attitude and awareness. Enterprises should establish a good awareness of the integration of in-depth production and education, so as to provide necessary support for actively creating a good social environment. Enterprises need to realize that the integration of industry and education can improve the conversion rate of research results. It can not only provide teachers and student teams for technology research and development of enterprise, but also provide places and equipment for teachers and students. Enterprises should also be aware of the necessity of cooperating with application-oriented universities to build majors and courses, because jointly building majors, courses and discussing talent training programs can help enterprises to understand the current situation of talent training and master the basic situation of talent training, and at the same time improve the quality of talent training by making talent training objectives that are more in line with the actual needs of enterprises. And increase the enterprise's own human capital. In order to raise the awareness of enterprises, the government should encourage and commend enterprises with deeper integration between industry and education and set up exemplary units to deepen the cooperation between industry and education.

3.3 Strengthen the construction of teaching staff and create a "double-qualified" teacher team

Under the background of the integration of industry and education, the teacher training mode of vocational colleges should take advantage of the cooperation between schools and enterprises to build a teacher team construction mode of mutual training and mutual employment, and promote the multi-level and three-dimensional development of school teachers. This requires a set of effective teacher training mechanism between schools and enterprises, so as to promote teachers to actively participate in the teacher training organized by enterprises and improve their skills. The school can regularly invite well-known experts at home and abroad to conduct in-depth academic exchanges and discussions with teachers. At the same time, the school can employ well-known entrepreneurs, enterprise engineers and outstanding talents in various aspects to serve as part-time teachers. This is not only conducive to the cultivation of students, but also can improve the teacher's project-based teaching ability. Schools can also send teachers to work as interns in enterprises during winter and summer vacations, and formulate preferential promotion policies for teachers who participate in on-the-job practice. At the same time, young teachers are encouraged to conduct academic visits to higher level universities, study for doctor's degree and study abroad. While improving themselves, they can also introduce advanced teaching concepts to the school and improve the overall teaching ability of teachers.

3.4 Optimize the course structure

With the continuous development and changes of the social economy, it is necessary to improve the professional curriculum system, timely update to meet the needs of different professions, highlight the cultivation of students' vocational skills, promote the development of curriculum teaching, so that students fully understand the professional knowledge and the knowledge and ability structure of corresponding positions. From the perspective of curriculum setting, the curriculum setting of higher vocational colleges should be forward-looking, actively connect with the industrial structure and future planning of the local area, explore and establish the three-level curriculum system: that is, the first-level curriculum is taught by teachers, teachers will not only teach professional theoretical knowledge, but also stimulate students' learning interest and initiative; The second-level curriculum is a combination of theoretical teaching and practice to strengthen the in-depth discussion between teachers and students; The third level courses are practical training courses. In the practical training courses, the work content in real industries and enterprises is simulated and restored, so that students can focus on solving practical problems and fully exercise and cultivate their practical operation ability.

4 Summary

The integration of production and education is an important direction for higher vocational colleges to carry out education reform at present. By carrying out the integration of production and education, it is helpful to promote students' understanding and absorption of theoretical knowledge. As an important base for conveying technical talents to the society, higher vocational colleges shoulder the important mission of cultivating diversified outstanding talents. With the gradual expansion of the scale of higher vocational colleges, talent training plans should also be constantly improved and innovative, combined with the needs of the development of society and enterprises for talents, targeted to develop the talent training mode, to cultivate excellent theoretical knowledge, outstanding technical ability of high-level talents, to make contributions to social development.

1. The 14th Five-Year Plan for National Business Education and Research in 2022, Research on Talent Cultivation in local Business Colleges under the background of integration of Industry and education, Project No.: SKJYKT-220706.
2. Innovation Training Program for College students Shandong Province in 2022, Coal mine gas detector based on FTIR, Project No.: S202213324011.

References

1. Ye Zhongliang. Research on the construction of vocational education teachers under the background of the integration of Industry and education[J]. Modern Vocational Education, 2021(15):70-71.
2. He Sha. Construction of Secondary Vocational Education Quality Evaluation System from the Perspective of Production-Education Integration[J]. Vocational Education, 2020,19(22):36-40.

3. MengLi. The Implementation of "1+X Certificate Background "and the Design and Thinking of Talent Training Program in Higher Vocational Colleges[J]. Cultural and Educational Materials, 2020(35):3.
4. Shang Yitong, Yang Yong. The dilemma and strategic choice of higher vocational innovation and entrepreneurship education in the new era[J]. Journal of Ningbo Vocational and Technical College, 2021,25(2):22-26.

Research on the construction of good family style in the context of rural revitalization

Chen Ru*

ShandongXieheUniversity, Jinan, Shandong, Research direction:Software Engineering, China

Abstract. Family style reflects the value pursuit and spiritual aspiration of a family, and is an important part of China's traditional culture with great characteristics.Based on the combing of concepts related to the rural revitalization strategy and the construction of good family ethics in rural areas, this paper firstly points out the background related to the rural revitalization strategy and the construction of family ethics, and on this basis reveals the relationship between the two.Then, the current situation and problems of family style construction in the context of rural revitalization are explained. Finally, it is refined that the construction of good family style in rural areas should follow the family members' alignment, pay attention to the requirements of sustainable development, inherit and carry forward the content of traditional excellent family style, pay attention to the use of new media technology, adapt to the development of the times, strengthen the propaganda and education of family style construction, so that the construction of good family style in rural areas can help the implementation of rural revitalization strategy.

1 Research background

Good family culture is the concrete implementation of the policy of rural revitalization, and rural revitalization is an important carrier for the cultivation of excellent family culture. The 19th Party Congress has clearly put forward the strategy of revitalizing socialist countryside culture, and one of its visionary tasks is "to reach a new height of countryside civilization". General Secretary Xi Jinping emphasized that "we should promote the revitalization of rural culture by cultivating civilized countryside, good family style and simple folk style". With the introduction and implementation of the national rural revitalization strategy, the importance of promoting rural revitalization with the construction of civilized family style has become more and more prominent. Under the background of the national rural revitalization strategy, promoting the construction of family style will be the actual development requirement and realistic power choice for rural revitalization, and the rural revitalization strategy also brings a brand-new development opportunity for the construction of family style[1]. To sum up, in the context of revitalization of the new countryside, a good family style construction is the inevitable result of normal development according to the realistic logic.

* Corresponding author: 1172886050@qq.com

2 The current situation and problems of building good family culture

At present, with the changes in the world's economic and social development, human production and life style and family composition have been greatly changed.Under the influence of various factors, the following problems have arisen in the construction of family culture in China.

2.1 Weak awareness of family tradition inheritance

In today's society, with the transformation of society and the evolution of family structure, the old family ties, which were defined by blood family ties, are gradually broken, and the traditional social structure of large families and extended families is gradually disintegrated. Families of three or two have gradually formed the most basic family social unit.The following data can be analyzed based on the seven censuses between 1953 and 2020, as shown in Figure 1.First, in terms of the number of households, the results of the seventh census show that there are 494,157,000 households in China, an increase of more than 248,074,000 households compared to the 13,411,000 households in the first census in 1953. Taking the data from the five censuses between 1982 and 2020 as an example, the proportion of one-person and two-person households has been increasing, the proportion of three-person households began to decline after reaching a peak in 2000, and the proportion of four-person, five-person, and six-person households and above has been gradually decreasing.After the introduction of the fertility policy, three-person households became the dominant household size, and although their share has been declining since 2000, they are still the dominant household type[2]. The proportion of one-person and two-person households has been maintaining an upward trend. To sum up, the small household has become the main type of family household. Everyone is taking care of their own small family life, slowly diluting the inheritance of family customs.

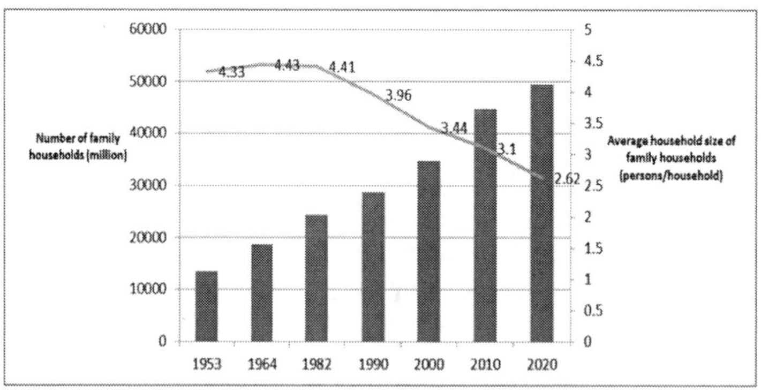

Fig. 1. National census household and average household population data chart.

2.2 The moral effect of family ethics is weakened

The greatest ability of human beings is imitation, and parents are the best role models for their children to learn from, so family education is crucial. At present, due to the obvious gap between urban and rural economic development in China and the unbalanced economic growth within the region, most of the young and middle-aged laborers in rural areas are gradually moving from the less developed areas to the developed areas to work, and because they cannot afford the higher cost of living and teaching in the local families, they have to leave their children behind in their hometowns, thus creating many left-behind children.The team used a self-administered questionnaire in the rural area where the team members are located to survey the lower grade left-behind children in a certain village who are between the ages of 7 and 10 and have been left behind for 3 months or longer[3]. 103 questionnaires were distributed and 96 valid questionnaires were returned. Among the valid survey samples, 46 were boys and 50 were girls; 51 were left behind in the first grade and 45 were left behind in the second grade.The highest proportion of survey respondents, 61.4%, had both parents working outside the home, and 41.8% of the parents worked outside the home for more than 6 months in a year, which made the responsibility of caring for and raising left-behind children need to be assumed by the actual guardians. For children left behind in a certain village, intergenerational guardianship is the most common form of guardianship (56.3%). This is followed by single-parent guardianship (27.1%), and the lowest proportion of guardianship by relatives (3.1%), as shown in Figure 2.

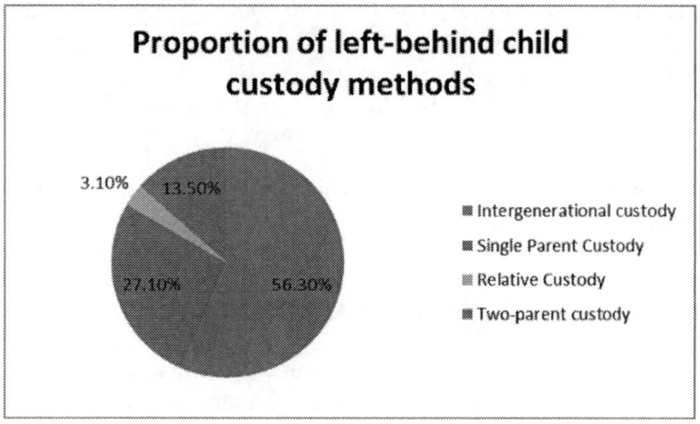

Fig. 2. Questionnaire survey on the proportion of left-behind children in custody.

Through the analysis of the questionnaire data, for the left-behind children, the basic parental companionship and family education are difficult to meet, and the implementation of family moral education is even more difficult. On the contrary, there are also some families with high living standard, overindulging their children, not quarreling a word, not admonishing them, pampering them, letting them know no manners, no etiquette, parents cannot correct them in time, and cannot play a good role in exemplary education, thus family ethics cannot be well inherited.

2.3 The form of passing on family traditions has not kept pace with the development of new technologies in society

In ancient times, family traditions were mostly codified in the form of family rules and regulations. However, in rural areas today, there is a serious lack of family style texts, and the construction of family style in rural areas is constrained and difficult to carry out. On the one hand, in terms of quantity, there are fewer texts of family traditions handed down in rural areas, and the transmission of family traditions is insufficient. On the other hand, the rise of the Internet has led to a change in the way culture is disseminated, no longer limited to the dissemination of paper books, e-books have gradually become the mainstream of the market because of the convenience of portable reading and low prices, resulting in the neglect of text-based family customs.

3 Research on the transmission of family traditions abroad

Through the collection of data, we found that the study of family ethics in Western countries is mainly reflected in family education, while a small number of texts on family ethics and family training exist in Japan and Korea.Japan is seen as the country most deeply influenced by Confucianism in China, and some Japanese families have long held family traditions as the principles and values of a family's activities. The earliest Korean family tradition was the "Family Model" written by Shin Hyun at the end of the Goryeo Dynasty, followed by the "Seventeen Rules of Family Discipline" written by Park Adjoin at the beginning of the Lee Dynasty, after which more family tradition texts emerged, reflecting the early tradition of Korean families to cultivate family traditions of respect for the elderly and love for the young and family harmony. cholars in Western countries have not developed direct research results on the issue of family ethics, but have put forward many theoretical concepts that are related to family ethics and are relatively mature. The focus can be examined in two categories. The first category is modern Western family education ideas, which advocate the need to pay attention to the psychological condition of youth, mostly based on empiricism and pragmatism, etc. The second category is Western moral education theories, which focus on disciplines such as pedagogy and psychology.

4 Suggestions for passing on good family traditions in the context of rural revitalization

4.1 Strict family rules and exemplary leadership

In family education, parents, as teachers of their children, should pay attention to teaching by example, be people-oriented, lead by example, and form an influence on the whole family with persuasive and inspiring words and actions, so as to lay a solid foundation for the cultivation and construction of excellent family culture[4]. On the other hand, each family member should supervise each other, strictly implement family rules, strictly guide, strictly supervise and strictly require their family members, so as to further enhance the moral quality of the family and the concept of law and discipline, and consciously make the whole family act reasonably and legally.

4.2 Empowerment of the times to enhance the new meaning of family traditions

The economic and social development of the countryside can not rely on external economic assistance, to develop a long-term plan for the development of good family customs in rural areas, we must focus on the development of "old civilization and new consciousness" innovation, so that the majority of people take the initiative to explore the unique meaning of the local customs and family life stories, remove the red tape of old customs, maintain the old civilization of the historical heritage of cultural development, respect the basic laws of rural social development, and Based on their own traditional cultural development characteristics to create a rural flavor, with modern significance of the excellent family style.

4.3 Multi-link integrated development to reduce population movement

The construction of traditional family ethics under the perspective of rural revitalization strategy should first ensure that the family structure is complete and family members are all together. Therefore, it is necessary to revitalize rural culture through education, spread the family culture through the news media and focus on the influence of family education to drive the main body of the family back to its place.First, the development of tourism can be strongly supported, especially to promote the great development of rural family style tourism, driving the overall level of economic development in rural areas. Build a number of key family style demonstration bases, clan shrines of family style representative figures, family style celebrity hometowns, family style museums and other family style tourist attractions, create a well-known brand of rural family style, and develop a number of family style branded B&B, residential and catering industries.Secondly, the state actively revitalizes rural industries, develops a number of rural assured farms, key agricultural leading enterprises, rural specialties, and creates local industries, farmers can realize employment at home, accumulate more material wealth for their families, and the construction of rural family style naturally comes to fruition.

4.4 Systematic propaganda, play the role of media propaganda guidance

Since the emergence of the media, it has assumed the important task of disseminating information and guiding social opinion. Therefore, to vigorously carry out the construction of rural family ethics and guide rural parents to return to their villages to take responsibility for family education, we must use the media as a powerful tool to vigorously promote the importance of family ethics to human growth, family harmony and social stability in the whole society.In addition, the media should enhance people's awareness of family ethics education through publicity and reports on the deeds of typical family ethics figures, especially the excavation and publicity of typical deeds of grassroots people, educate and influence the masses with the advanced model deeds around them, and increase the enthusiasm and initiative of farmers to participate in the construction of family ethics. In addition, we can also develop a propaganda system for the construction of good family ethics, and use multimedia and network technology to upload the cases of excellent family ethics role models to the system to create an example effect, so that people will consciously approach the role models, and subconsciously the construction of family ethics will be deeply rooted in people's hearts.

5 Concluding remarks

This paper analyzes the problems and causes in the process of building good family ethics, explores how to better build good family ethics in rural areas in the context of rural revitalization, and takes a multi-pronged approach to continuously enhance the ethical culture and moral concepts of rural people, so as to build a beautiful and civilized countryside.

1.2022 special project on traditional culture and economic and social development in Shandong Province: modern inheritance and development of traditional family style in the context of rural revitalization. Project number: L2022C10170115.

References

1. 1.Liu Xinze. Research on the construction of family style in the new era under the change of family structure[D]. Guilin University of Electronic Science and Technology, 2022.

2. Li Rui. Research on the construction of excellent family style in rural areas under the perspective of rural revitalization strategy[D]. Kunming University of Science and Technology, 2021.
3. Chen Ni. Research on the construction of good family culture in rural areas under the perspective of rural revitalization strategy[D]. Jiangxi University of Technology, 2020.
4. Wang Weiming,Wang Songqing. A study on the current situation of media dependence of rural left-behind children and countermeasures--a field study based on N village in southeast Guizhou[J]. Journal of Youth, 2022(04):41-46.

Reconfiguration of college physics teaching based on the "Trinity" education model

Hao Lv, and *Guanghai* Guo*

School of Mathematics and Science, Qingdao University of Science and Technology, Qingdao, Shandong, 266061, China

Abstract. College physics not only carries the task of learning basic knowledge for science and technology students, but also plays a deep role in educating students through thinking and politics. It has irreplaceable nurturing functions in cultivating students' ideals and beliefs, cultivating national sentiments and strengthening scientific thinking. In the process of education and teaching, we insist on the "trinity" education mode of ideologies, mindset and knowledge, cultivating people with ideologies, reshaping people with thinking and enlightening people with knowledge. Thus, we maximize the effect of "teaching" and "learning". A new form of university physics teaching is built by optimizing teaching resources and reforming the teaching mode, based on the characteristics of the curriculum and the students. Therefore, we realize the knowledge transfer to value leadership from teaching knowledge, and truly implement the fundamental task of moral education.

1 Cultivating students by curriculum ideology and politics

College physics is based on improving the physical ability and thinking of students majored in science and engineering, inspiring their innovative consciousness and spirit of exploration. It takes physics knowledge as the carrier, is driven by the two wings of "physics history + philosophical thinking", and takes the six main lines of "physics spirit, academic frontier, scientific and technological innovation, cultural inheritance, value concept and historical materialism" as the approach. It contains the dialectical unity of physical thoughts such as overall analysis and synthesis, induction and deduction, abstraction and concrete, history and logic. We take the classroom as the battlefield, the integration of ideological and political elements as the method by the 'student-centered' vision. Many teaching methods are taken to create a strong momentum of ideological and political education in the course, resulting in the achievement of the effective education effect. Therefore, it cultivates the professional talents of science and technology with both virtue and ability.

1.1 Selecting ideological content to sublimate physics

(1) The role model of scientists to achieve ideological and political education. We introduce the famous physicists' life stories and scientific research processes into the course, to cultivate

*Corresponding author: ghguo@qust.edu.cn

the scientific spirit of loving science, courageous spirit and perseverance of the students. (2) Scientific and technological achievements at the forefront of the world are introduced, such as aerospace, quantum communication, deep-sea exploration and other leading scientific achievements. These can enhance students' national pride and sense of national honor, stimulate students' patriotic enthusiasm, and guide them to learn more knowledge. (3) Exploration of the philosophical principles in physics knowledge. The research content of physics comes from the Marxist concept of matter, such as relative motion, and the relationship between time and space. We use the philosophical principles contained in the knowledge to train students' historical materialism effectively. (4) Pay attention to the cultivation of students' innovative spirit. The dynamic frontier of science and the application of physics knowledge in production and life are brought into classes. It broadens students' vision and leads them to establish the connection between basic knowledge and practical application.

1.2 Expanding the civics method into teaching

We explore the ideological and political thinking in college physics courses from 2016. With "three minutes in class" as the main approach, we diversified curriculum knowledge and three-dimensional class gradually. Then we integrated different teaching methods according to the teaching content and ideological and political elements. For example, in relative motion learning, the scene of automatic rendezvous and docking between Shenzhou-11 manned spacecraft and Tiangong-2 space laboratory is created for students. During students' "immersive", we simulated the process of docking of the two relative speeds, motion state, motion trajectory, etc. The students could "control" to achieve data fitting and complete the docking between Shenzhou and Tiangong. In the teaching process, students can not only feel the advanced aerospace technology of the motherland, but also have a deeper understanding of the speed of circular and relative motion of objects, leading to the silent education effect in diversified teaching.

1.3 Improve the effectiveness of education to help students achieve success

In the ideological and political implementation, we always adhere to the "student-centered" principle and give full play to the main role of students in the setting of teaching content and the selection of ideological and political elements. (1) Both knowledge and teaching methods are included to serve the goal of talent training. (2) The ideological and political elements are properly integrated into the teaching process. Whereby, the course research is the "support", the course material is the "carrier", and the ideological and political implementation is the "method", to form a three-dimensional curriculum. (3) Think what students think, to produce the course ideological and political education process into a vector based on the characteristics of students' personalized growth, such that students are easy to accept, resulting in the improvement of their growth.

2 Mindset reconfiguration shapes students

In college physics teaching, the research and practice of teaching reform based on mindset-based education (MBE) are explored to consolidate students' basic knowledge and shape their physical thinking. In the process of knowledge teaching, the training of physical thinking mode is targeted, the modular teaching content is designed, the role of basic physics discipline is given, the science and technology literacy of students is cultivated, and the thinking reconstruction is shaped to educate students, respectively.

2.1 Highlight MBE physical teaching concept

The teaching concept based on mindset-based education (MBE) is explored centering on the curriculum goal of combining "knowledge imparts" and "value leads". We research physics teaching content optimization, teaching module reorganization and teaching evaluation. We pay attention to the physics connotation and thinking elements of courses in the education process, and try to build an education system combining "physics knowledge" and "physical mindset". Finally, we build physics teaching into a logical and mindset-oriented course.

2.2 Advancing knowledge modules to build mindset connections

With the characteristic of modularization of college physics knowledge, the teaching partition is reset, and the knowledge system is reconstructed according to the classification of different knowledge corresponding to different thinking modes, to promote students' knowledge learning and thinking ability. According to the content of physics knowledge, we help students to shape their thinking frame from the perspectives of mathematical quantification thinking, model-building thinking, induction and summary thinking, and special general thinking. For example, when teaching the concept of "velocity" in particle kinematics, the introduction from average velocity to instantaneous velocity requires an infinite reduction of time, which is related to the limit of mathematics and the derivation of differentiation. Therefore, "calculus" is taken as the main line to connect the physical phenomenon and essence, make the physical phenomenon mathematical and quantitative, and guide students in quantitative analysis. The use of calculus tools to achieve the understanding of physics knowledge.

2.3 Expanding teaching methods to promote the development of mindset

The cultivation and exercise of mindset can't only rely on one-way linear transmission, but must be combined the characteristics of knowledge chapters and students' learning mentality. Through cases, interaction, reversal and other methods, students can take the initiative to learn, establish connections and shape their thinking in the process of participation. We guide students to build a course knowledge tree, and fill contents in them after each part of knowledge. The students can break through "two veins" of physics learning, and classify the thinking methods contained in physics knowledge through horizontal and vertical integration. By combining knowledge with new methods and ideas, students can improve their learning initiative and timeliness.

3 Knowledge transfer to enlighten people

Basic knowledge of science and technology is taught in college physics, with the classroom as the main channel, teaching resources as the basis, and knowledge transfer as the way. Such that the foundation of science and technology knowledge and literacy of students are consolidated.

3.1 Optimize teaching resources to improve the relevance of professional programs

We optimize the teaching resources suitable for the personal development of different science and technology students. Updating the rigid textbooks into a dynamic and diversified system of "textbooks-Internet resources-discussion materials-papers" to encourage students to master the knowledge and stimulate creativity through independent thinking and data retrieval. For example, for students majoring in environment and chemistry, when teaching electromagnetic fields with a mass spectrometer, we introduce the application of such testing equipment in isotope testing and soil remediation testing, so that students can feel the practical use of learning.

3.2 Reforming the teaching model and advocating the integration of physics into the times

According to students' development needs, we set up videos of knowledge points that are integrated with current technology applications, and dynamic static course knowledge, insist on corresponding video points for difficult chapters taught in class to give students flexible materials for review in class. During the educational process, we promote students' understanding and application of knowledge through exercises and training, group discussions, microlearning resources, and student explanations. Quantum physics contents involve Compton scattering, photoelectric effect, etc., which are interesting knowledge points, so we assign the teaching task of the lecture to students. Students prepare in advance, then they teach and explain the knowledge points, background and physical scenes in groups, which not only increases students' mastery of knowledge, but also improves students' ability to sort course knowledge, prepare lecture PPTs and express themselves in the class.

3.3 Reinforce classroom teaching and focus on real-time feedback

As a basic course of science and engineering, college physics is still mainly taught in class. During the teaching process, we rely on internet platforms such as Rain Class and Super Star to interact with students, including 1. The storage and playback functions of courseware enable students to access the platform at any time; 2 Exercises in class after explanation of difficult knowledge points, and check the students' general results with feedback in real-time; 3 online testing after the end of a module to let students evaluate their learning effect; ④ Inter-evaluation of course papers can not only help students to learn with each other, but also check their learning Status. Which promotes the dynamic learning process, and improves the participation of students and knowledge mastery degree effectively.

4 Conclusion

College physics not only carries the task of learning basic knowledge for students majored in science and engineering, but also plays a deep role in educating them in the basic course of thinking and politics. It has irreplaceable significance in educating students in cultivating scientific knowledge, ideals and beliefs, cultivating national sentiment and strengthening scientific thinking. The course teaching is like a battle, which requires not only pre-battle preparation, but also battlefield struggle and post-battle summary. We should insist on the "student-centered" concept, teach knowledge to enlighten them with mindset, thinking and knowledge of the "trinity" education model. Therefore, we teach students with curriculum ideology and politics, physical mindset and useful knowledge. What's more, we want to create a course of education full of energy and enthusiasm, to achieve the effect of training students in silence. By creating a new form of college physics teaching, we could realize the key task of establishing moral education from knowledge transmission to value leadership.

This research is funded by the 2022 Teaching Reform Research Fund of Qingdao University of Science and Technology.

References

1. W. Y. Zhang, D. H. Xu, L. Duan, J. Zhang, Physics and Engineering, **31**, 6 (2021)(in Chinese)
2. Y. J. Chen, Z. X. Huang, X. Zhan, L. Zhang, Physics and Engineering, **32**, 3(2022) (in Chinese)
3. L. Z. Mu, Physics and Engineering, **32**, 2(2022) (in Chinese)
4. M. G. Qi, Physics and Engineering, **32**, 3(2022) (in Chinese)
5. X. X. Han, Y. Z. Zhu, C. H. Jiao, L. Ma, Physics and Engineering, **32**, 1(2022) (in Chinese)
6. W. Y. Zhang, D. H. Xu, L. Duan, J. Zhang, Physics and Engineering, **31**, 6(2021) (in Chinese)
7. H. Lv, X. Wang, G. H. Guo, L. H. Teng, P. Gao, Education Modernization, **8**(2021) (in Chinese)

Exploration and practice of aviation manufacturing talent training mode based on "practical ability-oriented and industry-education integration"

Zheng Hu[1], *Shiping* Sun[1,*], and *Lan* Cheng[2]

[1]School of Aeronautical Manufacturing Engineering, Nanchang Hangkong University, Nanchang 330063, China
[2]Office of Teaching Affairs, Nanchang Hangkong University, Nanchang 330063, China

Abstract. The aviation manufacturing industry is a key area for innovation-driven development. In order to adapt to the new requirements for aviation manufacturing talents put forward by the transformation and upgrading of the aviation industry, Nanchang Hangkong University and AVIC Hongdu Group continue to explore and practice the talent training channels urgently needed for tooling design positions. The university and enterprise jointly built an aviation manufacturing talent training model based on "practical ability-oriented and industry-education integration." The effective method formed from four aspects: the determination of talent training methods, the establishment of professional curriculum system, the innovation of teaching methods and the improvement of university-enterprise collaborative management mechanism. Thus, the win-win cooperation between the university and enterprise has been realized, and valuable experience has been accumulated for exploring a new aviation manufacturing talent training model.

1 Introduction

At present, under the guidance of the national policy, the integration between industry and education, as a very important work of the central and local governments and various industries, has become an important policy to promote the development of vocational education and higher education, and to strengthen the training of innovative talents and technical talents. Moreover, the integration between industry and education is an important institutional arrangement to promote the comprehensive reform of education [1]. Deepening the integration of industry and education has become the need of epoch development and social consensus [2]. In order to implement the important decision and deployment of the CPC Central Committee on "deepening the industry-education integration, school-enterprise cooperation," Jiangxi Province is taking the government as the leading force to build a high-quality integrated development platform for industry-university-research-use [3]. The construction of industry-education cooperation between aviation enterprises and

* Corresponding author: shipingsun@163.com

aviation universities aims to expand the aviation industry and strengthen aviation education, and support Jiangxi aviation's strategy of strengthening the province from the education chain, talent chain, and industrial chain.

Nanchang Hangkong University is the only aviation university in Jiangxi Province that undertakes the task of training aviation professionals, serving the aviation industry, and serving the economic development of Jiangxi. With the successful first flight of C919 in China, aviation manufacturing enterprises such as AVIC Hongdu Group have entered the stage of preparation and implementation of aircraft mass production. At this stage, a large number of advanced craft equipment and technology are put into use, and aviation enterprises urgently need aviation manufacturing talents who master advanced manufacturing technology [4-5]. In order to promote the rapid development of Jiangxi's aviation industry and serve the local economic and social development, Nanchang Hangkong University signed the "Cooperation Agreement on the Integration of Industry and Education Platform for Tooling Design" with AVIC Hongdu Group. As a major specialized in cultivating manufacturing talents in the aerospace field, the aircraft manufacturing engineering specialty [6] has actively cooperated with the Tooling Technology Center of Hongdu Group to establish an aviation manufacturing class that integrates industry and education. It aims to explore the cultivation of specialized talents for aviation tooling design and manufacturing posts, and realize the accurate supply of aviation manufacturing talents.

The aircraft manufacturing engineering specialty of Nanchang Aviation University is a brand specialty and characteristic specialty of colleges and universities in Jiangxi Province. More than 60 percent of the graduates of the major work in aviation enterprises. After nearly 20 years of development, the major has built a continuous engineering practice education system of practice, training, and practice by virtue of the university-enterprise cooperation practice education platform, which has improved the students' engineering ability. After nearly 20 years of development, the major has built an engineering practice education system integrating practice, training, and internship by virtue of the university-enterprise cooperation platform, which has improved the students' engineering ability. Nanchang Hangkong University and the tooling technology center of Hongdu Group jointly carry out the training of aviation manufacturing talents urgently needed for aviation tooling design positions. This move not only responds to the national policy requirements and implements the university-enterprise cooperation education strategy between the university and Hongdu Group, but also is an inevitable trend for the major to adapt to the development of the aviation industry, innovate the talent training mode, and enhance students' employment competitiveness. Based on the practice of integration of industry and education in the past three years, this paper discusses and summarizes from four aspects: the formulation of the talent training plan for the integration of industry and education in aviation classes, the construction of a professional curriculum system facing the needs of aviation tooling design, the development of practical teaching methods that adapt to the production environment, and the improvement of the management mechanism of university-enterprise cooperation education, which provides a reference for the school to further promote the industry-education integration and university-enterprise collaboration.

2 Formulation of talent training programs for the integration of industry and education

At present, a large number of advanced equipment and new processes integrating informatization, digitalization, and intelligent technology have been gradually put into aircraft manufacturing. The rapidly developing aviation industry urgently needs aviation manufacturing professionals. While the aviation manufacturing positions that integrate new technologies put forward new and higher requirements for professional competence [7]. Therefore, in order to cultivate professional talents that are compatible with the needs of the industry, it is necessary to embed the talent needs of the aviation industry into the talent training process, and universities and enterprises jointly formulate professional talent training goals for positions. Through the integration of industry and education, students' job competence can be enhanced and the social fit of talent training goals can be improved.

According to the cooperation agreement signed between the university and Hongdu Aviation Industry Group, the School of Aeronautical Manufacturing Engineering and the Tooling Technology Center of Hongdu Group established the "Teaching Steering Committee of Industry-Education Integration Aviation Manufacturing Class." Combined with the development of the aviation industry and the demand for aviation manufacturing talents of Hongdu Group, a training program revision seminar attended by professional teachers, technical supervisors, and aviation experts was convened. After investigation, the university and enterprise jointly compiled an undergraduate talent training program for the integration of industry and education aviation class. With the goal of being competent for the aviation tooling design and manufacturing job requirements, graduates are required to "have good engineering practice ability in aviation tooling design and modeling. Through various practical teaching training, students can apply the knowledge and skills they have learned, and the ability to analyze and solve practical problems in complex aircraft manufacturing engineering. Therefore, the goals and requirements of the training of aviation manufacturing talents integrating industry and education were determined.

Focusing on the talent training objectives and requirements, both the school and the enterprise will put competency, professional ethics and engineering practice ability through the whole process of talent training, and jointly design the professional curriculum configuration and experimental practice content. In addition, a professional curriculum system that meets the needs of aviation tooling design and manufacturing has been built to support the talent training goal of industry-education integration.

Combined with the advantages of university-enterprise collaborative education, the teaching operation mode of the industry-education integration aviation class has been formulated. The "2.5+1.5" training model of basic knowledge learning on campus in the first 2.5 years and professional practice learning in enterprises in the last 1.5 years is adopted. This mode can give full play to the advantages of theoretical teaching and enterprise practical training in the school, thereby strengthening the combination of theory and practice of students and greatly improving their engineering practice ability. At the same time, the training model ensures the natural connection of teaching links such as subject foundation, professional courses and professional practice from the time arrangement. In addition, this model is conducive to selecting students from the third grade for university-enterprise joint training.

3 Establishment of professional curriculum system for the integration of industry and education

The curriculum is the basic unit to support the goal of talent training. Only by combining the professional curriculum with the expected job requirements of the training goals, professionals with rapid post-competence can be cultivated [8]. Focusing on the training goal of "aviation tooling design and manufacturing" in the industry-education integration aviation class, a model oriented to the development of tooling design engineering capabilities for aircraft parts forming and assembly was developed. This model combines professional theoretical courses with technical post-ability requirements to increase the proportion of practical learning hours. In addition, this model strengthens the practical ability of computer-aided engineering, and builds a professional curriculum system that integrates industry and education from professional theory, design simulation, production practice and other links.

According to the two professional ability course groups of aircraft sheet metal and aircraft assembly, two professional course groups integrating sheet metal forming process and assembly digital application of manufacturing technology are set up. For examples: "Aircraft Sheet Metal Forming Principle," "Aircraft Parts Forming Process," "Aircraft Sheet Metal Tooling Design and Manufacturing," "Aircraft Parts Forming Simulation," "Aviation Tooling Production Skills Training," "Professional Course Design," "Professional Comprehensive Practice" to "Graduation Internship" and "Graduation Project." These courses range from theory, and practical training to comprehensive practice, thus building a curriculum system that supports the knowledge and ability of aircraft sheet metal tooling.

Based on the practical ability training of talents, each course makes full use of the production conditions of enterprises for theoretical and practical teaching. Set up experimental and practical learning hours according to the course objectives, and promote the parallel of theoretical learning and field practice, so that students can master knowledge and skills on time. For example, "Aircraft Parts Forming Simulation" allocates theoretical and practical hours according to 1:3, while "Aviation Process Equipment Production Skills Training" arranges production procedure learning and practical operation hours according to 3:1. This model can promote the cultivation of engineering practice ability. The proportion of practical hours in the industry-education integration curriculum system reached 28.2%, which provided a guarantee for achieving the goal of talent training with a solid foundation and strong practical ability.

4 Project/task-driven shaping of educational scenarios

The production tasks of Hongdu Group's tooling technology center include: tooling R&D design, analysis and improvement, trial production test and final production. These production tasks involve knowledge of the entire tooling design and manufacturing process. In addition, the technical center has rich tooling design, manufacturing and production resources, which provides a guarantee for practical teaching. However, the production tasks of the technical center are characterized by small batches and multiple types, and the main goal of the technicians is to complete the scientific research and production tasks. Therefore, in this kind of practical training that needs to complete production tasks, it is important for students to master complete professional theoretical knowledge and cultivate students' engineering practical ability. It involves how to form practical solutions to engineering problems in theoretical teaching, and comprehend the application of professional theories in production practice, which require teachers to design a teaching process carefully. Moreover, students have different professional knowledge points due to the different engineering tasks completed during the practice stage. Therefore, how to assess the professional courses decomposed into task practice and how to evaluate the acquisition of students' engineering practice ability, we need to establish a scientific and reasonable quality evaluation system to ensure the quality of teaching, so as to ensure the quality of education.

According to the division of production tasks of each department of the tooling technology center, a model with project/task as the main line is proposed. By sorting out professional theoretical knowledge and production practice content, the systematic professional theoretical knowledge is fragmented and modularized. And disperse the above content into the production practice tasks, and guide students in practice with professional knowledge. Professional knowledge is used to guide students in practice, and students apply professional theories in practice. Promote professional ability training with enterprise production tasks and strengthen problem-driven learning and practice. Therefore, this model can quickly cultivate students' engineering practice ability, thereby constructing a new teaching method and scenario for teacher teaching and student learning. Take a project/task completed by a student as an example, as shown in Fig. 1. The task was to design a tooling for the cutting edge of the aircraft skin. In the design scheme, the vacuum absorption method is selected to fix the aircraft skin, and high stiffness and lightweight curved platform is used to support and position the aircraft skin. The following tasks need to be completed according to the actual skin material properties, appearance characteristics and trimming process: overall design of tooling platform, vacuum adsorption scheme planning and calculation, connection method between platform and adsorption fixture, etc. The whole task process involves the content knowledge of many professional courses, such as "Aircraft Sheet Metal Forming Principle," "Aircraft Parts Forming Process," "Aircraft Sheet Metal Tooling Design and Manufacturing," "Aviation Manufacturing Technology and Application," "CATIA Modeling and Application," "Aircraft Assembly Simulation" and so on, which belong to the nature of professional course design. The traditional "professional course design" is carried out after the student has completed the professional course. However, the integration of industry and education is to use professional production tasks to guide and drive students to take the initiative to learn, learn while applying, and cultivate students' ability to solve complex engineering problems in the process of completing projects/tasks.

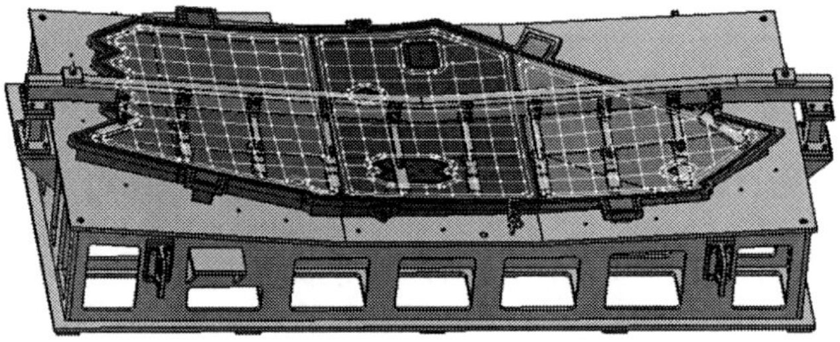

Fig. 1. A tooling for the cutting edge of the aircraft skin.

Combined with the diversity of students' practical tasks, the university and enterprise jointly formulated the following assessment methods: use the process performance of completing projects/tasks to assess students' professional quality; Assess the mastery of modular knowledge with the completion of projects/tasks; Fragmented expertise strung together with project/task summary reports; Use project/task reporting defense to test job competency. By shaping project/task-driven professional education scenarios, students can complete learning effectiveness checks and course assessments.

5 Formation of a standardized management mechanism for university-enterprise collaborative education

The industry-education integration and education and university-enterprise cooperation are order-based talent training models that adapt to social and economic development and solve the urgent needs of enterprise positions. By introducing enterprises into the supply side of talent training, we can use the enterprise's on-site practical teaching resources to cultivate professionals who meet the needs of enterprises. In this way, the pertinence and competitiveness of talent training can be improved, and the "supply and demand" coordination of talents can be achieved [9]. However, in the process of talent cultivation in the integration of industry and education, due to the great differences in the objects of concern and management mechanisms between universities and enterprises, the enthusiasm of universities and enterprises for educating students is different [10]. Therefore, in order to successfully realize the integration of industry and education in the cultivation of innovative talents, it is necessary to establish a set of talent training management mechanisms based on practical education consensus. Moreover, from the aspects of management institutions, teaching operation management, student and teacher management, teaching quality evaluation and guarantee, etc., to ensure the training quality of industry-education integration engineering application talents.

According to the strategic cooperation agreement signed between the Nanchang Hangkong University and AVIC Hongdu Group, the teaching steering committee of the industry-education integration aviation manufacturing class was established, including the chief teacher of the tooling technology center, the training director, the teaching dean of the college, and the professional leader. In addition, the charter document for the teaching management of the industry-education integration aviation manufacturing class has been formulated. The aircraft manufacturing engineering specialty has established a teaching management group headed by the department leader, which standardizes the management methods of student selection and class formation, curriculum teaching arrangement, and teaching quality assessment; The tooling technology center has set up a practical teaching group headed by the training leader and composed of the heads of various departments, which conducts practical content arrangement, leading teacher management and student practice site teaching management; The department leader and the training leader negotiate the process supervision and task adjustment of teaching. Focusing on the training goals of aviation manufacturing talents, the two sides clarified their respective management responsibilities and formed a standardized management mechanism for university-enterprise collaborative education, as shown in Fig.2.

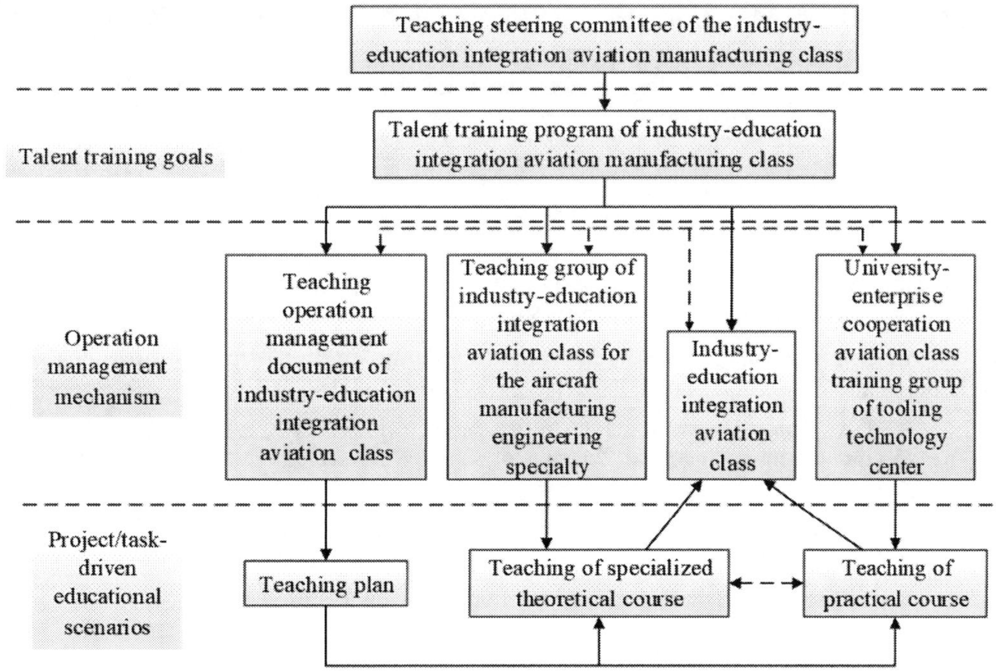

Fig. 2. Block diagram of the management mechanism of school-enterprise collaborative education.

6 Conclusions

Focusing on the new requirements for aviation manufacturing talents put forward by the transformation and upgrading of the aviation manufacturing industry, and taking the initiative to meet the urgent needs of AVIC Hongdu Group's manufacturing positions, we have carried out the exploration and practice of aviation tooling design and manufacturing talent training integrating industry and education with the tooling technology center of Hongdu Group. In addition, a set of methods has been formed that can be continued and promoted. The graduates of the two previous aviation classes integrating industry and education are all employed in aviation companies, which has improved the school's ability to serve national defense aviation and local economic construction, and highlighted the school's aviation characteristics.

This work was created under the support of the Research on Teaching Reform of Colleges and Universities in Jiangxi Province (Grant No. JXJG2286) and University-level teaching reform project in Nanchang Hangkong University (Grant No. JY21022)

References

1. The relevant responsible person of the National Development and Reform Commission answered a reporter's question on "Several Opinions on Deepening the Integration of Industry and Education". http://www.gov.cn/zhengce/2017-12/19/ content 5248610.htm
2. C.H Jiang. Deepening Industry-Education Integration: Theoretical Foundation, Practical Basis and Implementation Mechanism. Journal of Ningbo Polytechnic. **25**, 6-11 (2021)
3. The International Cooperation Conference on Industry-University-Research Utilization Helps Jiangxi's High-quality Development. http://ce.jxcn.cn/system/2019/06/14/ 017530850.shtml
4. L. P. Jiang. Hot Topic and the Latest Advances in Manufacturing Technology of C919. Aerospace manufacturing technology. **22**, 26-31 (2013)
5. Y. Q. Zhu, N. R. H. Ding, J. J. Wang. Aircraft manufacturing technology professional develop international research and analysis. Journal of Huzhou Vocational and Technological College. **3**, 12-14 (2016)
6. B. He, G. Liu, Z.Q. Liu. Research on the training mode of aerospace professionals in Europe and the United States. Theory Research. **30**, 145-146 (2015)
7. Y. Y. Du. Analysis on demand of aviation technical and skilled talents under background of made in china. Journal of Chengdu Aeronautic Polytechnic. **33**, 4-6 (2017)
8. C. Gui. Study on Five-in-one Business English Talents Cultivation Mode Based on College-enterprise Collaboration. Journal of Changchun University. **28**, 46-49 (2018)
9. J. Fang. Research on the mechanism of industry-education integration and school-enterprise cooperation in colleges and universities on promoting the employment of college students. Industrial Innovation.**16**, 183-184 (2020)
10. X. L. Li, W. H. Lu, X. Hao. The Mechanism Construction of University-Enterprise Cooperative Education. Journal of Shenyang Jianzhu University (Social Science).**19**, 205-209 (2017)

Design of MTI graduation examination syllabus and test paper

Shan Liu*

School of Foreign Languages, Wuhan Textile University, 430200 Wuhan, China

Keywords: MTI graduation test syllabus, Translation competence construct, Test design.

Abstract. At present, there is not any MTI graduation test system in China, although the enrollment of MTI students witnesses an increase. This paper presents MTI graduation written test construct and design of syllabus. It then elaborates on the test construct, modules, which is intended to clarify the purpose, significance and contents of MTI graduation test and shed new light on future large-scale test development and improvement of cultivation quality of MTI graduates.

1 Introduction

At present, there are 316 universities with MTI programs in China, cultivating and training advanced translation talents in China. However, there is no MTI graduation examination system in China. MTI graduation examination is a summative evaluation of MTI graduates' translation ability, measuring whether graduates achieve learning effect and evaluating their knowledge and skills, which is an evaluation of macro translation ability. In China, there are two kinds of summative evaluation methods for MTI graduate students: one is CATTI examination, and the other is MTI dissertation. However, CATTI mainly focuses on bilingual ability, but fails to comprehensively examine the subjects' translation ability, professional knowledge and instrumental ability. Also, there are some doubts about the form of MTI dissertations in China. Dissertations focus on theory, translation knowledge and language proficiency itself, and cannot comprehensively examine graduates' instrumental ability, strategic ability and psychological and physiological factors.[1] This paper puts forward the design scheme of MTI graduation examination syllabus, interprets and analyzes its structure and module, which is intended to clarify the purpose, significance and content of MTI graduation examination, and also provides valuable reference for future research and development of MTI examination and MTI teaching.

*Corresponding author: susanliu212@126.com

2 Construction of translation ability in MTI graduation examination

MTI students' translation ability includes "language proficiency (foreign language and mother tongue)" and "translation ability (interpretation or translation)", as well as relevant professional knowledge (politics, economy, culture, science and technology, etc.) required to develop and improve these two abilities (Ping Hong, 2019). [2]

By referring to the PACTE model [3], China English Proficiency Scale (CSE), Evaluation Index System of Translation Master's Degree Training Units, China Translation Competence Evaluation Grade Standard (2022 Edition),this study set the core elements of translation competence in MTI graduation examination, that is, the competence that can be evaluated through the examination, including eight sub-competences of communicative language competence, encyclopedic knowledge, translation professional knowledge, translation strategy competence, instrumental competence, professional competence, international communication competence and physiological and psychological factors. MTI graduates should fully understand the core elements of translation task situation.

3 Design of MTI graduation examination syllabus

The examination is designed by different classification and modules. According to the MTI Graduation Examination Index System, a general module shared by universities across the country is set up, corresponding to the first-level index. According to the specialty of MTI universities, we design several special modules such as law, medicine, economy and trade. Universities can also design their own modules with their own professional characteristics. Each module is divided into sub-modules, corresponding to the second and third levels of indicators.

Examination syllabus plays an important role in guiding the development of MTI graduation examination. The establishment of examination syllabus is the premise and foundation of the development and compilation of examination papers, and its examination content, nature and requirements will play a decision-making role in the development, implementation and verification of further tests. The formulation and publication of MTI graduation examination syllabus is one of the necessary factors to ensure the reliability of the examination. The exam syllabus helps test takers and other people related to the exam to understand the exam correctly and comprehensively (Li Xiaoju, 2001: 78) [4] . MTI graduation examination syllabus plays an important role in the design, development and implementation of MTI graduation examination. The examination syllabus stipulates that the measured index elements can help to realize the construct validity test of the test, and help to test the validity of the test in the test evaluation stage (Yan Ming, 2016: 252) [5]. The following part is a detailed description of the examination purpose, examination nature and scope, and examination paper composition in MTI graduation examination syllabus.

3.1 Purpose of examination

MTI graduation examination evaluates the learning results of MTI students, measures the acquisition of relevant abilities and knowledge, and judges whether the training objectives are achieved, which is a summative evaluation of translators' macro abilities. The purpose of this exam is to assess whether MTI graduates meet the graduation requirements stipulated in the Evaluation Index System of Translation Master's Degree Training Units-Graduate Requirements Index, examine whether graduates meet the teaching requirements stipulated by the National Teaching Committee of Master of Translation scientifically, fairly and effectively, test the teaching quality of Master of Translation, ensure the teaching effectiveness, promote the improvement of teaching quality, and accurately measure the translator's macro ability of graduates. The examination results provide reference for the evaluation of graduates' professional ability, the evaluation of MTI universities and the employment of language service enterprises.

3.2 Scope of examination

This examination belongs to the standard reference academic examination, which includes seven first-class indicators: communicative language ability, encyclopedic knowledge, translation professional knowledge, translation strategy ability, instrumental ability, professional ability and physiological and psychological factors. With reference to the Chinese Translation Competence Evaluation Grade Standard (2022 Edition), "international communication ability" is included in the examination scope.

3.3 Examination time and test takers

This exam is held once a year in the graduation semester of MTI students. The subjects of the examination are MTI graduates. The general module of this examination is organized by the National Master of Translation Professional Teaching Committee. The first-level index of encyclopedia knowledge is tested by universities according to their professional characteristics, which also design their own characteristic modules.Universities with similar characteristic modules, such as legal, medical, economic and trade can share the same characteristic modules.

3.4 Examination form

In order to effectively assess the macro-ability of MTI graduates with a view to the objectivity and feasibility of the examination, this examination includes written examination and computer operating examination so as to fully ensure the reliability and validity of the examination.

3.5 Modules of test paper

The examination adopts the design principle of classification and sub-module, and adopts the form of general module + characteristic module. According to the index system, a general module shared by colleges and universities all over the country is set up, which corresponds to seven indexes in the first-level index: communicative language ability, encyclopedic knowledge, translation knowledge, translation strategy ability, instrumental ability, professional ability and physiological and psychological factors. The general module includes seven parts: communicative language ability test, translation ability test, translation knowledge test (including translation knowledge + translation strategy ability), professional ability , instrumental ability, international communication ability and physiological and psychological factors. Ability level requirements refer to A-memorization, B-understanding, C-analysis, D-application, E-evaluation (Krathwohl, 2002: 2) . [6]

4 Test paper design

4.1 Communicative language ability

Communicative language ability refers to language comprehension ability and language expression ability of language learners and users when they use their own language knowledge, non-language knowledge and various strategies to participate in language activities on a certain topic in a specific situation (Fang Xiucai, 2021) [7]. In addition to the commonly used reading comprehension questions, this syllabus adopts abstract writing to comprehensively evaluate cross-language comprehension and expression ability. This type of question originates from real communication tasks. In real life situation, there are usually some reports and article whose main points need to be summarized, in which cross-language conversion is realized. The input text of this question is about 1500 Chinese words, and test takers need to write 300-word English abstract. The examination materials cover the fields of politics, economy, culture, society, science and technology, etc. The styles of reading materials include narration, explanation and discussion, and the genre includes news reports, journal articles and speeches. Cross-language abstract writing evaluates graduates' ability to understand Chinese and express in the target language, and examine their ability to analyze, synthesize and evaluate information across languages.

4.2 Translation ability

Translation Competence Test examines graduates' ability to perform code-switching effectively. The present translation test items are simple, comprehensive and subjective, and most of them adopt the form of text translation, and the scores are mostly overall impression scores, which inevitably affects the reliability and validity of translation competence test. MTI graduation examination should adopt subjective questions of translation test as far as possible, so as to effectively achieve the training goal of "advanced" senior talents of translation major. The forms of items are phrase translation, paragraph translation, translation modification and translation commentary. In order to ensure the authenticity and practicality of the topic, the translated texts mainly come from real translation projects in the language service industry.

4.3 Translation knowledge

Part of the translation knowledge questions mainly examine graduates' translation knowledge, including multiple-choice questions, blank-filling and matching. The content covers declarative knowledge related to translation profession, including translation theory knowledge, translation practice knowledge, professional ethics standards, basic behavioral norms, pre-translation, during-translation and post-translation behavioral norms, translators' social roles, etc. Matching test examines the test takers' ability to judge the translation skills used in the translation process, including addition, deletion, part-of-speech conversion, concretization, perspective conversion and so on.

4.4 Professional ability

Professional ability refers to the moral standards and behavioral norms that all learners and practitioners in the translation industry must abide by, including reasonable handling of the relationship between social and economic benefits, faithful interpretation, abiding by contracts, respecting and protecting the intellectual property rights of texts or discourse, keeping trade secrets, safeguarding the right to know, interpersonal communication skills and problem-solving skills of authors, customers, clients and readers, etc., most of which is declarative knowledge. We refer to NATTI exam in Australia, and adopt multiple-choice questions, blank-filling and question-and-answer to test graduates' relevant abilities.

4.5 Instrumental ability

Instrumental ability refers to graduates' ability to improve translation efficiency and quality by means of information technology, network platform, digital resources, computer-assisted translation, machine translation and other technical means. The assessment methods can be software-oriented and task-oriented. Objective questions can be used for software use, based on modular knowledge.

4.6 International communication ability

According to China Translation Competence Evaluation Standard (2022 Edition), international communication ability refers to the ability of cross-cultural information exchange and communication by integrating Chinese and foreign countries, telling Chinese stories and spreading Chinese voices. Graduates of Master of Translation should be able to publicize and explain Chinese ideas, Chinese wisdom and Chinese solutions in foreign languages. The items of this part include translation of terms with Chinese characteristics, translation of Chinese stories and texts, etc.

4.7 Physiological and psychological factors

Physiological and psychological factors, including cognitive factors, attitude factors and other ability factors, affect the whole process of translation and have a profound influence on translation ability. Richter scale is used to evaluate them.

4.8 Encyclopedia knowledge (Characteristic module)

Encyclopedia knowledge module is set by each university according to its own professional characteristics, which mainly examines the knowledge of a related discipline or a certain field and the knowledge of source language and target language culture.

5 Conclusion

The development and validity research of MTI graduation examination is of far-reaching significance to the development of MTI discipline, training talents to meet the needs of the industry, improving the teaching level of MTI, etc. It will better promote the development of China's high-level translation talent training system and provide measurement basis for the talent demand of language service industry.

Future research will focus on the research, development and promotion of MTI graduation examination assisted by modern educational technology. We will carry out small-scale pilot tests, collect validity evidence, and analyze the collected validity index evidence. We will further develop tutoring materials related to graduation examination, and give full play to the wash-back effect of graduation examination in the training of MTI students.

Supported by National MTI Education Research Project "A Study on MTI Graduation Examination Indicator System based on PACTE Model" (No.MTIJZW202018)

Reference

1. Han Shuqin.Integrated system of"teaching evaluation"for the cultivation of MTI translation ability--based on PACTE model.Shanghai Translation,**2**(2020)
2. Ping Hong.Strengthen quality awareness and promote the development of MTI education.Chinese Translation,**7**(2019)
3. PACTE.Results of the validation of the PACTE translation comparison model:Translation problems and translation comparison.In Alvstad,C.,Hild,A.&Tiselius E.(eds).*Methods and Strategies of Process Research:Integrated Approaches in Translation Studies*.Amsterdam:John Benjamins(2011)
4. Li Xiaoju. *The Art of Language Testing*. Changsha: Hunan Education Press(2001)
5. Yan Ming. Construction, Evaluation and Validity Verification of Business English Discourse Practical Ability. Harbin: Heilongjiang University Press(2016)
6. Krathwohl, David R.A revision of Bloom's taxonomy: An overview [J]. Theory into practice, **4**(2002)
7. Fang Xiucai. Test Framework of ESP competence under the background of new under the background of new Liberal Arts. Journal of Xian International Studies University, **2**(2021)

Exploring the gamification of cybersecurity education in higher education institutions: An analytical study

Hanyu Xiao [1], *Hao* Wei [1], *Qichen* Liao [2], *Qiongwei* Ye [1,*] *Changlin* Cao [3], and *Yawen* Zhong [3]

[1]Yunnan University of Finance and Economics, Kunming, China
[2]Beijing Foreign Studies University, Beijing, China
[3]Guangzhou Institute for Industrial Development in Greater Bay Area, Guangzhou, China

Keywords: Higher education institutions, Cybersecurity education, Cyberattacks, Gamification.

Abstract. Our world has become increasingly dependent on electronic technology. As most economic, cultural, and social activities are conducted in cyberspace, how to protect data from cyberattacks has arisen as a prominent challenge. Cybersecurity education and training that improves awareness among personnel is recognized as an effective approach. Higher education institutions (HEIs) have become prime cyberattack targets as they hold vast amounts of valuable research and personal data. This paper analyses the state of cybersecurity in HEIs and the problems of cybersecurity education, and proposes the solution of gamification of cybersecurity education. A detailed feasibility analysis and recommendations for developing cybersecurity education games are provided. This paper expands the theories of gamified cybersecurity education in China, and sheds light on enhancing the effectiveness of cybersecurity education in HEIs through games.

1 Current state of cybersecurity in HEIs

Currently, individuals, businesses, organisations, and government agencies conduct most of their economic, cultural, and social activities and interactions in cyberspace. How to protect data from cyberattacks has arisen as a challenging issue. In recent years, China has encountered an exponential increase in cyberattacks, with malicious actors changing up their techniques and exploiting system vulnerabilities, misconfigurations, the Internet of Things (IoT), cloud computing and other emerging technologies [1]. On June 22nd, 2022, the Northwestern Polytechnical University in China reported cyberattacks from foreign attackers. The investigation report showed that phishing emails and multiple types of cyber weapons were used during the attacks, including jump servers, proxy servers and backdoors. These attacks have brought the issue of cybersecurity at key universities in China to the

* Corresponding author: yeqiongwei@163.com

fore. The rapidly changing cybersecurity landscape requires organization departments at all levels to keep pace with new threats to defend against cyberattacks [2].

On June 1st, 2017, the Cybersecurity Law of the People's Republic of China came into force. Following that, a series of laws and regulations were promulgated, which helped establish important systems for protection of critical information infrastructure security, network security, security assessment of cloud computing services, and data security management. Over 300 national standards for cybersecurity have been adopted [3], which play a guiding role in identifying and assessing the risks that cyberattacks pose to different organizations and assets.

One important aspect to consider when developing cybersecurity policies is to improve cybersecurity awareness of the personnel involved. No matter how much money an Internet organization pours into building firewalls, intrusion detection systems, or encryption, as long as the attackers have someone on the inside, those efforts will be of no avail. This prioritizes cyber education of staff in organizations that face cyber threats, as even simple understanding of cybersecurity and knowledge of how to make safe decisions can help avoid or at least mitigate cybersecurity risks [4]. An effective way to increase cybersecurity awareness is through education and training. Current training programs may have provided a good starting point for cybersecurity capacity building, but they are far from sufficient.

2 Cybersecurity challenges in HEIs in the new era

Because cybersecurity often involves the defence industry, up to now, most cybersecurity education programs have been led by national government units or agencies responsible for defence contract management [5]. In the information age when the risk of cyber conflict between nations is rapidly increasing, national infrastructures, businesses, and institutions have fallen victim to cyberattacks [6]. Cybersecurity threats are not limited to data theft and service disruption, but they also pose a menace to world peace – cyber war was included in the 60 cybersecurity predictions for 2019 [7].

Academic institutions are prime cyberattack targets as they hold vast amounts of valuable research and personal data which attract cybercriminals. HEIs are confronted with serious cybersecurity challenges, notably a shortage of expertise, funding and resources. The rapid technological change brings new cyber risks, which warrant new resolutions [8]. HEIs need to improve cybersecurity competencies of students and the faculty to defend against cyberattacks. Through a comprehensive analysis of the current state of cybersecurity in HEIs, the following challenges are identified.

2.1 Lack of innovation

First and foremost, despite being in the age of fast technological iteration, cybersecurity education in HEIs still follows superficial learning of cyberattacks through traditional teaching methods, such as lectures, seminars, and lab sessions. Current approaches to cybersecurity education have not utilized comprehensive theories, standards, or methods, and they fail to envision innovative strategies using underlying learning theories [9].

Secondly, the cybersecurity textbooks and learning materials used in HEIs still focus on how to respond to common risks. They are outdated, failing to address the real threats brought about by Internet technology developments and updates in the field of cybersecurity. Instead of adapting to the new cybersecurity ecology and environment, they are in effect more likely to cause mismatch between cybersecurity education and reality.

Thirdly, the content, mechanism and method are not innovative enough. To be specific, the content is not practical enough and cybersecurity training and practice are largely absent. As for the mechanism, HEIs fail to establish a management system suitable for cybersecurity education in the mobile Internet era. As most HEIs don't have a special department for cybersecurity education and awareness, a unified organizing system is missing. Also, cybersecurity roles and responsibilities are not clearly defined and assigned [10]. Therefore, the practical cybersecurity education is in urgent need of a self-contained yet interesting teaching mechanism to encourage student engagement.

2.2 Lack of immersion

Firstly, HEIs appear to be unimaginative when it comes to cybersecurity education. The educational style is monotonous, emphasizing theory over practice. It puts students, the supposedly agents of their own learning, to a passive role, and fails to create a gamified learning environment to stimulate students' immersion. As a result, students lack the motivation to acquire knowledge of cybersecurity.

Secondly, studies have shown that games can be an effective tool not only for training but also for encouraging behaviour change [11]. With the development of virtual reality (VR) technology and digital games, immersion brings a virtual interactive environment that gives users a gaming experience. In contrast, there have been few encouraging developments of immersive learning experience in the education mode of HEIs, which impedes the effective and deep integration of educational games and classroom teaching.

Thirdly, college students are usually unaware of the importance of safeguarding national and university cybersecurity in the cyber world. They are used to the concept of knowledge acquisition, but not to the conscious participation in national and university cybersecurity practices. Therefore, there is an urgent need to propose innovative curricula and teaching methods in cybersecurity education. One of the rapidly growing areas in computer science education is "game-based learning". It encompasses VR games, network-based games, multi-user virtual environments, massively multiplayer online games, and simulations [12].

2.3 Lack of interaction

There is a lack of positive interaction mode in HEIs. In the educational mode of colleges and universities, educators are in the absolute, dominant position, and cybersecurity education follows a mechanical pattern of knowledge transfer that focuses solely on the teachers, without paying enough attention to the development needs of the students. The solidified identities of teachers and students further push the two groups apart, the most typical result being the lack of interaction among teachers, students, and between the two groups. When applied in cybersecurity education, this mode that lacks interaction will make students' learning stay only at the theoretical level, devoid of deep understanding or empathy for the cyber culture and cybersecurity education.

2.4 Lack of comprehensiveness

In general, the institution and mechanism of cybersecurity education in China's HEIs is gradually improving, and so is the overall cybersecurity awareness of students. However, given the exponential growth of cyberattacks, cybersecurity education in HEIs is not on track with the "prevention-oriented" principle and lacks comprehensive considerations. Although cybersecurity awareness has been included into the ideological and political education in HEIs, there are no full-time teachers to provide professional guidance to students. Meanwhile, the top-level design of cybersecurity education remains somewhat staid. There are no formal documents to guide the exploration of cybersecurity education games, which explains why HEIs are not willing to take the risk of innovating new approaches. In addition, HEIs are too dependent on teaching materials and overemphasize knowledge of cybersecurity. This has led to deary indoctrination, in which gamification, a new teaching aid that is able to provide a new learning experience where interaction and entertainment are combined and effectiveness enhanced, is completely disregarded.

3 Feasibility analysis of applying gamification to cybersecurity education

Games as a new medium can complement and guide computer-based cybersecurity education and training. They provide an interesting and enjoyable educational environment where participants learn theories and concepts of cybersecurity and put them into practice. In particular, participants learn how to exploit the vulnerabilities in a dynamic environment and respond to attacks by developing defences and countermeasures on the spot. This way of learning enables participants to learn and master cybersecurity concepts at a more rapid rate [4]. In 2016, Awojana and Chow proposed incorporating a game-based learning system into the field of cybersecurity. This medium, they argued, would be attractive to young people, and help build a method for learning the basics of information security, and create a form of passion within the faculty and students, who could have some fun while receiving the training to become the next generation of cybersecurity professionals [13].

Similarly, courses that create gamification effects through simulation and imagination in teaching are common in HEIs. For example, the accounting courses at Yunnan University of Finance and Economics in Kunming, China have introduced business role-playing games and ERP sand table simulation business training. The game has incorporated practical business knowledge throughout the mechanics and is very well received among students [17]. In the sand table game, players accumulate assets by simulating business and business-related life behaviours, and they are ranked at the end according to their final asset totals. The competition combines the knowledge from macro finance, economics and accounting, which makes learning comprehensive and interesting. From the game developer's perspective, cybersecurity education allows participants to compete by following a set of rules and making vague and intrinsically meaningful choices [18]. For example, different sectors can choose different defence strategies when facing cyberattacks, similarly, different attackers with different targets can choose different attacking strategies.

3.1 Game frameworks applicable to cybersecurity education innovation

Usually, the game analysis frameworks use the elemental tetrad that splits games into four elements – mechanics, aesthetics, story, and technology — all of which can be closely integrated with cybersecurity education [14]. The basic stakeholders of cybersecurity activities, namely the attacker and the defender, are binary opposites, between which a simple, goal-oriented competition or confrontation relationship can be established. The stakeholders can be multiple opposing parties with both offensive and defensive functions who carry out offensive and defensive exercises, which can be a microcosm of the current global cybersecurity outlook. More broadly, the stakeholders can involve participants from different sectors in a certain cybersecurity environment, their positions corresponding to different cybersecurity events, such that attacking and defending simulations can be conducted in that very cybersecurity environment.

Cybersecurity education creates an environment where the educators output content to one or more persons. It is suitable for the framework of multiplayer games such as board games, card games, turn-based board games, and etc. The difficulty and value settings can be adjusted according to the player's mastery of cybersecurity knowledge. It is also possible to create and design complex and difficult games featuring interaction and confrontation specifically for teachers and students of certain majors. In the game, the player can either write code to attack the system in the role of a hacker, or troubleshoot system vulnerabilities and manage risks as a cybersecurity administrator. For players who just want to have a smattering of cybersecurity, the game can be adjusted to a less challenging level and focus more on simulation and demonstration of narrative content. More complex game frameworks are capable of exploring cultural, moral, and philosophical themes through the cultural context of cybersecurity related content.

3.2 Student (player)-centred education

From the game developers' point of view, games must bring something to the player. This belief is consistent with the educators' faith of bringing knowledge to their students. The concept of student player-centred education game has two objectives: to design interesting cybersecurity games and to educate. Besides entertainment, this type of game can give participants a sense of gaining knowledge and accomplishment. The attitude of students towards knowledge is similar to that of gamers: some are willing to follow the rules and devote effort to learning; others ignore the rules and try to get the best result quickly by cheating; still others, who are not interested in the results at all, ignore the rules altogether. Developers and educators find a common goal here: to give students/players a good mindset, and to respect, rather than take advantage of them.

Generation Z students are tech-savvy at a very young age, and they have become used to short, efficient, and eye-catching media. Educators who follow the same routine will not be able to stop students from voting with their feet. Applying gamification and introducing eye-catching methods, such as creating conflicts, confrontations, and competitions give participants the chance to test their knowledge level. The autonomy in setting attack and defence targets and role-playing in cybersecurity-related scenarios are new experiences for students. They can promote students to gain joy and intrinsic motivation from competitions or creative contents, and encourage them to pay attention to the topic of cybersecurity while playing their roles. In particular, experiential learning and understanding of knowledge, including the background information of the defending and attacking sides of cyberattacks and threats, can only be obtained by letting participants restart, time and time again, new rounds or processes with different roles in the game.

3.3 Providing an immersive and interactive space for educational practices

Multiplayer games are interactions between players and content within the limits of game mechanics. In the embedded content of cybersecurity and under the set goal of positive education, the simulation of knowledge is transformed into the motivation of the players. Through the narrative adaptation of cybersecurity-related cases, the players' emotions are evoked: the desire to win is elevated to cybersecurity awareness, and they begin to vicariously think about the process according to the game mechanics. The immersive interaction allows players to achieve the goals set by the mechanics with the help of certain emotional feedback. The combination of immersion and interaction can evoke the internal drive for learning, transforming case studies into case experiences. To create a cybersecurity game, certain art designs need to be considered, including visual elements such as symbols, icons, characters, scenes, props, etc., which help enhance the vividness of the narrative and give a basis for the players' imagination. Gamification creates a virtual environment that provides participants (players) with an experience filled with emotionally charged story and various interaction ways, which yields an immersive learning experience.

In terms of single-player games, the players can create characters, participate in cybersecurity events, continuously earn cybersecurity-related achievements in the process, thereby understanding, learning, reinforcing, and applying the knowledge, and even developing new relevant strategies and discovering new vulnerabilities. After the game, educators can facilitate discussion among players by reviewing their attack or defence strategies, providing immediate feedback on the correctness and effectiveness of the strategies, thus facilitating the construction of cybersecurity-related knowledge.

3.4 Foreign research on cybersecurity education games

Over the past decade, countries around the world have been actively engaged in the research on gamification of local cybersecurity education content. In 2015, Gestwicki and Stumbaugh summarized over 20 educational games on cybersecurity, both digital and non-digital, across Europe and the U.S., and drew the conclusion that all the games had advantages and disadvantages – they either had too little professional knowledge or had too high skills thresholds – but pointed out that the drawbacks might as well be transformed into development opportunities for cybersecurity education games [15].

Microsoft was the first to release "Elevation of Privilege (EoP)" in 2014 [16], a card game that helped improve identification of threats using the STRIDE methodology, i.e., spoofing, tampering, repudiation, information disclosure, denial of service, and escalation of privilege [17]. Similar board games that focus on cybersecurity education are: "Play2Prepare" [18], "Cyber Security-Requirements Awareness Game"[19], "Decision & Disruption" [20], and etc. Games that are targeted at cybersecurity education in schools include: "[d0x3d!]", a board game that aims to teach cybersecurity basics to K-12 students who have no access to a computer science curriculum or STEM education [21]; "The Security Cards", a card game that supports different types of educational activities in academic environments [22].

Although there have been many cases of gamification of cybersecurity education abroad for our reference, most of them are not suitable for China's realities, ideologies, and values, and therefore lessons cannot be directly borrowed. For example, Haggman set the UK and Russia as mutually hostile countries between which cyber warfare happens [23]. Such a hostile ideology that creates an "imaginary enemy" runs counter to the purpose of education and is not in line with the value of "a global community of shared future".

4 Recommendations for developing cybersecurity education games suitable for HEIs in China

4.1 Prioritizing education-oriented game mechanics

It is proved that incorporating games into learning will improve learning outcomes, and the effect is most prominent in multiplayer games [24]. However, due to the negative impact of gaming addiction, the promotion of gamification has been highly controversial in China. As games for pedagogical use, their mechanics should be designed in such a way that they are more like "tools". The class hours of the course should be considered when deciding the settlement period of the game results. It is recommended that all rounds or tasks be completed within 2 class hours and that the route of serious games be followed. The ideological orientation should be properly guided to prevent excessive stimulation and to prevent the transformation of cybersecurity education of students into training of malicious actors. To better manage the class, the teachers may start with board game and card game, and expand to single-player game or online multi-player game.

4.2 Keeping up with the times and follow China's cybersecurity standards

Introducing national cybersecurity standards is an important way to achieve the educational goals of cybersecurity education games. Game scenarios should be designed to facilitate, simulate and recreate complex events in real life. This coincides with the suggestion of Awojana and Chow: "Also, an improvement on the existing game based learning system is recommended to include the added features on awareness, defensive and attacker strategies. For future research, we would recommend an introduction of naturality to further improve on the existing features on the Multiplayer Game category for maximum effectiveness" [24]. Therefore, the preferrable approach to enhance the authenticity of cybersecurity education games is to combine regulations and moral ethics in the real world [24].

In 2020, the National Information Security Standardization Technical Committee of China released 26 national standards, which provided whole-field regulation of and guide to information security. The provisions are highly valuable and can be used as direct references for games to set values, devise mechanics, and design cultural backgrounds. Only by incorporating the national cybersecurity standards, can the games initiate a dimensional collapse strike against the one-sided negative opinions on games, establish the meaning of games as teaching tools, and achieve the goal of entertaining for learning and learning for practice.

4.3 Assembling a comprehensive talent team for effective management

The content and form of gamification vary depending on the target audience of cybersecurity education. Therefore, a game design cannot be regarded as the one-size-fits-all solution to different educational situations. Gamified cybersecurity design should adhere to the five principles of environment dependence, target values, characteristic differences, scientific tasks, and group dynamics, set different environments and goals, combine different game elements, and transform complex tasks into comprehensible and engaging narrative content. The members of the game development team, as needed, should be from various disciplines, including cybersecurity, gamification design, pedagogy, psychology, graphic design, screenwriting, law, game programming, etc. Mechanics, play rules and narratives should be designed according to the target students' knowledge of cybersecurity and the level of learning they are required to achieve to promote effective learning. Since a game needs to go through numerous rounds of modifications and tests, a certain amount of research on the game process and participants' feedback is also warranted to facilitate the improvement of the game and enrich the theory of gamification education in China.

4.4 Incorporating cultural settings with Chinese characteristics to enhance influence

Drawing lessons from the existing cybersecurity education games made by foreign firms is beneficial to conducting independent research and production of gamified cybersecurity education tools in China. However, as different games are created on country-specific contexts, ideologies and social systems, we should avoid direct copying and plagiarism when learning from them. Our ultimate goal is to create cybersecurity education games suitable for Chinese college students. It naturally follows that stricter criteria and standards are set in terms of the original quality of game content and mechanics. The setting of the games should be embedded with culture featuring excellent Chinese characteristics, tell China's story, innovate Chinese game mechanics and technology, and pay more attention to improving the discourse system of Chinese culture. For example, organizations such as the Red Hackers' Alliance, Internet Security Base, and China Eagle Union have fought against hegemony by "hacking", protecting national security, upholding justice, and forming the Chinese "hacking culture". These are positive and high-quality themes for the design of cybersecurity education games, and are the support for strengthening the players' sense of justice and evoking the feeling of patriotism.

This work was supported by the Prominent Educator Program: Yunnan [2018]11, Kunming E-Business and Internet Finance R&D Center (KEIRDC[2020]).

References

1. Y. Li and Q. Liu, Energy Reports **7**, 8176-8186 (2021)
2. https://baijiahao.baidu.com/s?id=1743132415536145988&wfr=spider&for=pc (2022)
3. Editorial Board, China Cyberspace, **6** (2022)
4. E. Trickel, F. Disperati, E. Gustafso, F. Kalantari, M. Mabey, N. Tiwari, Y. Safaei, A. Doupé, G. Vigna, *2017 USENIX Workshop on Advances in Security Education (ASE 17)* (2017)
5. G. C. Kessler and J. Ramsay, Journal of Homeland Security Education, **2**, 35 (2013)
6. E. Johnson and N. Willey, IEEE Security and Privacy, **9**, 18-25 (2011)
7. Y. Kolli and A. Y. Javaid, *Proceedings of the International Conference on Frontiers in Education: Computer Science and Computer Engineering (FECS)* 23-29 (2019)
8. D. Miles, *2011Second Worldwide Cybersecurity Summit (WCS)* 1-3 (2011)
9. B. Martini and K. K. R. Choo, *Proceedings of Twenty Second European Conference on Information Systems* (2014).
10. Q. Liu, Y. He and S. H. Yang, Journal of Chongqing University (Social Science Edition), **5**, 218-226 (2018)
11. M. Salazar, J.Gaviria, C. Laorden, et al., *2013 IEEE Global Engineering Education Conference (EDUCON)* 602-607 (2013)
12. A. Kumar, S. Gupta, A. Rai and S. Sinha, International Journal of Scientific and Research Publications, **3**, 1-5 (2013)
13. J. L. Qin and H. L. Leng, Journal of Guangxi College of Education, **2**, 144-151 (2022)
14. J. G. Bond, *Introduction to Game Design, Prototyping, and Development* (Addison-Wesley Professional, 2017)
15. P. Gestwicki and K. Stumbaugh, *2015 Computer Games: AI, Animation, Mobile, Multimedia, Educational and Serious Games (CGAMES)* 131-137 (2015)
16. A. Shostack, *Summit on Gaming, Games, and Gamification in Security Education* (2014)
17. B. Potter, Network Security, **1**, 15–18 (2009)
18. I. Graffer, M. Bartnes and K. Bernsmed, Norsk Informasjonssikkerhetskonferanse (NISK), 58-69 (2015)
19. A. Yasin, L. Liu, T. Li, R. Fatima, J. Wang, IET Software, **13**,159–169 (2019)
20. S. Frey, A. Rashid, P. Anthonysamy, M. Pinto-Albuquerque, S.A. Naqvi, IEEE Trans. Software Eng, **45**, 521–536 (2019)
21. M. Gondree, Z.N. Peterson, *CSET* (2013)
22. http://securitycards.cs.washington.edu/

23. A. Haggman, *Cyber wargaming: Finding, designing, and playing wargames for cyber security education* (2019).
24. T. Awojana and T. S. Chou, *2019 Conference for Industry and Education Collaboration. American Society for Engineering Education* (2019)

Courses reform of mould courses based on field augmented reality facing engineering education certification

Hui Zhang*, *Yao* Chen, *Weiming* Che, *Zhen* Guan, *Xiaoyang* Zhu, and *Chengshun* Zhu

School of Mechanical Engineering, Jiangsu University of Science and Technology, 212100 Zhenjiang, China

Abstract. Mould courses are crucial components of the mechanical manufacturing course system, and their innovation and reform can inspire new approaches to college education reform, as for the engineering education certification process. The augmented reality mould disassembly and assembly teaching scheme that is proposed in this paper can help students master the structure and processing of complicated moulds, and thus make comprehensive use of the relating learning knowledge and skills. By understanding of the typical structural design and assembly of moulds, students can learn actively by interaction of the three teaching strands of instruction, case study, and assessment. This will raise the level of instruction throughout the courses as well as student participation and interest. The proposed AR auxiliary system is a new approach to essentially foster students' capacity for independent learning, knowledge understanding, and innovation and production in the age of digital learning and engineering education certification.

1 Introduction

The Washington Agreement, known as the international pact for reciprocal recognition of engineering education, provides the inspection criterion for engineering education and serves as the internationally recognized quality assurance system. With China's entry into the agreement in 2016, new standards for the calibre of China's higher education were also established. This effectively promoted the fusion of domestic engineering education with global standards.

In our domestic schools and universities, there are currently no effective and systematic plans to provide a sequence of courses leading to professional engineering certification or mechanical manufacturing and automation majors. The standard PPT teaching method combined with the chalkboard method makes it tough to arouse students' interest and is ineffective for encouraging them to take initiative and improve their mobility. One of the areas of curriculum teaching reform study is how to convey the curriculum content in a more vivid manner.

* Corresponding author: zimmerman@just.edu.cn

This study focuses on mould-related courses, such as mould design, and proposes an assisted teaching technique based on field augmented reality projection for disassembly and assembly, and offers suggestions for teaching reforming and building.

2 The existing problems in mould teaching

Mould course feature rich knowledge points, high background curriculum system requirements, and high practical operability since they are crucial courses in mechanical specialization [1]. Mould assembly practice can help students in schools and universities develop their practical skills as well as their analytical and problem-solving abilities, enabling them to use newly acquired information skills and abilities to finish the design and installation of standard mould structures [2]. The following flaws are identified in the current mould design course operation and current traditional mould design teaching practices:

(1) The teaching approach is somewhat traditional. The teaching strategies are rather dated. There aren't many case studies and evaluation points sprinkled throughout the classroom, practice, and assessment in the standard teaching practice, which combines multimedia course ware instruction with mould disassembly and assembly practice teaching. Additionally, because of the small experimental class size, students were unable to become comfortable with the mould assembly fast. This had an impact on the teaching outcomes and made it difficult to help students develop their practical skills and creative design thinking.

(2) There is little usage of new information technology in the mould teaching classroom. 3D and 2D modelling software [3] is used in other mechanical courses. And there is no relationship between the disassembly experiment and the general curricular design, making it challenging to pigue student's interest in something comparable. Because modern information technology is not integrated into the courses, the traditional teaching approach cannot accurately reflect the background features of the mould courses.

(3) There is a broad instructional gap for teaching and practicing. The connection between teaching and experiment is not strong enough, students cannot use the knowledge they have gained in a flexible manner, and the teaching effect cannot satisfy the teaching requirements since there are many set procedures in classroom teaching.

Due to the typical teaching approach, pupils lack conceptual understanding and possibilities for application of the course material [4]. The problem of the mismatch between theoretical knowledge and practical application and the students' failure to properly comprehend professional knowledge and practical application of knowledge are both caused by the constrained experimental class hours.

3 Researches on reforming of mould courses

Due to the significance of mould courses, numerous schools and universities have established mould design, mould design and manufacturing, or mould CAM courses [5]. Some institutions have even established specialized mould majors. In response to the necessity for educational reform, many educators or scholars have also proposed their own approaches or ways for the mould design course's teaching mould change.

(1) From the standpoint of professional engineering certification [6], it is essential to adhere to the paradigm and standards of the Sydney Agreement, to carry out professional construction for international certification, to implement result-oriented education, and to develop results-oriented curriculum systems. It is also necessary to carry out the full process, comprehensively evaluated professional courses in a scientific and reasonable

manner, and to enhance the professional connotation. The referenced indicator should be process-oriented, student-centred, and results-driven.

(2) From the perspective of project teaching [7], the importance of project teaching approach in vocational education is clarified, and the project teaching evaluation standard is presented from the course setting. By emphasizing the manufacturing, assembly, debugging, maintenance, and other skills, the effective and practical training and teaching techniques are investigated to grow the first-line skill talents in the mould industry. The steps of 'task', 'plan', 'implementation', 'check', and 'evaluation' for teaching is adopted.

(3) The teaching should be carried out by using online and offline mixed classroom teaching [8], to increase the depth and breadth of instruction and to improve students' understanding of the fundamental structure and components of stamping dies. These methods are combined with mould module of NX. Alternatively, a set of process methods spanning the mould design process also exist on the CATIA or other modelling software. This type of strategy is sophisticated and information-based.

(4) New techniques for teaching classes on mould using augmented or virtual reality are proposed [9,10]. Many are based on the interactive design of computer web pages or mobile phone applications. The knowledge material is simulated, and instructions are carried out in the simulated environment, in a virtual learning environment. Some are created using the Unity 3D virtual reality platform, and they apply the human-computer interaction education method to create simulation training systems that can expose the system's structure, function, and important technology.

These teaching strategies and ideas serve as a fantastic resource for our mould course's upcoming teaching redesign. An essential thinking difficulty in the reform of mould design teaching is how to enable students to create the knowledge system of mould design in a shorter teaching period due to the restricted amount of time allotted for the course.

4 The application of case teaching method assisted by field augmented reality projection

An information projection assisted mould disassembly and assembly teaching platform was created with the use of self-made experimental equipment projection to address the drawbacks of conventional mould teaching. In Figure 1, the framework of the system is displayed. The framework is built after an analysis of the characteristics of the experiments for mould based on augmented reality. The actual assembly site and virtual assembly information are integrated.

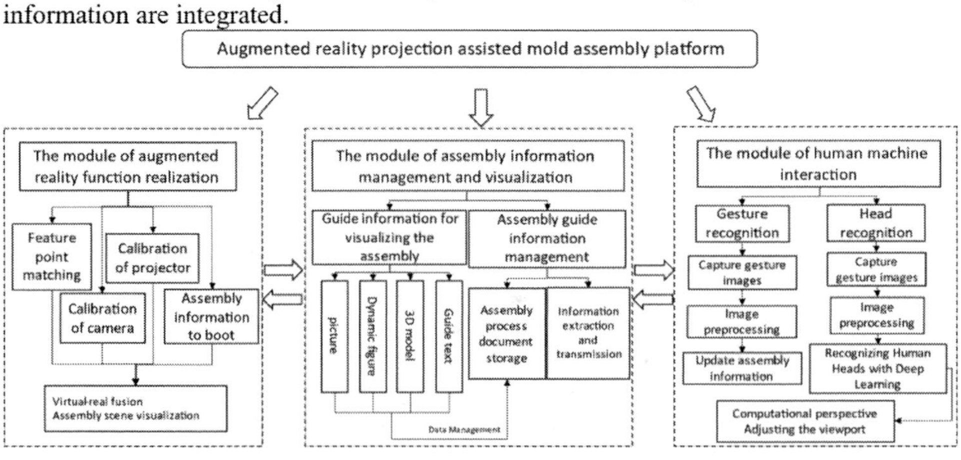

Fig. 1. Framework of augmented reality assisted assembly system.

The following are the specific function modules. It primarily consists of the human-computer interactive module, the assembly information management and visualization module.

The picture acquisition and processing, joint calibration of the camera projector, recognition and matching of image features are all included in the realization module. The real-time positioning of 3D models in actual assembly scenes are established and serves as the foundation for the projection of supplemented guiding data onto the assembly site. All types of guidance information can be precisely projected onto the specific position of the site. The display position of the 3D model can be updated with the movement of the assembly parts.

Data support for the visual components is provided by the assembly information management and visualization module. The mould components are organized into blocks, with a list of details about the procedure by XML files. In order to optimize the description of complicated information and clearly convey the assembly phases, the platform is enhanced by 3D model, voice, assembly animation, and image combination.

The platform can interact more easily thanks to the human-computer interface module. The update of on-site assembly information and the rationalization of the observation model perspective are realized with the implementation of gesture recognition and head recognition services. The software interface for the auxiliary assembly platform is shown in Figure 2. The part structure tree is shown on the left side of the diagram, and the assembly text description is shown on the right. The assembly phase information including animation and model would be projected onto the desktop when the students choose the mould setting phase. The projector will display text, image, animation, and 3D content.

After the on-site posture registration, the 3D model is projected to the corresponding position of the workbench. The location image of the field operator is gathered during the 3D presentation in order to update the model display angle using head recognition. To make it easier for pupils to acquire assembly attention information during process, the guidance voice is played simultaneously in each disassembly/assembly step. In Figure 3, the assembly example is displayed.

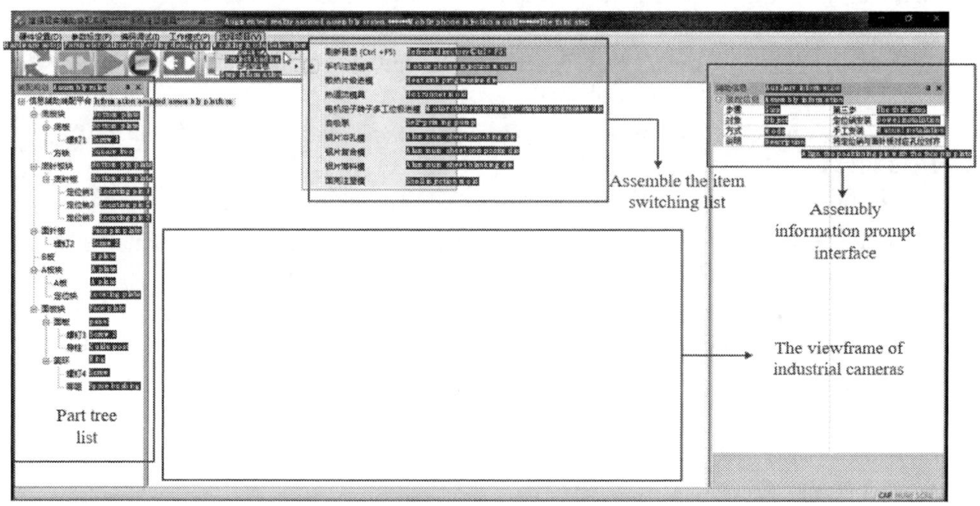

Fig. 2. Software interface diagram of auxiliary assembly platform.

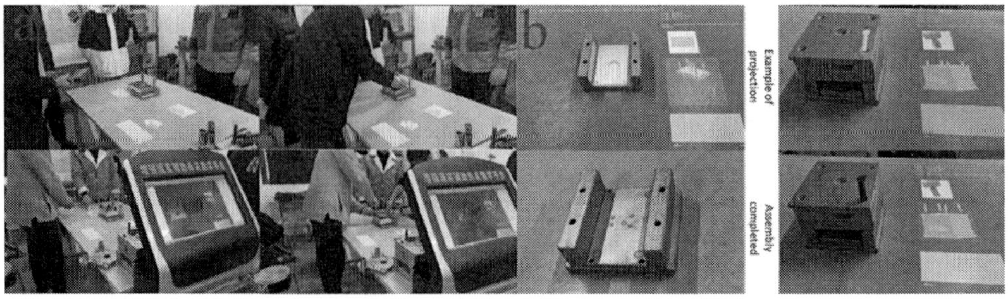

Fig. 3. Examples of experimental course operations (a) Examples of student field operations (b) Example of projection guided assembly.

5 Conclusion

The direction of future development is toward the fusion of information technology and curricular instruction. New forms of interaction include virtual reality and augmented reality. This paper evaluates the inadequacies of conventional mould education and actively investigates curriculum reforming strategies based on the study of various mould teaching techniques and ideas. The mould design course was taught using an augmented reality example that produced specific results with a benchmark value. At the same time, emerging technologies like augmented reality are in a constant state of development. Additionally, we'll keep enhancing the quality and delivery of mould courses.

This work was supported by the Self-Made Experiment Project of Jiangsu University of Science and Technology180813102004.

References

1. Gerdenitsch C., Sackl A., Hold P. International Journal of Industrial Ergonomics. J. 92,(2022)
2. Eswaran M., G. A. Kumar, I. A. Kumar, R. Bahubalendruni M.V.A. Expert Systems With Applications. J. (to be published)
3. HU B.F., WANG X. R., WANG X. F., Journal of Machine Design. J. 39(01):159-163,(2018).
4. Yang Y. L. Education and Teaching Forum. J. (13):155-158,(2021)
5. K. Pritam, B. Rajesh. International Journal of Virtual and Personal Learning Environments. J. (IJVPLE), 12(1),(2021)
6. Jie D., Yong W., H. Yang. Abstracts of the 7th International Conference of Pioneering Computer Scientists,Engineers and Educators(ICPCSEE 2021)Part I. C. (2021)
7. Huang K. T., Ball C., Francis J., Ratan R., Boumis J., & Fordham, Cyberpsychology, Behavior, and Social Networking. J. 22(2), 105-110. (2019).
8. K. Guo,L. L. Liu,S. B. Yuan,M. C. Yang,S. Z. Liu,T. Xu,F. Wu. International Workshop of Advanced Manufacturing and Automation. C. (2020)
9. Kaur D. P., Mantri A., & Horan B., IETE Journal of Research. J.67(2):155-164. (2021)
10. Tsai C. Y., Liu T. Y., Lu Y. H., & Nisar H. Multimedia Tools and Applications.J. 79(43), 31981-32009. (2020)

Exploration of teaching reform of network security experiment course under the background of emerging engineering education

Xiaoming Ye[1,2,*], *Zhibo* Du[1,2], and *Gang* Gan[1,2]

[1]Chengdu University of Information Technology, School of Cybersecurity, 610225, Chengdu, China
[2]Advanced Cryptography and System Security Key Laboratory of Sichuan Province, 610225, Chengdu, China

Abstract. Given the practical needs of network security professionals against the background of emerging engineering and guided by principles of cultivating stronger innovation ability and frontier problem-solving ability, this paper, a case study of a network security experiment course, proposes to build an open training platform with multidisciplinary cooperation and multi-party participation in order to provide solutions to existing problems. It attempts to enhance school-enterprise cooperation and jointly determine the complex engineering problems of network security. Following the pattern of the post-role competency, typical engineering problems, and hierarchical experimental projects, this paper explores the teaching reform of a network security experiment course by realizing individualized and differentiated evaluation of the course's teaching effectiveness.

1 Introduction

It is crucial to develop high-quality, compound emerging engineering talents in the new environment and circumstances who are in line with the development of national strategic emerging technologies, who can handle the demands of building new infrastructure and developing interdisciplinary collaborative innovations, and who possess both cutting-edge theoretical knowledge and comprehensive application ability[1][2].There is an urgent need for the assistance of diverse and excellent engineering and technology specialists during this crucial time of new scientific and technological revolution and industrial change, particularly since China's new economy is developing quickly[3].

Students majoring in network security are required to meet new standards based on the evolving engineering background[4]. Electronic information technology, the digital economy, and network security all require a lot of technical abilities to develop[5]. As a result, this paper investigates and establishes a teaching reform model of student immersive participation, scientific research innovation challenge, and whole-process project progression, followed by thorough application in the network security experiment course, based on the practical needs of network security professionals in the context of emerging

* Corresponding author: yexm@cuit.edu.cn

engineering and guided by the goal of cultivating stronger innovation ability and frontier problem-solving ability.

2 Analysis the teaching of experiment course

The network security experiment course aims to enable students of information security majors to apply knowledge from multiple courses to solve practical network security problems after taking elementary theoretical courses in computer network, operating system, program design, cryptography, information security architecture, and OSI network protocol analysis. It is a course that thoroughly combines theory and practice in the information security major's training program and curriculum structure.

This course covers the full process of security data collection, data preparation, data analysis, and solution creation, which includes numerous abstract ideas, models, and algorithms [6]. As a core engineering practice course for junior students majoring in information security, it plays an important transitional role. On the one hand, it focuses on developing students' abilities to solve difficult engineering issues based on basic theoretical knowledge. On the other hand, it lays the foundation for a comprehensive practice course and graduation design that come in the fourth year [7] [8]. Consequently, the current network security experiment course must be improved in the following three ways.

1) Cross-integration of teaching contents and the construction of an engineering scenario experiential teaching and students' independent participation

Emerging engineering focuses on developing the ability to address complex engineering challenges. However, in the real world of teaching, teachers lack practical expertise in project technology development and operation management. Because of this, only a small part of the engineering scenario can be found in the open modules of the enterprises, and the majority of the projects are out of date and lack critical technical modules [9]. As a result, teachers have difficulty keeping up with the times in terms of project design and updating, as well as accurately understanding and grasping the new characteristics of complicated engineering challenges, causing them to lose touch with reality.

2) Experiential teaching and students' independent participation

At the moment, teachers continue to use traditional classroom teaching methods rather than student-centered research-based teaching approaches [10]. There are several issues: the classroom environment is dull and boring; the teaching effect is polarized; a small number of active students can fully understand the network security framework through independent learning; most students only aim to pass course exams; and they complete experiments solely on the basis of experimental instruction without taking the initiative to think critically and creatively.

3) Objective and diversified teaching evaluation and overall feedback of students' ability

Curriculum assessment continues to rely on conventional evaluation methods. There is no professional method for evaluating the effectiveness of educational courses. Particularly lacking in teaching effectiveness evaluation is a breakdown of the students' ability index into its component parts [11].

3 Exploration of teaching reform

As for network security experiment course reform in the context of emerging engineering, efforts should focus on optimizing and improving teaching contents and methodologies, as well as completing process assessment methods.

3.1 Design of course teaching contents

We can address difficult network security engineering problems by collaborating with schools and businesses. First, it should conform to the development of cutting-edge technology, consider talent demands for the development of strategic emerging industries, and emphasize that graduates can effectively meet the requirements for the development of emerging industries in terms of both theoretical knowledge and engineering skills. As a result, reform should focus on professional curriculum systems to build an open training platform with multidisciplinary collaboration and joint participation as well as encourage school-enterprise collaboration to jointly determine the complicated engineering problems of network security.

The course's top-level design should emphasize practical network security engineering scenarios, incorporate the post-role and competency model, and create hierarchical elementary, intermediate, and advanced-level engineering challenges by setting professional scenarios by varying levels. In addition, the experiment must be paired with corresponding fundamental training units, comprehensive analysis projects, challenging research projects, and competitions in order to form the project chain course mode of fundamental experiment mainline, node-based innovation experiment, and project-based innovation experiment. Using the function of an information security management engineer as an example to design the course content, as illustrated in Figure 1.

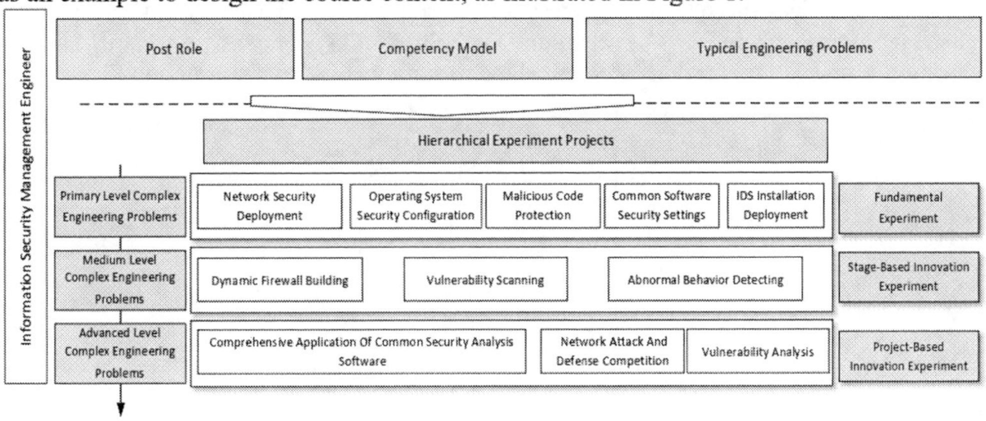

Fig. 1. A case of network security experiment design.

In the network security experiment course, teachers construct a library of innovative projects. Cooperative businesses and frontline educators determine the innovation content of complex network security engineering problems jointly. The project environment should progress from simple to complex. Projects must have a clear sequential association, along with stated research objectives and technical evaluation indicators. The source of the project is closely related to the enterprise innovation practice. Project practice can be directly applied to scientific research or competitions, such as the Challenge Cup, the national college student information security challenge, and the college student computing competition, among others.

3.2 Course teaching reform

Implement the above-mentioned designed teaching content and further optimize teaching methods. This paper proposes combining the content of experiments, applying simulation technology, and developing an online simulation experiment platform to manage students' practice processes dynamically [12-13].

1) Teachers employ cloud desktop technology to manage experimental equipment resources in a centralized manner, allowing students to complete the experiment procedure independently.

2) To effectively accomplish the flipped classroom effect, teachers track and record students' experimental data. Meanwhile, during the experiment, teachers and students can communicate in real time.

3) The simulation experiment platform based on the B/S framework allows students to perform experiments while professors dynamically monitor the process, breaking the constraint of time and space for teaching and learning.

4) To increase the teaching effect of the network security experiment course, each group of students can record and share videos of their experiment findings with their peers. Students have been tremendously motivated to participate in online classes as a result of such contact. Several groups have created videos to share with the class. Students can truly become devoted and thrilled about pursuing solutions in this manner. It has played a vital role in education and has boosted students' information absorption rates.

3.3 Improvement of teaching assessment

Regarding course evaluation, we have highlighted student-centered evaluation methods that are also in line with the teaching process and lesson plans. Additionally, a professional course teaching effectiveness evaluation method should concentrate on the three-dimensional views of profession, accomplishment, and practice, as illustrated in Figure 2.

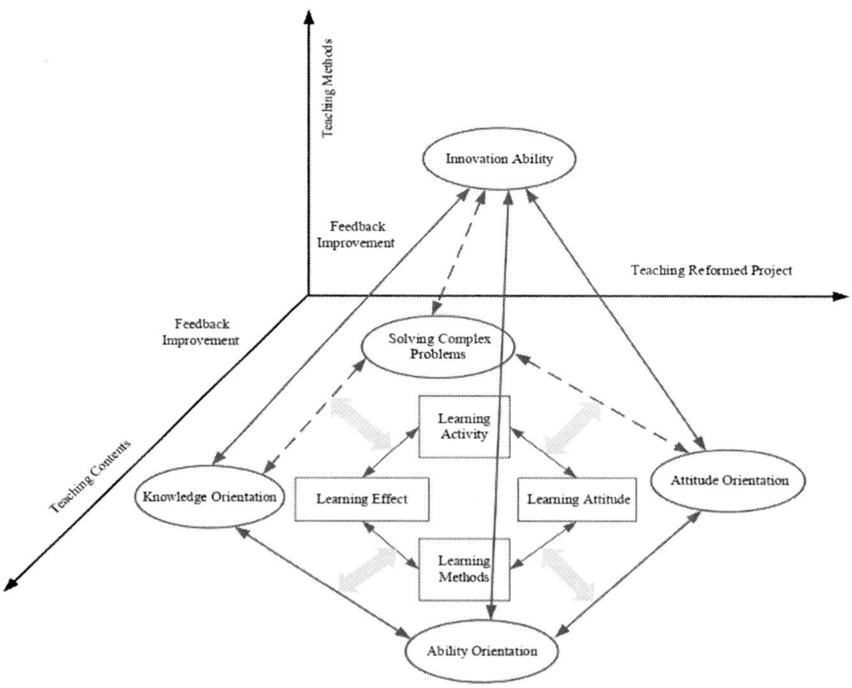

Fig. 2. Teaching effectiveness evaluation system.

The course teaching effectiveness evaluation method can operate in the two modes listed below. On the one hand, it emphasizes the improvement of students' professional quality and professional skills through course teaching and achieves the effect of feedback and improvement closed loops during the teaching and learning process so as to enhance the quality of course teaching; on the other hand, teachers can conduct horizontal and vertical comparative analyses of project completion indexes of the same grade in different years to improve course teaching content, experiment design, and assessment methods.

4 Conclusion

This study, which is grounded in emerging engineering and makes reference to the network security business and other associated emerging industries, focuses on three key issues: teaching content, teaching methodology, and teaching assessment. This study examines the teaching reform of the integration of emerging engineering thinking and network security experiment course, keeping students at the center and guided by the principle of developing greater innovation capacity and frontier problem-solving ability.

Following the pattern of the post-role, competency, typical engineering problems, and hierarchical experimental projects, this paper designs and expands the open training platform with multidisciplinary cooperation and multi-party participation while focusing on the professional curriculum system. It also attempts to improve school-enterprise cooperation so that they can jointly determine the complex engineering problems of network security. This paper aims to enhance students' ability in fundamental theory, engineering practice, and innovative application at the same time so that they can gradually adapt to the constant development and changes of network security technology in the future by continuously improving the teaching content, experiment projects, and teaching methods of the network security experiment course.

This work is supported by Teaching Research and Reform Project of Chengdu University of Information Technology (No. JYJG2022126, JYJG2023083), College Students' Innovative Entrepreneurial Training Plan Program of Chengdu University of Information Technology (No. 20201062125, 202110621224, 202110621225), the Sichuan Philosophy and Social Sciences (No. SC21B034), and the Sichuan Science and Technology Program (No. 23ZDYF0380).

References

1. M. Ye, L. Sun and J. Shen, EEIT, 62-65 (2022)
2. H. Yan, H. Ao and Z. Chen, EEIT, 54-57 (2022)
3. H. Zhang and F. Zhang, GCRAIT, 381-383 (2022)
4. Z. Ting, AEECA, 1104-1108 (2022)
5. P. Xia, IWCMC, 199-203 (2020)
6. W.P. Chen, Y.X. Lin, Z.Y. Ren, D. Shen, Comput. Appl. Eng. Educ, 114-129 (2021)
7. M. Luo, Z.Cheng, J. Shen, HSMET, 336-341 (2019)
8. X. Yang, CSIA, 928, 1432-1436 (2019)
9. D.Y. Baskakova, O.Y. Belash, S.O. Shaposhnikov, T and QM and IS, 783-787 (2021)
10. L. Xu, S. Fang, L. Hobbs, Int. J. Sci. Math. Educ, 667-689 (2023)
11. M. Tian, G. Lu, L.Li, H. Yin, Front. Psychol. 12, 2139 (2021)
12. Y. Wang, H. Li, ITMS,34, 891-893 (2015)
13. J. Zhang, ICMSOA ,2173, 12013-12015 (2022)

Application of data analysis in product selection of cross-border e-commerce

Aling Luo*, *Lanruoyun* Long, and *Yue* Wang

School of Information Management and Business Administration, Neusoft University, Chengdu, China

Abstract. In order to better understand the relationship between data analysis and cross-border selection, and apply the practical application skills of cross-border selection better. The author sorted out several commonly used analysis tools, analysis the steps and the methods of cross-border e-commerce. This paper mainly introduces the role of cross-border e-commerce product selection and the application of data analysis in cross-border e-commerce product selection. At the same time, this paper also analyzed three techniques of data analysis in cross-border e-commerce product selection. Cross-border selection is the basis of cross-border e-commerce operation. In the process of scientific selection, it is necessary to judge the potential of products through data analysis. Correct selection can not only save time, the most important is to improve the efficiency and effect of product operation.

There is still a saying circulating in the cross-border e-commerce industry: seventy percent depend on the selection of products, thirty percent depend on operation.

1 The important role and significance of cross-border e-commerce product selection

For a successful cross-border e-commerce seller, the choice of products is very important. Because products are related to storage and shipping costs, search engine optimization and marketing strategies, pricing strategies and potential profits. Therefore, the product determines the whole business development of a cross-border e-commerce seller. Overall, the role of cross-border e-commerce products selection is mainly manifested in the following aspects:

(1) Cross-border e-commerce product selection can reduce the trouble caused by infringement. Consider the infringement problem in advance when selecting products on Amazon, which can avoid the account being closed due to infringement after the products are put on the shelves.

(2) Good cross-border e-commerce product selection is conducive to store operation. To operate an Amazon store well, it is necessary to have a certain grasp of the market situation and development, which is essential in the selection of products. The better the sales

* Corresponding author: luoaling@nsu.edu.cn

volume, the better the product operation will be, the higher the ranking will be, the more traffic will be brought, and a virtuous cycle will be formed, which is definitely beneficial to the operation.

(3) Product selection analysis improves the scientific rationality of marketing activities of cross-border e-commerce enterprises. Product selection analysis collects and collates relevant marketing data, and then makes relevant marketing management decisions. It improves the scientific rationality of marketing activities of cross-border enterprises, makes marketing activities carried out accurately, and points out the direction for the development of cross-border e-commerce.

(4) Products selected by cross-border e-commerce can deeply match audience needs and product experience. Good products can serve the needs of specific consumer groups, and can deeply explore the real needs of people;

(5) Good product selection is conducive to improving after-sales service efficiency. For example, in the early stage of product selection, focusing on customer experience and paying special attention to product quality, customer satisfaction and retention rate will be relatively high in the later stage, thus reducing the return rate of cross-border e-commerce and improving the efficiency of after-sales service.

2 Application of data analysis in product selection of cross-border e-commerce

Every country has its own traditional culture, and everyone has their own lifestyle and consumption habits. How to select products that meet the needs of different buyers is the most fundamental purpose of data analysis in the application of cross-border e-commerce product selection.

2.1 Market selection

Market selection, starting from the website category data, through filtering and comparing all kinds of multidimensional data, to determine the product track. Market data analysis is the analysis of market capacity, market price, market trend, market concentration and other relevant data. Through comprehensive analysis, a large number of scattered market information is formed as a whole, which can judge the supply and demand situation of certain commodities in the market and provide reference for the development of the market in the later period.[1]

Market capacity analysis is helpful in formulating sales and operational plans and objectives. Industry trend analysis can understand the life cycle state of the industry. Market potential analysis can understand the future development space of the industry.

In the selection, market capacity is a very important indicator. If a product has no market capacity, it will lose the foundation to build. Google Keywords and Google Trends can be used to judge the market trend and market capacity of this product, so as to understand the stage of this product and make better judgments.

2.2 Product selection

Product selection is based on the data of the product itself, through the analysis of the operating data of the existing products on the platform, copy on the shelf.

2.3 Keyword selection

Through keyword information insight into the real needs of buyers, and then to find products to meet the needs.

3 Skills of data analysis in product selection of cross-border e-commerce

There are a variety of techniques for cross-border e-commerce selection, but not all of them are suitable. Sellers can try different selection techniques first, and through trial and error, then find their own selection techniques. Here are some common selection techniques:

3.1 Analysis of negative rating data

Poor review data analysis means to find out customer dissatisfaction mainly by grasping the poor review data of hot selling goods on the platform, and then carry out product improvement or select the supplier's products that can solve customers' pain points. The analysis of bad evaluation data focuses on capturing bad evaluation data, and also pays attention to the analysis of good evaluation data of goods, and analyzes the real demand points and expectations of customers. In other words, bad review data analysis not only finds references from good reviews of products, but also mines useful information from bad reviews. Choose products that can meet customers' pain points, products will naturally get considerable exposure, and sales can start quickly. However, it is not easy to obtain these data. It takes a lot of time to collect and spend a lot of time on data analysis.[2]

When doing data analysis, we can use various data research tools, such as Terapeak, Trendsamazon, Digital Chief, etc., or we can entrust data analysts to do analysis with data mining tools.

3.2 Selection combination analysis

Selection combination analysis method means to select products through the thinking of product combination. That is to say, when the sellers of newly opened stores establish product lines, it is suggested that the stores set up three product combinations: core model, popular model and normal product.

Table 1. Product Portfolio Analysis.

Product type	**Core product**	**Explosive product**	**Normal product**
Combination ratio	20%	10%	70%
Product characteristics	High quality, niche, high price, high profit, low sales	Hot commodity, low cost, low price, low profit, high conversion rate, high sales	Cost-effective, moderate price/ profi/sales
Product action	Represent the product image and characteristics, used to enhance the brand image	Store drainage	Regular sales
Corresponding commodity	The Best product in the store	Clearance style, old style, popular new style	Products normally sold

Planning 20% of core products to achieve high profit; Planning 10% of explosive products to obtain traffic; Plan 70% normal products to coordinate sales. Products should be selected according to the needs of different target customers, not all the products in the same price segment and the same quality, a certain price and quality ladder can produce more orders.

3.3 Google trend analysis method

Google trend analysis method refers to the use of Google's data analysis tools to analyze the external industry information and internal business information, and dig out valuable information as a reference for product selection.

Through these search data, we can check the popularity and search trend of a certain keyword within a certain time range, so as to understand our market, audience information and future marketing direction and other relevant information. Google Trends Analysis analyzes the cyclical characteristics of categories by Google Trends tool, finds the search popularity and keywords of categories by Keyword Spy tool, obtains the sales information of products on the shelf by Google Analytics tool, analyzes which products are selling well, and the overall sales rate.

Google Trend analysis should look at the overall data and changing trend of the industry, the sales situation of various brands in the industry, the sales and distribution of categories, the sales data and price of a single product, as well as the sales data (traffic, conversion rate, bounce rate, customer price, etc.) of at least 3 core stores and major competitors in the industry. In addition, Google Trends emphasizes gaining experience from both successful and unsuccessful products and gradually becoming an expert in product selection.

Type in a search term or topic on the search page and hit Enter to get the Google Trends Index for that term from 2004 to date. The number of accurate searches divided by the average number of searches at a given time ranges from 0 to 100, with higher numbers being hotter). You can also set comparison items for him, up to five keywords at a time.

The keyword research function can play the following roles: to understand the performance of keywords in different countries, different cities and different times; Understand key words, the main market of the product; Understand the topics related to the keywords to further understand the characteristics of the audience; Compare the performance of different keywords in the same country and at the same time; Use specific searches for more insight.

3.4 Seller Sprite analysis

Seller Sprite is an Amazon seller tool SAAS software, based on big data and artificial intelligence technology, to help Amazon sellers discover the blue Ocean market, create potential products, etc.

The Seller Sprite is a data interface for querying Google trends in real time. It supports both web and shopping modes, supports historical trends in the last 5 years, and can be used in China without climbing the wall.

The Seller Sprite features 3 modules and 16 tools. You can choose products, optimize keywords, research the market and analyze competitive products. It achieves one-click acquisition of detailed product data, one-click generation of 16+ dimension market analysis report and one-click mining of all relevant keywords of the target market. One click download product reviews, QA, main image and other functions.

4 Conclusion

Reasonable analysis tools, steps and methods can help us choose products better. Proper selection can not only save time, but most importantly, reduce detours in the operation of cross-border e-commerce enterprises and improve the operation efficiency and effect of products. Therefore, we must do a good job of data analysis before cross-border operation.

Project source 1: General project of Sichuan Private Education Association, "Research on the Reform and Construction of Applied Curriculum in Private colleges and Universities: Taking Cross-border E-commerce as an example", Sichuan Civil Education Association [2022] No.4, project number: MBXH22YB40;
Project source 2: General project of Sichuan Education Development Research Center, "Research on Applied Curriculum Reform of Private Colleges based on OBE Education Concept and Blended Teaching Mode", Sichuan Education Development Research Center [2021] No.65, project number: CJF21065

References

1. Zhichao Deng. Analysis Strategy of Cross-border E-commerce platform Selection based on Big Data. Special Zone Economy, **6**, 135-137(2009).
2. Liuhong Jiang. Thoughts and Skills of selecting Products in cross-border E-commerce export trade. Shopping Mall Modernization, **6**, 58-59(2019).
3. Hao Liu, Zhijian Mai. The application of big data analysis technology in cross-border e-commerce. Digital Economy, **1**, 191-192 (2021).

Multimodal discourse analysis of the external publicity documentary four seasons of China

Jiaxin Lv*
Beijing International Studies University, Beijing, China

Abstract. As one of the effective forms of cultural exchange between China and foreign countries and the shaping of national image abroad, the external publicity function of documentaries has been increasing. The paper argues that the mutually reinforcing relationship between the images and text modes in the documentary objectively conveys to foreign audiences that China upholds the ecological concept of caring for nature and advocating the harmonious coexistence between man and nature. Meanwhile, the paper finds that the image of a big country has been established, including the image of respecting nature, adapting to nature, and protecting nature in the Four Seasons of China. The implications of this study are relevant for proposing an MDA framework for external publicity documentaries from the cultural, context, content, and expression levels, to explore the multimodal strategy of external publicity documentaries to help China project a good national image internationally.

1 Introduction

Since the 18th Party Congress, President Xi has emphasized the need to enhance the creativity, appeal and credibility of foreign discourse, to tell the Chinese story and spread the Chinese voice in a way that overseas readers can readily accept and in a language that is easy to understand. At the same time, the development of globalization and digitalization has brought many new opportunities and challenges to the external publicity of China's national image. Film historian Richard Bassam argues that documentaries serve a dual political and social purpose, eliciting an emotional response and social effect by conveying a message (Bassam, 2013). At the same time, as a mixed product under the interaction of multiple modalities, documentary is an ideal research object for multimodal discourse analysis.

Existing multimodal research focuses on following topics, including multimodal critical discourse analysis (Tian Hailong, Pan Yanyan 2018), multimodal aesthetic discourse analysis (Dong Mei, Yuan Xiaolu 2021), multimodal metonymy and image meaning construction (Feng Dezheng, Zhao Xiufeng 2017), multimodal stylistic research (Yan Yun et al. 2021), multimodal translation research (Wu Jianguo et al. 2021; Ji Wenkai 2021). However, in the process of image establishment and external communication, there is a lack of practical operation on how to externalize the "shallow meaning" of each mode in the

* Corresponding author: Dearlvsuper@163.com

external publicity documentary, to achieve the purpose of disseminating culture and establishing good national image level-specific recommendations.

Therefore, this paper constructs a multimodal analysis framework for external publicity documentaries by applying the system function grammar of Halliday, the visual grammar of Kress & van Leeuwen, and a comprehensive framework for MDA of Zhang Delu. It aims to explore how the external documentary completes meaning integration through the two symbols of images, texts, and the cooperation between these two symbols. The documentary *Four Seasons China* shaped the national image of China following the ecological concept of "respecting nature", "adapting to nature" and "protecting nature". In this way, this paper inspires the production of external publicity documentaries that project China's good national image, and disseminate Chinese culture globally in the future.

2 The analytical framework of four seasons China

2.1 System functional grammar

Halliday (2014) proposed three meta-functions of language, namely conceptual function, interpersonal function and textual function. The concept function can explain the experience of the world and establish the logical semantic relationship between clauses, which is composed of transitivity and phonetic system. Interpersonal function focuses on embodying complex social relationships, which reflects that in a social context, language can not only be used to explain experience and reality, but also express the speaker's attitude, maintain interpersonal relationships, and influence the recipient's response and behavior. The three meta-functions of the above languages can be used to analyze the relationship of textual modalities.

2.2 Visual grammar

Kress & van Leeuwen carried out further research on functional grammar, extending it to visual patterns. At the same time, by analogy to the meta-function of language and drawing on the relevant theories of film studies, Kress & van Leeuwen proposed a visual grammar analysis framework. This grammar includes the reproduction meaning, the interaction meaning, and the compositional meaning of the images. In representational meaning, Kress & van Leeuwen differentiated images into two categories, narrative and conceptual. According to the presence or absence of projections of image participants, actions and reactions and mental and verbal processes are distinguished, where no projections exist for the first two processes. In the meaning of interaction, the main concern is the subtle and specific relationship between the audience and the image participants, which can be reflected in three aspects: (eye) contact, distance, and perspective. (Li Zhanzi, 2003).

2.3 Comprehensive framework for MDA

Zhang Delu (2009: 27-28) proposed a multimodal comprehensive theoretical framework, which distinguished the relationship between the language text mode and the image mode, that is, the complementary relationship and the non-complementary relationship. Complementarity means that a mode cannot fully express its meaning, and needs to be supplemented by other modes to ensure the integrity of meaning. This is a typical multimodal discourse pattern, which can be further divided into reinforcing relationship and non-reinforcing relationship. Therefore, using the multimodal discourse analysis framework can better analyze the interactive relationship between language modality and image modality and the effect achieved.

3 Research design

3.1 Research objects

The research object in this study is the CNC documentary *Four Seasons of China*, which was broadcast on the CNC overseas platform and YouTube on February 4, 2019. The documentary is divided into 24 episodes. This paper selects the four episodes of the documentary *the Beginning of Spring*, *Rainwater*, *the Waking of Insects*, and *the Spring Equinox*, which are the most played on YouTube, as the research objects. Once the program was aired, it was well received by audiences in Israel, the United Kingdom and other countries. At the same time, Tang Guoqiang, a Chinese diplomat in Norway, also praised the program. It can be seen that the broadcast of this program is a successful case of "Chinese culture going global".

3.2 Research questions

The following questions are answered in this paper: 1) How does the image mode in *Four Seasons of China* construct China's ecological image of "respecting nature", "adapting to nature" and "protecting nature"? 2) How does the text mode in *Four Seasons of China* *c*onstruct the ecological image of "respecting nature", "adapting to nature" and "protecting nature"? 3) How do image and text modes interact to construct the ecological image of "respecting nature", "adapting to nature" and "protecting nature" in this documentary?

3.3 External publicity MDA framework:

To answer the three questions in 3.2, a multimodal analysis framework for external publicity documentaries is proposed in this paper to analyze how image and text modes conduct an ecological image of China and the complementary relationship among image and text modes in the documentary.

4 Results

4.1 Image mode

4.1.1 Representationa meaning

In the sense of representational meaning, Kress & van Leeuwen (2006) believed that it can represent the construction of the experience of the external world, and distinguished two types of narrative process and conceptual process of images according to the characteristics of images with or without vectors.

Symbolic processes represent what the participants are or mean (Kress & van Leeuwen, 2006). In image 1 of the documentary, both the vector and the symbolic ecliptic theodolite and astrosphere appear. Image 1 shows the scene when the host observes the instrument around the astronomical instrument. The host's gaze (vector) is set on the celestial instruments (target), which is an action process. Through the action process in the narrative concept, the documentary shows the awe, love, and exploration of nature in today's China. Therefore, these various astronomical instruments and the working principles behind them reflect the important idea that respecting nature is always important in Chinese ecological concepts.

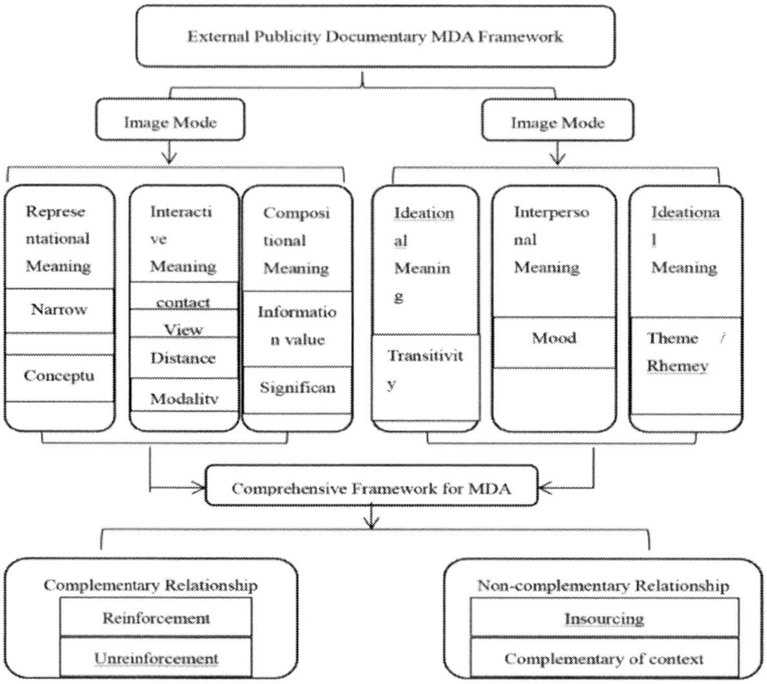

Fig. 1. External publicity documentary MDA framework.

The process of conceptual meaning in the representation of meaning proposed by Kress & van Leeuwen (2006) just corresponds to the descriptive relationship and existential relationship in functional grammar. The analytical process involves a "part and whole" relationship (Kress & van Leeuwen 2006). There are two kinds of actors involved in this process: the carrier (the whole) and the owned property (the part). Image 2 reflects the analysis process of conceptual meaning, which belongs to the non-structural analysis process. It demonstrates to the audience the overall construction and layout of the Dujiangyan Water Conservancy Project, to make sure the audience understands the names of the various parts of the Dujiangyan Water Conservancy Project and their specific locations. In this way, the audience can understand the great water conservancy project in ancient China. At the same time, through the construction principle of Dujiangyan, the audience can understand the ecological philosophy of "adapting to nature" runs through the blood of Chinese culture.

Image 1

Image 2

4.1.2 Interactive meaning

Kress & van Leeuwen (2006) proposed three methods to examine the interactive meaning in images, namely contact, social distance and perspective. The first is "contact", which contains two images of "offering one" and "requesting one". In the "requesting" images, the participant's eyes usually look at the viewer, which means that the participant asks the audience for attention and approval, and invites the audience to participate.

Image 3 was taken from Rainwater and belongs to the "requesting" image. In the image, the old woman looks at the audience with a smile on her face It seems that she wants to convey the joy of starting farming to the audience through the screen so that the audience can also feel her joy. By requesting similar images, the audience can easily feel the emotions that the documentary wants to convey, achieve emotional communication with the audience through images, and establish the image of a country that respects nature in the minds of the audience.

Another concept in visual grammar is perspective, also called attitude, which is divided into horizontal perspective and vertical perspective (Kress & van Leeuwen 2006). Image 4 applies the process of shooting from a top-down perspective, giving the viewer a certain symbolic authority, surpassing the participants themselves, and making the image display more objective. This process is an action process, reflecting that people's daily life operates by the laws of nature. So it makes the foreign audience understand the importance of the philosophy of adapting nature to people's daily lives.

Image 3

Image 4

4.1.3 Compositional meaning

Compositional meaning examines how representational and interactive meanings function as a whole, a way of representing the relationship between documentary participants and viewers. Applying significance is to attract the audience's attention, including the use of colour, relative size, perspective, and foregrounding or background. In this documentary, the images are always highlighted with colour, foregrounding, and size. For example, in image 5, a lovely giant panda slowly walks toward the audience from a green bamboo forest, reflecting the fact that endangered species such as the giant panda have been largely removed from the danger of extinction under Chinese protection measures. These images make the audience an impression that China is a country that has made good achievements in environmental protection, thus building up the image of a great nation that protects the environment.

4.2 Text mode

The main manifestation of the text mode of the documentary is the subtitles appearing on the screen. According to the three meta-functions of language proposed by Halliday, namely, ideational function, interpersonal function, and textual function. This paper will analyze text mode in the *Four Seasons of China* by applying this theory. The examples are as follows:

Image 5

Water has always been a crucial resources for the Chinese people. This is why the Rain Water solar term holds such an important place in Chinese culture.

Man and nature were one and the same.

The brilliance of Dujiangyan is that it takes full advantage of the local terrain.

The fields are showing a little green and peasants who follow the solar terms have begun their hard work.

Precious medicinal herbs are often hidden in the deepest forest.

4.2.1 Ideational function

Halliday believes that the function of language concepts is mainly expressed by the transitivity of sentences (Halliday, 1994). Transitivity is a semantic system that expresses the function of concepts, "it is to divide what people see, hear and do in the real world into several kinds of 'processes', as well as the 'participants' and 'environmental components' related to various processes.'"(Hu Zhuanglin, Zhu Yongsheng, Zhang Delu, 2009). The relational process expresses the relationship between the objects, and the sign of the judgmental relational process is the existence that contains "is".

The main clauses of example 1 and 2 contain copulas "been", "is" and "were", which are typical sentences representing relational processes. Among them, the first sentence of example 1 and example 2 belong to the modified type, while the second sentence of example 1 belongs to the identification type. In example 2 shows that for the Chinese nation whose main mode of production in agriculture, rainwater is like a gift from nature. In example 3, the painter's description of the connotation behind the creation of Chinese ink painting, that is, "the integration of man and nature." It can be seen that Chinese people have always advocated the concept of harmonious coexistence between man and nature.

Table 1. Relational process analysis form.

Water	has always been	A crucial resources for the Chinese people.
Carrier	**Process: containing**	**Attribute: characteristic**
This	is	Why the Rain Water solar term holds such an important place in Chinese culture.
Identified	**Process: containing**	**Identifier**

4.2.2 Interpersonal function

The interpersonal function of language involves the speaker's attitude, intention, and judgment, and is mainly realized through tone. There are three basic types of tone in interpersonal functions: declarative sentences, imperative sentences, and interrogative sentences (Halliday, 2014). And according to Halliday's definition of the nature of declarative sentences in his framework as "giving of information" rather than "giving of goods or services", "question of information" and "order of goods and services" (Halliday & Matthiessen 2014, Hu Zhuanglin et al. 2017). Whereas the main purpose of a declarative sentence is to provide information. It found that this documentary tends to use declarative sentences, for example, the above five sentences are all declarative sentences. There are large differences in Chinese and Western cultures, so the use of declarative sentences helps to clearly explain some difficult cultural concepts to foreign audiences, helping them understand and eliminate the difficult problem of viewing movies due to lack of cultural background knowledge. And the expression of declarative sentences makes the content expression more objective and real, so that the audience can feel the authenticity of the content, so that they are more willing to accept the good ecological concept conveyed in the film, and establish a good national image of China in the minds of the audience.

4.2.3 Textual function

Textual function is mainly realized through topic structure and information structure, emphasizing the organization of discourse. This paper takes example 3, example 4 and example 5 as examples, and mainly discusses the topic structure including theme and rheme. As shown in the table below:

Table 2. Textual function analysis form.

Theme	Rheme
The brilliance of Dujiangyan	Is that it takes full advantage of the local terrain.
The fields/ peasants	Are showing a little green/ have begun their hard work
Precious medicinal herbs	Are often hidden in the deepest forest.

Through the above table analysis, it is found that these examples employ objects as themes instead of people to emphasize the philosophy of adapting to the nature of Chinese people. This way of expression highlights the guiding role of natural objects in human activities and shows that people arrange their daily production and living activities by natural laws. Following the laws of nature will help human beings create a better life, and it is a clever way for human beings to resolve various problems in nature. Thus, the audience acquires and establishes the image of China as a country that respects the philosophy of adapting to nature through the text mode in the documentary.

4.3 Comprehensive framework for MDA

Zhang Delu (2009:26) proposed that the two kinds of relationships between various modalities are complementary relationship and non-complementary relationship. The main function of the documentary text mode is to present specific information that cannot be expressed through the image mode. The subtitle commentary in this documentary assumes the main function of the image mode, expressing the meaning of the content in the most direct way. And Image mode in image 3 introduces the overall picture of the Dujiangyan Water Conservancy Project and the names of each part, with the text mode "Waijiang is used for flood discharge". The complementary relationship is manifested between image mode and text mode, where the image mode serves to strengthen the text mode. In the image 4, the text mode "The fields are showing a little green and peasants who follow the solar terms have begun their hard work." is the main mode to make the audience understand the importance of the philosophy of adapting to nature in Chinese people's daily life, while the image mode "farmers are spreading medicine among the fields" strengthens the idea. Therefore, the relationship between image and text mode is a strengthened relationship among complementary relationships, which is conducive to establishing good China's image in the audience's mind.

5 Conclusion

Combining systemic functional grammar, visual grammar theory, and Zhang Delu's comprehensive framework of multimodal discourse analysis, this paper, from the aspects of culture, context, content, and expression, conducts multimodal discourse analysis on the CNC documentary *Four Seasons of China*. The meaning construction of the international communication image of "respecting nature", "adapting to nature" and "protecting nature" is conveyed by China's twenty-four solar terms and its related customs and customs, and its multimodal discourse. The research found that through close-ups of the characters and shooting from a bird's-eye view, the harmonious composition, color matching, and harmonious complementarity of images and texts in the documentary together, the documentary completed the construction of the tone of the discourse, presenting the objectivity and truth of China's cities and villages featured by characteristics of traditional customs to foreign audiences. At the same time, in the documentary *Four Seasons of China*, the relationship between the image mode and the text mode is presented as a complementary relationship. The coordination of each mode shows a national image of "respecting nature", "adapting to nature" and "protecting nature" in which history and modernity are combined, scientific and technological progress is inclusive and open, man and nature are in harmony, and diversity coexists.

References

1. M.A.K.Halliday, & C.M.I.M.Matthiessen, Construing Experience Through Meaning: A Language Based Approach to Cognition. London: Cassell, (1994).
2. M.A.K.Halliday, & C. M. I. M. Matthiessen, An Introduction to Functional Grammar. London: Routledge (2014).
3. G.Kress, & T.van Leeuwen. Reading Images: The Grammar of Visual Design. London: Routledge (2006).
4. F.Dezheng,Zhao Xiufeng.Multimodal Metonymy and Image Textual Meaning Construction. Journal of Foreign Languages, (6): 8-13 (2017).
5. H.Zhuanglin,Z.Yongsheng,Z.Delu, L.Zhanzi.Introduction to Systemic Functional Linguistics. Beijing: Peking University Press (2017).
6. L.Zhanzi.A sociosemiotic analysis of multimodal discourse. Foreign Language Studies, (5): 1-8. (2003).
7. R.Bassam, translated by Wang Yawei (2013). Records and Reality:Criticism of Non-Fiction Films in the World . Taiwan: Taiwan Yuanliu Publishing House.
8. P.Yanyan, L.Zhanzi. A review of domestic multimodal discourse analysis (2003-2017) -Taking CSSCI source journals as the research object. Journal of Fujian Normal University (Philosophy and Social Sciences), (5): 49-59 (2017).
9. Z. Delu. Exploration on the Comprehensive Theoretical Framework of Multimodal Discourse Analysis. Chinese Foreign Languages, 6(1): 24-30 (2009).
10. Z.Delu. A Comprehensive Framework for Multimodal Discourse Analysis from the Perspective of System Function Theory. Modern Foreign Languages, 41 (6) (2018).

Research on curriculum ideological and political design based on online and offline mixed teaching

Yulong Cheng*
Jiuquan Vocational and Technical College Gansu China

Abstract. "Curriculum ideological and political education" is to integrate ideological and political education elements into professional courses, imperceptibly influence students' ideology and behavior, and give full play to the function of cultivating virtues and cultivating people. This paper explores ideological and political elements deeply, according to the requirements of curriculum standards, centering on teaching objectives and teaching content, carries out curriculum ideological and political design based on blended teaching mode, runs ideological and political education throughout education and teaching, implements the goal of "three-in-one education", and cultivates students' good professional quality and professional skills.

1 Introduction

On May 8, 2020, the Ministry of Education issued the Guiding Outline of Curriculum Ideological and Political Construction in Colleges and Universities (JG [2020] No. 3), which raised the curriculum ideological and political construction to the level of strategic measures to implement the fundamental task of establishing morality and cultivating people, and pointed out that "this strategic measure affects and even determines the long-term stability of the country, the national rejuvenation and the rise of the country."

As a higher vocational college, how to excavate the ideological and political elements in the professional courses, organically integrate the ideological and political content into the professional course teaching, give full play to the educational function of the professional courses, guide the students silently, and realize the "all-staff, all-process, all-around" education. The author believes that the best model is to organically integrate ideological and political elements into the teaching process before, during and after class through the combination of online and offline teaching. Adopt a variety of teaching methods and means, such as project-based teaching, case teaching, flipped classroom, micro-class, video, etc., to guide students to love their country, love their home, and cultivate patriotic feelings, so as to cultivate compound high-skilled talents with feelings of home and country for the construction of socialist modernization with Chinese characteristics.

* Corresponding author: 983647317@qq.com

2 Overview of mixed teaching

In the era of information technology, there are multiple ways to learn knowledge, and the combination of online and offline hybrid teaching emerged as the times require. This teaching model is student-centered, combines the advantages of traditional learning methods with the advantages of digital or networked learning, and carries out personalized learning independently according to the needs of students, without time and space constraints. Teachers have changed from former knowledge imparters to designers and instructors of learning activities. Teachers and students can communicate and interact online, forming a new type of partnership learning relationship. In the teaching process, teachers recommend the network resources screened on the learning platform to students, enriching the teaching content. The classroom teaching under the line is mainly to break through the key and difficult points, answer questions and solve doubts, effectively help students solve problems and carry out discussions, which is conducive to improving students' self-learning ability, expression ability and communication ability, and comprehensively improve students' comprehensive quality.

3 Curriculum ideological and political design based on mixed teaching

3.1 Overall design idea of curriculum ideological and political

The course "Building Mechanics and Structure" is an online high-quality course of vocational education in Gansu Province completed in 2019. This course is the core course of civil engineering majors in higher vocational colleges. It plays an important role in the professional course system as a link between the preceding and the following. The course content and overall design ideas are shown in Figure 1 and Figure 2:

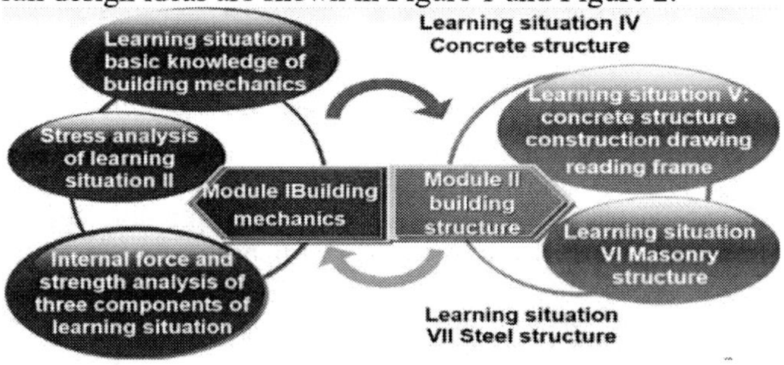

Fig. 1. Course content.

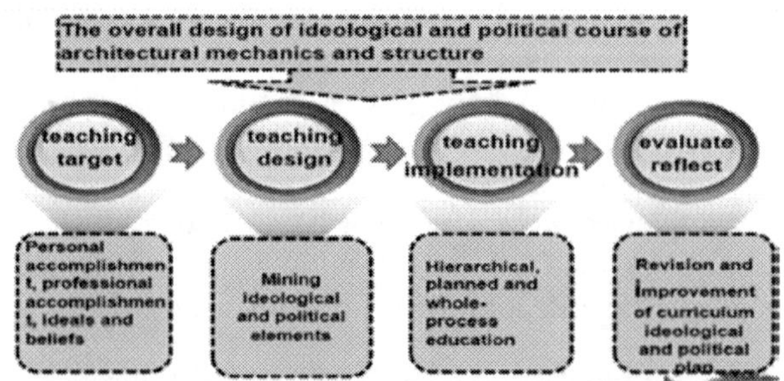

Fig. 2. Overall design ideas of curriculum ideological and political.

Table 1. Course content and mapping points of ideological and political elements.

Learning situation	**Mapping point of ideological and political elements**
Learning situation I basic knowledge of building mechanics	When learning the basic knowledge of the course, introduce the videos of Huoshen Mountain and Leishen Mountain Hospital. It reflects that in the face of emergencies in China, the people of the whole country worked together, united and cooperated to overcome difficulties, stimulate students' strong patriotism, enhance national pride, establish a sense of professional honor and social responsibility, and firmly adhere to the "four self-confidence".
Stress analysis of learning situation II structure Stress analysis diagram and balance conditions	In the process of learning component force analysis, take the force analysis of Chinese athletes in horizontal bars, Trojan horses, rings and other sports as an example, integrate the spirit of athletes' hard work, hard training, love for the motherland, and win glory for the country into the teaching content, and cultivate students' patriotism.
Internal force and strength analysis of three components of learning situation Internal force, stress and strength	Integrating the feelings of family and country - the influence of the penetration of "external forces" on us under the great changes that have not occurred in a century, and the interference of "external forces" is reflected in all aspects of life; Especially since the outbreak of the COVID-19 epidemic, it has had a great impact on our production and life. Through group discussion, students can understand that since "external forces" are beyond our control, we can keep our "Chinese heart" to cope with the interference of "external forces".
Learning situation IV Concrete structureDesign principles and methods, concrete materials, flexural members,compression members	Play the video of structural collapse and building collapse during the earthquake. Through social hot events, educate students to be scientific and rigorous, practical and realistic, safety first and quality first at all times, always take people's life and property as their own responsibility, abide by professional ethics, keep improving, and be meticulous.
Learning situation V: concrete structure constructiondrawing reading frame structureconstruction drawing	Firmly adhere to the "four self-confidence" and enhance the sense of national pride - science and technology will make the nation prosperous, and science and technology will make the country strong. Science and technology is the foundation of the development of the motherland, and science and technology can lead in all directions;Through the study of 3D flat method atlas 16G101-1 and the application of BIM technology in the construction drawing reading, students can establish the ideal belief of a powerful country in science and technology.
Learning situation VI Masonry structure Masonry materials	Taking Zhaozhou Bridge as an example, the case teaching method is used to guide students to understand and identify with national policies, establish environmental awareness, achieve sustainable development, live in harmony with nature, establish environmental awareness, and understand that green waters and green mountains are golden mountains and silver mountains.
Learning situation VII Steel structure Steel structure material, type selection and construction requirements	Introduce world-famous steel structure engineering videos such as Beijing Daxing International Airport, Hong Kong-Zhuhai-Macao Bridge, Sea-crossing Bridge, and Deep-sea Tunnel. Through the application of a large number of new materials and new technologies in super projects, let students understand the importance and urgency of technological innovation. Core technologies should be in their own hands, break through themselves, move forward in continuous innovation, and cultivate students' awareness of innovation and entrepreneurship.

3.2 Mining of ideological and political elements of the course

According to the talent training plan, the goal is to cultivate compound high-skilled talents with all-round development of morality, intelligence, physical fitness, beauty and labor. The teaching content is student-centered, and the teaching content is reconstructed based on students' cognitive ability and students' characteristics according to the analysis of learning situation. In the process of teaching design, we should pay attention to the organic integration of teaching content and ideological and political education elements. See Table 1 for the mapping points of ideological and political elements of the curriculum:

3.3 Course ideological and political teaching design

3.3.1 Select teaching content

According to the teaching standards of the course, the learning situation IV concrete structure and learning task I structural requirements of reinforced concrete beam are selected as examples. The teaching objectives are as follows:

Knowledge objectives: understand the section size and material requirements of reinforced concrete frame beams, and master the structural requirements of upper and middle full-length reinforcement, lower full-length reinforcement, erection reinforcement, stirrup and side structural reinforcement of frame beams.

Competence objectives: be able to correctly read the types of reinforcement in the frame beam, and be able to read and turn over the construction drawings of beam plane method in the given project drawings.

Ideological and political objectives: through the study of the structural requirements of reinforced concrete beams, especially the reinforcement of beams, cultivate students' rigorous and conscientious scientific attitude, establish the sense of responsibility of safety first, quality first, and the ideal belief of innovation and progress, and the power of science and technology.

3.3.2 Teaching content design

Before class, release learning tasks on the learning platform of the online excellent course "Building Mechanics and Structure", set up discussion questions, urge students to independently study the basic theoretical knowledge of the teaching content of this lesson, and complete the corresponding discussion and question and answer. Guide students to learn independently, make good knowledge reserves, and lay a foundation for further in-depth study. Focus on cultivating students' ability of independent inquiry, independent thinking and problem finding.

In the class, case teaching, BIM technology and other methods are used to break through the key and difficult points and answer questions. Key knowledge When explaining the structural requirements of frame beam reinforcement, play the video of building structural damage and the pictures of structural damage during the earthquake, so that students can have a perceptual understanding of the huge loss caused by building structural damage. Integrating professional spirit, we should first ensure the safety of the structure, be rigorous, meticulous, keep improving and abide by professional ethics when designing and calculating the structure.

After class, publish assignments and expand learning resources on the teaching platform, consolidate and expand the knowledge learned, and submit learning results in groups. Cultivate students' team spirit and communication skills, and carry out self-learning management.

4 Conclusion

To sum up, as a front-line professional course teacher in higher vocational colleges, we should constantly explore the ideological and political elements of the curriculum and improve the ability to integrate them. Based on the mixed teaching mode, the ideological and political education content is organically integrated into the professional course teaching, and the main channel of classroom teaching is well used, so that the ideological and political education of the curriculum is throughout the education and teaching, reflecting the educational value of the professional course.

References

1. New Era (ZBF [2019] No. 47)
2. F. Qiangqiang, Zh. Ya. Curr and Po: Back, Con and Path .J. China, Agr, Edu, (2020.4)
3. D. Xiaoli, T.Mingqin. Cur, Ide, Pol, Des, Practice based. Tea, Mod mode.J.Hig, Edu, (2021-26)
4. Y.Lian. Logic, Pra, path, Curriculum Ideo, quality Edu, direction .J. Univ, Edu, (2020 (3): 121-123)
5. Ch. Gen. Prac, Res, Integra, Ideological, Political Cou, Ideo, Higher Edu .J. Edu, Exp, (2021.4: 69-72)

Teaching reform of "production planning and control" for modern manufacturing industry

Jun Hou*, *Feng* Li, *HuiHui* Zhou, and *Hairu* Yang

Hubei University of Automotive Technology, Mechanical Engineering Department, 167 Checheng West Road, Shiyan City, Hubei, China

Keywords: Production planning and control, Teaching reform, Modern manufacturing industry.

Abstract. "Production Planning and Control" is one of the major courses in Industrial Engineering, and its cross-cutting, adaptable, and practical characteristics require that the course should well integrate technology and management to meet the evolution of modern manufacturing industry. Through the study of the traditional teaching effectiveness of "Production Planning and Control", this paper pointed out the issues, including insufficient interaction, unappealing content, and lack of systematization of the knowledge. By introducing teaching reform approaches for the course, it proposes to combine various teaching methods, rearrange the teaching material, systematically plan the practical teaching links, and assess the learning effect through a diversified evaluation system, in order to promote students' motivation and learning enthusiasm, meanwhile improve the teaching effect of the course to meet the requirement of modern manufacturing industry for talents.

1 Introduction

Industrial Engineering is a new cross-cutting discipline covering engineering and management. It aims at optimizing the performance, economic efficiency and productivity of industrial systems and engineering projects through scientific and rational organization and coordination of relevant production factors, taking human resources, materials, information, energy and production organization as the elements in the system.[1] Throughout the teaching practice of industrial engineering at home and abroad, it can be divided into two major categories: those established in management disciplines, which are oriented to management methods, and those established in mechanical engineering disciplines, which are oriented to engineering.

"Production Planning and Control" course is one of the core professional courses in Industrial Engineering. By learning the course, students will be familiar with the theoretical framework of the operation of the production planning system, master the planning and

* Corresponding author: derekhou@163.com

control of the supply of materials and other resources [2], the main indicators of production planning, production capacity balance and production planning steps and methods. The students will have better understanding of the content and role of production operations planning, the principles and methods of production operations planning as well as inventory control, equipment maintenance planning and the corresponding control work.

However, with the rapid development of China's modern manufacturing industry, there is an obvious lag in the course content, such as the outdated cases with focus only on the traditional manufacturing fields, meanwhile the teaching methods are relatively monotonous, which ignore the practical problems, consequently making the teaching effectiveness of the course difficult to achieve expectation [3]. Therefore, it shows great significance to analyse the characteristics of the course, put forward the reform countermeasures, and sum up suggestions on teaching theory and practice for improving the teaching and learning efficiency.

2 Characteristics of "production planning and control" course

"Production Planning and Control" is a comprehensive intersection of engineering and management science, manufacturing technology and production planning science, the objectives of this course are, to familiarize students with modern enterprise production operation system, and ensure that the students can master the basic ideas and principles of production planning, while utilize or apply methods in the operation and management of production systems. This course exhibits unique characteristics, mainly in the following three areas.

2.1 Interdisciplinary

The cross-disciplinary character of the course is obvious. The objects of study, lie in the production process, operations planning, production line balance, inventory control and other technical learning based on the penetration of management concepts with an assist of time management, human resources management, and financial management.

2.2 Application-oriented

This course shows close connection between theory and practice, throughout the production operation process, facilities layout, enterprise resource planning and other aspects of a systematic and comprehensive understanding. It is focusing on the enterprise production process of integrated production planning, material requirements planning, assembly and production operations plan development methods and inventory control strategies.

2.3 Contemporary

The modern manufacturing industry and economic transformation show a significant impact on this course. As the traditional manufacturing industry is facing transformation and industrial upgrading, which requires enterprises to change from a production management system aimed at cost minimization to a production management system that places equal emphasis on cost, quality, and customer experience, therefore, the "production planning and control" course must also keep pace with the times.

3 Issues of "production planning and control" curriculum

Although this course shows significant importance in Industrial Engineering, the learning effectiveness is not as good as expected in many colleges where the course is offered.

3.1 Insufficient interaction

The traditional teaching method of "a chalk, three feet podium" still occupies a place in classroom lectures, and teachers instil a lot of knowledge into students through detailed explanations, while students just listen [4]. The learning is boring even annoying and may lead to lack of learning enthusiasm from the students.

First of all, in many situations, it is the teacher alone on the podium, while students may not have the chance to ask any questions, which resulted in the great creative ability loss and creative ability is mercilessly stifled. The classroom becomes boring, as students can only passively accept the knowledge. Some teachers prefer to read from books, also do not know how to activate or expand the students' thinking, making the classroom dead and weird.

In some cases, students are afraid of the teacher and do not dare to ask questions, especially for Chinese students. Hence. The teacher is unaware of the students understanding level, and the classroom has become a one-man show for the teacher only.

3.2 Unappealing content

The modern manufacturing industry and economic transformation development have a significant impact on this course. Due to the rapid development of China's economy, traditional manufacturing industries and service industries are facing transformation and industrial upgrading, and products are changing from the traditional single-variety, high-volume, stock-ready production method to multi-variety, small-volume, customized order-based production method.

In addition, some of the textbooks have been published earlier, and the case descriptions are slightly outdated compared with the current economic development. At present, the textbooks on the market are generally based on traditional manufacturing industries, which cannot reflect the ever-changing modern enterprise management methods and innovations in processes, methods, and tools.

When students graduate and enter the plants, they may feel a big difference between what they have learned in school and the actual application in the enterprise, which makes it impossible for them to use their existing knowledge to deal with production management-related work in a short period of time.

3.3 Lack of systematization

Most of the experiments of "production planning and control" are simple process simulations of a certain object of a production system, while the actual production site process changes are extremely complex. The traditional experimental means and methods are single and lack of systematization, and most of the course experiments are validation experiments, with few hours of practical teaching. Due to lack of practical system comprehensive use of analysis process, the knowledge points are independent of each other, lacking the necessary connection.

In this case, students can't establish a professional system-level concept in their mind after doing the experiments. Many professional knowledge is poorly understood. And most experiments only meet the requirements of verifying the theory of classroom teaching. It is difficult to connect with the actual production site of enterprises.

The problems of disconnection of theory and practice are especially prominent, for example: theoretical teaching is separated from the real application; the experimental time is too little; the experimental projects are scattered; the content and form are single; instruments and equipment are in shortage; the experimental funds are insufficient, and etc. To get rid of this serious situation, a scientific and systematic practical teaching mode of "Production Planning and Control" needs to be resolved.

4 Innovations in curriculum reform

In view of the unique characteristics of the course, the main problems faced by the current teaching, and the author's practical teaching experience, this paper aimed at optimizing and adjusting, to make the teaching and learning in line with the current requirements of enterprise production operations, with focus in below four approaches.

4.1 Diverse the teaching methods with integrated approaches

The teaching method of multi-method integration is adopted in teaching nowadays, which is also be suitable in the teaching of "Production Planning and Control".

First of all, an inspiring and guiding way should be used, as the course involves a wide range of professional knowledge. Most of the chapters are with intrinsic connection, so it is difficult to talk about all the knowledge in a short time. Therefore, teachers should devote themselves to transforming the "injection" teaching mode into "inspiration", mainly guiding students, and changing the long-formed passive learning state of students. The most important knowledge should be pointed out in class by teacher, while it is better to guide students to study by themselves, solve problems after class by assigning relevant topics and consult relevant information next time.

Afterwards, discussions can be held in class, and students' understanding can be further expanded through mutual expressions and interactions. This could be a good solution to the problem when facing complex contents with limited class time nowadays. It can also stimulate students' learning enthusiasm and initiative, and improve their comprehensive ability of searching information, finding, analysing solving problems, and summarizing into conclusions. The teaching system is summarized in the following figure.

The teaching system can be disassembled and analysed in the lesson preparation, and made into a courseware animation, which can be shown and unfolded step by step in the classroom. In this way, students can understand the lecture content intuitively, with the teacher's explanation, and a better learning effect can be achieved. The courseware can add with animation, pictures, and other factors, which is conducive to the activity of classroom atmosphere and bring students' interest in learning.

Moreover, the concepts related to production management and advanced production technology (such as JIT production, flexible manufacturing system, enterprise production planning, etc.) should be covered in the course through relevant videos.

4.2 Rearrange the contents

The course materials should be rearranged or self-edited to make them better match the production characteristics of modern enterprises. As an important carrier, the course textbook is the main tool and reference for students to pre-study before class and review after class. Teachers need to deliver the course systematically through a combination of textbooks and cases, to achieve the teaching objectives. Therefore, the selection of teaching materials should be consistent with the development objectives of the course. The content of the current textbook is mainly organized according to the three decision-making levels of strategic decision, operational decision, and control decision in the production operation of enterprises. The content is relatively small, which to a certain extent limits the space for students' independent learning and the depth of the course lectures. Therefore, the content and teaching methods of "Production Planning and Control" need to be adjusted with the progress of economy and society, to meet the changing needs of today's enterprise operation process and production planning.

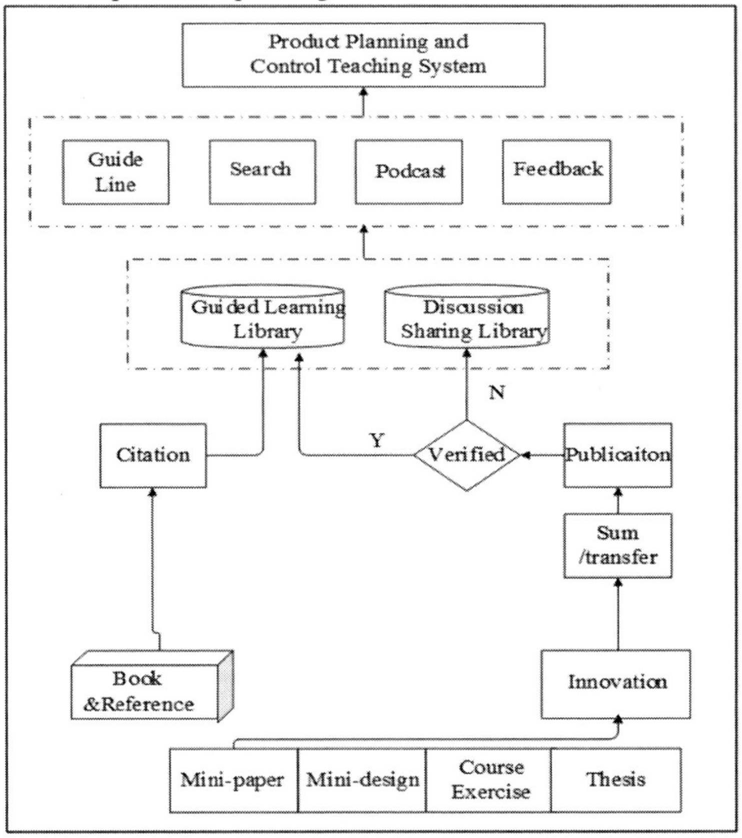

Fig. 1. "Production planning and control" teaching system.

Secondly, the curriculum reform focuses on the combination of theory and practice, highlighting the practical problem-solving skills training. Considering the content of the course "production planning and control", the combination of theory and practice is essential. The content of the textbook is highly condensed, and usually may not be easy for the college students, who are the lack of practical production experience. Therefore, it is especially important to combine theoretical learning with practical operations in certain actual production processes to broaden students' horizons and strengthen their theoretical basis.

At last, many actual production cases are collected from enterprises and a case library was prepared with supporting courseware, which is in line with the employment objectives of industrial engineering students. During the course, students are guided to apply the basic principles and methods of production planning and control to solve practical problems by combining rich case studies to improve their cognitive ability of practical production problems. In addition, in order to enhance students' sensory understanding of the actual production, the course is interspersed with short videos of the production process, such as a short video of the production process of an automobile factory, which visually describes the whole process of stamping, welding, painting and final assembly, so that students have a deeper impression of the overall or local production process of the automobile, which helps to link the subsequent theoretical learning with the actual production.

4.3 Strengthen "industry-academia-research" trinity

Suitable manufacturing enterprises (such as Dongfeng, the biggest commercial vehicle manufacturer in China) are selected, in order to establish teaching system and management system of industry-university-research cooperation, with relocating experimental projects to enterprises, with the targets of "finding problems, proposing solutions, collecting and analysing data, testing and optimizing new solutions, and solving problems".

To strengthen students' ability to solve practical engineering problems with relevant theoretical knowledge, excellent graduates were created with innovative spirit, consciousness, and ability. As the opportunities of real internship in a factory are limited, a teaching software can also be used to simulate and demonstrate the functions of basic data, inventory management, production planning, operation management, equipment management, etc. Systematic reform and innovation were carried out through in-depth internship arrangement with enterprises, and virtual software system at the same time, by rearranging contents, innovating teaching methods, which help build up the undergraduate major of Industrial Engineering with higher level and continuous improvement.

4.4 Optimize the course assessment system

Although the learning contents of each subject and practice in Industrial Engineering are different, the assessment method basically adopts the examination plus course design. Under the requirement of curriculum reform, this course focuses on the "sequencing" of explicit knowledge and "manifestation" of tacit knowledge.

Table 1. Curriculum assessment and evaluation system.

Appraisal Items	Appraisal requirements	Ratio
Final Exam	Assessment of the mastery of basic knowledge and concepts, calculation ability, comprehensive analysis and application ability, independent learning ability, etc.	60%
Classroom Seminars	Assessment of understanding of complex engineering problems, mastery of research methods, data processing and analysis ability, etc. Study reports to be completed after lectures	20%
Course mini-paper / mini-design	The ability to calculate and analyse, the ability to think independently, and the ability to synthesize and design will be assessed. (Multiple assignments, can be combined to take the average score)	20%

In addition to the traditional assessment methods, this course adds the following:

(1) Through the course mini-paper/design, course design, graduation design, let students "summarize" their achievements and feelings, and "convert" into a standardized model and "publish" into "Discussion and Sharing Library". So, the database becomes bigger and richer after several rounds running. The computer knowledge base is added to the "backstage" so as to realize the "manifestation" of tacit knowledge.

(2) For the innovative designs, cases or short papers written by the students, the excellent cases are selected and transferred into the library, with multiple experimental

projects and micro-factory projects in the "Guided Learning Library", in order to provide continuous updating and progress of the curriculum. Fig.1 shows the teaching system logic.

Total evaluation score of 100 points = closed-book examination score of 60% + process assessment score of 40%.

(1) Closed-book examination 60%: According to the teaching objectives of the course, which are focusing on assessing students' understanding and application of basic knowledge and knowledge of important and difficult points. It can reflect students' ability to analyse problems and apply what they have learned; the content and type of assessment should be able to support the achievement of the course objectives.

(2) Process assessment 40%: including classroom seminar 20%, course mini-paper / mini-design 20%

The classroom seminar mainly assesses the students' attitude, the operability of the conclusions, and integration ability of data processing and team management, and etc. The assessment process should also emphasize the importance of completing assignments independently and cultivating students' ability to apply knowledge to solve problems.

5 Summary

In this paper, constructive approaches were proposed of course teaching reform to fit for the characteristics of "Production Planning and Control", and the current teaching situation. Various teaching methods were explored, and a talent training mode with close cooperation between industry, academia and research were established. This paper emphasizes the combination of theoretical teaching and engineering practice, supplemented by an efficient course assessment system, in order to adapt to the development of modern manufacturing industry. The approaches improve students' learning efficiency and practical problem-solving ability, and finally make necessary paving for students when they are transferring to the workplace. The curriculum reform ideas listed in this paper, may not only be used for Industrial Engineering but other related professional courses as a reference.

Supported by HUAT Doctoral Scientific Research Fund - BK202223

References

1. Zonghong Huang, Long Wu. *Contemporary Education Theory and Practice*, **2**, 105-107(2012)
2. Wei Wang, Jing Wang, Yujie Zhu, et al. *Forest Engineering*, **6**, 184-186, (2013)
3. Jingcai Li, Wenli Xu, Jiafu Yang. *Popular Science and Technology*, **1**, 94-96(2020)
4. Jingli Fan, Yunbing Hou, Zhang Hao. *Curriculum Education Research*, **1**, 253, (2020)
5. Wenlong Gui, Zhenhua Wu. *Popular Science and Technology*, **8**, 124-126, (2020)

Exploration and practice of ideological and political education in biochemistry and molecular biology for cultivation of ethical and medical talents

Chunjing Zhang[1], *Ying* Liu[1], *Xiaodan* Qi[2], *Xiaolong* Wang[1] and *Zhenglin* Zhao[1,*]

[1]Department of Biochemistry, Qiqihar Medical University, Qiqihar 161006, Heilongjiang, China
[2]Department of clinical Biochemistry, Qiqihar Medical University, Qiqihar 161006, Heilongjiang, China

Abstract. Combine the learning characteristics of medical specialty and the core socialist values. Ideological and political education is integrated into the teaching of biochemistry and molecular biology. We will strive to cultivate medical talents of the new era with excellent medical skills, noble medical ethics, the patriotism, concern for the people's livelihood and dedication for the society, guided by "professionalism", "practicing ability" and "social adaptation".
The talent training of medical university bears the important task of training medical workers with noble medical ethics, exquisite medical skills and humanistic spirit [1]. Biochemistry and Molecular Biology is an important basic and compulsory course for medical majors. Its relevant theories and technologies have penetrated into all fields of basic medicine and clinical medicine. This course contains rich ideological and political education elements, which are closely combined with clinical practice and daily life, so that students can more vividly and concretely grasp the knowledge and feel the essence of the thought. The implementation of curriculum ideological and political education is helpful to improve the humanistic quality of medical students and professional ethics of doctors. This paper explores and practices the implementation methods of curriculum ideology in biochemistry and molecular biology. It also integrates the elements of moral education into daily teaching guided by "professional spirit", "practicing ability" and "social adaptation", aiming to continuously improve the effect of education and ultimately contribute to the cultivation of medical talents with both moral and medical skills.

1 The importance and necessity of carrying out curriculum ideological and political education

Biochemistry and Molecular Biology is a professional basic course for medical students.

* Corresponding author: mdj6612@163.com

Studying biochemistry and molecular biology will help medical students understand the mechanism of disease occurrence and development, as well as the principle of disease diagnosis and prevention at the molecular level, and lay the foundation for learning other basic medical courses and clinical medicine courses [2]. Find the entry point of ideological and political education in the teaching content, and integrate patriotism, professional quality, speculative ability, benevolence, scientific quality, doctor-patient relationship, legal awareness, etc. into the biochemistry curriculum as ideological and political elements, leading the medical students' social responsibility, life values, and improving the students' professional identity, social responsibility, humanistic quality, professional ethics and legal awareness. It is helpful to train medical talents of the new era with excellent medical skills and noble medical ethics for the country and society [3].

2 Specific teaching implementation of ideological and political education

2.1 Design of ideological and political elements in biochemistry and molecular biology

It is very necessary and important to integrate ideological and political elements in the course of Biochemistry and Molecular Biology. The excavation of ideological and political elements is the core link of ideological and political education [4].

In the specific teaching process, in view of the characteristics of the discipline and the needs of medical personnel training, we should take "professional spirit", "practicing ability" and "social adaptation" as the guidance, and take hot topics or related events related to professional knowledge as the entry point of ideological and political education. Focus on professional quality and scientific spirit education, cultivate students' medical mission and responsibility, scientific rigorous and practical scientific spirit; Carry out humanistic care education to address the correlation between ideological and political elements and daily life and life health. Table 1 lists the design of ideological and political elements of biochemistry teaching content.

2.1.1 Humanistic quality education guided by "professional spirit"

In the training process of medical students, we should not only impart medical professional knowledge, but also establish lofty political beliefs, strengthen life consciousness, and cultivate people through cultivation. In the teaching of humanistic quality education guided by "professional spirit", ideological and political elements such as national self-confidence, professional quality, dedication, team spirit and scientific quality can be integrated. Cultivate students to establish correct professional values, and stimulate students' thirst for knowledge and internal learning motivation, so that students can reflect on their responsibilities and better serve the society. For details sees table 1.

2.1.2 Professional quality training oriented by "practicing ability"

Taking the intersection and integration of clinical cases and knowledge points as the main line, taking the cultivation of clinical thinking ability as the goal, and on the basis of full investigation and analysis of post competency requirements, pay attention to the integration of basic knowledge and clinical practice, and give consideration to innovative training and discipline progress. Cultivate students' scientific, rigorous and realistic scientific spirit guided by "practicing ability". Make students realize the importance of biosafety, integrating theory with practice, updating knowledge and doctor-patient communication to doctors. Improve students' ability to promote health and solve practical clinical problems as well as their lifelong learning ability. It is committed to cultivating medical professionals with noble medical ethics and professional competence. For details sees table 1.

Table 1. Design of ideological and political elements of some teaching contents guided by professionalism, professional ability and social adaptation.

Ideological and political objectives of the course	Elements of ideological and political education	Chapter	Theoretical knowledge points	Design of ideological and political content
Humanistic quality education guided by "professional spirit"	Patriotism; National self-confidence	Introduction	China's contribution in the field of biochemistry	The deeds of famous scientists and scholars in China, such as Tu Youyou.
	Social responsibility; Dedication	Transmission of genetic information	Polymerase chain reaction: PCR technology	Medical staff and scientific researchers on the front line of COVID-19 epidemic prevention.
	Professional quality; Team spirit	Structure and function of protein	Three-dimensional structure of protein	Three dimensional structure analysis of protein complex of COVID-19 receptor ACE2.
	Professional quality; Ethics	Gene diagnosis and gene therapy	In vitro DNA recombination technology	Gene editing technology.
Professional quality training oriented by "practicing ability"	Scientific rigor	Common molecular biological techniques	Determination of optimum pH of salivary amylase	The addition amount of trace reagents should not be neglected during the experiment.
	Update knowledge in time	Structure and function of protein	Relationship between protein structure and function	The structural analysis of COVID-19 receptor-ACE2 can promote the development of COVID-19 therapeutic drugs.
	Integrating theory with practice	Glycometabolism	Sugar intake and utilization	As the new youth of the new era, the importance of strengthening physical training.
	The importance of biosafety	Common molecular biological techniques	Plasmid DNA extraction and identification	Biological materials should be properly disposed and should not be arbitrarily discarded to prevent biosafety incidents.
	Doctor-patient communication	Amino acid metabolism	Abnormal ammonia metabolism	For hyperammonia, attention should be paid to communication with the patient's family members.
	Patients' privacy	DNA damage and repair	DNA damage	Cases of xeroderma pigmentosum.

Cultivation of physical and mental quality guided by "social adaptation"	Social responsibility	Structure and function of protein	Molecular composition of protein	Melamine is added to Sanlu milk powder.
	Establish correct values	Vitamins and inorganic salts	Vitamin	Diet and health, such as "junk food" and "canned food".
	Cultivate legal awareness	Eukaryotic gene and genome	Basic structure of eukaryotic gene	Pay attention to the protection of genetic resources and patents.
	Professional identity	Lipid metabolism	Cholesterol metabolism	Use theoretical knowledge to guide relatives in daily diet.
	Humanistic care education	Biosynthesis of DNA	Telomere and telomerase	China has gradually entered the stage of aging society.

2.1.3 Cultivation of physical and mental quality guided by "social adaptation"

Take the intersection and integration of life examples and knowledge points as the main line, take the cultivation of social adaptability as the goal, and pay attention to the combination of theory and practice. The events such as the addition of melamine in Sanlu milk powder and the addition of plasticizer in alcohol, which have received widespread attention so far, will be discussed with students in combination with physiology, biochemistry, pathology, immunity and other disciplines to strengthen the sense of justice, responsibility and destiny of medical students. The cultivation of physical and mental quality guided by "social adaptation" is guided by values in knowledge teaching and ability training, helping students to shape correct world outlook, outlook on life and values, and cultivating students to become medical professionals with good physical and mental health and social adaptation.

2.2 Exploring the teaching methods of ideological and political education

Now we are in the era of "Internet+". We should make rational use of network resources to carry out ideological and political education in biochemistry and molecular biology. Build a mobile learning environment through "online"+"offline" mixed teaching [5]. For example, upload rich teaching resources on the online teaching platform, including videos, cases, network links, etc. At the same time, a variety of teaching methods are mixed in the classroom, such as case review, discussion and debate and group discussion, to achieve the organic combination of quality education and professional education. Take diabetes as an example. Before class, guide students to consult relevant literature and collect cases of diseases; In class, teachers guide students to discuss and speak in groups, and integrate ideological and political elements such as concern for life and health, professional quality and care education into teaching; After class, students are encouraged to combine biochemistry knowledge with moral education elements to make micro-video. Therefore, professional knowledge and ideological and political education are integrated through a variety of teaching methods to achieve value leadership in knowledge dissemination.

2.3 Optimize the assessment system

On the basis of the original basic course assessment system, a diversified assessment system under various classroom models is implemented. The humanistic knowledge and professional knowledge will be included in the theoretical examination questions, and the humanistic quality evaluation standard will be included in the skill operation evaluation standard. Through the questionnaire survey, we can understand the students' evaluation of the mixed teaching effect integrated with ideological and political education. Such an evaluation mechanism will strengthen the internalization effect of students' knowledge and ideological and political education in the learning process, and realize the essence of educating.

3 Effects of ideological and political education in biochemistry and molecular biology

The ideological and political education of biochemistry and molecular biology courses in our university has been practiced for nearly three semesters, and the teaching objects include the students majoring in medical laboratory technology in 2020, 2021 and 2022. The integration of ideological and political education has triggered students' humanistic thinking and received positive feedback from students. From students' classroom interaction, face-to-face class and TBL report, we learned that students can use the basic knowledge of biochemistry and molecular biology to guide the study of clinical knowledge and apply it to daily life. Through the symposium, we learned that students generally believed that integrating ideological and political education into the curriculum improved their interest and enthusiasm in learning biochemistry and biology. Through the anonymous questionnaire on the subject of ideological and political education, from the evaluation feedback of 231 students in three sessions of medical laboratory technology major, we learned that students gave high evaluation on ideological and political education in biochemistry and molecular biology courses, which indicates that the goal of education is achieved in the teaching process. For details sees table 2.

Table 2. 231 medical laboratory technology students' evaluation for the teaching effect of ideological and political education.

Ideological and political education content	Positive evaluation proportion (%)	Average weight (full score of 5 points)
Professional identity	97.40	4.75
Patriotism National self-confidence	93.07	4.40
Scientific spirit	92.64	4.29
Establish a correct outlook on life and values	94.37	4.57
Dialectical thinking	91.34	3.96
Social responsibility	92.64	4.23
Dedication	95.24	4.62
Legal consciousness	93.51	4.52
Professional quality	95.67	4.28
Medical ethics	97.84	4.34

Note: The options include 6 items: totally disagree, disagree, general, relatively agree, agree and very agree. The weight score is 0-5 points. Positive evaluation refers to 3 items: relatively agree, agree and very agree.

4 Summary

The ideological and political education in medical universitys is of great significance for training medical workers with high academic level and humanistic quality. Medical university and universities are the bases for training medical professionals. With the transformation of medical service mode from "disease centered" to "human centered" [6], the society has put forward higher requirements for the professional quality of medical workers. The application of ideological and political education in the teaching process of biochemistry and molecular biology has endowed ideological education with fresh vitality. Combining medical professional knowledge with moral education will not only help to improve the teaching quality, but also help to shape the noble medical ethics of medical students and establish correct socialist core values. It plays a vital role in cultivating medical talents with excellent medical skills and noble medical ethics.

This research was financially supported by 2020 higher education teaching reform research project (No.SJGY20200823)

References

1. X.J.Shi, C.X.Jin, H.B.Tian, J.Li, C.Zhang, L.Xu, L.X.Lv, Med. Educ. Res. Pract 28(4):637-639 (2020)
2. C.Q.Li, H.Z.Liu, X.L.Li, S.M.Li, H.X.Wang, Educ.Teach. For 37:68-69 (2020)
3. H.Gao, C.J.Zhang, S.Y.Li, H.Y.Guo, J.Xing, Y.Liu, S.B.Wang, X.Gao, Chinese. High. Med. Rduc 3:77-78 (2020)
4. J.H.Shi, X.Y.Niu, Z.J.Wang, L.Shen, J.Ma, L.Shao, Med. Educ. Manag 8(6):677-680 (2022)
5. L.Cao, L.Wang, B.He, B.L.He, J.Lin, J. High. Educ 35:67-69 (2022)
6. L.W.Liang, New. West 9:152-153 (2019)

Teaching reform and practice of database principle and application

Junshan Li*, and *Yi* Hu

School of Computer, South China Business College, Guangdong University of Foreign Studies, Guangzhou 510545, Guangdong, China

Abstract. Aiming at the characteristics that the content of database principles and applications is difficult to understand and master, this paper first analyzes the comprehensive and practical characteristics of database principle and application course, and then systematically introduces some innovative practices of the author in textbook construction, teaching content reform and design ability training, including the construction of systematic case teaching content system; The reform of curriculum content system keeping pace with the times; The construction of innovative design ability training system; The practice of curriculum design that is closely integrated with application; The introduction of typical entrepreneurial innovation cases; The guidance of famous sayings and aphorisms compatible with the curriculum. The author's beneficial attempts and innovative practices in the construction of database principle and application courses and the training of applied computer talents are expected to play a certain enlightening role in the teaching of computer majors, teachers and courses in relevant colleges and universities.

1 Introduction

Use Database technology is an important support and guarantee technology in the construction of national information infrastructure and information society. The research and development of various information system platform software based on database technology has become a necessary knowledge and basic skill for technology and management personnel in computer and related professional fields, therefore, database technology has become one of the core technologies that computer, electronic information and related to management students must master and apply flexibly.

As a required backbone professional course for undergraduates majoring in computer and related electronic information, database principles and applications cover relational operation, functional dependency theory and relational standardization theory, involving logical organization, physical organization, query strategy and control mechanism of databases; The design method should follow the phase division and design principles of the software life cycle; The design process requires strong programming ability; Designers should generally have some business knowledge or practical experience in the application field of user organizations, so the course of database principles and applications has always

* Corresponding author: lijunshan403@163.com

been difficult to learn, understand and master; The design of database based application software system (hereinafter referred to as database application system) has been a challenging problem for a long time[1]. Therefore, it is very necessary to actively carry out the teaching reform of the database principle and application course, which is obviously of great practical significance for the training of application-oriented and innovative talents.

2 Comprehensive and practical characteristics of database course

The learning of the course of database principle and application needs discrete mathematics and program design as the basis. Although some of the contents of this course are highly theoretical, the essence of the course is a practical design technology. The core of the design technology is mainly the conceptual structure design, logical structure design, physical structure design of the database, and the manipulation and application of the database. It is the physical structure design of the database and the requirements for the operation and application of the database that make the design of the database application system and the programming ability of the designer and the ability to combine with the domain knowledge become the key to the success of the system design, which also makes the course of database principles and applications seem not only a professional course, but also a comprehensive design and practice course based on database principles and design methods [2-4]. That is to say, if the course of database principle and application only explains the knowledge of database principle and the design method of database application system, most students may still not understand the operation mechanism of the database, and still cannot fully understand and master the design method of the database, but only truly guide and lead students to carry out the logical structure of a typical database application system through comprehensive and in-depth explanation After the whole process of physical design and database application behavior programming design, it is possible for students to truly understand and master the basic principles, overall architecture and design methods of databases. This is the reason why the teaching organization system of database principles and application courses is difficult to build, and it is also the core and key that teachers have always felt that the course is difficult to teach and students have always believed that the course is difficult to learn.

3 Some teaching and practice methods of the course of database principle and application

After decades of teaching practice in the course of database principles and applications, the author has compiled and published database course textbooks in several publishing houses. In particular, the first to fourth editions of Database Principles and Applications (SQL Server) published in Tsinghua University Press have been adopted by dozens of universities across the country, and have been praised by many teachers and students. The course of database system principle and application, which the author is responsible for building, has also been selected as the national excellent course and national boutique resource sharing course. The following introduces some teaching practices and reform practices of the author around the database principle and application course.

3.1 The systematic case based teaching content system and teaching mode highlight the characteristics of the combination of theory and application

In the teaching process of database principles and applications, it is necessary to use real design cases and reliable experimental data to support the implementation of design methods and the verification of design results. Therefore, in the content organization of the textbook of the course of database principle and application, a case data set of the university teaching information management system is introduced, which is composed of seven database tables and their data, such as student information table, course information table, student course score table, etc., and based on the case data set of the university teaching information management system, in relation operation, SQL language and its query application, database integrity constraints, database (file) creation The case course teaching content system is constructed in the contents of data table creation, data entry in the table, database application system design, etc. Based on the data set of teaching cases of the university teaching information management system, the teaching materials are organized with the teaching cases of the "university teaching information management system" as the main line; The discussion teaching is based on the teaching case of "University Teaching Information Management System"; The course experiment is organized and implemented around the relevant contents and design modules of the case of "University Teaching Information Management System"; The independent curriculum design is designed by students to select information management cases in their familiar application fields to design the database application system. The multi-level and multi link teaching case guidance and case based teaching mode highlight the distinctive characteristics of the combination of theory and application of database principles and application courses.

3.2 The continuous reform of the curriculum content system has realized the characteristics of keeping pace with the times in the reform of the teaching content

Although the basic content system of the database course has been basically formed, from the perspective of deepening students' understanding of the course content, the presentation methods and teaching methods of the relevant content of the course will never end. Therefore, in the evolution from the first edition to the fourth edition, the textbook "Principles and Applications of Database (SQL Server)" has reformed and improved the expression and organization methods of related contents in many aspects. For example, in order to enable students to intuitively understand the core knowledge point of the overall architecture of the database management system, which is the mapping of the logical mode to the external mode in the three-level model of the database system, the textbook uses the definition sentence of the external mode (user view):

```
CREATE VIEW CG
AS SELECT S.S#, SNAME, C#, CNAME, CLASSH, GRADE
FROM S, SC, C
WHERE S.S# = SC.S# AND SC.C# = C.C#
```

It explains that the values of the table (external mode) CG are queried (SELECT) from the three tables S, SC, and C. Then, by constructing the "Mapping Example of Table S, SC, and C External Mode CG" as shown in Figure 1, it intuitively illustrates the association between the values in the data records "S256, Wang, C5, Database, 50, 80" queried from the table CG and the tables S, SC, and C, That is, the complete data record "S256, Wang, C5, database, 50, 80" does not exist in the database. The values in the data record are queried from three tables S, SC, and C, and are spliced together. There are many examples of such novel expressions of relevant contents in the content of the textbook, such as the addition of the design method of "combined E-R diagram" in the content of database conceptual structure design. This novel expression method and the supplement and improvement of teaching content that keep pace with the times have not been seen in other existing database textbooks.

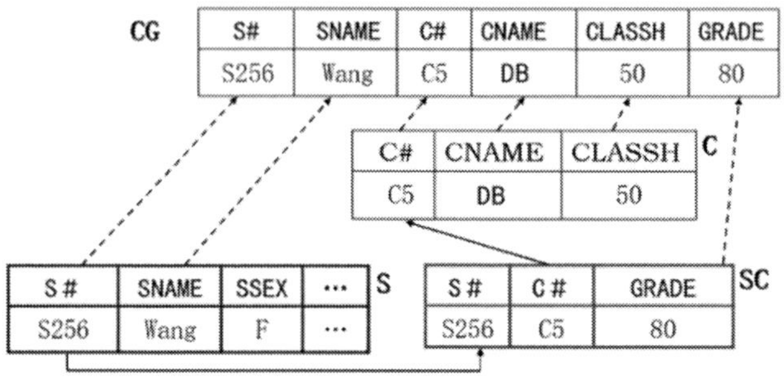

Fig. 1. Mapping example of outward mode CG of tables S, SC and C.

3.3 Innovative design ability content system, highlighting the characteristics of practice and design ability training

Database technology is essentially a practical technology. The ultimate goal of database course teaching is to enable students to master the design technology and design methods of database application systems [5]. For this reason, in the content organization of the database principle and application course materials, the construction methods of data flow diagram and data dictionary, the sorting methods of user data management requirements, and the analysis methods of system functional requirements and performance requirements are systematically introduced around the needs of user demand analysis. This paper systematically introduces the database conceptual structure design method based on E-R diagram, the database logical structure design method based on E-R diagram to relational schema conversion rules, and the database physical structure design method based on SQL Server2012 relational database management system. Focusing on the implementation requirements of the database application system, taking the design of the university teaching information management database application system as a case, this paper introduces the design process and programming methods of user login and student learning information maintenance modules in detail. The contents are organized in combination with actual cases. The design methods and steps are clear, the design process is connected step by step, the design results are verified and the operation results are displayed, and the relevant design contents are described in detail. This not only facilitates the organization of the design practice teaching content, but also facilitates the case demonstration and law following of the students' independent design process, highlighting the characteristics of practice and design ability training.

3.4 The supporting curriculum design practice and organization links have improved the students' design innovation ability

As the training of database design ability involves the analysis ability of management information requirements in certain fields, a certain high-level language programming ability, the comprehensive application and experience of database design knowledge, etc., the general listing and explanation of some design steps and design methods obviously fail to meet the needs of improving students' comprehensive design ability [6]. For this reason, in the textbook "Database Principle and Application (SQL Server)", the author first gives detailed system function analysis, database creation based on SQL Server, data table structure design and table creation method based on SQL Server around the design and implementation of university teaching information management database application system, and then gives a new project method based on Visual Studio programming development environment according to the system and programming needs, Then from the aspects of function description, interface layout and object and attribute setting, related control and attribute design, program code and its design ideas and programming methods, program module debugging and running, and based on SQL Server database management system development environment and Visual Studio VB NET programming language. The design steps and methods of login module, student information addition module, student information query module, score information query module, score information maintenance module and main interface module are given in detail and systematically, It enables students to understand and learn the design process and design and programming methods of a practical database application system in an immersive way, and then through the design process experience of relevant course experiments, it not only enables students to understand and basically master the relevant design technology and design methods, but also improves their practice and design ability.

3.5 The integration of typical entrepreneurship and innovation cases has improved students' confidence in design innovation

The integration of typical entrepreneurship and innovation cases has improved students' confidence in design and innovation. The main teaching goal of the course Database Principle and Application is to cultivate the practical design ability of database based information systems. The cultivation of practical design ability not only requires students to master the basic design technology and design methods of the database, but also requires students to have strong programming and application ability for a high-level language, The latter is where many students' weaknesses and deficiencies lie, so it is inevitable that there is a fear of difficulties among students. For this reason, the author not only inspires and enhances students' interest in learning through the explanation of some programming cases in the course teaching, but also inspires students' enthusiasm and initiative in curriculum practice design through relevant typical cases and the employment annual salary and success path of some excellent graduates with strong design ability of the college. In addition, students are also actively encouraged to take part in the annual examination of software designers and database engineers organized by the Ministry of Personnel of the People's Republic of China. The number of students taking part in the examination of software designers and database engineers is not only increasing every year, but even some students have obtained certificates of senior software designers, which has greatly improved the students' confidence in practical design and innovation.

3.6 The introduction of famous sayings and aphorisms integrated with classroom teaching meets the classroom teaching requirements of ideological and political education

In the process of students' four years of learning and the formation of their life values and aspirations, course teaching plays a crucial role. Course teaching not only teaches students knowledge, but also involves the cultivation of their life values and aspirations [7]. For this reason, in addition to introducing some ideological and political elements of the course in real time in the teaching of database principles and applications, the author mainly gives one or two famous aphorisms around a certain theme in the classroom every week to shape students' value orientation related to the characteristics of the course and enlighten them on the way of life. For example, in view of the characteristics of database courses that are difficult to learn and understand, we give famous aphorisms that are determined to tackle difficulties and dare to climb; According to the characteristics of the overall structure required by the course content, the famous aphorisms of the importance of establishing the grand ideal and goal of life are given; In view of the characteristics that curriculum design and programming should start from the big and focus on the small, the famous aphorism of realizing the relationship between grand goals and small goals is given; In view of the situation that individual students play with their mobile phones instead of attending classes in class, the famous aphorism of the relationship between self-discipline and career success is given. Through the natural integration of these targeted aphorisms in classroom teaching, it has played a certain role in inspiring, guiding, encouraging and demanding students.

4 Conclusion

The database principle and application course plays an important role in the training of new engineering applied talents. The improvement of the content system of the database principle and application course, the innovation of the practical teaching content system, the training of the design innovation ability, and the ideological and political exploration of the course of teaching and educating people are always on the way. We look forward to the author's practice of organizing teaching materials and teaching contents around case based teaching, building a teaching material content system of Database Principles and Applications (SQL Server) (4th Edition) that integrates theory and design ability training, and the exploration in course teaching and practice can be used for reference by peers in improving database course teaching methods and improving practical design ability, And then it plays a positive role in promoting the teaching quality of computer specialty and training applied talents to adapt to the information society.

References

1. Junshan Li, Xia Ye. Database Principle and Application (SQL Server) (Version 4) [M]. Beijing: Tsinghua University Press, 2020.7
2. Xiaojie Du, Bin Yang. Discussion on the teaching reform of Database Principle and Application under the background of new engineering [J]. Information System Engineering, 2021.5.20:151-152, 155
3. Yongping LIU, Xiaobo GUO. Research on the Teaching Reform of Database Principles and Applications [J]. Computer Knowledge and Technology, 2020, 16 (6): 118-120
4. Ge Zhu. Research on Teaching Reform of Database Principle and Application Course [J]. Heilongjiang Education(Theory & Practice), 2018, No.7～8:82-83
5. Ting Wang, Maoyang Zou, Xi Wu. Teaching Research and Practice on the Course of "Database Principle and Application" in Computer Specialty [J]. Wireless Internet Technology, 2019, N0.21:100-101
6. Mingyong Li, Yingde You. Teaching Research on the Cultivation of Innovation Ability in the Course of Database Principle and Application [J]. Computer Education, 2020, No.1:33-36
7. Xiaoli Zhang, Qiuxia Hu. Exploration and Practice of Ideological and Political Education in the Course of Database Principle and Application [J]. Computer Education, 2022, No.1:88-91

The exploration and practice of BIM technology in the teaching reform of civil engineering courses in higher vocational colleges

Yulong Cheng*

Jiuquan Vocational and Technical College Jiuquan, Gansu Province

Abstract. The information wave has promoted social development, but also promoted a lot of technological innovation. BIM technology is based on the development of computer information technology, virtual simulation of the building entity, so that its digital presentation. The three-dimensional visualization model established by BIM technology can comprehensively display the structural requirements, reinforcement configuration and other parameters of building columns, beams, plates, walls and other components in a three-dimensional way. It is convenient to calculate the steel bar and concrete engineering quantity accurately and compile the project valuation documents. This paper takes the course "Measurement and Valuation of Construction Engineering" as an example, with the help of Glodon BIM software to help the teaching, deepen the teaching reform, and provide reference for the peers.

1 Introduction

BIM (Building Information Modeling) is the building information model, which is an engineering data model based on information technology and integrates various related information of construction projects, and is the digital expression of the entity and functional characteristics of construction project facilities. Its development is divided into three stages: primary stage, intermediate stage and advanced stage. The primary stage is mainly used for design, modeling cost calculation, collision detection and other special applications. Intermediate stage is mainly used in design, construction integration, management, operation and maintenance and other systematic application stage; The advanced stage reflects the construction, operation and maintenance of smart cities and other smart applications. Currently, the BIM technology in our country is in the primary stage from the cognition, understanding and popularization of the concept and gradually transitioning to the intermediate stage of systematic application.

The course "Measurement and Valuation of Construction Engineering" is the core course of the major of construction engineering technology and engineering cost in higher vocational colleges, which is highly practical. The teaching goal is to study this course, can carry out engineering quantity calculation, engineering valuation, mainly train in the

* Corresponding author: 983647317@qq.com

engineering cost, construction, project management company and other departments engaged in construction budget, bidding and bidding documents compilation and other aspects of senior technical personnel. In the teaching process, according to the project drawings, Glodon BIM civil engineering measurement platform and cloud pricing software are used for modeling calculation and pricing, which can greatly improve the accuracy of engineering measurement and pricing.

2 Application characteristics of BIM technology

BIM technology is a tool to build a three-dimensional architectural model according to the engineering data information of project drawings. Its essence is to use software to establish a two-dimensional model of engineering project through point, line and surface, and carry out three-dimensional presentation of the model. With the help of digital technology, a complete and accurate engineering model consistent with the building entity is provided for the entire construction project to complete the integration and sharing of building information model.

At the same time, through the BIM database, the computer can quickly carry out statistical analysis of various components, greatly reduce the manual operation and potential errors, easy to achieve the engineering information and the design scheme is completely consistent. The accurate engineering quantity statistics obtained through BIM can be used for cost estimation in the preliminary design process and the engineering quantity budget before the construction and the engineering quantity final accounting after the construction.

2.1 Integrity of model parameters

BIM software not only makes attribute editing and parameter description for building foundation, wall, column, beam, board, roof and other components according to project drawings, but also includes complete engineering information description, such as project name, information of participating units, structure type, material attribute, engineering use, engineering characteristics and other basic design parameter information. It can fully reflect all the information of the construction project.

2.2 Correlation of model attributes

All components in the 3D model established by BIM software are automatically identified and interrelated. The software identifies and checks all parameters of each construction of the building model, screens out the wrong and missing items, further summarizes and calculates, and forms the corresponding model and engineering quantity calculation report. If the attributes of a component in the model are modified, the attributes of all components associated with it in the corresponding positions of other graphs will also be automatically changed, and the calculated data of the engineering quantity report will be automatically updated.

Thus, it can be seen that using BIM software to establish a calculation model for engineering quantity calculation, not only can save time, but also can check whether the parameters of components are correct, to achieve the purpose of automatically checking the attributes of components.

2.3 Unity of model attributes

In different stages of the whole life cycle of a construction project, such as design, construction, operation and maintenance management, the attributes of the BIM model are always consistent, and the parameters of the same component do not need to be edited repeatedly in different stages. The parameter attributes of each component in the model only need to be modified or extended in different stages of construction projects without re-establishment, which avoids the problem of inconsistent component attributes.

3 Application of BIM technology in the course teaching of building engineering measurement and valuation

3.1 Selection of project cases

According to the course content and teaching standards, the case teaching method is adopted. The selected project case is: the construction project of an employee dormitory. Project description: the construction area is 1107.91m2, the building has seven degrees of seismic fortification, the structure form frame structure, the civil building engineering design grade 3, and the building design service life is 50 years. The building has three layers. The height of the first ~ third layer of the building is 3.30 meters. The total height of the building starts from the outdoor natural floor to the roof cornice 10.350 meters, and the indoor and outdoor height difference of the building starts from the outdoor natural floor to the indoor 0.450 meters. Indoor environmental pollution control class is Class Ⅱ, mainly used for dormitory, project No. 2019J-98.

3.2 Creating a project

First of all, according to the engineering drawings, create the project by using the BIM civil engineering measurement platform, edit the engineering information, the project overview, the number of floors, the storey height setting, the property editing of reinforcement and concrete materials, and complete the engineering information setting and the establishment of the shaft network.

Secondly, the foundation, column, beam, plate quantity calculation, this part of the quantity calculation is the weak link of learning, students because of the lack of engineering practice experience, no intuitive perceptual understanding, can not correctly understand the geometric characteristics of the component, more can not correctly read the structure of the construction drawing of the reinforcement configuration and anchorage, lap, According to the drawing calculated steel and concrete engineering quantity deviation is large.

The foundation is modeled by using the civil construction measurement platform of Guanglian BIM. Through 360 degree rotation of the model, the actual state of the foundation is presented in three dimensions. The parameters and attributes of the reinforcement configuration of the foundation as well as the requirements for the lap and anchorage of the details are randomly checked from different angles and different parts, and all geometric characteristics of the foundation are visually displayed in an all-round way without dead corners. Help students correctly read the basic construction drawings, establish three-dimensional space model, greatly change the students' cognition of "boring, obscure" learning content, reduce the deviation of engineering quantity calculation.

In the study of the structure of the main stress component column, beam, plate reinforced concrete engineering calculation, reinforcement engineering calculation is the priority among priorities, but also difficult, and the correct reading structure construction drawing is the premise of accurate calculation of engineering. The traditional construction drawing of building structure is composed of point, line and surface elements. Students often cannot correctly read the structure construction drawing. In order to understand the construction drawing, they must have strong basic professional knowledge, or need experienced construction technicians to interpret and disclose. BIM technology converts 2D drawings into 3D visual virtual models, making point, line and surface elements in drawings virtually displayed as solid components such as foundation, wall, column, beam and board, greatly reducing the difficulty of reading structural construction drawings, cultivating students' spatial imagination and thinking ability, and reducing the difficulty of reading drawings.

In practical operation, the structure model of column, beam and plate is established by using the civil construction measurement platform of Guanglian BIM (Figure 1). From different dimensions, it can be seen in detail whether the configuration of steel bars in the construction of column, beam and plate structure meets the design requirements of the construction drawings, and whether the link mode, joint position, joint length and anchorage requirements of steel bars meet the standards and specifications. Whether the deduction and increase are correct in the calculation of steel bar engineering quantity.

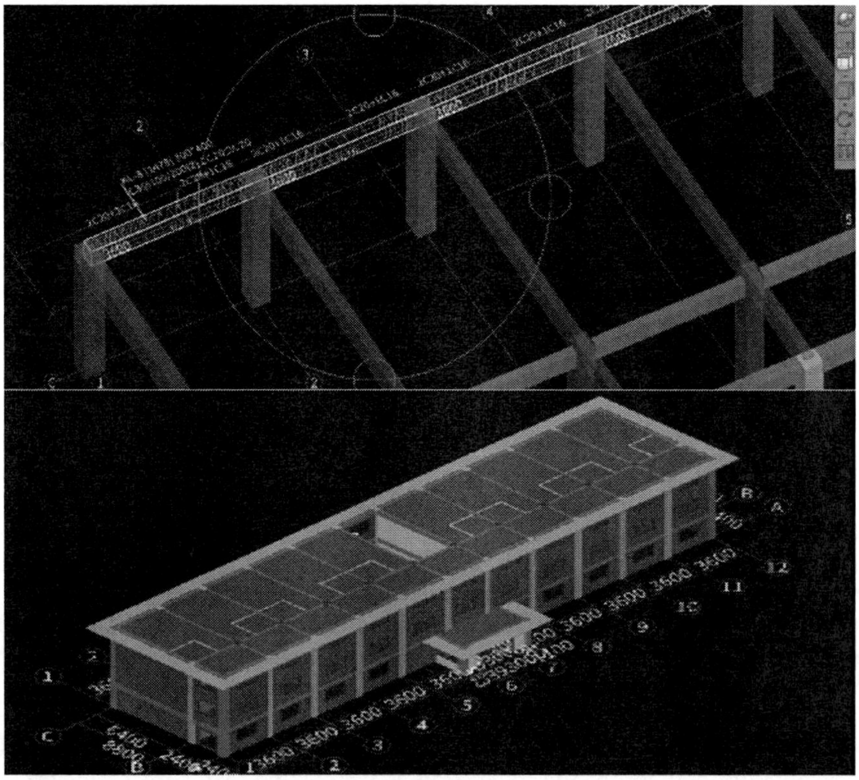

Fig. 1. Structure model of column, beam and plate.

3.3 Timeliness and convenience of project pricing documents

Project pricing is affected by regional differences, quota prescription, government pricing and material market price fluctuations. Moreover, students have not been exposed to the construction industry market and do not understand the basic cost information of engineering projects and the policies and regulations of project pricing issued by the government and related industries. Therefore, it is difficult for students to make the pricing documents to be operable.

The Glodon BIM cloud pricing platform can be used to update the price of materials in real time and inquire the relevant provisions of the latest pricing policy; It can timely reflect the price information changes of labor, materials and machinery platforms in the industrial market of various regions and the requirements of the pricing documents issued by relevant government departments, so as to ensure the timeliness and market competitiveness of the project pricing documents compiled.

4 Conclusion

In order to solve the difficulty of calculating the quantity of structural construction drawing, crack the difficulty of reading structural construction drawing, correctly calculate the quantity of reinforced concrete and compile the engineering valuation document in the course of "Measurement and valuation of Building Engineering".

The BIM technology is organically integrated with the identification and calculation of structural construction drawing, and the three-dimensional model of construction drawing of building structure is established through BIM technology to display the configuration parameters of steel bars in structural components in detail. The previous single 2D drawing is transformed into a three-dimensional teaching mode based on information technology to display the solid model of building and enrich the image, which ADAPTS to the needs of contemporary information and digital development.

Reference

1. Wenshan.WU the Devt and Application Pro of BIM Tech [J]. Grassroots Construction, 2019 (5)
2. Bing.Sun Application of BIM Tech in Energy Building Stru Des [J]. New Bui Ma, 20, 47(9): 186
3. Xiao Li, App of BIM Tech of Meas and Valu Eng [J]. City Arc, 2020.11
4. Jiayin, WangBian Xiaohan. Res between pre and cast-in-place bui on BIM tech [J] Green Buil Mat, 2021 (2) : :17-138
5. Tu Jinsong, Liu Yunlin, Appli Res Pro for pref structure Des and Cons BIM Technology [J]. Jou of Anhui Jianzhu Un, 2019,27 (1) :1-5

On the construction of characteristic specialty of the local applied undergraduate for the talent training of new engineering course

Tian Ji*, *Xiuhan* Jia and *Guibing* Pang

School of Mechanical Engineering and Automation, Dalian Polytechnic University, Dalian, Liaoning, China

Abstract. Combine the requirements of new engineering construction and required by China 2025 for professional personnel training, and meet the industry's demand for high-quality technical personnel. This paper takes the mechanical major as an example, puts forward the construction of characteristic specialty for the construction of new engineering course. Reforming the original talent training mode, strengthening the training of engineering application ability and innovative practice ability, and building a characteristic professional teaching and practice system that meets the needs of enterprises and serves local industries. Throughout the project teaching method and the whole teaching process, which is based on engineering practice education center, furthermore, it deepen cooperation between colleges and enterprises, production and education integration, which establishing an all-round quality guarantee and monitoring system. And it cultivates application-oriented engineering practice and innovation ability of the foundation.

1 Introduction

As China's economy has entered a new normal, and the "Manufacturing in China 2025" guideline has been put forward, China is making every effort to implement the strategy of building a strong manufacturing country, and the manufacturing industry as a whole is facing the historical task of transformation and upgrading. The global outbreak of the "COVID-19" epidemic has made this transformation even more urgent. At present situation, in order to promote the realization of the strategic goal of "Manufacturing in China 2025" and accelerate the transformation and upgrading of the manufacturing industry, it is imperative to reform the existing talent training system, which poses a challenge to the training of traditional engineering professionals.

Compared with traditional engineering talents, emerging industries and new economies need high-quality compound novel engineering talents with engineering practice capability, innovation capability and international competitiveness. "We urgently need to develop novel engineering talents to support the development of the new economy. At present, the goal orientation of engineering talents training in China is not clear, engineering education

* Corresponding author: jitian@dlpu.edu.cn

is too divorced from the reality of industrial enterprises, and engineering students have defects in comprehensive quality and knowledge structure." Zhang Daliang, director of the Higher Education Department of the Ministry of Education, commented on China's engineering education. Wu Aihua, director of the General Department of Ministry of Education of the People's Republic of China, also put forward "five deepening" to promote the implementation of new engineering education. Industry-education integration is an important part of the new engineering education, focusing on the cultivation of engineering education to meet the needs of the industrial field, which requires the coordinated promotion of universities and enterprises.[1]

The reform of integration of production and education was clearly put forward at the The 19th National Congress of CPC. In July 2019, at the ninth meeting of the Central Committee for Comprehensively Deepening Reform, the National Pilot Implementation Plan for the Integration of Industry and Education was adopted.[2]

Training methods of new engineering construction mainly include interdisciplinary, school-enterprise cooperation, repositioning of local universities, and evaluation of engineering majors.[3] This is of great significance to improving the quality of professional talent training and realizing the training requirements of "industry demand orientation, cross-border cross-integration, support and leading industry" for the training of new engineering talents.[4]

The employment situation of many engineering graduates is not optimistic because they don't meet the employment standards of enterprises. The reason for this phenomenon is that there is no practical ability training in the training of engineering professionals.[5] The practice places of universities in China are generally limited, students are not trained, and their hands-on ability is very poor, which can not meet the requirements of enterprises.[6, 7]

As a local university, Dalian Polytechnic University's graduates' scientific research ability is not as good as that of students from double-class universities, and their practical ability is not as good as that of students from vocational and technical colleges, which leads to the problem of low employment rate. Therefore, in the professional construction, it is necessary to meet the requirements of the construction of new engineering disciplines, promote the order-based training of talents, strengthen students' practical ability, and integrate production and education. Make the school's talent training goals consistent with the job needs of the enterprise, and suit the industrial characteristics and needs of the local economy. In this way, students can quickly adapt to the job position after graduation and meet the market demand for applied professionals[8].

2 Construction of teaching and practice system for mechanical specialties

Reform the talent training mode, formulate talent training programs that meet the needs of the machinery industry, optimize the knowledge structure system, strengthen practical teaching, and cultivate students' professional basic knowledge and engineering practice ability. In order to meet the needs of talent training for the coordinated development of knowledge, quality, ability and literacy, the proportion of credits in practical teaching should reach more than 30% of the total credits, and a teaching system for special professional talent training suitable for the requirements of new engineering construction will be constructed.

Actively promote the combination of talent training for mechanical majors with production practice and social practice. Efforts should be made to form a practical teaching system based on experiments and engineering practice, with engineering design and production as the main line, relying on scientific research and engineering training, and boosted by comprehensive practice. Strengthen the integration of production and education, rely on the Engineering Practice Education Center, further deepen school-enterprise cooperation, and establish a stable off-campus practice base. Finally, a practical teaching mode of "school-enterprise cooperation, combination of curricular and extra-curricular integration" is formed.

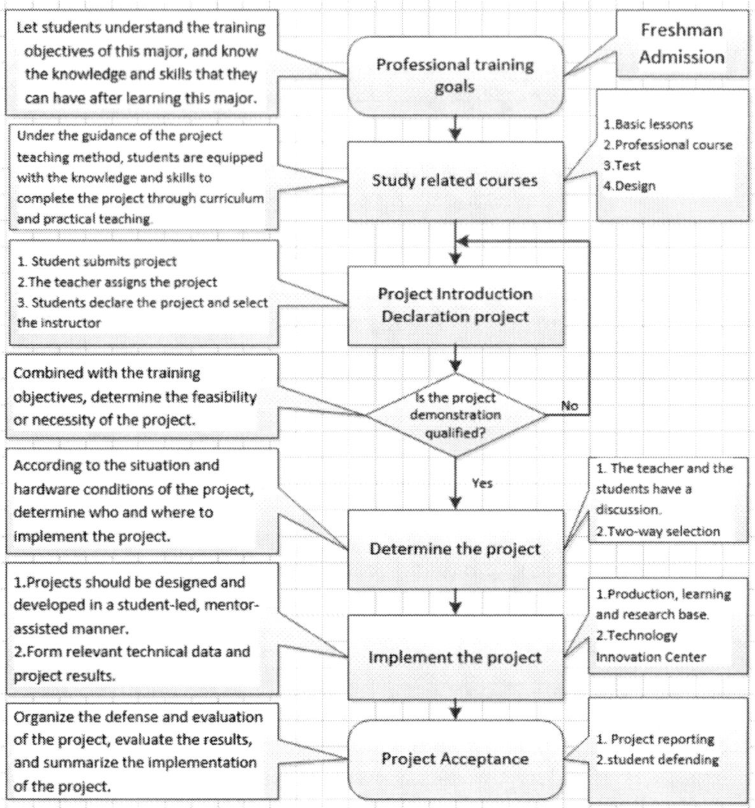

Fig.1. Project teaching method process.

2.1 Constructing a training mode of characteristic professional talents that meets the requirements of new engineering construction

"Mechanical Engineering" is one of the majors involving a wide range of knowledge and strong practicality. Mechanical design and manufacturing itself is a process, and each stage involves different aspects of knowledge, all of which are related to the teaching content of a certain course. Therefore, in the process of professional construction, according to the professional training objectives, an overall teaching project is formed, and each teaching link is an independent project, serving the overall project and realizing the unity of project and ability. The specific flow is shown in Fig. 1.

In order to expand students' knowledge and improve students' innovation ability and engineering practice ability, the professional curriculum system is divided into four levels: First of all, set up the necessary professional basic courses, build a basic professional knowledge and theoretical foundation platform for students, and guide students to enter the professional field initially. Then set up a series of systematic and professional elective courses to lead students to a deeper and broader field of expertise. Secondly, on the basis of the professional elective course group, special lectures are set up to further enrich and refine the professional knowledge and theories of students, making them truly become "professionals". Finally, experts inside and outside the school will give various academic reports on the latest research results and applied technologies, so that students can enjoy the infinite scenery of the academic frontier, and demonstrate the basic procedures and methods of academic research for students.

Adopt broad basic education, fine professional knowledge and training characteristics that are closely combined with practical innovation. Focus on cultivating students' self-learning ability, able to find problems, analyze problems, solve problems and carry out innovative work. In the course setting, professional courses and practical teaching links with obvious industry characteristics are set up to strengthen the training of professional skills and practical ability, so that students can quickly be competent for technical work in the industry after employment.

Through this new application-oriented talent training model, it focuses on cultivating students' basic quality, professional quality, engineering practice ability and innovation ability, and improving their employment competitiveness and entrepreneurial ability.

2.2 Constructing a Practical Teaching System Supporting the Cultivation of Applied Talents

In order to meet the requirements of new engineering for talent training, strengthen the connection with the production practice of enterprises, and play the role of combining production, education and research, a practical teaching system as shown in flow chart 2 is constructed.[9, 10]

The reformed practical teaching system focuses on solving the problems of short, scattered, and unsystematic practical teaching and training, and the quality of practical teaching cannot support the cultivation of higher-level innovative and applied talents required by the construction of new engineering disciplines.

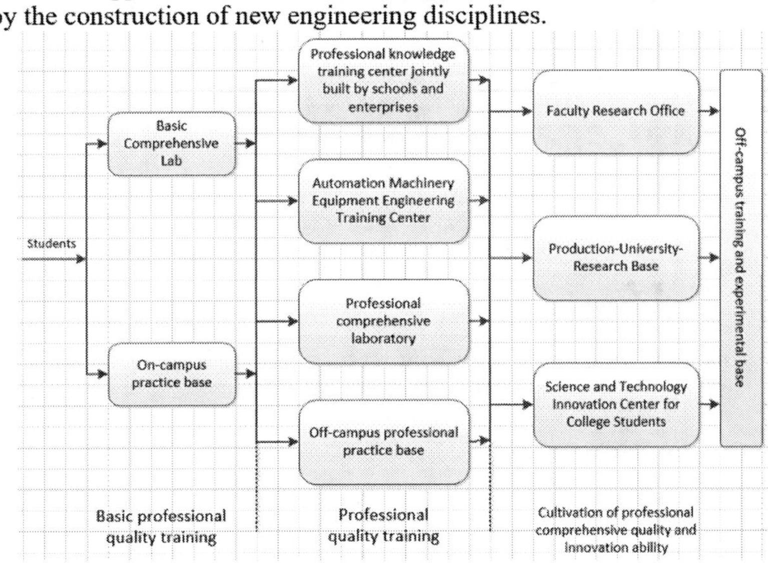

Fig.2. Practical teaching system.

3 Construction of teaching guarantee and monitoring system

The construction of teaching quality assurance and monitoring system has played an important role in improving the quality of personnel training.

3.1 Quality assurance model and system structure

The teaching quality assurance system structure is shown in flow chart 3.The teaching quality monitoring and guarantee system is constructed by teachers' evaluation of learning, students' evaluation of teaching, and leading experts' listening to lectures.

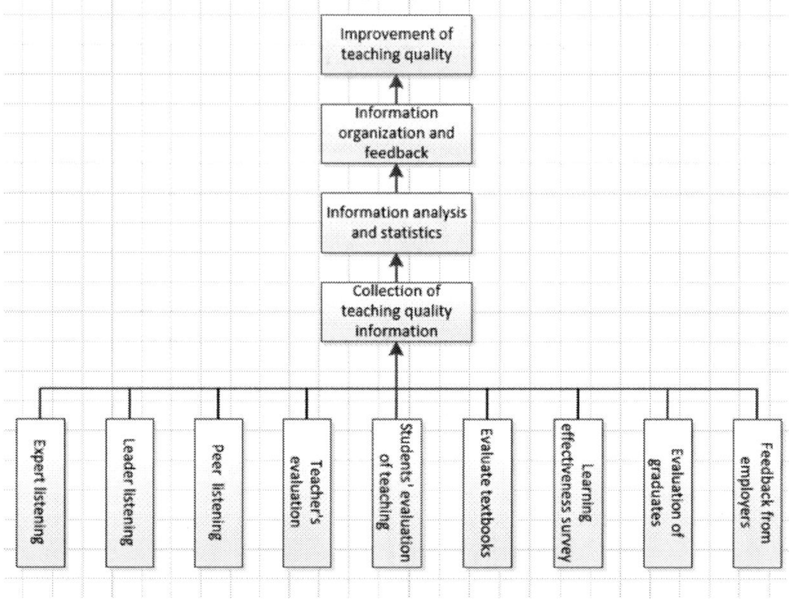

Fig. 3. Teaching quality assurance system structure.

3.2 Monitor the teaching quality of teachers

According to the quality supervision system, clear requirements are put forward for each teaching link. Make the teaching process have rules to follow, and the quality of work in each link is guaranteed.

The implementation of quality standards is collected from five perspectives, including leadership, supervision, students, peers, and graduates. Collect a lot of information through different monitoring planes.

3.3 Improve the teaching quality of teachers

The college verifies the collected teaching feedback information, and then gives feedback to each major or the corresponding teachers, and requires timely correction.

4 Conclusions

The construction and development of new engineering courses provide local colleges with new school-running direction and transformation goals. Through benchmarking the construction of mechanical specialty of new engineering courses, the professional characteristics of "adapting to the needs of enterprises, serving the development of local industries and deeply integrating production and education" are created. Implementing application -oriented education reform by implementing project teaching method; Relying on the construction of engineering practice education center by schools and enterprises, the cooperation between schools and enterprises will be deepened, production and education will be integrated, students will be guided to actively innovate, and an all-round and multi-angle quality assurance and monitoring system will be established, which will lay the foundation for cultivating high-level applied engineering and technical talents with engineering practice and innovation ability. The next step is to constantly sum up and improve in the process of new engineering construction, so as to realize the high-quality development of mechanical specialty education.

The authors are very grateful to the Education Branch Foundation of China Light Industry Federation (under grant No. QGJY2019019), the Province Educational Science Planning Foundation of Liaoning (under grant No. JG17DB050) for its financial support for this project.

5 References

1. General Office of the State Council, Several Opinions of the General Office of the State Council on Deepening the Integration of Industry and Education. Issued by the State Council (No. 95, 2017)
2. National Development and Reform Commission, Ministry of Education, Ministry of Industry and Information Technology, A total of six ministries, National implementation plan for the pilot project of integration of production and education. Notice on Printing and Distributing the Pilot Implementation Plan of the National Industry-Education Integration Construction (Development and Reform Society, No.1558, 2019)
3. M. Y. Chen, S. Y. Pan, Z. J. Xie, Practical exploration of the integration of production, teaching and research in apparel engineering with new engineering concepts (Experimental Technology and Management, **35(10)**, 144-147, 2018)
4. L. Guan, J. H. Liang, Exploration and practice of school-enterprise collaborative education model under the background of new engineering (Computer Education, **11**, 100-103, 2018)
5. S. L. Wu, S. Y. Zhao, C. Z. Huang, Research on the quality assurance path of the construction of new engineering majors in local undergraduate colleges (College Education, **6**, 18-21, 2018)
6. X. L. Wei, Z. H. Fan, J. N. Wang, Research on the practical teaching system of mechanical majors based on the cultivation of innovation ability (Journal of Hebei University of Technology (Social Science Edition), **33(3)** 103-106, 2016)
7. X. W. Wang, B. F. Wang, Construction and Application of Trinity Practice Teaching Platform in the Transformation and Development of Newly-built Undergraduate Colleges (Experimental Technology and Management, **35(11)**, 164-166, 216, 2018)
8. C. P. Du, B. L. Chen, Practical Teaching and Its Enlightenment in German University of Applied Sciences (Contemporary Educational Science, **(2)**, 80-83, 2017)
9. X. Z. Ming, C. L. Tang, J. Zhou, etc, Discussion on the Reform and Construction of Applied Undergraduate Practice Teaching Mode for Mechanical Majors (Experimental Technology and Management, **28(9)**, 18-21, 24, 2011)
10. H. Zeng, H. X. Wang, D. Q. Zhang, Reform and practice of training mode for applied talents in mechanical specialty (Journal of Liaoning University of Technology (Social Science Edition), **(2)**, 99-103, 2015)

The practical teaching design of illustration design course based on OBE concept

Yanfei Chen*, and *Zhijie* Lu

School of Design & Arts, Jingdezhen Ceramic Institute, Jingdezhen, Jiangxi, China

Abstract. Based on the concept of OBE education and taking the course of Illustration Design as an example, this paper expounds in detail how to apply the concept of OBE to practice teaching design by focusing on teaching objectives, teaching contents, teaching methods, teaching modes, teaching resources, course assessment and achievement evaluation. This can be used for reference to solve the problems existing in the course teaching and effectively improve the quality of the course teaching.

1 Introduction

Outcomes-based education (OBE for short) is an educational concept that is oriented towards students' learning outcomes. It believes that the goal of instructional design and instructional implementation is the final learning outcome of students through the educational process. At present, domestic research on outcomes-based education mainly focuses on how schools or majors use the OBE education concept to carry out the reform of talent cultivation model, the design of training program and professional certification at the macro level, but there are still some deficiencies in the specific operability [1]. This paper focuses on these three aspects, taking the course of illustration design as an example, to carry out the course design.

2 Defining output

Figures and tables, as originals of good quality and well contrasted, are to be in their final form, ready for reproduction, pasted in the appropriate place in the text. Try to ensure that the size of the text in your figures is approximately the same size as the main text (10 point). Try to ensure that lines are no thinner than 0.25 point.

Defining output is to define the learning outcomes of the course according to the graduation requirements in the training program, that is, the teaching objectives.

The following principles should be reflected in the formulation of teaching objectives based on the concept of OBE: (1) teaching objectives should reasonably support graduation requirements. (2) The coverage of teaching goals is multi-dimensional. (3) The teaching objectives should reflect the concept of "student-centred" and be expressed by explicit

* Corresponding author: icychenyanfei@163.com

action verbs, such as students' ability to describe, explain, analyse, design... (4) Teaching objectives need to accurately describe the cognitive level of students and be measurable and evaluable [1, 3]. Based on the above principles, this article reversely combs the teaching goals of the Illustration Design course based on the graduation requirements and professional positions in the visual communication design talent training program (refer with: Table 1).

Table 1. Teaching objectives of illustration design.

Styles Level	Specific Objectives
Knowledge Layer	Objective 1: Students can state and explain the basic knowledge and theory of the definition, classification, generation and development of illustrations, the comparison and transformation between literary art and painting art, the conception and technique expression of illustration creation.
	Objective 2: Students can apply the basic procedures of illustration design, understand the expression and aesthetic consciousness of illustrations, and interpret, analyze and evaluate the application of illustrations with different themes and styles; Be able to summarize and explain the current situation and trends in illustration design.
Ability Layer	Objective 3: Students can apply the knowledge of illustration design to analyze, conceive, design and implement specific operations on related topics; Be able to apply the theoretical and practical knowledge of illustration design to design a preliminary solution for the enterprise.
Quality Layer	Objective 4: Students can make use of online learning courses and resources such as MOOC and micro-courses, as well as Chinese and English materials query, literature retrieval and other means to carry out independent learning and cooperative learning, write research reports, conduct results demonstration and effective communication and exchange.
	Objective 5: Students can understand and abide by relevant professional ethics and norms and fulfill their responsibilities in the practice of illustration design.

3 Achieve output

The achievement of output refers to the use of reasonable teaching strategies (including the selection and integration of teaching contents, the design of teaching methods and modes, and the construction of teaching resources) to enable students to achieve learning outcomes in teaching goals [2].

3.1 Selection and integration of teaching content

According to the teaching objectives of Illustration Design (refer with: Table 2), the teaching contents are divided into 3 modules and 9 units, which are expanded in the logical order of “basic - theory – practice”. Each module corresponds to 1-2 teaching objectives. However, non-technical goals such as students' learning and teamwork ability cannot be directly reflected in the course teaching content, but need to be reflected through the reform of teaching models.

Table 2. Module Division and Corresponding Teaching Objectives of Illustration Design.

Module	**Main Teaching Content (unit)**	**Teaching Objectives**	**Student Achievement**
Basic Knowledge Module	1. The concept and historical evolution of illustrations 2. Illustration expression methods and tools 3. Function, value and application area of illustration design	Objective 1	Students can state and explain the basic knowledge and theory of the definition, classification, generation and development of illustrations, the comparison and transformation between literary art and painting art, the conception and technique expression of illustration creation.
Theoretical Knowledge Module	4. Design the categories and forms of illustrations 5. Aesthetic features of illustration design 6. The development trend of modern illustration design	Objective 2	Students can apply the basic procedures of illustration design, have a deep understanding of illustration performance and aesthetic consciousness, explain, analyze, and evaluate the application of illustrations on different topics; Be able to summarize and explain the current situation and trends in illustration design.
Practical Knowledge Module	7. Design criteria of illustration design 8. Design orientation and conception of illustrations 9. Artistic expression of illustration design	Objective 3	Students can apply the knowledge of illustration design to analyze, conceive, design and implement specific operations on related topics; Able to apply the theoretical and practical knowledge of illustration design to design a preliminary solution for the enterprise.

3.2 The design of the suitability of teaching methods and learning activities

Based on the teaching needs of OBE concept, teachers choose appropriate teaching methods or learning activities according to the knowledge type and teaching objective level of "learning output". Table 3 shows the main knowledge types, levels of teaching objectives and corresponding teaching methods and learning activities of each unit of the course of Illustration Design. On the one hand, different teaching methods are adopted for different types of knowledge. For factual or conceptual knowledge, self-learning and classroom teaching are mostly adopted. Regarding procedural knowledge, "integration of knowledge and action" and "learning by doing" can be emphasized. Experiential teaching, simulated practice teaching, and case teaching can be used more; for metacognitive knowledge, we should pay more attention to the cultivation of students' way of thinking, such as discussion, collaborative inquiry learning, problem solving, etc [3]. Different levels of teaching goal, on the other hand, also should adopt different teaching methods, such as memory and understanding of the teaching goal of the two low-order can use part of classroom teaching and autonomous learning, and the analysis, evaluation, the teaching aim of creating these higher-order needs more using collaborative inquiry learning, the discussion, case teaching, the teaching method based on the problem or project.

Table 3. Corresponding table of knowledge type, teaching objective level and teaching method of Illustration Design.

Module	Main Knowledge Type	Teaching Goal Level	Teaching Method and Learning Activities
Basic knowledge module	Factual knowledge Conceptual knowledge	Memory Understanding	Self-learning Lecture Case study
Theoretical knowledge module	Factual knowledge Conceptual knowledge	Memory Understanding Application Analysis	Self-learning Lecture Case study
Practical knowledge module	Procedural knowledge Metacognitive knowledge	Understanding Application Analysis Create (design)	Self-learning Lecture Project teaching Collaborative learning
Basic knowledge module	Factual knowledge Conceptual knowledge	Memory Understanding	Self-learning Lecture Case study

3.3 Flexible design of teaching mode

The teaching based on the concept of OBE emphasizes "student center", in which teachers are the guide and leader of learning [4]. In the teaching design of Illustration Design (refer with: Figure 1), the teacher adopts a mixed teaching model of online learning before class, offline interaction on the middle line of class and online learning after class. Students achieve the role of cognitive knowledge and sublimation knowledge through independent and cooperative learning before and after class, and the role of consolidating and deepening knowledge through classroom learning. In the classroom teaching, the main teachers check the learning effect before class, summarize and sort out the knowledge points, arrange the classroom tasks and explore the learning together through group discussion, group cooperation and online teaching platform interaction. Course evaluation is based on the learning output data of students to achieve the teaching objectives of the course, including online and offline learning and the overall evaluation of the final design work [5].

This teaching mode not only reflects the dominant position of students' learning, but also is conducive to cultivating students' autonomous learning ability and cooperative inquiry ability, so as to achieve the non-technical teaching objectives, as mentioned above, teaching objectives 4 and 5 [6].

3.4 Optimization and integration of teaching resources

Based on the course teaching objectives, the teacher designs the teaching content of the online and offline courses as a whole, constructs a practical, project-based, and modular integrated curriculum system that meets the professional qualification standards, and clearly design project-oriented course teaching content. There are two types of projects -- classroom projects and extracurricular projects. Classroom projects are specific cases that cover teaching knowledge points, and extracurricular projects are open cases (such as competitions and topics) that guide students to study independently and develop knowledge independently [7].

Under the concept of outcomes-based education, curriculum teaching resources cannot be blindly piled up. Both online and offline resources need to be introduced, optimized, integrated and constructed around the realization of curriculum learning outcomes (i.e., teaching objectives). Attention should be paid to the diversity of resource design to meet the needs of students for different types of teaching resources. Teaching resources need to be dynamically optimized, integrated and updated to evaluate the effectiveness and utilization of teaching resources; Attention should be paid to intellectual property issues in resource utilization.

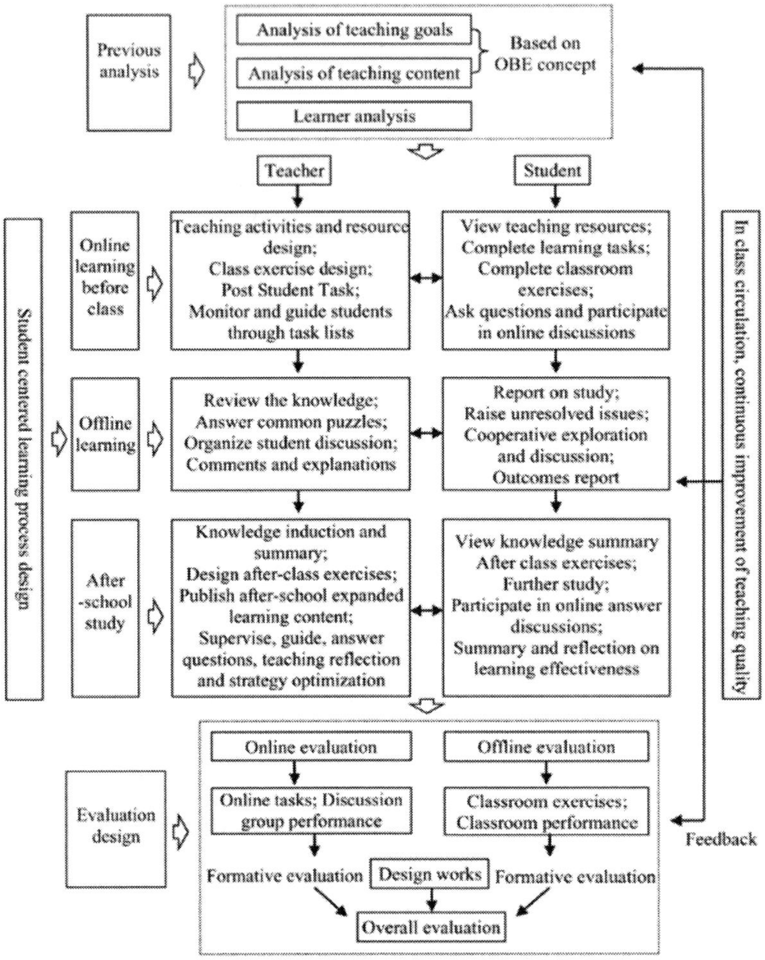

Fig. 1. Teaching design of illustration design based on OBE concept.

4 Evaluation output

Under the concept of OBE education, evaluation output refers to the adoption of diversified evaluation methods, focusing on whether learning outcomes are achieved. The following principles should be paid attention to in the course assessment design: First, pay attention to the combination of process assessment and summative assessment. Second, the content of the examination should be closely related to the teaching objectives of the course, and emphasis should be laid on knowledge examination, ability examination and quality examination. Third, the main body of assessment should be diversified, encourage teacher-student mutual assessment, student self-assessment, and student-to-student mutual assessment, etc., and change the past form of teacher-based assessment [8]. According to the above principles and steps, this paper designs the assessment program of Illustration Design course (refer with: Table 4).

Table 4. Corresponding relationship between assessment methods and teaching objectives.

Assessment Type	Assessment Method	Proportion (%)	Corresponding Teaching Objectives
Process Assessment	1. Practice in class	20	1, 2
	2. Class attendance and online learning	10	4
	3. Design work (project or competition design scheme)	20	3, 5
	4. Research report (on problems arising from independent learning, creative thinking and process of design scheme)	10	2,4
Summative Assessment	5. Final design work (schoolwork exhibition)	40	3,4,5

When the assessment method of learning achievement belongs to quantitative evaluation (such as test and final exam), teachers should clear the relationship between teaching objective, teaching content and work form, so as to determine the quality of learning achievement and avoid the proposition deviating from teaching objective. When the assessment method of learning achievement belongs to qualitative assessment (such as project achievement display and exchange, practice report, etc.), teachers need to design a "two-way form of assessment scale", which consists of assessment dimension, assessment scale and dimension description.

5 Summary

In a word, the course teaching design based on OBE idea subverts the traditional mode. It is a reverse design process based on students' learning outcomes, which effectively solves the problems of "what to learn (goal)", "why to learn (need)", "how to learn (process)", "how to prove to learn (evaluation)" and so on. However, dogmatism should be avoided in practical applications, because from a static perspective, not all learning outcomes can be clearly expressed, and some hidden learning outcomes (such as personality qualities, learning habits, thinking traits, etc.) cannot be accurately measured; From the perspective of dynamics, learning outcomes are changing, and it is a difficult problem to describe "future learning outcomes" prospectively in the era of rapidly changing social environment.

References

1. Z. Li, CUT, **8** (2020)
2. P. Gu, W.Hu, P. Lin, N. Bao, X. Lu, G. Xiong, Y. Chen, RHEE, **7** (2021)
3. H.Zhou, F. Dong, J. Chen, DCE, **25** (2019)
4. Y. Yuan, FER, **35** (2019)
5. D. Zheng, L. Chen, X. Wang, ETM, **34** (2020)
6. B. Dai, W. Ji, J. Liu, L. Zhang, N. Liu, RHEE, **6** (2021)
7. X. Zheng, J.Zhangg, S. Bai, G. Guo, CUT, **2** (2017)
8. L. Han, Q. Fu, R.Zhao, FER, **8** (2020)

Research on the teaching reform of the course web front-end design based on the emerging engineering education model

Xiaosong Wang*

Shandong Technology and Business University, Management Science and Engineering Department, 264005 Yantai City, China

Abstract. Web Front-end Design is a basic professional course of information management and information system major. The course mainly trains students' ability of web design and website development. This paper attempts to change the traditional teaching mode that teachers are the main body. It tries to build a new teaching mode that students are the main body and teachers are the guiders. In the process of curriculum reform, the complete project-driven teaching method is adopted to complete the teaching of course knowledge points. At the same time, the reform references to the emerging engineering education model with the whole life cycle of the system's conceive, design, implement and operate (CDIO) as the background. By the reform, students can change passive learning into active learning, improve their practical ability, and further enhance the practical development ability of Web page design projects.

1 The existing problems in traditional teaching

Carefully analyse some problems and deficiencies in the current teaching process of Web Front-end Design, in order to make students more proficient in the corresponding professional skills, it is urgent to carry out teaching reform.

Firstly, the teaching method is outdated. In the teaching process, teachers often only explain some impart knowledge or simply train students' single skills, ignoring the cultivation of students' professional knowledge, personal ability, interpersonal ability and creative ability.

Secondly, evaluation method is single. Most of the practical engineering courses tend to use the traditional combination of usual results plus experimental results and final results to complete the assessment and evaluation of students, which can't stimulate students' interest in learning, and the teaching effect is poor, which is obviously inconsistent with the current evaluation standard of emerging engineering education.

Thirdly, teaching hours are insufficient. The course of Web page design involves many aspects, such as the early conception, images processing, web effect design and dynamic

* Corresponding author: morningpine@163.com

effect design, website publishing and post-maintenance. However, due to the limitation of curriculum hours, teachers cannot complete the connection of many abilities in a limited time. As a result, students cannot fully grasp and use the knowledge that they have learned to solve the actual project development.

Finally, the website design is incomplete. In the practical teaching process of web page design and production, teachers mainly provide students with a single page design experiment based on the distribution of knowledge points, without providing a complete website project development, unable to cultivate students' ability to analyse and design a complete website system.

2 The specific measures for teaching reform

2.1 Teaching content reform

Teachers make teaching tasks according to teaching objectives. First of all, teachers formulate detailed teaching tasks according to the syllabus, and adopt the flipped classroom mixed teaching task to formulate independent knowledge points as the unit, so as to facilitate students' independent learning. Therefore, the whole course is organized into several modules according to the knowledge structure, and each module is divided into several small knowledge points.

Based on the above ideas, the course content of Web Front-end Design is adjusted and divided into three modules. Each module is composed of several small knowledge points, which is convenient for students to learn independently. There is coupling between modules. Each module is connected in series to form a complete system. The course structure is shown in Table 1.

2.2 Teaching mode and teaching organization reform

2.2.1 Teaching mode reform

According to the design concept of CDIO engineering education mode, the project is divided into four stages in combination with the software project development process. Demand analysis corresponding concept, project design corresponding design stage, project realization corresponding implementation stage, test and maintenance corresponding operation stage, and design teaching content and process based on these four stages [1]. At the same time, taking project teaching as the main line, the task-driven teaching method and learning by doing teaching method are adopted to enable students to master the knowledge and operating skills of website planning, design, production and release in the process of completing project development, as shown in Table 2.

2.2.2 Teaching organization reform

In teaching, teachers divide the content into different steps according to the four stages of CDIO and the development process of software projects [2].

In the concept stage, the teacher guides students to analyze the needs, functions and functions of the project according to the specific requirements of the project, and complete the sorting and classification of the materials. At the same time, according to the requirements of software engineering development projects, complete the preparation of requirements analysis documents and detailed analysis documents.

Table 1. The structure of course.

Teaching modules	Knowledge points	Learning contents
HTML	7	Text and Paragraph, List, Hyperlink, Table, Frame, Form, Multimedia applications in web pages.
CSS	7	Definition and use of style sheets, definition selectors, use of text and layout styles, use of background and colour styles, setting of beautifying web pages and hyperlinks, concept and use of rectangular modules, and use of list styles.
JavaScript	5	Identifiers and variables, operators and expressions, JavaScript program control structures, common objects, event programming.

Table 2. Practical project: specific teaching content design of a website.

CDIO	Website project development process	Tasks in each stage
Conceive	Requirement analysis	Task 1: Design idea of website construction Task 2: Complete the needs analysis of the website
Design	Website project design	Task 1: Website style design Task 2: Website column design Task 3: Material collection and sorting Task 4: Design the overall rendering of the webpage
Implement	Project implementation	Task 1: Web page Slicing Task 2: Web page production Task 3: Comprehensive website production
Operate	Test and maintenance	Task 1: Space and domain name application Task 2: Website upload, test and maintenance

Table 3. The implementation process of six-step teaching method.

Teaching steps	Main content	Teaching organization
Project import	Describe project functions Demonstrate the final effect of the project Distribute materials required for the project	Teacher demonstration project Explain the key points and difficulties of task completion
Knowledge teaching	Teaching of new knowledge points in the project	Teachers explain and demonstrate by simple cases
task allocation	Instruct students to receive different tasks according to the division of work	The teacher instructs the students to complete by themselves
Complete the task	Team members complete the tasks received The project leader completes the summary of tasks The connection of various projects The project leader completes the test of the project	The teacher should explain the common problems that students encounter in time, and learn while doing.
Submit task Project presentation	Submit the project, demonstrate and explain the gains, deficiencies and knowledge points that need to be supplemented by teachers	Students submit complete projects and demonstrate
Project Summary	Summarize the problems in the project development	Teachers summarize and propose ideas for improvement

In the design stage, the teacher first teaches the knowledge points needed to complete the project, then guides the students to decompose the project, and assigns the relevant tasks to the students, so that the students can complete the design of graphics, Flash dynamic effects, logos, etc. required for web page design. Students complete the design of different functional modules according to the needs of the project, and finally form their own renderings for use in the implementation stage. In the process of completing their respective tasks, teachers should give guidance according to the situation of students. In this way, the boundary between the theoretical teaching and practical teaching of the course is weakened, and the reform of the integrated teaching method of doing in learning and learning by doing is realized. Students can master theoretical knowledge and improve practical ability in the process of completing each project.

In the implementation stage, teachers guide students to complete the design of a single web page with different functional modules (including static and dynamic effects), and combine the individual tasks organically to form the completed project.

In the operation stage, teachers mainly guide the test and running of the website, find problems and solve them in time, and finally form products (including instructions for use) that can be delivered to customers.

In order to facilitate teaching and management, the teaching process can adopt the six-step teaching method of project introduction, knowledge teaching, task assignment, task completion, project demonstration, and project summary to complete the organization of teaching for each project [3]. The details are shown in Table 3.

2.3 Reform of evaluation and examination methods

The final assessment is carried out from three aspects: the usual performance, the project task assessment, and the project submission and reporting, which respectively account for 30%, 50% and 20% of the total performance. Finally, the comprehensive assessment results of the students are calculated. The teacher gives the usual assessment results according to the students' attendance and learning attitude. The project task assessment is given by the teacher according to the students' task completion. The project submission and project report assessment are completed at the same time, and this part is completed by a combination of teacher evaluation, self-evaluation of the student, and the project team mutual evaluation. The teacher gives each student's overall evaluation score according to the effect, workload and quality of the project report and demonstration.

3 The teaching reform results

The application of CDIO emerging engineering education mode in the teaching reform of Web Front-end Design course, and the integration of online and offline mixed teaching methods, and the use of task-driven teaching methods in the specific implementation process will stimulate students' interest in learning, make students become the main body of teaching. Students not only master the professional knowledge of web design and production, but also improve their web design ability, team cooperation ability, organization ability and communication ability. Through the effectiveness of teaching reform, the links among different courses are connected, and the ability of students to practice project engineering is enhanced. Good teaching effect improves the quality of talent training of information management and information system specialty.

References

1. Haiying. M, Web front-end development teaching practice based on CDIO concept. Information system engineering. 160-162,**04**(2021)
2. Yan. W, Jialin. M., The application and practice of Web programing based on CDIO. Software engineering. 50-51,**19**(2016)
3. Junqing. M, Xiaolong. M, Research on countermeasures of integrating CDIO engineering concept into Web Front-end Development Technology course. Computer Era. 74-76,**6** (2021)

Exploring the innovation of Chinese cultural education practice from the perspective of inter-subjectivity theory

Xuling Chen*

Jinan University, Guangdong Province, China

Keywords: The inter-subjectivity theory, Chinese culture, Educational pr a-ctice, Educational innovation.

Abstract. The theory of inter-subjectivity, which emphasizes the sharing of equal subjects through communication and interaction, contains a rich educational philosophy. The theory of inter-subjectivity guides the innovation and reform of Chinese cultural education practice, which is an important initiative to enhance students' sense of Chinese cultural identity and contains the logic of theory, action and thought. In the face of the practical difficulties of Chinese cultural education practice in universities, on the one hand, we can promote the intercultural communication of educational subjects by creating cultural environment and improving educational management. On the other hand, we can explore the intercultural common ground of educational subjects by designing practical activities and focusing on cultural knowledge to promote the high-quality development of Chinese cultural education reform in the new era.

1 Introduction

The theory of inter-subjectivity is a theory introduced into the field of education based on a re-examination of students' subjectivity to adapt to the laws of educational development. In order to further implement the strategic plan of the 20th Party Congress about inheriting the excellent Chinese traditional culture, guiding students to actively carry out cultural exchanges and cultural practices is a natural choice to enhance their sense of Chinese cultural identity.[1] However, Chinese cultural education practices often lack the highlighting of intersubjective dialogue and interaction. In this regard, using inter-subjectivity as a theoretical guide to carry out Chinese cultural education practices helps to confirm the equal and coexistent status of educational subjects and construct a knowledge community based on cultural integration. But what are the key elements of the educational implications of inter-subjectivity theory? Further, what is the logical reasoning behind the

* Corresponding author: cxl13760585454@163.com

practice of Chinese cultural education in the context of inter-subjectivity theory? How can concrete and innovative changes in education be implemented? To clarify these questions, it is necessary to start from the basic connotation of the theory of inter-subjectivity and clarify the logic of its role in educational practice to derive feasible ways to promote the innovative development of Chinese cultural education.

2 The educational concept of inter-subjectivity theory

2.1 The inter-subjectivity theory

The inter-subjectivity theory is a new relational structure that has emerged from contemporary western philosophy in the field of philosophical studies of subjectivity by reflecting on the conflict of subject-object relations. In terms of its development, the theory of inter-subjectivity is both a reflection on the subject-object dichotomy paradigm and a positive response to the social crisis in recent times. The subject-object model can deal with the relationship between man and nature and man and things. However, in dealing with man and man, this model will fall into the dilemma that man is not an object. It can be seen that the theory of subjectivity based on the subject-object relationship is an incomplete interpretation of subjectivity. For this reason, the research trend in philosophy shows a shift from the dissolution of subjectivity to the construction of the theory of inter-subjectivity. This shows that the theory of inter-subjectivity has certain inspirational implications for the construction of cognition and interpersonal interaction in the field of education.

2.2 Features of the educational philosophy of inter-subjectivity theory

The educational concept features of intersubjectivity theory include three aspects. First of all, inter-subjectivity theory emphasizes the co-existence and sharing of interactive subjects. The theory of inter-subjectivity transforms the unidirectional orientation of subject-object relationship into symbiotic inter-subject relationship without restricting the internal relevance of object as intermediary. It emphasizes the characteristics of interactive subjectivity and common subject. Secondly, the theory of inter-subjectivity emphasizes that the dialogue between subjects should be equal. The educated and the educator from the perspective of the theory of inter-subjectivity are in a shared context, providing favorable basic prerequisites for developing an equal exchange between them. In the mutual relations between subjects, people are in mutual need, constantly making two-way predictions.[2] Each subject exists both as an object of the other and as a degree of objectivity, determining the existence of the self through the mutual observation of subjects. Thirdly, the theory of inter-subjectivity emphasizes that the micro subject should show subjectivity. What Marx called "human dependence", "human independence based on material dependence" and "free individuality based on the full development of the individual and their common social production capacity as their social wealth" are the three social aspects.[3] These three stages of social and human development are both the three stages of development of subjectivity and the three stages of development of the theory of inter-subjectivity. Marx's idea of the theory of inter-subjectivity emerged with the second major turn in the process of forming a new vision of history. The second turn, which took place between 1845 and 1865, was a deeper study of the practical view of interaction through philosophy and economics towards the stage of materialism of interaction practice.[4] The paradigm shift in understanding from a practical anthropology to a social relations theory of interaction essentially initiated the study of the inter-subjectivity theory of interaction. Overall, the basic connotation of inter-subjectivity theory can be summarized into three elements. The first is practicality. The interaction between subjects is the product of practice, which should be carried out and improved in practice. The second is equality. The theory of inter-subjectivity is based on the monism of teachers and dualism of teachers and students. It emphasizes the equality of communication mechanism, communication emotion and communication status. The third is interactive subjectivity. Under the theory of inter-subjectivity, the subject is co-existent and there is no possibility of accidental conversion. Both sides promote each other and jointly act as the core subject of education.

3 Innovation embodiment of Chinese cultural education practice from the perspective of the inter-subjectivity theory

Chinese culture is the root cultural resource of university cultural education. The integration of the two is an inherent requirement of university Chinese cultural education. The Chinese culture education is faced with such challenges as college students' weak sense of identity with excellent traditional Chinese culture, weak construction of professional teachers and the lack of effective connection between content and form.[5] It has become one of the focuses of the academic circles to grasp the dilemma of Chinese excellent traditional culture education scientifically, and promote the solution of the problem pertinently and efficiently. To this end, the inter-subjectivity theory has been proposed and applied in the field of education, mainly to solve the dilemma faced by the theory of subjectivity in education. In terms of educational values, the academic circle has reached a consensus of "student-oriented development". Taking students as the subject of education is the primary value orientation of the concept of student-oriented development.

3.1 Theoretical logic: the turn towards conformity to the subject position

The educator is seen as the subject of the whole teaching activity, and the educatee is regarded as the object to be reformed. The crisis facing subjective education can be attributed to three specific problems. Firstly, subjectivity is limited to the subject-object relationship in the objectified activity, which leads to an incomplete interpretation of subjectivity. Secondly, the subject-object relationship leads to the possessive personality of the subject. Thirdly, subjectivity under the subject-object relationship is unable to cope with the educational trend of the dual subject. On this basis, the theory of inter-subjectivity does not dissolve the existence of the subject, but rather transforms the way of understanding. It emphasizes the establishment of interactive relations between two subjects in the act of educational interaction, thus resolving the crisis of subjectivity.

3.2 Logic of action: developing a two-way communication between subjects

The Inter-subjective communication between teachers and students involves the following three breakthroughs and advantages. Firstly, the research object is advanced from single subject to synchronic double subject. Both the educator and the educated are educational subjects. The subjectivity of them exists in the simultaneous education process. Secondly, the object is common. In the educational community, the mental world of the educated, the educational content, and the educational environment serve as the common object in the education of inter-subjectivity theory. The common object is the premise and foundation of the interaction of the two subjects.[6] Thirdly, the education of intersubjectivity theory focuses on the dialogue, communication, understanding and resonance between the two subjects. The subject relation in teaching activity changes from tension to harmony.

3.3 Ideological logic: focus on the holistic development of human beings

The inter-subjectivity theory of teacher-student coexistence contains the value pursuit of the good state of true education. The field of education requires inter-subjectivity theory to have the following qualities. The first property is human nature. The interaction between the educator and the educated must be human-centred. The second property is developmental. The subject reconstructs the old cognitive system and explores new contents. The development of one side of the interaction will lead to the development of the other side. The third property is initiative. This theory actively motivates the educatees to carry out more inter-subject communication, so as to highlight the subject status of the educatees thereby improving the educational effect.

4 Innovative practices of Chinese cultural education from the perspective of inter-subjectivity theory

Based on the discussion of the logic of Chinese cultural education practice from the perspective of intersubjectivity theory, how should educators mobilize the various elements of the current Chinese cultural education system to construct an educational mode dominated by teachers and students? It is necessary to make concerted efforts from the dimensions of educational environment, educational management and educational activities to enhance the overall identification effect of Chinese cultural education.

4.1 Respect for difference: intercultural exchange of educational subjects

Based on cultural differences, the development of interculturality is a key element in the construction of intercultural identity. According to the logic of identity construction, when there is a high degree of unity between the integration of oneself and the identification of otherness, a sense of conscious identification with cultural values will emerge within the individual.[7] In this context, intercultural communication based on the theory of inter-subjectivity emphasizes the integration of multiple cultural perspectives. On the one hand, educators should build cultural exchange scenes guided by the concept of harmony. There is a need to allow for the existence of multiple cultures and to seek common ground while preserving differences in a multicultural context and to develop a sense of cultural belonging. While adhering to the dominant direction of Chinese cultural education, educators allow the existence of distinctive cultures and give them full respect so as to create the favourable atmosphere for the gradual strengthening of Chinese cultural identity. On the other hand, educators should take equal education as the principle and guarantee students' dominant position in educational management. On the institutionalization of education management, educators need to formulate scientific and clear regulations to ensure the standardized and institutionalized development of Chinese culture education. In the uniformity of education management, educators should strengthen unified management on the basis of respecting differences, and push forward the common goal of cultivating talents. In terms of the flexibility of teaching management, educators should bring the different factors of college students' educational background, growth experience and thinking mode into the category of educational preparation. In the autonomy of educational management, educators should give college students more opportunities to participate in educational activities in educational management.

4.2 Building consensus: exploring the intercultural common ground of educational subjects

Inter-subjectivity requires that teachers and students focus on the meeting of minds, the exchange of ideas and the harmonious discussion of views. For this reason, it is necessary to tap into a common cultural base in order to harmonise and unify the will of the members of the community. On the one hand, educators should aim at cultivating practical skills and guide subjects to communicate in multiple directions. In terms of academic activities, colleges and universities need to actively carry out academic competitions to promote exchanges and learning, so as to deepen college students' understanding of the content of Chinese culture. In terms of practical activities, educators should realize the diversification of activity themes, and combine with the current educational mainstream of the new era, which attaches importance to Party construction, Party history and red culture learning, to carry out more red research activities, such as re-walking the red line, watching red movies, and national conditions education. On the other hand, educators need to focus on cultural knowledge as the main purpose, adjust the education curriculum system. Inter-subjectivity theory emphasizes student-orientation. As two subjects, teachers and students act on the common object of classroom in an efficient, scientific and sustainable way. Educators should first establish a student-centred educational value orientation and adhere to the principles of representativeness, richness and relevance in the selection of Chinese cultural teaching content. At the same time, teachers should take the lead in professional teaching and guidance, while students should actively explore, think and give feedback as the main form. Educators should pay attention to listening to students' voices and insist on equal dialogue interaction to create a harmonious teaching atmosphere.

Research achievements of "Research on Chinese Cultural Identity Education for Hong Kong and Macao College Students" (Project No. S202210559143) and "Research Model of Red Cultural Education for Hong Kong and Macao College Students" (Project No.22211011), a "Challenge Cup" competition project of Jinan University in 2022.

References

1. Jinping Xi. Hold high the great banner of socialism with Chinese characteristics and unitethe struggle for the comprehensive construction of a modern socialist country [N]. People's Daily, 2022-10-17(2).
2. Jing He. Generative inter-subjectivity: bidirectional prediction and meaning construction [J]. Philosophical Analysis, 2022, 13(4): 111-122+198.
3. Marx. The complete works of marx and engels [M]. Beijing: People's Publishing House. 1979.
4. Ping Ren. Towards a materialism of interaction practice[M]. Beijing: People's Publishing House: 2003, 3-4.
5. Jiahui Cui, Zu Tong. The integration of excellent Chinese traditional culture into theideological and political education of college students[J]. Talent, 2022(32).
6. Benyan Zhao. The function of inter-subjectivity theory ideological and political educationand its realization[J]. Journal of Shandong Youth Political College, 2021, 37(1), 56-60.
7. Jonathan Friedman. Cultural identity and global processes[M]. Beijing: The Commercial Press, 2003: 109.

Application and exploration of virtual simulation experimental platform in the experimental teaching of clinical testing instruments and techniques

Yucheng Peng , *Yishan* Huo , *Abibula* Madinaimu, *Jie* Lv, *Yangchun* Feng, *Jia* Yang, *Wenbin* Qiao, *Fan* Guo, *Zhenzhen* Cheng, and *Xiumin* Ma*

Clinical Laboratory Center, the Third Clinical Medical College of Xinjiang Medical University (Affiliated Tumor Hospital), Urumqi, Xinjiang Uygur Autonomous Region, China

Keywords: Virtual simulation experiment platform, Clinical laboratory instruments and technology, Teaching reform, Online teaching.

Abstract. Clinical laboratory instrumentation and technology is a multidisciplinary, multi-technology, multi-disciplinary cross-discipline, with strong application, theoretical and experimental teaching methods are single and boring, and it is difficult for students to master and understand the abstract content. The laboratory has cooperated with a company to complete the experimental teaching for undergraduate students, and analyzed the advantages of this teaching method and the problems that need to be solved through the questionnaire and formative evaluation, and analyzed and summarized them, so as to provide relevant experience for this kind of courses to adopt the virtual simulation experimental platform and provide directional guidance for the construction and development of the virtual simulation experimental platform.

Clinical laboratory instrumentation and technology is a multidisciplinary, multi-technology, multi-disciplinary course, which is highly applied, rapidly developing, and has a short update cycle, and is one of the main professional courses in medical laboratory technology.

Since the epidemic in 2020, universities across the country have been actively responding to the call of the Ministry of Education to "suspend classes without stopping school" and adopting various teaching methods such as online teaching, catechism teaching, virtual simulation teaching, etc. As a new applied subject course with a high degree of knowledge and technology intensity and a unique application goal, Clinical Laboratory Instruments and Technology has undergone After nearly three years of continuous integration and exploration, our teaching and research department is currently using Shandong Zezhong virtual simulation platform to conduct laboratory classes, replacing the online teaching method adopted by most institutions, and improving teaching quality and implementing teaching reform by continuously developing the teaching

* Corresponding author: 365319938@qq.com

mode of this course. In accordance with the spirit of document [2001] No. 4 of the Ministry of Education, combined with the teaching requirements of this course and the construction standards of the national high-quality courses, constantly adhere to the development and practice of the teaching methods of the course, the reform and innovation of teaching methods, so that it can adapt to the teaching needs of the current situation is the focus of this paper.

1 Current problems faced by the traditional teaching methods of clinical laboratory instrumentation technology in the faculty

The current situation of teaching mode: This course takes the basic instruments and advanced professional instruments commonly used in clinical medicine laboratories as the learning content, reflecting the current situation of the rapidly developing laboratory medicine instruments, which plays an important role in the cultivation of the practice induction ability, clinical application ability and professional expansion ability of laboratory medicine students[1]. The course is composed of multidisciplinary intersection, with more knowledge points and more boring learning content, which brings certain challenges to students' learning. The traditional teaching mode and the common online teaching mode easily lead to low motivation of students and unsatisfactory teaching effect, coupled with the change of the teaching environment and mode by the epidemic, it is urgent to perfect and improve the teaching mode of this course.

Necessity of teaching reform: Since the beginning of 2020, the sudden epidemic has brought an unprecedented impact on Chinese higher education. In a very short period of time, the teaching in universities nationwide changed from "offline teaching" to "online teaching". This comprehensive online teaching is a big review of the achievements of "Internet+education" reform in China's higher education, and it also lays a rich practical foundation and ideological foundation for the future online teaching reform to continue to lead to more important status. The "Clinical Laboratory Instruments and Techniques" laboratory course contains five parts: blood, urine, coagulation, biochemistry, chemiluminescence, covering most of the instruments that students need to master in their internship and future work, the traditional teaching method uses PPT lectures in the laboratory, and then takes students to visit the medical testing center according to the conditions of the undertaking college; this teaching method faces several disadvantages, such as the influx of large numbers of students into the department at the same time It will affect the daily work of the staff, the medical laboratory center in a wide range of instruments, valuable, strict requirements of the laboratory environment, students in the department to visit will bring an increase in uncertainty may be infected with the normal operation of the instrument accident; and students in batches will bring the extension of the teaching time and different teachers to lead the teaching can not ensure homogeneous teaching and other issues; at the same time, students can only be in the laboratory class to observe and listen to the teaching The teacher's explanation loses the meaning of "laboratory class" and brings problems such as boring, single, abstract and incomprehensible content. Therefore, the teaching and research department is currently cooperating with Shandong ZeZhong virtual simulation platform to make the necessary teaching reform attempts.

2 Feasibility of building a virtual simulation platform

2.1 From the perspective of historical evolution

The development of educational technology has roughly gone through four different stages of development: the traditional 1.0 era based on oral and oral transmission; the 2.0 era of electrification education based on slides; the 3.0 era dominated by multimedia teaching; and the 4.0 era which is currently in between moving from the 3.0 era to digital teaching. Looking at this historical evolution, we can find that each breakthrough in education technology has brought about changes in teaching mode, which will drive the deepening development of university teaching theory and in turn guide the teaching reform practice. In the old days of traditional oral teaching, university lectures were conducted in the form of traditional fixed classes, and students needed to adapt to the needs of lecture-based classroom teaching, and the typical characteristics of the university learning space were fixed seats, fixed lecterns and fixed blackboards. With the development of education technology, multimedia learning and computer-assisted learning have emerged, and the space for students to learn has also changed. Classroom seating has changed from fixed to mobile, the teacher's podium has become changeable from front and center, the classroom blackboard has changed from fixed on the wall to a movable whiteboard, and multimedia equipment has been installed.

From a global perspective, computer-assisted education, marked by digitalization since the 1970s, has greatly promoted the change of university teaching mode and the continuous iteration of university students' learning style. One typical example is the promotion and application of the "active learning" teaching model. According to this theory, learning is a process in which the cognitive subject interacts with the learning environment and gradually constructs a cognition about the external world, thus developing its own cognitive structure. Based on this theory, the introduction of virtual simulation platform in our teaching department can reflect the emphasis on student-centered, problem-oriented, and teacher-student interaction and student-student interaction.

2.2 Guidance of national policy

The spirit of the document "Several Opinions of the Ministry of Education on Comprehensively Improving the Quality of Higher Education" (Education High [2012] No. 4), based on the "Ten-Year Development Plan for Education Informatization (2011-2020)" (Education Technology [2012] No. 5), the Ministry of Education issued the "Notice on the Construction of National Virtual Simulation Experimental Teaching Center (No. 94 [2013]) and launched the first batch of national virtual simulation experimental teaching centers in August 2013, up to now there are 300 national virtual simulation experimental teaching centers in China. The construction of national-level virtual simulation experimental teaching center is the key point of university education informatization and the extension of the construction of experimental teaching demonstration center [2].

2.3 Service undergraduate teaching

Whether it is experimental teaching demonstration center, or virtual simulation experimental teaching center, are for undergraduate services, so the landing point must fall on undergraduate teaching. Whether it is the acquisition or development of virtual simulation projects, there must be a broader application prospect, especially for medical undergraduate applications, the best can be applied in a number of medical-related professional undergraduate students. Only such a project can really serve undergraduate teaching well.

2.4 Consistent with school-school sharing

The Ministry of Education advocates that experimental teaching resources should be shared between schools to improve the utilization rate of instruments and equipment. The nature of the virtual simulation project is especially in line with the requirement of school-school sharing [3]. The amount of investment in virtual simulation projects is generally large, if each university independently invests funds in research and development, and the research and development is only used by students in their own schools, there will be repeated investment and waste of resources. Therefore, universities should not only cooperate with relevant virtual simulation development enterprises, but also establish inter-school sharing mechanism with other universities, so that virtual simulation resources can be promoted and applied efficiently.

3 Virtual simulation platform combined with course development

3.1 Integrating the virtual simulation platform into traditional experimental lectures Traditional offline teaching is teacher-led face-to-face lectures

Online teaching we follow the principle of student-centered teaching, and cultivate the ability of students to learn independently. Using virtual simulation experiments to explore the teaching model, the teaching and research department in the traditional physical experiments based on virtual simulation experiments into the virtual reality teaching model, for example, in the clinical laboratory instrumentation experiments, physical operations are currently being used or will be used in medical testing centers more advanced instruments, purely theoretical lectures on the principles of medical students is relatively boring, the content is also more abstract is not easy for students to understand, so the teaching department in the experimental lectures on the principle of boring, abstract content is not easy for students to understand. Therefore, the laboratory must focus on the actual operation in order to help students understand the key points, and the virtual simulation platform can not be limited by time and space, so that students can use it flexibly through pre-course pre-study, interspersed in class, and after class consolidation. The instructor completes the instrument explanation in the classroom, and the teacher assists the students to learn the corresponding virtual simulation integrated experiments and connects the corresponding principles, sources and extensions of the instrument experiments. For example, the principle of routine blood testing inside the clinical hematology instruments, the development and iteration of the instruments and the improvement of the testing principles and methods are taught one by one in the classroom as the main line. The traditional laboratory class can only give students a tour and demonstration, while the virtual simulation platform can show all the relevant testing principles of the machine and the methodological iteration of the operation process of the relevant instrument to students, through the timely guidance of the teacher, students operate on the virtual platform to practice or view the operation video in the system at any time, especially you can view the whole process of instrument development, it is easier to grasp the focus and difficulties of the experiment, more can continue to watch after class, if it is too late to extend the learning. By interspersing the virtual simulation platform with traditional laboratory operations, students can deepen their understanding of concepts, develop systematic thinking, and appreciate the practical role of the latest testing technologies and methods in clinical practice. In this mode, students can make full use of classroom and classroom time to strengthen their memory and achieve "virtual" and "real" complementarity.

3.2 Transformation of student-directed learning

The virtual simulation platform of my teaching department is open and shared to undergraduate students, breaking the time and space restrictions. Students can enjoy the high-quality online resources at any time through cell phones and computer networks, and experience the experimental process by clicking on the required experimental supplies and instruments with the mouse and following the steps[4].In addition, in order to improve the students' participation, the teaching and research department assisted the company to optimize the platform management functions, adding self-test questions, online Q&A interactive communication forum, learning statistics and other functions; some experimental steps are also set up in the middle of the question, only the correct answer can continue the experimental process, the wrong answer needs to find the reason, like a breakthrough game, this mode can increase the fun, but also to carry out formative evaluation of students.

Laboratory instrumentation and technology is a relatively boring course, but through the faculty lecturers to issue discussions, to inspire students' active thinking and innovation, as well as in the class session in addition to online question and answer, and interspersed with a combination of various forms of teaching, such as flipped classroom, group discussion, etc.. Depending on the characteristics of the content students are learning, undergraduate teaching should focus on the people. All in all, there is a method for teaching, but there is no definite method, and it is important to get the right method.

4 Implementation effect and problems

4.1 Virtual simulation platform implementation effect

Based on the actual lecture of the laboratory class, the teaching and research department relies on the virtual simulation teaching platform, in order to meet the characteristics of the course experimental content of strong theory, abstract content is not easy to understand, for example, the experiments related to "automatic biochemical analyzer" in just three hours of time, only using traditional lectures can not guarantee the quality of students' listening, and at the same time, because the experiment The content of the experiment is many, involving electrolytes, proteins, enzymes and other important and difficult knowledge covering all the theoretical content of "Clinical Biochemistry Laboratory Technology", which also brings great pressure to the laboratory teachers, and it is also a great challenge for students to recall the relevant knowledge points and master the new content in a short time. Therefore, in this experimental teaching, a combination of "virtual" and "real" teaching mode is implemented, in which students are allowed to log into the virtual simulation platform before class to practice the operation of the instrument and recall and review the testing principles and meanings of the relevant items; during the class, the teacher takes the form of micro-lessons and demonstration lectures in the virtual simulation platform to help students deepen their impression and master the important and difficult points; after the class, students then check and fill in the gaps through the experimental operation of the virtual simulation platform, and interact with the teacher online to improve learning efficiency. After 2 years of teaching practice in the undergraduate and post-secondary classes undertaken by the faculty, especially the large-scale online teaching at the time of the new crown epidemic, students in the classes undertaken by the faculty participated in the whole experimental process by using the virtual simulation platform[5] to make up for the limitation of long experimental materials and experimental cycles.

The teaching and research department surveyed a total of 169 students in Medical Laboratory Technology (College Preparatory) 2021-1, Medical Laboratory Technology 2019-1 and Medical Laboratory Technology 2019-2 by questionnaire star, and came to the conclusion that 90% of the students think that the effect of adopting virtual simulation platform is better than traditional laboratory teaching, more than 88% of the students think that the mode can increase learning interest, enrich learning resources and broaden their horizons, more than 83% of the More than 83% of the students think that virtual simulation teaching is beneficial to the cultivation of independent learning ability and the formation of scientific thinking, and 87% of the students think that the form of virtual simulation is convenient for review and pre-reading after class, which can help to understand and consolidate abstract theoretical knowledge. Meanwhile, through the analysis of the formative evaluation of 169 students in the class of 2021 and the undergraduate class of 2019, we can learn that the passing rate of the exams after adopting virtual simulation teaching reaches more than 95%, and the percentage of students who scored 80 or above also reaches 38%, which shows that the virtual simulation teaching has been well evaluated by most students, and also makes the teaching quality improve year by year.

At the same time, the teaching and research department and the universities in Kashgar region are cooperating with each other, planning to build our own virtual simulation platform that meets our own needs by relying on the resources of the existing virtual simulation platform and the policy advantages of the state and autonomous region, and combining the advantages of the resources between the cooperating clinical medical schools and universities, so as to expand the advantages and avoid the poor information caused by our own "closed door", communicate and cooperate with related institutions, make full use of the resources, build and use the virtual simulation platform more rationally, and carry out the teaching reform of the curriculum in a deeper way.

4.2 Existing problems

First of all, compared with traditional experiments, the opening of virtual simulation experiments brings new challenges to teachers and students, and requires good cooperation and dedication of teachers and students. The conceptualization, writing, production and teaching application of virtual simulation integrated experiments in every aspect is a careful process that requires repeated refinement and improvement, and the faculty team needs to carefully plan and continuously learn all aspects of knowledge in order to continuously optimize the experimental content and teaching methods[6].Secondly, when students run virtual experiments with cell phones, the font and items are smaller and inconvenient to select and operate; when the lab computer is running, there may also be difficult problems such as network lag, which is related to the stability of the platform and computer hardware support, more school policies are needed to support and maintain to ensure safe operation and management[7]. Again, in order to fully mobilize students' motivation, it is also necessary to enhance the data management functions of the platform, such as the number of logins and browsing time of students, the interactive function between students and teachers, the online test area, etc. Teachers can accordingly give students suitable formative assessments[8], and increase the proportion of such formative assessments in the total grade of the subject, which can improve students' motivation for online learning, broaden their horizons and expand their thinking, and help improve their overall quality ability.

5 Conclusion

This teaching and research department assists traditional physical experimental teaching through the constructed virtual simulation experimental platform of laboratory instrumentation, through the deep integration of modern information technology and medical professional knowledge. The teaching mode of combining virtual and real, online and offline teaching is adopted to help students integrate the abstract and profound principles of test instrumentation, which has a profound impact on the composition of students' knowledge system[9].At the same time, the use of virtual simulation platform also helps students to increase the access to knowledge and facilitate the improvement of students' independent learning ability; the core requirement of higher quality education is to strengthen the cultivation of students' independent learning ability. At present, the virtual simulation experiment platform has gained some experience, but how to further improve the teaching effect and the quality of classroom teaching must be further explored. In the future, based on the enhanced physical experiments and the syllabus, the teaching and research department will design comprehensive experiments with independent characteristics that are more suitable for students, use information technology to constantly update the educational concept and reform the educational model [10], and cultivate high-quality medical talents who can keep up with the times.

Undergraduate Education Teaching Research and Reform Project of Xinjiang Autonomous Region (PT-2021021), Education Research and Teaching Reform Project of Xinjiang Medical University (YGS2021009) Education Reform Project of the Third Clinical Medical College of Xinjiang Medical University (No.SLC202004).

References

1. Zhang Lili, Qiao Sen, Chen Zehui, et al. Health Professions Education, 2019, 37(2):41-42.
2. Wang Weiguo. Laboratory Research and Exploration, 2013, 32(12):5-8.
3. Li Ping, Gao Dongfeng, Xu,Jin et al. Experimental Technology and Management, 2014, 31(7):1-5.
4. Wang Shuai.. China Continuing Medical Education, 2018, 10(18):28-30.
5. XuFei, Nie Zhiyan, Jin Lei, et al. Chinese Journal of Immunology, 2021, 37(2): 231-234.
6. Shurong Ren, Bei Zhang, Jing Wang, et al. Chinese Journal of Immunology, 2020, 36(2):236- 240.
7. Fucai Wang, Junsheng Lin. Chinese Journal of Immunology, 2020, 36(19): 2312-2315.
8. Song Ying, Zhang Yongmei. China Continuing Medical Education, 2020, 12(25): 16-20.
9. Zhang Xiaobo, Liu Ruyi, Lei Yanjun, et al. Northwest Medical Education, 2015, 23(1):119- 121.
10. Ministry of Education. Modern Educational Technology, 2021, 31(2):1.

An emergency rescue analysis of a hazardous chemical deflagration accident

Zhiguo Zhang, *Kunpeng* Cu* and *Xinyi* Tao

Department of Emergency Rescue, China Fire and Rescue Institute, No. 4, Nanyan Road, Changping District, Beijing, China.

Abstract. The hazardous chemical explosion and combustion accidents have the characteristics of wide scope, high risk, complex situation, and difficult to deal with. After the occurrence of accidents, timely, accurate, and efficient response is an urgent need to protect the safety of people's lives and property. This article takes a hazardous chemical deflagration accident in North China in 2020 as an example. It conducts research from three aspects, including the basic situation of the case, the handling of the explosion accident, the successful experience of handling of the explosion accident. The rapid response and efficient disposal methods of accidents, the enhancement of disaster prevention and disaster relief capabilities, and the formation of a long-term mechanism to ensure the safety of people's lives and property are expounded in this article, in order to provide a reference for similar accident management..

1 Introduction

At least 158 people were killed, more than 6,000 people were injured and 300,000 people were homeless by a deadly explosion at the port of Beirut, the capital of Lebanon, at 18:00 on August 4, 2020. Lebanese Prime Minister Hassan Diab stated that the explosion was caused by the ignition of about 2,750 tons of ammonium nitrate ignited by combustible and explosive materials, which were stored in the port warehouses since 2014 but never had been properly disposed. At approximately 14: 48 on March 21, 2019, the Tianjiayi Chemical Co, Ltd, located in the ecological chemical park of Xiangshui County, Yancheng City, Jiangsu Province, suffered a particularly serious explosion, causing 78 deaths, 76 serious injuries, and 640 hospitalizations, the direct economic loss rise to 1.986 billion yuan. The explosions of hazardous chemicals, such as the explosions in Beirut, Lebanon and Xiangshui, sounded the alarm once again about the control of dangerous chemicals.

Hazardous chemicals refer to highly toxic chemicals and other chemicals which are toxic, corrosive, explosive, combustible, and combustion-supporting, meanwhile, they are harmful to humans, facilities, and the environment. Hazardous chemical explosion accidents have the characteristics of wide scope, complex situation, high casualties, high risk and difficult to deal with [1-5].

* Corresponding author: cuikunpeng2004@163.com

The control of hazardous chemicals is a global problem, and accidents occur frequently due to mismanagement or other reasons. According to incomplete statistics, in the past 30 years, it is as many as 295 serious and typical safety accidents involving hazardous chemicals in China, including 262 explosion accidents, accounting for 88.9%, resulting in heavy property damage and casualties.

A hazardous chemical deflagration accident occurred in North China in 2020, which is the most complicated, highest safety risk and the most difficult to dispose of in the field of hazardous chemical gases at home and abroad recent years. The following takes this accident as an example to discuss the emergency response to this hazardous chemical explosion accident, hereinafter referred to as "North China X explosion accident".

2 Basic situation of the accident

In this article, it analyses the background of the "North China X explosion accident" from various aspects such as the construction and situation of the accident institution, and the situation of explosive materials. The details are as follows:

The accident house was located in a district in North China. It was built of brick and wooden beam structure. There were lights in the house, no one was guarded on site, and no video surveillance equipment.

The site of the accident house was basic farmland, after the accident, a total of 757 gas cylinders of different specifications was cleared out on site. Among them, there was an ethylene oxide 800L tank, two 40OL tanks; three 10OL ethylene oxide gas cylinders; In addition, empty bottles and recycled waste gas cylinders were mainly stored in the house during the incident.

Considering the test results of 100 L ethylene oxide cylinders, combined with the flammable and explosive properties of ethylene oxide (The boiling point of ethylene oxide is 10.7 degrees Celsius, the explosion limit is 3%-100%, and the minimum ignition energy is 0.065 mJ), the expert group tentatively determine that the first explosive combustion material in this accident was the ethylene oxide.

3 The handling of explosion accidents

In this article, it analyses the background of the "North China X explosion accident" from various aspects such as the construction and situation of the accident institution, and the situation of explosive materials. The details are as follows:

1) There were many types of gas cylinders, and the situation was complex and changeable. The person in charge of the enterprise concealed the situation and was unable to provide details of the gas cylinders on site.

2) There were many ways of harm and high safety risks. The cylinder body and safety accessories were damaged after the explosion impact. Once improperly handled, there was a great possibility of instantaneous explosion, fire and poisoning.

3) The disposal was difficult and professional. The accident site was a dangerous explosion area. Special explosion-proof equipment must be used and professional protective clothing must be worn. Gas cylinders must be handled carefully.

4) The social influence was wide and the political influence was great. In the process of eliminating accident hazards, it was bound to affect the normal activities of nearby enterprises, such as production, residents ' lives, and transportation, and affect the safety and stability of the area.

Facing the task of emergency disposal, all party responded quickly, assembled quickly, studied and judged scientifically, and launched the special emergency response plan and on-site handling work plan for hazardous chemicals immediately. The emergency response to this accident was divided into four stages:

3.1 The first stage: emergency rescue

After the accident, the Municipal Emergency Command Centre immediately mobilized the Municipal Emergency Management Bureau, the Municipal Fire Rescue Teams, the X District Emergency Management Bureau and other institutions, as well as 13 fire trucks to be on the scene for disposal. According to the material characteristics of the gas cylinders and the fire situation, firefighters controlled the spread of the fire to prevent the situation from expanding, and they implemented long-distance water spraying to cool down, avoided explosions, and they isolated the scene to prevent unrelated personnel from approaching.

After the open fire was extinguished urgently, there were still a number of gas cylinders leaking at the scene, a large amount of unknown gas and smoke were produced, and there was a risk of secondary explosion. In order to prevent secondary accidents, the police blocked the roads to the accident site and conducted emergency evacuation of nearby villagers; and the environmental protection department simultaneously monitored the accident site and the surrounding environment in real time; firefighters continued to spray water to cool the gas cylinders to prevent gas and the smoke spread to the surrounding area; the Municipal Emergency Management Bureau mobilized hazardous chemical experts to rush to the scene to participate in the disposal work.

3.2 The second stage: preparation for disposal

Directed rescue and disposal work on the spot, set up an on-site headquarters. The Municipal Emergency Management Bureau communicated with the professional rescue teams and experts, researched and drafted preliminary professional disposal work recommendations, and reported preliminary opinions on emergency handling to the experts on the scene command.

The on-site headquarters fully dispatched all forces, fully studied and judged the situation on the spot, thoroughly studied the emergency response plan according to the accident site, and coordinated all relevant institutions to do a good job of the site. After thorough research, the working idea of "disposing on-site and storing off-site" for gas cylinders was determined, and the tasks and responsibilities of each institution were basically clarified.

The on-site headquarters sent professional technicians and experts into the accident site to investigate and further study and judge the accident. At the same time, they sent unmanned aerial vehicles to take real-time aerial images of the scene to pay attention to changes in the situation on the scene. They organized a work scheduling meeting to re-research and analysis of the scene situation and development situation, listen to the opinions and suggestions of experts from all parties, refine the on-site disposal work plan, expand the professional disposal force, clarify the division of tasks for all parties, reconfirm the necessary emergency material supplies ready in place, once again comb the on-site gas cylinder disposal process, and once again clear on-site emergency response measures.

The on-site headquarters held a meeting to deploy the next stage of on-site disposal work: First, each institution should formulate a detailed work plan based on the division of tasks; second, each institution should fully consider the unexpected situations that may occur at the accident site, and formulate targeted emergency measures. Third, the fire brigade, health committee, public security bureau, traffic management bureau, weather bureau, environmental protection bureau and other relevant departments in district X must arrive at the designated place at the designated time and prepare for the gas cylinder disposal site.

3.3 The third stage: cylinder cleaning

All on-site emergency response personnel and required emergency rescue materials were ready, and all on-site preparations were in place.

The on-site headquarters of the Municipal Emergency Bureau issued an instruction to organize personnel to enter the scene to carry out accident site disposal in accordance with the disposal principle of " safety first, adequate protection, easy first then difficult, classified disposal".

According to the division of responsibilities, the fire rescue team was responsible for on-site emergency command and emergency disposal. The emergency management department and hazardous chemical experts should provide on-site technical support; departments of environmental protection, health, public security, meteorology and more should do a good job of relevant guarantees, and the local governments should do a good job of disposal cooperation and logistical guarantees.

Under the unified command of the on-site headquarters, various departments worked together to clean up a total of 757 gas cylinders of different specifications, with a total volume of 27,000 liters, involving 41 hazardous chemicals such as ethylene oxide and acetylene. Explosive and toxic gases accounted for 68.3%, and other compressed and liquefied gases accounted for 31.7%. The gas cylinders were initially cleaned and classified and placed in safe areas around the site.

Fig. 1. Cylinders cleaned out on site.

3.4 The fourth stage: cylinder disposal

The on-site headquarters held a meeting to deploy the gas cylinder disposal work and put forward the "three point in place" worked requirements of personal protection in place, monitoring and detection in place, and disposal measures in place. On-site disposal personnel adopted the highest level of protection. Peripheral cleaning personnel wore activated carbon masks, safety monitoring personnel in absorption and disposal work wore self-priming gas masks, and X area personnel who participating in the bottle opening test wore air respirators and filter gas masks for safety protection. They entered the site in batches to calibrate and appraise the gas cylinders, found out the bottom number of the gas cylinders on site, mastered the main components of all the gas cylinders, stored the sorted gas cylinders in zones and categories, and disposed of them one by one.

The emergency response sited headquarters coordinated emergency response, fire protection, public security, publicity, environment, meteorology, health, local governments, professional social forces, and industry experts and other resources. A total of more than 30 institutions and more than 2,000 people participated in the on-site disposal. Fifteen hazardous chemical productions and management enterprises and hazardous waste disposal enterprises were mobilized to carry out on-site disposal. The fire rescued departments successively dispatched 19 fire rescue stations, 59 fire trucks, and 352 officers to the scene for disposal.

The public security departments evacuated and resettled more than 500 surrounding people, and the environmental protection departments monitored the environment of the surrounding residential areas. After 6 day and night of intensive and orderly joint disposal work by multiple departments, no secondary accidents occurred during the disposal period, the disposal personnel were in normal health, all the gas cylinders were disposed of, and the on-site emergency disposal work was all over.

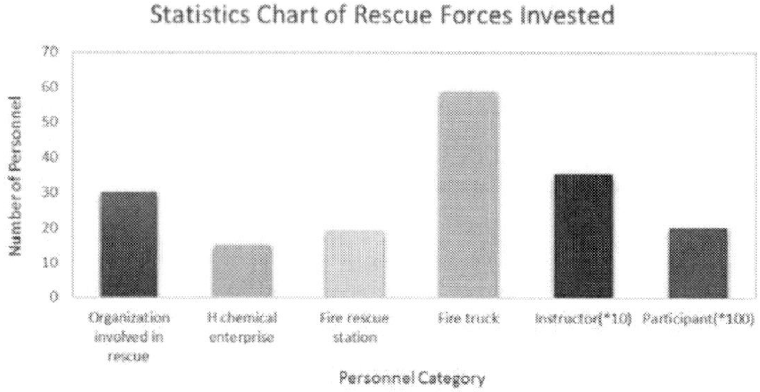

Fig. 2. Statistics chart of rescue forces invested.

4 The Problems and Lessons of the accident

Considering the existing evidence materials and expert opinions, the accident investigation team believes that the direct cause of the accident is mainly due to the following two possibilities: One is that the ethylene oxide gas cylinder has a physical explosion under high temperature conditions, resulting in leakage, burning and explosion when encountering a fire source; second, under high temperature conditions, self-polymerization reaction occurs in the ethylene oxide cylinder and directly explodes. One of the reasons for accelerating the self-polymerization of ethylene oxide may be that the ethylene oxide cylinder is not evacuated or filled with stable gases such as nitrogen, resulting in the mixing of air and other impurities in the ethylene oxide cylinder. The main problems reflected in the accident are as follows.

4.1 The problem of operating beyond the scope of the business license

The involved institution was suspected with the problems such as engaging in hazardous chemical business activities beyond the business method approved by the business license, illegally repackaging, and illegally storing hazardous chemicals.

4.2 The problem of illegal modification of gas cylinders

After conducting extended investigations and surprise inspections of the institution, it discovered that the institution was suspected of illegally modifying gas cylinders, filling non-dedicated gas cylinders with mixed gas, and illegally storing ethylene oxide, etc. problem.

4.3 The problem exposed in the transportation of hazardous chemicals

The institution involved used ordinary vehicles that were not qualified to transport chemical products to transport chemicals for a long time, and distributed hazardous chemicals through logistics units or freight software that was not qualified to transport hazardous chemicals.

4.4 The problem of insufficient supply on critical moments with the low frequency use equipment

Fire and rescue teams are equipped with a certain number of combustible gas detectors, toxic gas detectors and other instruments, but they are used low-frequency, which objectively causes the insufficient situation of the equipment to meet the disposal needs or even cannot be used regularly during an emergency. Relevant departments are not professional enough, their work is not solid enough, and the training and use of equipment in grassroots organizations are lacking. In the case of relative lack of funds, we can consider the establishment of commercial companies to sell various testing ceremonies, and in an emergency, call and purchase directly from commercial companies, so as to be prepared and take precautions.

5 Conclusion

The rescue and disposal work of this accident was a complete success. The specific successful experience includes: the disposal command and dispatching, coordinated and orderly cooperation, professional and scientific disposal, and close cooperation.

References

1. Z.X. Mo, T.X. Wu, F. Xie, and W.H. Song, Simulation and the emergency measures study of the transient leakage of liquid ammonia transient based on MATLAB. *Acta Scientiarum Naturalium Universitatis Nankaien*, 2014, vol. 4, pp. 1–5.(in Chinese).
2. Y.E. Shuliang, S. Zhang. A method of hazardous chemical materials deflagration identification based on multi-parameter and feature-level fusion. *Chinese Journal of Sensors and Actuators*, 2011, 24 (04):620-623.
3. Z.X. Wang, Eakage simulation analysis and diffusion model optimization of hazardous chemicals. Dalian University of Technology, 2016, (in Chinese).
4. P.Murray-Tuite, B. Wolshon. Evacuation transportation modeling: an overview of research, development, and practice, *Transportation Research Part C: Emerging Technologies*, 2013,vol. 27, pp. 25–45.
5. Fire Department of the Ministry of public security. Notice on firefighters' sacrifice in fire fighting of puyong high speed refrigerator truck in Xianyou County, Putian City, Fujian Province. 2017.06.09
6. 360 safety. Why learn some fire dynamics. http://www.360doc.com/content/17/0131/10/26447790_625574789.shtml. 2017.07.13.
7. L. Xu, H.P. Zhang, Y. Yang, W. Wang, W.B. Zhu. Experimental study on full scale fire of waste tires. *Journal of applied basic and engineering sciences*. 2006.14 (1): 33-39.
8. J.J. Su, Z.L. Fang, K. Tian. Analysis on the causes of refrigerator truck deflagration accident and fire fighting and rescue measures. Proceedings of science and Technology Annual Meeting of China Fire Protection Association, 2018.11.
9. Y. Shen, Q. Wang, W. Yan, and J. Sun. An evacuation model coupling with toxic effect for chemical industrial park. *Journal of Loss Prevention in the Process Industries*, 2015,vol. 33, pp. 258–265.

An empirical study of the factors affecting moral hazard for doctors based on fraud theory

Yaohui Wang[1], *Tongxian* Chen[2] and *Xiaohan* Chen[2,*]

[1]Zhejiang Shuren University, Research Institute of Modern Service Industry, Zhejiang Province, China
[2]Taizhou Second People's Hospital, Clinical Psychology Department, Zhejiang Province, China

Abstract. Doctor moral hazard behavior is a topical and sensitive issue in medicine. Recognition of the factors that influence doctor moral hazard behavior is fundamental to controlling or preventing it. Researchers have identified the factors that influence doctor moral hazard behavior based on models of fraud risk. In this present study, these factors were categorized into five dimensions: motivation, opportunity, rationalization, exposure, and punishment. A literature review and in-depth interviews with experts led to the development of a scale of the factors that affect doctor moral hazard. The scale has good reliability and validity. Data were obtained by interviewing medical staff. By using IBM SPSS 20.0 and AMOS 20.0, nine factors with strong explanatory power were extracted: economic pressure, pressure to undertake scientific research, decision-making autonomy, patient participation, treatment uncertainty, systemic deficiencies, probability of exposure, threat of hospital punishment, and threat of social punishment. The development of the scale and the extraction of the key influencing factors clarified the scope and the nature of factors that influence doctor moral hazard behavior. The analysis also provides a basis for governments and hospitals to govern doctor moral hazard behavior.

1 Introduction

Moral hazard is an insurance-related term used in economics that describes a type of opportunistic behavior[1] in which an individual who takes on a financial risk does not bear the downside costs. Moral hazard is inevitable in medicine because of information asymmetry. The idea that there is moral hazard in medicine was first published by Arrow in "Uncertainty and the welfare economics of health care" in 1963[2]. Moral hazard includes both moral hazards for the demander and the supplier of medical services. The central agent in supplier moral hazard is the doctor. In the 1970s, Victor Fuchs of Stanford University and Robert Evans of the University of British Columbia separately proposed a theory of induced demand and the concept of doctor-induced demand[3,4]. Tancredi and Barondess introduced the concept of defensive medical behavior in 1978[5], which then was defined as

* Corresponding author: nooorachen@163.com

"the use of diagnostic and end-treatment measures explicitly for the purposes of averting malpractice suits[6]". It can be seen that medical decisions are not always made entirely in a patient's interest.

Previous research has shown that moral hazard in health care is mainly found in patient examinations, hospitalization and drug administration[7]. Evans found that doctor moral hazard behavior was manifest in unnecessary or expensive examinations and the prescription of expensive or overused drugs[7]. More recent studies have shown that overcharging and receiving financial gifts unrelated to treatment were also aspects of doctor moral hazard[8,9]. Doctor moral hazard has led to the rapid growth of medical expenses in various countries. For example, medical expenditure in the United States increased from $26.9 billion in 1960 to $1149.1 billion in 1988, accounting for 14% of GDP[10]. On March 23, 2010, President Barack Obama signed the Patient Protection and Affordable Care Act (ACA) to reduce medical costs for individuals and governments[11]. In April 2009, China launched the New Medical Reform and introduced a series of measures to rebuild the country's medical system and, in so doing, emphasized government leadership of public welfare organizations. The control of medical expenses and the close supervision of medical procedures have gradually become the principal targets of medical reform. These are activities that are closely related to doctor moral hazard. Thus there is an urgency to the reformation and control of doctor moral hazard.

Information asymmetry, opportunity and rationalization are generally considered to be necessary conditions for doctor moral hazard to obtain[12]. For example, A common rib fracture patients, in general, through the ordinary chest film can be diagnosed. But doctors can also say that in order to make a better diagnosis, they guide patients to do CT or even 3D reconstruction, because he will say that ordinary chest films may cause missed diagnosis. In this case, doctors will consider it reasonable to reduce the rate of missed diagnosis. Researchers have offered different perspectives on doctor moral hazard by studying specific factors that affect it. For example, Zhang et al. found that third-party payment was a principal driver of doctor moral hazard in the medical field and that it increased management costs. They suggested that appropriate incentives and restraints should be adopted to minimize the likelihood of doctor moral hazard. Research into moral hazard as experienced by farmers and project managers suggests that a lack of effective government supervision will lead to a high incidence of moral hazard[13,14].

Doctors are the principal providers of medical services and therefore play a decisive role in how medical services are allocated. They are therefore key to the prevention and control of doctor moral hazard. There are individual differences in doctor moral hazard: doctors in different hospitals and different doctors in the same hospital experience moral hazard to different degrees. Previous research has focused on the macro level rather than on the behavior of individual doctors and what influences them. Macro causes and institutional factors influence doctor behavior by exploiting individual differences between doctors. Thus, the key to resolving problems of moral hazard is to explore the factors that affect doctor moral hazard and the mechanisms by which they exert influence on individual doctors.

2 Theoretical framework

There has been no authoritative literature on the connotation of fraud. After referrence, the explanation of fraud in Longman Dictionary is "the illegal act of deceiving others in order to obtain something, such as money, goods, etc."Oxford Dictionary defines it as "illegal or criminal deception for financial or personal benefit". Cambridge Dictionary defines it as "the crime of obtaining money by cheating others". In Collins dictionary is fraud defined as "deliberate deception, fraud or cheating in order to gain an advantage". The definition in modern Chinese dictionary is "to do things against the law and discipline in a deceitful way". It can be seen from the above that many definitions emphasize the two essential characteristics of fraud, namely, the subjective intention of the fraud perpetrators and the illegal nature of the behaviour itself. Its subjective intention contains the intrinsic and tractive characteristics of moral hazard, and the illegal nature is tantamount to the characteristics of harming others and benefiting doctors themselves[7].

For patients in the process of diagnosis and treatment, the essence of doctor moral hazard behaviour is fraudulent behaviour, which, in other words, is the speculative behaviour at the expense of others. From this point of view, the analysis of doctor moral hazard behaviour can refer to fraud theory. For the antecedents of fraud, there have been a series of research results, including related theories and influencing factors of fraud. The main theories and contents are as follows.

W.Steve Albrecht put forward the triangle theory of fraud, which attributed the emergence of corporate fraud into three elements, pressure, opportunity, and rationalization[8]. Bologna et al further developed the "GONE" theory on the basis of the fraud triangle theory. The four factors referred to greed, opportunity, need and exposure[9]. According to the theory, the motivation of fraud can be divided into general factors and individual factors. General factors are from the organizational level, including the opportunity of fraud, the possibility of exposure, the probability and intensity of punishment, etc.; individual factors are from the level of fraud conductors, including the moral level and fraud motivation of managers, etc[10]. Wolfe and Hermanson further developed the fraud triangle theory in 2004[11]. The core of this theory was to put forward the factors of fraud ability. Gbegi and adebisi (2013) put forward a new diamond theory of fraud from the perspective of legal accounting, based on a detailed study of Wolfe and Hermanson's diamond theory of fraud, combined with the relationship between other theoretical models of fraud motivation and the fraud motivation theory[12]. And Tugas (2012) summed up the fifth factor of accounting fraud, namely external supervision[13], so as to develop the Pentagram theory of fraud based on Wolfe and Hermanson's diamond theory of fraud (2004). The main connotation of external supervision is exposure and punishment.

To sum up, the pertinent research of fraud theory has demonstrated that the influencing factors of fraud can be divided into five aspects, motivation, opportunity, rationalization, exposure and punishment,as shown in the Figure 1. An examination of previous studies enabled us to abstract the factors that affect doctor moral hazard. In-depth interviews with experts and empirical research on medical staff were conducted to examine the degree to which these factors influence doctors. SPSS 20.0 and AMOS 20.0 were used in empirical research to determine the characteristic factors of moral hazards for individual doctors. Then, an understanding of medical behavior of doctors can be gained for governments and hospitals to develop a management framework for preventing or controlling moral hazard. Then, the questionnaire survey was used to propose the specific influencing factors of each dimension of doctor's moral hazard, and exploratory and confirmatory factor analysis was carried out.

3 Methods

3.1 Questionnaire design

In order to obtain the influencing factors of doctor's moral hazard as much as possible, the interview focused on the possible factors of doctor's moral hazard, including motivation, opportunity, self rationalization, exposure, punishment and so on. The interviewees fully expressed the internal and external factors that may affect the moral hazard of medical students. Finally, we interviewed 10 hospital managers, 10 doctors, and medical science There are 5 professors, 5 nurses, 10 patients and their families, and 5 people from all walks of life. A large number of influencing factors were obtained through interviews.

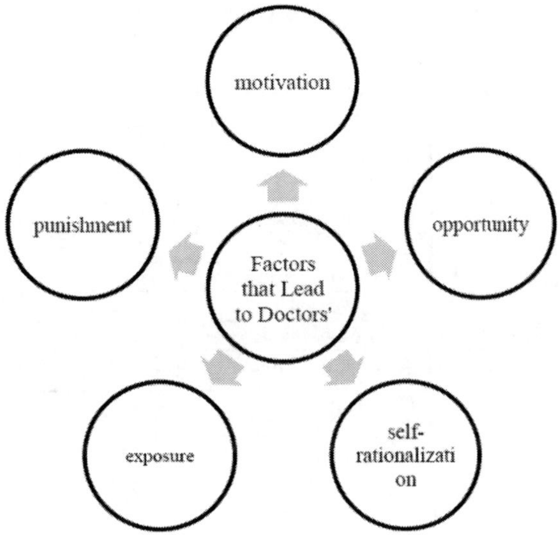

Fig. 1. Conceptual model of doctor's moral hazard intention factors.

According to the interview results, more than 50 specific factors affecting doctors' moral hazard were determined. The first draft of the questionnaire was formed, and 10 managers who had a better understanding of doctors' moral hazard were selected to conduct a pre test. In the prediction test, the respondents were required to complete the pre-test questionnaire according to the normal survey status. After the questionnaire was completed, they were asked how they felt in the process of answering the questionnaire, whether there were any understanding problems, and whether there were suggestions for the improvement of the questionnaire. Finally, a formal questionnaire was formed. The questionnaire collected basic information and used a five-point Likert scale as a metric for additional data-gathering questions: 1, the impact is not significant; 2, the impact is general; 3, the impact is relatively significant; 4, the impact is very significant; 5, the impact is extremely significant.

3.2 Data collection

Because the purpose of this study is to grasp the specific content of the influencing factors of doctor's moral hazard under the Chinese medical situation. The research population is mainly doctors, taking into account the hospital managers who have a better understanding of doctors' medical behavior. Doctors may be more sensitive to the investigation of this topic. Therefore, the questionnaire is completed by the way of on-site distribution, and the respondents can leave no trace. For the selection of hospitals, in order to ensure the coverage of hospitals of different levels and regions, the study was carried out in Zhejiang, Jiangsu, Beijing, Guangxi and other provinces.

The scope of the survey involves 800 questionnaires distributed in this survey, 608 of which are recovered, with a recovery rate of 76%; for the first time, 17 questionnaires with missing items are deleted; for the second time, 11 questionnaires with obvious self contradictory options are deleted. After twice screening, 580 valid questionnaires were obtained, and the effective rate was 95.4%. The descriptive statistical results of the samples are shown in Table 2. The gender, age, professional title and education background of the samples are reasonable, and the type and nature of the units are also in line with the actual situation of Chinese hospitals, so they are generally representative. According to the research needs, 290 out of 580 valid questionnaires were used for exploratory factor analysis and 290 for confirmatory factor analysis.

Table 2. Descriptive statistics of valid samples.

Basic information		Sample size	Proportion (%)
Gender	Male	382	65.9
	Female	198	34.1
Age	Less than 25 years	16	2.8
	26-35 years	62	10.7
	36-45years	318	54.8
	46-55years	168	29.0
	Over 56years	16	2.8
Education	Associate degree	26	4.5
	Undergraduate	410	70.7
	Master's degree	120	20.7
	Doctor's degree	24	4.1
Hospital grade	First class hospital	370	63.8
	Second class hospital	92	15.9
	Other	118	20.3
Public or private hospitals	Public hospitals	552	95.2
	Private hospitals	28	4.8
Titles of doctors	Preliminary	290	50
	Vantage	74	12.8
	High	182	31.4
	Higher	34	5.9

4 Results

4.1 Reliability

A reliability test evaluates the internal consistency and stability of the scale by calculating the alpha coefficient. We used the criteria which were given in Devillis (1991): the alpha coefficient of the total scale is required to be above 0.8, but an alpha coefficient between 0.7 and 0.8 is acceptable; the alpha coefficients of the sub-scales are required to be above 0.7, but alpha coefficients between 0.6 and 0.7 are acceptable[17]. The consistency test showed that the alpha coefficient of the total scale was greater than 0.9 and the alpha coefficients of each subscale were greater than 0.8. The specific values are shown in Table 3. For each scale, if, after deleting a measurement item, the alpha coefficient of the scale did not improve significantly, thus showing that the reliability of the scale was unchanged, the deleted item was not considered. Each scale was found to be reliable, and therefore the questionnaire was reliable.

4.2 Validity

Content validity and construct validity are commonly used to establish the validity of a questionnaire. The measurement items were reviewed by individuals with backgrounds in the medical field and they were modified and improved many times over four rounds of reviews. The first round focused on the comprehensiveness of the questionnaire to ensure it covered all aspects of doctor moral hazard. In the second round, the experts combined items that repeated statements to emphasize key points. In the third round, expressions that were easy to misunderstand or difficult to understand were amended and optimized. Finally, hospital managers, clinical experts and retired doctors were invited to assess the questionnaire. Thus the questionnaire used in this study has a high degree of content validity.

Table 3. Alpha coefficient of each scale.

Scale	Alpha coefficient in pre-investigation stage	Alpha coefficient in formal investigation stage
Total scale	0.961	0.965
Scale of motivation dimension	0.897	0.908
Scale of opportunity dimension	0.919	0.908
Scale of rationalization dimension	0.867	0.871
Scale of exposure dimension	0.922	0.923
Scale of punishment dimension	0.889	0.941

Construct validity includes convergent validity and discriminant validity. The construct validity of a questionnaire is usually determined using exploratory factor analysis. The evaluation criteria are: when a measurement item becomes unrelated to any factor, it should be deleted; when the loading of a measurement item for a particular factor is greater than 0.5, it has convergent validity; if the loading of each measurement item for a particular factor is large but is small for other factors, then there is good discriminant validity; and if the loadings of a measurement item for all factors are less than 0.5 or the loadings for two or more factors are greater than 0.5, the item is a cross factor measure and should be deleted. We combined exploratory factor analysis with confirmatory factor analysis to determine the validity of the questionnaire.

4.3 Exploratory factor analysis

The Kaiser–Meyer–Olkin test (KMO) and Bartlett's test were used to ensure that the questionnaire data were suitable for exploratory factor analysis. Factor analysis was carried out for the five dimensions of the factors that affect doctor moral hazard according to the method described in Bentley and Chou (1987)[18].

KMO and Bartlett's test were calculated using IBM SPSS 20.0. The KMO values for each dimension were 0.774, 0.845, 0.862, 0.816 and 0.843; all values are >0.5. The significance level of the Bartlett test was $0.000 < 0.001$, indicating that there was a strong correlation between variables. The correlation matrix was not a unit matrix, indicating suitability for factor analysis. However, values of 1.6 in the motivation dimension and 2.7 in the opportunity dimension were too low on average ($P < 0.5$), indicating that they should be deleted. After recalculation, the KMO values of each dimension were 0.771, 0.838, 0.852, 0.816 and 0.822; all values are > 0.5. The significance level of the Bartlett test was $0.000 < 0.001$, indicating that each dimension scale was suitable for factor analysis.

We used principal component analysis to extract common factors by orthogonal rotation when the eigenvalue was > 1 and the cumulative variance contribution was $> 60\%$. Two common factors were extracted from the motivation dimension, with a cumulative variance contribution of 73.414%; two common factors were extracted from the opportunity dimension, with a cumulative variance contribution of 65.796%; two common factors were extracted from the rationalization dimension, with a cumulative variance contribution of 69.188%; one common factor was extracted from the exposure dimension, with a cumulative variance contribution of 73.661%; two common factors were extracted from the punishment dimension, with a cumulative variance contribution of 70.430%. Each common factor was named according to its specific content. The common factors extracted from each dimension are shown in Table 4.

Table 4. Common factors extracted and the definition of common factors for each dimension.

Motivation dimension	Scientific research pressure	Economic pressure	Opportunity dimension	Decision-making autonomy	Patient partici-pation	Rationali-zation dimension	Treatment uncertainty	System defect	Punishment dimension	Hospital punishment	Social punishment	Exposure dimension	Probability of exposure
1.2	0.900		2.5	0.673		3.1	0.792		5.1	0.918		4.1	0.740
1.3	0.855		2.6	0.828		3.2	0.797		5.2	0.902		4.2	0.848
1.4	0.647		2.8	0.581		3.3	0.698		5.3	0.643		4.3	0.911
1.9	0.649		2.9	0.693		3.4	0.756		5.4	0.623		4.4	0.898
1.10	0.893		2.10	0.813		3.5	0.839		5.5	0.772		4.5	0.861
1.11	0.880		2.11	0.862		3.6	0.527		5.6		0.705	4.6	0.753
1.1		0.554	2.1		0.735	3.7		0.843	5.7		0.872	4.7	0.764
1.5		0.743	2.2		0.782	3.8		0.786	5.8		0.902	4.8	0.664
1.7		0.733	2.3		0.669	3.9		0.787	5.9		0.853		
1.8		0.677	2.4		0.824				5.10		0.914		
			2.7		0.620				5.11		0.902		

The results of validity testing showed that all loadings for each item in the questionnaire were greater than 0.5 and that no item loading was for a single factor or cross factors. The results also showed convergent validity and discriminant validity for each dimension scale, and thus each dimension showed construct validity.

Table 5. Goodness-of-fit of confirmatory factor analysis.

Model	Chi-square value / Degree of freedom		GFI	AGFI	CFI	RMSEA
Motivation dimension	2.493		0.978	0.943	0.989	0.072
Opportunity dimension	2.656		0.968	0.930	0.976	0.076
Rationalization dimension	2.930		0.975	0.934	0.970	0.082
Exposure dimension	2.297		0.992	0.962	0.996	0.067
Punishment dimension	3.421		0.971	0.923	0.985	0.092
Models meet the verification criteria	<3		>0.9	>0.85	>0.9	<0.1

4.4 Confirmatory factor analysis

We used AMOS 20.0 to analyze the second set of 290 data items to eliminate invalid terms and to evaluate the goodness-of-fit of the model and the validity of each variable.

Chi-square values (χ^2) for degrees of freedom (DF), goodness-of-fit index (GFI), adjusted goodness-of-fit index (AGFI), comparative goodness-of-fit index (CFI) and root mean square of approximate error (RMSEA) were used to evaluate the confirmatory factor analysis. When χ^2 / DF < 3, GFI > 0.9, AGFI > 0.85, CFI > 0.9, and RMSEA < 0.1, the model has a high goodness-of-fit. We used AMOS 20.0 to perform confirmatory factor analysis on the five dimensions,as shown in Figure 5. We deleted terms with poor goodness-of-fit. The parameter values were significant, and the overall effect of the model was ideal. Overall, the measurement items for each dimension measured that dimension well, showing that the scale of each dimension had good structural validity.

Table 6. Confirmatory factor analysis of the second half of samples (N=290).

Dimension	Items	Standardized load	CR	AVE
Motivation dimension				
Economic pressure	Economic pressure from medical groups	0.894	0.811	0.594
	Economic pressure from departments and hospitals	0.77		
	Economic pressure from peer comparison	0.625		
Scientific research pressure	Pressure of technical innovation in practice	0.827	0.915	0.783
	Pressure to obtain research funding and publish papers at all levels	0.893		
	Pressure to improve academic status	0.932		
Opportunity dimension				
Decision-making autonomy	Academic authorities have corresponding treatment guidelines	0.721	0.861	0.611
	Degree of treatment consistency	0.899		
	Transparency of treatment	0.835		
	Patients have no decision-making abilities	0.647		
Patient participation	Decision-making autonomy in diagnosis and treatment	0.703	0.753	0.507
	Degree of information asymmetry in diagnosis and treatment	0.629		
	Doctors are fully authorized by patients to diagnose and treat diseases and other medical conditions	0.794		
Rationalization dimension				
Treatment uncertainty	Uncertainty of treatment outcomes	0.677	0.820	0.534
	Traceability of diagnosis and treatment behavior	0.747		
	Patient initiatives to operate on diseases or lesions without indications	0.78		
	Severity of moral hazard behavior	0.715		
Systemic deficiency	The belief that most doctors who offend will face no punishment	0.755	0.653	0.487
	The system is not optimal, and doctor's incomes are not high enough	0.635		
Exposure dimension				
	Frequency of inspection by hospital	0.906	0.872	0.637
	Frequency of inspection by society	0.919		
	Frequency of patients voluntarily reporting adverse events	0.689		
	Frequency of peers voluntarily reporting adverse events	0.638		

Punishment dimension				
Hospital punishment	Poor evaluation of patient satisfaction	0.645	0.891	0.737
	Punishment of departments	0.935		
	Punishment by medical groups	0.96		
Social punishment	Media exposure	0.828	0.912	0.776
	Individual doctors may be threatened by patients in various ways	0.888		
	Individual doctors may be punished by law	0.924		

It can be seen from Table 6 that the normalized loading of most items on the common factor is > 0.7. Among the items that failed to meet this standard, the items that met the minimum standard (e.g., under economic pressure, the pressure of peer comparison) also reached 0.625. Therefore, the convergence validity of the scale is good and the whole scale is acceptable. In addition, the construction reliability (CR) of most variables was > 0.8, and the average extraction variance (AVE) was also > 0.5 (except that systemic deficiency in the rationalization dimension is slightly less than 0.5). Therefore, the variables in the scale have good construct validity.

5 Discussion

We derived five dimensions of factors that affect doctor moral hazard from a comprehensive worldwide literature study supplemented by in-depth interviews with experts: motivation, opportunity, rationalization, exposure and punishment. We extracted the common factors of each dimension using exploratory factor analysis. When we had defined the factors, we found that the factors affecting doctor moral hazard that we had extracted from the empirical data were essentially the same as those identified in the theoretical analysis and the interviews; only the rationalization dimension was different.

5.1 Motivation dimension

Exploratory factor analysis identified two factors in this dimension that affected doctor moral hazard: economic pressure and scientific research pressure. Pressure for technological innovation or staff development was not included. During interviews, doctors responded that the main pressures they felt were economic pressure and pressure to conduct scientific research. Scientific research can include technological innovation. Personnel development is the responsibility of senior doctors, who have taught and trained their juniors, completed performance evaluations, and led scientific research and education.

5.2 Opportunity dimension

We found two factors in this dimension that affected doctor moral hazard: decision-making autonomy and patient participation. Information asymmetry was not included. The degree of information asymmetry between doctor and patient is an economic factor which, for an individual doctor, presents them with opportunities to decide on non-indicated treatments. It is also an opportunity to expand their decision-making autonomy with respect to the treatment they recommend, which is often restricted by the government and hospital management. Patient participation enables a patient or their family to have some say in the recommended treatment, but that say can be limited by lack of information. Information asymmetry can reduce patient participation and increase doctor autonomy in determining treatment.

5.3 Rationalization dimension

We found two factors in this dimension that affected doctor moral hazard: system defects and treatment uncertainty. System defects included the beliefs of medical staff that clinical services were not properly remunerated due to social factors, such as governmental support for therapeutic drug use. Treatment uncertainty arises because a particular medical treatment does not necessarily lead to good or bad outcomes, and bad outcomes are not necessarily a consequence of bad treatment. Thus doctor moral hazard behavior can be difficult to identify from treatment outcomes.

5.4 Exposure dimension

We found one factor in this dimension that affected doctor moral hazard: the probability of exposure. For an individual doctor, audits of their behavior, spot checks or investigation of their reports are internalized as the probability that their moral hazard behavior will be discovered. This was the only common factor found by orthogonal rotation. It is perhaps appropriate to combine the probability of exposure with the threat of punishment into one dimension.

5.5 Punishment dimension

We found two factors in this dimension that affected doctor moral hazard: hospital punishment and social punishment. We found no threat of punishment from patients in this dimension, contrary to our original Hypothesis 5. Although patients can threaten doctors through complaints, prosecutions, and even medical injuries, doctors we interviewed thought that being threatened by a patient was the act of an individual patient rather than an act of punishment by the hospital or by society.

To summarize our findings, the factors that affect doctor moral hazard were categorized into five dimensions, and nine principal characteristic factors were identified. Through identification and analysis of the characteristic factors of each dimension, we are able to explore the mechanisms of influence and devise measures to prevent and control doctor moral hazard behavior.

6 Conclusion

Moral hazard is usually seen as an economic concept rather than a moral one. However, doctor moral hazard has a considerable ethical component because doctors have a duty of care towards their patients. We categorized the factors that influence doctor moral hazard behavior into five dimensions that we had identified from analysis of the literature and in-depth interviews with experts: motivation, opportunity, rationalization, exposure and punishment. We developed a questionnaire to gather empirical data and used exploratory factor analysis to identify the factors that principally influence doctor moral hazard behavior. We found that economic pressure, pressure to undertake scientific research, autonomy in decision-making, patient participation, treatment uncertainty, systemic deficiencies, the probability of exposure, and threats of hospital and social punishment had significant effects on the occurrence of doctor moral hazard behavior. It was also found that the pressure for scientific research was greater than economic pressure, which showed that although doctor moral hazard behavior was affected by economic pressure, regulating and controlling doctors economically may not be an efficient way to reduce doctor moral hazard behavior. Instead, regulating the pressure to conduct scientific research might provide more control.

This paper contributes to the theory of doctor moral hazard in the following ways: it provides a theoretical analysis and summary of the research on factors that affect doctor moral hazard; it gives a comprehensive analysis of doctor moral hazard using the five dimensions of motivation, opportunity, rationalization, exposure and punishment; it identifies fifteen characteristics of the influential factors and recognizes nine principal characteristic factors. From the data we obtained, we developed a scale of the factors that influence doctor moral hazard behavior, using IBM SPSS 20.0 and AMOS 20.0 to establish the reliability and validity of the scale in each dimension. We extracted the nine major factors that influence doctor moral hazard behavior from the empirical data by exploratory factor analysis to provide the groundwork for government departments and medical institutions to prevent or control doctor moral hazard behavior.

The theoretical hypotheses of the paper were verified by analysis of the empirical data. However, the analysis also identified shortcomings that need to be further studied. These include improvement of the measurement scale, using additional software to refine and optimize measurement, and incremental revision of the questionnaire; and expanding the scope of the research and increasing the sampling capacity in subsequent research to gather more data, which will improve the accuracy of empirical analysis. These latter activities will enable us to conduct multi-level factor analysis of the factors that affect doctor moral hazard, so that we can better determine the importance of these factors, identify additional factors, and further analyze the mechanisms by which these factors influence doctor moral hazard behavior.

References

1. Ross, S. A. (1973). The economic theory of agency: The principal's problem. *The American economic review*, **63**(2), 134-139.
2. Arrow, Kenneth.1963. Uncertainty and the Welfare Economics of Medical Care. *American Economic Review*. **53**(5):941-73.
3. Fuchs, V. R. (1978). *The supply of surgeons and the demand for operations* (No. w0236). National Bureau of Economic Research.
4. Evans, R. G. (1974). Supplier-induced demand: some empirical evidence and implications. In *The economics of health and medical care: proceedings of a conference held by the International Economic Association at Tokyo* (pp. 162-173). Palgrave Macmillan UK.
5. Tancredi, L. R., & Barondess, J. A. (1978). The problem of defensive medicine. *Science*, **200**(4344), 879-882.
6. Ali, A. A., Hummeida, M. E., Elhassan, Y. A., M. Nabag, W. O., Ahmed, M. A. A., & Adam, G. K. (2016). Concept of defensive medicine and litigation among Sudanese doctors working in obstetrics and gynecology. *BMC medical ethics*, 17, 1-5.
7. Doran, E., Robertson, J., & Henry, D. (2005). Moral hazard and prescription medicine use in Australia—the patient perspective. *Social Science & Medicine*, **60**(7), 1437-1443.
8. Lundin, D. (2000). Moral hazard in physician prescription behavior. *Journal of health economics*, **19**(5), 639-662.

9. Cheraghi, R., Esfandnia, A., & Vaisi, H. (2018). The study of induced demand done CT scan services in Imam Reza Hospital 2015. *Revista Publicando*, **5**(16 (2)), 427-434.
10. Einav, L., Finkelstein, A., Ryan, S. P., Schrimpf, P., & Cullen, M. R. (2013). Selection on moral hazard in health insurance. *American Economic Review*, **103**(1), 178-219.
11. Cheraghi, R., Esfandnia, A., & Vaisi, H. (2018). The study of induced demand done CT scan services in Imam Reza Hospital 2015. *Revista Publicando*, **5**(16 (2)), 427-434.
12. Einav, L., & Finkelstein, A. (2018). Moral hazard in health insurance: what we know and how we know it. *Journal of the European Economic Association*, **16**(4), 957-982.
13. ZHANG, L. G., LI, L. L., & LI, X. R. (2017).An Analysis of the Factors Affecting Farmers' Moral Hazard Behaviors: An Empirical Study Based on Structural Equation Model. Journal of Jiangxi University of Finance and Economics, (06),77-86.
14. Zhang Ping， Ma Li.(2018).Empirical Study of Influential Elements of Project Managers' Moral Hazard-Towards Construction Enterprises. *Journal of Technical Economics & Management* ,**3**: 15-19.
15. Aghghaleh, S. F., & Mohamed, Z. M. (2014). Fraud risk factors of fraud triangle and the likelihood of fraud occurrence: Evidence from Malaysia. *Information Management and Business Review*, **6**(1), 1-7.
16. Farahmand, F., & Spafford, E. H. (2013). Understanding insiders: An analysis of risk-taking behavior. *Information systems frontiers*, **15**, 5-15.
17. Steiger,J. H. (1990). Structural model evaluation and modification: An interval estimation approach. *Multivariate behavioral research*, **25**(2), 173-180.
18. DeVellis,R. F.,& Thorpe,C. T. *Scale Development:Theory and applications* [M],Newbury Park:Sage,1991:47.

Analysis of a hazardous factory explosion accident

Shihui Guo, *Zhiming* Wang, *Kunpeng* Cui* and *Chuan* Xiao

Department of Emergency Rescue, China Fire and Rescue Institute, No. 4, Nanyan Road, Changping District, Beijing, China

Abstract. Factory explosion accidents not only cause damages of factory facilities and equipment, or casualties usually, but also cause fire disaster due to various reasons, resulting in larger losses. After the occurrence of accidents, timely, accurate, and efficient response is an urgent need to protect the safety of people's lives and property. A hazardous Factory Explosion accident in North China in 2019 was taken as an example by this paper. It conducts research from four aspects, including the basic situation of the accident, the handling of the explosion accident, and the analysis of the cause of explosion accident. The useful advice and efficient disposal methods of accidents, the enhancement of disaster prevention and disaster relief capabilities, and the formation of a long-term mechanism to ensure the safety of people's lives and property are expounded in this paper, in order to provide a reference for similar accident management.

1 Introduction

In the winter of 2019, a gas explosion accident occurred in the production workshop of a foreign-funded enterprise in a region in North China, causing 4 deaths, 10 injuries and direct economic losses of 14.29563 million yuan. After the accident, the emergency forces of public security, fire protection, emergency management, health and other departments coordinated and worked together to deal with the accident, and immediately carried out the rescue and treatment of the wounded. At the same time, the stability maintenance and public opinion control of the casualties and their families were well-handled. Due to the timely handling of the accident, the loss of national property has been reduced, showing the achievements of the construction of the emergency rescue system for work safety accidents and disasters in a certain area of North China in recent years. At the same time, it also puts forward higher requirements for the on-site emergency response capabilities of the urban area[1-4].

The following takes this accident as an example to discuss the emergency response to this hazardous factory explosion accident, hereinafter referred to as "North China X factory explosion accident".

* Corresponding author: cuikunpeng2004@163.com

2 Basic situation of the accident

In thispaper, the background of the "North China X factory explosion accident" from various aspects such as the company composition and architectural layout of the accident, gas facilities and cold storage conditions wasanalyzed. The details are as follows:

The enterprise involved is a foreign-funded enterprise, which was located in a district in North China. Its business scope includes bean paste, pastries, raw and auxiliary materials for pastries, food seasonings, and self-produced food packaging products. The company has a total of 662 employeesand 12 departments, including life department and production department. The life department is responsible for the company's fire protection, safety and security, training and education. The production department is responsible for organizing production and production equipment management and production in accordance with the production plan. It is also is responsible for Revising of management system, training and education of operating personnel's safety in production and operating procedures.

The main buildings of the company's factory area include office buildings, phase I production workshops, phase II production workshops (untapped), warehouses, attached rooms and sewage treatment facilities. The accident area is located in the middle of the north side of the first production workshops (see Figure 1) , The workshop is a single-story main frame structure building with a partial two-story west side. The accident area mainly involved the gas cylinder room, cold storage, raw material storage, frying flour room, sieving room, additive storage, sugar storage, steam frying flour room and some rooms in the pastry workshop (see Figure 2).

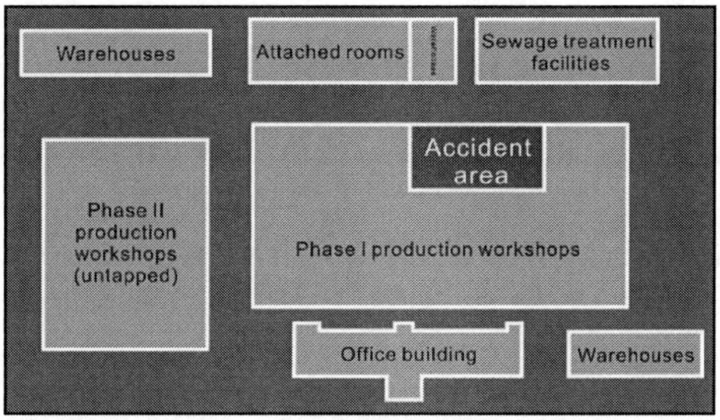

Fig. 1. Location of the accident.

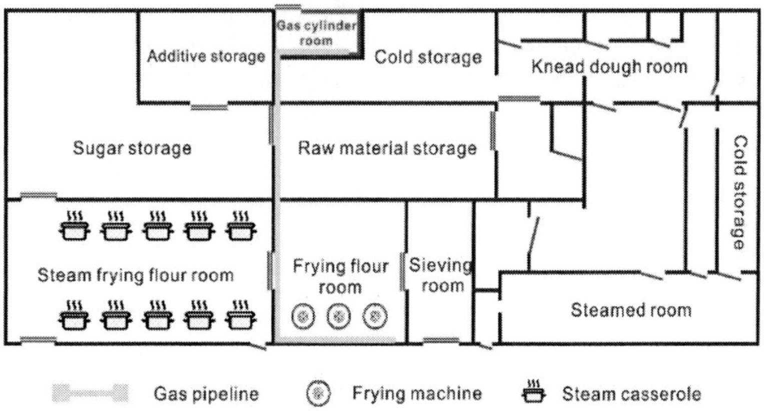

Fig 2. Regional room layout diagram of accident occurrence.

The gas cylinder room is located on the north side of the phase Iphase Iproduction workshop, about 6 meters long from east to west, 3 meters wide from north to south, and 3 meters high from ground to ceiling. The north wall of the cylinder room contains doors, thermometers, explosion-proof lighting switches and windows from west to east. The other walls are solid partition walls with no door or window openings and connected to the roof; there is a ventilation pipe in the northeast corner to exhaust air to the outside of the room. Liquefied petroleum gas cylinders are placed in the southeast corner. The gas cylinders are connected to the gas pipeline through the manifold through the pressure reducing valve and the hose.

The gas pipeline was built by a relevant company in 2006. The diameter of the pipeline is 80 mm and the operating pressure is about 200 KPa. The gas pipeline is fixed horizontally at a distance of 1.2 meters from the ground on the south wall of the gas cylinders, and a pressure gauge is installed on the west side. The gas pipeline passes through the south wall of the gas cylinders from the pressure gauge to the south, and then bends upward, which is about 1.4 meters from the ground. Set the main pipeline valve (DN80 flange ball valve), and bend to the south about 3.5 meters above the ground, extend horizontally along the west wall shared by the gas cylinder room and the raw material warehouse, across the top of the cold storage, and pass through the southern partition of the cold storage and the south wall of the raw material warehouse enters the fried noodle room. The gas pipeline runs from the west wall to the south wall of the noodle room. The south wall of the noodle room is divided into 3 vertical branch pipes, extending to about 30 cm from the ground, and connected to 3 low-pressure stir-frying machines through hoses. The type of gas used in the stir-frying machine is liquefied petroleum gas, with a rated pressure of 1.96 to 3.23 KPa.

3 The handling of explosion accidents

After the accident, the involved company evacuated people from the factory area, reported the accident information, and cooperated with relevant departments to carry out emergency rescue and after-care work.

Seven minutes after the explosion, the Municipal Fire Rescue Corps received an alarm and then dispatched 54 fire trucks, 200 commanders and 6 search and rescue dogs to the scene to search and rescue the trapped people. The district emergency center sub-center has sent 10 ambulance teams and 14 vehicles to the accident site to treat the injured.

After the accident, the local committee and district government organize relevant departments and the local town government to carry out emergency response, dispatch emergency rescue teams and equipment to assist in emergency rescue work, and do a good job in zoning control of the accident site and isolation of surrounding areas. The local government established an accident handling temporary headquarters, formulated an accident emergency response work plan, and coordinated and organized the rescue of the injured, the comfort of the families of the injured and the dead, the aftermath treatment, and the release of follow-up information about the accident.

Relevant leaders of the Municipal Party Committee and Municipal Government rushed to the scene to direct emergency rescue work as soon as possible. The relevant departments such as the Municipal Public Security Bureau and the Municipal Emergency Bureau were present to coordinate and guide emergency response work. The Traffic Management Bureau of the Municipal Public Security Bureau, together with relevant local authorities, carried out traffic diversion and management around the accident site. The Municipal Emergency Bureau synchronously activated the emergency response mechanism and coordinated the relevant departments to do a good job in the release of accident information.

Fifty minutes after receiving the alarm, the open fire was extinguished; all the 5 people trapped in the accident were rescued, but 4 of them died and 1 was injured. A total of 108 people were injured and hospitalized in the accident. After 14 days , all the injured were discharged.

4 Analysis of the cause of the accident

After comprehensive analysis of relevant technical appraisals, site surveys, inquiry transcripts and video data by the public security organs and expert groups, the suspicion of deliberate arson and explosions was ruled out. The company's gas explosion accident was determined to be a major production safety responsibility. The specific causes of the accident are as follows.

The flange gaskets (Figure 3, A and B) of the main valves of the gas pipeline in the phase I production workshop are made of methyl vinyl silicone rubber, which is subject to long-term corrosion by the mixed gas of liquefied petroleum gas and dimethyl ether in the pipeline. Physical and mechanical performance of the flange gaskets declines. The small cracks develop and gradually grow on the flange gaskets, resulting local breakages. The B gasket is torn and a leak is formed, under the action of the internal pressure of the pipeline. A large amount of gas leaks into the gap between the outer wall of the refrigerator and the surrounding wall in the cold storage, which spreads to the inside of the cold storage, the top space and adjacent areas such as the mixing room, the batching room, the raw material storage, etc.. An explosive mixture of gas in the inner and outer spaces of the cold storage was formed. Meanwhile, the fan in the cold storage also accelerates the mixing of the leaked gas and the air. When an ignition source such as an electric spark explodes, a high-voltage shock wave is quickly formed and spreads around, igniting the combustibles at the scene, leading to an accident. The accident was judged to be a liquefied petroleum gas explosion, and the explosion center was located in the cold storage area.

The involved institution was suspected with the problems such as engaging in hazardous chemical business activities beyond the business method approved by the business license, illegally repackaging, and illegally storing hazardous chemicals.

Fig. 3. Gas pipeline main valve and flange gasket diagram.

5 Conclusion

Generally speaking, it's was a complete success of the rescue and disposal work in this accident. In this rescue operation, the authors participated in the accident disposal. This paper mainly discusses from the perspective of management and command. In view of the accident's leakage diffusion radius, cause of death and injury, LPG explosion equivalent, building model, etc., further detailed research will be carried out, and comparison with other accidents will be carried out to further summarize relevant experience and lessons.

References

1. Roux T L . The Grenelle Gunpowder Factory Explosion. *Acculturating to Industrial Hazard in France*, 2018:1790-1810
2. Z. X. Mo, T. X. Wu, F. Xie, and W. H. Song, Simulation and the emergency measures study of the transient leakage of liquid ammonia transient based on MATLAB[J]. *Acta Scientiarum Naturalium Universitatis Nankaien*, 2014, 4: 1–5.(in Chinese).
3. Romano E , Elklit A . Rescue workers and trauma: Assessing interaction among risk factors after a firework factory explosion[J]. *J Emerg Manag*, 2017, 15(5):311-323.
4. Yuan J W , Zhao X D , Jiang C M , et al. Study on impact zone for dispersion and explosion accident in coal gasification factory[J]. *Journal of Safety Science and Technology*, 2012, 7(8):432-439.
5. Fall T . Crisis after explosion at Chinese factory[J]. *International Dyer*, 2019, 204(2):18-19.
6. Chang S C , Cheng Y C , Zhang X H , et al. Effects of moisture content on explosion characteristics of incense dust in incense factory[J]. *Journal of Thermal Analysis and Calorimetry*, 2021, 12: 26-34.
7. YE Shuliang, ZHANG Sheng. A Method of Hazardous Chemical Materials Deflagration Identification Based on Multi-Parameter and Feature-Level Fusion[J]. *Chinese Journal of Sensors and Actuators*, 2011, 24 (04):620-623.
8. Z. X. Wang, eakage simulation Analysis and Diffusion model optimization of Hazardous Chemicals[D]. *Dalian University of Technology*, 2016,:15-21(in Chinese).
9. Xu Liang, Zhang Heping, Yang Yun, Wang Wei, Zhu Wuba. Experimental study on full scale fire of waste tires [J]. *Journal of applied basic and engineering sciences*. 2006,14 (1): 33-39.
10. Liao D G, Fang C , Wang X , et al. Investigation of a liquefied petroleum gas explosion in a factory building. *Fire Science and Technology,* 2018, 11 (3): 134-140.

A comprehensive evaluation of power suppliers

Ye Chen[1,*], *Ping* Chen[2], *Huawei* Xiao[3] and *Yutong* Xiao[2]

[1]State Grid Wuhan Power Supply Design Institute Co. LT, Hubei, China
[2]State Grid Hubei Electric Power Co. LTD. Technical Training Center Scientific Research Department, Hubei, China
[3]State Grid Hubei Electric Power Co., LTD. Material Department, Hubei, China

Abstract. Aiming at the shortcomings in current power equipment supplier evaluation, this paper is designed for different types of project comprehensive evaluation models. First of all, starting from the type of project and engineering needs, the indicator system was established in four aspects: qualification ability, process control, operation quality, and service quality. Then, the subjective weight and objective weight of each evaluation index were calculated by the fuzzy analytic hierarchy process (AHP) and factor analysis method. The final weight was obtained by a combination weighting method. The supplier category was determined according to the principle of maximum membership, and the final evaluation was completed. Finally, the evaluation model was verified by the distribution transformer supplier, and the results proved the objective rationality of the evaluation model.

1 Introduction

The power grid material supplier is the core link of the power grid material supply chain. The performance evaluation of suppliers can strengthen the ability of material supply guarantee, improve the level of material intensive management, and facilitate the selection of suppliers. It is of practical significance to conduct supplier behavior analysis and supplier comprehensive evaluation [1-2].

At present, the evaluation of suppliers is mainly studied from two aspects: the construction of an evaluation index system and the evaluation method. Literature [3] and [4] constructed evaluation indexes from the aspect of social responsibility, and literature [5-9] used multiple discriminant analysis (MDA), grey clustering trigonometric method, neural network, and support vector machine to evaluate. Due to the particularity of power supply, different types of projects have different material supply objectives. When suppliers need to supply multiple projects at the same time, their bidding standards should be different. The existing methods do not consider this problem. The index design is either too single or too broad and lacks pertinence, resulting in the difference between the evaluation results and the actual situation.

Based on this, this paper first analyzes the demand characteristics of different types of substances for power projects, constructs a comprehensive evaluation index for suppliers,

* Corresponding author: 512070331@qq.com

and constructs an evaluation model based on the fuzzy analytic hierarchy process (FAHP). The effectiveness and feasibility of the model are verified by example analysis.

2 Construct a comprehensive evaluation index system

The power grid material supply chain is determined by the operation demand of the power grid, which can be divided into engineering demand and non-engineering demand. The engineering demand is determined by the specific power construction project. The non-project category refers to the operation and maintenance of the power grid, which is the demand formed by the operation accident and emergency. As for two types of projects, in addition to quality assurance, the former need to strictly control the supply time, and supplies to strictly match the project schedule; the latter is highly uncertain and requires corresponding speed[10].

Combining the characteristics of these two types of projects, ECP, enterprise resource planning (ERP), manufacture scheduling platform (MDS), power production management system (PMS), and other platforms' various dimensions of data, evaluation indicators[11,12] are established based on the supplier's qualifications and capabilities, process control, product quality, and service support. The evaluation indicators are shown in Table 1.

Table 1. Evaluation system for power grid material supplie.

The primary indicators	The secondary indicators	Indicator description	Indicator type	The data source
Ability of qualification	Qualification of credibility	Assign the value according to the corresponding credit level of the supplier	Semantic phrases	Original data
	engineering performance	Proportion of engineering projects of suppliers in one year	Accurate number	Calculated by formula
	Shipment inspection performance	Proportion of supplier's inspection items in one year	Accurate number	Original data
Process control	Degree of contract fit	Reflect supplier contract signing and performance process	Semantic phrases	Expert scoring
	Sample inspection pass rate	Pass rate of sample inspection	Semantic phrases	Expert scoring
	Progress of production schedule	The supplier completes the schedule of the whole planning process	Accurate number	Original data
	Timeliness of delivery	To reflect the delivery as agreed	Semantic phrases	Expert scoring
Operation quality	Defect rate	The proportion of familial defects in equipment	Accurate number	Calculated by formula
	Failure rate	The percentage of devices that fail	Accurate number	Calculated by formula
	Equipment service life	Normal operating year of the device	Accurate number	Calculated by formula
Service quality	Installation quality	The degree of field support during installation	Semantic phrases	Expert scoring
	Debugging quality	Commissioning and commissioning of equipment	Interval number	Original data
	After-sales quality	The degree of support for equipment repair and maintenance	Semantic phrases	Expert scoring

(1) Ability of qualification: Qualification of credibility, performance of R&D and design engineering projects, and performance of operation and inspection projects are taken as evaluation indicators. Qualification of credibility refers to the credit rating of the supplier. The proportion of annual R&D expenses of R&D design suppliers: engineering project performance, the proportion of engineering projects in one year; performance of inspection projects, the proportion of inspection projects within one year.

(2) Process control: Degree of contract fit, sample inspection pass rate, the progress of the production schedule, and timeliness of delivery. Degree of contract fit and user satisfaction refers to reflect the supplier contract signing and performance process. Based on the progress of the production schedule, the supplier completes the whole planning process with the schedule. The progress of production schedule (qualified) refers to the qualified rate of spot inspection of the arrival of goods and inspects the quality of production. The timeliness of supply reflects the delivery in accordance with the agreement.

(3) Operation quality: Defect rate (the proportion of familial defects in equipment), failure rate (the percentage of devices that fail), equipment service life (normal operating year of the device).

(4) Service quality: Installation quality (the degree of field support during installation), debugging quality (commissioning and commissioning of equipment), and after-sales quality (the degree of support for equipment repair and maintenance)[12].

3 Comprehensive evaluation model

The fuzzy analytic hierarchy process (FAHP) and Factor Analysis (FA) were used to calculate the subjective and objective weights of indicators. Then, combined weights were assigned based on game theory.

3.1 Fuzzy Analytic Hierarchy Process

Fuzzy analytic hierarchy process (FAHP) uses a fuzzy consistency matrix for subjective weighting, which can not only maintain the advantages of traditional AHP, but also ensure the consistency of the judgment matrix.

The fuzzy complementary matrix is constructed, and the n evaluation indexes selected are compared pairwise. Based on the membership degree of the fuzzy relationship between 0.1-0.9, the fuzzy relationship between indexes is quantified to form a fuzzy matrix. Clearly, matrix A is a fuzzy complementary matrix.

$$A = \left[a_{ij} \right]_{n \times n}, \quad a_{ij} + a_{ji} = 1 \tag{1}$$

The fuzzy complementary matrix is transformed into the fuzzy consistent matrix. The fuzzy complementary matrix A is summed by row, and the fuzzy consistency matrix T is obtained by mathematical transformation using the following formula.

$$T = \left[t_{ij} \right]_{n \times n}, \quad t_{ij} = (t_i - t_j)/2n + 0.5 \tag{2}$$

Calculate the weight coefficient. By substituting fuzzy consistent matrix T into AHP, the weight of fuzzy hierarchy ω= (ω1, ω2..., ωn)

$$\omega_i = \frac{2}{n(n-1)}(\sum_{j=1}^{n} t_{ij} - 1) \qquad i = 1, 2, \cdots, n \tag{3}$$

Modify the index weight coefficient. Formula (4) is used to calculate the similarity degree (Rij) of evaluation weights of each expert index and the deviation degree (Pij) of expert evaluation. In Formula (5), the scores with large deviation degrees are discarded.

$$R = 1 - \sqrt{\frac{\sum_{j=1}^{n}(\omega_{ik} - \omega_{jk})^2}{n}}, \qquad i = 1, 2, \cdots, n \tag{4}$$

$$X_i = \sum_{j=1}^{n} R_{ij}, \quad P_i = \frac{X_{\max} - X_i}{X_{\max}} \times 100\% \tag{5}$$

Consistency test. The consistency check is made according to the weight matrix of the division calculated above, and the judgment basis is CR<0.1.

$$\lambda_{\max} = \sum_{j=1}^{n} \frac{(T\omega)_i}{n\omega_i} \tag{6}$$

$$CI = \frac{\lambda_{\max} - n}{n-1}, \quad CR = \frac{CI}{RI} \tag{7}$$

3.2 Establish the fuzzy relation matrix

Determine the evaluation index, assuming n evaluation objects, C ={c1,c2... cn}, where c1, c2... cn is n evaluation factors participating in the evaluation.

Establish supplier evaluation standard set V, standard set V= {v1, v2... , vm}, where v1, v2... , vm has m evaluation levels. In this paper, suppliers are divided into three levels: A, B, and C (A> B> C).

Establish the fuzzy membership matrix r, r = $(r_{ij})n\times m$, membership r_{ij} is:

$$r_{ij} = \begin{cases} 1 & x_i \le s_i \\ (s_{j+1} - x_i)/(s_{j+1} - s_i) & s_i < x_i < s_{i+1} \\ 0 & x_i \ge s_{i+1} \end{cases} \tag{8}$$

Factor analysis

Based on the index system constructed above, the collected sample data of power material suppliers are standardized and processed to form the original index data set.

The common factor is extracted, and the eigenvalue and eigenvector are calculated through the covariance matrix. The principal factor is extracted according to the variance contribution degree, and the cumulative variance contribution degree is usually selected to be greater than 90%.

2) The variance-maximizing orthogonal rotation method is used to differentiate the factor loading coefficients of the common factors.

3) The maximum likelihood and least square methods were used to estimate the factor scores and calculate the scores of each index.

$$\omega_j^2 = \frac{\beta_j}{\sum_{j=1}^{n} \beta_j} \tag{9}$$

(4) Game theory combinatorial weighting

The combined weighting method of game theory can fully combine subjective consciousness with the internal distribution of objective data and improve the scientific rationality of weight to a certain extent [12]. Combined weighting method of game theory is used to optimize subjective weight and objective weight.

Table 2. Weight matrix of performance evaluation index of distribution transformer supplier.

Primary indicators			Secondary indicators			Weighted Weightiness
Number	Name	Weightiness	Number	Name	Weightiness	
1	Ability of qualification	0.198	1	Qualification of credibility	0.367	0.072666
			2	Engineering performance	0.313	0.061974
			3	Shipment inspection performance	0.32	0.06336
2	Process control	0.314	4	Degree of contract fit	0.234	0.073476
			5	Sample inspection pass rate	0.282	0.088548
			6	Progress of production schedule	0.228	0.071592
			7	Timeliness of delivery	0.256	0.080384
3	Operation quality	0.227	8	Defect rate	0.324	0.073548
			9	Failure rate	0.361	0.081947
			10	Equipment service life	0.315	0.071505
4	Service quality	0.261	11	Installation quality	0.343	0.089523
			12	Debugging quality	0.336	0.087696
			13	After-sales quality	0.321	0.083781

The analytic hierarchy process and factor analysis method are used to weigh the evaluation index of the supplier, respectively, and the comprehensive weight vector of the evaluation index of the supplier is obtained. ω={ω1,ω2}, where ω1 is the subjective weight vector determined by the analytic hierarchy process, ω2 is the objective weight vector determined by the factor analysis, and the comprehensive weight vector is:

$$\omega = \alpha_1 \omega_1^T + \alpha_2 \omega_2^T \tag{10}$$

According to the idea of the game aggregation model, with the goal of minimizing deviation, the two linear combination coefficients α1 and α2 of the above equation are optimized, and the most satisfactory weight of ω is obtained.

$$f = \min \left\| \omega - \omega_k \right\|_2, \quad k = 1,2 \tag{11}$$

1) According to the properties of matrix differentiation, the linear system of optimal first-order derivative conditions equivalent to Equation (6) is:

$$\begin{bmatrix} \omega_1\omega_1^T & \omega_1\omega_2^T \\ \omega_2\omega_1^T & \omega_2\omega_2^T \end{bmatrix}\begin{bmatrix} \alpha_1 \\ \alpha_2 \end{bmatrix} = \begin{bmatrix} \omega_1\omega_1^T \\ \omega_2\omega_2^T \end{bmatrix} \tag{12}$$

2) The optimal linear combination coefficient is obtained from the above formula. After normalization, the comprehensive weight ω based on the combination weight of game theory is finally obtained as follows:

$$\omega = \alpha_1^*\omega_1^T + \alpha_2^*\omega_2^T \tag{13}$$

Among them , $\begin{cases} \alpha_1^* = \alpha_1/(\alpha_1+\alpha_2) \\ \alpha_2^* = \alpha_2/(\alpha_1+\alpha_2) \end{cases}$.

(5) Comprehensive evaluation model

The comprehensive evaluation model is established, the fuzzy comprehensive evaluation vector is calculated, and the supplier grade is selected by the maximum membership principle max{pj}.

$$P = \omega \cdot R \tag{14}$$

4 The example analysis

In order to verify the feasibility and scientificity of the method proposed in this paper, the distribution transformer is taken as the object, and the data of 7 suppliers in a bidding process is selected for comprehensive analysis. In the example, the data of distribution transformer material suppliers of a State Grid company in a province were used to verify the method in this paper. The suppliers that continuously supplied from 2001 to 2018 were selected as the analysis objects, and an evaluation index system was established.

Table 3. The final layer weight.

Indicator layer	Subjective weight (%)	Objective weight (%)	Comprehensive weights (%)
Qualification of credibility	7.2666	7.942	7.314
Engineering performance	6.1974	5.725	6.164
Shipment inspection performance	6.336	6.643	6.357
Degree of contract fit	7.3476	9.716	7.513
Sample inspection pass rate	8.8548	9.372	8.891
Progress of production schedule	7.1592	8.913	7.282
Timeliness of delivery	8.0384	6.153	7.906
Defect rate	7.3548	5.237	7.207
Failure rate	8.1947	9.587	8.292
Equipment service life	7.1505	9.319	7.302
Installation quality	8.9523	5.372	8.702
Debugging quality	8.7696	6.528	8.613
After-sales quality	8.3781	9.495	8.456

There are different data sources and types of indicators, such as qualification of credibility, degree of contract fit, sample inspection pass rate, timeliness of delivery, installation quality, after-sales quality, and other indicators are semantic indicators; engineering performance, shipment inspection performance, the progress of production schedule, defect rate, failure rate, and equipment service life are accurate figures. After deliberation by experts and decision-makers, the value range of each index is determined, and the value of each index is normalized.

The weight matrix of the performance evaluation index of distribution transformer suppliers is shown in Table 2. The final weight is shown in Table 3.

The final evaluation result can be achieved, which is consistent with the actual situation. Taking the supplier with the code T-04 as an example, the membership degrees of A, B, and C are 0.243, 0.693, and 0.064, respectively, and the supplier is evaluated as B level. The evaluation results of suppliers are shown in Table 4.

Table 4. Statistics of supplier scores.

Supplier	A	B	C	Level
T-01	0.643	0.295	0.062	A
T-02	0.763	0.180	0.057	A
T-03	0.045	0.264	0.691	C
T-04	0.243	0.693	0.064	B
T-05	0.032	0.361	0.607	C
T-06	0.692	0.305	0.003	A
T-07	0.231	0.761	0.008	B

The results of the proposed method and the traditional fuzzy analytic hierarchy process are compared, and the results are shown in Table 5. The evaluation results of T-03, T-04, T-06, and T-07 are different. Evaluated in a traditional method, T-03 and T-07 are A, T-04 is C, and T-06 is B. While evaluation in this method, T-03 is C, T-07 is B, T-04 is B, and T-06 is A. This indicates that the traditional method will omit the internal rules between the data, resulting in the difference between the evaluation results and the actual situation.

Table 5. Comparison of evaluation methods.

Supplier	Evaluation result	
	The traditional AHP	The Present Paper
T-01	A	A
T-02	B	A
T-03	A	C
T-04	C	B
T-05	C	C
T-06	B	A
T-07	A	B

5 Conclusion

This paper first established the indicator system in four aspects: qualification ability, process control, operation quality, and service quality, for different engineering needs of different projects. Then, the subjective weight and objective weight of the evaluation index were calculated by AHP and factor analysis, respectively. Then the combined weighting model of game theory is used to calculate the comprehensive weight of the index. In the end, the suppliers are graded by comprehensive evaluation. Examples verify the effectiveness and practicability of the model.

References

1. ZHOU Qinghua, WANG Qi. Research on Low Carbon Supplier Selection Based on Intuitionistic Fuzzy Sets and VIKOR[J]. Science and Technology Management Research, 2017, 5(10): 233-237.
2. Zhang Y. TOPSIS method based on entropy weight for supplier evaluation of power grid enterprise[C]//2015 International Conference on Education Reform and Modern Management. Atlantis Press, 2015: 334-337.
3. MEN Yekun1 QIAN Mengdi1, YU ZhaoFuzzy. A comprehensive evaluation of power equipment suppliers based on game theory and combination weighting[J]. Power System Protection and Control, 2020, 48(21): 179-186.
4. WANG Tao, ZHOU Pengcheng, WU Nannan. Research on Supplier Selection of Hydropower Enterprises Based on Grey Relational TOPSIS Method[J]. Water Power, 2018, 44(03): 74-76,93.
5. PENG Zhanglin, ZHANG Qiang, YANG Shanlin. Overview of comprehensive evaluation theory and methodology[J]. Chinese Journal of Management Science, 2015, 23(S1): 245-256.
6. ZHANG Mengzhong, MARCHOZE R. An overview on qualitative research methods[J]. Chinese Public Administration, 2001(11): 39-42.
7. LI Fuxiang, LIU Qiqi. The comprehensive evaluation of China's regional financial development — based on panel data empirical research by factor analysis and TOPSIS[J]. Journal of Industrial Technological Economics, 2016, 35(3): 152-160.
8. TANG Xiaoling, TAN Zhuling. A comprehensive evaluation of the development level of Shanxi's real estate industry based on factor analysis and cluster analysis[J]. Applied Mechanics and Materials, 2014: 3335.

Research on reform of practical teaching system for applied undergraduate engineering students

Zhongju Wei*, *Fangfang* Yu, and *Xiaoping* Xie

School of Minning and Mechanical Engineering, Liupanshui Normal University, Liupansuhi, Guizhou, 553004, China

Abstract. In response to the low quality of practical teaching in engineering majors, particularly in terms of the effectiveness of experimental teaching, lack of innovation, and other issues, this paper summarizes and analyzes the problems that exist in experimental teaching and innovative practices for cultivating applied undergraduate students, based on the requirements for graduate abilities and knowledge from corporate employers, as well as the situation of engineering practical teaching in China. It explores the composition of various elements in the practical teaching system, standardizes and innovates various elements of experimental teaching activities, and cultivates students' innovative thinking and practical abilities through a multilevel disciplinary competition system, thus constructing an innovative practical teaching system for cultivating applied undergraduate students. The practice has proved that students' practical and innovative abilities are significantly enhanced, their innovative abilities are significantly improved, the quality of graduates' employment is improved, and the social feedback is positive. A large number of high-quality applied undergraduate students have been cultivated for local economic construction.

1 Problem statement

The undergraduate students cultivation goal of local newly established undergraduate institutions is to cultivate applied high-level specialized talents. In recent years, it has been found that students' mastery of professional knowledge and skills is not strong enough, based on graduation thesis defense and feedback from employers [1]. This phenomenon should be given sufficient attention by educators and managers.

The reasons for this phenomenon are as follows: firstly, the traditional practical teaching model, teaching content and methods, as well as practical assessment system, no longer fully meet the requirements of students' practical ability and knowledge enhancement under the current situation of engineering majors. Secondly, from the perspective of practical teaching content, some content is too outdated, some content lacks relevance and fails to integrate well with local realities, and needs to be updated. Thirdly, the traditional practical teaching system lacks clear guidance on students' skills training and knowledge enhancement, and most practical teaching activities lack corresponding

* Corresponding author: weizj2010ck@163.com

operational training methods and assessment systems. Most teachers only give examination scores based on experiment reports or course design instructions, failing to reflect students' real performance and level. Fourthly, the innovation ability of most students is insufficient. The overall quality of practical teaching in engineering majors is not high, especially the effect of experimental teaching, which is not very good. Therefore, it is urgent to establish an innovative practical teaching system for the cultivation of applied talents, so as to enhance students' practical and innovation ability [2].

2 Principles and ideas for research on practice teaching reform

2.1 Principles for research on practice teaching reform

Practical teaching is a critical component of improving teaching quality in applied local undergraduate colleges and universities, and is essential for cultivating students' practical abilities and innovation spirit [3]. The construction of the practical teaching reform system should generally embody the following principles:

(1) The practicality principle: It should conform to the actual situations of Liupanshui in Guizhou Province, and provide standardized guidance for students' practical activities.

(2) The operability principle: The establishment of the practical teaching system must be easy to operate, applicable, and easy to form habitual management patterns.

(3) The innovation principle: The establishment of the practical teaching system should not only focus on system innovation but also emphasize students' innovative thinking.

(4) The standardization principle: It should be conducive to the implementation of standardized and standardized management.

(5) The promotability principle: The establishment of the practical teaching system can be used for mining majors and can also be promoted to other engineering majors.

2.2 Research ideas for the reform of practical teaching

Based on research on the ability and knowledge requirements of graduates by employers, combined with the advanced experience of practical teaching modes in other domestic universities' engineering majors, and carefully summarizing the experience of our college's school-enterprise cooperation in engineering majors, as well as the various problems encountered by students when applying theory to practice, we seek new models of school-enterprise cooperation and new mechanisms for on-the-job internships, and explore the reform of practical teaching content and modes. The guidebooks for practical teaching in engineering majors had written, propose specific internship teaching reform measures, and formulate internship teaching standards based on these measures, standardizing and institutionalizing the management of internship teaching. Teaching materials had publishde to guide student practical teaching, while cultivating students' innovative thinking and practical skills through multi-level discipline competitions.

In response to the situation where the practical teaching content is somewhat outdated, lacks relevance to local circumstances, we will develop internship syllabi and guidebooks that are both relevant to local circumstances and advanced. These materials will be based on local economic and social realities.

In response to the practical problem of the lack of corresponding operational training methods and assessment systems in most practical teaching activities, the assessment method has been reformed to focus on process assessment, taking into account the assessment results from enterprises. This objective evaluation of the effectiveness of practical teaching will guide the requirements for the next practical teaching step.

To address the problem of non-standard experimental teaching, regulations have been introduced to strengthen teaching management, standardize the management of student experiments, ensure the achievement of internship teaching objectives, and urge students to learn and consolidate their knowledge, improve their application ability, and further improve the quality of internship teaching.

By implementing reform measures in practical teaching and combining them with changes in the methods of practical teaching assessment, the students' practical activities are objectively and truthfully reflected. This fully stimulates students' enthusiasm for learning and their proactive initiative, transforming practical activities from passive to active, and thus cultivating students' innovative practical abilities.

With the focus on enhancing students' practical and innovative abilities, a "multi-level and three-dimensional" subject competition system covering mining engineering has been gradually established through exploration and practice, consisting of four stages, four levels, three categories, and three abilities. Meanwhile, the competition is combined with practical teaching, integrating the subject competition work with experiments, professional course design, and concentrated practice to form a practical teaching format based on subject competition and aimed at cultivating applied innovative talents, further improving students' practical and innovative abilities.

Ultimately, an innovative practical teaching system for cultivating applied talents, centered on the innovative practical teaching system and "multi-level and three-dimensional" subject competition system, has been established. It comprises a complete practical teaching system from goals to content to methods to assessment and evaluation, covering recognition internships, production internships, course design, graduation internships, graduation design, and subject competitions.

3 The significance of practical teaching reform

3.1 The need for practical teaching in the school's educational positioning

As a local applied undergraduate university, the school has clearly defined the objectives and ideas for cultivating applied talents based on its educational positioning, which is of great significance for the development of the local economy and society. Practical teaching is the core content of applied undergraduate education and plays a vital role in cultivating applied talents. To cultivate applied talents, it is essential to emphasize the importance of practical teaching, emphasizing the need for students to have a solid theoretical foundation, strong practical skills, innovative spirit, and cooperation awareness. Practice is an important means of training for the comprehensive ability and innovative capacity of talent cultivation. Therefore, the reform of the practical teaching system and the cultivation of students' innovative abilities are particularly important [4].

3.2 The need for building a practical teaching guarantee system

Practical teaching is an important part of the higher education teaching system and an effective way to cultivate students' basic skills, practical abilities, and innovative spirit. Serving the local economic and social development and meeting the practical needs of the industry is the foundation of local applied undergraduate colleges [5-6]. Cultivating students' knowledge application and practical operation abilities is the fundamental starting point for talent cultivation in local applied undergraduate colleges. Applied talents with deep basic knowledge and stronger practical abilities than vocational college students and traditional undergraduate students are the advantages of local applied undergraduate talent cultivation. Therefore, practical teaching plays a crucial role in the talent cultivation process of local applied undergraduate colleges. Currently, there are still many problems in the practical teaching of engineering majors in colleges, and students' practical application abilities cannot be effectively improved. The normal operation of practical teaching is not guaranteed, and students cannot carry out practical operations and on-site practices in a timely manner. The construction of the practical teaching system is not reasonable, the formulation and implementation of teaching plans, and the evaluation of teaching quality are not in place. There are no unified standards for practical teaching, and monitoring and management are not standardized enough [7-8]. The evaluation of practical teaching is unscientific and cannot truly reflect students' practical teaching level, which greatly dampens students' initiative to engage in practical learning. Therefore, educational reform is of utmost importance for building a practical teaching guarantee system for cultivating applied talents and developing students' innovative ability [9].

4 The implementation process of practical teaching reform

4.1 Research and surveys on universities and enterprises

Conducted research on the status and effectiveness of practical teaching in three engineering majors at universities in China, and surveyed four employers' requirements for the knowledge and abilities of graduates from engineering majors. The contents includes the status and effectiveness of practical teaching in engineering majors at universities in China, as well as the requirements of employers for the knowledge and abilities of graduates from engineering majors.

4.2 Organizing and discussing of practical teaching content

According to the research results, the organization and discussion of practical teaching content were mainly conducted from the following aspects:

Determine the qualities, skills, and knowledge that students should possess through each practical stage and form a systematic practical teaching content, i.e. what skills and knowledge students need to acquire through practical activities.

Through internships, students can understand the production technology and development status of enterprises, recognize and understand the production process and major production links of enterprises, lay the foundation for production in combination with the study of professional courses. Through internships, students can strengthen their perceptual understanding of the main production links of enterprises, clarify the important position of engineering industry in the national economy, understand the important role played by engineering and technical personnel in enterprises, further cultivate and improve students' ability to identify, analyze and solve problems, learn some scientific and technological and management knowledge in production, and establish a professional thinking to contribute to the industrial modernization.

Through experiments, students can systematically verify the basic theoretical knowledge and professional theoretical knowledge they have learned, consolidate and expand their knowledge, skills in calculation and drawing, cultivate and improve their ability and quality to analyze and solve practical problems, and cultivate and exercise their good ideological style of loving labor, connecting theory with practice, and respecting science and practice.

4.3 Constructing the multilevel discipline competition system

Centered on improving students' practical and innovative abilities, a multilevel discipline competition system has been gradually established, consisting of four stages, four levels, three categories, and three types of abilities, guiding students to participate in practical work competitions and complete college innovative practice projects.

The main measures to construct a multilevel discipline competition system are as follows:

(1) Strengthen the construction of discipline competition projects at the four levels. From the departmental level to the national level, the construction of discipline competition projects at the four levels is strengthened. A layered competition project is constructed, including departmental, university-level, provincial (municipal)-level, and national-level competitions, forming a multi-level selection mechanism.

(2) Combination of competition and practical teaching. We integrate discipline competitions into daily practical teaching activities, and organically integrate discipline competition work with experiments, professional course design, and concentrated practice to form a practical teaching form based on discipline competition and aimed at cultivating applied innovative talents. The ultimate goal is to promote teaching, learning, and training through competitions.

(3) Combination of competition and laboratory opening. Combining various discipline competitions, open experimental projects are designed to attract more students to participate in discipline competition activities through elective open experiments, and closely integrate laboratory opening with discipline competitions.

(4) Combination of foundation and specialty. We emphasize the role of discipline competitions in combining basic knowledge and professional knowledge, especially comprehensive competition projects are the best carrier for combining foundation and specialty. Through the training of comprehensive competition projects, students combine the basic and professional knowledge they have learned, achieve systematic integration of knowledge, and achieve knowledge integration between various courses. Students' design ability, innovation ability, and application practice ability have been greatly improved.

5 Summary

After years of effort, research on the practical aspect was conducted, content was determined, and reforms were implemented to standardize and innovate laboratory teaching. At the same time, through the multi-level subject competition, innovative thinking and practical abilities were developed among students. Both practical teaching and subject competitions were explored and practiced to enhance students' practical and innovative abilities. Finally, an innovative practical teaching system was established for the training of applied talents in engineering majors. After years of research and practice, the social effects have been excellent, and students' practical and innovative abilities have significantly improved. Professional students have won numerous awards in national competitions, and the employment rate and social feedback have been positive. A large number of highly qualified applied talents have been trained for local economic development.

The authors thank for the support from the Reform projects of teaching content and curriculum system in colleges and universities in Guizhou Province (2020194, 2022284), First-class specialty cultivation project of mining engineering of first-class universities in Guizhou Province, and First-class undergraduate course construction project of Liupanshui Normal University(LPSSYylkz -2020 -08).

References

1. L. Qingzhuo, Frontiers in Educational Research, **5** (2022)
2. Z. Fan, W. Yuchan, S. Yu, Curriculum and Teaching Methodology, **5** (2022)
3. Z. Lida, R. Tianyu, X. Peihua, International Journal of Technology Enhanced Learning, **15** (2023)
4. Y. Chunlei; Y. Shuai; B. Yingchao, et al., SHS Web of Conferences, (2023)
5. S. Qin, T. Xiaoming, Journal of Physics: Conference Series,**1213** (2019)
6. D. Liling. International Journal of New Developments in Education, **4** (2022)
7. W. Xianjun. Frontiers in Educational Research, **5** (2022)
8. W. Renlan. Curriculum and Teaching Methodology, **5** (2022)
9. L. Ruini. Curriculum and Teaching Methodology, 5(2022)

Study on the model of university-enterprise cooperation in cultivating applied mining engineering graduates

Zhongju Wei*, *Fangfang* Yu, and *Junwei* Yang

School of Minning and Mechanical Engineering, Liupanshui Normal University, Liupansuhi, Guizhou, 553004, China

Abstract. Due to society's biased perception of coal enterprises, Mining Engineering students' cultivation faces problems such as students' unwillingness to engage in mining work and the decoupling of graduates' abilities from job demands. The teaching and research team conducted in-depth research and exploration on the cultivation model of applied mining engineering professionals, and constructed a university-enterprise cooperation model for talent cultivation guided by the spirit of "hard work, innovation, unity and selflessness." This model effectively solves the bottleneck of mining engineering talent cultivation in local colleges and universities and meets the new requirements of the current era's development. After years of exploration and practice, mining engineering students not only love enterprises but also significantly improve their comprehensive innovation abilities.
Coal is an important guarantee of energy security, and energy enterprises urgently need a large number of applied technical and management talents who love their jobs and can adapt to the needs of modern industry development. However, the talent cultivation of mining engineering majors has faced problems such as the decoupling of graduates' abilities from job demands due to society's biased perception of coal enterprises [1]. The teaching and research team adheres to the educational philosophy of "demand-oriented, student-centered, and quality-based" and conducts in-depth research and exploration on the talent cultivation model of applied mining engineering professionals. With the establishment and practice of the practical teaching system for cultivating applied mining engineering talents and the construction of an intelligent mining engineering course system for regional coal industry transformation needs, the team has constructed a university-enterprise cooperation model for talent cultivation guided by the spirit of "hard work, innovation, unity, and selflessness."

1 Teaching problems faced by engineering majors

The mining industry is one of the key industries in many countries, and mining engineering major in universities is aimed at cultivating professionals for this industry.

* Corresponding author: weizj2010ck@163.com

However, there are several problems in training students in mining engineering major that need to be addressed [2].

(1) Mining university students generally have insufficient professional identification, sense of professional mission, and social responsibility due to traditional professional understanding, and the teaching system construction is not yet perfect.

(2) Enterprise participation in talent cultivation is insufficient, and students' research literacy, innovation consciousness, and ability are weak. It takes a long time for them to adapt to job requirements, and their potential for career development is insufficient.

(3) The teaching resources for the transition from traditional mining to intelligent mining are relatively scarce, the teaching content is relatively backward, information technology and education have not been deeply integrated, and the course construction does not sufficiently drive the development of the profession. The teaching methods lack innovation, and there is a lack of evaluation methods for the effectiveness of talent cultivation through the integration of industry and education [3].

2 Solutions to teaching issues

To improve the quality and relevance of mining engineering education, we need to adopt a comprehensive and strategic approach that addresses the following issues.

(1) Establish a curriculum system that combines moral education with professional education, runs through the entire cultivation, and fosters a love for the industry.

The curriculum system is designed from two perspectives: historical commonality and industry characteristics. Industry characteristics are based on professional attributes and school positioning, and constructing knowledge points that are the same as those of engineering education certification. The curriculum system runs through the four years of university and employment [4-5].

(2) Cooperate with universities and enterprises to cultivate students' scientific spirit.

University-enterprise cooperation builds research platforms, cooperates in tackling technological problems, and integrates achievements into teaching materials, courses, and projects [6-7]. To meet the needs of enterprises for intelligent transformation and upgrading, teaching resources such as intelligent mining simulation are developed, and an intelligent mining class is established.

(3) Cooperate with universities and enterprises to cultivate students' innovation consciousness and ability.

With representative enterprises, establish a professional construction guidance committee and build an "industry-university-research" innovation and entrepreneurship base to provide project sources for students' major innovation projects and subject competitions based on practical production problems [8]. By building a dual-tutor team through forms such as enterprise secondment training, scientific and technological envoys, and hiring enterprise experts, guide students to participate in activities such as the "Panjiang Cup" and compete with frontline production technicians.

3 University-enterprise cooperation in talent development practical process

(1) Universities and enterprises carry out extensive communication and cooperation to jointly cultivate engineering majors. The mining engineering major is closely aligned with the school's positioning and the needs of socio-economic development. Education experts in the mining engineering field and production management experts in coal mining enterprises were invited to revise and review the training plan.

The specific skills required by enterprises for engineering talents, as well as theoretical knowledge and engineering practical scenarios, are included as teaching content to enhance students' skills. The need of enterprises to solve engineering technical problems is used as technical research and development topics for teachers and students, which are closely related to actual engineering problems.

The laboratory is jointly built by the university and enterprise, and equipment is shared. A basic experimental platform is built, such as the mining pressure and rock control laboratory, rock mechanics performance laboratory, and well and roadway engineering laboratory. A virtual simulation platform is jointly built, such as VR laboratory, virtual simulation laboratory for coal mining and tunneling machines. A physics simulation platform is jointly built, such as physical models.

(2) Take the industry's difficult development process as spiritual belief and cultivate students' morality.

Through the "commonality of history" and "characteristics of the industry," the curriculum design for ideological and political education with the "five development goals" of morality, intelligence, physical fitness, aesthetics, and labor education was completed. Based on the outcomes-based education (OBE) concept, a set of indicators were formulated, and the entire curriculum became the main channel for education, enhancing the organic integration of knowledge transmission and value guidance. This meets the training goal of "attracting and retaining students to study mining and work in the mining industry," and effectively realizes the goal of nurturing talent silently and promoting moral education. Five years after graduation, the employment rate in the industry is as high as 60%, leading the country, and the major has been rated as a five-star first-class applied major in China.

(3) We have constructed an integrated curriculum system and teaching platform that combines teaching, research, and training, to integrate scientific research with professional education.

We have collected a large number of typical coal mine-related case materials, including preliminary mine design, geological data, training videos on responding to the major disasters in mines, advanced mining machinery.

In response to the requirements of intelligent mining, we have added relevant courses such as unmanned mining technology, constantly updated the core course content, and developed lecture notes on mining and mining machinery and equipment that are tailored to the characteristics of coal mining in Guizhou. We actively carry out teaching reforms, select high-quality textbooks, and use online and offline mixed teaching methods such as MOOC to develop an intelligent mine virtual simulation training system and build a first-class curriculum.

Research results are continuously fed back into teaching content and teaching methods, and teaching methods such as "interactive communication, case-based discussion, and virtual simulation training" are used to achieve a "student-centered" approach. Student course design, graduation design, and practical works are all based on the actual production of coal mining enterprises, and students' scientific literacy and lifelong learning abilities are enhanced.

(4) We have constructed a progressive innovation and practice teaching platform and competition system, realizing the integration of innovative education and professional education.

Focusing on improving students' practical innovation ability, we have gradually built a four-level competition system including department-level, school-level, provincial-level, and national-level competitions, to cultivate students' professional basic skills, comprehensive abilities, and innovative abilities. We guide students to participate in various academic competitions and innovation and entrepreneurship competitions to further enhance their practical and innovative abilities.

Through this practice and competition system, we have achieved a comprehensive and progressive training of practical skills that are interconnected and mutually reinforcing. By participating in the "Panjiang Cup" coal mine safety regulations and measures competition, students' professional abilities to analyze and solve complex engineering problems have been further developed. Students' innovation and entrepreneurial awareness have significantly improved, and they have maintained first place in the school for years in participating in academic competitions and innovative projects, ranking at the forefront of the southwest region.

4 Talent cultivation effectiveness

4.1 Significant improvement in talent cultivation quality

The sense of professional identity and social responsibility of students has significantly improved, and graduates are willing to engage in related work in the challenging mining industry. According to third-party employment quality reports, the first-time employment rate of graduates has maintained a leading level in the past four years. A survey of graduates 5 to 7 years after graduation showed that a large proportion of them are still engaged in the mining industry, ranking among the top in the country, and have reached the promotion standards for intermediate professional titles, with a significant increase in their average salary compared to their initial employment.

Students' innovative and practical abilities have significantly improved. Students have strong practical abilities, and many outstanding graduates have emerged who are proficient in production work and have become technical backbone of their respective industries, earning high praise from enterprises. Students have expressed that it is because of the education provided by their alma mater and the leading examples set by their teachers that they came to understand, love, and ultimately devote themselves to the coal mining industry, leading to their current achievements.

4.2 Outstanding achievements in discipline and specialty construction

Since the application of these achievements, the only academician workstation in the mining engineering field of local universities in Guizhou province has been established. The construction of the discipline research team has made significant progress, with the introduction of multiple doctoral students, and many individuals being awarded the title of outstanding teacher, innovation and entrepreneurship mentor, innovative talent, "double-qualified" teacher, and other honorary titles.

4.3 Significant demonstration effect

Since the application of the achievements, special reports have been made at academic conferences to introduce and promote the results, and multiple domestic academic exchanges have been attended. A monograph on innovative and practical interactive teaching methods, "Interactive Teaching Method Innovation and Practice," has been published. The achievements have been borrowed and applied by multiple universities, playing a good demonstration role. The school has tailored the mining engineering major to local conditions and has developed characteristics and advantages through school-enterprise integration. Multiple news media platforms have reported on the effectiveness of applied talent training, and batches of excellent mining professionals with high-quality skills have emerged from here and gone out into society.

5 Summary

Focusing on the modern energy industry and the new demand for high-quality applied talents in the automation and intelligent upgrading of regional coal pillar industries, and facing the practical difficulties in training mining engineering students in a challenging field, the university has explored and practiced a talent cultivation model through collaboration with enterprises, based on the current educational situation, the construction of new engineering disciplines, and innovative talent cultivation. This has effectively solved the teaching difficulties such as the insufficient professional identity and sense of mission of students, inadequate scientific literacy and innovation awareness, lack of information teaching resources, and weak innovation in teaching methods. The cooperation has significantly improved the level of talent cultivation and professional construction, and explored the successful path for local universities to train applied talents in challenging majors.

The authors thank for the support from the Reform projects of teaching content and curriculum system in colleges and universities in Guizhou Province (2020194, 2022284), and First-class undergraduate course construction project of Liupanshui Normal University (LPSSYylkz -2020 -08).

References

1. W. Chenggang, L. Tiansen, Adult and Higher Education, **4** (2022)
2. W. Yuan, W. Xueyu, L. Yingyan, Journal of Physics: Conference Series, **1992** (2021)
3. D. Rui, International Journal of Education, Culture and Society, **5** (2020)
4. Z. Li, International Journal of New Developments in Education, **2** (2020)
5. L. Quanzhen, Z. Qi, Z. Jianchang, American Journal of Engineering and Technology Management, **4** (2019)
6. M. Chen, J. Tan. Journal of Education and Practice, **10** (2019)
7. D. Haibin, International Journal of e-Education, e-Business, e-Management and e-Learning, **8** (2018)
8. D. Lu, J. Mei, Frontiers in Educational Research, **5** (2022)

Practice OBE concept and innovate the guidance method for graduation design of electrical engineering

Xiaofang Meng, *Lidi* Wang*, *Youwen* Tian, *Nannan* Zhang, and *Hui* Wang

Shenyang Agricultural University, Information and Electrical Engineering, Liaoning Shenyang 110866, China

Abstract. In order to improve the quality of undergraduate graduation design, this paper studies and improves the guidance method of electrical engineering graduation design based on the OBE concept. The graduation design teaching process was discussed around the topic selection stage, the topic opening stage, and the design stage. The main goal is to expand students' knowledge, enhance their engineering knowledge and improve their ability to solve practical engineering problems. The process inspection and guidance methods were optimized from the three levels of instructors, majors and colleges. The process inspection and guidance of colleges and specialties were online or offline. After the student selected the topic, the graduation design guidance and inspection of the instructor was conducted face to face or online. Through the questionnaire survey, this paper completed the achievement degree analysis of graduation design goals. The method proposed in this paper is beneficial to improving the practical ability and innovation ability of electrical engineering undergraduates.

1 Introduction

Undergraduate graduation design is an important teaching link of electrical engineering, a basic training to integrate and improve the knowledge learned by undergraduate students of electrical engineering, and a basic method to cultivate innovative thinking and practical ability of undergraduate students. Therefore, it has been highly valued by all colleges and universities [1]. Through graduation design, undergraduates can comprehensively apply their relatively independent professional knowledge, promote the combination of theory and practice, and cultivate their ability to analyze and solve practical problems and conduct scientific research [2].

At present, the new economy represented by new technologies, new models and new industries is developing vigorously, which puts forward higher requirements for engineering and technical personnel [3]. It has become the consensus of the whole society to accelerate the construction and development of electrical engineering specialty, and cultivate electrical engineering professionals under the background of new engineering

* Corresponding author: xfmeng123@syau.edu.cn

disciplines leading the future technology and industrial development [4]. However, there are a series of problems in the graduation design at present. The quality of the graduation design is not high [2], and the training effect on students' comprehensive quality and engineering practice ability is not good. This makes it urgent to improve the guidance method of the graduation design for electrical engineering majors.

Based on Outcomes Based Education (OBE for short), according to the requirements of engineering education certification standards and training programs, this paper analyzes the problems faced by the graduation design of electrical engineering specialty and the corresponding measures, and makes an in-depth discussion from the aspects of teaching process design, process inspection, guidance reform and optimization.

2 Problems and countermeasures of undergraduate graduation design teaching

2.1 Problems in undergraduate design teaching of electrical engineering

The graduation design of electrical engineering specialty is faced with a series of problems from planning to implementation and guidance of graduation design. How to guide students to complete the design work in a time tight, task heavy and high-quality way? How to implement the guidance direction and quality requirements of graduation design and form verifiable documents while preparing for professional certification? How to improve students' ability to solve complex engineering problems with graduation design? These are the problems that must be faced and solved in the graduation design of electrical engineering major.

2.2 Countermeasures

In view of the above problems, first of all, we need to unify our thinking, enhance confidence in the face of difficulties, and strengthen the guidance of graduation design. Discuss at all levels of colleges, majors, teaching and research offices and instructors, reach a consensus on the important role of graduation design in the training of engineering applied talents, fully consider and plan the problems that may be faced in the graduation design, and then formulate the graduation design guidance plan. According to the requirements of the Graduation Design in the Engineering Education Certification Standards, and in combination with the actual engineering problems of the electrical engineering specialty, cultivate the students' engineering awareness, cooperation spirit, and the ability to comprehensively apply the knowledge learned to solve practical complex engineering problems [5]. In addition, the college and the major timely track and regularly check the guidance work of the graduation design, and timely adjust the guidance plan to effectively promote the graduation design.

3 Design of graduation design teaching process based on OBE concept

The undergraduate graduation design of electrical engineering should be student centered, focusing on students' learning achievements, educational practicality and students' adaptability to social production and life [6]. In order to effectively solve the problems encountered in the graduation design, based on the OBE concept, in accordance with the requirements of the engineering education certification standards and training programs, we need to carefully design the "graduation design" teaching process, as shown in Figure 1.

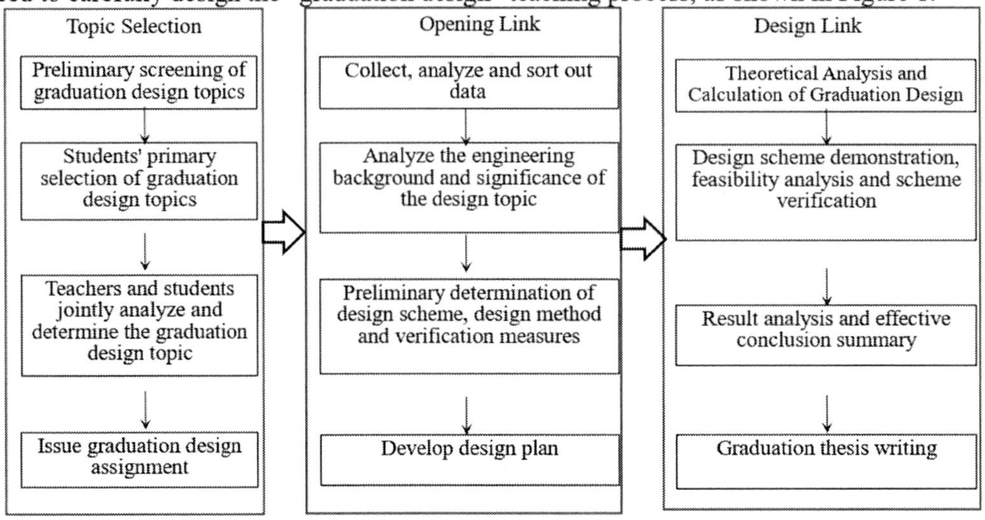

Fig. 1. Graduation design teaching flow chart.

3.1 Topic selection

Before selecting the topic, it is necessary to investigate the needs of relevant enterprises in the field of electrical engineering, understand the employment needs of enterprises, and determine the graduation design topic based on the needs of enterprises. In order to improve students' comprehensive ability to solve practical problems in a limited time, it is recommended to start the topic selection before the graduation design time period uniformly planned by the school. It is a good choice to select the topic at the end of the semester before the graduation design officially starts.

In the process of topic selection, the method of two-way topic selection is adopted, and the final completed topic is related to students' work or future planning, so as to stimulate students' interest in autonomous learning. After the students select the topic, the instructor explains the tasks and requirements of the graduation design specifically according to the students' conditions, so that the students have an overall understanding of the graduation design and establish the design goals.

3.2 Opening link

First of all, we should collect data and research, and complete data analysis and sorting. Make full use of the vacation time, students carry out research work in combination with the actual production, collect and analyze relevant data. Clear the engineering background and significance of the design topic, as well as the current situation and development trend, and then complete the literature review. On this basis, further analyze the design topic, preliminarily determine the design scheme, design methods and verification measures, formulate the design plan, and form the framework of the graduation design thesis.

3.3 Design link

First, carry out theoretical calculation and analysis, apply the methods of modeling, calculation, simulation, experiment, data analysis and information synthesis to study the engineering problems of the graduation design, and complete the demonstration of the graduation design scheme and feasibility analysis. Draw relevant design drawings, sort out theoretical calculation and analysis, experimental or simulation research results, method application and actual problem solving effect, and complete effective conclusion summary. Write papers based on comprehensive analysis. In the process of writing the thesis, we will form a deeper understanding of the theoretical or practical problems related to design, generate new insights, and improve students' innovation ability.

4 Optimization process inspection and guidance

Process inspection and guidance are carried out at three levels, namely, instructors, professionals and colleges. In order to facilitate contact and communication, each instructor has established a QQ group or WeChat group for graduation design guidance. The process inspection and guidance of the college and specialty shall be carried out in an orderly manner in the semester when the graduation design officially starts, and the online or offline centralized mode shall be adopted.

Professional guidance is aimed at all students of the major, with the main goal of expanding students' knowledge, enhancing engineering knowledge, and improving their ability to solve practical engineering problems. The guidance is completed through school enterprise cooperation guidance and inviting experts to make relevant reports. The guidance content includes requirements, steps, common modeling methods, verification methods, and writing methods of design papers. The graduation design guidance of the instructor is aimed at the students. He/she needs to publish the relevant information required for the completion of the design in the contact group at the right time in combination with the students' completion topics, as well as the specific schedule for regular meeting or online communication guidance. Instructors can complete the guidance of graduation design through face-to-face or online communication. The specific guidance contents include: data collection, analysis and sorting, and writing of literature review; The determination of design scheme, design method and verification measures, the formulation of design plan, the writing of design outline, the determination of graduation design thesis structure, and the writing of graduation design proposal report; Determination of design contents, analysis and calculation methods, and rationality and effectiveness of conclusions; Instruction and guidance of the school on the format and requirements of graduation design.

The graduation design process inspection is indispensable, including weekly inspection, mid-term inspection, pre defense and defense. The instructor inspects and supervises the completion of students' graduation design every week, and the specialty checks the progress of some students' graduation design every week to find and solve problems in a timely manner. The college and professional association will organize the mid-term examination. The pre oral defense is conducted before the formal oral defense. Students are instructed to prepare the oral defense report materials. Through the pre oral defense, the students' abilities in sorting out the research results, writing, oral presentation, summary and analysis are mainly exercised. The oral defense shall be conducted by professional groups and the oral defense committee shall be formed. According to the defense process, the defense committee members of each group organize the defense process and adhere to the tutor avoidance review system. Through the defense work, students can exercise and improve their comprehensive abilities in time concept, thinking and politics, summary, expression, mentality, and social responsibility.

Through specific guidance and supervision of design progress, students have made great progress in research methods, simulation tools, system development, engineering design, experimental means, data collation, conclusion formation and comparative research.

5 Questionnaire

After the college organizes the oral defense, it conducts a questionnaire survey on the subjective satisfaction of the graduation design and the achievement of the graduation goals participated by all students for the students of this major through online questionnaires, which can complete the analysis of the achievement of the graduation design goals, and summarize the shortcomings in the graduation design, so as to facilitate the further improvement of the graduation design.

6 Summary

Graduation design is an indispensable teaching link. With the help of graduation design, students can use the basic theories, basic knowledge and basic skills of their major to analyze and solve relevant theoretical and practical problems, which can cultivate students' ability to carry out research independently. Based on OBE concept, student-centered, this paper discusses the design of graduation design teaching process, the optimization of process inspection and guidance methods, the implementation of questionnaire survey, and the optimization of electrical engineering graduation design guidance methods, which can improve the quality of graduation design and is of great significance to the cultivation of students' comprehensive quality and engineering practice ability.

References

1. Meng Xiaofang, Park Zailin, Tian Youwen. Research on Strategies for Improving the Graduation Design of Electrical Engineering [J]. China Electric Power Education, 2011, (27): 130-131.
2. Wang Yuanyuan, Zeng Xiangjun. Reflections on Several Issues of Undergraduate Graduation Design of Electrical Engineering [J]. China Electric Power Education, 2013, (23): 103111.
3. Zhang Jianhui, Wei Baoquan, Zeng Jianjun. Research on the Training Mode of Electrical Professionals in the Context of New Engineering [J]. Journal of Electrical and Electronics Education, 2020, 42 (5): 18-22.
4. Yu Lei, Fei Shumin. Research on the Training of Electrical Engineering and Automation Professionals in the Context of New Engineering [J]. Journal of Electrical and Electronics Teaching, 2019, 41 (5): 17-21, 25.
5. Ma Lina, Ning Guixia, Han Feng, et al. Research and Practice of the Graduation Design under the Joint Guidance of the School and Enterprise of Civil Engineering Specialty Based on the OBE Concept [J]. China Modern Education Equipment, 2022, (5): 79-81.
6. Luo Zhen. Exploration of Teaching Reform of Graduation Design Course in Application-Oriented Universities Based on OBE Concept [J]. Industrial Design, 2021, (12): 46-47.

Design of power control system for student dormitory

Chunyan Liu[1,*], *Shujiao* Wang[1], and *Yanshan* Sun[2]

[1]Shandong Xiehe University, Computer Department, 250107, Shandong, China
[2]Shandong Special Equipment Inspection Institute Group Co., Ltd, 250101, Shandong, China

Abstract. This design is based on the residential building of boarding school as the research object. The STC89C52RC single-chip microcomputer is used as the main control chip, and the clock chip, temperature chip, smoke collection module, A/D conversion, LED digital tube display circuit, matrix keyboard, infrared wireless remote control and other controllers are used to control the power system and adjust the access control system. This system is applicable to all kinds of colleges and universities that have strict management on students' electricity consumption. It can automatically control the electricity consumption of students' dormitories according to the school management regulations, and can automatically make emergency response to emergencies such as fire.

1 Introduction

With the sustained and rapid development of the economy and the remarkable improvement of people's living standards, the requirements of boarding students on the management level of electricity use are also increasing. The intelligentization and humanization of dormitory can improve students' good feeling for dormitory life and improve the quality and safety of dormitory life [1]. If we only rely on human resources to achieve the management level required by these requirements, we often need to pay a huge cost. Therefore, the automation of building power system and access control system is particularly important. This design can realize the basic functions of the system, and the cost is low. It can expand the functions according to the needs, and has a certain market prospect and promotion value.

2 System design scheme

The design uses STC89C52RC as the core control chip, in combination with the work and rest time management regulations of the student dormitory, uses the clock chip as the time basis chip of the power system control, uses the 8-bit common anode 7-segment digital tube as the display circuit, and can display the date, clock and temperature information through

*Corresponding author: skdlcy123@163.com

the digital tube, Drive the corresponding relay through the drive circuit to meet the requirements of controlling each circuit (use led lamp to display the working status of each relay). The design can also realize the startup and shutdown of the dormitory access control system, and use the smoke sensor module, photosensitive resistor, A/D conversion and other circuits to realize the emergency plan.

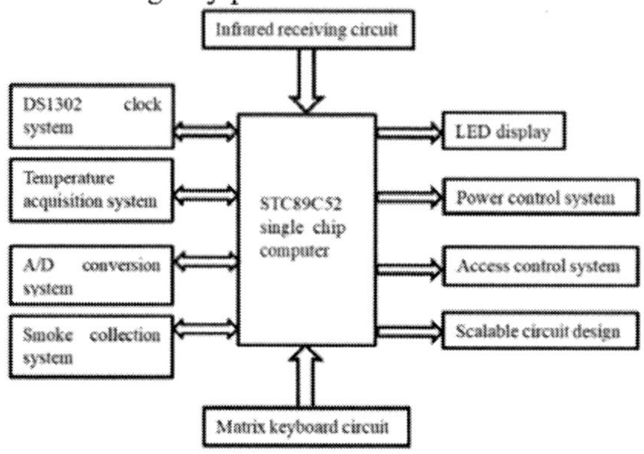

Fig. 1. General drawing of circuit design.

3 Hardware design

3.1 Minimum system design of single chip computer

STC89C52 is a low-power, high-performance CMOS 8-bit microcontroller produced by STC, full-duplex serial port communication.[2]. The minimum system is mainly composed of power supply, reset circuit, oscillation circuit, etc. Since there are many external devices connected to the P0 port of the single chip computer in the later stage, in order to enhance its driving ability and ensure accuracy and stability, 8x10K pull-up resistor is used here.

3.2 Power circuit input and output design

The control board of this design adopts DC5V power supply, and directly uses the power adapter with the input Vi of AC220V and the output Vo of DC 5V for power supply. Because STC89C52RC single-chip microcomputer is the core control element, it is easy to be subject to electromagnetic interference. Therefore, several 0.1uF capacitors can be connected in parallel to enhance the filtering ability of the power supply circuit as a protective measure to improve its anti-interference ability.

3.3 LED display

In order to visually display the current time, so as to accurately judge the current working state of the controller, you can choose to display the current time using a 8-bit red LED with a total anode.

3.4 Clock circuit

DS1302 clock chip is a low-power, high-performance real-time clock chip launched by an American company, with 31 bytes of static RAM attached. It transmits multiple bytes of clock signal and RAM data in a burst mode, and uses SPI three-wire interface to synchronize with MCU [3]. The design is powered by the filtered power supply of the power adapter DC5V. At the same time, in order to ensure that the chip can save data in case of power failure, so that it can continue to work when the power supply is restored, the design uses DC3V button battery as the backup power supply energy.

3.5 Relay control circuit

Because the single-chip microcomputer system is a DC 5V weak current control system, and the dormitory building is powered by AC 220V and 50Hz current, the single-chip microcomputer cannot be directly used to control the power system and access control system in the dormitory building. In addition, because there are many rooms in the dormitory building of boarding school, the whole dormitory building consumes a large amount of power, reliable isolation technology must be used to separate the mains part from the controller circuit part. This design uses optocoupler isolation technology here.

3.6 Matrix keyboard circuit

The matrix keyboard is a keyboard group with a layout similar to the matrix used in the external equipment of the single chip computer. When there are many keys in the keyboard, in order to reduce the occupation of I/O ports, the keys are usually arranged in a matrix form. The keyboard is designed to adjust the manually input DS1302 clock, and also to manually control the access control and power system in case of emergencies. This design uses matrix keyboard instead of directly connecting with P3 pin of single chip computer, which is not only to save the number of I/O ports, but also to prepare for the expansion of functions when necessary later.

3.7A/D conversion circuit

A/D conversion is a circuit that quantizes analog quantity or continuously changing quantity and converts it into corresponding digital quantity. Due to the use of smoke sensors, photoresistors, etc. in this design, the single-chip microcomputer needs to convert the analog signals collected by the smoke sensor module, photoresistors and other sensors into digital signals for analysis through the A/D conversion chip, so that the controller can react to the system. In this design, the AT2402 chip is used as the external memory chip EEPROM, When necessary, it can save the working data that the single chip computer needs to store, which is convenient to call.

3.8 Sensor circuit

The sensor can convert the detected danger signal into electrical signal (usually analog value), and then convert it into digital signal that can be recognized by the computer through A/D, and make corresponding response after analysis. In this design, considering that high-power power consumption is likely to lead to sudden fire and other unexpected situations, smoke sensor module, photosensitive resistor and temperature chip are used as sensors for detection, so that emergency response can be made in time in case of special circumstances, and digital tube can be used to display the current temperature condition at a fixed time.

3.9 Infrared wireless receiving circuit

Infrared wireless receiving remote control is a widely used means of communication and remote control, which is widely used in real life. The infrared wireless remote control circuit includes a transmitting circuit and a receiving circuit. This design adopts infrared wireless remote control mode, directly uses the single chip computer for decoding, uses the common DIY electronic remote controller as the transmitter, uses the VS838 infrared remote control receiver as the receiver, and transmits the command signal to the single chip computer for analysis and corresponding execution.

3.10 Drawing of control board and relay drive board PCB

In order to save space and resources, the control board in this design uses patch packaging. In order to improve the anti-interference ability of PCB design, in addition to basically meeting the frequency characteristics of each device, the PCB board in this design should be arranged as evenly as possible, and large linewidth should be used for wiring. The copper-clad surface of the bonding pad and the bottom layer of the top layer shall be optimized accordingly.

4 Software design

The design of system software is to make each part of hardware run by writing the program of corresponding module. The corresponding program can be divided into main program and subprogram of each part. In this system, three modes of manual, automatic and infrared wireless remote control can be used to realize the functions of power supply/power off and door opening/closing at the corresponding time.

5 Conclusion

As an intelligent building power consumption system, the power consumption control system can monitor the temperature, smoke and other conditions of the equipment at all times, and also make emergency response to emergencies such as fire. In addition, the control mode of the system in this design is also very flexible, which can meet the control requirements of the electrical system in the student dormitory. A series of low-power devices are adopted, which has low cost. It not only effectively saves the use cost, but also effectively strengthens the management of the electrical system and access control system in the student dormitory, and ensures the use safety.

References

1. C.Y. Shi, Communication World, Design of intelligent dormitory system based on 51 single chip computer, 08, 263-264, (2018)
2. Y.L. Bi, Shanghai University of Applied Technology, Design of GSM based remote alarm system for children's anti-lock in the car, (2018)
3. X. Zhou, Nanjing University of Information Engineering, Design of low hysteresis pressure sensor and acquisition system (2014)
4. J. Lu, Journal of Chifeng University (Natural Science Edition), Research on software and hardware design of infrared electronic code lock, 11 ,32-36, (2015)

SHS Web of Conferences **166**, 01059 (2023) https://doi.org/10.1051/shsconf/202316601059
EIMM 2022

Exploration and research on transforming the traditional working methods of college student affairs in the post epidemic era

Yimeng Xu[1], *Chunjing* Zhang[1], *Yan* Wang[2], *Dongdong* Li[1], *Jiawei* Guo[1], *Ruchao* Li[1], and *Siwei* Nao[1,*]

[1]Medical Technology School Qiqihar Medical University, Qiqihar 161006, Heilongjiang, China
[2]Basic Medical Science School Qiqihar Medical University, Qiqihar 161006, Heilongjiang, China

Abstract. In the post epidemic era, although the COVID-19 epidemic is becoming stable under the strong control of the country, the complexity of the COVID-19 epidemic situation has brought great impact on the life and learning of college students. Therefore, the work of counselors is also facing great challenges in the post epidemic era today. The sudden COVID-19 epidemic has changed the actual work situation of college counselors. The work object requires refinement from face to point, the work position impacts the traditional mode from offline to online, and the difficulties in work face problems and contradictions. Faced with such a situation, college counselors need to change their work strategies, improve their work efficiency, study and judge the corresponding methods of emergencies, emphasize professional and role positioning and subdivide their work responsibilities, adhere to the fundamental and strengthen the ideological guidance in special periods. At present, college counselors should cultivate their internal skills, firm their beliefs, keep the "unchanged" and lead the "change". Through a comprehensive discussion on the work challenges faced by counselors during the COVID-19 epidemic and the main problems of college students, new ideas are provided for the work of counselors in the "post epidemic era".

1 Challenges faced by counselors in the "post epidemic era"

Although the post epidemic era has not had a great impact on colleges and universities, it has brought various impacts on college students in terms of employment, postgraduate entrance examination, daily study and life. As the front-line staff of colleges and universities, the counselors, facing the mode of combining the post epidemic era with the scattered student groups, are in line with the need to let students self-discipline in the process of home or online learning at school, and relieve the psychological pressure of students in the post epidemic era, as well as graduate employment and postgraduate entrance examination, which are the primary problems that college counselors need to face.

* Corresponding author: xym569837111@163.com

1.1 The counselor's working style is constantly changing

Since the outbreak of COVID-19, the work mode of counselors also needs to be adjusted from offline face-to-face communication to online communication based on the new media platform according to the actual situation. Since the outbreak of COVID-19 in 2020, COVID-19 has been controlled to a certain extent. After nearly three years of online teaching mode, college students have been accustomed to online home learning to a certain extent, and face-to-face communication between offline teachers and students or students will also be limited, so the work of college counselors is limited by space conditions, Then how to do a good job in "online" management for counselors has become a new challenge .With the impact of the COVID-19 epidemic, the pace of non graduating students returning to school is blocked. Under the circumstances of college students' self-management at home, self-study, etc., due to time and space constraints, the workload of college counselors has correspondingly increased the difficulty. On the premise that the COVID-19 epidemic situation has been controlled to a certain extent, counselors need to break through the limitations of existing conditions to remotely manage students, such as through WeChat, Tencent Conference and other new media platforms.

On the one hand, counselors not only need to monitor students' health and travel conditions, but also need to carry out ideological and political education, mental health counseling, employment and entrepreneurship counseling and other work remotely. The communication mode between instructors and students needs innovation urgently. Due to the increasingly powerful function of new media, the function of new media network has developed to basically meet the needs of home learning and home office. However, for the work of counselors, only through "cold" network communication, it is impossible to truly understand the real psychological situation, learning state and ideological dynamics of students. Therefore, college counselors should rely on online education as the basis, and develop and create a communication mode of "advancing with the times" based on the post epidemic era, so as to carry out student work more conveniently and efficiently. The author learned through interviews that, Some students are on "hang up" for online teaching" In addition to the occasional questions from the teachers, the students' concentration ratio in most of the online classes is very small, which leads to an increase in the rate of students failing grades, leading to a series of problems such as demotion, which also adds a certain challenge to the difficulty of college counselors' work, so the counselors' work style also needs to keep pace with the times.

1.2 The difficulty of counselors' work continues to increase

In the post epidemic era, many students, especially medical students and science students who need offline experimental courses, have affected their academic progress because of the epidemic. In the post epidemic era, it is more difficult to obtain employment, so it is difficult to graduate, which is followed by the pressure of going to school and obtaining employment. The spread of the epidemic worldwide has made it difficult to go abroad for further education. Although some foreign schools have launched online teaching mode, some students or parents want to experience life abroad because of the epidemic, considering that such teaching mode is difficult to be certified or some students want to experience life abroad, Therefore, more and more college students choose to study in China, but some students will face the situation of "no study to go to" when the number of postgraduate enrollment remains unchanged. At the same time, due to the COVID-19 epidemic, it is not uncommon for recruitment units to reduce quotas or even cancel recruitment, and the employment situation of college students has become increasingly grim. Then the following problem is the increasing difficulty of college counselors' work.

In the post epidemic era, facing such a tense employment environment, it is particularly important to solve the difficulties of graduates, help them graduate smoothly and implement their graduation destination.

Similarly, the psychological problems of college students in the post epidemic era are particularly prominent. The fear caused by COVID-19 has also caused collective anxiety to some extent, and this anxiety and fear will also appear in college students; Long term home isolation will make some family conflicts become increasingly prominent, thus increasing the negative impact on college students' psychology. In the face of the epidemic, many college students showed panic due to lack of scientific prevention and control knowledge. Moderate panic is normal, but many college students showed excessive tension and anxiety. The author interviewed students of different grades through interviews. The degree of psychological anxiety caused by the epidemic among freshmen is equivalent to that of students from junior to graduating, In particular, the students who are about to graduate are facing employment pressure, homework pressure, online class pressure, postgraduate entrance examination and re examination and other influences, and their psychological problems are becoming increasingly prominent. What needs to be vigilant is that these psychological problems are not transient. After the full resumption of work, production and schooling, they still need to be guided. When necessary, they should be guided to conduct psychological counseling or medical treatment to ensure the stability of their psychological state after returning to school, which adds some difficulties to the work of college counselors.

2 Change of counselor's work strategy in the "post epidemic era"

In the post epidemic era, college counselors should have political literacy, always pay attention to the latest trends of the epidemic and also recognize the impact of the epidemic on college students, so that they can improve their professional skills in a targeted way and better "prescribe the right medicine" for students in different situations. Fans economy and online celebrity economy are prevailing. With the advent of the epidemic, from Zhu Guangquan and Li Jiaqi's live broadcast of Hubei to General Secretary's arrival at the online live broadcast room of Qinling agricultural products, the power of the network economy has already affected the whole society. Only by grasping the key points shown by the times, discovering the problems existing in students, and understanding what students need, can we change students' concepts. Although the pandemic test was cruel, the dedication of countless medical staff turned the "battle of epidemic prevention and control" into the appearance of "patriotic education".

2.1 Improve work efficiency and study and judge emergency response methods

The COVID-19 epidemic has put forward higher requirements for college counselors' ability to deal with emergencies. The epidemic is coming fast, and it is in the winter vacation. Students are scattered all over the country, making management more difficult. To complete the sorting of large quantities of student health data in a short period of time is the first hurdle. Counselors must have the emergency ability to quickly handle transactions and all-around collaborative operation. Specifically, diseases threaten the life safety and health of college students. Home isolation may also cause a series of family conflicts and psychological crises. Online teaching can lead to poor learning results, network addiction and even extreme thinking. Although similar problems are also encountered in daily student work, in the context of the epidemic situation, the problems are concentrated, the work tasks of counselors are urgent and large, and the working methods have been completely changed. We must adapt to various changes brought about by emergencies, improve our personal ability to deal with crisis events and information processing, and explore new working methods. Specifically, we should make good use of the network to speed up the information sorting; Make good use of student backbones and party and league organizations to improve the accuracy and height of work; Attention should also be paid to communication methods to improve the working temperature.

2.2 Emphasis on specialty, role orientation and job responsibilities

In order to meet the challenges brought by the COVID-19 epidemic and turn the crisis into an opportunity, college counselors need to clarify their work responsibilities and assume multiple roles. College counselors play the following roles in epidemic prevention and control: first, they are educators of faith, organizers of prevention and control work, do a good job of students' information sorting, strengthen guidance and publicity, guide students to treat the epidemic rationally and jointly overcome the epidemic; Manage the service providers, do a good job in daily class management, do a good job in the employment of graduates under special background, and do a good job in online teaching academic support; Psychological facilitators should do a good job in psychological health education, pay attention to the psychological health of college students, and relieve students of psychological problems caused by epidemic situation and other reasons; The public opinion guider should do a good job of information reception and integration processing, transmit the network information with attitude and temperature to college students, guide college students to treat the complicated network speech rationally, and do not believe, spread or fabricate rumors. The new role requires new breakthroughs. The challenges brought by the COVID-19 epidemic objectively put forward higher requirements for the professional ability of college counselors, and also prompted the counselors to re-examine themselves, especially in management and service capabilities, psychological counseling capabilities, network application capabilities, and public opinion response and guidance capabilities. The repositioning of counselors' roles and the subdivision of their responsibilities are new requirements for the ideological and political education of college students in the special context, which are based on the situation, the times and the situation. They are also the political responsibilities of college counselors, which directly affect the effectiveness of college students' work in emergencies, and also relate to the overall development of college students' work.

2.3 Adhere to the fundamental principle and strengthen the ideological guidance in special periods

No matter when, the core of ideological and political education is always unchanged. In the face of the epidemic, counselors need to first do a good job in self ideological education, improve their ideological and political position, always pay attention to the specific work deployment of the Party Central Committee, obey the command of the Party, take unified action, strengthen confidence, take the initiative to speak, and carry out ideological guidance work for college students as required. On this basis, counselors should seize the opportunity of ideological and political education provided in the special period, use bellicose "epidemic" materials, focus on strengthening the education of ideals and beliefs, patriotism, focus on the fundamental task of building morality and cultivating people, and grasp the "root" problem of educating people for the party and the country. At the level of daily words and deeds, counselors should focus on guiding college students to consciously comply with epidemic prevention requirements, trust the leadership of the Party and the country, establish correct epidemic prevention concepts and put them into action. Counselors should guide students to firmly believe that the party and the state can lead the people throughout the country to win the fight against epidemic prevention and control, so that students can consciously regulate their words and deeds in accordance with epidemic prevention requirements and drive others. At the ideological level, counselors should explore the materials of fighting "epidemic", guide college students to correctly understand the advantages of the socialist system with Chinese characteristics in focusing on major events, and achieve the unity of loving the party, patriotism and socialism. The war epidemic has written the "Chinese spirit", "Chinese speed", "Chinese value", "Chinese power" and "Chinese plan". The counselors should guide students to "look at the epidemic out of the epidemic", correctly view the Communist Party of China and the socialist system with Chinese characteristics, compare the development trend of the world and China, and carry out education in ideals and beliefs, patriotism. Students should be aware of the advantages of the system, learn from the heroes of anti epidemic, and understand the spirit of dedication, and strengthen the guidance and education of students through online second class, cloud politics and other forms.

3 Work innovation of counselors

3.1 Firm belief

Listening to the Party's words and following the Party is the fundamental principle of college counselors' daily work. In the face of major tests and challenges, we need to stand firm, obey the unified command and coordination of the Central Committee of the Party, implement the policy requirements of the school and college party committee, standardize our own behavior with the highest party spirit, be ready to fight at any time, and carry out all work at the height of political tasks. Only in this way can we be fearless, calm, shoulder heavy burdens, and bite the bullet. Secondly, we should clarify the main line of work: to ensure the life, health and safety of students in an all-round way, and to do a good job in management, service and education. In any case, counselors should closely focus on the job responsibility requirements in the regulations, solve students' actual difficulties, and ensure students' basic life needs, academic and personal development needs during the epidemic prevention and control period. This management and service awareness should also be extended to daily student work. Finally, we should implement the fundamental task: to cultivate morality, educate people for the Party and the country. While comprehensively protecting the physical and mental health of students, we should carry out the education of ideals and beliefs, patriotism, and responsibility throughout the work, continue to give play to the power of the war "epidemic"` story, tell a good story about the Chinese road and system, establish a model of war "epidemic", let life come first, the whole country unite, sacrifice their lives, respect science The great anti epidemic spirit of shared destiny has become an important source of ideological and political education for college students. At the same time, we should take this opportunity to mobilize college students to actively move closer to the party organization and develop a group of student party members who are truly learned, understand and believe.

3.2 Weaknesses

A comprehensive understanding of the basic situation of students is the basis for all student work. Counselors should go to dormitories, canteens, and classrooms to strengthen regular contact with students, implement the "one-on-one" conversation requirements, master student information in daily work, establish work accounts, and understand the situation of each student, especially the psychological situation, so that they can better deal with emergencies in the face of. The work ability and energy of a counselor is limited. While managing services and guiding all students with ideas, the counselor should also focus on building a backbone team of students, and drive a group of people in terms of ideas and behavior. When it comes to the critical time, the counselor can be reliable and useful. In daily work and emergencies, a group of student backbones can take responsibility and be ahead of others, Counselors should give full play to the subjective initiative of student backbones, and urge them to promote collective development while making personal progress. At the same time, counselors should clearly realize that the epidemic prevention and control work is long-term, and the post epidemic era does not mean that the epidemic has completely ended, but has entered the stage of normalization of epidemic prevention, the global epidemic is still spreading, and the domestic sporadic and local cluster epidemic in early 2021 has also sounded an alarm for us. Counselors should strengthen learning and lifelong learning, constantly adapt to the development of the times and changes in the environment, arm themselves from multiple angles and in all directions, make learning a habit, strive to make themselves become "generalists" in work, and forge ahead on the road of cultivating new youth in the new era.

3.3 Stand on the foundation of ten thousand changes

The importance of the network has shown itself thoroughly in the prevention and control of the epidemic, so the sensitivity of college counselors to new media and the ability to handle online business are also crucial. First of all, the ability to skillfully use the network should be improved. With the rapid development of the Internet, counselors should keep up with the situation and make full use of the advantages of new media. For example, they can take some simple short videos to warn students how to improve their psychological quality in the post epidemic era and how to correct negative emotions such as stress and anxiety. College students are young, and may not be able to accurately judge the network information. The network information is rich in content, so there will be different voices. So college counselors must be rational, mature, and objective to screen from it, and pass the correct and positive information to students, Let the national official voice be heard and seen by students. Not only that, counselors should also be able to speak, be able to speak, explain the truth to students, and explain the truth while emphasizing the authenticity of information. In a word, college counselors should firmly grasp the initiative of the network education position, carefully study the network behavior habits of contemporary young students, create a network atmosphere that students like and full of positive energy, and let the party flag fly high in the cyberspace.

This research is a project of the Heilongjiang Provincial Education Science Planning Office (No.GJB1422446)
This research was financially supported by 2021 higher education teaching reform research project (No.SJGY20210977)

Reference

1. Wang Zhuli. How should education transform in the post epidemic era [J]. Research on Audio Visual Education, 2020,41 (4): 13-20
2. Zhu Yanjia, Chen Jun. College counselors' responsibility in the fight against "epidemic" [J]. Journal of College Counselors, 2021,12 (1): 48-51

3. Guo Yujuan. The situation and innovation of employment of college graduates in the context of epidemic prevention and control [J]. China Higher Education, 2021 (Z2): 76-77
4. Zhu Jun, Li Jiahua. Precision Service Helps College Students' Employment [J]. China Higher Education, 2020 (7): 48-49
5. Pang Deying. Exploring the Path for Counselors in the New Era to Improve Their Ideological Leading Ability [J]. Journal of Guangxi Youth Cadre College, 2020,30 (1): 23-25
6. Zhang Pengsheng, Wang Yinghua. Practice of applying positive psychology to carry out ideological and political education in the context of normalized epidemic prevention and control - taking the ideological and political education of nursing students in Huanggang Vocational and Technical College as an example [J]. Journal of Huanggang Vocational and Technical College, 2021,23 (1): 52-55
7. Li HongweiExploration and research on employment and entrepreneurship of college students under the background of normalization of epidemic prevention and control [J]Modern Commerce and Trade Industry, 2021 (25): 69-71
8. Guo Xiaona. Concept and path selection of employment guidance for college counselors in response to the COVID-19 epidemic [J]. Humanity World, 2020 (24): 157-159
9. Wang Jian, Gong Yi, Wang WanxinResearch on the employment problems and countermeasures of foreign language college students in the context of trade restrictions in the post epidemic era [J]Chinese Business Review, 2022 (11): 152-154
10. Liu Fang. Research on Strategies for Promoting College Counselors' Professional Identity under the Background of Great Ideological and Political Policy [J]Science and Education Guide, 2019 (35): 78-79

The temperature and pressure Remote intelligent control system for biogas digester based on STM32

Shuyi Wei*, *Xiuxia* Zhang, and *Qiangming* Cheng

North Minzu University, School of Electronics and Information Engineering, Yinchuan, 750021 China

Abstract. The application of biogas digesters in modern life has become more and more extensive. However, the current level of automation in biogas management was too low. and people are afraid of odor and dirty when operating biogas fermentation. In order to solve the shortage of modern energy and improve the safety and efficiency of biogas digesters, a temperature and pressure remote intelligent control management system based on STM32 for biogas digesters was designed. This system took STM32 as the main control chip, through the DS18B20 and PMS pressure measurement module for temperature and pressure measurement, combined with ESP 8266 01sWiFi module and cloud platform for data transmission communication and storage, and then displayed to the user by the QT software interface, the remote intelligent control of the biogas digester in the cloud was realized, so that the efficiency and safety management of the biogas digester were could improved. This management system of the biogas digester would promote the energy industry and sustainable development of human beings and facilitated rural revitalization.

1 Introduction

Energy is an important resource for national development, and also a guarantee for national industrial development and people's livelihood. With the shortage of non-renewable energy in China and the implementation of the rural revitalization policy, the promotion and application of biogas digesters has become an important way to ensure the energy supply of rural villages and towns [1]. The biogas digester using animal manure and crop straw fermentation can not only save energy and generate energy for cooking and boiling water in people's daily life, but also generate biogas for power generation. The biogas digester produced by the biogas digester can be used as organic fertilizer to save fertilizer and pesticide, which can not only improve the food safety of crops, but also promote and drive the development of rural aquaculture industry [2]. Therefore, the utilization of biogas digesters will provide vast fertile land for the development of rural areas and aquaculture. However, at present, the automation level of biogas management is too low, and people are afraid of odor

* Corresponding author: wsyvivi@163.com

https://doi.org/10.1051/shsconf/202316601060

and pollution when operating biogas fermentation. The biogas digester is sensitive to the internal temperature and pressure. Reasonable biogas digester temperature and pressure can quickly and effectively improve the working efficiency of the biogas digester, enabling people to use the biogas digester safely and effectively [3]. Therefore, how to effectively and intelligently monitor and regulate the temperature and pressure in the biogas digester is also the main problem. This paper proposes an intelligent temperature control and pressure control system for biogas digesters based on cloud platform technology, which can not only be realized; Realize the sharing of state information and data of the Internet of Things, and can also control pressure and temperature efficiently and high-quality, which is of great significance to energy conservation and low-carbon sustainable development [4].

2 Overall design architecture of remote temperature control system

2.1 Overall structure of the system

The system used STM32 as the main controller of the system, combined with DS 18B20 temperature and PMS pressure measurement module, LED display, Alibaba Cloud server, ESP 8266 01s Wi-Fi module and QT interface[5] , designed to form a remote intelligent biogas digester temperature control system. First, the DS18B20 temperature sensor and PMS pressure sensor are a sensing layer that collects the biodigester temperature and pressure analog signal and converts it into a digital signal to the main control STM32 chip. The STM32F103C8T6 acts as the central hardware, responsible for receiving and transmitting the signals required by each device, forming a central processing and provisioning. The Wi-Fi module built a bridge between the hardware and the user, had realized the interconnection between the user and the hardware device. Finally, there is the temperature and pressure control module we need. This temperature and pressure control module consists of triac voltage regulator module and an electric heating element, which consists of a voltage stabilization control box, and controls the conduction angle of the triac with PWM waves to control the output power. The overall structural framework of this system is shown in figure 1.

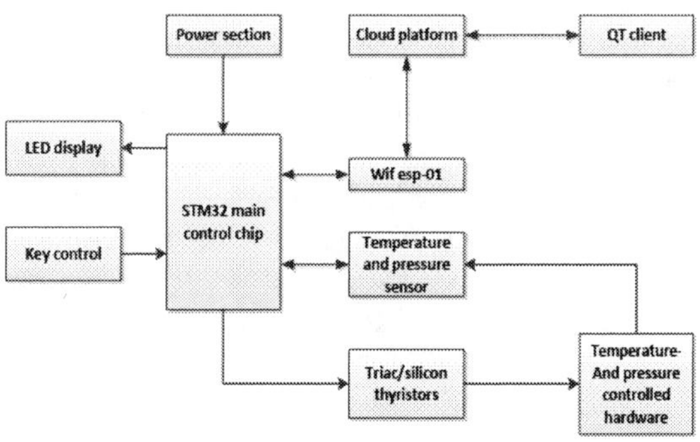

Fig 1. Overall structural framework of the system.

2.2 Overall program flow design of the system

The system programming process mainly includes MCU control, WiFi ESP-01s transmission module, button setting and display modules. First of all, the temperature and pressure sensor collects the temperature and pressure data of the biogas digester and transmits it to the MCU for processing and judgment. if it is the target temperature pressure, it returns to the starting point, if not, sends a command to start the PWM output to adjust the temperature and pressure of the digester. The system program flow is shown in figure 2 below.

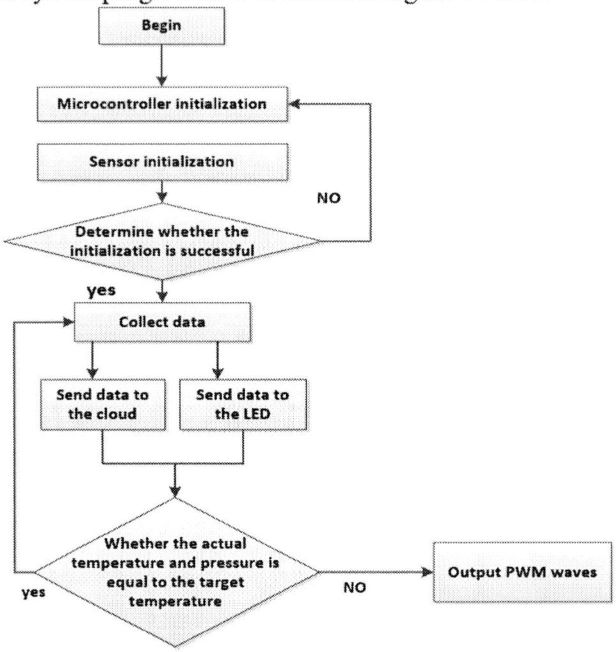

Fig 2. System program flow.

3 Temperature and pressure control system hardware design and temperature regulation method

3.1 Hardware structure design of temperature and pressure control equipment

The hardware equipment of this system is a multi-functional temperature and pressure control box, and the box structure is divided into 3 parts, namely the placement area, the control equipment area and the intelligent control area. The placement is divided into three layers, which is convenient for storing more biological reagents, and each layer contains a fan, and in the box, the exhaust plate is equipped with a pressurized fan, which is used to place the circulation exchange of carbon dioxide and other gases in the environment inside and outside the layer and the adjustment of the air pressure temperature inside the box. The structure diagram of temperature and pressure control box is showing in figure 3.

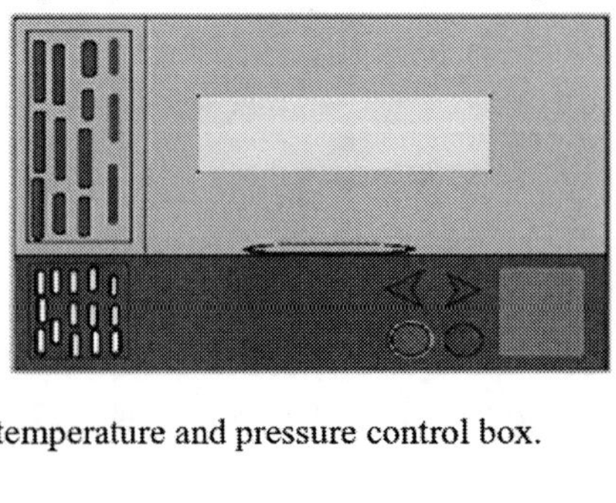

Fig. 3. Structure diagram of temperature and pressure control box.

3.2 Temperature and pressure control equipment temperature regulation mode

In this system, incremental digital PID temperature regulation is selected in the temperature regulation mode. PID control algorithms mainly include digital control and analog control [7]. Figure 4 shows the basic structure of a digital PID control system, where the roles of resistors, capacitors, and operational amplifiers are replaced by computer software operation.

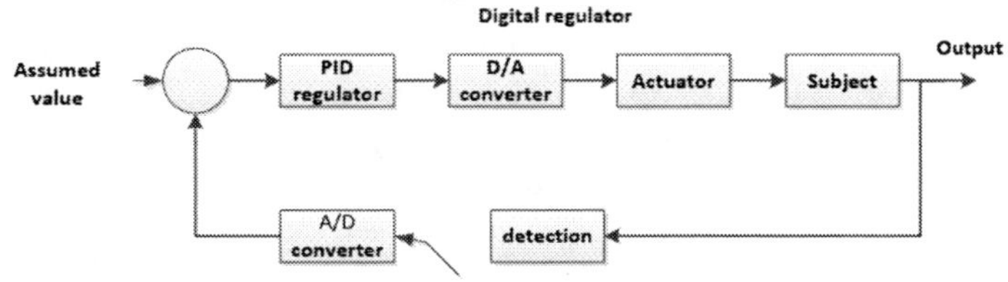

Fig. 4. Block diagram of a digital PID control system.

Equation (1) below is the discrete output of the PID incremental control algorithm:

$$\Delta u(k) = Ae(k) + Be(k-1) + Ce(k-2) \tag{1}$$

4 Temperature and pressure control system software design and communication construction

4.1 Cloud platform construction

For remote storage and processing of data, combined with user needs, this paper selects Alibaba Cloud IoT Cloud Platform to build and develop it[9], and the following are the detailed steps for building this system cloud platform.

(1) First register an account and activate IoT Platform: Then open the console of IoT Platform to create a "temp" product.

(2) Continue to add devices according to the prompts, "temp" is to connect to the device, "temp_control" is to connect to the QT client for data transmission, These two devices communicate with each other, and single-chip microcomputer and QT communication can be realized.

(3) Set up and add device service functions to realize the connection of things.

(4) Create rules to realize data information exchange and storage between the cloud platform and remote devices, and realize the construction of the cloud platform.

4.2 QT software interface settings

QT is a cross-platform C++ graphical user interface application development framework developed by Qt Company in 1991.This system combines QT development to visualize system data, which is convenient for users to view and manage. The following are the main steps for developing the QT interface of this system.

(1) User subscription interface design: first carry out the page layout, and then carry out coding regulation to realize the basic functions of MQTT such as Connect, Publish, Subscrible, UnSubscrible, Disconnect, etc., and set the information area to display debugging information in real time.

(2) Design of temperature and pressure control display interface: the control interface is mainly composed of the main functions of "target temperature and pressure", "real-time

 https://doi.org/10.1051/shsconf/202316601060

temperature and pressure" and "start" button. The start button is the start button for temperature and pressure regulation.

5 Test validation

This system used stm32 master chip, cloud platform and QT client. Combined with PID incremental control algorithm, the temperature and pressure of biogas digester are monitored and controlled in real time. After testing, the system functions can operate normally and stably and reach the expected functions. The following figure 5 show the temperature curve diagram under the control of PID increment algorithm.

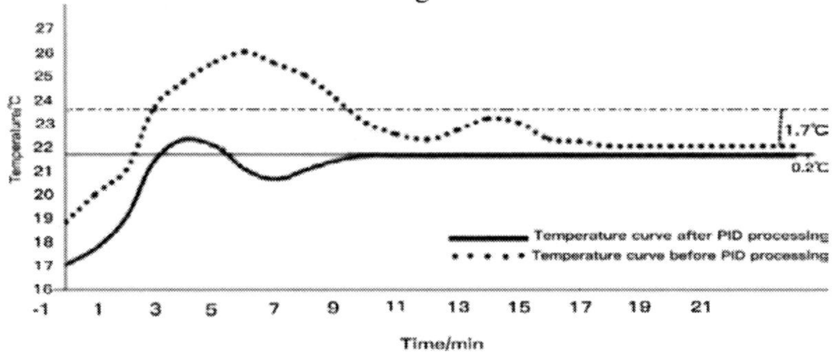

Fig. 5. Temperature curve of the PID control.

6 Conclusion

This system used STM32 master chip, cloud platform and QT client. Combined with PID incremental control algorithm, the temperature and pressure of biogas digester are monitored and controlled in real time. The biogas digester temperature and pressure control system combined with cloud platform technology, whith alized the remote intelligent monitoring and management of biogas digester by users. The application of this system greatly improved the efficiency and safety of biogas digester, and provided more intelligent and digital development direction and path for our national rural revitalization. The intelligent and digital temperature control management system has great potential for development in the rural and aquaculture industries now and in future.

References

1. Binbin Wang,Zebo Hu,Yucai Lu. Design of household biogas digester heated by solar energy[J].Chemical Engineering Design Letters, 2022, 48(08): 162-164.)
2. Lei Zhang. Design of intelligent gas storage system based on cloud platform[J].Automation Instrument, 2023.
3. Jijun Wang,Xiao Zhou,Yan Li, Fangyuan Li, Songlin Yu. Analysis and correction of external temperature measurement error of portable infrared thermal imager[J].Infrared, 2021, 42 (10): 28-32.)
4. Mingxia Yang. Design of high-precision platinum resistance temperature measurement system[D].Tianjin Polytechnic University, 2019.
5. Qingna Lai,Yanying Zheng.Construction and thinking of large-scale instrument and equipment sharing management in ordinary universities[J].Equipment Management and Maintenance,2022 (05): 21-23.)

6. Peng Wan. Research on solar energy-power generation waste heat heating biogas digester system based on TRNSYS[D].Qingdao University of Technology, 2018.)
7. Tianqi Zhang. Analysis of DS18B20 digital thermometer[J].Science and Technology Innovation, 2021 (22): 165-166.)
8. Junjie Xu, Weijie Zhang,Muquan Lin. Design of intelligent crib control system [J].Information Technology and Informatization, 2019 (11): 78-80+84.)
9. Huixian Song. Construction status and suggestions of rural household biogas digester in Dali County[J].Modern Agricultural Science and Technology, 2022 (03): 155-157.)

Design of remote monitoring system for 3D printing nano diamond film

Shuyi Wei*, *Xiaoyue* Chen, and *Xiuxia* Zhang

North Minzu University, School of Electronics and Information Engineering, Yinchuan, 750021 China

Abstract. The rapid development of the 3D printing industry has had a positive impact on all walks of life. Compared with the traditional manufacturing industry, 3D printing could not only shorten the design and manufacturing cycle, but also had great advantages in manufacturing accuracy. With the rapid development of cloud computing in recent years, the combination of cloud services and 3D printing had produced a new production model. This paper proposed to use single-screw extrusion 3D printer to prepare nanodiamond films. In order to monitor the printing process, cloud servers were used to monitor 3D printing remotely. This paper designed a remote control and monitoring system based on cloud platform, Alibaba Cloud server was used to integrate information resources, and finally made remote control of 3D printing equipment, remote video monitoring of printing process, and used image processing to preliminarily judge the integrity of printed objects.

1 The preface

3D printing technology was a new construction technology adapted to digitalization and intellectualization, which can greatly improve the construction efficiency and reduce the loss of raw materials [1]. 3D printing was called additive manufacturing due to its manufacturing characteristics. According to the product digital model, 3D graphics could be formed by using slicing software to print a certain part and the overall advanced manufacturing technology[2]. The research of Chinese academician Lu Bingheng showed that 3D printing has obvious advantages and practical value in many industries [3-4]. The technology achieved complex and diversified production structure, intelligent and automatic production process, saves raw materials and labor costs, so it was widely used in major manufacturing industries.

Cloud computing was not only a way of data storage and processing, but also a new way of thinking. To be exact, cloud computing can provide a service platform for configuration, computing and storage according to the needs of users. Cloud computing, as a new service method, needed to be fully automated and highly stable central server support when facing a lot of data [5]. Based on cloud platform technology, intelligent development can be achieved in different product areas [6].

* Corresponding author: wsyvivi@163.com

Like diamond, nano-diamond has special properties due to its unique structure [7]. Diamond has been widely studied for its excellent physical properties, such as good optical transmission, chemical stability and high mobility of electrons and holes [8-9]. In response to the CPC Central Committee's call for innovative, coordinated, green, open and shared development, in this design, nanocrystalline diamond with large surface area advantage was used to replace monocrystalline silicon, and 3D printing technology was used to replace high energy consumption and high pollution monocrystalline silicon preparation technology. Remote control and monitoring of printing equipment based on cloud platform.

2 Overall scheme design of the system

2.1 Overall design of the system

In order to reduce the idleness of a large number of manufacturing resources and break away from the stand-alone mode, users could choose 3D printers independently to meet the needs of private customization and more humanized services. The overall design of system functions was as follows:

The upper computer was started by software and transplanted to the cloud server. The FDM type 3D printer could access remote control through the whole network of the cloud server.

Real-time monitoring of working parameters enabled the system to set and monitor printing parameters in real time.

The system could monitor the printing condition of printed matter by using sensors and make preliminary judgment.

The cloud server was established, and the client could access the equipment operation, personnel management, video monitoring and other resources through the web page. Based on the above functional requirements, the system was composed of control system, video acquisition system, cloud platform, etc., as shown in Figure 1.

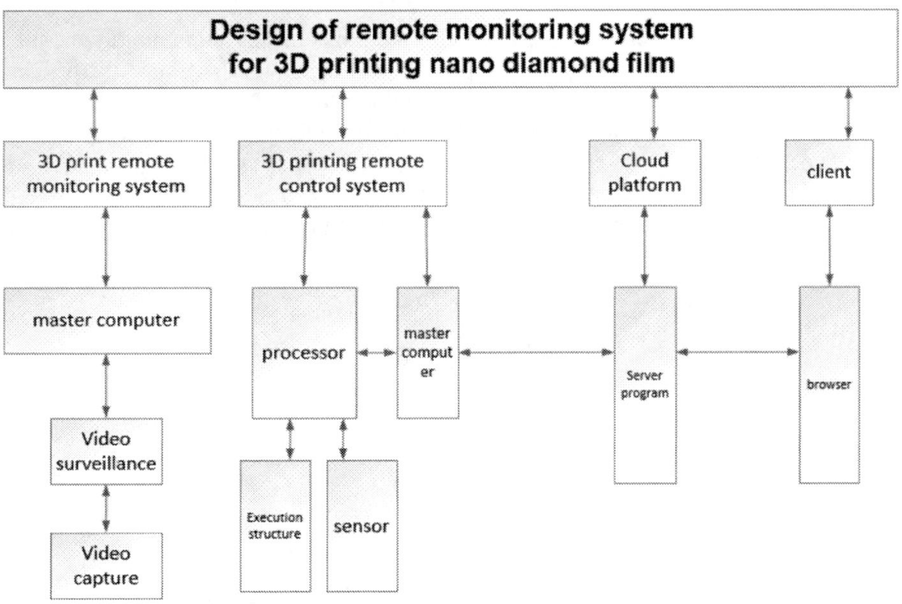

Fig. 1. Overall design drawing of the system.

2.2 Selection of 3D printer related devices

The 3D printer processor determined the accuracy and processing speed of the printer. In this paper, the ARM series 32F407 chip was used. This control chip had low power consumption and fast speed in information processing, which can meet the requirements of system timeliness. The temperature sensor adopted NTC thermistor, which is characterized by high sensitivity, fast response, compact structure, simple installation, wide temperature range, good stability and high reliability. Stepper motor was an important part to execute the commands of the upper computer system, which controls the movement of the XYZ axis of the printer. Its accuracy and response ability affected the printing speed and the quality of finished products. Therefore, 42 closed-loop stepper motor was adopted in this design.

2.3 Selecting the server and client

This paper used a small cloud service lightweight server provided by Alibaba Cloud. Lightweight servers included all resources, such as instance specifications, block storage, mirrors, snapshots, bandwidth, and security groups. Lightweight application servers could be configured through management or API. The running speed and processing speed could meet the requirements of the system, and the development was simple and the maintenance was convenient.

The web version client design used HTML technology for web page development, mainly used HTML and CSS for web page construction, used HTTP protocol data transmission, and used GET for login verification, and accessed the resources stored on the cloud platform, all used open source.

3 Design of remote control system

3.1 Control system structure

The FDM3D printer processor used STM32F407, and the control system mainly included the processor STM32F407, 220V AC power supply, DC motor, motor drive module, print nozzle, thermistor, material breakage detection module and cooling fan. The system structure was shown in Figure 2. The control system was mainly used to execute the command of the upper computer. For the setting of parameters, the upper computer used the WiFi serial communication to set the temperature of the printer's print nozzle and the temperature of the hot bed, and used the parameters returned by the sensor to correct.

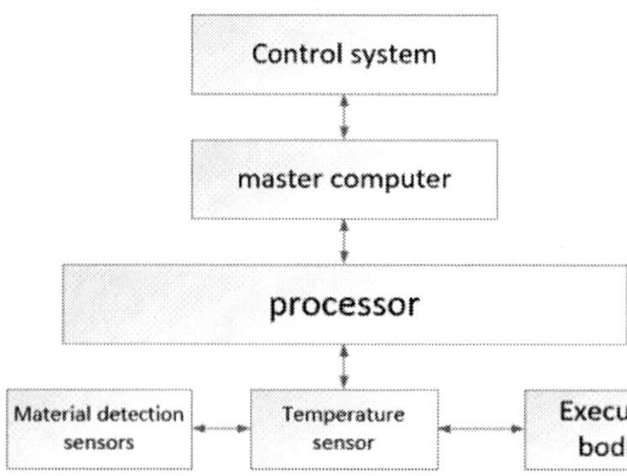

Fig. 2. System structure block diagram.

3.2 Master computer and communication of control system

The communication between the upper computer and the cloud server was to use the WiFi transmission module ESP0809, and established a connection with the cloud platform through the WiFi module to complete the data transmission and control command execution with the cloud server. Figure 3 was the data transmission flow chart. The data receiving was based on the monitoring of the port, whether the data request receives the request, then received the data packet, saved it to the local server, and then called the data in the packet.

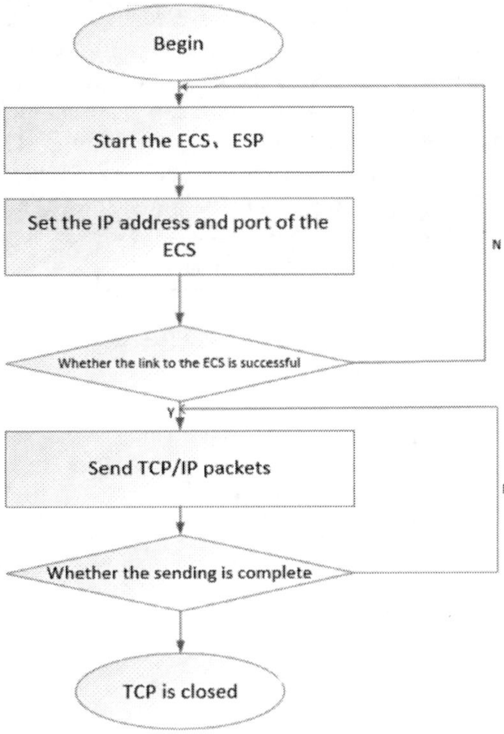

Fig. 3. Data transmission flow chart.

4 Construction of cloud server and design of client

4.1 Construction of ECS

The lightweight server of Alibaba Cloud used in this article is the simple application server selected according to the system requirements. It is characterized by fast processing speed, easy to build cloud servers, rapid establishment of cloud servers that adapt to the system, and fully meets the system needs.

After the MySQL database was established, it connected with local data, completed the editing environment, installed and used browsers and servers, and migrated the web-based web page monitoring system to the cloud platform, including the establishment of APIs. Then the control system was ported to the cloud server through API, and for the sake of network security and port call, the web page security settings and port opening settings were completed, and the required cloud platform was finally built.

4.2 Design of web client

The client of this design adopted B/S architecture. Compared with the traditional C/S architecture, the B/S architecture can cross platforms, and does not need specific clients. The B/S architecture mode based on web technology, simple software installation, maintenance and update. At the same time, users only needed a browser to access the system. Because all function additions only needed to be operated and completed in the background, the system had good scalability [10].

Using the B/S architecture, the system was divided into four modules. The first was the login module, which is used for user login. After successful login, the system entered the main interface. The main interface was divided into equipment management, personnel management, parameters and monitoring interfaces. The equipment management mainly included equipment list and equipment operation record group. The personnel management included personnel list, and the parameters and monitoring module included print data setting and video monitoring. The system function module was shown in Figure 4.

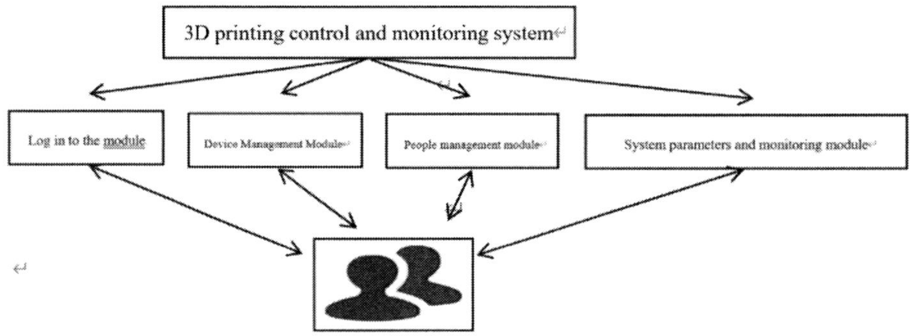

Fig. 4. System function module diagram.

5 Summary

Based on the relevant technology of the 3D printing remote control and monitoring system of the cloud platform, this paper developed a process that could be used to print nano-diamond films in 3D, and could realize remote monitoring of printers through the cloud platform. This design realized the remote control of FDM type 3D printers through the whole network access of ECS. In order to better and more intuitively display the operation of the device and facilitate client maintenance, HTML+ssc+js language and zend and MySQL database software were used to design the web client database. This article used Alibaba Cloud as the system's cloud server, and installed Apache, Tomcat, JDK, eclipse, and MySQL software to build the cloud server for remote control and monitoring of 3D printers. The safety settings of the firewall, the port settings, the settings of the communication HTTP and TCP were performed, and the remote access function of the cloud server was completed.

Reference

1. Qingxuan Shi, Jian Huo, Xikai Wu, et al. Research progress of 3D printing raw earth architecture technology [J/OL] Industrial building: 1-13 [2023-0310] https://doi.org/10.13204/j.gyjzG22042612.
2. Regulatory Considerations in the Design and Manufacturing of Implantable 3D - Printed Medical Devices[J].Robert J.Morrison, Khaled N. Kashlan, Colleen L.

Flanangan, Jeanne K.Wright, Glenn E. Green, Scott J. Hollister, Kevin J. Weatherwax. Clinical And Translational Science .2018 (5).

3. Hongbo Lan, Dachen Li, Bingheng Lu. Micro-nano scale 3D printing [J] Science in China: Technical Science, 2015, 45: 919 - 940.
4. Kai Cheng, Hongbo Lan, Bingheng Lu, etc. Research on active hybrid nozzle for multi-material and multi-scale 3D printing [J]. Chinese Science: Technical Science, 2017, 47: 149-162
5. Fei Yan. Research on school service platform based on cloud computing architecture [D]. East China Normal University, 2011
6. Yuhu Xu Design and Research of Intelligent Industrial Booth Based on Cloud Platform [D]. Shanghai University of Engineering and Technology, 2021. DOI: 10.27715/d.cnki. gshgj.2021.000916
7. Ao Bai. Study on the preparation of large area optical-grade nano-diamond films [D]. Wuhan University of Engineering, 2018
8. Stepan Stehlik, Lukas Ondic, et al. Silicon-Vacancy Centers in Ultra-Thin Nanocrystalline Diamond Films.[J]Micromachines 2018, 9(281)1-11; doi:10.3390/mi9060281
9. Jihan Yang, Yongping Zhang. "Nanocrystalline Diamond Films Grown by Microwave Plasma Chemical Vapor Depositionand Its Biocompatible Property [J] Inventi Impact - Microwave, 2019, 2019.
10. Xingrong Huang. Design and implementation of three-layer structure based on B/S architecture [J]. Computer Knowledge and Technology, 2015,11 (32): 52-53

Research on the promotion path of labor education in local colleges and universities from the perspective of the integration of five disciplines

Qian Zhang* and *Min* Cheng

School of Economics and Management, Hubei University of Automotive Technology, Shiyan, Hubei China

Keywords: Labor education, Five disciplines integration, All-round development.

Abstract. Labor education is an important part of college and primary education, which directly determines the labor spirit, labor value orientation and labor skill level of the cultivated workers. Through the quantitative analysis of the current situation of labor education in local colleges and universities, the path of optimizing labor education in local colleges and universities is put forward in this paper, so as to promote the development of labor education in local colleges and universities.

1 Introduction

At the 2018 National Education Congress, the General Secretary Xi Jinping stressed, "Train socialist builders and successors with all-round development of virtue, intelligence, physical conditions, mind status and community service, speed up the modernization of education, build an educational power, and build up the satisfying education of the people", which involves "labor" into the comprehensive education development concept and puts forward the general requirements of "virtue, intelligence, physical conditions, mind status and community service". In March 2020, the CPC Central Committee and the State Council issued the *Opinions on Comprehensively Strengthening Labor Education in Universities, Primary and Secondary Schools in the New Era*, requiring that "labor education should be included in the whole process of talent training, run through all sections of universities, primary and secondary schools, run through all aspects of family, school and society, and integrate with moral education, intellectual education, physical education and aesthetic education." Labor education directly determines the labor's spiritual outlook, value orientation and skill level of socialist builders and successors, and provides the fundamental guideline for comprehensively strengthening labor education in the new era. In July 2020,

* Corresponding author: 441558585@qq.com

the Ministry of Education issued the *Guidelines for Labor Education in Universities, Primary and Secondary Schools (Trial)*, proposing to strengthen the education of Marxist labor concept in colleges and universities, to focus on innovation and entrepreneurship, carry out productive labor and service labor combining disciplines and specialties, accumulate professional experience, and cultivate creative labor ability and honest and trustworthy legal labor consciousness. The *Opinions* and *Outline* give comprehensive guidance on how to build an education system that combines virtue, intelligence, physical conditions, mind status and community service, and set specific requirements on what and how to teach labor education and how to grade it. As the new generation of national rejuvenation, whether contemporary college students have the correct labor values is related to the all-round development and healthy growth of hundreds of millions of young people, the improvement of comprehensive quality of the people, and the prosperity of the Party and the country. Therefore, it is urgent and important to study college labor education in the new era.

2 The value implication of labor education

2.1 Implement the fundamental task of promoting moral education in colleges and universities

As the most concentrated manifestation of human's practical activities, labor is an important carrier to systematically carry out the education of world outlook, outlook on life and values, and an important way to realize the all-round development of human beings. Our Party always adheres to the guiding position of Marxism in the educational front and adheres to the educational policy of combining education with productive labor and combining theory with labor practice. On the new journey, we must give more prominence to the guiding role of the all-round human development of Marxist theory according to the current social and educational reality, and lay more stress on the political, ideological, social and practical nature of labor education, so as to better play its function of cultivating virtues and educating people.

2.2 Give full play to the value of comprehensive education

Virtue, intelligence, physical conditions, mind status and community service are the basic criteria of students' quality orientation, the overall goal of all-round development for a person, and also an education system. In this system, moral education is in the dominant position, labor education is not only an important support of moral education, but also a necessary carrier for moral education, intellectual education, physical education and aesthetic education to play a role in educating people. Labor can cultivate morality, improve wisdom, strengthen physique and cultivate aesthetic. Labor education is an important part of the national education system and a necessary way for students to grow up. It can help students establish correct labor concept, master the necessary labor ability, cultivate positive labor spirit, and form good labor habits and quality to carry out labor education in the new era. Labor education plays an irreplaceable role in the cultivation of students' comprehensive quality.

2.3 Cultivate students' ability of innovation and creation

Labor education can improve the creative ability of college students. Influenced by traditional educational concepts, most college students study hard and have strong examination ability, but lack practical ability. The socialist modernization has entered a new stage, the transformation of economic mode has put forward new requirements for the quality and ability of talents, and the cultivation of innovation and creation ability has become an important content of future talent training. Colleges and universities should change according to the situation, advance according to the time, and innovate according to the circumstances. They should strengthen labor education, build internship and training platform for students, provide labor opportunities, guide students to test theoretical knowledge in practice, deepen their understanding of theoretical knowledge, give full play to students' subjective initiative and creativity, and stimulate students' innovation , creation and entrepreneurial ability.

3 Analysis of current situation of labor education in local colleges and universities

In order to ensure the authenticity and validity of the research results, the research team conducted a questionnaire survey among college students in some local universities in Hubei Province. The survey objects included undergraduate students and master students in 8 universities, including Hubei University of Automobile Industry, Huanggang Normal University, Hubei University of Science and Technology, Hubei University of Engineering, and so on. The survey adopted random sampling. There were totally 435 questionnaires being collected, and 426 of them were valid. SPSS software was used for statistical and quantitative analysis of sample data to study the labor cognition of students in local colleges and universities and the status quo of labor education development, and then to analyze the promotion path of labor education in local colleges and universities.

3.1 Students' consciousness of independent labor is weak

The independent consciousness of labor refers to the consciousness that college students participate in labor by self-organization, love labor by self-motivation and carry out labor with self-restraint. Under the far-reaching influence of exam-oriented education, many primary and secondary schools, parents and media take test scores as the only standard to measure students' ability, while the education not included in the scope of examination or difficult to quantify, such as moral education, aesthetic education and labor education, is marginalized. Influenced by the growth environment, "post-00s" college students have a high degree of recognition of labor spirit, but their awareness in participating in labor actively is not high enough. When asked "Do you agree that 'work is the source of all happiness'?", 92.58% of the students "strongly agree" that hard work is the only way to achieve personal ideals and national development. When asked "Will you take the initiative to sign up for labor practice in your life?", only 25.23% of the students choose "yes", and 64.02% choose "comply with the arrangement", indicating that most of the students take labor as a task to carry out, it can be seen that college students lack the concept of self-labor, and their enthusiasm and subjective initiative of self-work need to be further strengthened.

3.2 The phenomenon of valuing labor over education is widespread

The purpose of labor education in colleges and universities is to guide college students to establish the values of respecting labor, develop honest and law-abiding labor quality, cultivate the labor spirit of struggle and dedication, and improve the labor ability of innovation and creation. Some colleges and universities still equate labor education with simple manual labor, life labor and housework when carrying out labor education. Although more than 60% colleges and universities have set up compulsory courses for labor education, students believe that the form of labor courses is greater than the content, and students' labor consciousness and labor awareness have not been really improved. When the students are asked "What problems do you think exist in current school labor education?", the top three answers are "labor education is rigid in form" (64.49%), "labor education is one-sided in content and form" (63.32%), "college students do not really understand the meaning and purpose of labor education" (53.5%). "Value on labor over education" or even "there's only labor without education" phenomenon is still widespread in colleges and universities.

3.3 The curriculum system of labor education is not sound

Firstly, teachers, funds and places for labor education are lacking. For a long time, the weakening of labor education in colleges and universities has resulted in the shortage of labor education teachers. The lack of labor education teachers is not only difficult to meet the development of regular labor education, but also difficult to meet the requirements of setting up high-quality labor education courses. According to the survey, in most colleges and universities, counselors, ideological and political teachers, and student administration personnel concurrently teaching labor education courses, and only a few colleges and universities have full-time teachers to teach labor courses. In addition, labor education funds are insufficient, the lack of material and hardware site support, many colleges and universities can only guarantee the daily teaching needs, the places for labor education are seriously lacking, and labor education can only be rigid in form. Secondly, the labor education curriculum is not perfect. Although most colleges and universities have set up labor education courses, many colleges and universities simply replace the content of the labor education curriculum with the second classroom activities such as social practice, voluntary service and work-study, lacking the construction of a complete curriculum system.

3.4 Labor education management is absent

Firstly, some colleges and universities do not have clear rules and regulations on which department is responsible for labor education, leading to unclear division of work, inadequate management, buck-passing and poor educational result. Secondly, labor education assessment mechanism is lacking. Some colleges and universities just collect the statistics of the times of labor education and look up labor course teaching records. For the specific development process and effectiveness, there are no clear assessment indicators, and assessment results are quite different from the actual situation, which cannot mobilize the enthusiasm of workers. "Contribution is not necessarily rewarded, and fault is also not necessarily punished", so that some teachers and students just simply do it, and labor education cannot be implemented.

4 Study on optimal path of labor education in local colleges and universities

4.1 Enhanced top-level design

Labor education is not only an important part of the "Educating Five Domains Simultaneously", but also an important starting point to implement the "three-wide education". College students' labor education in the new era is a top-down systematic project. The premise of ensuring the project landing is to make overall planning and proper layout. Firstly, the organization and leadership of labor education should be strengthened. A leading group of labor education work led by school leaders, coordinated by key departments, and implemented by grassroots units should be established. Under the guidance of national policy spirit and implementation opinions, documents on the labor education system with school-based characteristics should be issued to provide policy guidance and paths for schools to carry out labor education. Secondly, the construction of teaching staff should be strengthened. A team including full-time and part-time labor education teachers should be provided with enough full-time teachers and employ part-time teachers in various forms, and improve the mechanism for the evaluation and recruitment of labor teachers, assessment, excellence evaluation, and training, so that labor teachers enjoy the same resources and benefits as other teachers. In addition, funding and site security should be improved. Adequate funds are an important guarantee for the sustainable development of labor education. Schools should actively strive for the policy support from superiors, allocate funds for school labor education as a whole, actively expand labor education sites inside and outside the school, and promote the effective implementation of labor education.

4.2 Improving the labor curriculum system

Labor curriculum is an important way of labor education and plays a leading role in labor education. Labor education not only needs practice, but also needs labor courses to impart theoretical knowledge and strengthen students' cognition of labor. Labor courses in colleges and universities should set up a curriculum system that combines with professional courses, practical education, innovation and entrepreneurship, integration of production and education, and set up corresponding course outline and required credits. In addition to implementing the national curriculum, we will innovate and develop the local curriculum of labor education, integrate labor education into the curriculum of other disciplines, form educational synergy, and make labor education become routine and daily. The labor education curriculum should have integrated design to form an overall pattern of labor education with "living labor, production labor and service labor" as the main form, and "vocational experience labor and creative labor" running through it.

4.3 Improving the mechanism for ensuring labor education

Make overall arrangements for investment in labor education, strengthen the construction of labor education facilities in schools, actively attract social forces to provide labor education service, and improve the mechanism for replenishing labor education equipment and consumables. Establish the evaluation system of labor education to evaluate and the process and results of labor education quantitatively, effectively improving the effect of curriculum construction. Schools should strengthen the construction of labor education atmosphere, innovate the way of labor education, improve the safety guarantee mechanism of labor education, and strive to promote the orderly and effective implementation of labor education.

4.4 Integrating labor education, professional education and innovation and entrepreneurship education

Based on the characteristics of local colleges and universities, we should strengthen the integration of labor education with professional education, innovation and entrepreneurship education. Firstly, the proper way and content of labor education should be chosen to realize the combination of them. Secondly, the ways and methods of integrating labor education with professional education should be attached with attention. When students receive professional education, teachers imperceptibly implant labor related knowledge to realize the coordinated development of labor education and professional education in the same direction.

4.5 Constructing the trinity model collaborative education of "family, school and community"

School, family and society bear the irreplaceable responsibility of labor education respectively. The leading role of school labor education should be given full play to excavate off-campus labor education resources, expand off-campus practice bases, and guide students to increase their knowledge and talents in social practice, professional practice and skill training. Combined with the characteristics of "net generation" students, the social level can make full use of the "WeChat, Weibo and WeSee and one end" platforms to spread labor education knowledge, publicize the advanced deeds of model workers, guide young people to establish a correct concept of struggle and happiness, and create a positive social atmosphere. To give full play to the role of family labor education, schools should keep close communication with families, strengthen the guidance of family education, and encourage the home-school community to work together to carry out social welfare labor, so as to integrate labor education into family daily life and form a joint force for labor education.

5 Conclusions

Youth is the future of a country and the hope of a nation. In the new era, college students should show their spiritual outlook, correct their value orientation and improve their skill level in labor. Colleges and universities should firmly grasp the strategic task of training new people who take on the great task of national rejuvenation, fully implement the Party's educational policy, implement the fundamental task of fostering virtue through education, and train socialist builders and successors with all-round development in areas such as morals, intelligence, physical fitness, work and aesthetics

Subject Source: 2021 Teaching Research and Reform Project of Hubei Institute of Automotive Technology- Construction and Implementation of College Labor Education Curriculum System under the Concept of "Knowledge-action Unity" (JY2021053)

References

1. Cui Yanqiang, Chen Xiaosheng. Marx's thought of labor education and its contemporary value [J]. Journal of Soochow University (Educational Science Edition), 2022, 10(01):67-74.DOI:10.19563/j.cnki.sdjk.2022.01.007.
2. Jin Zhe, Chen Enlun. Exploration on the logic and practice path of labor education in the new era [J]. Journal of Guizhou Normal University (Social Science Edition), 2021 (06):53-60.DOI:10.16614/j.gznuj.skb.2021.06.007.
3. Shi Guihong, Feng Jiangying. Exploration of labor education into ideological and political education [J]. School Party Construction and Ideological Education, 2022(04):48-50.DOI:10.19865/j.cnki.xxdj.2022.04.014.
4. Lin Kesong, Xiong Qing. Towards cross-border integration:the value, understanding and practice of labor education curriculum construction in the new era[J]. Journal of Educational Science, Hunan Normal University, 2020, 19(02):57-63.DOI:10.19503/j.cnki.1671-6124.2020.02.008.

Current situation and reflections of IT teaching in junior high school--taking the learning of excel as an example

Huansong Yang, *Mengting* Shen, and *Caixia* Liu*

School of Information Science and Technology, Hangzhou Normal University, Hangzhou, China

Abstract. With the rapid development of the Internet and mobile information technology, the state has made it clear that "Internet¬+" education has become an important development project for national education. Information technology education is also playing an increasingly important role in the development of students, and online and offline hybrid teaching is a teaching mode that is very suitable for information technology. Online and offline blended teaching is a new teaching model that has emerged in the mobile internet era, and is a combination of online learning and the advantages of traditional teaching. However, there are still problems with online and offline blended teaching such as uncertainty in the use of educational resources, so a more appropriate teaching process system needs to be tapped to achieve better teaching results.

1 Introduction

Promoting the integration and development of information technology and education into the classroom has become the trend of education nowadays. Online and offline hybrid teaching is a new teaching mode that has emerged in the mobile Internet era, and a teaching mode that combines the advantages of online learning on the Internet with traditional teaching. In this model, online teaching entails teachers uploading course learning resources on education platforms via the internet, and students using resources in online learning platforms such as laptops and mobile phone clients to complete various tasks. This paper takes the junior high school information technology course as an example and examines a suitable process system to adapt to the diversity of educational software to achieve better teaching results.

2 Investigation of the teaching situation of information technology in junior high school

The object of this research is the seventh grade students, and the content of the research is selected from the seventh grade information technology course on Excel, using "Formulas

* Corresponding author: 2332206722@qq.com

and Functions" as a reference. The course is taught in the same way before and after, and the subject is taught by the same teacher to achieve the same conditions as far as possible.

2.1 Student learning

Before students learn about Excel data processing, they receive teaching resources from textbooks only and are unfamiliar with this piece of data processing knowledge. Most students do not do pre-reading work before class, so in class, they will not be able to keep up with the teacher's progress. According to the survey, students' concentration is not sustained for long periods of time and can be very distracting, resulting in infrequent interaction with the teacher; completion of homework after class is determined by the severity of the teacher, and most students have little self-control. The survey was conducted to determine how well students received what they had learnt by observing how well they completed their homework and how often they interacted in class. As the survey in Figure 1 shows, students' homework is not well completed; the time and content of their studies in school are not well distributed. In addition, due to the heavy tasks assigned by teachers, students spend more energy on their studies and neglect sports, resulting in a low level of physical fitness for the majority of students; long hours of inefficient learning prevent students from developing physically and mentally.

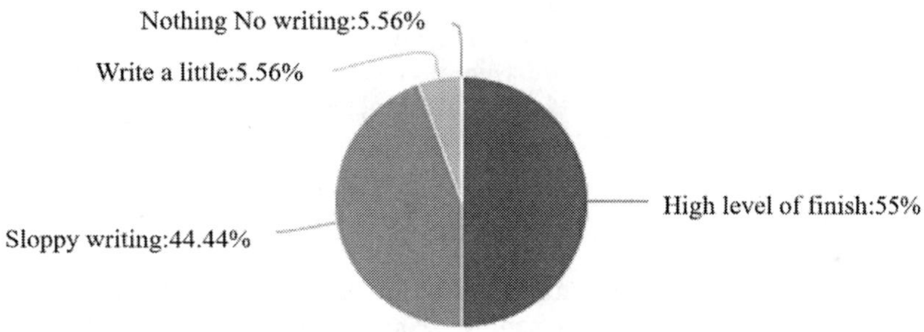

Fig. 1. Assignment completion.

2.2 Teachers' teaching

Teachers are already familiar with the courseware of "Formulas and Functions" in Excel, but the progress of the teachers' lessons has to be relatively slowed down due to the lack of pre-study of the students before the lessons. The multimedia room in the school is equipped with computer software versions for students that do not meet the requirements needed for teaching, which also creates some problems in teaching. It was found that the most commonly used version of Office related software did not match the syllabus and therefore needed to be upgraded. In addition, most of the teachers' lesson plans used old lesson plans from previous years, which lacked new ideas. Throughout the lessons, teachers mostly used the lecture method, leaving very little time for students to think and discuss and no time for students to explore on their own. Moreover, teachers rarely set stage tasks for students in the classroom, resulting in the completion of students' post-lesson assignments and the quality of their completion falling short of expectations, as shown in Figure 2.

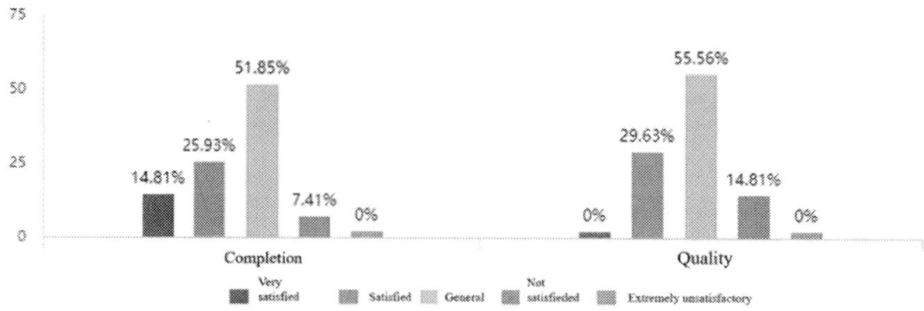

Fig. 2. Assignment completion and satisfaction.

3 Analysis of the problems of teaching information technology in junior high school

3.1 Teaching resources are not up to standard

The survey shows that the teaching tools provided by schools are outdated and the computer software versions are low, making it difficult for the teaching process to keep up with the ideas of teaching design and for the quality of teaching to reach the expected results. Teachers mostly use a single lecture method, and it is difficult to attract students' interest with pure text-based courseware. Slightly more advanced teaching resources cannot be presented, resulting in students not being able to get a full sense of classroom experience and participation.

3.2 Rigid teaching implementation process

Under the demand of examinations and the situation that IT courses are not taken seriously, teachers always passively teach students all the examination points within the time given by the Ministry of Education, and teachers' teaching tasks are heavy and teaching time is tight, which leads to the majority of teachers adopting the form of "one word", telling students the examination points directly and making them memorise them, rather than This has led to the majority of teachers adopting a 'one-liner' approach, telling students the test points and making them learn them by rote, rather than letting them explore and master them on their own. This creates a dependency mentality and is not conducive to active learning. In the classroom, teachers tend to fill up the classroom [2], leaving little time for students to communicate, discuss and think. Students are passive recipients of knowledge, and interaction with the teacher is infrequent and almost non-existent, which is not conducive to students' mastery of knowledge and the cultivation of a spirit of enquiry.

3.3 Inadequate feedback on teaching evaluation

The extent to which students have received knowledge cannot be judged solely on the basis of post-lesson quizzes, but also on the basis of how well they have listened to the lesson, how well they have participated in the lesson and how well they have completed the post-lesson assignments. Single post-lesson quizzes prevent teachers from tracking student learning and there is insufficient feedback between teachers and students to develop and implement appropriate post-lesson improvement tasks for students.

4 Analysis of the development of online and offline hybrid teaching mode of junior high school information technology

4.1 Feasibility analysis of the online and offline hybrid teaching mode of junior high school information technology

The junior high school IT course is a highly operational and practical course. With the continuous development of technology, the content of IT courses is constantly updated. As a new teaching mode, the online/offline hybrid teaching mode can play an effective role in the IT classroom, which also requires specific teaching design. The application of online and offline hybrid teaching mode in junior high school IT classrooms requires both theoretical support of the hybrid teaching mode and a stable teaching environment [13].

4.2 Overview of the online and offline hybrid teaching mode of information technology in junior secondary schools

With the rapid development of mobile Internet, the teaching mode of school curriculum has also changed. The use of big data, mobile Internet and other information technology has enabled the information transfer of course content, thus realising accurate teaching and greatly improving teaching quality. All secondary schools are actively adopting the online and offline hybrid teaching model, of which there are many teaching systems, but the most common one is Nails.

4.3 Construction of a hybrid online and offline teaching mode for junior secondary IT

The extent to which students have received knowledge cannot be judged solely on the basis of post-lesson quizzes, but also on the basis of how well they have listened to the lesson, how well they have participated in the lesson and how well they have completed the post-lesson assignments. Single post-lesson quizzes prevent teachers from tracking student learning and there is insufficient feedback between teachers and students to develop and implement appropriate post-lesson improvement tasks for students.

4.3.1 Online independent pre-study before class

Before the class starts, the teacher will upload the courseware related to the course to the pinned file and upload the links to the relevant web pages, and release the pre-study tasks and task notifications. Students check the task notifications and confirm the pre-reading tasks, then do independent study online according to the needs of the task, complete the pre-reading tasks and submit them to expand their knowledge base for offline learning in class.

4.3.2 In-class offline classroom teaching

In class, students are invited to share their pre-reading, and the teacher will explain the relevant knowledge points in a targeted manner and design various consolidation questions that students will answer as they go along. At the same time, the teacher designs guided topics to address key teaching points and organises offline discussions with students, and uses pinned activities such as "voting" and "countdown" to organise online interaction with students. Through interesting interactions, students' desire to master knowledge is enhanced. In the classroom, teachers can selectively address students' questions. For problems that are common to students, the teacher can explain them systematically and slow them down to ensure that they are solved; for individual problems that exist among students, the teacher can play the role of group discussion and encourage students to discuss and communicate with each other, and then the teacher can guide them, which can largely improve students' ability to think about and solve problems.

4.3.3 After-school mixed extension training

After the lesson, teachers can assign after-school homework for students based on the lectures in the lesson. After the students have completed their homework, they can upload and submit it through their home school book. At the same time, teachers need to reflect on the implementation of the lesson and optimise the lesson plan. Teachers can also upload resources for tasks that need to be extended according to the learning needs of different students so that students can learn independently. At the end of the lesson, teachers can take simple quizzes on what students have learnt in class, count the scores and understand the common problems that students have and answer them in a group, or chat directly with students about individual problems to help them better grasp what they have learnt. Teachers can also design questionnaires to find out how satisfied students are with the blended learning model and what they think about it [14].

5 Analysis of the practice and effectiveness of the online and offline hybrid teaching mode of junior high school information technology

5.1 Design and practice of online and offline hybrid teaching mode in junior secondary IT

Take "Formulas and Functions" as an example, and develop in detail the specific implementation process of the online and offline hybrid teaching mode in the IT curriculum.

5.1.1 Teaching analysis

1) Teaching analysis

The target students of the course "Formulas and Functions" are Year 7 students, who have a strong interest in learning information technology, and each student has a different level of mastery of basic information technology knowledge and skills. After a period of study, students have already had some experience and ability in independent inquiry learning, cooperation, communication and discussion, and have a certain mastery of basic operation and basic skills. In addition, students need to be encouraged to conduct independent inquiry, online and offline discussion and exchange, hands-on practice, and teacher-student cooperation to summarise and summarise knowledge together and experience the learning process [15].

2) Teaching objectives

- Knowledge and skills: Students will be able to master the use of Excel formulas through the study of Formulas and Functions and will be able to master the application of basic functions such as SUM and AVERAGE in Excel.

- Process and Methods: Students will develop their independent learning skills and hands-on skills through teacher-led explanations and student hands-on operations.
- Emotional Attitude and Values: Students will experience the use of formulas and functions in Excel and develop the ability to think and explore on their own. At the same time, they will experience the joy of success in the process of completing tasks and be able to apply the knowledge they have learnt to solve practical problems in life.

3) Teaching focus and difficulties

- Key points: the use of Excel formulas and functions
- Difficulties: the basic format and integrated use of formulas and functions

4) Teaching preparation

- Multimedia room
- "Formulas and Functions" PPT
- "Formulas and Functions" exercise form

5.1.2 Teaching design

1) Online independent pre-reading before the lesson

Before the lesson starts, the lesson materials and the tables used in the exercises are uploaded to the pinned file for students' reference. Students will be given a pre-reading task to complete and submit within a set time frame through independent study. The teacher uses the submitted assignments to determine what problems the students have, as shown in Figure 3.

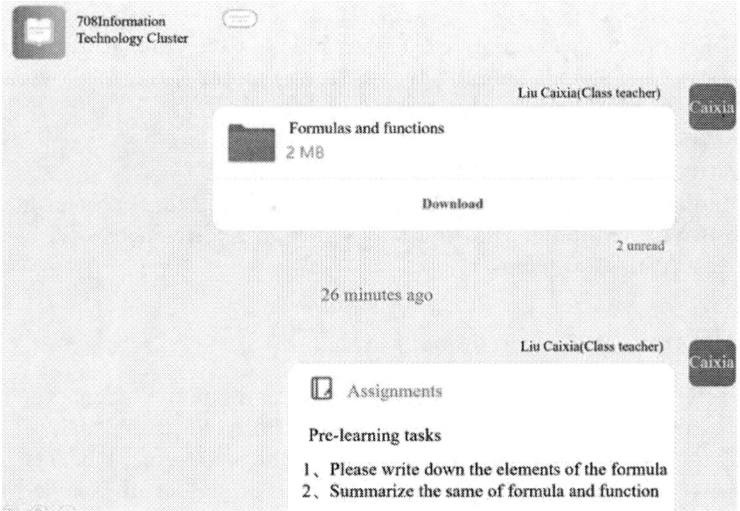

Fig. 3. Pre-lesson tasks.

2) In-class offline classroom teaching

- Context creation, introducing new lessons

Teacher: What do students usually do at weekends? (PPT show home page)

Students: watch TV, brush Jitterbug, read novels, play badminton

Teacher: According to the answers given by students just now, the teacher found that children nowadays are addicted to mobile phones, tablets, etc. and have become proper internet users. This shows that the number of Internet users in our country is increasing year by year. So now we can see a table of "the scale of the number of Internet users in China", through this table, students, we want to quickly sort out these data, through the calculation of the information we want to know, which will need to use the formula we are about to learn. (Board book "formulas and functions")

- Task-driven, independent exploration

Teacher: Issue Task 1: Calculate the usage rate of instant messaging in 2011. Ask students to demonstrate. (Show the "Formulas and Functions" table)

Students: Explore independently and complete Task 1 (students actively demonstrate on stage)

Teacher: Ask a question. In the demonstration, we can see that the calculated usage rate is a decimal, but what do we generally say about usage rates in mathematics?

Students: The percentage form.

Teacher: Issue Task 2: Convert all usage rates into percentage form. Ask students to demonstrate and go around the table, giving help to students who have problems.

Students: Complete Task 2 and share and discuss in small groups, giving guidance to each other.

Teacher and students: summarise the elements of the formula and the steps for using it. (PPT shows page 2)

Teacher: Launch a polling activity on pins for a small exercise on formulas, leaving time for students to discuss and exchange ideas in small groups before starting. (Show the pinned poll topic)

Students: Students think carefully and complete their answers based on what they have learned.

Teacher: Explain the mini-exercise and post Task 3: Calculate the total number of Internet users in 2011. And ask students to demonstrate. (PPT show page 5)

Students: Work in groups to complete Task 3 and have the group leader demonstrate.

Teacher: Post Task 4: Calculate the average usage rate in 2011. Walk around the stage during this time and help students who are having difficulty.

Students: Work in small groups to complete Task 4.

- Cooperative communication and classroom summary

Teacher and students: Summarise the components of the function and how it is used, and compare it with the formula to find similarities and differences, and ask students to share their ideas. (PPT show page 6)

3) Post-lesson mixed extension training

Post-lesson assignments are posted for students in the nail group. Students need to complete and submit them within a specified time, and the teacher collects the students' assignments and checks the students' mastery of knowledge. At the same time, students can ask their teachers for answers at school if they are struggling, or stay on the pinned page to chat privately with the teacher if they are too late to ask. The teacher sees the message and solves the problem for the student. Teachers reflect on themselves based on the completion of students' homework, optimise lesson plans and highlight important and difficult points.

5.2 Analysis of the effectiveness of the online and offline hybrid teaching mode of information technology in junior secondary schools

5.2.1 Design of questionnaire

The experiment was carried out in a middle school, and after the practice, questionnaires were administered to classmates as well as teachers. The questionnaire mainly concerned the students' learning status, the degree of receiving knowledge and the concentration of attention under the online and offline hybrid teaching mode. The questionnaires were distributed to students in a class of Year 7 at the end of the teaching implementation, and the students were allowed to fill in and return the questionnaires centrally.

5.2.2 Survey results and analysis

1) Students' acceptance of knowledge

According to the survey, under the online and offline hybrid teaching mode, students paid more attention to the pre-study work before class, which prompted them to study purposefully in class, focus on listening to the lectures for the knowledge they did not understand, and have a general understanding of the knowledge points through the pre-study process. Secondly, as the lesson plans are updated in class, it greatly engages students' interest in learning. At the end of the lesson, the teacher will answer questions online in addition to tutoring in school, making it easier for students to receive their knowledge.

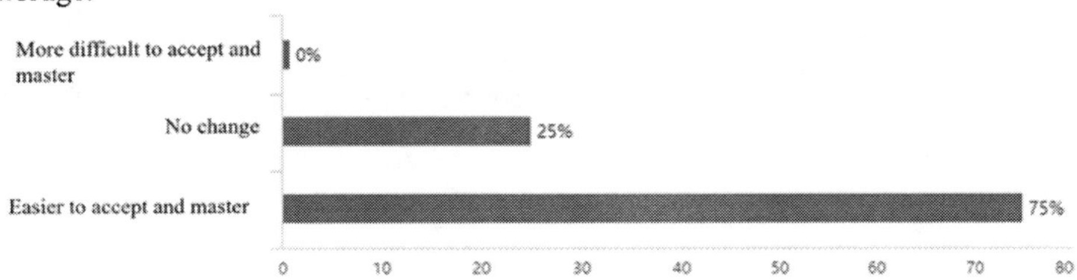

Fig. 4. Level of student acceptance of knowledge.

2) Students' means of problem solving

According to the survey, when students are faced with a problem, most of them choose to learn independently, explore their knowledge as well as ask their classmates and work in groups. With the online and offline hybrid teaching model, most students overcome their dependency on learning, enhance cooperation with their peers and develop their cooperation skills. It also develops students' ability to think independently to solve problems. The number of people who ignore problems and do not go to solve them is basically zero, indicating that students' motivation to learn is greatly enhanced and can effectively improve their learning efficiency.

3) Completion of students' homework

After investigation, students' homework completion in the IT class using the online and offline hybrid teaching mode was much better compared to before because they had pre-reading in place before class and could keep up with the progress in class, plus the messages sent in the pinned group would be reminded when it was time, which could prevent students from forgetting to hand in their homework and served as a reminder.

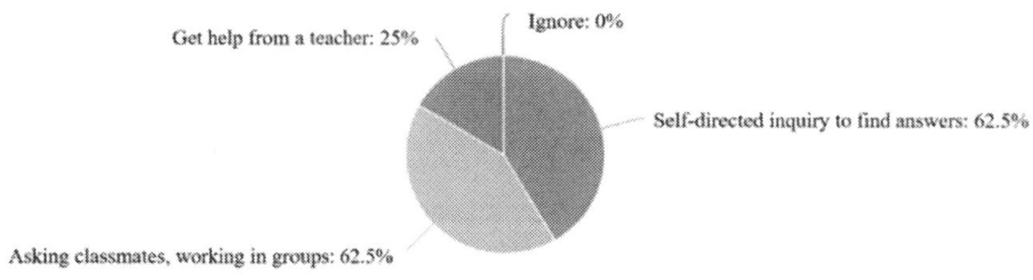

Fig. 5. Student problem solving tools.

6 Conclusion

Based on relevant theoretical research and practical mapping, this project has explored and researched the integration of junior high school IT and offline hybrid teaching models, and found that the existing online and offline hybrid teaching models have substantially improved the learning outcomes for students. Novel lesson plans were researched, in-depth junior high school IT classrooms were practised, and initial evaluations were conducted through questionnaires. The online/offline blended teaching model has been a major trend and is not only limited to IT courses, but other subjects can also adopt this model and bridge the communication gap between parents, students and teachers with the help of pegging. However, this study is only an attempt on a small lesson in Excel, and due to the objective conditions, the subjects of this study are only individual classes, there are certain limitations, so we need to further expand the scope of the experimental subjects for further research.

References

1. Ming Li. A Study on the Blended Teaching Mode of College English from the Perspective of POA. 2020, 2(3)
2. Dong Luo. Based on Online and Offline Hybrid Teaching in College Mathematics Courses. 2020, 3(3)
3. Liu Xiuling. Research on Online and Offline Hybrid Teaching in Information Technology Courses [J]. Liaoning Institute of Economics and Vocational Technology. Journal of Liaoning Institute of Economic Management Cadres, 2019(01):124-126.
4. Chen Guinan. The application and implementation of online and offline hybrid teaching mode in computer courses [J]. Computers and Telecommunications, 2015(12):99-101.
5. Li Yan, Wang Lin. Exploring the problems and countermeasures of offline learning in distance education [J]. China Education Technology Equipment, 2012(12):128-130.
6. Tian Yang, Du Jing, Huang Ronghuai. Exploration of learning and social collaboration strategies for blended learning [J]. China e-learning, 2018(05):8-14.
7. Cheng Wangkai, Li Nannan. Exploration and practice of online and offline hybrid teaching mode based on cloud classroom in teaching microbiology in higher education [J]. Microbiology Bulletin,2018,45(04):927-933

Application of metabolic GM $(1,1,t^h,p)$ power model in fresh e-commerce prediction

Jiefang Liu*, and *Rongrong* Yang

School of Management and Economics, Tianjin University of Technology and Education, Tianjin 300222, China

Abstract. Aiming at the prediction problem of fresh e-commerce industry, this paper attempts to combine the metabolic theory with the improved GM (1,1) power model. The article introduces the traditional GM (1,1) power model to enhance the adaptability of the model to the data series, and at the same time, a new parameter is introduced when constructing the background value, the background value is represented as a linear function of adjacent sequence points, and the form and solution method of the two specific models are given, with the goal of minimizing the average relative error, and the power exponential and new parameters are co-optimized by genetic algorithm. The optimal modeling dimension is determined through model testing, and on this basis, the metabolic GM $(1,1,t^h,p)$ power model is established, and the model is applied to the prediction of the transaction scale of the fresh e-commerce industry. The results show that the improved GM (1,1) power model can significantly improve the fitting accuracy compared with the original model, and the metabolic GM$(1,1,t^h,p)$ power model has good performance in the prediction problem of fresh e-commerce.

1 Introduction

Fresh e-commerce is currently in a more complex and changeable environment, although favorable policies and customer demand provide a better development environment for it, but how to accurately grasp the development direction and growth trend of fresh food e-commerce has become a problem that plagues the development of fresh food e-commerce enterprises.

Among the existing forecasting studies in the field of fresh e-commerce, more scholars focus on the forecast research of fresh product demand and cold chain logistics demand. Zhang Y L analyzed and predicted the sales volume of four fruits on the Ganfuyuan platform[1]. Ma J Y constructed the ARIMA-SVM combination prediction model based on the Sharp value weight allocation method, and analyzed the sales volume of fresh e-commerce agricultural products[2]. Li K used time series theory to establish several potato demand fluctuation forecasting models[3]. Du X F forecasts demand for perishable agricultural products based on the support vector machine (SVM) method[4]. Huang L uses

* Corresponding author: liujf101@126.com

the GM (1,1) model and the BP neural network model to simulate and predict logistics demand[5]. Li Y provided appropriate sales and supply solutions for the fresh food e-commerce platform[6]. As the "last blue ocean" in the e-commerce field, fresh e-commerce is very important to predict its industry transaction scale, but most of the existing predictions on industry transaction scale come from industry analysis reports. GM(1,1) power model can achieve better fitting of data series due to the flexibility of power exponential value, and has been widely used in many fields, so this paper attempts to use GM(1,1) power model for the first time to predict the industry transaction scale and user scale of fresh e-commerce.

2 Traditional GM(1,1) power model

Let the non-negative original sequence be $X^{(0)}=(x^{(0)}(1),x^{(0)}(2),...x^{(0)}(N))$,whose primary accumulation generates a sequence of $X^{(1)}=(x^{(1)}(1),x^{(1)}(2),\cdots,x^{(1)}(N))$, where $x^{(1)}(k)=\sum_{i=1}^{k}x^{(0)}(i)$, $k=1,2,\cdots,N$, noting the background values $z(k)=\frac{1}{2}(x^{(1)}(k)+x^{(1)}(k-1)$, $k=2,3,\cdots,N$

Definition 1 Set $X^{(0)}$, $X^{(1)}$ and $z(k)$ as defined above, the grey differential equation for the GM(1,1) power model is

$$x^{(0)}(k)+az(k)=b(z(k))^{r},\quad k=2,3,\cdots N$$

Where r is the power exponent, a and b are constants.

Definition 2 The whitening equation for the GM(1,1) power model is

$$\frac{dx^{(1)}(t)}{dt}+ax^{(1)}(t)=b(x^{(1)}(t))^{r}$$

When $\hat{x}^{(1)}(1)=x^{(1)}(1)=x^{(0)}(1)$, the time response function is

$$\hat{x}^{(1)}(t)=\{\frac{b}{a}+[x^{(1)}(1)^{(1-r)}-\frac{b}{a}]e^{a(r-1)(t-1)}\}^{\frac{1}{r-1}} \tag{1}$$

Following the least squares method for the grey differential equation, we obtain $(a,b)^{T}=(B^{T}B)^{-1}B^{T}Y$,

of which

$$B=\begin{bmatrix}-z(2) & (z(2))^{r}\\ -z(3) & (z(3))^{r}\\ \vdots & \vdots\\ -z(N) & (z(N))^{r}\end{bmatrix}\qquad Y=\begin{bmatrix}x^{(0)}(2)\\ x^{(0)}(3)\\ \vdots\\ x^{(0)}(N)\end{bmatrix}$$

Power exponent r, which is generally found by optimization methods. Combining a, b, and r substitute into formula (1). The simulated value of the original sequence is obtained by $\hat{x}^{(0)}(k)=\hat{x}^{(1)}(k)-\hat{x}^{(1)}(k-1)$, $k=2,3,\cdots,N$. The predicted value of the q-step of the original non-negative sequence is obtained by $\hat{x}^{(0)}(k)=\hat{x}^{(1)}(k)-\hat{x}^{(1)}(k-1)$, $k=N+1,N+2,\cdots,N+q$.

3 Metabolic GM (1,1,t^h,p) power model

3.1 GM(1,1,t^h,p)power model

Definition 3 Set $X^{(0)}$, $X^{(1)}$ and $z(k)$ are defined above, then the grey differential equation for the GM(1,1,t^h,p) power model is

$$x^{(0)}(k)+az(k)=(b_0+b_1t+b_2t^2+\cdots+b_ht^h)(z(k))^r,\quad k=2,3,\cdots,N.$$

Definition 4 The whitening equation for the GM (1,1,th,p) power model is

$$\frac{dx^{(1)}(t)}{dt}+ax^{(1)}(t)=(b_0+b_1t+b_2t^2+\cdots+b_ht^h)(x^{(1)}(t))^r \tag{2}$$

When $h=0$, formula (2) is the traditional GM(1,1) power model.
When $h=1$

$$\frac{dx^{(1)}(t)}{dt}+ax^{(1)}(t)=(b_0+b_1t)(x^{(1)}(t))^r \tag{3}$$

is the whitening equation for the GM(1,1,t,p) power model.
Let $y=(x^{(1)}(t))^{1-r}$, then

$$\frac{dy}{dt}+a(1-r)y=(b_0+b_1t)(1-r) \tag{4}$$

When $\hat{x}^{(1)}(1)=x^{(1)}(1)=x^{(0)}(1)$, the ordinary differential equation tells us

$$y(t)=e^{\int_1^t -a(1-r)d\partial}[(x^{(1)}(1))^{1-r}+\int_1^t e^{\int_1^\theta a(1-r)d\partial}(1-r)(b_0+b_1\theta)d\theta] \tag{5}$$

Further

$$y(t)=e^{-a(1-r)(t-1)}\{(x^{(1)}(1))^{1-r}+(1-r)e^{-a(1-r)}[\frac{b_0e^{a(1-r)t}}{a(1-r)}-\frac{b_0e^{a(1-r)}}{a(1-r)}+\frac{b_1te^{a(1-r)t}}{a(1-r)}-\frac{b_1e^{a(1-r)t}}{a(1-r)}-\frac{b_1e^{a(1-r)t}}{a^2(1-r)^2}+\frac{b_1e^{a(1-r)}}{a^2(1-r)^2}+\frac{b_1e^{a(1-r)t}}{a(1-r)}-\frac{b_1e^{a(1-r)}}{a(1-r)}]\} \tag{6}$$

The time response function is

$$\hat{x}^{(1)}(t)=\{e^{-a(1-r)(t-1)}[(x^{(1)}(1))^{(1-r)}+(1-r)e^{-a(1-r)}g(t)]\}^{\frac{1}{1-r}}$$

of which

$$g(t)=\frac{b_0e^{at(1-r)}}{a(1-r)}-\frac{b_0e^{a(1-r)}}{a(1-r)}+\frac{b_1te^{a(1-r)t}}{a(1-r)}-\frac{b_1e^{at(1-r)}}{a^2(1-r)^2}+\frac{b_1e^{a(1-r)}}{a^2(1-r)^2}-\frac{b_1e^{a(1-r)}}{a(1-r)}$$

Integrating formula (3) on the basis of $[k-1,k]$ get

$$\int_{k-1}^{k}\frac{dx^{(1)}(t)}{dt}dt+\int_{k-1}^{k}ax^{(1)}(t)dt=\int_{k-1}^{k}(b_0+b_1t)(x^{(1)}(t))^r dt$$

Note $z^{(1)}(k)=\int_{k-1}^{k}x^{(1)}(t)dt$, $z^{(2)}(k)=\int_{k-1}^{k}(x^{(1)}(t))^r dt$, $z^{(3)}(k)=\int_{k-1}^{k}t(x^{(1)}(t))^r dt$

Then

$$z^{(1)}(k)=\int_{k-1}^{k}x^{(1)}(t)dt=px^{(1)}(k)+(1-p)x^{(1)}(k-1)$$

,

$$z^{(2)}(k)=\int_{k-1}^{k}(x^{(1)}(t))^r dt=p(x^{(1)}(k))^r+(1-p)(x^{(1)}(k-1))^r$$

$$z^{(3)}(k)=\int_{k-1}^{k}t(x^{(1)}(t))^r dt=pk(x^{(1)}(k))^r+(1-p)(k-1)(x^{(1)}(k-1))^r$$

Therefore

$$\hat{x}^{(0)}(k)+az^{(1)}(k)=b_0z^{(2)}(k)+b_1z^{(3)}(k)$$

For the given p and r , following the least squares method, we get $(a,b_0,b_1)^T=(G^TG)^{-1}G^TH$,of which

$$G=\begin{bmatrix}-z^{(1)}(2) & z^{(2)}(2) & z^{(3)}(2)\\ -z^{(1)}(3) & z^{(2)}(3) & z^{(3)}(3)\\ \vdots & \vdots & \vdots\\ -z^{(1)}(N) & z^{(2)}(N) & z^{(3)}(N)\end{bmatrix}\qquad H=\begin{bmatrix}x^{(0)}(2)\\ x^{(0)}(3)\\ \vdots\\ x^{(0)}(N)\end{bmatrix}$$

$$\min MAPE=\frac{1}{N-1}\sum_{t=2}^{N}\left|\frac{x^{(0)}(t)-\hat{x}^{(0)}(t)}{x^{(0)}(t)}\right|\times 100\%$$

$$s.t\begin{cases}\hat{x}^{(0)}(t)=\hat{x}^{(1)}(t)-\hat{x}^{(1)}(t-1)\\ \hat{x}^{(1)}(t)=\{e^{-a(1-r)(t-1)}[(x^{(1)}(1))^{1-r}+(1-r)e^{-a(1-r)}g(t)]\}^{\frac{1}{1-r}}\\ g(t)=\frac{b_1te^{a(1-r)t}}{a(1-r)}-\frac{b_1e^{at(1-r)}}{a^2(1-r)^2}+\frac{b_0e^{at(1-r)}}{a(1-r)}+\frac{b_1e^{a(1-r)}}{a^2(1-r)^2}-\frac{b_1e^{a(1-r)}}{a(1-r)}-\frac{b_0e^{a(1-r)}}{a(1-r)}\\ (a,b_0,b_1)^T=(G^TG)^{-1}G^TH\\ r\neq 0,1\end{cases}\tag{7}$$

When $h=2$,

$$\frac{dx^{(1)}(t)}{dt}+ax^{(1)}(t)=(b_0+b_1t+b_2t^2)(x^{(1)}(t))^r\tag{8}$$

is called the whitening equation for the GM(1,1,t²,p) power model. The same can be proved that its time response function is

$$\hat{x}^{(1)}(t) = \{e^{-a(1-r)(t-1)}[(x^{(1)}(1))^{1-r} + (1-r)e^{-a(1-r)}f(t)]\}^{\frac{1}{1-r}}$$

Where

$$f(t) = \frac{b_2 t^2 e^{at(1-r)}}{a(1-r)} - \frac{2b_2 t e^{at(1-r)}}{a^2(1-r)^2} + \frac{b_1 t e^{a(1-r)}}{a(1-r)} + \frac{2b_2 e^{at(1-r)}}{a^3(1-r)^3} - \frac{b_1 e^{at(1-r)}}{a^2(1-r)^2} + \frac{b_0 e^{at(1-r)}}{a(1-r)} - \frac{2b_2 e^{a(1-r)}}{a^3(1-r)^3} + \frac{2b_2 e^{a(1-r)}}{a^2(1-r)^2} - \frac{b_2 e^{a(1-r)}}{a(1-r)} + \frac{b_1 e^{a(1-r)}}{a^2(1-r)^2} - \frac{b_1 e^{a(1-r)}}{a(1-r)} - \frac{b_0 e^{a(1-r)}}{a(1-r)}$$

4 Example analysis

The transaction scale of the fresh e-commerce industry is very important to its industry development trend, so this paper models and analyzes the transaction scale of the fresh e-commerce industry to further promote the development of the fresh e-commerce industry.

Table 1. Transaction scale of fresh e-commerce industry from 2010 to 2019.

Unit: 100 million yuan

Year	2010	2011	2012	2013	2014	2015	2016	2017	2018	2019	2020	2021
Transaction scale	4.2	10.5	40.5	130.2	289.8	542	913.9	1402.8	1950	2554.5	3641.3	4658.1

Data source: Net Economics, Prospective Industry Research Institute

4.1 Select the dimensions of the best predictive model

In order to improve the accuracy of the model as much as possible, the optimal data dimension must be determined, this paper aims to predict the transaction scale of the fresh e-commerce industry in 2019, establish GM (1, 1, t^h, p) power model of different dimensions, and determine the most suitable data dimension by the size of the average error, the specific values are shown in Table 2:

Table 2. Comparison of accuracy of models with different dimensions.

Data dimension	Traditional GM(1,1) power model			GM(1,1,t^h,p) power model					
				GM(1,1,t,p) power model			GM(1,1,t²,p) power model		
	Simulation error	forecast error	average error	simulation error	forecast error	average error	simulation error	forecast error	average error
9 (2010-2018)	10.5%	2.1%	6.3%	2.3%	5.6%	4.0%	5.5%	1.5%	3.5%
8 (2011-2018)	3.4%	0.5%	2.0%	1.1%	5.4%	3.3%	1.2%	3.1%	2.1%
7 (2012-2018)	2.1%	2.2%	2.1%	1.3%	4.2%	2.8%	0.8%	1.7%	1.2%
6 (2013-2018)	2.2%	2.7%	2.5%	1.1%	3.2%	2.1%	0.4%	0.4%	0.4%
5 (2014-2018)	2.4%	3.2%	2.8%	0.4%	1.7%	0.3%	0.2%	1.5%	0.9%
4 (2015-2018)	1.8%	4.7%	3.2%	0.0%	0.3%	0.2%	0.7%	2.6%	1.6%

Note: (1) Forecast error refers to the prediction error in 2019;

4.2 The average error is the average of the simulation error and the prediction error.

It can be seen from Table 2 that the improved GM(1,1,th,p) power model can significantly improve the fitting and prediction effect of the model compared with the traditional GM(1,1) power model, so in this case, the GM(1,1,t,p) power model is used to establish the model, and the data dimension is 4 dimensions.

4.3 Establish a metabolic GM (1,1,t,p) power model

According to the results of Table 2, the data for the 2015 year is removed, the data for 2019 is added, and then the GM(1,1,t,p) power model is established, which is the first metabolic GM(1,1,t,p) power model, and so on for the second and third metabolic iterations. In 2022, the transaction scale of fresh e-commerce industry will reach 562.5 billion yuan.

5 Conclusion

In order to be more in line with the principle of new information first, the metabolism theory is combined with the GM $(1,1,t^h,p)$ power model, and it is applied for the first time in the prediction of the transaction scale of the fresh e-commerce industry, and the examples show that the improved model can improve the prediction and simulation error well, and further expand the application scope of the power model, which has certain practical significance and application prospects. In addition, although China's fresh e-commerce is still in its infancy, with the popularization of the Internet and the development of e-commerce, the future fresh e-commerce has great development prospects, fresh e-commerce practitioners should follow the trend of the times, keep pace with the times, continue to innovate, and enhance the core competitiveness of the brand.

Reference

1. Y. Zhang, Y. Liu. Rese. Model. J. Pres. Proc. **10**. 95 (2021)
2. J. Ma, Z. Sun. Rese. Model. J. Logi. Tech. **13**. 71 (2022)
3. K. Li. Rese. Proc. J. Shan. Agri. Econ. **17**. 134 (2021)
4. X. Du, S. Leung, J. Zhang. Dema. Mach. J. Inte. Scie. **3**. 556 (2013)
5. L. Huang, G. Xie, W. Zhao. Regi. Appr. J. Comp. Syst.1(2021)
6. Y. Li, Y. He, Z. Wu, H. Zheng. Fore. Epid. J. Shop. Mode. **16**. 1(2020)

Research of virtualized log management system in communication dispatching center of power grid

Jianwen Ling*, and *Yafei* Luo

Guangzhou Power Supply Bureau, Guangdong Power Grid Co., Ltd. China Southern Power Grid, P.R. China

Keywords. Log, Log management, Log system, Virtualization.

Abstract. Logs happen every day. They record all kinds of events of current network and its management facilities. Communication dispatchers can use it to aware network or facility failures. In the purpose of improving awareness of communication network and its management facilities, this research is focusing on a log management system for different types of communication devices and network management servers. From log system architecture, to actual situations of log collection. Then, the distribution of system, from bare-metal servers to virtual machines. Most a virtualized log management system is deployed and tested in a dispatching center of power grid.

1 Introduction

Device and system logs provide a huge amount of information of current network and its management facilities. They record noteworthy events, such as network link down, device hardware failure, unauthorized login, but also trivial events, such as customer port up/down, network path switching, periodically system updates.

Currently, communication dispatchers monitor more than a dozen networks via different network management systems. In order to aware the network failure and dispatch maintainers promptly, communication dispatchers check every network management system periodically. They spent a large amount of time in differentiating system logs to find out whether there is a failure in those networks or management facilities.

With complete logs, communication dispatchers can analyze current status of the network, also backtrace the past status. In conjunction with several properly rulesets, machines can automatically reconstruct events, detect network failures, and aware system intrusions. Furtherly, provide guidance to communication dispatchers to draw up a strategy to settle such events.

* Corresponding author: lingjw@guangzhou.csg.cn

Hence, a log management system can effectively reduce communication dispatchers' checking time, aware emergence or major failures when such events occur. Comparing to bare-metal deployment, virtualization technology is introduced in the last.

2 System design

In this research, the log management system is design and implemented in four major modules, including log collection, log aggregation and storage, log analyzing, and log monitor.

2.1 Log collection module

This module is focusing on collecting logs from different varieties of communication devices and network management facilities. For different types of communication devices use different logging interfaces, this module supports syslog, SNMP (Simple Network Management Protocol), CORBA (Common Object Request Broker Architecture), etc. Also, this module supports IPMI (Intelligent Platform Management Interface) events, Windows and Linux logs in order to monitor the status of network management servers.

For security reasons, computers and networks are divided into the production control zone and the management information zone in power grid enterprises. Production control zone and management information zone are isolated by forward and reverse isolation devices. [1] Hence, log collection module should be deployed in both zones separately.

2.2 Log aggregation and storage module

Since logs collected from different devices and facilities have different formats, saving them directly is not suitable for fast searching and analyzing. This module not only saves the original logs, but transforms them into a uniform data table.

Several key information is included in the data table.

(1) Event name, which can be extracted from alarm name or keywords in logs.

(2) Event source, which helps identify the event occurred from which network, which device and which part of the device.

(3) Event occurred time and resumed time, which helps analyzing related events and crucial to event monitoring and statistic.

(4) Comments, for communication dispatchers to add memorandum and link such events to operation records, failure records, or scheduled records.

2.3 Log analyzing module

Tens of thousands of logs generate every day. It's impossible for communication dispatchers to check every log to find out emergence or major failures. This module automatically analyzes related logs generated in a short period of time.

For transmission network and data network devices, e.g., SDH/OTN network elements, routers, and switches, several network links down at the same time or in a very short period of time, and related hardware does not report any hardware failure, that probably means the optical fiber cable, which carrying such network links, is broken.

For network management facilities, e.g., Linux servers and Windows servers, remotely login event occurred without authorized maintenance operation records, that probably means the system is breached.

After analyzing related logs, this module can identify the root of those logs, additionally provides guidance to settle such events.

2.4 Log monitor module

This module provides root logs view, emergence and major alarm logs view, and original logs view of each network and facility separately. When root logs occurred, this module plays a warning sound to remind communication dispatchers.

Both B/S (Browser/Server) and C/S (Client/Server) structures are allowed in the management information zone in power grid enterprises, but B/S structure is not recommended in the production control zone. Hence, log monitor module is based on C/S structure.

3 Log reporting and collecting

According to the provisions, networks and servers are divided into two zones, the production control zone and the management information zone, in communication dispatching center of power grid. Furtherly, the production control zone is divided into the control area (security area I) and the non-control area (security area II), the management information zone is divided into security area III and security area IV.

The control area (security area I) and the non-control area (security area II) are under logical isolation. Systems and devices in different areas of the production control zone can connect through firewalls. The same logical isolation happens between security area III and security area IV.

However, systems and devices in the production control zone and the management information zone can only transfer text messages through isolation devices.

Currently, SDH/MSTP (Synchronous Digital Hierarchy/Multi-Service Transport Platform) optical transmission network, power dispatching data network, communication network for power distribution grid, etc. and their management systems are deployed in security area I. Communication power supply supervisory control system is deployed in security area II. Power integrated data network, unified communication network and their management systems are deployed in security area III. [2] Log management system collects logs from those devices and systems in different ways.

SDH/MSTP optical transmission network devices report event logs and alarms to management systems, and the optical transmission network management system provides a northbound interface using CORBA. Log management system should connect to the northbound interface to get logs reported by network management system.

Data network devices, e.g., routers and switches, can be configured to report every log through syslog and SNMP Trap. Just set syslog and SNMP Trap target to log management system, and most of logs can be collected. However, syslog and SNMP are running over UDP (User Datagram Protocol) but not TCP (Transmission Control Protocol), the data packets maybe lost in transmission. Log management system should periodically acquire full logs from data network devices' log buffer.

Linus server can be configured to report logs through syslog, or log management system acquire log files through SSH (Secure Shell Protocol).

Windows servers can use SCOM (System Center Operations Manager) or WEF (Windows Event Forwarding) to gather logs. However, both SCOM and WEF are mostly deployed on Windows Server, not suitable for a unified log management system. Therefor to get Windows Event Logs third-party agents, e.g., Evtsys (Eventlog to Syslog Utility by Purdue University), Rsyslog Windows Agent and NXLog

Logs of network management facilities, e.g., physical servers, can be acquired through IPMI interface.

After gathering logs in the production control zone, log collection module should forward all the logs to the log aggregation and storage module deployed in the management information zone through isolation devices. Then, logs can be processed in the management information zone only.

4 Virtualized deployment

As already stated in previous sections, one log collection module is deployed in the production control zone, and a log management system, including all four modules, is deployed in the management information zone. They can be deployed on bare-metal servers or virtual machines.

If log modules and system are deployed on bare-metal servers, those physical hosting devices are dedicated. All computing resources, including CPU, RAM and disk space, are exclusively used for log modules and system. Although bare-metal server provides high performance, there are two major disadvantages of this deployment way in real world.

Firstly, there are more than one hundred network management and security monitoring services in communication dispatching center of power grid. If each service or system occupies one bare-metal server, there is not enough space for such large number of servers in the data center of communication dispatching center. Furtherly, even though there are enough space, the power consumption is huge, and the UPS (Uninterruptible Power Source) would not provide long-enough run time.

Secondly, in the data center of communication dispatching center, all of the bare-metal servers are high performance servers, e.g., hundreds of CPU cores, several Terabytes of RAM. Such a log module or system will not cost so many resources. It will be a huge waste of investment using bare-metal servers for log module and system deployment.

On the contrary, deploying on virtual machines provides more benefits.

Firstly, virtualization saves space and power. One high performance server is capable of hosting dozens of virtual machines. In each security area, only three or four high performance servers can provide enough computing resources for all network management and security monitoring services, including log management system.

Secondly, virtualization saves time. A new deployment of virtual machine only takes a few minutes, when ordering and setting up a new bare-metal server will take days. When hardware or software failure occurred, virtual machines protected with High Availability or Fault Tolerance can recover in minutes even seconds. However, it will take hours or even days for bare-metal servers.

Lastly, virtualization helps maintainers. When computing resources of a service is not enough, it only takes seconds for maintainers to assign more vCPU, RAM or disk space to the virtual machine on which running such service. But if the service is running on a bare-metal server, it will take hours.

In summary, it's better to deploy a log collection module on virtual machine in the production control zone and a log management system on virtual machine in the management information zone.

5 Summary

In this article, the need of communication dispatchers was identified. Then the architecture of a log management system was proposed, and log collecting methods were introduced. The practical application of a virtualized log management system was found. The reliability and stability of this system are tested. And it has been running in a communication dispatching center of power grid for more than two years.

References

1. Standardization Administration of the People's Republic of China, *Guidelines of cyber security protection for electric power system supervision and control*, **GB/T 36572-2018**, (2018)
2. China Southern Power Grid, *Technical specification for communication network management and service application system of CSG*, **Q/CSG 1204037-2018**, (2018)

Design and implementation of automatic sorting car based on OpenMV

Lin Zhu, and *Yan* Yang*

School of Computer and Information Engineering, Beijing Agricultural College, China

Abstract. The system uses the OpenMV algorithm module combined with the k-means framework through the Euclidean distance formula to facilitate the automation of logistics sorting, which identifies the color of logistics parcels in the LAB color space. It sends the identified color information to the motion drive module, which sorts and transports the logistics parcels to the designated storage area. The fusion of algorithms allows the system to identify colors and transportation accurately.

1 Introduction

The development trend for intelligent logistics is the logistics sorting trolley, which is significant for bottleneck issues like excessive human dependence and poor operational efficiency in e-commerce logistics[1]. Therefore, the research on this topic is carried out by automatically recognizing the pre-set tasks, activating the camera for image acquisition and color recognition, running the main control program in the vision recognition module, and sending the movement control command to the motion drive module to transport the sorted objects to the designated area. If the object color is not recognized, no movement command will be sent until the color of the sorted object is recognized, and this process is repeated until the object color is recognized. In order to facilitate the automation of logistics sorting, the motor module drives the logistics sorting to the appropriate storage space.

2 Overall solution design of automatic sorting trolley

The sorted objects are sorted using color recognition in this study. Red, yellow, and blue are the primary colors for the sorted objects, and red, yellow, and blue are also the three pre-determined fixed transport lanes for the three things to be sorted. When sorting items in a factory setting, the simplest sorting transport channel can significantly lower the factory operation cost[5]. This is taking into account the actual application background of the topic. In Fig1. the schematic diagram is displayed.

* Corresponding author: 20058010@bua.edu.cn

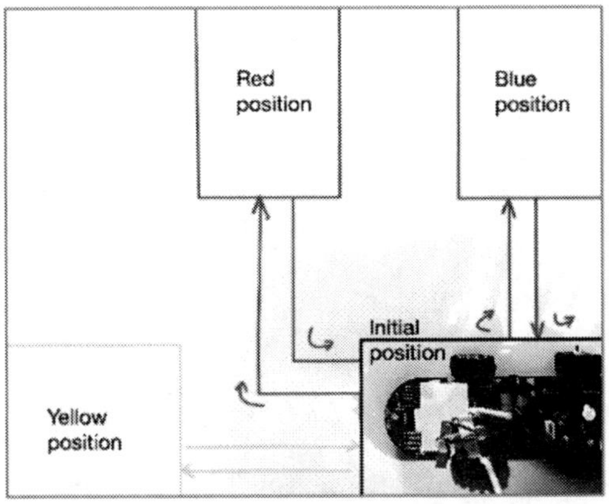

Fig. 1. Overall solution diagram.

2.1 Visual recognition module

The OpenMV3 Cam M7 model's machine vision module is used in this project to carry out the task of object classification and color recognition. The image processing module's CPU is an ARM Cortex M7 processor, which uses the module's sensors to transmit various image and video data to the microcontroller, which then processes, recognizes, and categorizes the images.

2.2 Electric drive module

The system, which is in charge of transporting the sorted objects to the prescribed placement area, uses the Arduino UNO R3 and L293D motor driver modules as the cart driving hardware. The L293D quad high-current half-H driver is used to connect the positive and negative terminals of the two DC motors in the motor drive circuit, which drives two DC motors using four PWM digital IO ports as the drive interface[9-10].Fig. 2 depicts the general hardware layout of the system.

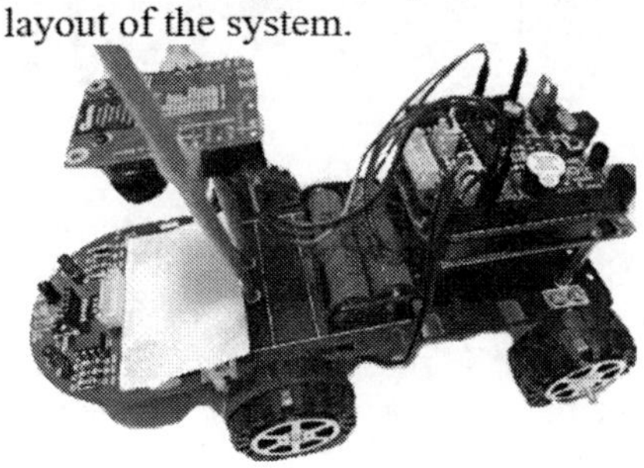

Fig. 2. Physical view of automatic sorting trolley.

3 Key technologies

3.1 Color recognition algorithm

To acquire photos of the target objects, a machine vision system based on OpenMV[4] is developed. The captured target images are then transformed from RGB to LAB color model space. To enhance the color segmentation of the target object, the K-means clustering technique is used in the target object image recognition and segmentation. When compared to conventional image segmentation methods for embedded system environments, this approach, which separates color blocks of the same color in the image, has the advantages of a small model and quick speed.

The lowest of these three distances is determined to be the color of the pixel point in the LAB color model by measuring the Euclidean distance between each pixel point and the average of the three colors (red, yellow, and blue)[2]. The following equation can be used to determine how far apart the red, yellow, and blue hues are from each pixel point:

$$\Delta E = \sqrt{(\Delta L)^2 + (\Delta a)^2 + (\Delta b)^2} \tag{1}$$

where E represents the color difference from the reference color and L/a/b represents, correspondingly, the color difference between the two colors in various components. By selecting the shortest distance out of the three distances, the color of the pixel is established to be one of these colors.

The fundamental idea behind the K-means clustering segmentation algorithm, which is an unsupervised learning technique[8], is to first randomly choose one pixel point from K pixel points as the initial cluster center, and then to compute th e Euclidean distance d2 by applying the Euclidean distance to the other pixel points. The computed pixel points are grouped into the class that corresponds to the location of the closest cluster center. The clusters are then divided again until the sum of squared errors within the class is minimized, at which time the mean value of the pixel points after categorization replaces the original center[6].As seen in Fig 3. the image is divided into pixel points of the same color.

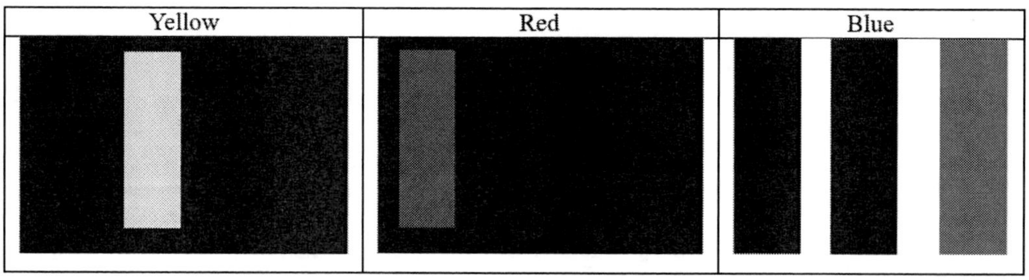

Fig. 3. Color segmentation results.

The majority of the image processing operations are included in the OpenMV vision module that was used in this project. The core algorithmic function in this project, find blobs[3], locates and returns all of the color blocks in the image. All of the returned objects will be merged by this function. It must be called multiple times in order to recognize additional colors. Set all of the aforementioned parameters in this system to their default levels, then just add color thresholds. Such as yellow, which the blobs y object receives from img.find blobs([yellow threshold]).

The find blobs function of OpenMV is used to compare the color value with the threshold during the color recognition process. If the color value is within the threshold, the color code r, b, and y are then sent to the motion driver module via the serial port. The color recognition process begins by counting the color that occupies the largest area in the current region of interest. No more color recognition will be carried out until the motion driver module idle instruction flag=0[7] is received in order to avoid control instruction conflict.

3.2 Serial communication design

Through a serial UART and a TTL level connection, the visual recognition module OpenMV and the motion driver module Arduino UNO R3 communicate. Set the baud rate to 19200 and activate UART1 in the OpenMV configuration for the visual recognition module. Enable softSerial1 and set the baud rate to 19200 in the motion driver module settings.

When a red paper jam is detected, the vision recognition module sends the character "r" over the serial port; when a yellow paper jam is detected, the character "y" is sent through the serial port; and when a blue paper jam is detected, the character "b" is sent through the serial port.

3.3 Motor drive circuit

The Arduino's analog IO port is used to output the motor's control signal as a PWM pulse-width modulated signal. L239D then amplifies the output signal to increase the current, which is then supplied to the DC motor's internal circuit to drive motor rotation. To meet the goal of offering low speed and great torque, a matching gearbox is additionally provided.

Since the amount of friction that a car's tires have with the ground changes depending on the scene, this system's motor drive design adjusts the PWM pulses' parameters using the enumeration method, and then sets the PWM pulse value of the control signal for the two motors to 130 (the Arduino analog port's PWM output range is 0–255).

When serial information is received in the serial port cache, the data is removed for command parsing, and the path is moved in accordance with the corresponding color code. The motion driver module serial port uses a soft serial port that is simulated by the IO port, and the baud rate is set to 19200.

4 Conclusion

The automatic sorting trolley built on OpenMV is designed using image processing, motor control, and serial communication technologies. A vision recognition module and a motion drive module make up the system. Serial communication is employed to communicate the target color information and regulate the motor, and the LAB color space model is used to realize the recognition of the color scale of goods.

The research work of this paper supported by the Beijing scientific research program: Research on Intelligent identification system Of peach pests based on Internet Of things(km201810020018) .

References

1. X.Y.Liu, Adhesion, **47**, 109-112 (2021)
2. H.J.Zhang, Fujian J, **27**, 146-147 (2011)
3. X.H.Wang, Zhejiang Sci-Tech University, **02**, 54 (2020)
4. N.N.Huang, Acta Agric.Univ.Jiangxi, **07**, 61 (2020)
5. D.Wang, *Manufacturing Automation*(WJST), **43**, 6-9+20 (2021)
6. K.Y.Chen, C.Y.Wu, Z.H.Guan, H.T.Li, G.Wang, Jiangsu J, **37**, 1425-1435 (2021)
7. S.J.Xia, H.Yang, W.Q.Ai, Journal of Changshu Institute of Technology, **35**, 59-64 (2021)

8. Q.R.Ge, Xidian University, **05**, 59 (2012)
9. T.G.Jiang, Shenyang University of Technology, **02**, 81 (2015)
10. Y.W.Tian, R.X.Lv, Y.J.Li, China Science and Technology Information, **02**, 81-83 (2020)

Application of structural rapid simulation technology in railway wagon equipment

Chunlei Zhao[1,*], *Xiangwei* Li[1,2] , *Qiang* Zhang[1,2] , *Shangchao* Zhao[1,3], and *Shuai* Wang[1,2]

[1]Simulation calculation analysis,Technology Department,CRRC Qiqihar Rolling Stock CO.LTD, China
[2]Rail vehicle engineering, College of Rolling Stock Engineering, Dalian Jiaotong University, China
[3]Material research, School of Materials Science and Engineering, Tianjin University, China

Abstract. In the traditional finite element simulation analysis, the designer spend a lot of time and energy to establish a reasonable finite element model. This approach is not suitable for rapid iterative updates and optimizations of products.Therefore, for the needs of rapid simulation of structure,this article introduced the basic principle of implicit boundary method and the characteristics of different analytical methods.The author explored and practiced the application of structural rapid simulation technology based on meshless method.Through the comparative study of simulation examples, The results of meshless analysis and finite element analysis are consistent. But the meshless method increase analysis efficiency by 92.5%.The research results have certain practical guiding significance for the application of structural rapid simulation in the engineering field.

1 Introduction

At present, the mainstream simulation software is based on the theory of finite element analysis. The most critical link in the traditional finite element simulation analysis is to establish a reasonable finite element model. The quality of the finite element model directly determines the accuracy of the result and the calculation run time[1]. For specific analysis objects, a finite element model of appropriate scale should be established in line with the actual situation. It is necessary to comprehensively consider the structural design, force transmission path, working conditions, material properties and other aspects of the equipment. The time taken is longer and typically accounts for about 70% of the entire finite element analysis process. Therefore, how to achieve rapid structural simulation by improving the efficiency of preprocessing is the key to shortening the entire structural simulation cycle. It is also an urgent problem to be solved in the field of engineering at present[2].

In view of the requirements of rapid structural simulation, this paper introduces the rapid structural simulation technology based on meshing. Taking the typical railway wagon body structure as the object, the result accuracy and solution efficiency of meshless fast simulation and traditional finite element simulation are compared[3]. It provides an

* Corresponding author: zhaochunlei123@163.com

engineering practice basis for the rapid simulation of complex railway wagon equipment structures.

2 The need for structural rapid simulation

At present, the complexity of railway freight car products is getting higher and higher, and the time span of the development process will be longer, and it will generally go through the process of scheme demonstration, preliminary design, detailed design, and test verification[4]. In the process of continuous refinement and iteration of product design schemes, multiple rounds of simulation analysis are generally carried out to ensure that the performance of the product is fully verified at the design stage. However, traditional finite element analysis methods require a lot of time and effort to build a suitable finite element model[5]. Once the design changes, it needs to be remodeled. This results in a great waste of manpower and material resources and time.

In the early stage of product development, it is the stage with the fastest frequency and the largest number of iterations of the design plan. Simulation analysis takes too long to affect the development progress of the entire product. Through the early rapid simulation iteration to drive the continuous optimization and improvement of the structural design, this stage does not have to be too rigid to the high precision requirements of the simulation results. The simulation results obtained quickly can verify the rationality of the design and make a preliminary evaluation of the structural performance of the product.

Therefore, in the early stage of product development where the scheme has not yet converged, the structure has subversive changes, and the design needs to be continuously updated and refined, a more time-saving structure rapid simulation technology is required than the traditional finite element simulation method. Faster and shorter analysis processes accelerate iterative optimization of designs. It can effectively improve the development efficiency of products and reduce the cost of manpower and material resources[6].

3 Structural rapid simulation technology based on meshless method

3.1 Simulation software based on meshless technology

MIDAS MeshFree is a new simulation design software developed based on the implicit boundary method (IBM)[7]. The software now supports static analysis, modal analysis, linear dynamic analysis, thermodynamic analysis and materials or geometric nonlinear analysis[8].

The software is mesh-free for the user. However, the software still meshes when it runs internally, but it uses a structured mesh generated based on the principle of implicit boundary method. As shown in Figure 1, the software generates a background area based on the size of the geometry and divides the mesh elements on this area. According to the different positions of the grid elements, they are divided into external elements, boundary elements and internal elements[9]. Among them, the external element does not participate in the calculation, the internal element adopts the processing method consistent with the finite element method, and the boundary element adopts the implicit boundary method. This method can solve the problem that the mesh is difficult to handle during the finite element analysis of complex structures. Very regular mesh elements can be generated without simplifying the model, greatly reducing the analysis cycle.

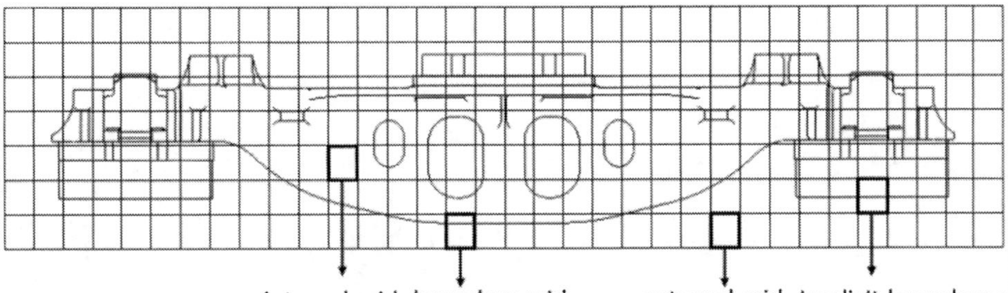

Fig. 1. Structured grids based on implicit boundary method.

3.2 The principle of implicit boundary method

MIDAS MeshFree uses the implicit boundary method.Firstly this method requires the construction of the D function.The D function is constructed as follows.

$$u = u^s + u^a = DNq^g + Nq^a \tag{1}$$

$$\sigma = \sigma^s + \sigma^a \tag{2}$$

u^a is the boundary value function; D Is Dirichlet function; N Is a shape function; q^g Is the mesh variable approximated on the mesh; q^a is the forced displacement of the node. The purpose of the constructor is to satisfy the boundary conditions.The expression of the D function is as follows:

$$D(\varphi) = \begin{cases} 0 & \varphi \le 0 \\ 1-(1-\dfrac{\varphi}{\delta}) & 0 \le \varphi \le \delta \\ 1 & \varphi \ge \delta \end{cases} \tag{3}$$

In the D function, φ function is an implicit equation used to describe the boundary. When this expression is $\varphi \le 0$, the value of the function is 0, indicating that the grid is on the boundary or outside the analysis domain; When this expression is $0 \le \varphi \le \delta$, δ is a smaller constant, generally $\delta \approx 10^{-5}$ or smaller, indicating that the grid is in a narrow band near the boundary; When this expression is $\varphi \ge \delta$, it indicates that the mesh is inside the analytical domain.

The calculation process of stiffness matrix is as follows.According to the virtual work equation, the following expression can be obtained.

$$\int_\Omega \{\delta\varepsilon\}^T \{\sigma\} \delta\Omega = \int_{\Gamma_t} \{\delta u\}^T \{t\} d\Gamma + \int_\Omega \{\delta u\}^T \{b\} d\Omega \tag{4}$$

In the above expression, $\{\sigma\}$ represents the stress tensor; $\{t\}$ represents quantity oriented; $\{b\}$ represents a force vector. Bring this expression into formula (2) to get the following expression:

$$\int_\Omega \{\delta\varepsilon\}^T \{\sigma^s\} d\Omega = \int_{\Gamma_t} \{\delta u\}^T \{t\} d\Gamma + \int_\Omega \{\delta u\}^T \{b\} d\Omega - \int_\Omega \{\delta\varepsilon\}^T \{\sigma^a\} d\Omega \tag{5}$$

The stiffness matrix expression can be obtained from the above formula.

$$[K_e] = \int_{V_e} [B]^T [C][B] dV \tag{6}$$

If the analysis problem is linear elastic, the strain matrix expression is as follows:

$$[B]=\begin{bmatrix} D_u\frac{\partial N_1}{\partial x}+N_1\frac{\partial D_u}{\partial x} & 0 & \cdots & D_u\frac{\partial N_n}{\partial x}+N_n\frac{\partial D_u}{\partial x} & 0 \\ 0 & D_v\frac{\partial N_1}{\partial y}+N_1\frac{\partial D_v}{\partial y} & \cdots & 0 & D_v\frac{\partial N_n}{\partial y}+N_n\frac{\partial D_v}{\partial y} \\ D_u\frac{\partial N_1}{\partial y}+N_1\frac{\partial D_u}{\partial y} & D_v\frac{\partial N_1}{\partial x}+N_1\frac{\partial D_v}{\partial x} & \cdots & D_u\frac{\partial N_1}{\partial y}+N_1\frac{\partial D_u}{\partial y} & D_v\frac{\partial N_1}{\partial x}+N_1\frac{\partial D_v}{\partial x} \end{bmatrix} \quad (7)$$

For the internal grid element, since the value of D function is 1, the strain matrix becomes the following formula:

$$[B]_{3x2m}=\begin{bmatrix} \frac{\partial N_1}{\partial x_1} & 0 & \cdots & \frac{\partial N_m}{\partial x_1} & 0 \\ 0 & \frac{\partial N_1}{\partial x_2} & \cdots & 0 & \frac{\partial N_m}{\partial x_2} \\ \frac{\partial N_1}{\partial x_2} & \frac{\partial N_1}{\partial x_1} & \cdots & \frac{\partial N_m}{\partial x_2} & \frac{\partial N_m}{\partial x_1} \end{bmatrix} \quad (8)$$

In the above expression, N_i is a shape function. m represents the number of grid element nodes. Therefore, the general finite element method is used to deal with the internal elements[10].

For boundary elements without boundary conditions, the value of D function is 1. This kind of element is divided into two parts, with and without materials. The element stiffness matrix is calculated by adjusting the weight coefficient and the position of the Gaussian integration point. The Gaussian integral formula of the stiffness matrix is as follows.

$$[K]_{2m\times 2m}=\sum_{j=1}^{n_y}\sum_{i=1}^{n_x}\omega_i\omega_j[B(\xi_i,\ \eta_i)]^T[C][B(\xi_i,\ \eta_i)] \quad (9)$$

In the above expression, n_x、n_y is the number of Gaussian integration points in the x direction and y direction of the element; (ξ_i,η_i) is the position of the Gaussian integration point.

For boundary elements with boundary conditions, the displacement expression contains the D function, so the strain matrix contains the derivative of the D function. Because the value of δ is very small, the influence of the derivative of D function and D function on the stiffness matrix cannot be ignored. The strain matrix is converted into two parts, and the expression of $[B_1]$ and $[B_2]$ is as follows[11]:

$$[B_1]_{3x2m}=\begin{bmatrix} D_1\frac{\partial N_1}{\partial x_1} & 0 & \cdots & D_1\frac{\partial N_1}{\partial x_1} & 0 \\ 0 & D_2\frac{\partial N_1}{\partial x_2} & \cdots & 0 & D_2\frac{\partial N_m}{\partial x_2} \\ D_1\frac{\partial N_1}{\partial X_2} & D_2\frac{\partial N_1}{\partial x_1} & \cdots & D_1\frac{\partial N_m}{\partial X_2} & D_2\frac{\partial N_m}{\partial x_1} \end{bmatrix} \quad (10)$$

$$[B_2]_{3x2m}=\begin{bmatrix} N_1\frac{\partial D_1}{\partial x_1} & 0 & \cdots & N_m\frac{\partial D_1}{\partial x_1} & 0 \\ 0 & N_1\frac{\partial D_2}{\partial x_2} & \cdots & 0 & N_m\frac{\partial D_2}{\partial x_2} \\ N_1\frac{\partial D_1}{\partial X_2} & N_2\frac{\partial D_2}{\partial x_1} & \cdots & N_m\frac{\partial D_1}{\partial X_2} & N_m\frac{\partial D_2}{\partial x_1} \end{bmatrix} \quad (11)$$

$$[B]=[B_1]+[B_2] \quad (12)$$

Accordingly, the stiffness matrix becomes as follows:

$$
\begin{gathered}
[K_e]=[K_1]+[K_2]+[K_2]^T+[K_3] \\
[K_1]=\int_{V_e}[B_1]^T[C][B_1]dV \\
[K_2]=\int_{V_e}[B_1]^T[C][B_2]dV \\
[K_3]=\int_{V_e}[B_2]^T[C][B_2]dV
\end{gathered}
\quad (13)
$$

The $[K_1]$ matrix only contains $[B_1]$ matrix. $[K_1]$ is related to D function itself and derivative of shape function. Only the entity part of the element is not zero. Therefore, the same calculation method as that of element matrix without boundary conditions can be adopted.

The $[K_2]$ matrix contains the derivatives of the D function and shape function, while the D function is non-zero only in the narrow band region, and its width is δ . The calculation of the $[K_2]$ matrix can be converted into line integral.

The calculation method of the $[K_3]$ matrix is similar to the $[K_2]$ matrix.

After calculating $[K_1]$、$[K_2]$and$[K_3]$, the sum of these matrices is the stiffness matrix of the boundary element with boundary conditions. In fact, for the principle of MIDAS MeshFree soft, the problems to be solved are all three-dimensional. The above derivation method can be extended to three-dimensional space.

The function of boundary function is to make the constructed displacement function meet the forced displacement. Using shape function to construct displacement function can ensure the completeness of solution.

$$
u^a=\sum_i N_i u_i^a \quad (13)
$$

N_i is the shape function of the element; u_i^a is the forced displacement of the i node of the element.When a forced displacement($u^a=\xi$) is imposed on the boundary of the structure, it is necessary to impose a forced displacement on all the element nodes through which the boundary passes. The forced displacement imposed by other irrelevant element nodes is zero.

3.3 Comparison with traditional finite element simulation analysis methods

In order to meet the requirements of rapid structural simulation, the meshless simulation has been reformed in principle. The pre-processing content in traditional finite element simulation is greatly reduced. As shown in Table 1, the finite element simulation is compared with the meshless simulation from the perspectives of method principle, specific operation, application occasions, etc.

Table 1. Comparison between finite element simulation and meshless simulation.

Project	Finite element simulation	Meshless simulation
Method principle	finit element method	the implicit boundary method
The geometry model	a lot of simplification is needed	the full model features are retained
Element type	select the element type based on the model simplified form	no element type
Mesh division	the density, shape, distribution of the mesh need to be controlled	no need to divide the mesh manually

Contact and connection	to define and create contact pairs or connection element for simulation	automatically create connections based on contact types
Boundary condition	created according to actual working conditions	created according to actual working conditions
Solution precision	high precision	medium high precision
Applicable occasions	in the middle and late stage of design	early design
Simulation tools	ANSYS	MIDAS Meshfree

As shown in Figure 2, geometric simplification and mesh generation in traditional finite element simulation require a lot of time. However, meshless simulation avoids these two tasks, so the time required for simulation has been greatly reduced as a whole. Designers can test more design iterations in a shorter time to analyze and verify the feasibility of more solutions[12].

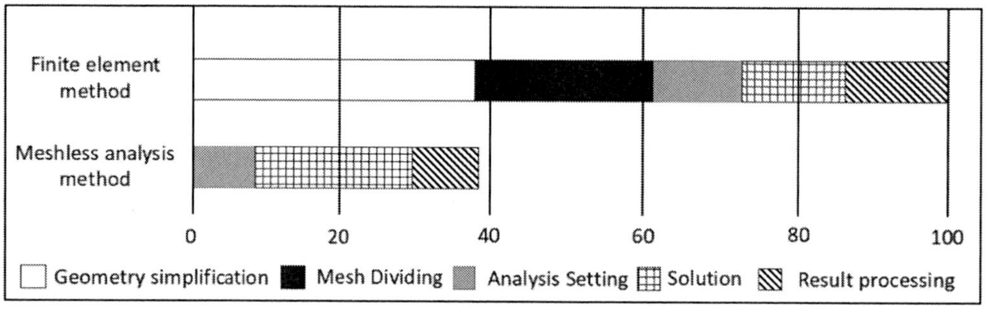

Fig. 2. Comparison of simulation time consumption.

4 Application examples of rapid structural simulation

4.1 Simulation analysis object

Taking the C70E body of railway freight car as the simulation analysis object, the car body has a typical railway freight car equipment structure. The car body is mainly composed of underframe, side wall, end wall and other structures. The car body is of welded structure. As shown in Figure 3. The equipment structure is made of stainless steel.

Fig. 3. Three dimensional model of C70E railway freight car body.

The stiffness and strength performance of the object are analyzed and verified by using the meshless simulation analysis tool MIDAS MeshFree and the traditional finite element simulation tool ANSYS. The accuracy of simulation results and the effectiveness of simulation work are compared.

4.2 Precision comparison of simulation results

According to TB/T3550.2-2019 Specification for Strength Design and Test Appraisal of Rolling Stock - Body, the calculation analysis of the static strength of the body are carried out[13][14].ANSYS and MIDAS MeshFree were used to calculate and analyze the static strength and stiffness of the model.In this specification, there are mainly four calculation conditions[15].The stress nephogram and displacement nephogram of calculation results are shown in Table 2 and Table 3.The maximum values of the four working conditions are compared in Table 4, and the relative error is calculated.

Table 2. Stress nephogram comparison.

Calculation condition	**Stress nephogram**		**Max stress position**
	ANSYS	MIDAS MeshFree	
Condition 1		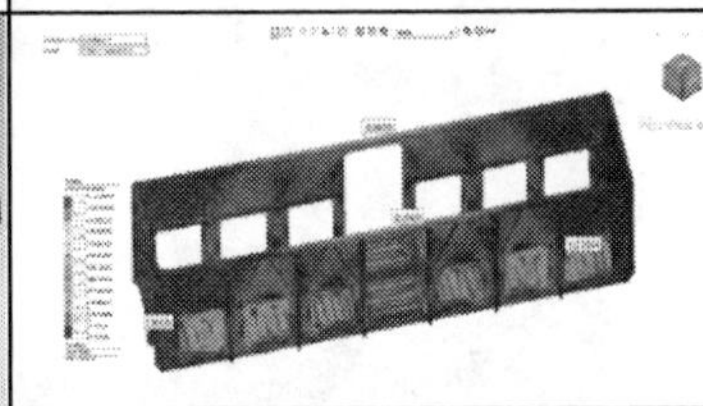	the same position
Condition 2	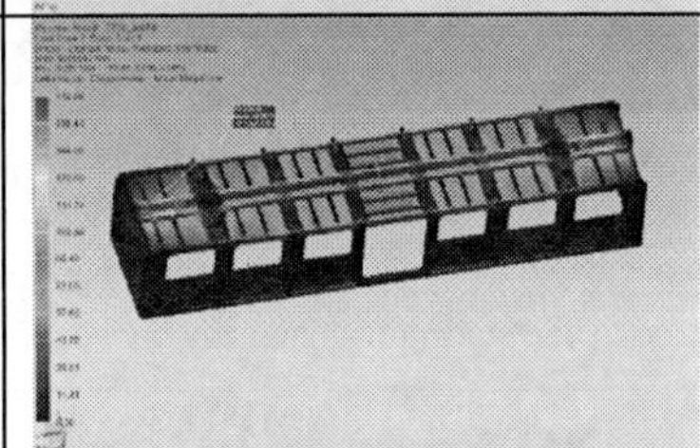	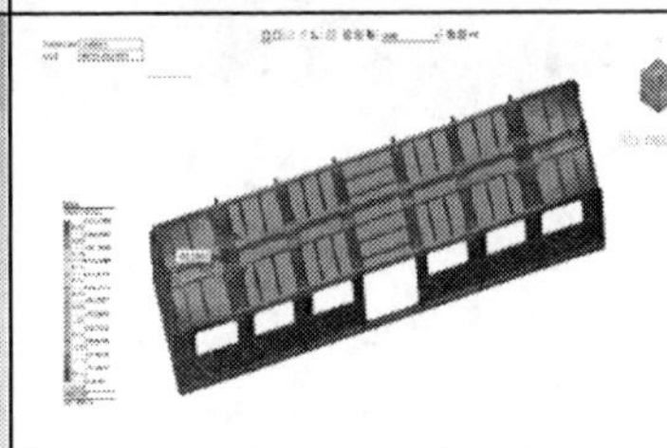	the same position
Condition 3	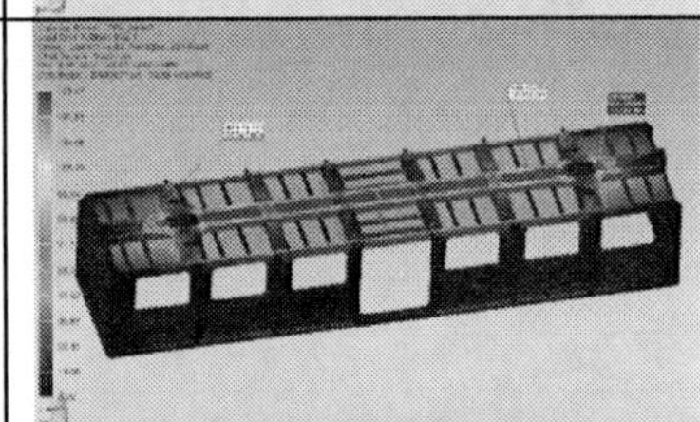		the same position
Condition 4	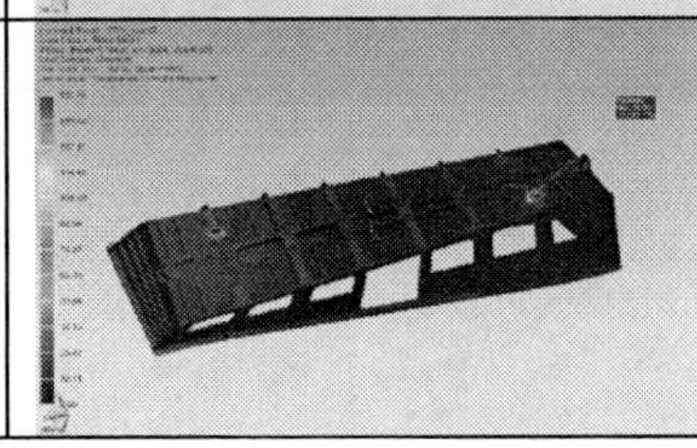	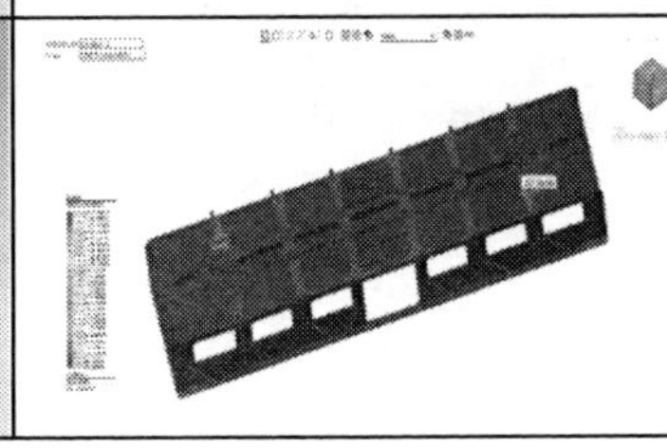	the same position

Table 3. Displacement nephogram comparison.

Calculation condition	**Displacement nephogram**		**Max stress position**
	ANSYS	MIDAS MeshFree	

Condition 1		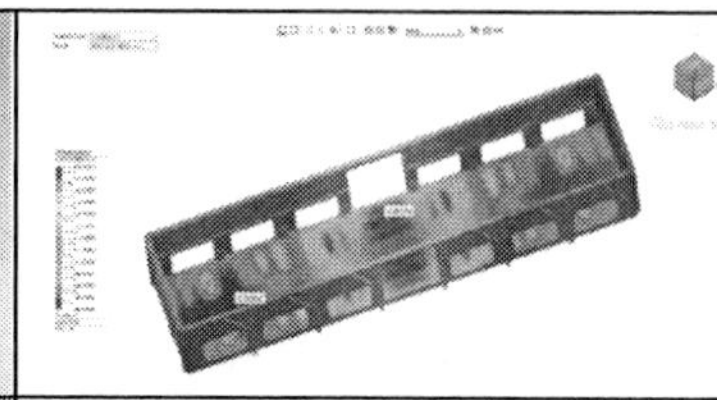	the same position
Condition 2		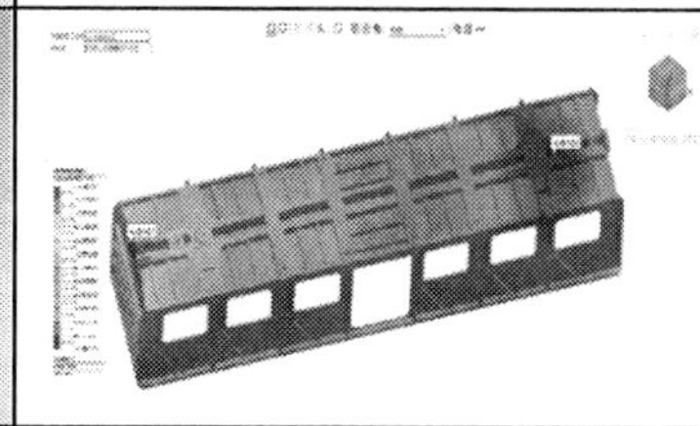	the same position
Condition 3	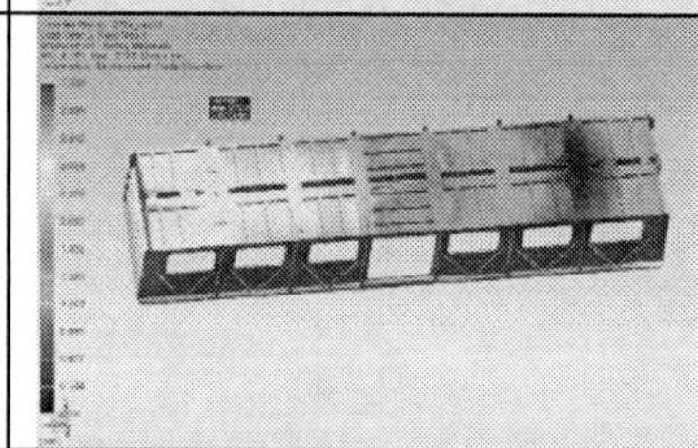	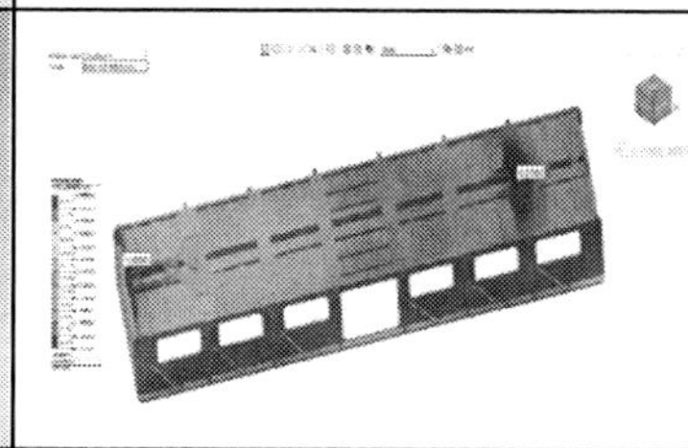	the same position
Condition 4	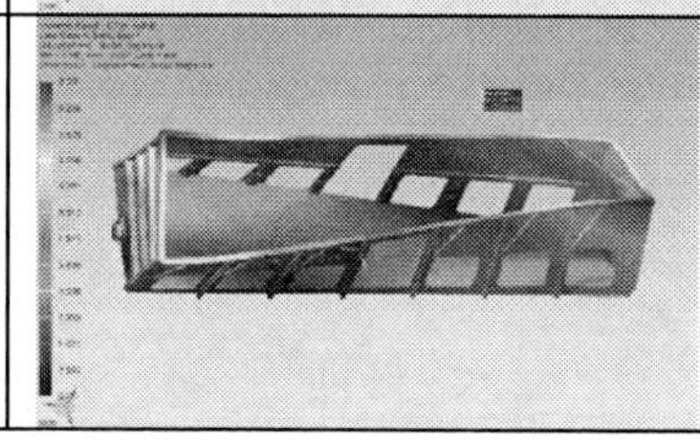	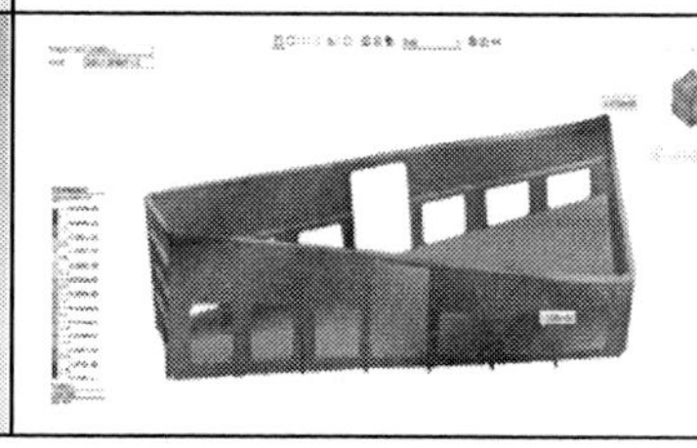	the same position

Table 4. Comparison of maximum displacement and maximum stress.

Calculation condition	Max displacement and max stress	ANSYS	MIDAS MeshFree	Relative error
Condition 1	max displacement (mm)	3.894	3.852	1.08%
	max stress(MPa)	118.84	112.3	5.50%
Condition 2	max displacement (mm)	4.03	4.08	1.24%
	max stress(MPa)	172	182	5.81%
Condition 3	max displacement (mm)	3.51	3.55	1.14%
	max stress(MPa)	143.5	147.3	2.65%
Condition 4	max displacement (mm)	9.00	9.34	3.78%
	max stress(MPa)	157.9	152.5	3.42%

It can be seen from the table that the stress distribution and the maximum stress position under different simulation methods are consistent, and the error of the maximum stress result is 5.81%. The results of structural stiffness calculated by the two methods are basically consistent. However, for strength analysis, the error of stress results is slightly larger, but within an acceptable range. There are several reasons for the large stress error of these two calculation methods.On the one hand, it may be that the shell element is used in the calculation of ANSYS, ignoring the influence of normal stress, while MeshFree fully considers the three-dimensional stress in the solid calculation. On the other hand, the accuracy of the stress results of traditional finite element simulation analysis is greatly affected by the number of grids and the quality of elements, and there may be some errors between the calculated stress and the actual stress. The displacement results tend to be more stable.In a word, the calculation error can meet the requirements of structural feasibility analysis in engineering design.

4.3 Timeliness comparison of simulation calculation

The simulation calculation time of different calculation methods is statistically compared, as shown in Table 5. Because there is no need to simplify the geometric model and mesh generation, and the optimization of the solution algorithm, the meshless simulation method is 92.5% more efficient than the traditional finite element simulation method.

Table 5. Simulation timeliness comparison.

Simulation work	Calculation condition	Time(minute)		Efficiency improvement rate
		ANSYS	MIDAS MeshFree	
preconditioner	geometric cleanup and simplification	480	60	87.5%
	mesh dividing	960	0	100%
	material property definition	7	5	28.6%
	connection or contact settings	240	20	91.7%
analytical solution	boundary condition setting	10	8	20%
	solution	5	20	-55%
Post processing	result extraction and processing	20	17	15%
the total time		1722	130	92.5%

The time of the pretreatment process has been greatly shortened, from 1687 min to 85 min, and the efficiency has been improved by 95%; The analysis solution time increased from 15 min to 28 min, and the efficiency decreased by 46.4%; The time of post-treatment process was reduced from 20 min to 17 min, and the efficiency was increased by 15%; The overall analysis time was reduced from 1722 min to 130 min.The time of each stage and the total time are shown in Figure 4.

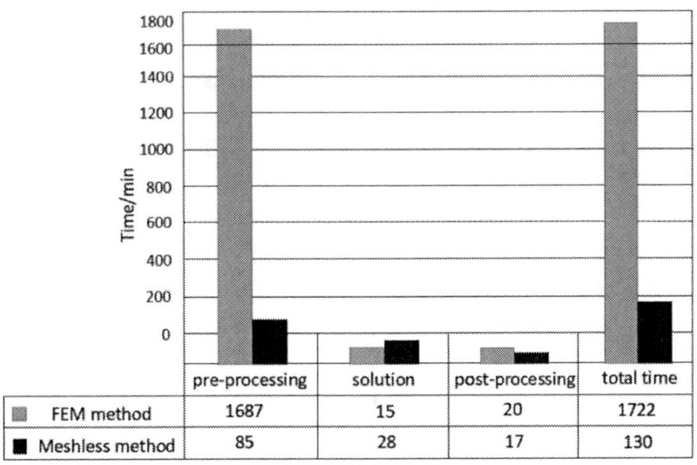

Fig. 4. Comparison of time consumed in each simulation stage.

5 Conclusion

In the early stage of the development of complex railway wagon equipment, due to the rapid iteration speed of the scheme and the great changes in structural design, the traditional finite element simulation method requires a lot of time and energy, which seriously affects the product development progress and design cost.In this paper, the calculation principle of MIDAS MeshFree software developed on the basis of implicit boundary method and the fast simulation technology of the structure are introduced to meet the requirements of fast structure simulation.Through the analysis of examples, the meshless analysis method greatly reduces the pre-processing time of traditional finite element simulation analysis while ensuring the analysis accuracy, and the overall simulation time efficiency is improved by 92.5%. The simulation analysis time is greatly saved, and the product design and development cycle is effectively shortened.

References

1. Andrew R J. Methodology for evaluating vehicle fatigue life and durability[D]. Knoxville:The University of Tennessee,2003.
2. Haiba M,Barton D.C,Brooks P.C. Review of life assessment techniques applied to dynamically loaded automotive components[J].Computers and Structures,80 (2002).
3. Ravi K.Burla and Ashok V.Kumar.Implicit boundary method for analysis using uniform B-spline basis and structured grid[J]. International Journal for Numerical Methods in Engineering,2008,76(13):1993-2028.
4. Liang Hua, Zhu Dejin. Structural analysis of portal crane based on MIDAS MeshFree [J]. Port Handling, 2018242 (5): 22-25.
5. Bai Shuping. Analysis and improvement of bolster cracks on K6 bogie of C80 type car on Daqin Line [J]. Railway Locomotive and Rolling Stock Workers, 2007 (05): 15-18.
6. CRIST J.Advantages of mesh free methods for structural and fluid analysis[R]. SAE,2019.
7. APANOVITCH V.The method of external finite element approximation[M].Minsk: Vyshehjshaya Shkola,1991.
8. China Railway Corporation,TB/T3550.2-2019.*Specification for Strength Design and Test Appraisal of Rolling Stock - Body*. Beijing: China Standards Press,2019-10-01.
9. Ren Zhen. Application of fixed grid method in shape optimization design of planar continuum structures [D]. Guangzhou: South China University of Technology, 2013.
10. Gu Zhangqi, Sun Mingqi, Chen Xiaofei. Fast Finite Element Modeling and Simulation of Rack Structure Based on SCDM and Workbench [C].Proceedings of the 2016 Mechatronics Academic Conference, 2016.
11. Zhao Junjie, Lu Zhaijun, Xu Cheng. Strength Analysis of Body Structure of New 108t General Freight Car[J].Rolling Stock Technology, 2006, (1):6-8.
12. Zhang Xiong, Liu Yan .*Meshless Method* [M] Beijing:Tsinghua University Press, 2005.
13. Wang Guiying, Han Junfeng, Li Hua. Development of 40T axle load stainless steel ore car exported to BHP Billiton Australia [J]. Rolling Stock, 2014, 27 (08): 43-46.
14. Ma Wentao,*Meshless method theory and MATLAB program* [M]. Ningxia People's Publishing House, 2019.

15. Gu Zhangqi,Xue fei,Chen xiaofei.Research on the application of structure rapid simulation technology in electronic equipment[J].Modern Machinery Xiandai Jixie,2021,(4):37-41.

Pattern segmentation method based on super-pixel multi-feature fusion

Xiaohong Gu, and Shuyuan Shang*

Beijing Institute of Fashion Technology, Beijing, 100029, China

Keywords: Clothing patterns, Super pixel, Image segmentation, Deep learning.

Abstract. The paper presents an optimized segmentation algorithm for clothing patterns. It uses the depth model to improve the image quality. Super-pixel pre-segmentation enhances the ability to capture the edge information of patterns.LBP texture information, HSV color information and image pixel space information are used to optimize the parameters of Gaussian mixture model. The energy function is optimized by maxflow/mincut to realize the fast segmentation of clothing patterns. The simulation results show that the segmentation accuracy and precision of the algorithm are improved.

1 Introduction

With the development of digital era, artificial intelligence, big data and real industry are deeply integrated. The transformation and upgrading of traditional industries realized the digital storage and display of intangible cultural heritage. At present, the means of extracting patterns mainly depends on manual copying. It is time-consuming and laborious. As one of the industries with the most commercial interests at present, the digital research of clothing patterns is of great value to the industry and fashion industry. Hou Xiaogang[1] made graying and binarization on the pre processed true color image. Combining morphological connected domain labeling and CV model contour evolution method. Realize the automatic segmentation of ethnic costume pattern gene sub map. Wang Hui[2] used bilateral filtering for image enhancement of printed fabric patterns. GrabCut algorithm uses saliency map as prior information input to realize pattern element extraction and reduce manual interaction. Zhao Lei[3] used Gaussian mixture model (GMM) clustering to achieve unsupervised segmentation by preprocessing image super pixels, combining HSV color information, spatial information and LC saliency map. Furthermore, on the basis of multi-scale, the edge connectivity is fused to optimize the saliency map, and the pattern is extracted using the graph cut method.According to the current research, the paper proposes an image segmentation algorithm based on multi-feature fusion for clothing patterns.

* Corresponding author:shang@bift.edu.cn

2 Image enhancement

In the process of image collection, images usually carry a lot of unnecessary information due to unavoidable environmental or technical limitations. Image enhancement can selectively highlight ROI areas or suppress unwanted features, and improve image effect to a certain extent. Traditional algorithms can be divided into histogram equalization based methods and Retinex theory based methods. The HE[4] method only optimizes a single pixel to achieve overall brightness improvement, ignoring the correlation between regional pixels and destroying image details. Retinex[5] theory considers the correlation of image area features, but it will cause color distortion artifacts for uneven lighting. LLNet[6] pioneered the use of stacked denoising self encoder to achieve weak light image enhancement and denoising. Its source code is difficult to achieve and is aimed at single channel gray image. Other CNN based methods, such as LLCNN, based on VSDR and ResNet[7], propose a dual branch and residual module. Although it is convenient to implement, it has color distortion, and can not handle brightness/contrast and denoising at the same time. LightenNet[8] will result in underexposure[9], as shown in Fig. 1.

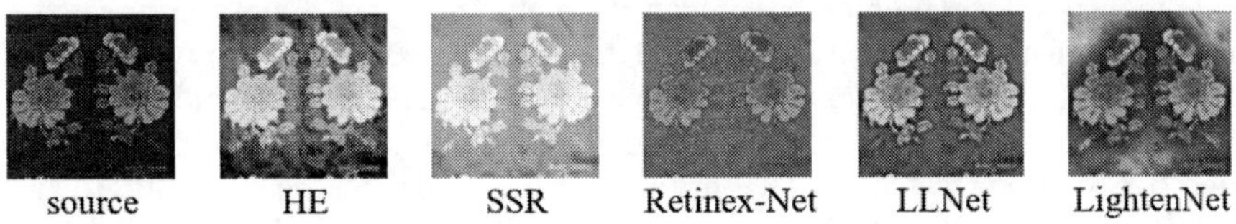

Fig. 1. Comparison of different enhancement methods.

It is difficult to achieve high quality image enhancement with simple network. MBLLEN[10] (Multi-branch weak light network enhancement model) decomposes the image enhancement problem into sub-problems of denoising, texture preservation, color correction, etc., and features are fused and output by multi-branches. Feature extraction module (FEM), enhancement module (EM) and fusion module (FM) constitute the core components of the network. The network structure is shown in Fig 2. The feature extraction module is a single branch network composed of 10 convolution layers. No pooling layer is added to deal with the image surface loss. The final enhancement effect is obtained by concatenating the output of all EMs modules to the color channel and using the weighted sum of 1 convolution kernel. Compared with other methods, MBLLEN can achieve satisfactory visual enhancement effect.

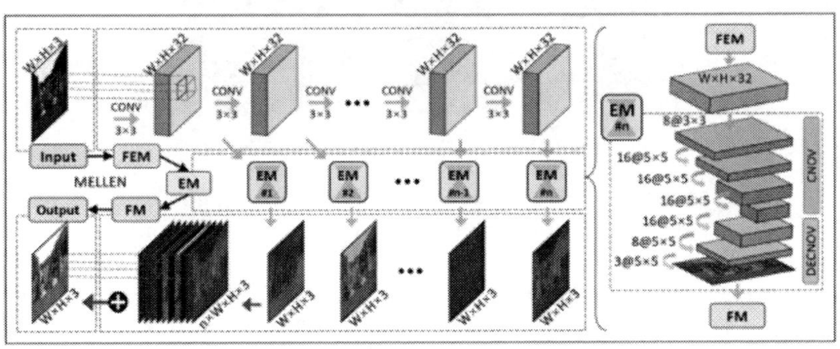

Fig. 2. MBLLEN Network Structure.

The weight of the whole network model is initialized with the pretrained VGG19 benchmark network and the parameters of the training model with Poisson noise provided by the author to reduce the training time cost of the neural network model. For clothing patterns of any scale I∈RW×H×3, the contrast is improved by adjusting the parameter percentage to 5% and 95% linear amplification network output. Set the gamma transform value to 8 to increase saturation. Obtain multiple 32 channel feature map weighted fused enhancement images $\hat{R} = \mathrm{F}(\mathrm{I};\theta)$, where F represents trainable parameters θ's network. Image enhancement effect is shown in Fig. 3.

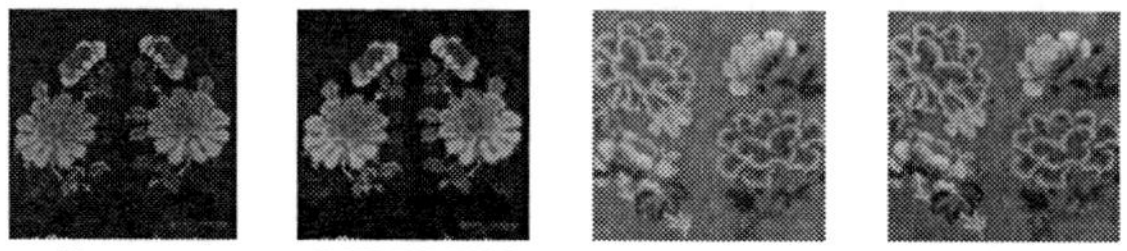

Fig. 3. MBLLEN image enhancement.

3 Prior knowledge

Since only rectangular boxes are determined, as long as a rough threshold value is taken, the requirements for rectangular boxes can be met. Therefore, binary connected domain analysis is carried out (Fig.4.). In terms of threshold processing, the threshold value is generally set as the empirical value of 127, but it will not always get better results in actual situations; OTSU is used to automatically generate a threshold to divide the image into target and background, which is suitable for the case of double peaks in the image. After threshold segmentation, the pixel value of the image background is 0, and the pixel value of the target is 1. The formula is:

$$g = w_0 \times (u_0 - u)^2 + w_1 \times (u_1 - u)^2 \tag{1}$$

wherein, u_0 is the mean of foreground pixels, and w_0 is the probability of pixels whose gray level is less than T;u_1 is the mean of the background pixels and w_1 is the probability that the gray scale is greater than T.u is the mean value of all pixels, and T is the best threshold when g is the maximum. The division is as follows:

$$dst(i,j) = \begin{cases} \max val, img(i,j) > threshold \\ 0, otherwise \end{cases} \tag{2}$$

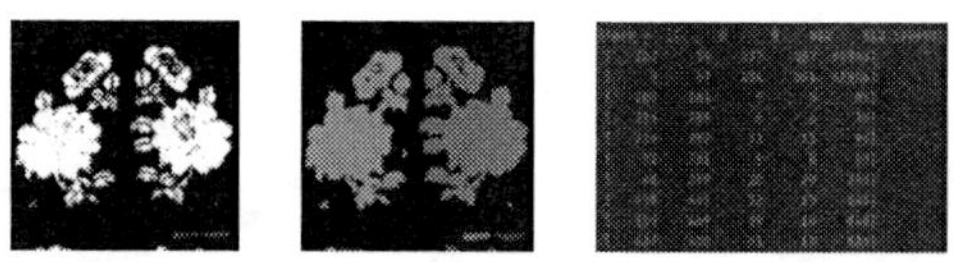

Fig. 4 Border coordinate acquisition.

After threshold segmentation, a black and white image is obtained, that is, each pixel on the image has only two possible gray levels. For any pixel *(x, y)* and its surrounding pixels to form a neighborhood, the Euclidean distance between each other is controlled within √2. Label distribution is carried out for different connected areas through connectivity analysis of binary images. The formula is as follows:

$$L_e = \begin{cases} 0, \cdots I_e = 0 \\ l, (l \leftarrow l+1), I_e \neq 0 \text{且} I_i = 0, \forall i \\ \min_{i|I_i=1}(L_i), I_e \neq 0 \text{且} I_i \neq 0, \exists i \end{cases} \tag{3}$$

where, I_e is the pixel value of pixel e, L_e is the label to be assigned, and i is the pixel in the 8 neighborhood of pixel e. In the array listed in the last figure in Fig. 4, the first row is the coordinate point of the entire image. Based on the image area information in the last column of the vectors, small areas of the connected area are filtered and the corresponding area-size coordinate vectors are extracted.

In order to improve the segmentation efficiency and reduce the complexity of the algorithm, the simple iterative clustering algorithm is used to segment the image, and the image processing is extended from the pixel level to the image block stage, and the image is characterized on the basis of superpixel area. At present, typical superpixel algorithms mainly include Superpixel Lattice, SLIC, Watersheds, TurboPixel, NormalizedCuts, etc. SLIC is ideal in terms of running speed, compactness of generating superpixels, edge dependence, etc[11].

SLIC greatly improves the execution speed of the algorithm by reducing the search space calculated by the distance between each cluster center. However, SLIC algorithm needs to manually configure the compactnes parameter size for all hyperpixels during image pre segmentation, especially when the texture feature areas are inconsistent, there will be hyperpixel blocks of different sizes. Due to factors such as production technology and fabric attributes, clothing patterns are basically highly textured, so it is necessary to use SLIC Zero to adaptively select the correct compactness parameters for pattern images, as shown in Fig. 5.

Fig. 5 Super pixel segmentation.

After simple iterative clustering, the super pixel edge can cover the image object edge (black solid line) in the given texture prominent area, and has good boundary adhesion. In terms of overall appearance, it is obviously different from the dense edges obtained by SLIC algorithm. At the same time, pixels with similar characteristics are aggregated to achieve image dimensionality reduction, which is helpful to eliminate abnormal pixels in the pattern background.

The essence of image texture features is to quantify the gray levels of different levels in the region composed of multiple pixels, which reflects the local texture information of the image. After constant repetition, the global characteristics of the object appear. Different objects show different regional characteristics. Through texture analysis, images can be better classified. LBP operator[12] constructs the relationship between the center pixel and its surrounding pixels, which is an operator to describe local texture features. The core idea is to assign labels according to the relationship between the pixel center threshold and its neighborhood gray value. LBP feature vector is represented by image block LBP histogram. Divide the image into N×N regions. Each sub block area $T=t(f_c, f_0, ..., f_{P-1})$ is composed of the central pixel point fc and its neighboring pixel values $f_0 \sim f_{p-1}$. In a defined 3×3 window, the center pixel fc of the window is taken as the threshold. When the gray value of eight adjacent pixels is greater than the center pixel value, the position is marked as 1, otherwise it is 0. The calculation formula is:

$$LBP(g_c) = \sum_{p=0}^{p-1} s(f_p - f_c) * 2^p \tag{4}$$

In which, p represents the neighborhood pixels; g_c is the coordinate of the central pixel c. Normalize and connect all image sub block histograms to obtain global texture features. s(i) is expressed as follows:

$$s(i)=\begin{cases}0, f_p < f_c \\ 1, f_p \geq f_c\end{cases} \tag{5}$$

HSV can perceive color more accurately than traditional RGB color space, and keep simple calculation. The super pixel basically retains the boundary information between the main regions and the basic topological structure. The K-means clustering algorithm is improved by combining the image position information after preprocessing. The dimensional feature is $x_i=[z_H, z_S, z_V, z_x, z_y, z_{LBP}]^T$, where Z_H, Z_S, Z_V represent color information; Z_x, Z_y represent the spatial position of the image; Z_{LBP} represents the pixel texture eigenvalue.

4 Gaussian mixture model

SLIC algorithm represents the image as a set of super pixel images $P=\{P_1,P_2,...,P_n\}$. The Gaussian mixture model is used to cluster the foreground and background of the pre segmented image. The model is:

$$p(x)=\sum_{k=1}^{k}\pi_k N(x \mid \mu_k, \Sigma_k) \tag{6}$$

means algorithm clusters foreground and background features to obtain the probability $p(x)$ and mean value of super pixel value in samples $\mu(\alpha, k)$, covariance matrix $\Sigma(\alpha, k)$ and weight $\pi(\alpha, k)$. The parameters of the model are obtained:

$$\theta=\{\pi(\alpha,k),\mu(\alpha,k),\sum(\alpha,k),\alpha=0,1,k=1...k\} \tag{7}$$

According to Gibbs energy term, S-T network diagram and the corresponding energy function are constructed. The formula is:

$$E(\alpha,k,\theta,z)=U(\alpha,k,\theta,z)+V(\alpha,z) \tag{8}$$

where: α is the pixel marker, K is the Gaussian component, θ is the foreground/background probability of the pixel, and Z is the image pixel. Due to the introduction of LBP texture features, a new region term is constructed according to the literature[13]:

$$U'(\alpha,k,\theta,z,\gamma)=\rho U_{hsv}(\alpha,k,\theta,z)+(1-\rho)U_{lbp}(\gamma,z) \tag{9}$$

U_{hsv} and U_{lbp} are the penalty values of color and texture at GMM respectively, and ρ is the weight. The smoothing term corresponds to the weight of the graph model n-link, which is the weighted accumulation of the color distances of all adjacent pixels. The final energy function is expressed as:

$$E(\alpha,k,\theta,z,\gamma)=U'(\alpha,k,\theta,z,\gamma)+V(\alpha,z) \tag{10}$$

Maxflow/mincut algorithm is used to minimize the energy function:.

$$\min_{\{\alpha_n : n \in T_u\}} \min_k E(\alpha, k, \theta, z, \gamma) \quad (11)$$

By introducing texture features and HSV color space into GrabCut algorithm, over segmentation results in true color images can be effectively improved. It improves the efficiency of the algorithm and reduces the number of iterations.

5 Experiment and analysis

5.1 Simulation experiment

The experimental environment is 64 bit Windows, CPU: Intel Core i5-6500, RAM: 8G. In order to verify the performance of the proposed algorithm, experiments were conducted on the collected clothing pattern samples (Fig.6.). The segmentation comparison test shall be conducted in Berkeley, DUTS and MSRA-B public data sets containing pixel level truth annotation. The segmentation performance of the algorithm is analyzed qualitatively and quantitatively.

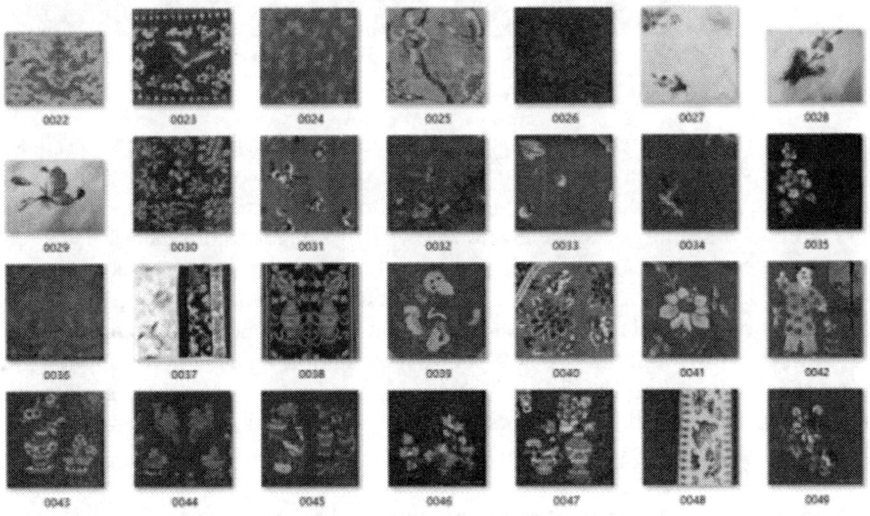

Fig. 6. Pattern data set.

Fig.7.shows the segmentation effect of patterns under different algorithms. GrabCut(GC)[14] has a good segmentation effect when the texture highlights and the contrast is obvious. Saliency Cuts(SC)[15] can better process the background in different situations by using Saliency map to obtain good edges, but cannot retain the complete image when the background is similar. FH[16] algorithm has a serious phenomenon of over segmentation and under segmentation in low contrast images. This algorithm can not completely remove the background when the main body color is light or blended into the background, but the segmentation effect is basically the same as GrabCut and FH algorithm when the boundary is clear and the pattern is single. It is superior to other algorithms in the integrity of pattern segmentation, edge detail preservation and other aspects.

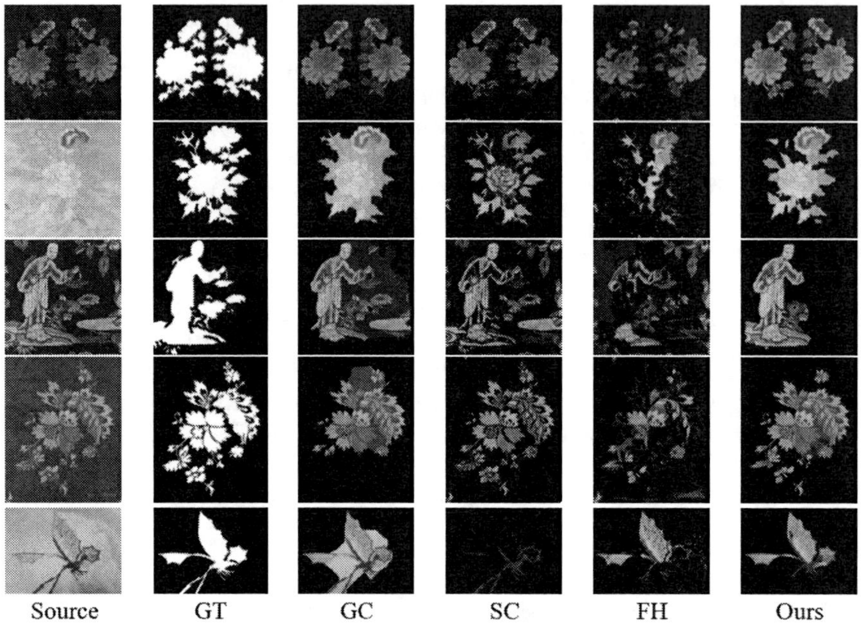

Fig. 7 Comparison of algorithm segmentation effects.

Select 6 images of different scenes in the public database for display (Fig.8.). The images listed cover a variety of situations, such as obvious objects touching the image boundary, simple background and the target is located in the image center, background and target are similar, multi target concentration, low light images, redundant objects, etc. The segmentation effect of this algorithm in different backgrounds is more accurate, closer to the true value image, and can effectively suppress the image background. GrabCut algorithm can not completely segment the target image when the image touches the boundary. SaliencyCuts algorithm has a poor segmentation result when the background is similar to the background before and after. In the end, the background is wrongly segmented when there is other interference. FH algorithm can not segment salient targets well in any of the scenes shown.

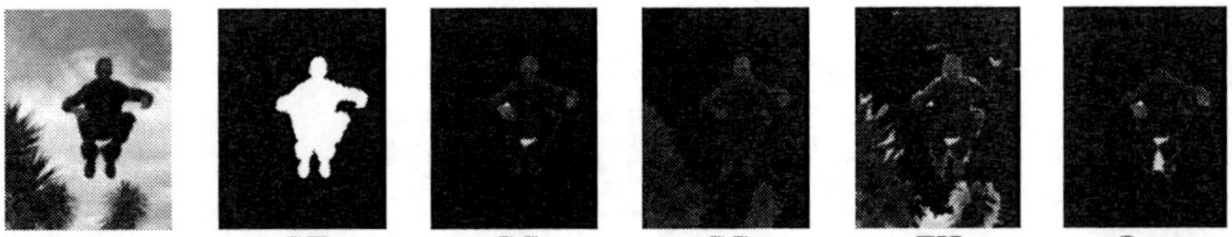

Fig. 8. Comparison of algorithm segmentation effects.

5.2 Analysis of results

The experimental results are analyzed separately, and the segmentation results are evaluated using evaluation indicators, namely Precision, Recall, F-measure, and aveMAE.

Table 1. Segmentation index of clothing pattern algorithm

Algorithm	Precision	Recall	F-measure	aveMAE
GC	0.701	0.825	0.725	0.138
SC	0.903	0.587	0.800	0.123
PH	0.482	0.482	0.720	0.187
Ours	0.872	0.883	0.865	0.065

It can be seen from Table 1 that the average F-measure results of other algorithms are 0.725, 0.800 and 0.720, respectively. The average F-measure results of the proposed method are 0.865, which is less accurate than SaliencyCuts, mainly because the SC can better highlight the target area by introducing the saliency map. Compared with GrabCut, SaliencyCuts and FH, this algorithm has good positioning performance for patterns with the minimum average absolute error, and the model performance is better than other methods.

Table 2. Algorithm segmentation indicators

Algo rithm	Berkeley			DUTS			MSRA-B		
	Precisi on	Recall	F-measure	Precisi on	Recall	F-measure	Precisi on	Recall	F-measure
GC	0.847	0.657	0.778	0.875	0.627	0.788	0.845	0.237	0.526
SC	0.751	0.529	0.335	0.368	0.602	0.306	0.649	0.348	0.100
FH	0.417	0.658	0.455	0.351	0.733	0.398	0.603	0.748	0.629
Ours	0.932	0.878	0.914	0.946	0.834	0.909	0.933	0.931	0.930

Compared with GrabCut algorithm, the segmentation accuracy of this algorithm is effectively improved under complex or single background.

6 Conclusion

The research improves the image quality by image enhancement and pre segmented region adjacency graph, reduces the scale of image post-processing, and improves the problem that the graphics cutting algorithm is based on pixel computing and has low interaction efficiency. According to the color, texture and position information of the pattern, it can be effectively segmented. The experimental results show that the algorithm in this chapter has a great improvement in the segmentation effect, and can accurately obtain significant objects in the image compared with other algorithms.

Fund project:Research Innovation Project for Postgraduates of Beijing Institute of Fashion Technology (X2022-114), Beijing Philosophy and Social Science Planning Research Project (No. 13JDWYA005)

References

1. HOU Xiaogang,CHEN Hong, & ZHAO Haiying (2019). The national costume pattern elements segmentation by incorporating morphology connected component and CVmodel. *Journal of Zhejiang University(Science Edition),*46(3), 288-294.(in chinese).
2. WANG Hui (2020). Elements Extraction of Apparel Patterns Based on Contrast and GrabCut Algorithm. *Zhejiang Sci-Tech University*.(in chinese).
3. ZHAO Lei (2021). Research on Traditional Ethnic Pattern Image Segmentation Algorithm Based on Saliency Detection. *Beijing University of Posts and Telecommunications*.(in chinese).
4. J.R. Jebadass, & P. Balasubramaniam (2022). Low contrast enhancement technique for color images using interval-valued intuitionistic fuzzy sets with contrast limited adaptive histogram equalization. *Soft Computing,*26 (10),1-12.
5. C. Wei, W. Wang, W. Yang, & J. Liu (2018). Deep Retinex Decomposition for Low-Light Enhancement. *BMVC,*1-12.
6. K.G. Lore, A. Akintayo, & S. Sarkar (2017). LLNet: A deep autoencoder approach to natural low-light image enhancement. *Pattern Recognition,* 61(6),650-662.
7. K. He, X. Zhang, S. Ren, & J. Sun (2016). Deep Residual Learning for Image Recognition. *2016 IEEE Conference on Computer Vision and Pattern Recognition (CVPR)*, 770-778.
8. C. Li, J. Guo, F. Porikli, & Y. Pang (2018). LightenNet: A Convolutional Neural Network for weakly illuminated image enhancement. *Pattern Recognition Letters*, 104, 15-22.
9. C. Li, C. Guo, L. Han, J. Jiang, M. Cheng, J. Gu, & C.C. Loy (2021). Low-Light Image and Video Enhancement Using Deep Learning: A Survey. *IEEE Transactions on Pattern Analysis and Machine Intelligence*, 1-20.
10. F. Lv, F. Lu, J. Wu, & C. Lim (2018). MBLLEN: Low-Light Image/Video Enhancement Using CNNs. *BMVC*, 220,1-13.
11. R. Achanta, A. Shaji, K. Smith, A. Lucchi, P.V. Fua, & S. Süsstrunk (2012). SLIC Superpixels Compared to State-of-the-Art Superpixel Methods. *IEEE Transactions on Pattern Analysis and Machine Intelligence*, 34(11), 2274-2282.
12. T. Ojala, M. Pietikäinen, & T. Mäenpää (2002). Multiresolution Gray-Scale and Rotation Invariant Texture Classification with Local Binary Patterns. *IEEE Trans. Pattern Anal. Mach. Intell.*, 24(7), 971-987.
13. S. Han, W. Tao, D. Wang, X. Tai, & X. Wu (2009). Image Segmentation Based on GrabCut Framework Integrating Multiscale Nonlinear Structure Tensor. *IEEE Transactions on Image Processing*, 18(10), 2289-2302.
14. C. Rother, V. Kolmogorov, & A. Blake (2004). "GrabCut": interactive foreground extraction using iterated graph cuts. *ACM Transactions on Graphics*,23(3),309-314.
15. M. Mukhiddinov, R. Jeong, & J. Cho (2020). Saliency cuts: salient region extraction based on local adaptive thresholding for image information recognition of the visually impaired. *Int. Arab J. Inf. Technol.*, 17(5), 713-720.

16. P.F. Felzenszwalb, & D.P. Huttenlocher (2004). Efficient Graph-Based Image Segmentation. *International Journal of Computer Vision*, 59(2), 167-181.

Pattern segmentation based on PoolNet and boundary connectivity

Xiaohong Gu, and *Shuyuan* Shang*
Beijing Institute of Fashion Technology, Beijing, 100029, China

Keywords: Significance test, Boundary connectivity, Pattern segmentation, PoolNet.

Abstract. Traditional image segmentation algorithms need to design features manually. Therefore, based on the advantage of PoolNet in object detection, this paper proposes a clothing pattern segmentation algorithm combining PoolNet detection and boundary connectivity. This algorithm has more fine edges than traditional segmentation. Especially in the case of similar background before and after, we can get more complete pattern elements, and have better results in segmentation accuracy.

1 Introduction

Traditional image segmentation algorithms have reached a bottleneck in image processing. Because of its dependence on the characteristics of manual design and higher mathematical ability requirements, the research[1-3] process has many limitations. In order to break through the original image data in precision, accuracy, recall and other aspects of the calculation results, researchers developed a series of model structures combined with the depth learning theory. The strong representation ability of the depth model structure makes the extracted image features have stronger generalization performance than the manually set ones[4], and have been applied in many fields such as image, voice and text. It is mainly to use depth learning to accurately locate patterns on the acquisition of deep semantics, as well as to accurately extract the edges of local significance, so as to make the edges of acquired patterns complete. The algorithm flow is as follows: 1) Input the pattern image of any size into the pre trained PoolNet model to obtain the global saliency map. There are some background information and virtualization problems in the saliency map, which affect the accurate extraction of patterns; 2) The background probability is obtained by using the super pixel background prior algorithm, the background information is suppressed and the target area is refined to obtain the local saliency image; 3) The obtained saliency map is weighted and fused to obtain highlighted saliency map; 4) Adaptive threshold segmentation transforms saliency image into binary image; 5) Morphological processing eliminates some background information in black and white images; 6) The

* Corresponding author:shang@bift.edu.cn

optimized image is used as a mask to obtain patterns by multiplying the image to be segmented.

2 Significance test

Traditional image segmentation algorithms capture local information and global context information separately through manually designed features and strict algorithm design. For example, threshold segmentation, super pixel, etc. mostly focus on the underlying information of the image, unable to capture high-level semantic information, and perform poorly for some images with complex background textures. CNNs can automatically learn features from large-scale datasets. Because of the smaller receptive field and overlapping area, shallow convolution can extract more fine-grained information and retain image details. Deep semantic knowledge can obtain more accurate location information of image object. However, when high-level semantic information is transmitted to a shallow level, the location information captured at a deeper level will be diluted. PoolNet[5] improved on the basis of CNN, applied simple pooling, and introduced GGM (global guidance module) and FAM (feature aggregation module) on the architecture of FPN, so as to generate detailed saliency mapping and further sharpen the details of the target object. Since the U-shaped structure of the model can still achieve better results when there are few training sets, this paper uses the pre trained PoolNet to generate the global saliency map. See Fig. 1 for the model structure.

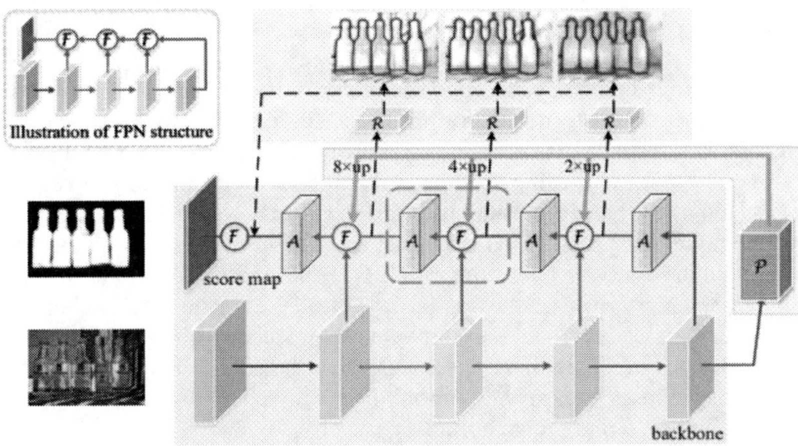

Fig. 1. PoolNetnet work structure.

The backbone network of the model is VGGNet16[6]. The last full connection layer is removed and all convolutional blocks are retained. For images with H×W , downsampling is performed according to decreasing spatial resolution, and the feature map of layer i is

$$\frac{W}{2^i}\times\frac{W}{2^i}\times C_i \quad (1)$$

Because the first layer convolution block can not extract useful information, it is easy to cause information redundancy, which greatly increases the computing cost. Therefore, only the features of conv2, conv3, conv4, and conv5 are used, and these features are marked as $\{Ci \mid i=2,3,4,5\}$. In order to improve the prediction of the object boundary, combined with edge detection training, the number of channels is compressed by 3×3 and 1×1 convolution layers in the top-down transmission process. By applying saliency detection and edge detection respectively, saliency features $\{Si|i=2,3,4,5\}$ and edge features $\{Di|i=1,2,3\}$ are obtained. Compress them to 48 channels and send them to the decoder network to obtain the saliency map.

In the network training process, the batch size is fixed to 1, so that images of different scales can be input. Therefore, the iter size parameter is equivalent to the batch size, and the parameter is set to 64. The amount of training data is increased by means of data enhancement.The model is micro tuned on the basis of the ResNet50[7] pre-training model.Through the control variable analysis and comparison with the optimizer SGD, the training under Adam has a better weight result. Adjust the input size of epoch to obtain the optimal solution in the whole model training process and obtain the pattern saliency map.

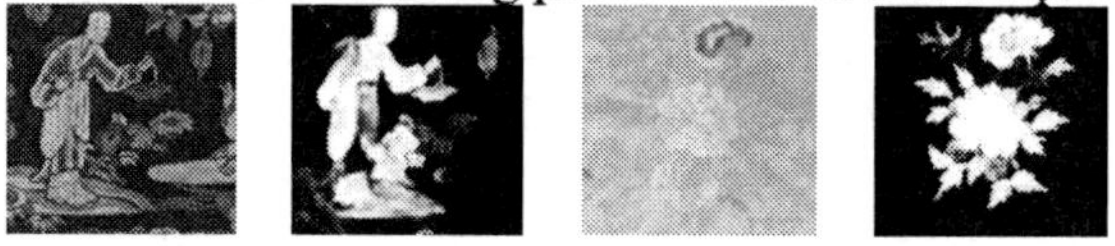

Fig. 2. Significance test results.

The deep learning saliency detection algorithm adopts an end-to-end approach. Because only features are extracted from RGB images, the information contained is limited. When the foreground and background are similar in color and texture, and the background is complex, there are problems such as difficult background suppression, incomplete saliency map, and blurry edges, as shown in Fig.2. Therefore, this paper uses a background prior method to fill and refine the target area.

3 Boundary connectivity

Because local features contain rich edge details of the image, it is unreasonable to completely discard this part of information in image segmentation, which will also lead to rough segmentation results. At present, most of them judge the background prior information of the region according to the correlation between the image region and the edge. Simply viewing all the edges as the background is easy to introduce foreground noise. The edge connectivity in the image is used to improve the robustness of the background prior. Boundary connectivity refers to the ratio of the perimeter of an area to the length of the entire image boundary, that is, the spatial layout of the image area is characterized by the image boundary[8]. Usually, there are few areas connected with the image edge, and the correlation between the area boundaries is small, then the significance value of the area is high, and the corresponding background probability is low. The formula for the connection tightness between region R and image boundary is as follows:

$$\mathrm{Bnd}Con(R) = \frac{Len_{\mathrm{bnd}}(P)}{\sqrt{Area(P)}} \tag{2}$$

where, p represents any super pixel in the image, Bnd is the collection of image boundary blocks, Len is the length associated with the area and image boundary, and $\sqrt{\mathrm{Area}(p)}$ is the area of the entire super pixel area. The formula is:

$$\mathrm{Len}_{bnd}(p) = \sum_{i=1}^{N} S(\mathrm{p}, p_i) \bullet \delta(p_i \in Bnd) \tag{3}$$

$$\mathrm{Area}\ (\mathrm{p}) = \sum_{i=1}^{N} \exp(-\frac{d_{geo}^2(p, p_i)}{2\delta_{clr}^2}) = \sum_{i=1}^{N} S(p, p_i) \tag{4}$$

$D_{geo}(p,p_i)$ represents the geodesic distance between any two hyperpixels.The experimental setting δ_{clr}=10, when $p_i \in$ Bnd, $\delta(.)$=1,otherwise, it is 0. According to the background contrast weight of the super pixel, the background probability w_i^{bg} is introduced as the connectivity mapping of the super pixel p boundary, which hovers between (0,1). The formula is as follows:

$$\mathrm{w}_{\mathrm{i}}^{bg} = 1 - \exp(-\frac{BndCon^2(pi)}{2\delta_{bndCon}^2}) \tag{5}$$

Generally, it is set δ_{bndCon}=1 according to experience. When $\delta_{bndCon} \in [0.5,2.5]$, the background weighted contrast is defined as:

$$\mathrm{w}Ctr(p) = \sum_{i=1}^{\mathrm{N}} \mathrm{d}_{app}(p,p_i) w_{spa}(p,p_i) w_i^{bg} \tag{6}$$

$d_{app}(p,pi)$ is the super pixel center distance, $w_{spa}(p,p_i)$ is the spatial distance weight. When the background probability of the target area is high, the contrast is enhanced, then vice versa.

4 Significant fusion

The PoolNet model produces a salient map that more fully highlights the target area in the image, while the background probability map obtained by boundary connectivity tends to be local to the image. Based on the global and local characteristics of the obtained salient map, the optimized salient map S_f is obtained by using the weighted fusion method. The formula is as follows:

$$\mathrm{S}_f = L_1(S_{1,}S_2) \tag{7}$$

Highlighted salient maps are obtained by linear fusion and binarized. Binary maps to an overall black and white image, visually highlighting the relationship between the part and the whole. The binarization of the saliency map not only highlights the edge structure of the target area, but also results in a small amount of data in subsequent image processing. At the same time, holes appear in the area of interest in the generated binary image. In subsequent processing, the image details of the internal area are not well presented. The binary image is filled with a hole filling algorithm in morphological processing. The basic idea of morphology is to use structural elements to measure or extract target shapes or features. Holes are background areas surrounded by foreground pixel borders and can be filled with a closed operation.Expansion increases the white highlight area before corrosion removes small non-critical areas, but a kernelsize needs to be set.Therefore, by constructing an array X_0 with an element of 0, the pixel value of the corresponding hole is 1, and the iterative process is used to fill all holes:

$$\mathrm{X}_k = (X_{k-1} \oplus B) \cap I^c, k = 1,2,3... \tag{8}$$

X_k is the Marker image, X_{k-1} is the Mask image, which is used to constrain the expansion result, that is, Mask $\geqslant$ Masker, and B is the structural unit SE, which is used to define connectivity.

5 Experiment and analysis

To verify the accuracy of this algorithm, we compared it with other significance detection algorithms using data sets including Berkeley, DUTS, MSRA-B and the collected images related to garment patterns. The effectiveness and robustness of the algorithm are evaluated through analysis from both subjective and objective aspects. This section from the Recall rate, Precision, F-measure and aveMAE evaluation indicators to analyze and compare segmentation performance. The experimental environment is configured for 64-bit Windows with CPU: Intel Core i5-6500 and RAM: 8G.

Fig. 3. Comparison of saliency maps of different algorithms.

The significant image effects listed in Fig.3. include FT[9], LC[10], HC[11], RC[11] all with background pixels, so it is not possible to get a more focused target. MR[12] has a better signature when it is a single target and it is inside the image. Background contrast weighted probability maps have the problems of incomplete salient maps and background virtualization for multiple targets with similar background before and after. The images obtained by PoolNet were the most significant in all experiments, but some edge information was ignored, such as dandelions in the second-to-last row of the graph. Obtaining the optimized salient map by using the linear fusion strategy effectively suppresses the corresponding background information and improves at the edge of the target..

Table 1. Algorithmic segmentation criteria.

Algorithm	Berkeley			DUTS			MSRA-B		
	Precision	Recall	F-measure	Precision	Recall	F-measure	Precision	Recall	F-measure
FT	0.275	0.224	0.141	0.599	0.397	0.373	0.718	0.224	0.330
HC	0.284	0.590	0.204	0.902	0.719	0.495	0.692	0.494	0.321
LC	0.265	0.157	0.100	0.592	0.396	0.382	0.716	0.227	0.322
RC	0.319	0.651	0.290	0.536	0.490	0.297	0.588	0.529	0.239
MR	0.917	0.413	0.712	0.896	0.499	0.667	0.905	0.473	0.566
wCtr	0.983	0.572	0.657	0.972	0.552	0.744	0.980	0.455	0.645
Poolnet	0.958	0.897	0.936	0.894	0.832	0.942	0.912	0.944	0.917
Ours	0.972	0.777	0.846	0.917	0.723	0.875	0.991	0.754	0.808

It can be seen from Table 1 that background probability significance images have higher accuracy because they calculate the regional distribution according to the boundary, while PoolNet network model has better global positioning of images according to high-level semantic information, so the recall rate is higher. On the other hand, due to the difference in the correlation between model training data sets and prediction samples, general data sets with similar types will have higher target positioning accuracy; The optimized saliency map combines the advantages of the two aspects to obtain a better result. It is applied to the clothing data set for training analysis to verify the effectiveness of this method.

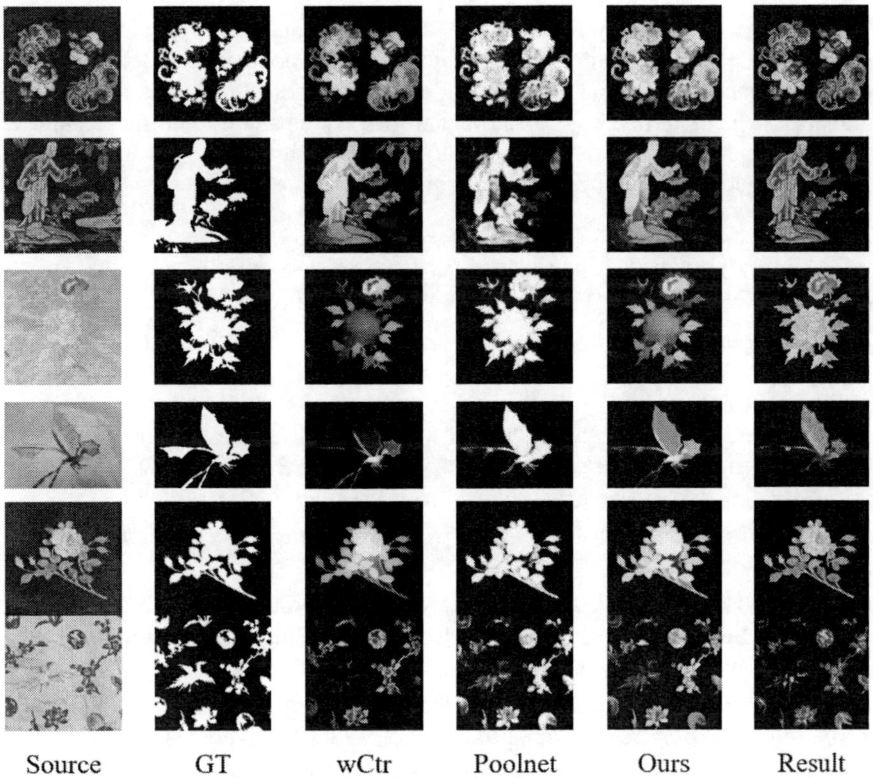

Fig. 4. Comparison of segmentation results on pattern dataset.

Fig. 4 shows the comparison of experimental results of different algorithms on the pattern dataset. It can be seen from the figure that the background robustness algorithm is relatively ineffective in preserving the integrity of significant targets, and the segmentation results in the fourth and sixth rows of images have more defects. Because PoolNet is an end-to-end training, the segmentation area obtained is relatively complete, but there is also a phenomenon of missing parts, such as the missing of flowers in the second picture. Compared with the first two algorithms,the algorithm proposed in this paper can maintain high segmentation integrity without manual labeling, while maintaining good edges. This shows that the method in this paper has certain competitiveness for a large number of multi-scale images with complex structures, and improves the performance of the model over other types when the background and target areas are similar.It can be seen from the data in Table 2 that the positioning accuracy of the algorithm for patterns has been improved, and the model performance has been greatly improved compared with other algorithms.

Table 2. Algorithm segmentation indicators.

Algorithm	Precision	Recall	F-measure	aveMAE
wCtr	0.948	0.734	0.885	0.095
PoolNet	0.870	0.784	0.845	0.105
Ours	0.934	0.847	0.910	0.066

6 Conclusion

Based on the edge connectivity of the image and the advantages of PoolNet in significant segmentation, the effective extraction of garment patterns is achieved. Because both global and local significance of the image are considered, the algorithm presented in this paper is more universal. The experiment is carried out from various angles, and the accuracy, recall rate, F value and MAE value are compared. The algorithm improves to some extent in obtaining the target image and improves the robustness.

Fund project:Research Innovation Project for Postgraduates of Beijing Institute of Fashion Technology (X2022-114), Beijing Philosophy and Social Science Planning Research Project (No. 13JDWYA005)

References

1. E. Shelhamer, J. Long, & T. Darrell (2017). Fully Convolutional Networks for Semantic Segmentation. *IEEE Trans Pattern Anal Mach Intell*, 39(4):640-651.
2. H. Zhao, J. Shi, X. Qi, X. Wang, & J. Jia (2017). Pyramid Scene Parsing Network. *2017 IEEE Conference on Computer Vision and Pattern Recognition (CVPR)*, 6230-6239.
3. Y. Wei, H. Hu, Z. Xie, Z. Zhang, Y. Cao, J. Bao, D. Chen, & B. Guo (2022). Contrastive Learning Rivals Masked Image Modeling in Fine-tuning via Feature Distillation. *ArXiv abs/2205.14141*, 1-17.
4. PAN Chenting (2020). Application of Deep Learning in Video Action Recognition. *Computing Technology and Automation*, 39(4), 123-127.(in chinese).
5. J. Liu, Q. Hou, M. Cheng, J. Feng, & J. Jiang (2019). A Simple Pooling-Based Design for Real-Time Salient Object Detection. *2019 IEEE/CVF Conference on Computer Vision and Pattern Recognition (CVPR)*, 3912-3921.
6. K. Simonyan, & A. Zisserman (2015). Very Deep Convolutional Networks for Large-Scale Image Recognition. *CoRR abs/1409.1556* ,1-14.
7. K. He, X. Zhang, S. Ren, & J. Sun (2016). Deep Residual Learning for Image Recognition. *2016 IEEE Conference on Computer Vision and Pattern Recognition (CVPR)*, 770-778.
8. W. Zhu, S. Liang,Y. Wei, & J. Sun (2014). Saliency Optimization from Robust Background Detection. *2014 IEEE Conference on Computer Vision and Pattern Recognition*, 2814-2821.
9. R. Achanta, S. Hemami, F. Estrada, & S. Süsstrunk (2009). Frequency-tuned salient region detection. *2009 IEEE Conference on Computer Vision and Pattern Recognition*, 1597-1604.
10. Y. Zhai, & M. Shah (2006). Visual attention detection in video sequences using spatiotemporal cues. *14th Annual ACM International Conference on Multimedia*, 815-824.

11. M. Cheng, N.J. Mitra, X. Huang, P.H.S. Torr, & S. Hu (2015). Global Contrast Based Salient Region Detection. *IEEE Transactions on Pattern Analysis and Machine Intelligence*, 37(3), 569-582.
12. C. Yang, L. Zhang, H. Lu, X. Ruan, & M. Yang (2013). Saliency Detection via Graph-Based Manifold Ranking. *2013 IEEE Conference on Computer Vision and Pattern Recognition*, 3166-3173.

Clock-offset computation method of space network aided by satellite clock prediction

Yachuan Bao[1,2*] , *Menghuan* Yang[1,2], and *Jianjia* Li[1,2]

[1] State Key Laboratory of Satellite Navigation System and Equipment Technology, Shijiazhuang 050081, China
[2] The 54th Research Institute of China Electronics Technology Group Corporation, Shijiazhuang 050081, China

Abstract. A novel network clock-offset resolution method for space network is proposed in the paper. In the process of clock-offset resolution based on the network inter-node measurement data, the prediction of satellite clock result is used as the priori information. A double weighted control is made with the consideration of the point clock performance and the measurement performance, and better measurement error suppression effect is achieved. The results of simulation experiment indicated that network clock-offset resolution result with better stability and accuracy is achieved compared with the traditional Least Squares method in different scenarios.

1 Introduction

Inter satellite link is an important means to proceed the communications and measure missions, and has been widely used in space information systems, because of its long-range, wide-visible, and large transmission capacity. In BDS and GPS systems, take satellites and ground stations as nodes, and using the satellite-ground and inter-satellite links as the communications and measurement ways, a satellite-ground cooperative network is constructed. The communications time synchronization and autonomous navigation network is undertaken by the net-work. The net assures the high-quality PNT service of GNSS systems.

The time synchronization of space net is the foundation of the space-time unification and effective cooperation of network nodes. The whole net time synchronization includes two key taches: clock offset measurement and clock offset estimation. When time synchronization precision requirement is high, two way time and frequency transfer method is used to fulfil the measurement of clock offset. When the precision requirement is low, the measure method can be common view or GNSS time synchronization. Based on the maximum measure principle, every nodes should have at least one range and relative clock offset measure, during the satellite operation period. As a result, the measure data will be redundant and relative. The purpose of the whole net clock offset estimation based on the measurement data, is to fulfil the reliability verification. The abnormal data can be discovered , and the obtained clock offset will be more accurate and stable.

* Corresponding author: baoyachuan@126.com

Traditional whole net clock offset estimation method include least square method and Kalman method. Kalman method is used in GPS system to accomplish the clock offset and orbit combined estimation. A method based on Kalman used for GNSS system is also proposed in China by Zhujun, and the autonomous time synchronization problem is also discussed based on the modern adjustment theory. Aimed at the limitation of traditional method, a brand new whole network clock offset combined estimation method aided by clock offset prediction is proposed in the paper. The method take clock offset prediction data as the priori information, and the double restrain of clock error and measure error is fulfilled. Compared with LS method, better accuracy and stability can be realized with the method. It also has lower computation and easy using superiority relative to Kalman method.

2 Whole network clock offset combined estimation method

After the clock offset measurement between the nodes in the network, whole network clock offset estimation can be made using the measure data, and more accuracy and stable clock offset can be obtained. Traditional method includes LS method and Kalman method.

The process of LS method is shown as followings:

The measurement formula is

$$\boldsymbol{V} = \boldsymbol{L} - \boldsymbol{AX} \tag{1}$$

In the formula(1), $\boldsymbol{L}$ is an m dimension measurement vector,

$\boldsymbol{A}$ is a $m \times n$ coefficient matrix, X is n dimension parameter vector need to be solved.

The solution of the measurement formula is based on the LS criterion, it can be written as

$$\boldsymbol{V}^T \boldsymbol{PV} = \min \tag{2}$$

$\boldsymbol{V}$ is the m dimension residual vector, the LS solution is

$$\boldsymbol{X} = (\boldsymbol{A}^T \boldsymbol{PA})^{-1} \boldsymbol{A}^T \boldsymbol{PL} \tag{3}$$

$\boldsymbol{P}$ is the symmetry weight matrix, and $\boldsymbol{A}^T \boldsymbol{PA}$ is the normal matrix.

σ_0 is the $m \times m$ parameter estimation error

$$\sigma_0 = \sqrt{\boldsymbol{V}^T \boldsymbol{PV} / (m-n)}, m > n \tag{4}$$

If the clock offset can be measured continuously, the sequential adjustment method can be used.

With the method, assuming that there are two measurement formula:

$$\boldsymbol{V}_1 = \boldsymbol{L}_1 - \boldsymbol{A}_1 \boldsymbol{X}, \boldsymbol{V}_2 = \boldsymbol{L}_2 - \boldsymbol{A}_2 \boldsymbol{X} \tag{5}$$

The measurement formulas are independent, and the needed vector $\boldsymbol{X}$ is the same. Measurement weight matrixes are $\boldsymbol{P}_1$ and $\boldsymbol{P}_2$. The solution method is using the

Added method.

$$(\boldsymbol{A}_1^T \boldsymbol{P}_1 \boldsymbol{A}_1 + \boldsymbol{A}_2^T \boldsymbol{P}_2 \boldsymbol{A}_2)\ \boldsymbol{X} = (\boldsymbol{A}_1^T \boldsymbol{P}_1 \boldsymbol{L}_1 + \boldsymbol{A}_2^T \boldsymbol{P}_2 \boldsymbol{L}_2) \tag{6}$$

The estimation result is

$$\boldsymbol{X} = (\boldsymbol{A}_1^T \boldsymbol{P}_1 \boldsymbol{A}_1 + \boldsymbol{A}_2^T \boldsymbol{P}_2 \boldsymbol{A}_2)^{-1} (\boldsymbol{A}_1^T \boldsymbol{P}_1 \boldsymbol{L}_1 + \boldsymbol{A}_2^T \boldsymbol{P}_2 \boldsymbol{L}_2) \tag{7}$$

LS method has the advantage of low complexity, and the whole net clock offset estimation can be made. But it lacks the using of the priori measurement information, and the continuous measure superiority cannot be utilized sufficiently.

Kalman method is to fulfill the combined clock offset estimation with the establishment of status model and measure model based on the measurement data. The stability of Kalman method is better than LS method, but it is weak in gross error restraint. Considering about the complexity of space environment and high-dynamic of inter satellite link, the abnormal measurement and atomic clock are possible to appear, the estimation of clock offset will be influenced. Kalman method also can be combined with the orbit estimation, but the complexity will be really high. When the nodes number of the space network is big, the computation pressure will be huge. More stable and low complexity method is needed for space information network composed of variable nodes

3 Space clock prediction aided clock-offset combined estimation method of space network

If the space clock has enough stability and can be simulated and predicted accurately, the time synchronization is no longer necessary or the time synchronization frequency can be lowered extremely. Clock offset modeling relies on clock offset observations that are generally based on long term offset observations and atomic clock models with strong stability and confidence

With the aid of clock modeling and extrapolation techniques, the estimation of clock error results can be realized, and the result of time alignment can be checked and corrected according to the prior information. Therefore, a better clock error calculation result should be obtained. Based on the above analysis, the whole network time synchronization algorithm based on satellite clock forecasting is proposed.

The algorithm includes two steps: clock error modeling and forecasting and clock error estimation.

- Clock offset modeling and prediction

The process of accurately simulating and forecasting the time varying features of atomic nodes in a space node includes four steps: clock error observation, clock error model fitting, clock parameter estimation, and satellite clock modeling.

Observing the satellites by the ground station can obtain the pseudo range observations of the satellites. On this basis, the known parameters such as precision orbit parameters, station coordinates, ambiguity parameters and tropospheric delay parameters can be solved to obtain satellites Clock difference observation sequence.

Based on the acquired clock observations, in order to achieve the optimal estimation of the clock parameters, we first need to construct a precise clock error model. Taking the quadratic polynomial model including phase, frequency and frequency drift as an example, the mathematical expression of the clock error model is

$$\Delta t_i = a_0 + a_1(t - t_0) + a_2(t - t_0)^2 + v_i \tag{8}$$

In the formula, a_0, a_1, a_2 are the satellite clock parameters, corresponding to clock, clock speed and bell drift, t_0 is the clock epoch reference epoch, Δt_i is the clock offset observation, v_i is the power law noise.

The accuracy of the clock-offset fitting model directly determines the accuracy of the clock model. When the data is collected, it is affected by the receiver failure or external interference, which causes the clock error observation data to be abnormal. Therefore, in order to reduce the impact of clock anomalies on fitting modeling, on the one hand, it is necessary to carry out the screening of outliers on the data of clock anomalies; on the other hand, the clock parameters estimation algorithm should have sufficient error suppression capability. The star clock parameters can be estimated using maximum likelihood or robust least squares.

- Whole network clock offset weighted estimation

Based on the sequence of clock offset observation excluding the abnormal values and the clock error forecasting after star clock modeling, the space information nodes are jointly estimated by the clock error. Specific steps include.

(a) Obtain relative clock observations from inter-satellite relative measurements;

(b) Pre-clock atomic clock offset $\boldsymbol{X}^*$ based on atomic clock model versus time base;

(c) Define the true clock offset $\boldsymbol{X}$, the clock offset error is $\delta\boldsymbol{X} = \boldsymbol{X} - \boldsymbol{X}^*$;

(d) Suppose $\boldsymbol{L}_u$ is the clock offset observation between satellite I and satellite j.

$$\boldsymbol{L}_u = g_u(\boldsymbol{X}_i, \boldsymbol{X}_j) + \boldsymbol{n}_u = \left|(\boldsymbol{X}_i^* + \boldsymbol{\delta X}_i) - (\boldsymbol{X}_j^* + \boldsymbol{\delta X}_j)\right| + \boldsymbol{n}_u \tag{9}$$

Suppose the network nodes number is n, independent observation data is m, $m \le C_n^2$.

The error formula is

$$\boldsymbol{V} = \boldsymbol{H}\delta\boldsymbol{X} - \boldsymbol{l},\ \boldsymbol{l} = \boldsymbol{L} - \boldsymbol{H}\boldsymbol{X}^* \tag{10}$$

In the formula, $\boldsymbol{V}_{m\times1} = (v_1, v_2, \cdots v_m)^T$, $\boldsymbol{\delta X}_{n\times1} = (\delta X_1^T, \delta X_2^T, \cdots, \delta X_n^T)^T$.

$$\boldsymbol{H} = \begin{bmatrix} \cdots & \cdots & \cdots & \cdots & \cdots \\ \cdots & \left.\dfrac{\partial \boldsymbol{g}_u}{\partial \boldsymbol{X}_i}\right|_{(X_i^*, X_j^*)} & \cdots & \left.\dfrac{\partial \boldsymbol{g}_u}{\partial \boldsymbol{X}_j}\right|_{(X_i^*, X_j^*)} & \cdots \\ \cdots & \cdots & \cdots & \cdots & \cdots \\ \cdots & \cdots & \cdots & \cdots & \cdots \end{bmatrix} \tag{11}$$

Based on the Bayesian estimation principle, take the predicted atomic clock skew $\boldsymbol{X}^*$ as the prior information. The estimation error is

$$\delta\hat{\boldsymbol{X}} = (\boldsymbol{H}^T\boldsymbol{P}_L\boldsymbol{H} + \boldsymbol{P}_X)^{-1}\boldsymbol{H}^T\boldsymbol{P}_L\boldsymbol{l} \tag{12}$$

In the formula, $\boldsymbol{P}_L = diag(\delta_0^2 / \delta_L^2)$ is the observation weight matrix, δ_0^2 is the mean error, and $\boldsymbol{P}_X = diag(\delta_0^2 / \delta_X^2)$ is the predict clock offset weight matrix.

For the clock error observation data that satisfies the normal distribution, the Bayes estimation can get the optimal estimation result of the whole network clock error. However, if there is any abnormality or gross error in the observed value of the clock, then the robust M estimation method can be used. Construct the following criteria function

$$\Omega = \min\left[\sum_{i=1}^{m}\sum_{j=1}^{m} p_{L_{ij}}\rho(v_i, v_j) + \sum_{k=1}^{g}\sum_{h=1}^{g} p_{X_{kh}}\beta(\delta\hat{X}_k, \delta\hat{X}_h)\right] \tag{13}$$

$\rho(v_i, v_j)$ is the extreme function of measurement error, $\beta(\delta\hat{X}_k, \delta\hat{X}_h)$ is the extreme value function of the correction number.

Based on the criterion, make

$$\sum_{i=1}^{m}\sum_{j=1}^{m} p_{L_{ij}}\rho(v_i, v_j) + \sum_{k=1}^{g}\sum_{h=1}^{g} p_{X_{kh}}\beta(\delta\hat{X}_k, \delta\hat{X}_h) = 0$$

It also can be written as

$$\sum_{i=1}^{m}\sum_{j=1}^{m} \boldsymbol{h}_i^T p_{L_{ij}}\phi(v_j) + \sum_{k=1}^{g}\sum_{h=1}^{g} \boldsymbol{e}_k p_{X_{ij}}\eta(\delta\hat{X}_h) = 0 \tag{14}$$

$\boldsymbol{h}_i$ is the i row of coefficient matrix $\boldsymbol{H}$, $\boldsymbol{e}_k$ is the k column of the unit matrix.

Make $\overline{p}_{X_{kh}} = p_{X_{kh}}\eta(\delta\hat{X}_h) / \delta\hat{X}_h$, $\overline{p}_{L_{ij}} = p_{L_{ij}}\phi(v_j) / v_j$.

Formula (14) can be written as

$$\boldsymbol{H}^T\overline{\boldsymbol{P}}_L\boldsymbol{V} + \overline{\boldsymbol{P}}_X\delta\hat{\boldsymbol{X}} = 0 \tag{15}$$

 https://doi.org/10.1051/shsconf/202316601070

Substitute the error equation $V = H\delta X - l$, the anti-error clock offset estimation is

$$\delta\hat{X} = (H^T \overline{P}_L H + \overline{P}_X)^{-1} H^T \overline{P}_L l \quad (16)$$

4 Algorithm simulation experiment verification

To verify the performance of the algorithm for simulation experiment design. In the experiment, a certain number of time nodes are used to construct the time alignment network. The network nodes obtain the clock atomic clock difference analog data based on the atomic clock skew difference method, time alignment is performed between the network nodes, and a certain amount of noise is added to characterize the comparison process Time alignment accuracy. By changing the network structure and comparing the measurement accuracy, different scenarios can be formed to verify the performance of the joint solution method of network clock error.

Simulate atomic clock and clock error data generation based on power model

$$x_i = x_{i-1} + \tau(y_i^{WP} + y_i^{WF} + y_i^{RW} + y_i^{FF}) + y_0\tau + \frac{1}{2}D\tau^2, \; i = 1,2,...,N \quad (17)$$

y_0 is the frequency drift rate; D is the linear frequency drift rate, for cesium clock and hydrogen clock, it is 0.

Cesium clock and rubidium clock analog data as shown in Figure 1. The rubidium clock frequency drift rate is taken as 10^{-12}, the linear drift rate is taken as 10^{-20}; the frequency drift rate of cesium clock is taken as the same as rubidium clock. Based on the above configuration of parameters, the cumulative clock error of the rubidium clock was 10 ns at the same time, and the cumulative clock error of the cesium clock was ns. It can be seen that the cesium clock has better frequency stability than the rubidium clock .

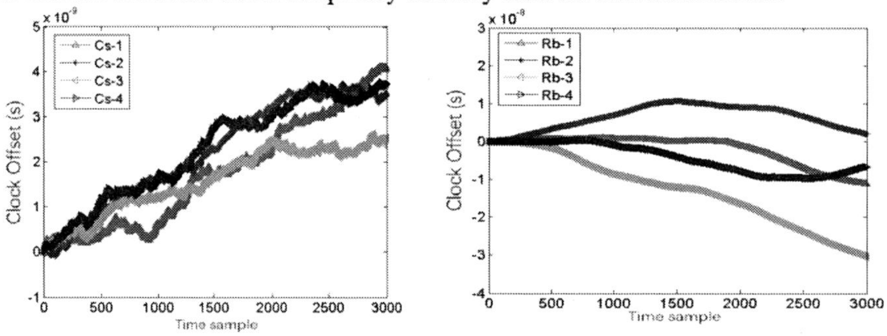

Fig. 1. Simulation of Atomic Clock Offset.

N-nodes are used to construct the clock difference observation network. Two way time comparison links are established between each other, and the number of the matching links is C_N^2 .

N is taken as 4, nodes are A, B, C, D respectively. Cesium clock model parameters is chosen for the node clock offset data simulation.

Experiment one: the whole network time comparison clock error estimation performance simulation

Suppose the accuracy of two way time alignment is assumed to be nanosecond, the number of matching links is six, and six sets of clock alignment data are obtained. Based on the cesium clock model described above, the clock error is modeled and predicted as the priori value.

Node clock error solution results shown in Figure 2.

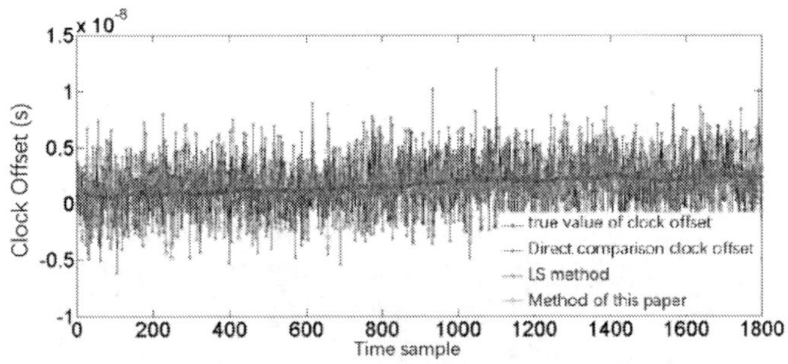

a) The clock offset estimation of node A and node B

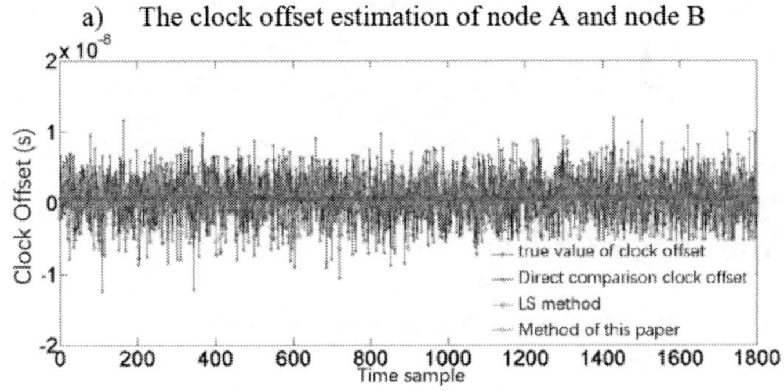

b) The clock offset estimation of node C and node D

Fig. 2. Simulation of Clock Offset Resolution Performance.

The node clock error resolution and error root mean square (RMS) are shown in the following table.

Table 1. Clock offset resolution precision.

	Direct comparison of clock	**Least square adjustment**	**This article method**
A-B clock offset(s)	5.0518e-09	3.0029e-09	2.3815e-09
C-D clock offset(s)	3.5279e-09	2.6376e-09	2.1576e-09

Table 2. RMS of clock offset resolution.

	Direct comparison of clock	**Least square adjustment**	**This article method**
A-B clock offset(s)	5.0487e-09	3.0035e-09	2.3690e-09
C-D clock offset(s)	3.5094e-09	3.4762e-09	2.1301e-09

Expariment II: impact of measurement accuracy

Reduce the accuracy of the comparison link (standard deviation) of 10 nanoseconds, to carry out the same experiment, the experimental results shown in Fig 3. The experimental results show that the accuracy and accuracy of the error correction can still be improved based on the whole network adjustment algorithm under the condition that the ratio measurement is decreased. However, the precision of the error ratio is still affected by the accuracy of the comparison measurement.

Table 3. Performance of clock offset resolution.

A-B	**Direct comparison of clock**	**Least square adjustment**	**This article method**
Standard error of comparison error (s)	4.8975e-08	2.9184e-08	2.2831e-08

Mean square error of comparison (s)	3.5198e-08	2.5258e-08	2.0678e-08

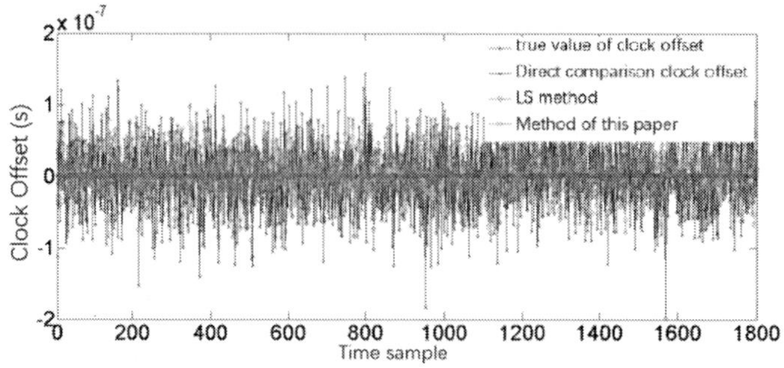

Fig. 3. Simulation of influence of measurement precision.

5 Conclusions

The satellite navigation systems represented by BeiDou and GPS all establish the measurement communication network based on the inter-satellite link. Based on the time alignment observation between the satellite and the ground nodes, the whole network clock error solution strategy can be used to achieve higher Accuracy and stability of the entire network time synchronization. In this paper, aiming at the limitations of the traditional algorithms, taking the clock modeling as a priori value of clock error, we double weighted the clock error of the atomic clock and the comparison link to achieve better performance of the whole network clock error resolution compared with the traditional algorithm. The algorithm can be applied to the whole network time synchronization of satellite navigation system and also can be applied in the future construction of spatial information network covering all kinds of satellite systems in order to meet the requirements of the unified spatial and temporal reference of spatial information network and the coordination of multi-system tasks.

References

1. LI Longlong, GENG Guotong, LI Zuohu. Study of the Development of the Inter-Satellite Links in Foreign GNSS[J]. Journal of Geomatics Science and Technology, 2016, 33(2):133-138.
2. LI Hewu, WU Qian, Xu Luo et al. Progress and tendency of space and earth integrated network[J], Science & Technology Review. 2016, 34(14): 95-106.
3. ZHAI Zaocheng. The Schedules of Space Clock Abroad and the Waves of Fundamental Physics Test[J]. World Sci-tech R@D, 2007, 29(5): 67-74.
4. LU Xiang, LIU Jian, CHENG Zijing, et al. The research of space network time synchronization technology is on the base of the orbit prediction[J]. Electronic Design Engineering. 2016, 24(5): 138-141.
5. LI Ruifeng, WANG Yuanming. Application of Two-Way Satellite-Ground Time Synchronization in COMPASS[J]. Geomatics and Information Science of Wuhan University, 2013, 38(7): 841-843.
6. SHI Leiyu. Research on the Key Technology on Inter-Satellite Network Contribution of GNSS[D]. Changsha: National University of Defense Technology, 2013.

https://doi.org/10.1051/shsconf/202316601070

7. HUANG Feijiang, LU Xiaochun, LIU Guangcan, et al. An Algorithm for Dynamic Satellite-Ground Two-Way Time Synchronization and Ranging[J]. Journal of Astronautics, 2014, 35(9): 1050-1057.

SHS Web of Conferences **166**, 01071 (2023) https://doi.org/10.1051/shsconf/202316601071
EIMM 2022

Rapid reconstruction of sparse multiband signals based on MMV-SWACGP algorithm

Nan Yu*

Da Lian University, Da Lian 116622, China

Abstract. In this paper, an MMV-SWACGP algorithm is proposed, in order to solve the problem of pseudo-inverse computation in the iterative process of OMPMMV algorithm for multi-band signal reconstruction by compressed sensing. This algorithm reduces the complexity and computation of OMPMMV reconstruction algorithm. It is of great significance to the fast reconstruction of sparse multiband signals. Theoretical analysis and simulation results show that the proposed algorithm has faster computation speed and better noise stability.

1 Introduction

In recent years, Compressive Sensing (CS) has brought a revolutionary breakthrough for data acquisition technology. In this theoretical framework, the sampling rate is no longer determined by the signal bandwidth, but by the signal structure and effective information. Therefore, as long as the signal is sparse in a transformation domain, the effective information of the signal can be obtained at a rate much lower than the Nyquist sampling rate, and the analog signal can be digitized, and the signal can be reconstructed through the optimization algorithm, which has a broad application prospect[1-7].

In the compressed sensing theory, the OMPMMV algorithm used for multi-band signal reconstruction needs to carry out pseudo-inverse operation in each iteration process, which has a large computational complexity and amount of computation, and is difficult to implement in engineering[8-15].Therefore, the OMPMMV algorithm is transformed into an unconstrained optimization problem, and the MMV Stagewise Weak Adaptive Conjugate Gradient Pursuit algorithm is proposed.The algorithm adopts greedy selection method which is similar to OMPMMV algorithm, and replaces pseudo-inverse operation by gradient optimization to reduce the computational complexity and computation amount in signal reconstruction process.

This algorithm reduces the difficulty of the engineering implementation of signal reconstruction and provides a more feasible method for the engineering implementation of multi-band signal reconstruction. In this paper, through the reconstruction simulation of multi-band signals, it is verified that MMV-SWACGP algorithm can accurately reconstruct sparse multi-band signals, and maintain a high probability of signal reconstruction and good noise stability while having a faster operation speed.

* Corresponding author: yu19830116@163.com

2 Basic theory of compressed sensing

Let X be a finite length discrete time signal which can be viewed as a $N \times 1$ dimensional column vector of space R^N. According to signal theory, any signal in R^N space can be represented by a linear combination of orthonormal basis vectors $\{\Psi_i\}_{i=1}^{N}$. That is, any signal X can be expressed as

$$X = \sum_{i=1}^{N} \alpha_i \psi_i = \Psi\alpha, \qquad i = 1, \cdots, N \tag{1}$$

where α is the column vector formed by the projection coefficient of the signal X on the Ψ domain. If the number of non-zero coefficients (or coefficients much larger than zero) of α is K, and K is much smaller than N, it indicates that the signal X is sparse or compressible in the domain Ψ, and its sparsity is K.

In the theoretical framework of CS, the signal is no longer collected, but the observation matrix Φ is used to project the signal X to the low-dimensional space for observation

$$Y = \Phi X = \Phi\Psi\alpha \tag{2}$$

where, Y is the $M \times 1$ dimensional observation vector ($K < M$), and Φ is the $M \times N$ dimensional observation matrix.

The main research contents of compressed sensing theory include:

Sparse representation: how to find the orthogonal basis Ψ so that the projection coefficient α of the signal is sparse;

Signal observation: how to design the observation matrix Φ to ensure that the important information is not destroyed when the signal dimension is reduced;

Signal reconstruction: How to design reconstruction algorithms to reconstruct original signals X from observation vectors Y with high probability.

3 MMV- stagewise weak adaptive conjugate gradient pursuit

3.1 Mathematical model

In practical engineering, in many cases, the signals processed are multi-band signals, which contain multiple signal components. The support set of its Fourier transform is N disjoint frequency bands (the position of each frequency band is arbitrary and unknown), and the bandwidth of each frequency band does not exceed B, as shown in Figure 1.

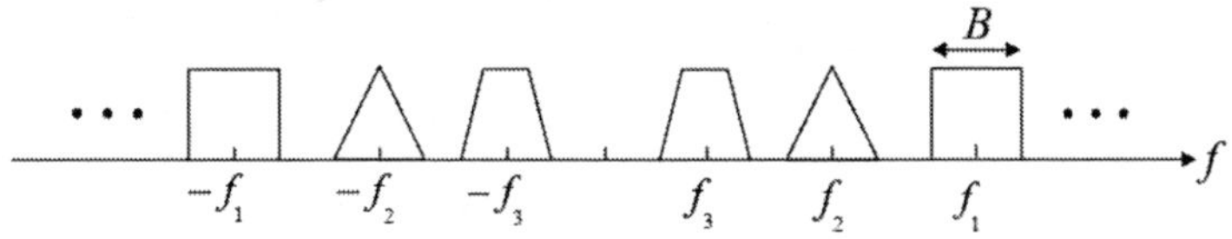

Fig. 1. Multiband signal model.

For compressed sensing acquisition and reconstruction of multiband signals, the sampling structure of Modulated Wideband Converter (MWC) was proposed[16-18], as shown in Figure 2. In this structure, the analog multi-band signals $x(t)$ enter N channels at the same time, and are multiplied by the mixing function $p_i(t)$ of each channel respectively. The $p_i(t)$ is an independent random function of Bernoulli distribution. After mixing, the signal passes through the low-pass filter with passband width of $1/T_s$. Then, low-rate sampling is realized through A/D with sampling frequency of $1/T_s$ to obtain compressed sensing data $y_i[n]$ of analog signals $x(t)$. Finally, the original signal is reconstructed by $y_i[n]$.

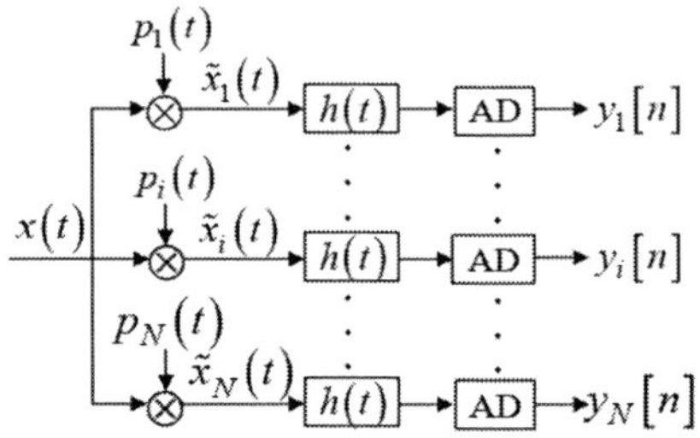

Fig. 2. Modulated wideband converter.

The output signal spectrum of MWC is shown in Figure 3, in which, c_{il} is the Fourier coefficient of the mixing function. The random sequence contains abundant frequency components, which can modulate all spectrum components within the monitoring bandwidth of the receiver to the baseband. The spectrum retained in the filter passband is a linear superposition of different spectrum components, which contains the complete information of the input signal. The output signal after low-pass filtering is sampled by Nyquist, and the observed value $y[n]$ contains each spectrum component of the input signal lossless, and the signal can be reconstructed from the baseband sampling value of multiple channels.

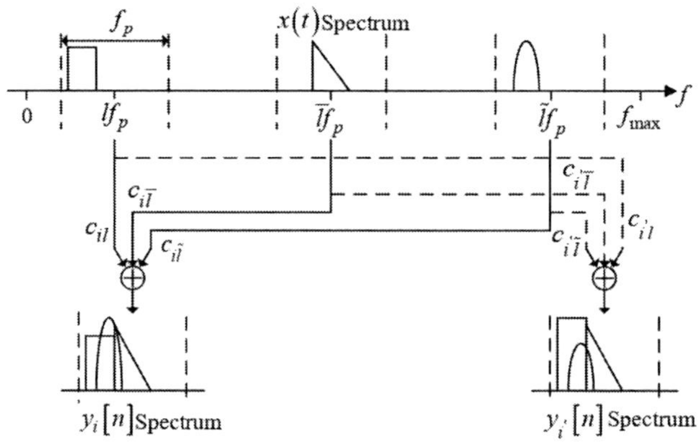

Fig. 3. The signal spectrum of MWC system.

3.2 Parameter selection

To analyze the relationship between sampling sequence $y[n]$ and unknown signal $x[n]$. First, define

$$f_p = 1/T_p, \quad F_p = \left[-f_p/2, +f_p/2\right]$$
$$f_s = 1/T_s, \quad F_s = \left[-f_s/2, +f_s/2\right] \tag{3}$$

The Fourier expansion of $p_i(t)$ for the ith channel is

$$p_i(t) = \sum_{l=-\infty}^{\infty} c_{il} e^{j\frac{2\pi}{T_p}lt} \tag{4}$$

In which,

$$c_{il}=\frac{1}{T_p}\int_0^{T_p}e^{-j\frac{2\pi}{T_p}lt}dt \tag{5}$$

The Fourier transform of $\tilde{x}_i(t)=x_i(t)p_i(t)$ is

$$\tilde{X}_i(f)=\int_{-\infty}^{\infty}\tilde{x}_i(t)e^{-j2\pi ft}dt=\int_{-\infty}^{\infty}x(t)\left(\sum_{l=-\infty}^{\infty}c_{il}e^{j\frac{2\pi}{T_p}lt}\right)e^{-j2\pi ft}dt \tag{6}$$

$$=\sum^{\infty}c_{il}\int_{-\infty}^{\infty}x(t)e^{-j2\pi\left(f-\frac{l}{T_p}\right)t}dt=\sum^{\infty}c_{il}X\left(f-lf_p\right)$$

It can be seen that the spectrum of $\tilde{X}_i(f)$ is a linear combination of $X(f)$ translation f_p, and its spectrum is very wide. Therefore, a low-pass filter is needed to filter out the high-frequency component to meet the inherent bandwidth limit of A/D.

After passing through the low-pass filter with cutoff frequency $f_s/2$, the signal $\tilde{x}_i(t)$ is sampled by A/D with the sampling frequency of f_s, and the discrete value $y_i[n]$ is obtained, whose discrete Fourier transform is

$$Y_i\left(e^{j2\pi fT_s}\right)=\sum_{n=-\infty}^{\infty}y_i[n]e^{-j2\pi fnT_s}=\sum_{l=-L_0}^{+L_0}c_{il}X\left(f-lf_p\right),\qquad f\in f_s \tag{7}$$

Writing matrix form

$$\boldsymbol{Y}(f)=\mathbf{A}\boldsymbol{Z}(f),\qquad f\in F_s \tag{8}$$

$$\boldsymbol{Z}(f)=\left[z_1(f),\cdots,z_L(f)\right]^{\mathrm{T}},L=2L_0+1 \tag{9}$$

$$z_i(f)=X\left(f+\left(i-L_0-1\right)f_p\right),\qquad 1\le i\le L,f\in F_s \tag{10}$$

L_0 is the smallest integer that guarantees all the spectrum of $X(f)$ goes into $\boldsymbol{Y}(f)$

$$-\frac{f_s}{2}+\left(L_0+1\right)f_p\ge\frac{f_{NYQ}}{2}\to L_0=\left\lceil\frac{f_{NYQ}+f_s}{2f_p}\right\rceil-1 \tag{11}$$

$$L=2L_0+1 \tag{12}$$

$\mathbf{A}$ is a matrix of coefficients c_{il}

$$\mathbf{A}_{il}=c_{i,-l}=c_{i,l}^{*},\qquad 1\le i\le m \tag{13}$$

The relationship between $X(f)$ and $\boldsymbol{Z}(f)$ is shown in Figure 4. It can be seen from the figure that $\boldsymbol{Z}(f)$ is sparse, which meets the basic condition of CS -- sparsity.

The CS method can be used to reconstruct $\boldsymbol{Z}(f)$ through Equation (8), and then $X(f)$ can be obtained from Equation (10) to complete the collection and reconstruction of multi-frequency band signals.

According to the spectrum analysis results of the signals collected by MWC, the process of multi-band signal reconstruction can be regarded as the reconstruction of sparse spectrum $\boldsymbol{Z}(f)$ through $\boldsymbol{y}(f)=\boldsymbol{AZ}(f)$, and then the reconstruction of $X(f)$ through $\boldsymbol{Z}(f)$.

where, A is an $N\times L$ dimensional observation matrix composed of the Fourier coefficient c_{il} of the ith channel $p_i(t)$, and $\boldsymbol{Z}(f)$ is a matrix composed of the original spectrum $X(f)$ of the signal.

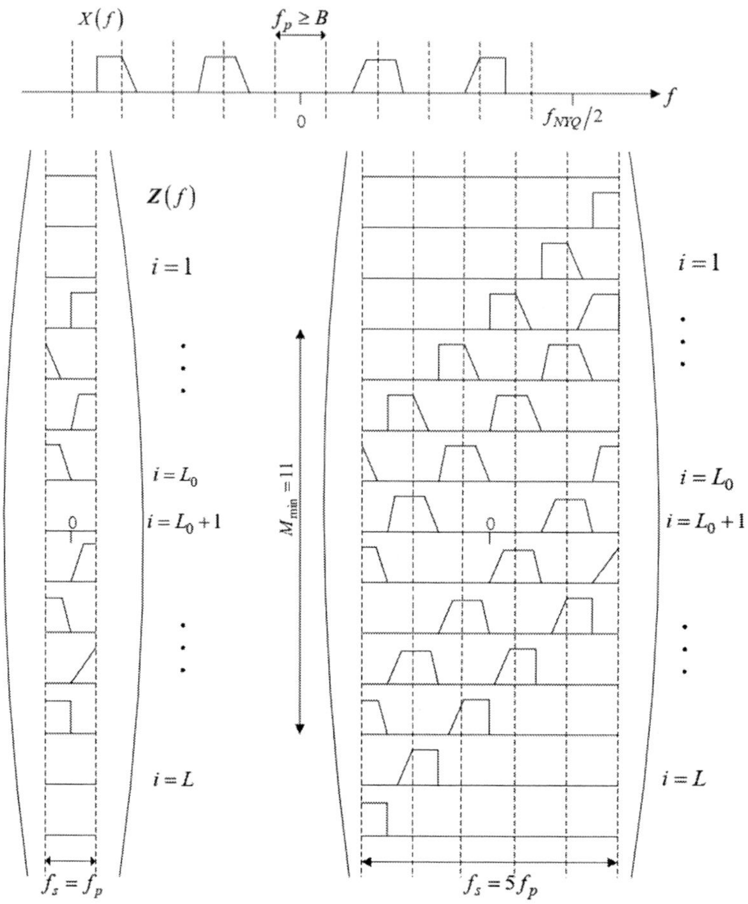

Fig. 4. The relationship of $X(f)$ and $Z(f)$.

The signal reconstruction process starts with the construction of framework $\mathbf{V}$

$$\mathbf{Q}=\int_{f\in F_s} y(f)y^{\mathrm{H}}(f)df=\sum_{n=-\infty}^{+\infty} y[n]y^{\mathrm{T}}[n] \tag{14}$$

$$\mathbf{Q}=\mathbf{V}\mathbf{V}^{\mathrm{H}} \qquad \mathbf{V}=\mathbf{A}\mathbf{U} \tag{15}$$

Then find the support set S of the sparsest solution $\hat{\mathbf{U}}$ for $\mathbf{V}=\mathbf{A}\mathbf{U}$. Reconstruct $\boldsymbol{Z}(f)$ by the following formula

$$\boldsymbol{Z}_S(f)=\mathbf{A}_S^{\dagger}y(f) \qquad z_i(f)=0, \quad i\notin S \tag{16}$$

3.3 OMPMMV algorithm

Typical multi-band signal reconstruction algorithms include the orthogonal matching tracking algorithm (OMPMMV algorithm), which firstly defines the vector set, namely the set of column vectors corresponding to the non-zero row of the sparse matrix in the observation matrix, and the initial value is defined as the empty set.

The residual is initialized as $\mathbf{V}$. In each iteration, the residual is correlated with each column of the observation matrix $\mathbf{A}$ to obtain a set of correlation vectors. The norm of each correlation vector is calculated, and the column of matrix $\mathbf{A}$ corresponding to the maximum norm is put into the set of vectors.

The residuals are projected into the vector space spaned by the set of vectors, the solutions and residuals are updated, and the above iteration process is repeated until the iteration stop condition is satisfied. The OMPMMV algorithm flows as follows:

Input: observation matrix $\mathbf{A}$, observation vector $\mathbf{V}$;

Output: Support set S_t;

Initialization: residuals $\mathbf{R}_0 = \mathbf{V}$, support sets $S_0 = \varnothing$;

Repeat steps 1-5:

Step 1: Select the k th column of matrix $\mathbf{A}$, which satisfies $k = \arg\max_k \|\mathbf{X}_k\|_q$, where $\mathbf{X}_k = \mathbf{R}_{t-1}^{\mathrm{T}} \mathbf{A}_k$;

Step 2: Update the support set $S_t = [S_{t-1}, k]$, and record the reconstructed vector set $\mathbf{A}_{S_t} = [\mathbf{A}_{S_{t-1}}, \mathbf{A}_k]$;

Step 3: Estimate $\hat{\mathbf{U}}$, $\hat{\mathbf{U}}_t = \mathbf{A}_{S_t}^{\dagger} \mathbf{V} = \left(\mathbf{A}_{S_t}^{\mathrm{T}} \mathbf{A}_{S_t}\right)^{-1} \mathbf{A}_{S_t}^{\mathrm{T}} \mathbf{V}$;

Step 4: Update residuals $\mathbf{R}_t = \mathbf{V} - \mathbf{A}_{S_t} \hat{\mathbf{U}}_t$, $t = t+1$;

Step 5: If the iteration stop condition is met, stop the iteration; If no, return to Step 1.

The selection of different vector norms in Step 1 has no great influence on the result. It only needs to meet $q \geq 1$, and $q = 2$ is generally chosen.

3.4 Improved algorithm

It can be seen from the process of OMPMMV algorithm that pseudo-inverse operation is required in each step of the iterative process, which is generally realized by QR decomposition or Cholesky decomposition. The main defect of the algorithm is that it has a large amount of computation and is difficult to meet the real-time requirements.

In order to improve the operation speed of OMPMMV-class algorithms, this paper proposed the MMV-gradient pursuit algorithm, and reduced the number of algorithm iterations according to the criteria selected by indexes. MMV-SWACGP algorithms is proposed.

3.4.1 MMV- gradient pursuit algorithm

The following equations need to be solved during each iteration of OMPMMV algorithm

$$\mathbf{V} = \mathbf{A}_{S_t} \hat{\mathbf{U}}_t \tag{17}$$

Construct the objective function (different from the one constructed in solving the SMV problem) :

$$J\left(\hat{\mathbf{U}}_t\right) = \frac{1}{2} tr\left(\hat{\mathbf{U}}_t^{\mathrm{T}} \mathbf{A}_{S_t}^{\mathrm{T}} \mathbf{A}_{S_t} \hat{\mathbf{U}}_t\right) - tr\left(\mathbf{V}^{\mathrm{T}} \mathbf{A}_{S_t} \hat{\mathbf{U}}_t\right) \xlongequal{\mathbf{B}_{S_t} = \mathbf{A}_{S_t}^{\mathrm{T}} \mathbf{A}_{S_t}} \frac{1}{2} tr\left(\hat{\mathbf{U}}_t^{\mathrm{T}} \mathbf{B}_{S_t} \hat{\mathbf{U}}_t\right) - tr\left(\mathbf{V}^{\mathrm{T}} \mathbf{A}_{S_t} \hat{\mathbf{U}}_t\right) \tag{18}$$

where, $tr(\cdot)$ is the trace of the matrix. According to the condition of function minimization, the gradient of the objective function with respect to the vector $\hat{\mathbf{U}}_t$ should be equal to zero

$$\nabla_{\hat{\mathbf{U}}_t} J\left(\hat{\mathbf{U}}_t\right) = \mathbf{A}_{S_t}^{\mathrm{T}} \left(\mathbf{A}_{S_t} \hat{\mathbf{U}}_t - \mathbf{V}\right) = 0 \Rightarrow \mathbf{V} = \mathbf{A}_{S_t} \hat{\mathbf{U}}_t \tag{19}$$

The above equation shows that the minimization of the objective function $J\left(\hat{\mathbf{U}}_t\right)$ has the same solution as the system of equations $\mathbf{V} = \mathbf{A}_{S_t} \hat{\mathbf{U}}_t$.

Using the steepest descent method to find the minimum value of the objective function $J(\hat{\mathbf{U}}_t)$, the negative gradient of the objective function is

$$\mathbf{G}_{S_t} = -\nabla_{\hat{\mathbf{U}}_t} J(\hat{\mathbf{U}}_t) = -\mathbf{A}_{S_t}^{\mathrm{T}}(\mathbf{A}_{S_t}\hat{\mathbf{U}}_t - \mathbf{V}) = \mathbf{A}_{S_t}^{\mathrm{T}}\mathbf{R}_t \tag{20}$$

The solution in the t th iteration is

$$J(\hat{\mathbf{U}}_{t+1}) = J(\hat{\mathbf{U}}_t + \alpha_t \mathbf{G}_{S_t}) = \min_{\alpha>0} J(\hat{\mathbf{U}}_t + \alpha \mathbf{G}_{S_t}) \tag{21}$$

α_t is the step factor, whose function is to make the solution vector start from $\hat{\mathbf{U}}_t$ and find a better solution vector along the $\mathbf{G}_{S_t}$ direction as the next iteration point, the requirement is

$$J(\hat{\mathbf{U}}_{t+1}) = J(\hat{\mathbf{U}}_t + \alpha_t \mathbf{G}_{S_t}) = \min_{\alpha>0} J(\hat{\mathbf{U}}_t + \alpha \mathbf{G}_{S_t}) \tag{22}$$

Making

$$\begin{aligned}\varphi(\alpha_t) &= J(\hat{\mathbf{U}}_{t-1} + \alpha_t \mathbf{G}_{S_t}) \\ &= \frac{1}{2} tr\left[(\hat{\mathbf{U}}_{t-1} + \alpha_t \mathbf{G}_{S_t})^{\mathrm{T}} \mathbf{A}_{S_t}^{\mathrm{T}} \mathbf{A}_{S_t} (\hat{\mathbf{U}}_{t-1} + \alpha_t \mathbf{G}_{S_t})\right] - tr\left[\mathbf{V}^{\mathrm{T}} \mathbf{A}_{S_t} (\hat{\mathbf{U}}_{t-1} + \alpha_t \mathbf{G}_{S_t})\right]\end{aligned} \tag{23}$$

To solve the optimal step is to find the α_t of $\varphi'(\alpha_t) = 0$

$$\begin{aligned}\varphi'(\alpha_t) &= \frac{1}{2} tr\left[\mathbf{G}_{S_t}^{\mathrm{T}} \mathbf{A}_{S_t}^{\mathrm{T}} \mathbf{A}_{S_t} \hat{\mathbf{U}}_{t-1}\right] + \frac{1}{2} tr\left[\hat{\mathbf{U}}_{t-1}^{\mathrm{T}} \mathbf{A}_{S_t}^{\mathrm{T}} \mathbf{A}_{S_t} \mathbf{G}_{S_t}\right] + \alpha_t \bullet tr\left[\mathbf{G}_{S_t}^{\mathrm{T}} \mathbf{A}_{S_t}^{\mathrm{T}} \mathbf{A}_{S_t} \mathbf{G}_{S_t}\right] - tr\left[\mathbf{V}^{\mathrm{T}} \mathbf{A}_{S_t} \mathbf{G}_{S_t}\right] \\ &= -tr\left[\mathbf{G}_{S_t}^{\mathrm{T}} \mathbf{G}_{S_t}\right] + \alpha_t \bullet tr\left[\mathbf{G}_{S_t}^{\mathrm{T}} \mathbf{A}_{S_t}^{\mathrm{T}} \mathbf{A}_{S_t} \mathbf{G}_{S_t}\right]\end{aligned} \tag{24}$$

$$\alpha_t = \frac{tr\left[\mathbf{G}_{S_t}^{\mathrm{T}} \mathbf{G}_{S_t}\right]}{tr\left[\mathbf{G}_{S_t}^{\mathrm{T}} \mathbf{A}_{S_t}^{\mathrm{T}} \mathbf{A}_{S_t} \mathbf{G}_{S_t}\right]} = \frac{tr\left[\langle \mathbf{R}_t, \mathbf{A}_{S_t} \mathbf{G}_{S_t} \rangle\right]}{tr\left[\langle \mathbf{A}_{S_t} \mathbf{G}_{S_t}, \mathbf{A}_{S_t} \mathbf{G}_{S_t} \rangle\right]} = \frac{tr\left[\langle \mathbf{R}_t, \mathbf{C}_t \rangle\right]}{tr\left[\langle \mathbf{C}_t, \mathbf{C}_t \rangle\right]} \tag{25}$$

In which $\mathbf{C}_t = \mathbf{A}_{S_t} \mathbf{D}_{S_t}$; $\mathbf{R}_t = \mathbf{V} - \mathbf{A}_{S_t} \hat{\mathbf{U}}_t$ is the residual

3.4.2 MMV-conjugate gradient pursuit algorithm

In order to improve the convergence rate of MMV-Gradient Pursuit, this paper proposed an MMV-Conjugate gradient pursuit (MMV-CGP) algorithm. The algorithm uses the gradient descent method to update the iterative search direction of the jth sampling point, and is

$$\mathbf{D}_{S_t}(:,j) = \mathbf{G}_{S_t}(:,j) + b(j)\mathbf{D}_{S_{t-1}}(:,j) \tag{26}$$

where, $\mathbf{D}_{S_t}(:,j)$ is the iterative search direction of the jth sampling in this iteration; $\mathbf{G}_{S_t}(:,j)$ is the gradient of the jth sampling in this iteration; $\mathbf{D}_{S_{t-1}}(:,j)$ is the iterative search direction of the jth sampling in the last iteration.

In MMV-CGP algorithm, the search direction of each iteration and the search direction of the last iteration are conjugate relative to $\mathbf{B}_{S_t}$, which is defined by conjugation

$$\mathbf{D}_{S_t}^{\mathrm{H}}(:,j)\mathbf{B}_{S_t}\mathbf{D}_{S_k}(:,j) = 0, \qquad k = 1,\cdots,t-1 \tag{27}$$

where, $\mathbf{B}_{S_t} = \mathbf{A}_{S_t}^{\mathrm{T}} \mathbf{A}_{S_t}$ is Hermitian positive definite matrix.

It's solved by conjugation

$$b(j) = -\frac{\mathbf{D}_{S_{t-1}}^{\mathrm{T}}(:,j)\mathbf{B}_{S_t}\mathbf{G}_{S_t}(:,j)}{\mathbf{D}_{S_{t-1}}^{\mathrm{T}}(:,j)\mathbf{B}_{S_t}\mathbf{D}_{S_{t-1}}(:,j)} = \frac{\langle (\mathbf{A}_{S_t}\mathbf{D}_{S_{t-1}}(:,j)), (\mathbf{A}_{S_t}\mathbf{G}_{S_t}(:,j)) \rangle}{\left\| (\mathbf{A}_{S_t}\mathbf{D}_{S_{t-1}}(:,j)) \right\|^2} \tag{28}$$

The solution in t th iteration is

$$\alpha_t = \frac{tr\left[\mathbf{D}_{S_t}^{\mathrm{T}}\mathbf{D}_{S_t}\right]}{tr\left[\mathbf{D}_{S_t}^{\mathrm{T}}\mathbf{A}_{S_t}^{\mathrm{T}}\mathbf{A}_{S_t}\mathbf{D}_{S_t}\right]} = \frac{tr\left[\left\langle \mathbf{R}_t, \mathbf{A}_{S_t}\mathbf{D}_{S_t}\right\rangle\right]}{tr\left[\left\langle \mathbf{A}_{S_t}\mathbf{D}_{S_t}, \mathbf{A}_{S_t}\mathbf{D}_{S_t}\right\rangle\right]} = \frac{tr\left[\left\langle \mathbf{R}_t, \mathbf{C}_t\right\rangle\right]}{tr\left[\left\langle \mathbf{C}_t, \mathbf{C}_t\right\rangle\right]} \tag{30}$$

In which $\mathbf{C}_t = \mathbf{A}_{S_t}\mathbf{D}_{S_t}$; $\mathbf{R}_t = \mathbf{V} - \mathbf{A}_{S_t}\hat{\mathbf{U}}_t$ is the residual.

3.4.3 MMV stagewise weak adaptive conjugate gradient pursuit algorithm

Similar to OMPMMV algorithm, MMV-conjugate gradient pursuit algorithm selects only one observation matrix column vector for sparse approximation in each iteration process, that is, MMV-conjugate gradient pursuit algorithm can also be improved through different selection criteria of support sets to reduce the number of iterations. By selecting three index selection criteria to improve MMV-CGP algorithm, MMV-RCGP, MMV-StCGP and MMV-SWCGP algorithms can be obtained.

In MMV-SWCGP algorithm, when β is fixed, the number of iterations increases or the support set is overestimated. Therefore, in this paper, MMV Stagewise Weak Adaptive Conjugate Gradient Pursuit (MMV-SWACGP) is proposed.

The algorithm adopts the conversion stage to gradually reduce β, divides each iteration into multiple stages, and determines the algorithm to enter the next stage or the next iteration by setting a threshold value. The initial value of β in each iteration process is the same.

Let ε_1 and ε_2 be thresholds for controlling iteration stop and stage conversion respectively. The specific steps of the algorithm are as follows:

Input: observation matrix $\mathbf{A}$, observation vector $\mathbf{V}$;

Output: Support set $\boldsymbol{S}_t$;

Initialization: residuals $\mathbf{R}_0 = \mathbf{V}$, weakening parameters $\beta_{start} \in [0.9,1)$, stage steps $step \in [0.5,1]$, support sets $\boldsymbol{S}_0 = \varnothing$, iteration counters $t = 1$;

Determine whether to stop the iteration. If $\|\mathbf{R}\|_2 / \|\mathbf{V}\|_2 \le \varepsilon_1$, the iteration will stop and the signal will be output. Otherwise, the iteration cycle will be performed in steps 1-5;

Step 1: Calculate the ℓ_2-norm of the correlation coefficients $\boldsymbol{\mu} = \left\{\mu_i \middle| \mu_i = \left\|\langle \mathbf{R}, A_i\rangle\right\|_2, i = 1,2,\cdots,L\right\}$;

Step 2: Calculate the threshold $h_{\text{MMV-SWACGP}} = \beta\left\|\left\|\langle \mathbf{R}, A_i\rangle\right\|_2\right\|_\infty = \beta \max_i |\mu_i|$ and update the index set $\boldsymbol{S}_t = \boldsymbol{S}_{t-1} \cup \left\{i : |\mu_i| \ge h_{\text{MMV-SWACGP}}\right\}$;

Step 3: (1) Calculate the gradient $\mathbf{G}_{S_t} = \mathbf{A}_{S_t}^{\mathrm{T}}\mathbf{R}_{t-1}$

If $t = 1$

$\mathbf{D}_{S_t} = \mathbf{G}_{S_t}$

$\mathbf{V}_t = \mathbf{A}_{S_t}\mathbf{D}_{S_t}$

Otherwise

$\mathbf{W}_t = \mathbf{A}_{S_t}\mathbf{G}_{S_t}$

$\mathbf{C}_t(:,j) = -\mathbf{V}_{t-1}'(:,j)\mathbf{W}_t(:,j)/\eta_{t-1}(j,j)$

$\mathbf{V}_t(:,j) = \mathbf{W}_t(:,j) + \mathbf{C}_t(:,j)\mathbf{V}_{t-1}(:,j)$

(2) $\eta_t = \langle \mathbf{V}_t, \mathbf{V}_t\rangle$

(3) $\alpha_t = tr\left(\langle \mathbf{R}_{t-1}, \mathbf{V}_t\rangle\right) / tr(\mathbf{Z})$

Step 4: Update residuals $\mathbf{R}_t = \mathbf{R}_{t-1} - \alpha_t \mathbf{V}_t$;

Step 5: If the conditions for stopping iteration are met, stop iteration; if not, determine whether β_t needs to be adjusted; if $\|\mathbf{R}_t\|_2 / \|\mathbf{R}_{t-1}\|_2 \le \varepsilon_2$, set $\beta_t = \beta_t - step$, return to Step 1; Otherwise, set $t = t+1$ and $\beta_{t+1} = \beta_{start}$, proceed to the next iteration.

Output signal

$$Z_S(f) = \mathbf{A}_S^{\dagger} y(f) \quad z_i(f) = 0, \quad i \notin S \tag{31}$$

4 Simulation analysis

4.1 Simulation signal

The mathematical expression of linear frequency modulation (LFM) signal is:

$$x(t) = A\exp\left[j2\pi\left(\frac{1}{2}kt^2 + f_c t\right)\right] \tag{32}$$

where f_c is the initial signal frequency, k is the frequency modulation slope, and A is the amplitude.

LFM signals are sparse in the frequency domain, and multiple signals can constitute sparse multi-band signals, which can be reconstructed by using CS algorithm. The experiment in this paper contains 6 narrow-band LFM signals, whose composition is shown in Table 1. The pulse width is 6us, and the spectrum is shown in Figure 5 (the lower band of each frequency band in the figure is the initial signal frequency, and the upper band is the initial frequency plus signal bandwidth). Multiple narrow-band LFM signals constitute sparse multi-band signals.

Table 1. The signal component.

	signal 1	signal 2	signal 3	signal 4	signal 5	signal 6
Amplitude	0.9	1	0.8	0.6	0.4	0.7
Initial frequency (f /MHZ)	60	140	220	300	380	460
Bandwidth(f /MHZ)	50	25	25	40	30	40
Frequency modulation slope(k /10^{12})	8.3333	4.1667	4.1667	6.6667	5.0000	6.6667

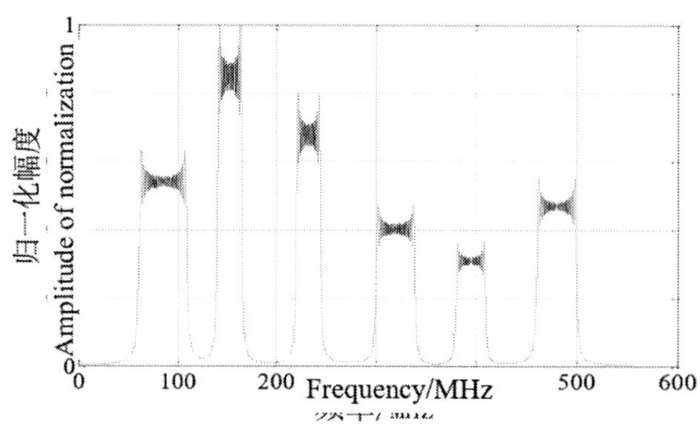

Fig. 5. Sparse multiband LFM signal.

4.2 Simulation experiment

In the experiment, OMPMMV algorithm and MMV-SWACGP algorithm were respectively used to reconstruct one-dimensional multi-band LFM signal (sampling rate is 51.282MHz), and the performance of the algorithm was compared and analyzed.

Experiment 1: In the noiseless environment

1) Verify the feasibility of multi-band signal reconstruction by MMV-SWACGP algorithm, and the reconstructed spectrum is depicted in Figure 6;

2) The signal was reconstructed through 12 iterations. The average CPU running time of each iteration of the algorithm was shown in Table 2. The reconstruction errors were 1.08% and 1.19%, respectively.

Experiment 2: In the environment containing additive white noise

1) Change the signal-to-noise ratio, run Monte Carlo simulation for 1000 times for the two algorithms, and count the reconstruction probability of the algorithm under different signal-to-noise ratios. The result curve is depicted in Figure 7.

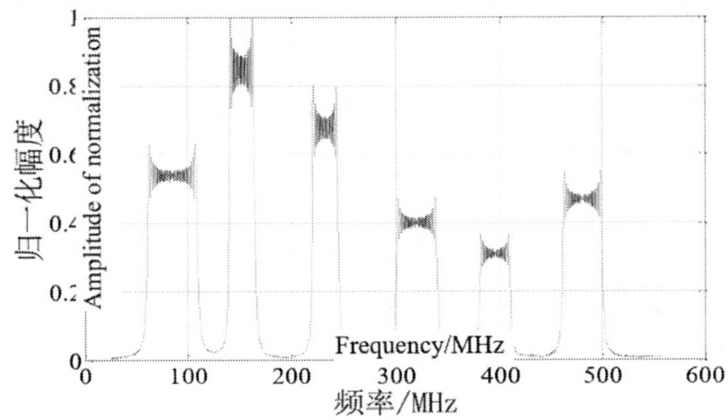

Fig 6. The multiband signal reconstruction spectrum of MMV-SWACGP algorithm.

Table 2. The average CPU operation time per iteration of the algorithm.

algorithm Number of iterations	first	second	third	fourth	fifth	sixth	seventh
OMPMMV(t/ms)	1.913	2.088	2.146	2.155	2.202	2.215	2.235
MMV-SWACGP(t/ms)	1.430	2.273	1.899	1.861	1.849	1.864	1.861

algorithm Number of iterations	eighth	ninth	tenth	eleventh	twelfth	Total time
OMPMMV(t/ms)	2.445	2.653	2.701	3.086	4.072	30.1
MMV-SWACGP(t/ms)	2.141	1.915	1.902	1.896	1.918	23.1

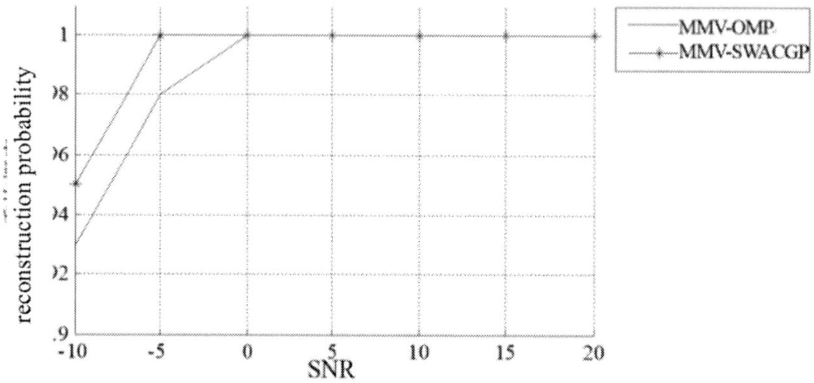

Fig. 7. The reconstruction probability on different SNR.

4.3 Simulation analysis

Based on the simulation results, the following conclusions can be drawn:

By comparing Figure 7 and Figure 6, it can be seen that the MMV-SWACGP algorithm proposed in this paper can accurately reconstruct multi-band signals;

Table 2 shows that the CPU running time of MMV-SWACGP algorithm is 76.7% of that of OMPMMV algorithm. In the two algorithms, as the number of iterations increases, the dimension of $\mathbf{A}_{S_t}$ increases, resulting in the OMPMMV algorithm iteration process, the solution of the pseudo-inverse operation of the complexity and operation time increased significantly. However, MMV-SWACGP algorithm does not require pseudo-inverse operation, and the dimension increase of $\mathbf{A}_{S_t}$ does not significantly increase the operation complexity. Therefore, the CPU running time of MMV-SWACGP algorithm is lower than that of OMPMMV algorithm.

As can be seen from Figure 8, both MMV-SWACGP algorithm and OMPMMV algorithm have good noise stability. When the SNR drops to -10dB, the reconstruction probability is still higher than 90%. In the two algorithms, the decrease of SNR has no significant effect on the reconstruction of signal support set. Therefore, both algorithms have good noise stability for the reconstruction of the original signal.

In conclusion, compared with OMPMMV algorithm, MMV-SWACGP algorithm can not only ensure the reconstruction accuracy and good noise stability, but also reduce the CPU running time of signal reconstruction. When the number of signals increases, the time decreases more significantly.

5 The conclusion

When CS theory is used to solve the reconstruction of multi-band signal, OMPMMV algorithm has the problems of engineering complexity and large amount of computation.

In this paper, a new algorithm is proposed, which transforms OMPMMV algorithm into unconstrained optimization problem, and MMV-SWACGP algorithm is proposed based on conjugate gradient principle. Theoretical analysis shows that this algorithm does not need pseudo-inverse operation, can reduce the complexity of signal reconstruction and the amount of calculation, and is easy to engineering implementation, more suitable for the application of high real-time requirements.In this paper, the simulation verifies that the algorithm can accurately reconstruct sparse multi-band signals, and the results show that the algorithm has faster operation speed while maintaining high reconstruction probability and good noise stability, which provides a more feasible algorithm for the engineering realization of multi-band signal reconstruction.

References

1. Donoho D L. Compressed sensing. Information Theory, IEEE Transactions on, **52**, 4 (2006).
2. Keying W, Xiaoyong G. Compressive sensing of digital sparse signals. Wireless Communications and Networking Conference (WCNC), (2011).
3. Qaisar, S., Bilal, R.M., Iqbal, W., et al. Compressive sensing: From theory to applications, a survey. Communications and Networks, Journal of, **15**, 5 (2013).
4. Candes, E., Becker, S. Compressive sensing: Principles and hardware implementations. ESSCIRC (ESSCIRC), 2013 Proceedings of the, (2013).
5. Qi-Fan Yang, Ke Fang, Yong-Jun Xie. Research on the Relation between the Number of Measurements and Signal Sparsity in Compressed Sensing. 2018 IEEE 3rd Advanced Information Technology, Electronic and Automation Control Conference (IAEAC), (2018).
6. Yuchen Shi, Pingyi Fan, Zheqi Zhu, et al. MIM-CS: Message Importance Measure for Compressed Sensing. 2021 IEEE International Mediterranean Conference on Communications and Networking (MeditCom), (2021).
7. Jiaqi Sun;Wenrui Dai, Chenglin Li, Junni Zou, et al. Compressive Sensing via Unfolded ℓ0-constrained Convolutional Sparse Coding. 2021 Data Compression Conference (DCC), (2021).
8. van den Berg E, Friedlander M P. Theoretical and Empirical Results for Recovery From Multiple Measurements. Information Theory, IEEE Transactions on, **56**, 5 (2010).
9. Blanchard, J.D., Cermak, M., Hanle, D., et al.. Greedy Algorithms for Joint Sparse Recovery. Signal Processing, IEEE Transactions on, **62**, 7 (2014)
10. Deepa, K G, Ambat, Sooraj K., Hari, K.V.S.. Modified greedy pursuits for improving sparse recovery. Communications (NCC), 2014 Twentieth National Conference on, (2014).
11. Mishali M, Eldar Y C. Blind Multiband Signal Reconstruction: Compressed Sensing for Analog Signals. Signal Processing, IEEE Transactions on, **57**, 3 (2009).
12. Majumdar A, Ward R K, Aboulnasr T. Algorithms to Approximately Solve NP Hard Row-Sparse MMV Recovery Problem: Application to Compressive Color Imaging. Emerging and Selected Topics in Circuits and Systems, IEEE Journal on, **2**, 3 (2012).
13. Xinquan Gao, Xuewei Wang, Jinglin Zhou. A Robust Orthogonal Matching Pursuit Based on L1 Norm. 2020 Chinese Control And Decision Conference (CCDC), (2020).
14. Blumensath T, Davies M E. Gradient Pursuits. Signal Processing, IEEE Transactions on, **56**, 6 (2008).
15. Blumensath T, Davies M E. Stagewise Weak Gradient Pursuits. Signal Processing, IEEE Transactions on, **57**, 11 (2009).
16. Iliadis, M., Watt, J., Spinoulas, L., et al. Video compressive sensing using multiple measurement vectors. Image Processing (ICIP), 2013 20th IEEE International Conference on, (2013).

17. Mishali M, Eldar Y C. From Theory to Practice: Sub-Nyquist Sampling of Sparse Wideband Analog Signals. Selected Topics in Signal Processing, IEEE Journal of, **4**, 2 (2010).
18. Hassan Mortada, Olivier Rabaste, Jonathan Bosse. Structured dictionary optimization: application to the modulated wideband converter. 2019 IEEE 8th International Workshop on Computational Advances in Multi-Sensor Adaptive Processing (CAMSAP), (2019).

SHS Web of Conferences **166**, 01072 (2023) https://doi.org/10.1051/shsconf/202316601072
EIMM 2022

Container network architecture and performance analysis of Macvlan and IPvlan

Liangbin Zhang*, *Yuanming* Wang, *Shibin* Liang, and *Ran* Jin
Zhejiang Wanli University, Ningbo, 315100, China

Abstract: Macvlan and IPvlan modes allow the host physical Network Interface Card (NIC) to create several virtual sub interfaces, which can meet the containers communication requirements across different network segment in complex application scenarios. The paper describes the architecture characteristics of these two modes in depth and builds container overlay network in single machine and multi machine environments. Around the key network indicators such as round-trip time (RTT), bandwidth and jitter, Ping and Iperf tools are used to test and analyse the end-to-end container communication performance. The experimental results show that IPvlan mode has better network performance and provides a comprehensive and rich application scenario for the container overlay network.

1 Introduction

Docker is the most popular lightweight virtualization container platform at present. Because Docker shares the host operating system, it greatly saves system resources such as CPU, memory and storage, and saves license and OS patch maintenance costs. Compared with traditional virtual machines, Docker has many advantages, such as less resources, fast startup and convenient migration. More and more applications are running in the form of container in the development, testing, and production environment [1-2].

However, Docker technology is not perfect, and container network has certain weaknesses. The background of modern application architecture is becoming more and more complex, and service provision often requires cooperation with multiple containers. How to build a secure and high-performance container network is the core problem to be solved in the industry. IPvlan and Macvlan are new modes of container overlay network [3], several virtual sub interfaces are allowed to be created from the host physical Network Interface Card (NIC) to interconnect the container, so that it is regarded as equal status of the container and the host in the physical network. Container can communicate with each other in Layer 2 and Layer 3 network between different hosts.

This paper constructs container overlay network environment for Macvlan and IPvlan within multi hosts, and uses Alpine and Iperf official container images to implement experimental testing and analysis of end-to-end container network transmission performance. IPvlan not only breaks through many limitations of Macvlan network in

* Corresponding author: zlb@zwu.edu.cn

application, but also has excellent network transmission performance across different network segments, providing useful reference for building high-performance and production level container network architecture in the future. The remainder of this paper is organized as follows. Section 2 introduces the related work. Section 3 describes container network architecture of Macvlan and IPvlan. Section 4 shows the experimental performance test and result analysis of Macvlan and IPvlan. Section 5 summarizes our work.

2 Related work

Docker containers are used in large-scale deployment, elastic scaling and other application scenarios. The degree of dispersion of container networks is significantly higher than that of traditional virtual machine network [4]. Management and control have become a difficult problem in large-scale container cluster deployment. Zhang weiqi [5] realized flexible adaptation and migration of container network based on Macvlan. Yang xin et al [6] pointed out that using the Macvlan network can solve the problem of docker network port conflict in the mesos cluster. Li wei et al [7] carried out experiments to verify that Macvlan container network does not cause significant loss of network transmission performance. Feng mingzhen [8] designed and implemented Docker container network system based on Macvlan, and the entire system can be seamlessly integrated with Docker daemon. However, Ipvlan is regarded as the upgrade iteration technology of Macvlan and there are few relevant references on IPvlan except the Docker official website. Therefore, research on the characteristics and performance of IPvlan and Macvlan can provide a better solution for container interconnection in complex networks.

3 Container network architecture of Macvlan and IPvlan

3.1 Network architecture of Macvlan

Typically, one host NIC can create only one Macvlan network to connect internal containers. Meanwhile, IEEE 802.1Q vlan trunk protocol allows one host NIC to create several virtual sub interfaces, and each virtual sub interface is bound to the designated Macvlan container network by labeling incoming and outgoing data frame of container with the designated Vlan Tag. With the route forwarding of network Layer device such as router or Layer 3 switch, Macvlan container can achieve cross Layer2 and Layer 3 network communication within multi hosts [9-11].

As shown in Figure 1, host 1 and host 2 create two new Macvlan networks with two sub virtual interfaces, host 3 creates two new sub interfaces as gateway of corresponding Macvlan network respectively, and host 3 enables routing and forwarding, which can realize container communication across different network segments within multi hosts. Docker network isolation method based on Macvlan can effectively use the bandwidth of the host NIC to achieve nearly lossless network performance, which is particularly suitable for applications such as network traffic monitoring. However, Macvlan network requires the host NIC to enable promiscuous mode, and allows uplink physical switch port associated with multi Mac addresses, which will bring certain hidden danger to the container's network communication security.

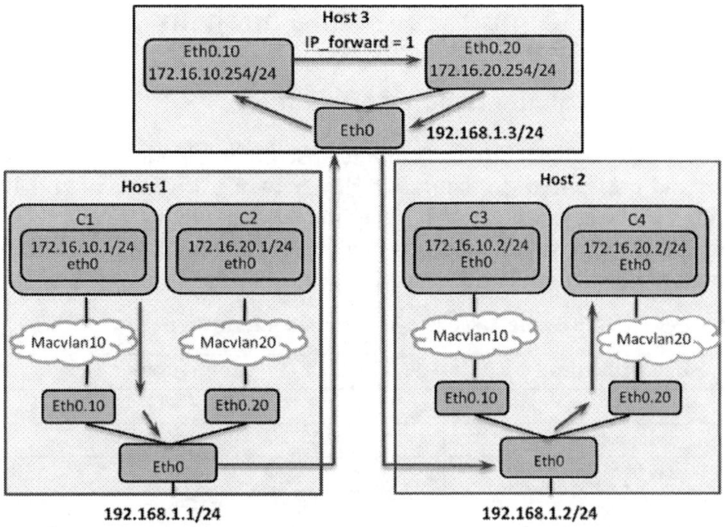

Fig. 1. Network architecture of Macvlan within multi hosts.

3.2 Network architecture of IPvlan

Because the application scenarios of Macvlan container network are subject to many restrictions, the new mode IPvlan network is generated iteratively to improve the performance and security of container network communication.

IPvlan requires at least 4.2 Linux kernel, and allows the host NIC to create several virtual sub interfaces to connect internal container of IPvlan network. All containers have the same Mac address. IPvlan network does not receive multicast or broadcast messages, and all ARP processes or multicast messages on the network are completed at the host NIC [12].

The working principle of the Layer 2 mode of the IPvlan is similar to that of the Bridge mode of the Macvlan. The Layer 3 mode of the IPvlan supports the message forwarding across network segments within current host. If the routing rule to reach the IPvlan container is configured on the external router, the IPvlan network can realize communication between the container and the external network. Figure.2 shows that different IPvlan network container can communicate with each other within the current host.

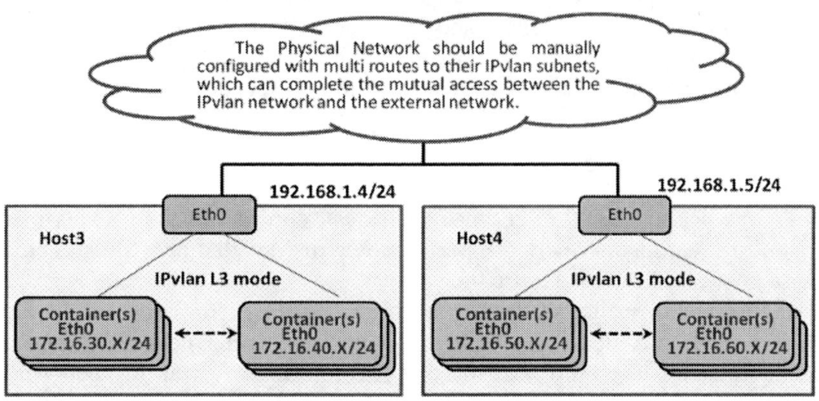

Fig. 2. Network architecture of IPvlan within multi hosts.

4 Experimental performance test and analysis

4.1 Experimental environment and test scheme

The experimental environment involves three host nodes. Node1 and Node2 install the Docker engine and create new container overlay network of Macvlan and IPvlan. Node3 creates two sub interfaces of the host NIC as the corresponding gateway of the Macvlan network respectively, and simultaneously enables routing and forwarding function. The node configuration information is shown in Table 1.

Table 1. Node configuration information.

Node properties	Configuration
CPU	Intel I7-11700
Memory	16G
Hard disk	2T
NIC	1Gbps
OS	Ubuntu 18.04.6
Docker	Docker-CE-20.10.7
Go	Go1.13.8
Test container image	alpine, clearlinux/iperf

The measurement of network performance includes availability, round-trip time (RTT), utilization, throughput and bandwidth. Ping command is an Internet packet explorer used to test network connectivity. Iperf is an open source tool developed by the University of Illinois to test network performance. Client and server modes are enabled at both ends of the test, TCP connection is tested bandwidth and transmitted data, UDP connection is tested jitter and packet loss rate [13-15]. For the two types of Macvlan and IPvlan container networks, our experimental test scheme is as follows: Ping command is used to test RTT, and Iperf tool is used to test bandwidth, throughput, jitter, packet loss rate and other network performance between end-to-end containers.

In our experimental test, the source container is set to send 100 ping request packets to the target container each time to get the RTT average, and the payload data size increases from 32 bytes to 32K bytes. The test parameters of Iperf are set as follows: the read/write buffer length option is the maximum allowed value, namely 63KB (UDP) and 1MB (TCP), Maximum Segment Size (MSS) of the transport Layer is set to 1460 bytes, and the numbers of concurrent threads is 1, 2, 4, 8, 16, and 32 in turn. One container runs the server side and the other container runs the client side. It outputs data communication statistics of the sending container and the receiving container within 10 seconds

4.2 Test results and analysis

For RTT, bandwidth, UDP jitter and other test dimensions, our experiment gives a comparison of the container network performance of Macvlan and IPvlan across different network segment as shown in Figure3-5.

The experimental results show that the transmission performance of IPvlan container network is significantly better than that of Macvlan container network. Macvlan relies on two sub interfaces of the third host to complete the route forwarding between containers across different network segments, which will inevitably increase the communication delay between end-to-end containers. In the Layer 3 mode of IPvlan, a router is added to current host to forward the routing message of each endpoint. As long as the parent interface is the same, containers in different network segments can also complete the message forwarding within the local host.

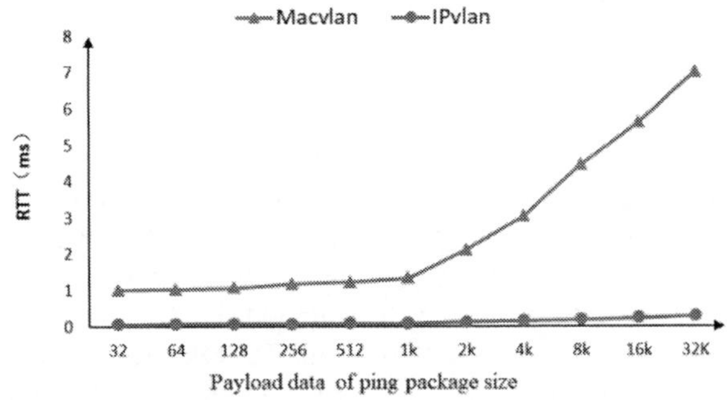

Fig. 3. RTT test of container across different network segment.

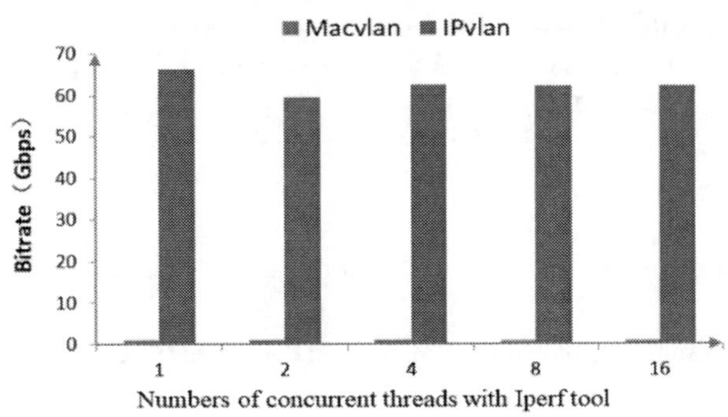

Fig. 4. Bandwidth test of container across different network segment.

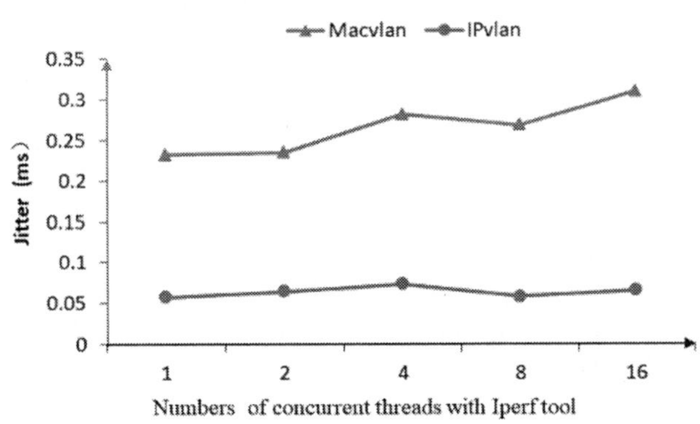

Fig. 5. UDP Jitter test of Container across different network segment.

IPvlan is a new twist on the tried and true network virtualization technique. The Linux implementations are extremely lightweight because rather than using the traditional Linux bridge for isolation, they are associated to a Linux Ethernet interface or sub-interface to enforce separation between networks and connectivity to the physical network.

For the following container application scenarios in the production environment, IPvlan should be used instead of Macvlan: (1) The uplink switch of the host NIC has set the binding between the current port and the designed Mac address; (2) The uplink switch of the host NIC has limited the numbers of Mac addresses associated with current port; (3)

Physical host NIC works on IEEE 802.11 wireless network protocol; (4) Constructing complex network topology, etc.

5 Conclusion

Macvlan is the main mode for multi host container overlay network. Without the help of traditional Linux virtual bridge devices, Macvlan can achieve nearly the lossless transmission performance of the local host. However, Macvlan is limited by port binding, the numbers of Mac addresses, and the lack of support for wireless networks. New mode IPvlan can better solve such problems instead of Macvlan, enabling administrator to fully control Layer 2 network, and even Layer3 network and has excellent network performance test across different network segment. Deeply exploring the special function of IPvlan and carrying out innovative application research on multi container network to better realize the system integration of user network, which will be our future research direction.

This work is supported by the Public Technology Research Project of Zhejiang under Grant No.LGF20F020005. and in part by Virtual Simulation Experiment Teaching Project of Zhejiang under Grant No.2019-250.

Reference

1. Wu Song, Wang Kun, Jin Hai. Journal of Computer Research and Development 56,58-68 (2019)
2. Wang Baosheng, Zhang Weiqi. Journal of National University of Defense Technology 41,142-152 (2019)
3. SEL Laboratory of Zhejiang University. Docker container and container cloud (version 2) ,108-127 (2020)
4. Zhang Qing, Liu Jian, Zhu Xiaomin. Telecom Engineering Technics and Standardization 28, 74-77 (2015)
5. Zhang Weiqi. National University of Defense Technology Master Dissertation,31-38 (2018)
6. Yang Xin, Wu Zhinan, Qian Songrong. Microcomputer Applications 32, 58-60 (2016)
7. Li Wei, Zhao Yongbin, Wang Ou, Gang Yining. Machinery Design & Manufacture 5,270-272 (2017)
8. Feng Mingzhen. Zhejiang University Master Dissertation,48-55 (2016)
9. Zang Di, Yang Zhigang, Wang Jing, Yao Zhicheng, Zhang Weigong. Computer Engineering 48,214-219 (2022)
10. Nigel Poulton. Docker Deep Dive,157-168 (2019)
11. Use Macvlan networks[EB/OL].https://docs.docker.com/network/macvlan (2022)
12. Use Ipvlan networks[EB/OL].https://docs.docker.com/network/ipvlan (2022)
13. Jian Caili. Huazhong University of Science & Technology Master Dissertation,44-52 (2020)
14. Wang Peng. Research on Digital Media 39, 67-71 (2022)
15. Iperf ultimate speed test tool for TCP, UDP and SCTP [EB/OL].https://iperf.fr (2022)

Research progress and prospect of gravity erosion in loess region

Jiaguo Gong[1,*], *Qianqian* Zhang[2], *Hao* Wang[1], *Yunzhong* Jiang[1], *Zheng* Ren[2], and *Liangjun* Ma[3]

[1] State Key Laboratory of Simulation and Regulation of Water Cycle in River Basin, China Institute of Water Resources and Hydropower Research, Beijing 100038, China
[2] School of Water Conservancy and Hydroelectric Power, Hebei University of Engineering, Handan 056038 China
[3] College of Energy and Power Engineering, Lanzhou University of Technology, Lanzhou 730050, China

Keywords: Gravitational erosion, Photogrammetry, Critical condition, Simulation of gravity erosion process, Loess region.

Abstract. Gravity erosion is one of the most important types of soil erosion in the loess region, and it is the focus and difficulty of the current erosion research in the loess region. This paper systematically reviews the research progress of gravity erosion experimental observation methods, gravity erosion occurrence critical conditions, the relationship between gravity erosion and watershed water sediment, and gravity erosion process simulation and so on, It points out that the lack of monitoring capacity of gravity erosion process caused by the random, sudden and rapid characteristics of gravity erosion is the bottleneck of gravity erosion mechanism research, It is proposed that new techniques such as photogrammetry with strong anti-interference ability and high spatial-temporal resolution should be introduced to strengthen experimental observation; Integrating the long-term and short-term influencing factors of gravity erosion process, revealing the control mechanism of infiltration on the occurrence of gravity erosion, and clarifying the critical law of gravity erosion; Strengthen the study of critical conditions and redistribution mechanism based on process, and reveal the mechanism of gravity erosion material stabilization and sediment yield differentiation; The combination law of influencing factors in the process of gravity erosion and sediment yield is explored, the uncertainty mechanism of the process of erosion and sediment yield is analyzed, and the zoning method of gravity erosion prone areas is explored; A watershed water sediment coupling simulation model with the physical mechanism of gravity erosion is developed to deeply reveal the coupling relationship between gravity erosion and watershed water

*Corresponding author: gongjg185@163.com

sediment process, and to provide reference for related research.

*Corresponding author:: gongjg185@163.com

1 Introduction

Gravity erosion is an important form of soil erosion in loess Plateau. Gravity erosion refers to the process in which the rock mass or soil mass loses its balance and displaces under the action of gravity [1]. According to the mechanical mechanism, material composition characteristics and scale of gravity erosion in loess area, gravity erosion can be divided into landslide, collapse, mud flow and other types. The main inducing factors can be divided into rainfall infiltration, vegetation root splitting, water erosion and so on. Gravity erosion is the main sediment yield mechanism in the Loess Plateau. Previous studies have shown that the contribution of gravity erosion to basin sediment is more than 20% [2-5]. If the contribution of hydraulic gravity erosion process is considered, the contribution of gravity erosion to basin sediment is more than 50% [4].

Gravity erosion is characterized by randomness, abruptness and rapidity, and its occurrence and development process is affected by many factors. The coupling response relationship is complex, resulting in the complex and changeable control mechanism of the occurrence, development and sediment yield process of gravity erosion [6-7]. Compared with hydraulic erosion research, the above reasons result in the lack of basic observation data for gravity erosion research, the lack of in-depth mechanism of erosion and sediment yield, and the slow progress of simulation research [8]. Therefore, it is urgent to systematically sort out the research results of the observation method of gravity erosion test, the critical mechanism of gravity erosion, the restabilization mechanism of gravity erosion material and the differentiation mechanism of erosion sediment production, and the simulation of gravity erosion sand production process, so as to explore to break the bottleneck of experimental research and to reveal the gravity erosion in depth. Erosion mechanism, as well as the research direction of research and development of gravity erosion simulation model, in order to achieve breakthroughs, provide scientific and technological support for scientific understanding of soil erosion in the Loess Plateau, construction of the Yellow River digital twin watershed and watershed/regional soil erosion control measures, control systems, governance decisions, et al.

2 Research progress

2.1 Observation method of gravity erosion test

2.1.1 Application of early monitoring technology in gravity erosion

My country's gravity erosion monitoring technology first started in the 1980s and was developed and applied in the Loess Plateau. Early monitoring techniques are widely used in field surveys, including filling methods, volumetric methods, stylus methods and pocket soil methods. Zheng [9] used the soil filling method and the volume method to monitor the erosion amount of the rill, and analyzed the monitoring accuracy of the two methods in terms of the erosion amount. It was found that the accuracy of the soil filling method was higher than that of the volume method, but the operation steps were less. The volumetric method is cumbersome and only suitable for indoor experiments. Yang et al. [10] used the stylus method to observe the occurrence types of small-scale gravitational erosion on the Qiaogou gully slope, and successfully observed three types of gravitational erosion: gully slip, small-scale collapse, and small-scale slump. Gao et al. [11] used the stylus method and the pocket soil method to observe the influencing factors and the amount of small-scale gravity erosion in the Xindiangou watershed. The observation frequency of additional measurements after heavy rain has successfully observed gravitational erosion types such as slop, small caving, and small slumps.

2.1.2 Application of new technology in gravity erosion

In recent years, with the development of measurement technology, 3D laser scanning technology, geomorphometer method, unmanned aerial vehicle (UAV) aerial measurement technology and photogrammetry technology have also received more and more attention in the field of gravity erosion research.

Zhang et al. [12] used high-precision GPS, 3D laser scanner and pinprick method to monitor and analyze rill erosion amount and rill erosion evolution process, and compared the observation accuracy of the three methods, and found that the calculation accuracy and DEM image generated by 3D laser scanner were superior to the other two methods. Zhang et al. [13] and Qin [14] used the method of combining 3D laser scanning technology and Cylone6.0 to monitor the terrain changes in the indoor simulated rainfall test process, and generated a terrain DEM accuracy of 2mm×2mm under gully erosion condition, and the calculation accuracy of erosion amount reached 96.85%. Huo et al. [15], Zhao et al. [16] using 3 d laser scanner to monitor the interior more than the same slope rill erosion under the condition of rainfall simulation, the dynamic process of using the generate DEM has realized the rill plane density, maximum average long groove depth, groove, groove more than average density and erosion intensity erosion topographic index calculation.

At the same time, the monitoring technology of regional topographic change with professional camera carried by UAV has also been gradually applied to the investigation and research of soil erosion. Gao et al. [17] used UAV aerial remote sensing technology to extract characteristic data of gravity erosion caused by heavy rain on July 26, 2017 in Xindiagou Basin, with an accuracy of 89.53%. Liao et al. [18] used UAV technology to obtain spatial distribution patterns and rill characteristics of rill with different slope and slope length in the field exposed plot under natural rainfall conditions as the research object. Compared with early detection technology, 3Dlaser scanner and UAV photogrammetry of high precision, high efficiency, no monitoring can take the initiative to contact, by repeating the same area to implement the dynamic monitoring of erosion process, but as a result of monitoring efficiency, and rainfall influence on the laser echo signal and the safety of (UAV), the technology is difficult to realize real-time dynamic monitoring of erosion process, Thus limiting the application of gravity erosion in observation. In view of the above shortcomings, Xu et al. [19] independently studied a set of MX-2010-G geomorphometer and gradually improved it, realizing the near-real-time monitoring and recording of gravity erosion process and using this system to achieve accurate monitoring of erosion amount, sliding volume, soil loss caused by slope flow erosion and other indicators in the process of gully slope gravity erosion.

In addition, the close-range photogrammetry technology is gradually maturing. Due to its advantages of large-scale synchronous observation, high timeliness, strong raindrop interference resistance and high measurement accuracy, some researchers have introduced it into the dynamic monitoring test of soil erosion. Guo et al. [20] and Jiang et al. [21] integrated UAV aerial survey and handheld photogrammetry to build a photogrammetry observation system, and realized near-real-time dynamic monitoring of rill erosion process under rainfall conditions. By using this system, the terrain change monitoring with time interval of 2min and spatial resolution of 1.5mm is realized, indicating that the close-range photogrammetry system has a good application prospect in the dynamic monitoring of erosional terrain. Due to the gravity erosion process has the characteristics of sudden, random, fast, and is often accompanied by interference factors such as rainfall, early gravity erosion monitoring is limited by technical means, mainly adopts artificial stationing, timely monitoring of the observed or encryption method of gravity erosion monitoring, difficult to capture the critical state of gravity erosion occurs, The timeliness and accuracy of measurement are relatively low (Table 1), and the gravity erosion data obtained by monitoring is difficult to match with influencing factors such as rainfall process and soil moisture content process to conduct accurate correlation analysis. With the development and application of new technologies, 3D laser scanning technology, UAV aerial survey technology, geomorphic method and photogrammetry technology have been continuously improving the accuracy, timeliness and anti-interference ability of gravity erosion observation tests (Table 2). Among them, 3D laser scanning and UAV aerial measurement technology have greatly improved the efficiency and accuracy of single and large area measurement. Combining the advantages of high speed photography, the geomorphic method can record and analyze the gravity erosion process at high speed by using laser to mark feature points and manual processing. Photogrammetry technology has been in an indoor slope rill erosion successful application in the measurement test, as the technology matures, the precision of matching, time response, and the other factors, measure performance in the rain, so on real-time with high advantage, it to achieve the real time dynamic measurement of the gravity erosion process laid a solid foundation.

Table 1. Comparative analysis of early observation methods.

The serial number	The name of the methods	The main measurement The principle of	precision	Time response	And other observational factors fit	Real-time measurement performance in rain	Real-time measurement performance in rain
1	Fill in the mill	Volume method	Centimeter level	time	Poor	generally	Poor
2	Volumetric method	Volume method	Centimeter level	time	Poor	generally	Poor
3	Measuring the stitch	Volume method	Centimeter level	time	Poor	generally	Poor
4	Bag making	Volume method	Centimeter level	time	Poor	generally	Poor

Table 2. Comparative analysis of new technology observation methods.

The serial number	The name of the methods	The main measurement The principle of	precision	Time response	And other observational factors fit	Real-time measurement performance in rain	Real-time measurement performance in rain
1	3D laser scanning	Principle of laser positioning	millimeter level	time	Good	Poor	Poor
2	Aerial photogrammetry by UVA	Principle of aerial triangulation	Centimeter level	time	Good	general	Poor
3	Method of sonar	Laser positioning, human eye recognition	Centimeter level	time	Good	Good	general
4	Close range photogrammetry	Principle of aerial triangulation	millimeter level	Second level	Good	better	Good

2.2 Study on the mechanism of gravity erosion

2.2.1 Research progress on factors affecting gravity erosion and its criticality

There are many factors affecting the process of gravity erosion on the Loess Plateau, including soil type, soil weathering degree, soil structure, soil bulk density, soil moisture content, slope, slope aspect, vegetation type, vegetation root system, soil animal activity, rainfall intensity, rainfall duration, earthquake, Freezing and thawing, human activities, et al. According to the time course of influence on gravity erosion, it can be divided into short-term influencing factors and long-term influencing factors. Short-term influencing factors include rainfall, earthquake and soil infiltration characteristics, while long-term influencing factors mainly include soil types, soil structure, topography and vegetation, et al.

Rainfall is an important driving factor of gravity erosion. Yang et al. [3, 22] analyzed the factors influencing the occurrence of small-scale gravity erosion and found that the higher the rainfall, the higher the frequency of gravity erosion. Yan [23], Liu [24], Xu et al. [25] found through indoor simulation tests that when the rain intensity was small, the proportion of large-scale gravity erosion events was large, and the topography development could be deduced from the side of the current generation. The rainfall duration has an obvious effect on the gravity erosion process in the early stage of topography development, and the effect gradually decreases with the topography development. There is no simple proportional relationship between gravity erosion and rainfall, which is affected by both rainfall intensity and rainfall. Xu et al. [26] analyzed the gravity erosion process and sensitivity and found that gravity erosion on gully slope is mainly manifested in three forms: landslide, collapse and mud flow. At the same time in the process of rainfall, with the same pattern and massive destruction of similar size will often appear adjacent, gravity erosion occurred frequency, scale and rainfall and rainfall intensity has a direct relationship, but in the early relief development, the influence of rainfall the obvious, therefore, no matter from gravity erosion test total peak, Rainfall duration is the main sensitive parameter affecting landslide and mud flow.

The influence of vegetation on gravity erosion is positively and negatively correlated. Sun et al. [27] used the grey correlation degree method to analyze the correlation between shear strength and soil parameters of landslide soil in Zhonggou Watershed, and found that the correlation between dry bulk density, water content, slope, root content and shear strength decreased successively. Zhang [28] analyzed the influence of vegetation restoration on gravity erosion from two aspects of soil moisture and root soil fixation, and found that with the increase of soil moisture, roots would inhibit gravity erosion. However, the root extrusion in the process of growth will promote the occurrence of collapse and landslide. Gao et al. [29] studied the effect of vegetation on the occurrence time, intensity and erosion rate of gravity erosion on the gully slope, and found that when the rainfall conditions on the gully slope model were consistent, the effect of vegetation on the occurrence of gravity erosion showed a time lag effect, which was different from that of the gully slope model. Compared with the bare land model, vegetation increases the distribution of small gravity erosion scales, but vegetation increases the gravity erosion rate in the short term and slows down the development of gravity erosion in the long run. Zhao et al. [30-31] analyzed the influence of vegetation on the gravitational erosion of gully slope under heavy rain conditions through the rainfall test of the bare soil model of the loess gully slope and the root-soil composite model, and found that the amount of secondary rainfall gravitational erosion in the root-soil model and the bare soil model was All showed a trend of rapid growth at first and then a gradual decrease, but the increase in the amount of gravity erosion in the root-soil model was smaller than that in the bare-soil model. Jiao et al.[32] and Wang [33] analyzed the soil erosion characteristics of different vegetation types based on the vegetation pattern characteristics of typical small watersheds in the loess hilly and gully area, and found that the erosion reduction ability of artificial shrubs is better than that of artificial trees, and with vegetation The increase in coverage achieves the effect of resisting the erosion of heavy rain. The above studies show that the influence of vegetation on the gravity erosion process is mainly manifested in two aspects: one is to change the mechanical properties between soil masses through root growth and interpenetration distribution; the other is to change the soil through the redistribution of rainfall and its infiltration process. The mechanical properties between the bodies affect the frequency, location, and amount of gravity erosion.

Geomorphic development stage determines the intensity of internal and external forces, and influences the action direction, occurrence frequency and erosion intensity of gravity erosion [27]. Xue et al. [34], Xin et al. [35], Wang et al. [36] analyzed the relationship between terrain fractals, river network channel fractals and gravity erosion, and found that the fractals can reflect the comprehensive factors of the basin topography and geomorphology, which can be used for The macroscopic prediction of gravity erosion, in which slope is the most important factor affecting the frequency, type and scale of gravity erosion [3]. Zhao [37] and Wang [38] based on the simulation test of gravity erosion on loess gully slope, found that the slope determines the type and scale of gravity erosion, and the slope height is an important factor affecting the occurrence of gravity erosion. When the gully slope has the same slope, the total gravity erosion is positively correlated with the slope height, but the slump erosion is less affected by the slope height, and the water content of the underlying surface is an important triggering factor for the gully slope gravity erosion. Yu et al. [39-40], Dong [41] took Baota District, Yan'an City, Shaanxi Province as the research object, analyzed the impact of topography and landform on gravity erosion, and found that slope is an important limiting factor for gravity erosion. With the increase of slope, the development of landslide at the foot of gully slope is accelerated, but for the landslide near the gully edge line, the impact of rainfall is higher than the slope. Ma et al. [42] found through the simulated rainfall test that the gravity erosion is the main driving force of the gentle slope land loss, and the correlation coefficient between the gentle slope land loss area and the gully side gravity erosion is 0.93. Tang et al. [43] found that landform is the congenital condition for the development and distribution of landslides, and geological structure is an important influencing factor for the centralized development and distribution of landslides. Earthquakes have a dual effect on the occurrence of landslides. In a short time, the structural zone affected by the release of seismic energy is easy to directly cause landslides; Over a long period of time, critical energy balance will be formed in some slopes affected by earthquake, and landslides will be more likely to occur in the future under other triggering factors of the same conditions.

Soil structure mainly affects gravity erosion by affecting the shear strength and mechanical stability of soil. Zhou et al. [44] analyzed the influence of freeze-thaw on the physical properties of soil samples and found that the changes of density and void ratio of soil samples showed "conjugate" changes, and multiple freeze-thaw cycles could change the internal structure and hydraulic properties of loess. Yao et al. [45] studied the erosion mechanism of arsenic sandstone and found that gravity erosion is closely related to the slope gradient and lithology of arsenic sandstone. When the slope Angle is larger than the critical slope Angle, gravity erosion is easy to occur. Yang [46] believes that all kinds of landslides will be affected by formation lithology and topographic structure. Due to the high content of clay minerals in Loess and strong hydrophilicity, it is easier to cause sliding, and the volume shrinkage of loess after water loss will cause soil fracture and loosening, which is very prone to gravity erosion. He et al. [47] and Xu et al. [48] believe that due to the existence of plant root pores, biological caves, bedding and pores in the Loess Plateau, with the seepage of water and the loss of particles, the pores can also continue to expand into caves, especially along the vertical joints, it is easier to produce caves and caves, and finally cause ground collapse. Li et al. [49] analyzed the impact of loess caves on loess landslides and believed that caves can accelerate the development of gullies, form landslide perimeter and free face, and intensify soil loss, fragmentation and local collapse. At the same time, the seepage conditions of the slope are changed, resulting in the concentrated infiltration of surface water, which induces the occurrence of landslides and the revival of ancient landslides.

The critical condition of gravity erosion in loess area is that the sliding force of unstable soil exceeds the shear resistance of sliding surface. The mechanical properties of soil such as structural strength, shear strength, cohesion and internal friction angle are mainly affected by soil type, dry density and water content of soil. Dang et al. [50-51] analyzed the influence of water content on the strength of unsaturated loess, gave a method to determine the structural strength of loess, and pointed out that the structural strength of unsaturated loess can be measured by the strength lost after its natural structure is destroyed, and there is a power function relationship between the structural strength and the initial water content; There is a good linear relationship between structural strength and unstable cohesion; The concept of ultimate strength moisture content of unsaturated loess is proposed. Zhang et al. [52] took the Loess in Yangling area as the research object, and found that with the increase of water content, its structural strength and shear strength showed a decreasing trend, but the ratio of shear strength to structural strength basically remained unchanged, and the cohesion of unsaturated loess was negatively correlated with water content. Fan [53] analyzed the shear strength of shallow undisturbed soil in the Loess Plateau and found that with the increase of <0.01mm physical clay content in the soil, the cohesion of the soil increases and the internal friction angle decreases; With the increase of dry bulk density, soil cohesion increased, internal friction angle decreased, and shear strength increased; With the increase of soil moisture content, the cohesion and internal friction angle of soil decrease, and the shear strength decreases. Yang et al. [3, 22] found through direct shear test that the cohesion and internal friction angle of loess decreased significantly with the increase of water content; For Malan loess, it is easy to collapse when the average water content of the soil near the collapse surface reaches 12%~15%. At this time, the internal friction angle is 30 ° ~35 °. The cohesion at the collapse surface is below 5kpa, which is far less than the measured cohesion of the undisturbed loess of about 25kpa under the same water content. Chen et al. [54] analyzed the relationship between water content and shear strength parameters of unsaturated loess in Lanzhou, Gansu Province, and found that the cohesion of unsaturated loess is greatly affected by water content. Guo et al. [55] analyzed the rapid shear test and believed that the dry density affects the shear strength by affecting the cohesion and internal friction angle, while the water content only affects the shear strength by affecting the cohesion.

2.2.2 Research progress on redistribution of gravity eroded materials

The redistribution process of gravity eroded material generally includes two forms: the first form is the process of rapid sliding and redistribution of gravity eroded soil under the action of gravity; The second form is the process of secondary erosion of gravity eroded soil under the action of rainfall and surface runoff. For the first redistribution process, there is no relevant research. For the second redistribution process, Guo et al. [56] found that gravity erosion has a significant impact on the particle size distribution of suspended sediment through field observation and analysis. With the occurrence of large-scale erosion, the proportion of sand particles in runoff sediment decreased from 71% to 51%, while the proportion of clay particles and silt particles increased from 1% to 7% and 28% to 42% respectively. According to this, when gravity erosion occurs, the suspended sediment load becomes smaller, and the sediment is easier to be transported to the gully flow. Gravity erosion makes the particle size distribution of suspended sediment more uneven and irregular.

2.2.3 Study on control mechanism of gravity erosion reduction

Water and soil conservation is an important basic national policy and an important starting point for the construction of ecological civilization in China. In the 1950s, various water and soil conservation projects, such as the construction of terraces, check dams, planting trees and grass, were implemented in the Yanhe River Basin; Since the 1990s, ecological restoration projects focusing on vegetation restoration, such as beautiful mountains and rivers and returning farmland to forest (grass), have been implemented successively [57]. Many scholars have explored and studied the regulation effect of soil and water conservation measures on gravity erosion. Yu et al. [58] considered that the erosion reduction effect of silt dam is stronger than that of vegetation in small watershed scale, while that of vegetation is better than that of silt dam in large scale. Chai et al. [59] taking Tianjiagou small watershed as the research object, the research shows that five control measures, namely, three-dimensional protection, landscape shelter, gully slope treatment, gully locking and foot fixing, have better control effect on erosion of red soil diarrhea sliding surface. Zhao et al. [60] proposed a method for selecting and optimizing combination of water and soil conservation plants on the Zhuanyaogou watershed of Hequ County, Shanxi Province, in the hilly and gully area of the Loess Plateau, by identifying four representative herbal plant roots to enhance soil shear strength. Hu [61] Research holds that artificial planting of seabuckthorn in arsenic sandstone Valley can gradually reduce or eliminate the influence of dry, wet, cold and heat changes, prevent the generation of new clastics layer, at the same time, the root system and litter have good protection to the existing clastics layer, so as to effectively block the diarrhea and reduce the occurrence of gravity erosion. Based on the above studies, gravity erosion in the loess area is characterized by soil destabilization under the combined action of soil and its structure, topography, vegetation, rainfall and other factors. The critical mechanism is that the sliding force of unstable soil exceeds the shear resistance of sliding surface. In the process, long time history influence factors including soil and its structure, topography, vegetation, etc., short-term factors mainly include rainfall characteristic parameters and the redistribution process, and the adjustment of the soil mechanics parameters, including rainfall, rainfall duration, rainfall intensity, soil moisture, soil infiltration rate and so on. The complex coupling effect of the above factors makes the sliding force and shear resistance of the sliding surface of soil in a complex dynamic adjustment, which makes the occurrence of gravity erosion sudden, random and rapid, and causes great difficulties to the observation and research. At the same time, the influence of gravity erosion on watershed water and sediment processes is coupled with the redistribution of erosion materials and the complex interaction with hydraulic processes after the occurrence of gravity erosion, which further aggravates the complexity of watershed water and sediment processes. At the same time, it is relatively weak to identify the mechanism of gravity erosion control from the perspective of soil and water conservation practice.

2.3 Research progress of gravity erosion simulation

2.3.1 Simulation of gravity erosion based on watershed water and sediment processes

The process of gravity erosion and sediment yield is an important part of the watershed water and sediment process. However, due to the lag of its mechanism research and the complexity of the process, most of the existing studies use indirect methods or generalized theoretical models to simulate gravity erosion and sediment yield. Cai et al. [62] based on the field observation and simulated rainfall test data of small watershed, a process model for predicting erosion and sediment yield of small watershed in Loess Hilly and gully region is established, which is composed of slope sub model, gully slope sub model and gully sub model. In the gully slope sub model, the power function relationship between gravity erosion and runoff depth is obtained by fitting. This study also provides a good reference for gravity erosion simulation in the process of watershed runoff and sediment. Li et al. [63-64] , Wang et al. [65] integrating three sub models of slope erosion, gravity erosion in gully slope area and unbalanced sediment transport in gully, a digital watershed model of the Yellow River is proposed and applied to the simulation of erosion and sediment production process in small watersheds. It is found that within the scale range of 10^5~10^6 m^2, the gravity erosion modulus increases with the increase of water flow, but at a larger watershed scale, the landform adjacent to the gully no longer exists, and gravity erosion no longer contributes to the total sediment transport. Wang [66] based on hydrological station network of gully and indoor simulated rainfall test data, an indoor general model of small watershed is established. Based on three time scales of annual, secondary flood event and secondary flood process, the water and sediment characteristics of geomorphic unit in different time and space scales of slope-gully-watershed system are obtained and applied in small watershed of Peijiamaogou and Qiaogou. Zhu et al. [67] the regional division of gravity erosion in West Shanxi is carried out by using fuzzy clustering method, and a typical small watershed is selected in each area to study the sediment yield mode, intensity and its proportion in total erosion. It is concluded that gravity erosion accounts for 35%~46% of total erosion. Zhang et al. [68] using quantitative geomorphology, the relationship between topographic factor of gravity erosion (A) and gravity erosion intensity is introduced and quantified. It is found that the gravity erosion intensity of loess sandstone, soft rock and hard rock will reach A severe degree when A value is greater than 0.8, 1.0 and 1.6 respectively. Fu et al.[69-70] based on the grey theory, a grey system prediction model based on the dynamic change law of gravity erosion is constructed to analyze the correlation between the predicted value series and the observed value series of gravity erosion. The core of the model is the correlation degree between the predicted value and the measured value. In essence, the grey system model belongs to the category of empirical regression model and does not directly involve the mechanical mechanism. Jin et al. [71] assuming that the occurrence of gravity erosion is controlled by internal and external factors, the internal and external factors are quantified by linear regression method and normalized comparison method respectively, and all channel units are queued according to the size of impact factors, so as to determine the channel unit where gravity erosion occurs. The above models are generally statistical models, which do not fully consider the mechanical mechanism and randomness of soil instability, and have poor applicability.

Wang et al. [72-74], Li et al. [2] the gully slope gravity erosion theoretical model based on soil instability is coupled and integrated with the slope rainfall runoff and soil erosion model and the gully unbalanced sediment transport model under the framework of DYRIM model. The simulation of watershed water and sediment processes including gravity erosion and sediment production process is realized and applied in Chabagou and Wuding River basins. Gong et al. [75] based on WEP model, the mechanism of raindrop splash erosion, thin layer flow erosion, stream erosion and gravity erosion is systematically considered, and the watershed water sediment coupling simulation model is established and applied in Nanxiaohegou watershed and Jinghe Watershed. The simulation of gravity erosion process is mainly to generalize the sliding soil mass into a triangular body, judge the gravity erosion critical by comparing and analyzing the sliding force and the shear strength of the sliding surface, and calculate the sediment production process by using the sediment carrying capacity of water flow and the principle of unbalanced sediment transport, which has achieved good simulation results. Liu et al. [76-77] a grid based small-scale continuous computing distributed hydrological model for arid and semi-arid areas is proposed, and the hydraulic erosion and gravity erosion sediment yield modules are reserved to realize the coupling calculation of water and sediment in the future research work, and establish the water and sediment yield and sediment transport model for the Loess Plateau. Cai et al. [78], Zhu et al. [79] A distributed water-sediment model (WEP-SED) was established to simulate the gravity erosion based on the collapse process, and the erosion soil was generalized as a four-prism to simulate the calculation. The results are in good agreement with the literature data.

To sum up, there are many uncertainties in the understanding of the critical mechanism of gravity erosion and the redistribution process of eroded substances, the understanding of the mechanism of gravity erosion is not unified, there are few studies on the redistribution mechanism of gravity eroded substances, and there are complex scale effects in the watershed water and sediment process, so the existing research results of gravity erosion simulation based on the perspective of watershed water and sediment process are basically: Indirect analysis of gravity erosion based on water sediment relationship; Quantitative analysis based on short-term and small-scale field observation data; Empirical model based on fuzzy clustering, regression analysis and grey system prediction model; Based on the physical mechanism model generalized in theory, the research results are speculative to some extent, and the representativeness is insufficient. Its reliability and multi-scale applicability are still in doubt. Watershed/regional scale water and sediment process analysis is the basis for large-scale water and soil loss control. It is urgent to carry out simulation research on gravity erosion water and sediment process based on physical mechanism, so as to provide basic scientific tools for watershed water and sediment coupling simulation based on physical process.

2.3.2 Gravity erosion simulation research based on Engineering Perspective

Gravity erosion is also an important form of geological disaster. Many scholars have carried out simulation research on gravity erosion based on soil mechanics, material mechanics and other principles for potential sites of gravity erosion. Cao [80] used the sliding arc method in traditional soil mechanics to analyze the force on the valley slope, and proposed the ratio of shear strength to shear stress of the soil on the sliding surface as the critical judgment condition for the occurrence of gravity erosion, and pointed out that whether the slope is balanced depends on the dynamic balance relationship between shear force and shear resistance. Yu et al. [81-82], Zhang et al. [83], Lu et al. [84], Jin et al. [85] used the finite difference FLAC3D software to study the gravity erosion mechanism of the generalized model of the small watershed on the Loess Plateau. It was found that the internal stress of the slope in the small watershed was mainly generated by the self weight of the rock and soil mass of the slope, and the yield of the internal soil mass was mainly in the "pressure shear" yield mode; At the same time, it is found that when there is vegetation coverage, the root reinforcement improves part of the stress of the shallow soil, weakens the stress of the root layer through the diffusion effect, enhances the sharing effect of the root system on the soil, effectively reduces the stress concentration of the slope soil, is conducive to controlling the deformation of the slope and improving the stability of the slope, and reduces the volume of the plastic yield zone and the tensile plastic yield zone through the shallow layer of the slope to varying degrees, The failure degree of gravity erosion is reduced, but the shear failure mode is still the main mode of gravity erosion yield. Based on the strength reduction theory, Zhang [86] used the finite element simulation software geo5 and ABAQUS numerical simulation software to study the mechanical mechanism of gravity erosion collapse process and pattern of coarse sand bank slope in desert in a small watershed, and compared it with the collapse characteristics of loess bank slope, pointing out that the sensitivity of bank slope stability to cohesion, internal friction angle and groundwater level decreased in turn, The longer the plastic deformation and complete instability of the bank slope soil take, the stronger the stability of the bank slope soil is, and the slope angle is the most dangerous part. Wei [87], Zou [88-89], Gao et al. [90-91] used the finite element software and the strength reduction coefficient method to establish the generalized model of the slope gully system in the nianzhuang gully basin and the generalized model of the Guandi gully slope gully system. By using the method of probability statistics and numerical simulation analysis, they studied the correlation between the residual slope length of the slope gully system and the siltation height of the dam site, and obtained that under the same siltation height, There is a binomial relationship between the amount of sediment deposited and the height; With the same sediment yield, the vertical siltation height on the dam site and the current siltation height on the dam site satisfy the power correlation.

The gravity erosion simulation research based on the engineering perspective, based on the mathematical and physical equations, takes the soil as a continuously changing material medium, uses a variety of mathematical methods to simulate and analyze the stress state and continuous deformation process of the soil, and establishes the continuous equation for mathematical calculation and description, which is quite different from the actual situation of loess with expansibility and joint structure development, and the scope of application is limited. In addition, this kind of model often focuses on the process of soil instability. Although it has certain advantages in the study of the critical characteristics of gravity erosion and is helpful for the in-depth understanding of the mechanism of gravity erosion, the research scale is relatively small and rarely involves the sediment production process. Therefore, it is difficult to meet the needs of the study of watershed water and sediment processes.

3 Analysis and Prospect

3.1 problem analysis

To sum up, some research achievements have been made in the aspects of experimental observation system and method, influencing factors, process mechanism, model simulation, etc. There are still some problems in gravity erosion research:

(1) The monitoring system of gravity erosion process is still the bottleneck of further mechanism research. Due to the sudden, random and rapid characteristics of gravity erosion process, the early gravity erosion monitoring technology mainly adopts the methods of manual point distribution, regular monitoring or intensive observation, which is difficult to make coupling and matching analysis with the influencing factors such as rainfall and soil moisture content process, and the timeliness and accuracy of measurement are difficult to meet the research needs for further revealing the critical characteristics of gravity erosion. The emerging three-dimensional laser scanner and UAV aerial photogrammetry have high precision, high work efficiency, no active contact, and can realize the dynamic monitoring of the erosion process by repeatedly monitoring the same area. However, due to the monitoring efficiency and the impact of rainfall on the laser echo signal and UAV safety, it is difficult to realize the real-time dynamic monitoring of the erosion process. Close range photogrammetry includes the advantages of the above technologies, as well as the advantages of large-scale synchronous observation and strong resistance to raindrop interference. However, there are still deficiencies in the application of gravity erosion, resulting in the lack of basic observation data. It has always been the bottleneck for the progress of gravity erosion mechanism and simulation research.

(2) The soil and its structure, topography, vegetation, rainfall and other factors are divided into long-term and short-term influencing factors. The complex coupling effect of long-term and short-term influencing factors makes the soil sliding force and the shear resistance of the sliding surface in complex dynamic adjustment. The complex dynamic changes make the erosion material redistributed after the occurrence of gravity erosion or coupled with the hydraulic process, further aggravating the complexity of the watershed water and sediment process. The main reason is that the existing erosion and sediment yield mechanism is not deep enough due to the numerous influencing factors of gravity erosion process, the complex coupling response relationship and the lack of basic observation data. Most of the research results focus on the qualitative relationship between gravity erosion and rainfall, topography, vegetation, soil and other factors. It is difficult to form a unified conclusion from the Angle,

depth and level of research. There are few quantitative research results, and the mechanism of gravity erosion is not clearly understood.

(3) The engineering perspective is mainly used to analyze the process of soil instability caused by gravity erosion. It has certain advantages in studying the critical mechanism, but the research scale is small, and the sediment production process is rarely involved; From the perspective of watershed water and sediment process, the relationship between watershed water and sediment is analyzed mainly based on the empirical model and the physical mechanism model after theoretical generalization, It is only a quantitative analysis of short-term and small-scale field observation data. Its representativeness is insufficient, and its reliability and applicability are still in doubt. The main reason is that most of the existing studies are based on the response relationship of gravity erosion influencing factors, so it is difficult to quantitatively reveal the occurrence, development and sediment yield process of gravity erosion, and it is difficult to support the research and development of gravity erosion simulation model based on physical mechanism. At the same time, due to the lack of effective observation data, it is difficult to judge whether the results of the existing gravity erosion simulation model can reflect the real situation, which makes the simulation research progress slow.

3.2 Prospect

In view of the above problems, it is urgent to reveal the mechanism of gravity erosion, the mechanism of gravity erosion material re stabilization and sediment yield differentiation on the basis of breaking through the monitoring means of gravity erosion process, On the one hand, it supports the uncertainty analysis of gravity erosion sediment yield process, and forms a scientific classification and zoning method of gravity erosion prone areas to provide support for gravity erosion control; On the other hand, support the research and development of gravity erosion simulation model based on physical mechanism, and improve the scientific research "Puzzle" of soil and water loss in the loess region.

(1) Break through the bottleneck of gravity erosion process observation. In the process of gravity erosion, the soil displacement is the main body, and the soil is a good light scattering body, so the photogrammetry observation method becomes a better choice, which can realize the dynamic monitoring with high time and space resolution under the condition of rainfall; By introducing photogrammetry technology, a terrain change process monitoring test system with large scene synchronous measurement, high time resolution and high spatial resolution is constructed. Through comprehensive configuration of terrain change monitoring, soil water content monitoring, vegetation, soil and other parameter characteristics, a gravity erosion process monitoring and test system is formed. Research and develop observation technology suitable for gravity erosion test. So as to "see" the process of gravity erosion sediment production, and lay a foundation for revealing the mechanism of gravity erosion and exploring the field monitoring method of gravity erosion.

(2) The control mechanism of infiltration on gravity erosion is revealed. The physical process of gravity erosion can be regarded as the instability process of erosion body. In this process, the soil, vegetation, terrain and other factors have a long action time process on the erosion body, while rainfall rapidly changes the mechanical properties of the sliding surface of the erosion body under the action of near ground wind speed, vegetation, terrain, soil hydrological characteristics and other factors, and the action time process is relatively rapid. It is necessary to grasp this key process, integrate different long-term and short-term influencing factors, use the gravity erosion process observation and test system to clarify the characteristics of gravity erosion sliding surface, study the coupling relationship between the critical terrain, soil moisture content, sliding surface characteristics, etc. of different types of

gravity erosion such as landslide, collapse and mud flow, and deeply reveal the control mechanism of infiltration on the occurrence of gravity erosion.

(3) Reveal the mechanism of gravity erosion material re stabilization and sediment yield differentiation. Among the existing studies, the research on the redistribution process of gravity erosion is relatively weak, which is difficult to support the analysis of the impact of gravity erosion on watershed water and sediment. The current research results on the process of gravity erosion on watershed water and sediment are mostly based on the qualitative or semi quantitative relationship obtained from the analysis of mutual relationship. Using indoor and outdoor monitoring tests, the coupling relationship between the moving process of erosion body to the downstream and the influencing factors such as rainfall, vegetation and topography is analyzed, and the proportion between the material quality directly entering the gully bottom and the contribution of secondary erosion is studied; It reveals the differentiation mechanism of gravity erosion and sediment yield, which directly converges into the watershed runoff, indirectly converges into the watershed runoff through the land surface hydrological process, and restabilizes the erosion body.

(4) The uncertainty mechanism of gravity erosion sediment yield process is analyzed, and the zoning method of gravity erosion prone areas is explored. On the basis of systematically identifying the characteristics of controlling factors in the occurrence and development process of gravity erosion, Based on indoor and outdoor tests, the variation range of characteristic values of different factors is analyzed, the combination law of influencing factors of gravity erosion sediment yield process is explored, the uncertainty mechanism of erosion sediment yield process is analyzed, and on this basis, the zoning method of gravity erosion prone areas is explored to provide scientific support for gravity erosion prevention and control.

(5) Research and develop a basin water sediment coupling model for the physical mechanism of gravity erosion. The existing gravity erosion simulation, on the one hand, focuses on the small-scale finite element method and soil mechanics method simulation, on the other hand, focuses on the generalized simulation of water and sediment process simulation model, which is still far from the demand for water and sediment coupling in the basin. Based on the physical process of gravity erosion and sediment yield, integrating the long-term and short-term influencing factors, and based on the requirements of distributed model driven by rainfall and DEM digital grid, the scale conversion law of DEM topographic characteristic parameters with different resolutions can be studied; A perfect basin water sediment coupling simulation model is established to quantitatively analyze the impact of gravity erosion on the water sediment process of small watershed under the comprehensive action of basin scale precipitation, vegetation and topography.

This work was supported by the National Natural Science Foundation of China Youth Fund Project (51209222) and the national key research and development program project (2018YFC0506904).

References

1. K. L. Tang. *Soil and Water Conservation in China*[M]. Beijing: Science Press. (2004)
2. T. J. Li, G. Q. Wang, C. Zhang, et al. Simulation of gravitational erosion in river basins on loess plateau[J]. Journal of Tianjin University, **41**(9): 6. (2008)
3. J. S. Yang, W. Y. Yao, S. B. Ma, et al. Analysis on the small gravitational erosion factors in gully region of the loess plateau[J]. Research of Soil and Water Conservation, **17**(6): 4. (2010)

4. J. S. Yang, W. Y. Yao, M. G. Zheng, et al. Analysis on gravitational sediment yield in the check-dam controlled basins of Chabagou Watershed[J]. Journal of Hydraulic Engineering, **48**(2): 5. (2017)
5. Z. Gao, F. Zhang, J. E. Gao, et al. Analysis and prediction of gravity erosion in typical small watershed in the fifthsub-region of huangtu hilly area[J]. Journal of Soil and Water Conservation, **32**(3): 7. (2018)
6. C. D. Gao, W. Q. Yao, P. F. Li, et al. Research progress of gravity erosion of the loess plateau[J]. Yellow River, **42**(6): 7. (2020)
7. H. Xue, W. C. Wang, P. H. He. Analysis on affecting factors of gravity erosion of the middle Yellow River region[J]. Yellow River, **30**(5): 3. (2008)
8. W. X. Lin, L. Q. Tang, D. B. Liu, et al. Gravitational erosion process and its simulation study progresses[J]. Water Resources and Hydropower Engineering, **42**(1): 5. (2011)
9. F. L. Zheng. A research on method of measuring rill erosion amount[J]. Bulletin of Soil and Water Conservation, (04): 41-45+49. (1989)
10. J. S. Yang, W. Y. Yao, L. L. Wang. Study on the regularity and mechanism of gravity erosion in the loess gully[J]. Yellow River, **36**(06): 93-96. (2014)
11. J. J. Gao, Q. S. Ai, L. Q. Han, et al. An observation-based dataset of gravity erosion of Xindiangou watershed in the first sub-region of Loess Hilly-Gully Region during 2017–2018[J]. China Scientific Data, **6**(03): 113-120. (2021)
12. P. Zhang, F. L. Zheng, B. Wang, et al. Comparative study of monitoring gully erosion morphology change process by using high precision GPS, leica HDS 3000 laser scanner and needle board method[J]. Bulletin of Soil and Water Conservation, (05): 11-15+20. (2008)
13. J. Zhang, F. L. Zheng, L. L. Wen, et al. Methodology of dynamic monitoring gully erosion process using 3D laser scanning technology[J]. Bulletin of Soil and Water Conservation, **31**(06): 89-94. (2011)
14. C. Qin. Quantitative researches on rill development on loessial hillslope based on photogrammetry[D]. Northwest A&F University.(2018)
15. Y. Y. Huo, S. F. Wu, H. Feng, et al. Dynamic process of slope rill erosion based on three-dimensional laser scanner[J]. Science of Soil and Water Conservation, **9**(02): 32-37+46. (2011)
16. X. K. Zhao, J. G. Gong, Z. Ren, et al. Experimental study on morphological evolution of rills on dark loessial soil slope[J]. Water Resources and Hydropower Engineering, **51**(02): 205-212. (2020)
17. J. J. Gao, Q. S. Ai, L. D. Hao, et al. Research on influencing factors of gravity erosion based on UAV technology[J]. Yellow River, **42**(10): 100-103. (2020)
18. Liao K T, Y. J. Song, J. Yang, et al. The extraction of rill erosion parameters on red soil slope[J]. Soil and Water Conservation in China, (02): 45-49+69. (2021)
19. X. Z. Xu, S. F. Wang, C. Zhao. Method to quantificationally measure the amount of gravitational erosion of the gully wall in the laboratory study[J]. Yellow River, **34**(10): 20. (2012)
20. M. H. Guo, H. J. Shi, J. Zhao, et al. Digital close range photogrammetry for the study of rill development at flume scale[J]. Catena, 143. (2016)
21. Y. M. Jiang, H. J. Shi, Z. M. Wen, et al. The dynamic process of slope rill erosion analyzed with a digital close range photogrammetry observation system under laboratory conditions[J]. Geomorphology, 2020, 350(C).

22. J. S. Yang, Zheng M. G, W. Y. Yao, et al. Landscape factors of gravity erosion in loess gully[J]. Soil and Water Conservation in China, (08): 42-45+69. (2014)
23. Q. Yan. Simulation of gravitational erosion in the loess gully wall based on various rainfall condition[D]. Dalian University of Technology. (2013)
24. Z. Y. Liu. Gravity erosion on the steep loess slope: Behavior, trigger and sensitivity[D]. Dalian University of Technology. (2016)
25. X. Z. Xu, C. Zhao. A Laboratory Study for Gravity Erosion of the Steep Loess Slopes under Intense Rainfall[C]//ICHE 2014. Proceedings of the 11th International Conference on Hydroscience & Engineering. 2014: 709-716.
26. X. Z. Xu, Z. Y. Liu, P. Q. Xiao, et al. Gravity erosion on the steep loess slope: Behavior, trigger and sensitivity[J]. CATENA, 135: 231-239.(2015)
27. S. H. Sun, S. Z. Zhang, F. Zhang. Gravitation erosion and its prevention measures in Zhonggou watershed [J]. Soil and Water Conservation in China, (09): 25-27+50+61-62. (1995)
28. G. H. Zhang, Research on soil erosion under the background of vegetation restoration needs to be strengthened[J]. Soil and Water Conservation in China, (09): 76-79. (2020)
29. H. Gao, X. Z. Xu, P. Q. Xiao, et al. Effects of vegetation on scale and rate of gravity erosion on the gully sidewall under heavy rainfalls[J]. Research of Soil and Water Conservation, **28**(06): 17-24. (2021)
30. X. Y. Zhao, X. Z. Xu, Y. Z. Jiang, et al. Effects of vegetation for gravity erosion on the loess gully sidewall under the intense rainfalls[J]. Journal of Soil and Water Conservation, 34(01): 58-63. (2020)
31. X. Y. Zhao. Effects of vegetation on gravity erosion on the gully wall under the intense rainfall[D]. Dalian University of Technology. (2018)
32. J. Y. Jiao, Z. J. Wang, Y. H. Wei, et al. Characteristics of erosion sediment yield with extreme rainstorms in Yanhe Watershed based on field measurement[J]. Transactions of the Chinese Society of Agricultural Engineering, **33**(13): 159-167. (2017)
33. Z. J. Wang. Characteristics of vegetation and erosion sediment yield in the Yanhe[D]. Watershed University of Chinese Academy of Sciences. (2014)
34. H. Xue, P. H. He, W. L. Wang. Studv on relations between river system shaping and gravity erosion of topography of the middle Yellow River[J]. Yellow River, (09): 67-68+70+108. (2008)
35. Z. B. Xin, J. X. Xu, Y. X. Ma. Hypsometric integral analysis and its sediment yield implications in the loess plateau, China[J]. Journal of Mountain Science, (03): 356-363. (2008)
36. H. Y. Wang, W. Q. Liu, Q. Q. Zhan. Quantitative analysis of landform development in the typical small watershed in Loess Plateau Based on Geographic Information System[J]. Journal of Xi'an University of Science and Technology, **34**(02): 210-215. (2014)
37. C. Zhao. A laboratory study on the gravitational erosion of loess gully[D]. Dalian University of Technology. (2011)
38. S. F. Wang. Mechanism analysis of the gravitational erosion from the gully wall on the loess plateau[D]. Dalian University of Technology. (2018)
39. L. Yu, X. Z. Xu, M. S. Zhang, et al. Sensitivity analysis of gravity erosion to topography factors on the loess plateau, China[J]. Journal of Soil and Water Conservation, **33**(04): 119-125. (2019)

40. L. Yu. Characteristics and sensitivities of the gravity erosion on the loess plateau, China[D]. Dalian University of Technology. (2019)
41. S. J. Dong. Spatial and temporal distribution of gravity erosion on loess gully sidewall [D]. Dalian University of Technology. (2021)
42. Y. L. Ma, X. Z. Xu, P. Q. Xiao, et al. Geomorphic natural hazard on loess terrain: expansion on the gully sidewall[J]. Natural Hazards, **109**(3): 2535-2555. (2021)
43. H. Tang, X. S. Zhao, F. Song. Types and spatio-temporal distribution of landslides in the area effected by "5·12" Wenchuan earthquake in Shaanxi province—a case study in Lueyang country[J]. The Chinese Journal of Geological Hazard and Control, **26**(01): 9-15. (2015)
44. H. Zhou, Y. Zhang, QIN Q, et al. Research on variability of basic physical properties of loess under freezing-thawing cycles[J]. Journal of Glaciology and Geocryology, **37**(01): 162-168. (2015)
45. W. Y. Yao, C. M. Li, P. Zhang, et al. Prospect and research on the erosion mechanism of pisha sandstone[J]. Yellow River, **40**(06): 1-7+65. (2018)
46. L. Z. Yang, G. F. Wang, A. J. Wang, et al. Landslides mechanization in the loess hilly area of eastern Gansu province—case study in Huan county[J]. The Chinese Journal of Geological Hazard and Control, **27**(02): 39-48. (2016)
47. W. S. He, Q. Xu, C. C. Liu. Ground deformation in Heifangtai loess yuan[J]. Journal of East China Institute of Technology(Natural Science Edition), **33**(03): 281-285+289. (2010)
48. L. Xu, H. J. Li, D. X. Wu. Discussion on infiltration of surface water and their significance to terrace loess landslides[J]. The Chinese Journal of Geological Hazard and Control, (02): 32-35. (2008)
49. Z. C. Li, G. Liu. Correlation and interaction mechanism between loess landslides and loess caves[J]. Journal of Lanzhou University (Natural Sciences), **50**(01): 21-25. (2014)
50. J. Q. Dang, J. Li. The structural strength and shear strength of unsaturated loess[J]. Journal of Hydraulic Engineering, (07): 79-83+90. (2001)
51. J. Q. Dang, J. Li. Strength characteristics of unsaturated loess[J]. Chinese Journal of Geotechnical Engineering, (02): 59-64. (1997)
52. B. P. Zhang, L. Wang, H. Z. Yuan. The quantitative analysis of effects of soil moisture upon the loess structure strength[J]. Acta Universitatis Agriculturalis Boreali-Occidentalis, (01): 54-60. (1994)
53. X. K. Fan, D. S. Jiang, H. L. Zhao. Analysis on anti-shear strength of shallow original state soil in loess plateau [J]. Journal of Soil Erosion and Soil and Water Conservation, (04): 70-76. (1997)
54. X. Q. Chen, Y. N. Ren, Y. Li, et al. Effect of water content on shear strength parameters of unsaturated loess[J]. Gansu Science and Technology, **34**(04): 88-90+106. (2018)
55. W. Z. Guo, Y. K. Liu, X. Z. Xu, et al. Sensitivity on shear strength of the loess in the ecotone of wind-water erosion[J]. Research of Soil and Water Conservation, **25**(03): 23-28. (2018)
56. W. Z. Guo, X. Z. Xu, Y. K. Liu, et al. Changes in particle size distribution of suspended sediment affected by gravity erosion on the Loess Plateau, China[C]//Egu General Assembly Conference. EGU General Assembly Conference Abstracts. (2017)
57. X. X. Xu, C. X. Gao, J. N. Zhao. Trends of runoff and sediment load of Yanhe River Basin and their related driving forces during 1956 -2009[J]. Journal of Sediment Research, (02): 12-18. (2012)

58. G. Q. Yu, Z. B. Li, M. S. Zhang, et al. Mechanisms of soil and water conservation measures regulating gravitational erosion in small watersheds on loess plateau[J]. Acta Pedologica Sinica, **49**(04): 646-654. (2012)
59. Y. F. Chai, B. Zhou, Z. M. Lv, et al. Control modes of red soil slipping surface in broken gully region of the loess plateau [J]. Soil and Water Conservation in China, (02): 49-51+69. (2014)
60. L. B. Zhao, B. G. Zhang, Z. Z. Su. Quantitative analysis of soil anti-shearing strength enhancement by the root systems of herb plants[J]. Chinese Journal of Eco-agriculture, (03): 718-722. (2008)
61. J. Z. Hu. Practice on planting hippophae rhamnoides in soft sandstone gullies for preventing gravity erosion[J]. Soil and Water Conservation in China, (05): 36-39+69. (2011)
62. Q. G. Cai, Z. X. Lu, G. P. Wang. Process-based soil erosion and sediment yieid model in a small in the hilly loess region[J]. Journal of Geographical Sciences, (02): 108-117. (1996)
63. T. J. Li, G. Q. Wang, H. Xue, et al. Spatial scale effects of sediment yield and transport characteristics in loess gully region[J]. Science in China(Series E) , **39**(06): 1095-1103. (2009)
64. T. J. Li, G. Q. Wang, H. Xue, et al. Soil erosion and sediment transport in the gullied Loess Plateau: Scale effects and their mechanisms[J]. Science in China Series E: Technological Sciences, (5): 10. (2009)
65. G. Q. Wang, T. J. Li, H. Xue, et al. Mechanism Analysis of Watershed Sediment Processes[J]. Journal of Basic Science and Engineering, (04): 455-462. (2006)
66. L. L. Wang. Runoff-sediment coupling mechanism of different geomorphic unit in the loess hilly-gully region[D]. Northwest A&F University. (2017)
67. T. X. Zhu, Y. Z. Chen. The primary study on sediment production of gravitation erosion in western Shanxi province[J]. Bulletin of Soil and Water Conservation, (02): 27-34. (1989)
68. X. B. Zhang, Z. X. Chai, Y. C. Wang. An analysis to the combined factors of topography and lithology in the gravitational erosion of loess plateau[J]. Bulletin of Soil and Water Conservation, (05): 40-44+57. (1989)
69. W. Fu. Research on establishment of the model for predicting soil erosion on loess hilly and gully areas [J]. Journal of Soil and Water Conservation, (03): 6-13. (1992)
70. W. Fu. Research on grey system model for soil gravity erosion in loess regions[J]. Journal of Soil Erosion and Soil and Water Conservation, **2**(4): 9-17. (1996)
71. X. Jin, Z. C. Hao, J. L. Zhang, et al. Distributed soil erosion model with the effect of gravitational erosion[J]. Advances in Water Science, **19**(2): 257-263. (2008)
72. G. Q. Wang, T. J. Li. The digital watershed model for the Yellow River Basin[J]. Sciencepaper Online, 2007(07): 492-499.
73. Wang G Q, Wu B S, Li T J. Digital Yellow River Model[J]. Sciencepaper Online, **1**(1): 1-11. (2008)
74. Wang G Q, Fu X D, Shi H Y, et al. Watershed Sediment Dynamics and Modeling: A Watershed Modeling System for Yellow River[M]. Advances in Water Resources Engineering. Springer, Cham, 1-40. (2015)
75. J. G. Gong, Y. W. Jia, J. J. Liu, et al. Study on water-sediment process and its coupling simulation in watershed[M]. Beijing: Science Press. (2018)

76. Z. Y. Liu, G. H. Ni, Z. D. Lei, et al. Study on hydrologic model of small scale distribution pattern for loess plateau region[J]. Yellow River, (10): 19-21. (2005)
77. Z. Y. Liu, G. H. Ni, Z. D. Lei, et al. Distributed hydrological model of small and moderate size watersheds in the Loess Plateau[J]. Journal of Tsinghua University (Science and Technology), (09): 1546-1550. (2006)
78. J. Y. Cai, Z. H. Zhou, J. J. Liu, et al. A distributed soil erosion model based on the three-process of runoff and sediment transport[J]. Journal of Hydraulic Engineering, **51**(02): 140-151. (2020)
79. Y. M. Zhu, Y. L. Lan, Z. H. Zhou, et al. Evolution mechanism of water and sediment processes in Daxia River Basin based on distributed water and sediment model[J]. Research of Soil and Water Conservation, **28**(04): 121-127. (2021)
80. Y. Z. Cao. Mechanism and prediction of gravity erosion in loess region[J]. Bulletin of Soil and Water Conservation, (04): 19-23. (1981)
81. G Q Yu, Z B Li, P Li, et al. Numerical simulation on gravitational erosion of small watershed system in Loess Plateau[J]. Transactions of the Chinese Society of Agricultural Engineering, **25**(12): 74-79+399. (2009)
82. G. Q. Yu, X. Zhang, M. S. Zhang, et al. Mechanism of vegetation regulating on gravitational erosion in the slope-gully system on loess plateau[J], Journal of Natural Resources, **27**(06): 922-932. (2012)
83. X. Zhang, Z. W. Zhang, Z. B. Li, et al. Stability evaluation of gravitational erosion for small watershed on the loess plateau[J]. Bulletin of Soil and Water Conservation, **32**(03): 236-239+301. (2012)
84. K. X. Lu, Z. B. Li, G. Q. Yu. Reliability analysis of gravitational erosion stability of small watershed in the Loess Plateau[J]. Arid Land Geography, **35**(04): 545-551. (2012)
85. X. Jin, Z. Liu, C. Z. Wang, et al. Numerical Simulation of Gravity Erosion on Artificial Loess Slope[J]. China Rural Water and Hydropower, (08): 40-45. (2020)
86. K. Zhang. Numerical simulation of gravity erosion characteristics of coarse sand bank slope in desert small watershed of upper yellow river[D]. Lanzhou University of Technology. (2020)
87. X. Wei, X. G. Li, Z. B. Li, et al. Study on the adjust-control effect of check dam on gravity erosion of slope-gully systems in the Loess Plateau[J]. Journal of XI'an University of Architecture & Techology, **41**(06): 856-861. (2009)
88. B. H. Zhou, J. Yuan, Z. B. Li, et al. Study on responding of feature evolution about slope-gully system erosion and check dam interception of small watershed on loess plateau[J]. Acta Agriculturae Boreali-occidentalis Sinica, **21**(10): 185-190. (2012)
89. B. H. Zhou, J. Yuan, Z. B. Li, et al. Spatial characteristics of gravitational erosion in slope-gully system on loess plateau as controlled by check dam[J]. Bulletin of Soil and Water Conservation, **33**(05): 55-59+86. (2013)
90. H. D. Gao, Z. B. Li, P. Li, et al. Quantitative evaluation of slope stability on check-dams at different siltation heights[J], Transactions of the Chinese Society of Agricultural Engineering, **28**(16): 127-132. (2012)
91. H. D. Gao. Hydro-ecological impact of the gully erosion control works in loess hilly-gully region[D]. University of Chinese Academy of Sciences. (2013)

A review of automatic coal volume measuring technologies

Dou Li [1] , *Haoxuan* Luo [2], *Lin* Wang [1], and *Jin* Gao, and *Li* Cheng[2*]

[1] Jiangsu Frontier Electric Technology Co., Ltd., Nanjing 211102, China
[2] Southeast University Jiangbei New Area Innovation Institute, Nanjing 210096, China

Keywords. Automatic coal volume measuring technology, Laser, UAV.

Abstract. In coal-fired power plants, how to timely inventory coal storage, in order to optimize the coal stock, and improve coal blending operation, and then carry out economic dispatch scientifically and reasonably, has always been an important topic. The traditional way of artificial method has big error, high cost and serious waste of resources. Ultrasonic measurement technology is greatly affected by time difference and dust. Measurement technology based on computer vision requires interpolation to fit the correction model. The above methods all have large measurement errors and have been eliminated by the market. This paper mainly introduces coal measuring technologies based on laser and uav tilt photography which have been researched and applied more recently. Their respective installation methods, characteristics and applicable working occasions are analyzed. They have the common characteristic that the 3d coordinate point cloud data of coal yard surface needs to be solved before the 3d model of coal yard can be generated and the coal storage amount can be calculated. In the case that the 3d coordinate point cloud data of coal yard of power plant cannot be obtained directly, 3d reconstruction can be carried out by using 2d images of coal yard in coal report, or by using neural network model, and then the coal volume can be checked. This research idea is of great significance to realize effective and accurate supervision of coal storage in power plants..

Nowadays, Electric Power Industry is dominated by thermal power generation, and the most important raw material for thermal coal-fired power plants is coal. According to statistics, fuel accounts for the largest share of the cost of power generation in coal-fired power plants, accounting for about 70-80% of the production cost of the whole plant [1].

In the current situation of rising coal prices and declining profits of power generation enterprises, coal-fired power plants generally adopt economic coal blending in order to reduce fuel costs and improve economic efficiency. Timely inventory of coal stocks of each coal type in coal yards can provide data support for accurate coal blending operations. At present, the statistical reporting of coal supply, consumption and storage in power plants has become the norm, but the coal information of each power plant in the dispatcher's

* Corresponding author: chengli@seu.edu.cn

possession is completely dependent on the power plant's independent reporting, and the credibility of the data is doubtful and the automation level is not high, especially for the vital coal storage data of each plant, the dispatcher lacks effective supervision means. The purpose of this paper is to investigate the measurement technology of coal storage in power plants in order to provide further research ideas for the automated monitoring and verification of the coal stockpile reported by the centralized power plants.

According to the different measurement principles, the published coal inventory technologies applied to thermal power plants include ultrasonic measurement technology [2-3], computer vision-based measurement technology [4-5], laser scanning measurement technology [6-8], and unmanned aircraft tilt photography measurement technology [9-10].

Since the time accuracy of ultrasound cannot be well controlled in the measurement process, it will inevitably cause measurement errors, especially when accurate measurement of points over a large area is required, ultrasonic measurement cannot meet the application requirements. In addition, the propagation speed of ultrasonic waves will change because of different transmission media, so the uncertainty caused will be even greater. Also, the presence of dust in the coal field can have a great impact on the measurement [2-3].

As for the measurement technology based on computer vision, due to too few effective coordinate points, the 3D model of the coal field obtained by this technique will be seriously distorted, and naturally there is a large measurement error [4-5].

With the rise of two-dimensional laser measurement technology, it has rapidly replaced the original measurement techniques and methods and gradually occupied the market. At present, it has been rarely seen in thermal power plants to use coal inventory instrument based on ultrasonic and computer vision measurement technology, and more and more mature are the coal inventory instrument based on laser scanning measurement technology and coal inventory instrument based on UAV tilt photography measurement technology, so this paper will focus on these two coal inventory technologies.

1 Laser coal inventory technology

When scanner working, the 2D laser scanner scans the surface of coal field in cross-section and obtains 2D coordinate data of coal field cross-section profile, which is matched with the position information obtained by displacement sensor or angle sensor, and finally obtains the surface form and 3D coordinate data of the measured target through software processing, and then carries out coal field storage calculation and 3D model establishment and display. According to different mounting platforms, the laser coal inventory instrument can be divided into portable laser coal inventory instrument, fixed laser coal inventory instrument and laser coal inventory instrument based on walking robot.

1.1 The portable laser coal inventory instrument

The measurement principle of the portable laser coal inventory instrument is shown in Figure 1, where the surveyor walks around the coal pile with the instrument in hand, the laser scanner dynamically measures the geometric information on the surface of the pile, the attitude measurement system simultaneously measures the spatial attitude data of the laser scanner, the GPS measures the spatial position of the laser scanner during the measurement process, and the 3D point cloud of the pile is formed through data fusion, and then the 3D model reconstruction and volume calculation are carried out. The GPS measures the spatial position of the laser scanner during the measurement process, and the data is fused to form a 3D point cloud, which in turn performs 3D model reconstruction and volume calculation.

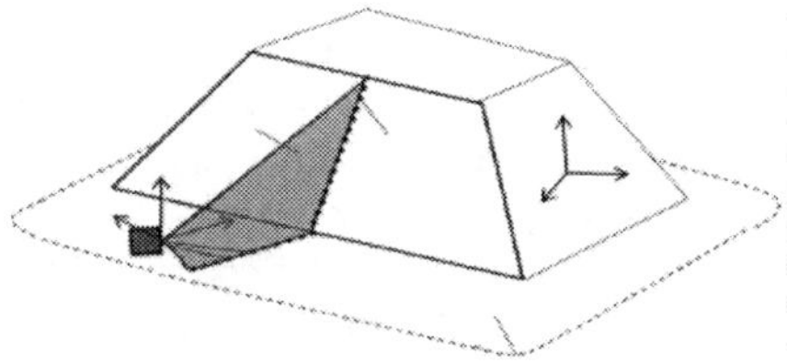

Fig. 1. Schematic diagram of measurement principle of the portable coal inventory instrument.

The Portable laser coal inventory instrument can be operated only by personnel handheld, with the advantages of easy and fast to use, but there are also the following problems.

1. It is greatly affected by the environment. The yard environment is complex, and there are often large reclaimers running back and forth on both sides of the yard, so the point cloud data collected will inevitably have foreign matter point clouds and noise point clouds, which will cause errors to the final measurement results.

2. There is an obvious scanning blind area. As can be seen from Figure 1, the laser scanner cannot scan the top of the coal pile during the measurement process, and the data can only be processed assuming that the top of the coal pile is a flat surface, which will certainly cause measurement errors.

3. Not conducive to the health of the surveyor. Large power plant coal yard and covers an area of large, uneven coal pile edge is difficult to walk, low efficiency and easy to inhale coal dust and toxic gases.

Therefore, the portable coal inventory instrument can only be used as a temporary or verification coal inventory device, not as a permanent coal inventory device.

1.2 The fixed laser coal inventory instrument

The fixed laser coal inventory instrument mounted on the coal yard traveling car or stacker reclaimer is used more often at home and abroad. The two-dimensional laser scanner and travel sensor are mounted on the coal yard traveling car or stack reclaimer and follow its movement, the laser scanner obtains the two-dimensional coordinate information of the surface of the measured coal pile, and the travel sensor obtains the position information of the laser scanner, then three-dimensional coordinates of the coal yard surface are solved, and then the three-dimensional model of the coal yard is established and the coal storage quantity of the coal yard is calculated. there are various installation methods according to the different forms of coal field [6].

1.2.1 Single strip coal yard - bucket wheel machine large arm side mounting

Fig. 2. Diagram of the installation of the coal inventory instrument on the side of the big arm of the bucket wheel.

As shown in Figure 2, the laser coal inventory instrument is installed on the side of the bucket wheel's big arm, which is a kind of installation method suitable for single strip coal field only. During the measurement, the bucket wheel's big arm is parallel to the track and lifted to the highest position; while the bucket wheel is walking forward, the laser scanner is activated to scan the coal field in section and get the coal field outline; at the same time, the bucket wheel's walking position is recorded to get the outline position. After the scanning, the 3D coordinates of the coal field surface are obtained, and then the 3D model of the coal field and the storage data are obtained. This way the coal inventory instrument is easy to install, but there are the following problems:

1. If the coal yard is stacked too high, the top of the coal yard cannot be scanned due to the limited height of the bucket wheel machine's large arm.
2. It can only scan the outline of the coal pile on one side of the coal pile near the bucket wheel, so it can only predict the outline of the other side of the coal pile based on the data scanned on one side, which will inevitably cause measurement errors.
3. Restricted to walking limit. Generally, a large amount of coal will be piled up outside the traveling limit of the bucket wheel, which cannot be scanned in this way and can only be estimated manually, which will inevitably lead to measurement errors.

1.2.2 Installation on single strip coal yard-door pickup bucket wheel

Fig. 3. Installation on single strip coal yard-door pickup bucket wheel.

Some power plants with a single strip coal yard are equipped with a portal pickup bucket wheel. Figure 3 shows a schematic diagram of the laser coal discograph installed on the portal pickup bucket wheel. The laser scanner and control box are mounted on the bucket wheel carriage, and a travel encoder is installed at the wheels underneath the bucket wheel to measure the travel distance of the bucket wheel. When the bucket wheel runs along the rails laid on both sides of the coal field at a uniform speed, the laser scanner scans the coal field to get a two-dimensional outline of the coal field, and the travel encoder gets the position of this outline. When the bucket wheel runs from one end of the coal field to the other end, the scanning of the whole coal field is completed, and the three-dimensional model of the coal field is obtained after data processing.

There is no scanning dead space in this installation, and the measurement process of coal inventory instrument scans vertically downward, thus high measurement accuracy can be achieved. Unfortunately, in order to improve the efficiency of the coal yard and the efficiency of coal stacking and pickup, most power plants adopt the way of arranging a strip coal yard on each side of the track, and few power plants adopt a single strip coal yard.

1.2.3 Installation on single strip coal yard-door pickup bucket wheel

For double strip coal field, if the coal field is not large and the coal pile is not high, coal inventory instrument can be installed in the centre of the front end of the bucket wheel machine's big arm, as shown in Figure 4. When measuring, the bucket wheel machine arm first swings to the left coal pile directly above and lifts to the highest position and scan the left coal field during the bucket wheel machine walking forward to get the section profile of the coal field, and records the bucket wheel machine walking position at the same time to get the profile position. After scanning, the three-dimensional coordinates of the coal field surface are obtained through data processing, and then the three-dimensional model of the left coal field and the volume data are obtained. Then, the bucket wheel rotates to the top of the right coal pile, and the right coal field 3D model and storage data are obtained in the same way.

Fig. 4. Diagram of the installation of the coal inventory instrument in the middle of the big arm of the bucket wheel.

There are some problems with this type of installation of laser coal inventory instrument.

1. It is only suitable for smaller scale strip coal yards.

2. There is a large scanning blind area. the top contour of the coal pile cannot be scanned completely.

3. It is not possible to scan the coal piled up outside the traveling limit of the bucket wheel, so it can only be estimated manually, which is another source of measurement error.

1.2.4 Double strip coal yard - bucket wheel middle crossbeam mounted

Fig. 5. Diagram of the installation of the coal inventory instrument on the middle crossbeam of the bucket wheel.

For double strip coal yards, in the case of larger coal yards and higher coal piles, the bucket wheel machine middle cross beam installation method is mostly used, as shown in Figure 5, where coal inventory instrument is installed at the highest point position of the coal yard, which is the bucket wheel machine middle cross beam or middle tower base. In this way, the entire contour of the left and right coal yards from the side near the bucket wheel to the outside of the top of the coal pile can be scanned within the bucket wheel's travel range.

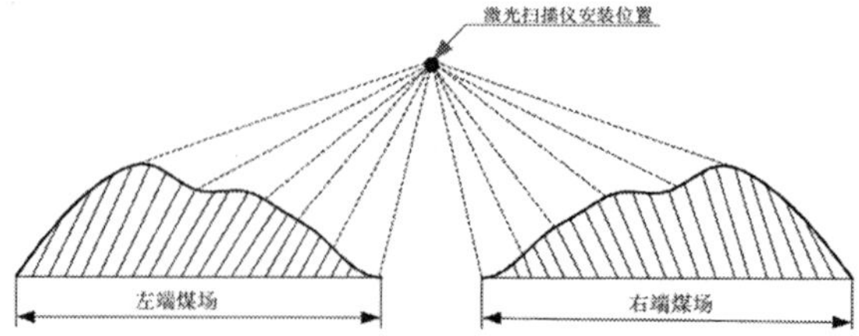

Fig. 6. Diagram of scanning left and right coal field of the coal inventory instrument.

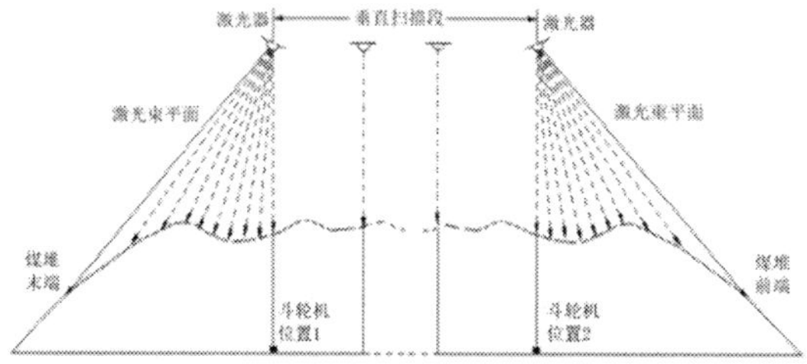

Fig. 7. The coal inventory instrument coal yard end scan schematic.

For the coal pile outside the front and rear walking limit position of the bucket wheel, the angle between the laser beam plane of the laser scanner and the vertical plane is changed by a rotating head, so that the laser beam is projected further away to complete the scanning of the coal pile outside the limit position of the bucket wheel, as shown in Figs. 6 and 7, so that the problem of scanning blind areas at the front and rear ends of the coal field, which exists in the middle installation method of the bucket wheel's arm, can be solved [6].Figure 8 shows the three-dimensional model of a coal field obtained from the omnidirectional scanning. However, when the coal pile exceeds a certain height, this method still cannot scan the outermost contour of the coal pile, and can only rely on the contour shape of the inner side of the coal pile to deduce the outer contour shape, which is the main source of measurement error of this type of the coal inventory instrument.

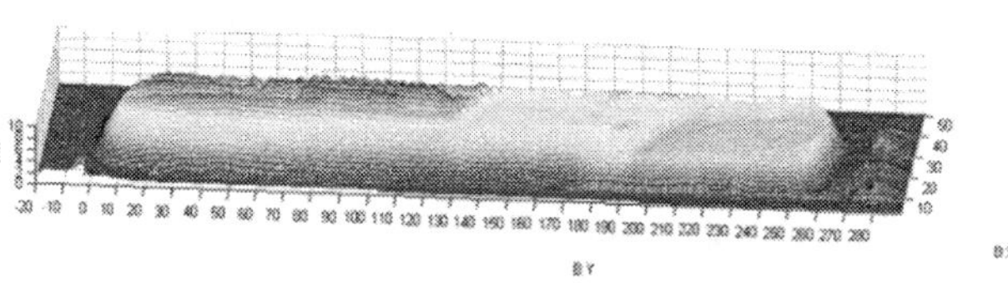

Fig. 8. 3D model of a coal field obtained by omnidirectional scanning.

1.2.5 Circular coal yard - bucket wheel middle crossbeam mounted

Circular coal yards are increasingly favored by coal-fired power plants because of their advantages of relatively small land area, large memory storage capacity per unit area, and resistance to harsh environments [11],as shown in Figure 9, a laser scanner is usually installed on the stacker-reclaimer's stacker arm or reclaimer arm for full-range scanning of the coal yard during stacking or rotation; a rotary encoder is installed at the rotation gear of the stacker-reclaimer's stacker arm or reclaimer arm to measure the rotation angle of the stacker-reclaimer arm [12].

Due to the limitations of the mechanical structure of the stacking arm and the retrieval arm of the circular coal yard, and the presence of concrete support columns inside the circular coal yard, the stacking arm and the retrieval arm of the stacking and retrieval machine cannot rotate 360 degrees individually, resulting in a blind scanning area.

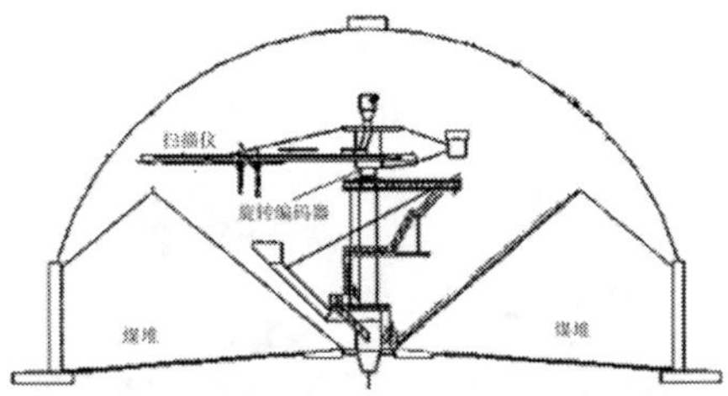

Fig. 9. Installation diagram of single probe the coal inventory instrument in round coal yard.

1.2.6 Circular coal yard - double probe stacking arm and pick-up arm mounted on

In order to eliminate the scanning blindness of the single probe coal inventory instrument, one solution is to install a laser scanner on each of the stacker arm and the reclaimer arm of the stacker reclaimer, and a set of rotary encoders at the rotating gears of the stacker arm and the reclaimer arm, as shown in Figure 10. The stacker arm and the reclaimer arm are rotated separately, and the data from both sets are finally integrated, then the full range measurement of a circular coal yard can be realized. Figure 11 shows the three-dimensional model.

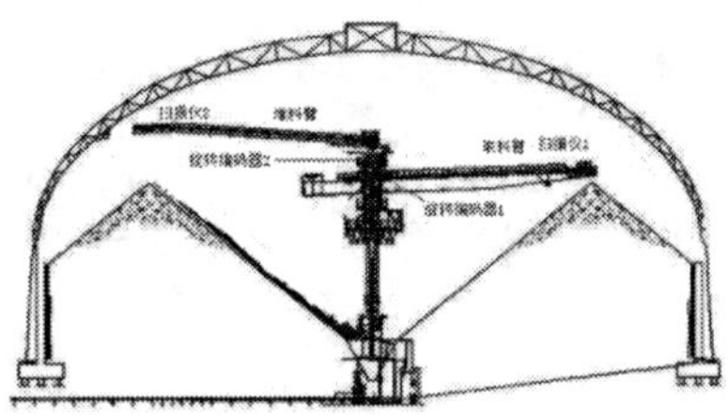

Fig. 10. Installation diagram of double probe the coal inventory instrument in round coal yard.

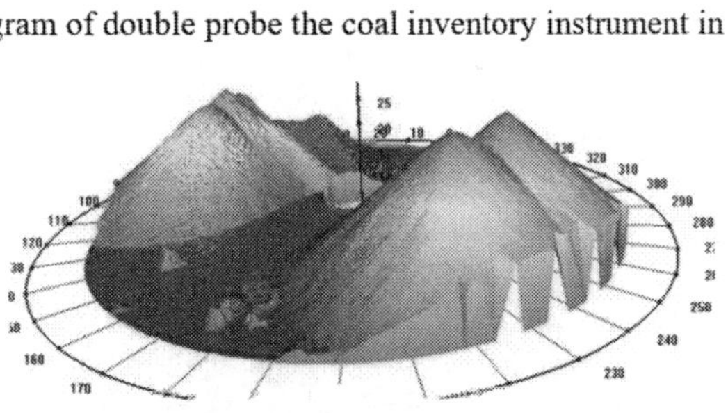

Fig. 11. Round coal yard 3D model

1.3 Walking robot-based laser coal inventory instrument

In recent years, more and more thermal power plants have started to adopt fully enclosed or semi-enclosed coal storage yards.

Under the dome of the closed coal yard, there exists a maintenance roadway, which runs through the whole coal yard and is usually used for maintenance. A sliding track is installed underneath the roadway, and a railcar or walking robot (containing a laser scanner, positioning encoder, wireless communication device, power charging device, cart drive device, etc.) is mounted on the track as shown in Figure 12.

 https://doi.org/10.1051/shsconf/202316601074

During the measurement, the walking robot slowly walks, and the laser scanner scans the coal field to obtain the surface contour of the coal field, while the position of the contour is obtained by the positioning encoder. After the measurement is completed, the scanned data is processed by the software to obtain a 3D coordinate point cloud of the coal field surface, and then the volume of the coal pile is calculated, and the data can be used to build a real-time 3D model of the coal pile.

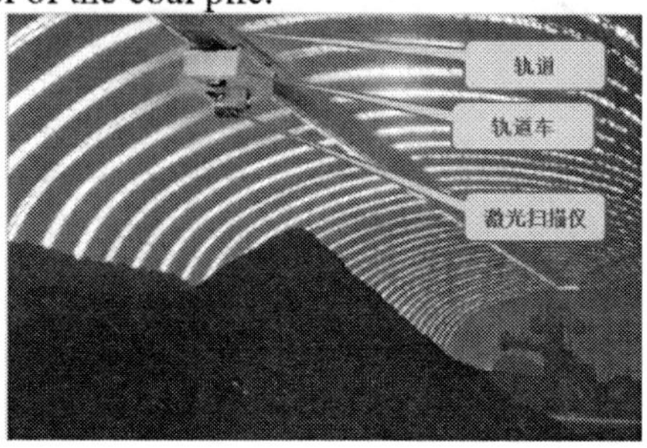

Fig. 12. Schematic diagram of the laser disk coal meter based on walking robot.

The coal inventory instrument based on walking robot can effectively solve various problems of measuring equipment installed on the bucket wheel, especially the scanning blind area problem, and the scanning degree is fast, no blind area in the scanning process, and high accuracy of the coal inventory instrument [13].

2 UAV tilt photography coal inventory technology

In recent years, with the development of UAV technology and 3D reconstruction technology, the difficulties of inventorying coal by manual measurement method and laser measurement method can be better solved by acquiring orthorectified image sequence of open coal storage site through UAV and then generating 3D realistic model of open coal storage site through 3D reconstruction algorithm.

The coal inventory system based on UAV tilt photography generally takes high-definition images of coal field by UAV sailing according to the planned trajectory first, then processes the images through motion recovery structure algorithm to get 3D coordinate point cloud of coal field surface, and then builds 3D realistic model of coal field and calculates coal storage volume.

2.1 UAV aerial photography to collect image data

UAV aerial photography acquisition of image data is done by relying on UAVs, HD cameras, and portable ground stations. Before the UAV collects data, the ground station is used to pre-plan the UAV's trajectory, flight altitude, flight speed, overlap between sampled images and the attitude angle of the camera during the sampling process. While the UAV carries HD cameras for data acquisition work, the ground station software monitors the UAV flight status in real time to ensure the safety of the sampling work [9].

A reasonable planning of the UAV sampling route is required after the flight area is determined. Figure 13 shows a UAV flight area trajectory planning map, where the blue area is the data acquisition area and the green line is the UAV flight route.

Fig. 13. UAV flight area trajectory planning.

The drone parameters mainly include the flight altitude, flight speed, vehicle yaw angle and drone movement after the completion of the task at the time of drone sampling. The camera parameters include camera orientation, photo mode, camera head pitch angle, image overlap and exposure at the sampling moment. Generally the vertical overlap and horizontal overlap should reach 70% and 50% or more respectively to meet the requirements of 3D real-world model reconstruction.

2.2 Reconstruction of 3D realistic model of coal field

The reconstruction of 3D real-world model of coal field is usually realized based on the Structure from Motion algorithm, which refers to the process of recovering the 3D structure of the scene by solving the camera parameters from the image sequences acquired from different angles. It is usually based on the pair-polar geometric relationship of feature matching points between two-view or multi-view images, and the 3D structure recovery of the scene is achieved by mapping a certain number of 2D image feature points onto the 3D spatial coordinate system to form a 3D point cloud [14]. The mapping relationship from the 2D plane to the 3D space is represented by a projection matrix composed of the internal camera parameters and the external camera parameters. The flow of the motion recovery structure algorithm is shown in Figure 14.

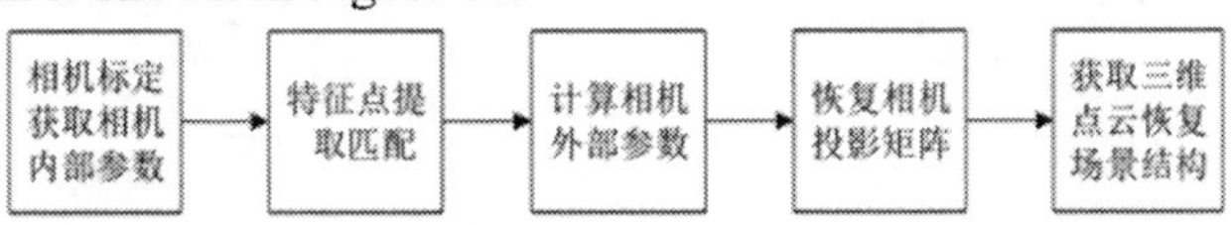

Fig. 14. Motion recovery structure algorithm flow.

2.2.1 Camera internal parameters acquisition

The internal parameters of the camera are determined by the internal structure of the camera, including camera focal length, image principal point coordinates, pixel size, etc. Camera calibration is usually used to obtain the internal parameters of the camera. Through the camera calibration process, the mapping relationship between the two-dimensional coordinates of the image and the three-dimensional spatial coordinates is found, and the camera parameters corresponding to each image are calculated.

With the development of camera calibration technology, many practical calibration methods have been proposed. Such as the planar template calibration method proposed by Zhengyou Zhang [15] takes multiple calibration plate images at different locations and solves the internal parameters of the camera according to the mapping relationship, which is highly accurate, robust, convenient and flexible, and has been widely adopted.

2.2.2 Camera external parameters acquisition

The camera motion can be decomposed into rotational motion and translational motion. The motion of the camera during shooting can be described based on the motion of the points between images, provided that there is a certain degree of overlap in the image content. That is, if the camera rotates and moves during shooting, the contents of the captured images will have the same rotation, translation, and other changes. Therefore, the motion trajectory of the captured contents between images can be found during camera shooting and the position pose at the moment of camera sampling can be recovered.

First, the image is pre-processed to eliminate the influence of interference on the image. Then, feature point extraction is performed, and the feature points are the points in the image with sharp changes in brightness (usually corner points, line intersections) or the extreme value points of curvature on the image edge curve. Then feature point matching is performed to identify the feature points corresponding to the same spatial object points in two or more images, find the relationship between images according to the feature points, and solve the external parameter matrix of the camera[16].

2.2.3 Coalfield 3D structure restoration

Based on the camera internal parameters and camera external parameters obtained above, the camera projection matrix can be recovered, the mapping relationship between 2D pixel coordinate points and 3D spatial coordinate points can be found, the 3D spatial coordinates corresponding to the image pixel points can be solved, and a 3D point cloud can be generated, and then the 3D structure of the coal field can be recovered. Figure 15 shows the 3D realistic model of a coal field obtained according to the above method.

Fig. 15. A three-dimensional realistic model of a coal field obtained by a drone coal inventory system.

3 Summary

This review mainly studies laser coal inventory technology and UAV tilt photography coal inventory technology, and summarizes the characteristics of portable laser coal inventory instrument, fixed laser coal inventory instrument, walking robot-based laser coal inventory instrument and UAV tilt photography-based coal inventory system, and their respective applicable operating occasions.

No matter which type of coal inventory instrument is used, the 3D coordinate point cloud data of coal field surface is finally solved, and then the 3D model of coal field can be generated and the storage capacity can be calculated. The most ideal way to monitor and check the coal stock reported by the centralized power plant is to directly obtain the 3D coordinate point cloud data of the coal inventory system of each power plant, and then re-establish the 3D model of the coal field of the power plant and perform the storage calculation. However, in practice, for various reasons, power plants are unwilling to provide, or the coal tray system does not disclose its coordinate point cloud data and thus the power plant is unable to provide, so the method of calibrating through the 3D coordinate point cloud data of the power plant coal field is almost impossible to achieve.

However, all coal inventory systems will eventually generate an inventory report for the user, which will record a two-dimensional image of the coal yard and storage data at the time of inventory. Therefore a feasible idea is to use the 2-D image of coal yard for 3-D reconstruction, or use the coal yard inventory image and stock quantity data to build a neural network model to calibrate the coal stock data of the power plant, which is important for establishing the optimal fuel blending model and storage model to realize the effective and accurate supervision of coal stock data of the power plant.

References

1. Li Guixian. Exploring fuel cost management in thermal power generation enterprises [J]. Value Engineering, 2020,39(7) :86-87.
2. Zhao Yinglin. Automatic measurement and mapping system for coal storage [J]. China Electric Power,1996(4):54-56.
3. Zong Weilin et al. Application of ultrasonic distance coal plant storage automatic measurement and mapping system[J]. China Electric Power,1999,32(4):80-82.
4. Liu Lei et al. Research on portable laser coal pan system based on computer vision[J]. Journal of North China Electric Power University,2005,32(2):62-66.
5. Qu Bin, et al. Research of Coal Storage system stocktaking Based on Binocular Stereo Vision. Proceedings of the 2011 Second ETP/IITA Conference on Telecommunication and Information (TEIN 2011 V2) 2011.
6. Wu, Hongfei. Automatic laser measurement system for coal field in thermal power plants [D]. Southeast University, 2014.
7. Ding Xinpin, et al. Application of cavity auto scanning laser system in surface mine gob detection [J].Coal Science and Technology, 2015,43 (10):46- 50.
8. Li Qingquan et al. Lidar measurement technology and its application research [J]. Journal of Wuhan University of Surveying and Mapping Science and Technology, 2000, 25(5):387-392.
9. Huang Zachun et al. Research and application of unmanned aircraft-based open-pit coal tray system [J]. Power Station System Engineering, 2020, 36(5):64-66.
10. Huang Jincai. UAV-based application of open pit coal storage yard storage measurement in thermal power plants[J]. Jiangxi Building Materials, 2020(11):58-59.
11. Zhang Z. Y. Exploration of structural design of large diameter closed coal storage yard[J] . Coal Engineering, 2015, 47(4):27-29.
12. Zhao Liang et al. Research and application of coal tray system in Shenbao Energy dome storage coal yard[J]. Coal Technology,2021,40(11):57-60.
13. Li Shaohui et al. Design of overhead rail coal tray robot system for closed coal storage yard [J]. Coal Science and Technology, 2019,47(9):208-213.
14. Li MJ. Research and application of 3D scene reconstruction of open coal storage yard based on motion recovery structure[D]. China University of Mining and Technology, 2019.
15. Zhang Z. A Flexible New Technique for Camera Calibration[J]. IEEE Transactions on Pattern Analysis and Machine Intelligence, 2000, 22(11).
16. Lowe D G. Distinctive image features from scale-invariant key-points[J]. International Journal of Computer Vision, 2004, 60(2):91-110.

Research on optimal supply decision of manufacturers considering futures purchase under deferred payment

Qingsong Xing*, and *Ying* Liu

School of Economics and Management, Chongqing Jiaotong University, Chongqing, China

Abstract. Taking the three-level supply chain consisting of a single supplier, a manufacturer and a strong brand as the research object, the manufacturer's optimal supply decision model is constructed, which considers the futures purchase under the deferred payment of the brand, and it is proved that the optimal solution not only exists but also is unique. Then, the influence of parameter variation on the optimal ordering strategy was analyzed by numerical example simulation and sensitivity analysis. The results show that when the period of deferred payment to the manufacturer is extended and the price discount is strengthened, the manufacturer can purchase from the futures market to lock the price and make up for its income loss through the supplier's delayed payment. Production rate should also be controlled, too high or too low production rate will affect the manufacturer's production cycle.

1 Introduction

Brand parties represented by well-known real estate companies occupy a dominant position in the supply chain. Faced with this situation, manufacturers often use price discounts and deferred payments to attract brand buyers, reduce costs through mass production, and optimize inventory through futures purchasing.

In combination with supply chain purchasing strategies, Zhai[1] et al. studied multiple procurement scenarios in which both retailers and manufacturers could derive benefits from the production time hedging strategy. Keynes[2]proposed the earliest hedging theory (futures risk avoidance theory), which believed that the hedges could effectively transfer the price risk in the market. Kouvelis[3] found that cash hedging technology could realize cost hedging under the condition of minimizing the hedging cost. The above studies are mostly based on the hedging theory, but they do not take into account the cash flow pressure brought by the strong brand in the supply chain to the manufacturer, and how to deal with the cash flow pressure. In this regard, the current representative achievements in the field of inventory optimization under deferred payment can be used for reference. Goyal[4]first proposed the deferred payment EOQ model, and Chu[5] et al. extended Goyal's model by studying the situation of spoiled products. Sundararajan[6] established EOQ model on the condition of

* Corresponding author: xingqingsong_2003@126.com

profit maximization per unit time, and discussed the impact of delayed payment and inflation on the model. Through the review of the representative results related to deferred payment and futures purchase, the current research mainly involves: the brand's optimal order quantity model with price discount under the deferred payment terms, does not combine the deferred payment and futures purchase strategy from the perspective of the manufacturer. In view of this, this paper constructs a three-level supply chain model of manufacturer futures procurement under deferred payment, and proposes the optimal strategy of the manufacturer. The influence of futures purchase price and price discount on the manufacturer's optimal strategy is analyzed by sensitivity.

2 Problem description and parameter description

2.1 Problem Description

Examine the three-tier supply chain system consisting of a single supplier, manufacturer and strong brand. When purchasing, the brand will ask for delayed payment and price discount. In order to ensure their own interests, manufacturers will reduce costs through mass production, deferred payments to upstream suppliers, and futures procurement. In the case of deferred payment, the manufacturer needs to adjust the deferred payment period and price discount coefficient to ensure stable operation. Supply chain structure is shown in figure 1:

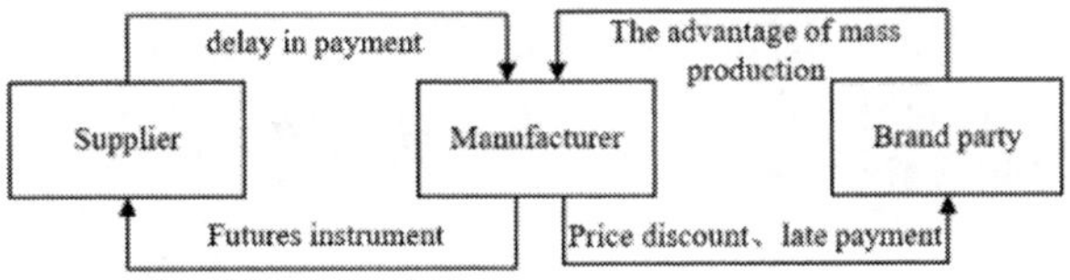

Fig. 1. Supply chain structure diagram.

2.2 Notations and assumptions

Notations used in the model:

D The total demand rate for the product, M Deferred payment period provided by raw material supplier, P Manufacturer's productivity, N Allow the brand party to delay the payment period, h Finished product storage costs, F_t Unit futures purchase price, m The number of times raw materials are delivered, A_{raw} Transportation costs of raw materials, B Storage costs of raw materials, H_a Carrying cost of finished goods, T The manufacturer's production cycle, w The purchase price of the brand, I_q Rate of return per unit time, I_p Interest rate paid per unit of time

Assumptions: No shortages allowed. The productivity and demand rate of manufacturers are constant values, and the productivity is greater than the demand rate. The deferred payment period given by the supplier to the manufacturer is no less than the deferred payment period given by the manufacturer to the brand. The futures contract of raw material commodities purchased by the manufacturer in the futures market can be delivered smoothly according to the provisions. Before the term M, the manufacturer deposits the income at interest rate I_q to earn interest. At the end of the term M, if the product in stock has not been sold, the manufacturer pays interest at interest rate I_p to the supplier.

3 Model establishment and solution

3.1 Mathematical models

The manufacturer starts to consume raw materials at $t=0$, the moment t_0 production is complete, the finished product reaches the highest level. With the sale to the brand, the inventory goes to zero at time T, at which point an order cycle ends, and the whole process repeats. Assume that the demand rate is D, the inventory cycle length of finished products is $T^{'}(T^{'}=T-t_0)$, T is the duration of the entire production cycle, and the productivity of the manufacturer is $P(t)=P(P>D)$, then the storage level $I(t)$ of finished products satisfies the equation and can be derived:

$$\begin{cases} \frac{dI(t)}{dt}=P(t)-D & 0\le t\le t_0 \\ \frac{dI(t)}{dt}=-D & t_0\le t\le T \end{cases} \qquad I(t)=\begin{cases} (P-D)t & 0\le t\le t_0 \\ -Dt+DT & t_0\le t\le T \end{cases}$$

Total inventory of finished products in time period $[0,T]$: $L(t)=\int_0^{t_0}[P(t)-D](t_0-t)dt+\int_0^{T}(t-t_0)Ddt$

Finished product inventory storage costs per cycle are: $C_h=hL(t)=h\left[\int_0^{t_0}(P-D)(t_0-t)dt+\int_0^{T}(t-t_0)Ddt\right]$ According to $\int_0^{t_0}Pdt=\int_{t_0}^{T}Ddt$, it can be concluded that: $t_0=\frac{DT}{P+D}$.

Through the futures purchase of financial derivatives, the risks caused by price fluctuations can be avoided to a certain extent. In addition, considering that the strong brand has the advantage of order volume, it requires more price discounts from the manufacturer during the purchase. It is assumed that the discount rate is $\tau(0<\tau<1)$, w_0 is the benchmark price without discount. Then the wholesale price of the brand party is: $w=\tau w_0$.According to the above assumptions, the profit function of the manufacturer in an order cycle is composed of the following parts:

Manufacturers' sales revenue per cycle can be divided into three situations:

1) $T^{'}\le N$.The brand must pay the rest at the end of term N, so the manufacturer's sales revenue: $S_r=wDT^{'}$ .2) $N\le T^{'}\le M.S_r=wDN+wD(T^{'}-N)$. 3) $M\le T^{'}.S_r=wDN+wD(T^{'}-N)$

Within each cycle, the manufacturer realizes scale effect by organizing mass production and reduces a series of additional costs caused by line change of product models and specifications, including equipment factor cost, quality factor cost, energy consumption factor cost, personnel factor cost and raw material consumption cost. These costs are represented by the following symbols. It can be seen that the indirect income obtained by the manufacturer is as follows: $\sum c_{f-x}=c_{f-mac}+c_{f-qua}+c_{f-ener}+c_{f-hum}+c_{f-mater}$.

The interest on the manufacturer's sales revenue per cycle exists in the following three situations: 1) $T^{'}\le N$. Brand Party shall make full payment at the end of term N, from time $N\sim M$. Therefore, interest earned by the manufacturer: $Y_a=wDI_qT^{'}(M-N).2)N\le T^{'}\le M.Y_a=wDI_q$ $\left[\int_N^{T^{'}}tdt+\int_{T^{'}}^{M}T^{'}dt\right]$.$3)M\le T^{'}.Y_a=wDI_q\int_N^{M}tdt$. Manufacturers' raw material consumption costs mainly include raw material purchase cost, transportation cost and inventory holding cost.

Where, if the storage level of raw materials is satisfied $dI_1(t)/dt = -P$, it can be derived $I_1(t) = -Pt + K$ (K is any constant value). As can be known from the initial conditions $I_1(t_0) = 0, K = Pt_0$, then the quantity of raw materials obtained by the manufacturer after delivery in the futures market is $Q' = Pt_0$, the inventory curve of raw materials is $I_1(t) = P(t_0 - t)$, the inventory of raw materials in time $[0, t_0]$ is $L_B = \int_0^{t_0} P(t_0 - t) = \frac{1}{2}Pt_0^2$, the storage cost of raw materials in each cycle is $W_B = \frac{1}{2}BPt_0^2$, and the total cost of raw materials consumed in each cycle is: $TC_{raw} = F_t P t_0 + A_{raw} + \frac{1}{2}BPt_0^2$. In addition, interest paid by the manufacturer on the amount of goods not sold after the expiration of each period of deferred payment is divided into three categories: 1) $T' \le N$. The manufacturer allows the brand party to delay the payment period n is less than the delay payment period and then the interest payable to the manufacturer is: Y_b=0. 2)$N \le T' \le M.Y_b$=0. 3)$M \le T'.Y_b = F_t I_P \int_M^{T'} I(t)dt$. To sum up, the manufacturer's net profit function in each cycle can be expressed as:

$$\Pi_{mi} = S_r + \sum c_{f-x} + Y_a - C_h - TC_{raw} - Y_b$$

After simplification, we can get:

(1)$T' \le N$

$$\Pi_{m1} = wD(T - \frac{DT}{P+D}) + \sum c_{f-x} + wDI_q(T - \frac{DT}{P+D})(M-N) - \frac{1}{2}h(P-D)(\frac{DT}{P+D})^2$$
$$-D\left[\frac{1}{2}T^2 - T(\frac{DT}{P+D})\right] - F_t P(\frac{DT}{P+D}) - A_{raw} - \frac{1}{2}BP(\frac{DT}{P+D})^2 \quad (1)$$

(2)$N \le T' \le M$

$$\Pi_{m2} = wD(T - \frac{DT}{P+D}) + \sum c_{f-x} + wDI_q\left[(T - \frac{DT}{P+D})M - \frac{1}{2}N^2 - \frac{1}{2}(T - \frac{DT}{P+D})^2\right] - \frac{1}{2}h(P-D)$$
$$(\frac{DT}{P+D})^2 - D(\frac{1}{2}T^2 - \frac{DT^2}{P+D}) - F_t P(\frac{DT}{P+D}) - A_{raw} - \frac{1}{2}BP(\frac{DT}{P+D})^2 \quad (2)$$

(3)$M \le T'$

$$\Pi_{m3} = wD(T - \frac{DT}{P+D}) + \sum c_{f-x} + \frac{wDI_q}{2}(M^2 - N^2) - \frac{h}{2}(P-D)(\frac{DT}{P+D})^2 - D\left(\frac{1}{2}T^2 - \frac{DT^2}{P+D}\right) - F_t P(\frac{DT}{P+D})$$
$$-A_{raw} - \frac{BP}{2}(\frac{DT}{P+D})^2 - F_t I_p D\left\{T\left[(T - \frac{DT}{P+D}) - M\right] + \frac{1}{2}\left[M^2 - (T - \frac{DT}{P+D})^2\right]\right\} \quad (3)$$

It is easy to verify: $\Pi_{m1}(N) = \Pi_{m2}(N), \Pi_{m2}(M) = \Pi_{m3}(M)$ So $\Pi_{mi}(T)$ is continuous on the interval $(0, +\infty)$.

3.2 Model solution

According to the necessary conditions for the existence of extreme values, the optimal value of T must satisfy: $\frac{d\Pi_{mi}(T)}{dT} = 0 \quad i = 1,2,3$. Thus, the following can be obtained:

$$\frac{d\Pi_{m1}(T)}{dT}=\frac{wPD}{P+D}+\frac{(P+D)(wDI_qM-wDI_qN)}{P+D}+\frac{D^2T}{P+D}-\frac{D+PDT+PDF_t}{P+D}-\frac{BPD^2T+hD^2(P-D)T}{(P+D)^2} \quad (4)$$

$$\frac{d\Pi_{m2}(T)}{dT}=\frac{wPD}{P+D}+\frac{wPDI_q(M-T)}{P+D}-\frac{PDT-D^2T}{P+D}-\frac{PDF_t}{P+D}-\frac{BPD^2T}{(P+D)^2}-\frac{hD^2(P-D)T}{(P+D)^2} \quad (5)$$

$$\frac{d\Pi_{m3}(T)}{dT}=\frac{wPD}{P+D}-\frac{BPD^2T}{(P+D)^2}-\frac{hD^2(P-D)T}{(P+D)^2}-\frac{PDF_t}{P+D}-\frac{PDT-D^2T}{P+D}-\frac{F_tI_pD(P^2T+2PDT-M(P+D)^2)}{(P+D)^2} \quad (6)$$

Firstly, the property theorem about the optimal solution of function $\Pi_{mi}(T)$ is given: **Theorem 1** (1)If $d^2\Pi_{m1}/dT^2<0$, then $\Pi_{m1}(T)$ increases strictly in the interval $(0,T_1^*)$ and decreases strictly in the interval $(T_1^*,+\infty)$, that is, $\Pi_{m1}(T)$ reaches its maximum value at T_1^* within $(0,+\infty)$.(2)(3)The same can be obtained. According to theorem 1, The optimal value T^* of $\Pi_{mi}(T)$ has been obtained. According to equations (4)~(6), $f_i(T)=d\Pi_{mi}/dT$ can be obtained: $f_1(N)=f_2(N)\,f_2(M)=f_3(M)$ For ease of expression, let $\varphi_1=f_1(N)=f_2(N)\,\varphi_2=f_2(M)=f_3(M)$, while $f_2(T)$ strictly monotonically decreases within $(0,+\infty)$, so $\varphi_1\geq\varphi_2$. The following theorem can find the global optimal solution T^*.**Theorem 2** If $\varphi_1<0\&\varphi_2<0,\Pi_{mi}(T^*)=\Pi_{mi}(T_1^*)$, therefore $T^*=T_1^*$.(2)(3)*The same can be obtained.*

4 Example analysis

In order to verify the feasibility of the model, specific parameters are set as follows: $M=20/360year, N=15/360year, I_p=0.15, I_q=0.09, F_t=24yuan/piece, P=7000piece/year, D=5000piece/year,$

$w_0=30yuan/piece$ $and\varphi_1=15609.26>0,\varphi_2=15317.90>0,\Pi_{m2}(M)=910.56,\Pi_{m3}(T_3^*)=6211.83,$

$B=4yuan/piece, h=6yuan/piece/year, \sum c_{f-x}=50yuan/time, A_{raw}=12yuan/piece, \tau=0.98,$

Through calculation, we can get: $d^2\Pi_{m1}/dT^2<0, d^2\Pi_{m2}/dT^2<0,\ d^2\Pi_{m3}/dT^2<0$ According to Theorem 1, the optimal production cycle of the manufacturer's inventory system is $T^*=T_3^*=0.7394$, and the maximum profit is $\Pi_m^*=6211.83$. According to Theorem 1, the optimal production cycle of the manufacturer's inventory system is $T^*=T_3^*=0.7394$, and the maximum profit is $\Pi_m^*=6211.83$. In order to directly show the influence of brand party's dominance on the manufacturer, M、N、τ、F_t are adjusted and the profit changes of the manufacturer are observed, as shown in Table 1:

Table 1. Influence of changes in M、N、τ、F_t on manufacturers' supply strategy.

M	F_t	N	τ	T^*	Π_m^*
20/360	24	5/360	0.98	0.7394	6222.04
30/360	23.8	5/360	0.98	0.7910	7069.03
20/360	24	15/360	0.97	0.7008	5581.64
35/360	23.7	5/360	0.98	0.8169	7511.56
25/360	23.6	5/360	0.98	0.8099	7374.16

Table 2. Effects of productivity P changes on manufacturers' production cycle.

D	P	η	T^*
5000	5500	0.91	0.7638
5000	6000	0.83	0.7513
5000	8000	0.63	0.7374
5000	10000	0.5	0.7467
5000	12000	0.42	0.7631
5000	14000	0.36	0.7814

As can be seen from the first and second sets of data in the table, when the period of deferred payment to the manufacturer is extended to half a month (15 days) and the price discount coefficient is increased from 2% to 3% (group 1 and Group 3 data), the manufacturer's profit will decrease by 10.29%. At this time, manufacturers can lock the price in the futures market and delay the payment for goods to make up for their own income loss, achieving a profit increase of 13.61%. The results of the fourth and fifth groups were adjusted $MandF_t$. However, consider that in real life, manufacturers not only buy cheap ($F_t = 24$) futures locked prices, but also buy raw materials on the spot market. If the manufacturer buys the futures contract at a low price in the futures market before production ($t = 0$), stores the raw materials in the warehouse after delivery, and buys the same amount of raw materials in the spot market at the price of 24.5 half a month (15 days) later when the price of raw materials in the spot market rises, and the storage cost of raw materials is 4, then the cost of buying futures is 1.35% less than that of buying spot. Therefore, the purchase of futures for enterprises to reduce the cost of procurement are beneficial. In addition, by changing the size of supplier productivity P, where η represents the ratio of demand rate D to productivity P, observe its impact on manufacturers' profits, as shown in Table 2:

As can be seen from Table 5, with the decrease of productivity, the production cycle of manufacturers becomes longer. The last three sets of data suggest that high productivity also leads to longer production cycles. This means that the manufacturer needs to control the production rate. Both too high and too low production rate will affect the production cycle of the supply chain, thus affecting the inventory cost.

5 Conclusion

Strong brands compress manufacturers' profit margins through delayed payment and wholesale price discounts, which deeply affects the sustainable circulation of manufacturers' own funds and the stability of production and operation. In this paper, a supply chain consisting of a single supplier, a manufacturer and a brand is considered, and an optimal supply decision model is constructed for the manufacturer considering futures purchase under the condition of deferred payment by the brand. The influence of futures purchase price, deferred payment period, price discount coefficient and other factors on the supply strategy of the manufacturer is further analyzed. The effect of manufacturer productivity on the optimal production cycle is also discussed.

References

1. Zhai Yue,Cheng T.C.E. Lead-time quotation and hedging coordination in make-to-order supply chain[J]. European Journal of Operational Research,2022,300(2):449-460.
2. Keynes J M. A Treatise on Money[M].London: Macmillan Publishers,1930.
3. Kouvelis Panos,Turcic Danko. Supporting Operations with Financial Hedging: Cash Hedging Vs. Cost Hedging in an Automotive Industry[J]. Production and Operations Management,2020,30(3):738-749.
4. Goyal, S. K. Economic Order Quantity under Conditions of Permissible Delay in Payments[J]. Journal of the Operational Research Society,1985,36(4):1069-1069.
5. Chu P, Chung K J, Lan S P. Economic order quantity of deteriorating items under permissible delay in payments[J]. Computers & Operations Research,1998,25(10):817-824.
6. Sundararajan R, Vaithyasubramanian S, Nagarajan A. Impact of delay in payment, shortage and inflation on an EOQ model with bivariate demand[J]. 管理分析学报(英文), 2021,8(2):28.

Decay model of energy storage battery life under multiple influencing factors of grid dispatching

Xiaorong Huang[*], *Jieming* Huang, *Jionghui* Wei, *Qingbo* Zhang, *Yuanjia* Li, and *Xiliang* Dai

Dongguan Power Supply Bureau of Guangdong Power Grid Corporation, Dongguan, Guangdong, China

Abstract. Energy storage batteries work under constantly changing operating conditions such as temperature, depth of discharge, and discharge rate, which will lead to serious energy loss and low utilization rate of the battery, resulting in a sharp attenuation of life, and the battery often fails before the end of its service life. Battery replacement leads to increasing energy storage costs, and in order to ensure the efficient, safe and reliable operation of batteries under complex working conditions of the power grid, effective management of batteries is required. The battery model is the theoretical basis of the management algorithm, and life prediction is the key technology to ensure battery safety. In view of the above practical application requirements, this paper studies the dynamic modeling of energy storage battery life based on multi-parameter information, and the results show that the proposed life model accurately reflects the battery life under multi-parameter information.

1 Introduction

Lithium-ion batteries have the advantages of high energy and power density, low discharge rate and high cycle life, and are an important choice for building microgrid-level energy storage systems. (Battery energy storage system ,BESS) .BESS plays an important role in improving power quality and ensuring the safe and stable operation of microgrids, and the life of the battery needs to be considered to evaluate the value of BESS[1]. At present, it is more important to consider the full life cycle of battery use to analyze the cost of energy storage. However, because the energy storage battery works under constantly changing operating conditions such as temperature, depth of discharge, and discharge rate, it will lead to serious energy loss and low utilization rate of the battery, resulting in a sharp attenuation of life, and the battery often fails before the end of its service life. The replacement of batteries leads to an increasing cost of energy storage, so it is necessary to study the battery life attenuation of energy storage based on different operating conditions [2].

* Corresponding author: 706360854@qq.com

2 Semi-empirical life decay modeling for lithium-ion batteries

At present, most of the battery life attenuation models of energy storage are based on the irreversible capacity of the battery, and the influence of many factors such as charge-discharge rate, charge-discharge cut-off voltage, temperature and the like on battery capacity is often considered and modelled [3].

The cycle aging and life decay of energy storage batteries are the common results of many factors such as temperature and depth of discharge, as (1):

$$t = t_{on} - t_{DOD} - t_{SOC} - t_T - t_s - t_N \tag{1}$$

The energy storage battery model constructed by Arrhenius equation only under the influence of temperature simulates its temperature dependence on the chemical reaction rate, and obtains the temperature model, as (2):

$$f_T(T) = \exp\left[g_T(T - T_{ref}) \cdot \frac{T_{ref}}{T} \right] \tag{2}$$

In formula: $f_T(T)$ -Lithium-ion battery capacity decay(%);

g_T -Temperature stress coefficient;

T_{ref} -Reference temperature.

2.1 The battery capacity decay model under the influence of multiple factors is considered

Using the solved temperature and multi-stress model to fit the data separately, it is found that there is still a large deviation in the data, which is that the battery life not only depends on the external stress factors, the battery degradation is a nonlinear process relative to the time and stress cycle, so a decay model combining nonlinear components and linear components is proposed, and the role of SEI film is simulated with nonlinear components, and then the impact of battery life on degradation is estimated, and the stress model under different conditions can be obtained by separating the mode[4].As fig1.

Battery life attenuation includes calendar decay and cyclic decay. The rate of calendar decay is determined by the temperature and SOC of the battery, so equation (3) can represent the aging decay model:

$$Q_{cal} = f_1\left(t, \overline{\sigma}, \overline{T_c}\right) \tag{3}$$

Cyclic attenuation refers to the loss of battery life during each charge-discharge cycle, and the loss is affected by factors such as depth of discharge, average SOC of cycles, average battery temperature, charge-discharge duration, and discharge rate, so equation (4) can represent the cyclic decay model.

$$Q_{cyc} = \sum_{i}^{N} n_i f_c\left(\sigma_i, \xi_i, T_i, T_s, C_i\right) \tag{4}$$

There into: N -Number of cycles in actual use; n_i indicates whether the loop i is a full cycle,the rain counting cycle algorithm is adopted.The above equations (3) and (4) are linearly integrated to obtain the attenuation function model Q_{loss}:

$$Q_{loss}\left(t,\xi,\sigma,T_c,T_s,T_i,C\right)=k_1f_1(t,\overline{\sigma},\overline{T_c})+k_2\sum_i^N n_if_c\left(\sigma_i,\xi_i,T_i,T_s,C_i\right) \quad (5)$$

Among them: $k_1+k_2=1$, the rain current counting algorithm can be used to simulate the estimation combined with the actual operation of the battery, which is more suitable for complex battery attenuation model[5].

2.2 Battery life attenuation model based on semi-empirical method

The decay rate of an energy storage battery is not a linear process, and the actual decay rate per cycle $\left(dL/d\left(Cycle\right)\right)$ is expressed as a function of L the linear decay rate over a cycle:

$$\frac{dL}{d\left(Cycle\right)}=\frac{dL}{dN}=f_L^{cyc}\left(L,f_d^{cyc}\right) \quad (6)$$

There into: L -The current life state of the battery is normalized by the ratio of the capacity lost by the battery to the rated capacity.

However, the resulting model in Equation (6) cannot simulate the rapid aging phase in the early cycle, and this rapid early decay may be caused by various mechanisms, but the main reason is the formation of solid interface films during the battery cycle. When a new battery starts working, it consumes a certain amount of active lithium ions to form this thin film. When a stable film is formed, the rate at which the film is formed decreases [6]. To model this theory, it is assumed that a certain portion of the battery's active material is consumed during the transient phase to form an SEI film. The rate of formation is inversely proportional to the already formed SEI film and stops at steady state [7].As fig 2.

Let be a portion of the charge capacity irreversibly consumed during SEI film formation. Divide the total normalized battery capacity into two parts: within the SEI section, and the rest decay at a rate proportional to the battery life. Equation (7) SEI formation is modeled, but with a different linear rate, the battery capacity decay is modeled as a double exponential function.as fig 3.

$$L=1-\rho_s esp(-Q_s)-(1-\rho_s)\exp(-Q_{loss}) \quad (7)$$

There into: Q_{loss} --Irreversible capacity decay rate(%); Q_s -Reversible capacity decay rate(%).

The parameters ρ_s depend on the internal design of the battery, and are related to the specific surface area of graphite and the layer formation conditions, generally taking 3% to 8%. Since use and temperature also contribute to the formation of SEI, Q_s is proportional to Q_{loss} (scale factor is φ_s):

The attenuation data shown also reveals the relationship between SOC and calendar life, and its trend of the fitted curve is an exponential model. The first number in the legend indicates the depth of discharge in the battery cycle, so this curve shows the battery capacity attenuation under the influence of different DOD, temperature and discharge[8].

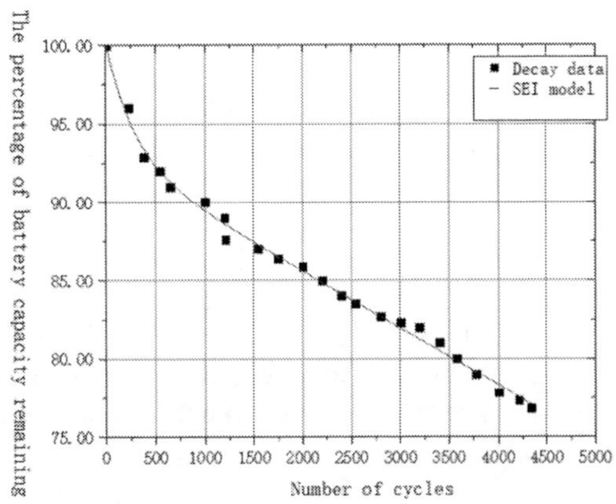

Fig. 1. SEI model fitting result.

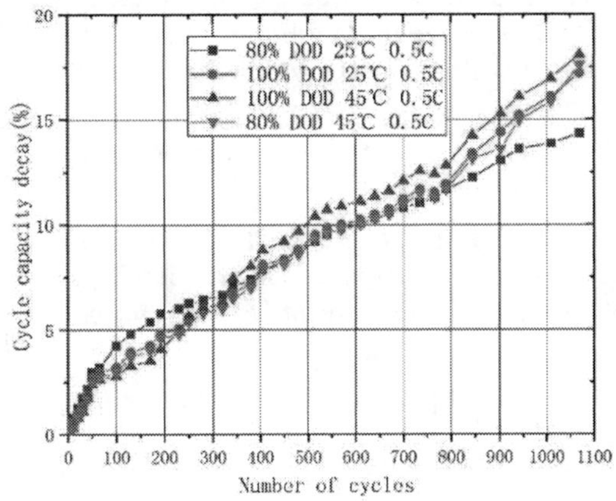

Fig. 2. Cycle capacity decay curve.

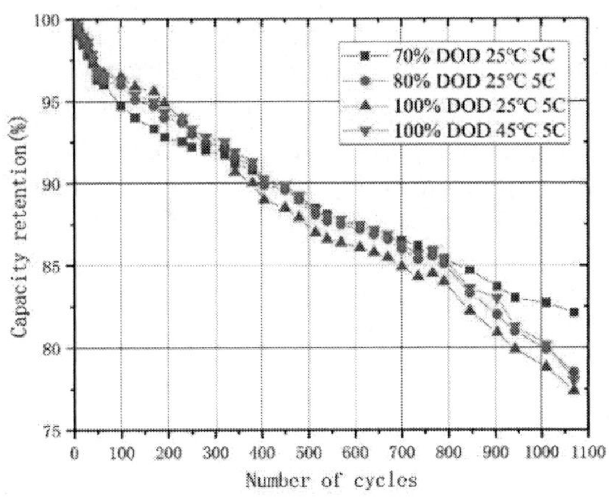

Fig. 3. Battery dynamic test data.

3 Result

Firstly, according to the modeling ideas of single influencing factor model and multi-stress model, a battery life capacity model considering multiple factors is established[9].Secondly, the overall attenuation characteristics of battery capacity are determined based on battery life attenuation experiments, and the results of multi-factor models are evaluated accordingly. The formation mechanism of SEI of lithium-ion batteries was mathematically modeled to solve the problem of inconsistency between the actual decay rate and the model description, and the SEI[10]. Finally, the multi-factor model is substituted into the overall model of SEI to obtain a semi-empirical life attenuation model, and the experimental results show that the model has a high degree of fitting to the attenuation data, and the estimation error of battery life attenuation is kept within 5%.

References

1. S. Maitreya, H. Jain and P. Paliwal, "Scalable and De-centralized Battery Management System for Parallel Operation of Multiple Battery Packs," *2021 Innovations in Energy Management and Renewable Resources(52042)*, 2021, pp. 1-7.
2. N. A. Sârbu and D. Petreuş, "State of Charge Estimation of Li-Ion Batteries using Artificial Neural Networks," *2022 45th International Spring Seminar on Electronics Technology (ISSE)*, 2022, pp. 1-8.
3. X. Li, R. Ma, L. Wang, S. Wang and D. Hui, "Energy Management Strategy for Hybrid Energy Storage Systems with Echelon-use Power Battery," *2020 IEEE International Conference on Applied Superconductivity and Electromagnetic Devices (ASEMD)*, 2020, pp. 1-2.
4. J. Xue, C. Yan, D. Wang, J. Wang, J. Wu and Z. Liao, "Adaptive Dynamic Programming Method for Optimal Battery Management of Battery Electric Vehicle," *2020 IEEE 9th Data Driven Control and Learning Systems Conference (DDCLS)*, 2020, pp. 65-68.
5. Y. Liu, T. Thiringer, N. Wang, Y. Fu, H. Lu and J. Liu, "Graphene based thermal management system for battery cooling in electric vehicles," *2020 IEEE 8th Electronics System-Integration Technology Conference (ESTC)*, 2020, pp. 1-4.
6. S. Dalvi and S. Thale, "Design of DSP Controlled Passive Cell Balancing Network based Battery Management System for EV Application," 2020 IEEE India Council International Subsections Conference (INDISCON), 2020, pp. 84-89.
7. N. A. -Z. R-Smith et al., "Multiplexed 16 × 16 Li-Ion Cell Measurements Including Internal Resistance for Quality Inspection and Classification," in IEEE Transactions on Instrumentation and Measurement, vol. 70, pp. 1-9, 2021, Art no. 2006109.
8. Schweiger, H.-G.; Obeidi, O.; Komesker, O.; Raschke, A.; Schiemann, M.; Zehner, C.; Gehnen, M.; Keller, M.; Birke, P. Comparison of Several Methods for Determining the Internal Resistance of Lithium Ion Cells. Sensors 2010, 10, 5604-5625.
9. N. NOURA, K. COS, L. BOULON and S. JEMEI, "Online Identification of Battery Internal Resistance under extreme Temperatures," 2020 IEEE Vehicle Power and Propulsion Conference (VPPC), 2020, pp. 1-5.
10. A. Benshatti, S. M. R. Islam, T. Link, S. Park and S. Park, "Design and Control of AC Current Injector for Battery EIS Measurement," 2020 IEEE Applied Power Electronics Conference and Exposition (APEC), 2020, pp. 3452-3455.

A flexible ensemble regression model of extreme learning machine for missing value imputation of DNA microarray data

Xiuwei Pan[1], *Wenlu* Dong[2], and *Hualong* Yu[2,*]

[1]Beijing Huanjia Communication Technology Co., Ltd, Beijing 100192, China
[2]School of Computer, Jiangsu University of Science and Technology, Zhenjiang 212003, China

Abstract. Missing value imputation (MVI) is important for DNA microarray data analysis because microarray data with missing values would significantly degrade the performance of the downstream analysis. Although there have been lots of MVI algorithms for dealing with the missing DNA microarray data, we note that most of them have a lack of robustness owing to only adopting the single model. In this paper, a flexible and robust MVI algorithm named EELMimpute is proposed to address missing DNA microarray data imputation problem. First, the algorithm constructs a relevant feature space for the missing target gene, where the relevant feature space only includes those co-expression genes of the target gene based on calculating their Pearson's correlation coefficients. Then, some fix-sized feature subspaces are randomly extracted from the relevant feature space to construct extreme learning machine (ELM) regression models between the extracted genes and the target gene. Furthermore, selecting those models without missing input gene values to construct the ensemble framework, and then imputing the missing gene by calculating the average output of all models included in the ensemble framework. Experimental results show that the EELMimpute algorithm is able to reduce the estimated errors in comparison with several previous imputation algorithms.

1 Introduction

In the past two decades, DNA microarray has been gradually developed to be one of the most important molecular biology techniques in the post-genomic era, and the microarray data has also been widely applied by biologists and medical experts to analyze various behaviors of life [1-2].

However, there may exist some missing gene expression values in microarray data, owing to various reasons, e.g., experimental errors, hybridization failures, the existence of dust or scratch on the chip surface, etc. [3]. The existence of missing values might significantly degrade the performance of some downstream analysis, thus, providing the complete gene expression data is necessary for the further downstream analysis.

* Corresponding author: yuhualong@just.edu.cn

To solve the problem above, a missing value imputation (MVI) strategy is required. Indeed, some complex MVI strategies have been developed for imputing the missing microarray data. The methods include K-nearest neighbors imputation (KNNimpute) [4], singular value decomposition imputation (SVDimpute) [4], Bayesian principal component analysis (BPCAimpute) [5], local least squares imputation (LLSimpute) [6], shrinkage local least squares imputation (SLLSimpute) [7], iterative locally auto-weighted least squares imputation (ILAW-LSimpute) [8], etc. In general, these methods can provide more accurate estimations for the missing values existing in the microarray data. However, all these methods adopt the single model, meanwhile we note the microarray data is generally small-sized, thereby the robustness of the imputing results by these methods can't be guaranteed.

In this paper, we propose a novel missing data imputation algorithm named ensemble regression model of extreme learning machine imputation (EELMimpute) for microarray data. Our EELMimpute involves three key phases. In the first phase, some co-expression genes whose expressions are strongly associated with that of the target gene are extracted from the original data to construct the relevant feature space. In fact, these co-expression genes could reflect the real values of the missing position of the target gene to some extent. Then, in the second phase, some fix-sized feature subspaces are randomly extracted from the relevant feature space to train some extreme learning machine (ELM) regression models. That means a lot of different mappings between a target gene and its several co-expression genes can be created. Here, the reason of selecting ELM as the regression modeling tool is that ELM is not only robust, but also time-saving [9-11]. Finally, the third phase takes charge of integrating all regression models into an ensemble framework, and further providing the estimated missing values by averaging the results from all models containing in the ensemble framework. Actually, this phase takes advantage of ensemble learning to further promote the robustness and accuracy of the imputing results. Experimental results on eight different DNA microarray data sets indicate that the proposed EELMimpute algorithm is able to reduce the estimated errors in comparison with several popular state-of-the-art imputation algorithms.

The contributions of this study can be concluded as follows,

A fast and robust regression model-ELM is adopted to address missing DNA microarray data imputation problem;

A robust ensemble learning framework based on the idea of feature subspace strategy is proposed to improve the imputation quality of missing DNA microarray data.

2 Method

2.1 Construction of relevant feature space

As we know, there exists a large number of noisy and irrelevant genes when specifying a target gene in DNA microarray data, which means these genes have no or very weak co-expression with the target gene. Obviously, it is unhelpful to use these genes for accurately impute the missing value of target gene. Therefore, a relevant feature space should be firstly extracted from the original gene space for reconstructing the missing target gene values. For this purpose, we adopt the Pearson correlation coefficient as the similarity metric between two genes, because of its accuracy and robustness on measuring the linear relationship between two equilong vectors. Without loss of generality, suppose the target gene is g_i, then the Pearson correlation coefficient r_{ij} that indicates the similarity between the target gene and the gene g_j is calculated as follows,

$$r_{ij}=\frac{\sum_{k=1}^{h}(e_{ik}-\overline{g_i})(e_{jk}-\overline{g_j})}{(\sqrt{\sum_{k=1}^{h}(e_{ik}-\overline{g_i})^2})(\sqrt{\sum_{k=1}^{h}(e_{jk}-\overline{g_j})^2})} \quad (1)$$

where $r_{ij}\in[-1, 1]$, and when it approximates 1 or -1 indicating there is a strong positive or negative linear relationship between two measured genes. As for e_{ik} and e_{jk}, they respectively denote the expression value of gene i and gene j on the kth instance, while $\overline{g_i}$ and $\overline{g_j}$ respectively represents the average expression of gene i and gene j across all h instances which don't include missing values on either of these two genes. Specifically, h is decided by the missing positions existing in both genes. For example, the expression pattern of two genes across 6 instances is given as follows,

$$\begin{bmatrix} 0.8 & ? & 1.0 & 0.7 & ? & 0.9 \\ ? & 1.2 & 0.8 & 0.5 & ? & 0.8 \end{bmatrix} \quad (2)$$

Then h equals 3 as the other three positions (1st, 2nd and 5th) hold missing values either on one gene or on both.

For a given target gene, m-1 Pearson correlation coefficients can be calculated. Next, the absolute values of these coefficients are ranked in descending sort to indicate which genes are strongly correlated with the target gene. The reason of adopting absolute values to sort the correlation coefficients lies in that no matter the strong positive correlation ($r\approx1$) or strong negative correlation ($r\approx-1$) indicates there is a strong linear relationship between the target gene and the investigated gene, which is very helpful for estimating the missing values.

Finally, we extract the genes corresponding to the first K top-ranked coefficients to construct the relevant feature space, which will be further used to recovery the missing target gene values. In general, K should be much smaller than m.

2.2 Construction of relevant feature space

Extreme Learning Machine (ELM) that was proposed by Huang *et al.*, [9-11], is a specific learning algorithm for training single-hidden layer feedforward neural networks (SLFN). The main characteristic of ELM that distinguishes it from those conventional learning algorithms of SLFN is the random generation of hidden nodes. Therefore, ELM does not need to iteratively adjust parameters to make them approach the optimal values, thus it has faster learning speed and better generalization ability. In this work, we consider ELM as a regression model.

Let us consider a regression problem with N training instances to approximating m continuous variables, and then the ith training instance can be represented as (x_i, t_i), where x_i is an $n\times1$ input vector, and t_i is the corresponding $m\times1$ continuous output vector. Suppose there are L hidden nodes in ELM, and that all weights and biases on these nodes are generated randomly. Then, for the instance x_i, its hidden layer output can be represented as a row vector $\mathrm{h}(x_i)=[\mathrm{h}_1(x_i), \mathrm{h}_2(x_i),..., \mathrm{h}_L(x_i)]$ by mapping with an activation function (the most popular sigmoid function is used throughout this paper). The mathematical model of ELM could be described as:

$$\mathrm{H}\beta=\mathrm{T} \quad (3)$$

where $\mathrm{H}=[\mathrm{h}(x_1), \mathrm{h}(x_2),..., \mathrm{h}(x_N)]^{\mathrm{T}}$ is the hidden layer output matrix over all training instances, β is the weight matrix of the output layer, and $\mathrm{T}=[t_1, t_2,..., t_N]$ denotes the regression target matrix. Obviously, in Eq. (3), only β is unknown, so we can adopt the least square algorithm to acquire its solution, which can be described as follows.

$$\beta = \mathrm{H}^{\dagger}\mathrm{T} = \begin{cases} \mathrm{H}^{\mathrm{T}}(\mathrm{H}\mathrm{H}^{\mathrm{T}})^{-1}\mathrm{T}, \text{ when } N \le L \\ (\mathrm{H}\mathrm{H}^{\mathrm{T}})^{-1}\mathrm{H}^{\mathrm{T}}\mathrm{T}, \text{ when } N > L \end{cases} \tag{4}$$

where $\mathrm{H}^{\dagger}$ denotes the Moore-Penrose generalized inverse of the hidden layer output matrix H, which can guarantee the solution is the least-norm least-squares solution of Eq. (5).

In our work, the instance x_i is a $q\times 1$ vector, where q denotes the selected relevant genes, and then it is used as the input in ELM to regress the value of target gene on the same instance. In other words, ELM models an approximate q-to-1 map between the selected relevant genes and the target gene. However, the map is non-linear but not linear as modeling by KNNimpute [4] or LSimpute family [7-8] algorithms.

2.3 Construction of relevant feature space

To further improve the robustness and accuracy of imputation results, we also introduce the ensemble learning to fill the missing gene expression values. Specifically, considering in general, DNA microarray data is small-sized but high-dimensional, it is easier to disturb the feature space but not sample space for generating diverse base learners, hence in this work, we adopt feature subspace but not bagging as the ensemble learning framework.

In the relevant feature space containing K co-expression genes, we randomly and independently extracted q genes for M times, where $q<<K$ and $M\geq 1$. Then combining each subspace with the target gene, and on each (q+1)-dimensional subset, we train an ELM regression model that using q relevant genes as input and the target gene as output. Specifically, the training data is required to be complete. Next, on each regression model, we input the expression values of the corresponding q relevant genes on the target instance s_j, and then run the model to acquire the corresponding output τ_{ij} which can be seen as an approximation for the missing gene expression value e_{ij}. Finally, the imputation value of e_{ij} can be calculated by,

$$\psi_{ij} = \sum_{k=1}^{K} \tau_{ij}^{k} \Big/ K \tag{5}$$

where τ_{ij}^{k} denotes the approximation value provided by the kth model, and ψ_{ij} represents the ensemble imputed value for the position e_{ij}.

It is clear that the ensemble learning model adopts the average value of outputs from all sub-models as the final imputation value. In comparison with the single regression model, this ensemble model is expected to provide an more accurate and robust result.

Combining the idea of relevant feature space construction, ELM regression modeling and feature subspace ensemble, a novel imputation algorithm named EELMimpute is proposed. Its procedure can be simply described as follows.

Algorithm. Pseudo-code description of EELMimpute

Input: A microarray data set $G \in \Re^{m\times n}$ with missing values, the number of hidden nodes L in ELM, the dimension of relevant space K, the dimension of feature subspace q, and the number of base regression models M.

Output: A complete microarray data set G' without missing values.

Procedure:

1. **For** i=1:m

2. **If** g_i does not contain the missing value in sample space
3. Put the copy of g_i into G' and return;
4. **Else**
5. Find K relevant co-expression genes for g_i by Eq.(1);
6. **For** j=1:M
7. Select q genes from K relevant genes randomly;
8. Train an ELM regression model using the instances with the complete q selected gene values and the target gene (i.e., g_i) values by Eq.(3) and Eq.(4);
9. **End for**
10. Find all missing positions for the target gene g_i;
11. Use the trained M regression models to approximate the value of each missing position, and impute them by using Eq.(5);
12. Put the imputed completely g_i into G';
13. **End if**
14. **End for**
15. Output the imputation microarray data set G'.

3 Experiments

3.1 Datasets

In our experiments, eight different DNA microarray data sets were used to evaluate our proposed algorithm and to compare with the other imputation algorithms. Table 1 provides the basic description for the used DNA microarray data sets.

Table 1. Datasets descriptions.

Dataset	Number of instances	Number of genes	Data Type
Colon	62	2000	Non-time series
SRBCT	83	2308	Non-time series
Leukemia	72	7129	Non-time series
Hepatocellular	22	10523	Non-time series
Drosophila	48	5070	Non-time series
Candida	9	16052	Non-time series
Saccharomyces	16	5282	Time series
Yeast	28	5716	Time series

3.2 Experimental settings

In the experiments, we compared the proposed EELMimpute algorithm with several popular and state-of-the-art imputation algorithms, including SVDimpute [4], KNNimpute [4], BPCAimpute [5], LLSimpute [6], SLLSimpute [7] and ILAW-LSimpute [8]. For each imputation algorithm, the parameters use the best default ones recommended in the corresponding references.

As for the proposed EELMimpute, the parameters are empirically designated as that K equals to be 200, q equals to be 5, M equals to be 100 according to the feedback of the a huge of experimental results. Considering q, which corresponds to the input dimension in ELM, is small enough, the number of hidden-layer nodes L is empirically set to be 10 as a default setting, because of some previous work have indicated that for low-dimension data, it is inappropriate for assigning an excess of hidden-layer nodes in ELM with two considerations as follows: 1) it would add unnecessary training time consumption; 2) the model tends to be overfitting.

We compared all imputation algorithms on eight data sets with different missing rates, 1%, 5%, 10%, 15% and 20%, respectively. That means 1%, 5%, 10%, 15% and 20% entries in the original complete data sets are randomly missed. In order to evaluate the imputation quality and compare the performance of various imputation algorithms, the normalized root mean square error (NRMSE), which is presented as follows, is used as the performance metric,

$$NRMSE=\frac{\sqrt{\text{mean}[(e_{\text{real}}-e_{\text{impute}})^2]}}{\text{std}(e_{\text{real}})} \tag{6}$$

where e_{real} and e_{impute} respectively indicates the real value and the estimated value of a missing position in the DNA microarray data, the mean function denote the mean square error of all missing positions imputed by an imputation algorithm, and the std function denotes the calculation of standard deviation.

In this paper, each experiment is randomly conducted ten times, then the average NRMSE is given to evaluate the quality of each imputation algorithm, which is also a popular practice used in the experimental settings of most previous work [5-8].

3.3 Results and analysis

Fig. 1 presents the NRMSE performance of each imputation algorithm at different missing rates on eight DNA microarray data sets. Overall, the proposed EELMimpute algorithm has better performance on nearly all data sets at most missing rates. Specifically, EELMimpute averagely reduces 26.26%, 6.95%, 2.96%, 9.44%, 7.70% and 3.95% NRMSE in comparison with SVDimpute, KNNimpute, BPCAimpute, LLSimpute, SLLSimpute and ILAW-LSimpute algorithms, respectively. Meanwhile, the proposed algorithm has also acquired 28 best results in 40 independent testing conditions (8 data sets × 5 different missing rates). The reasons for the success of EELMimpute algorithm may be attributed to the use of ELM regression model which provides a powerful nonlinear mapping ability, and the adoption of ensemble learning framework which provides a stronger generalization. Actually, EELMimpute can be seen as a multiple imputation algorithm for estimating the missing values.

Another interesting phenomenon that can be observed in Fig. 1 is that the proposed EELMimpute algorithm is more stable than the other imputation algorithms, i.e., its performance can be less impacted by the missing rate. We believe that its stability can mainly attribute to its feature space construction mechanism. As we know, no matter for KNNimpute or LSimpute family algorithms, its neighboring genes only come from those complete genes without missing values, thus with the increase of missing rate, the calculation of relevant genes will become less and less accurate, further degrade the quality of imputation. However, our proposed EELMimpute algorithm always uses the whole gene space to extract the relevant feature space, and when there exists missing values for one specific gene, only the positions without missing value participate in the calculation of Pearson correlation coefficient, thereby the useful information can be fully reserved. Another reason lies in that the use of ensemble learning framework, which has been testified to be effective for improving the stability of learning results.

Next, we tested the actual difference between the EELMimpute algorithm and the other imputation algorithms in statistics. Specifically, the critical difference (CD) metric is used to show the difference of various algorithms. Fig. 2 shows the CD diagram at a standard level of significance α=0.05, where the average ranking of each imputation algorithm is marked along the axis (higher rankings to the left). In CD diagram, if a group of algorithms are not significantly different under Nemenyi test [12], these algorithms will be connected by a thick line.

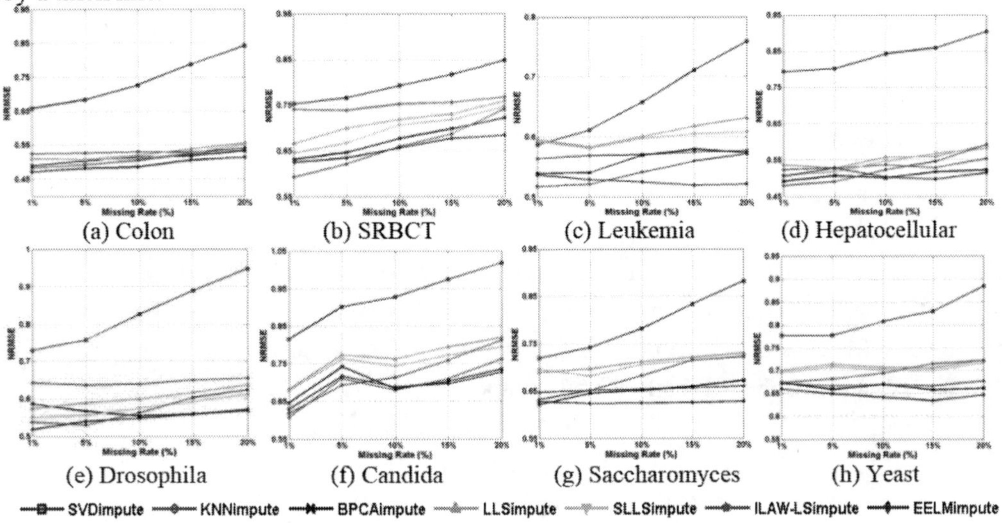

Fig. 1. Average NRMSE of the SVDimpute, KNNimpute, BPCAimpute, LLSimpute, SLLSimpute, ILAW-LSimpute and the proposed EELMimpute algorithms at different missing rates on eight DNA microarray data sets (a) Colon, (b) SRBCT, (c) Leukemia, (d) Hepatocellular, (e) Drosophila, (f) Candida, (g) Saccharomyces and (h) Yeast.

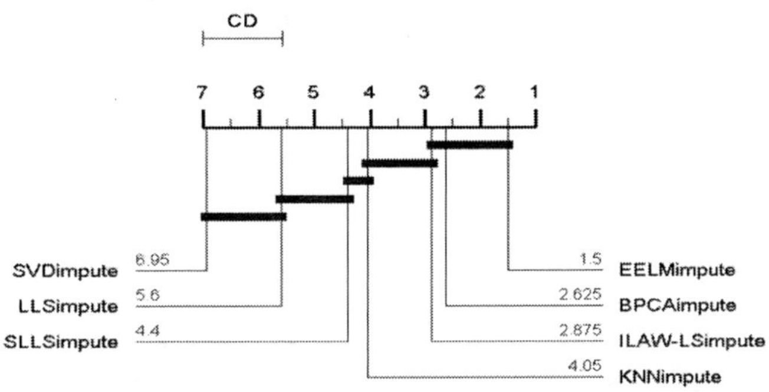

Fig. 2. CD diagram of various imputation algorithms at a standard level of significance α=0.05.

From the results shown in Fig. 2, we observe that the EELMimpute algorithm achieves the statistically superior imputation performance than SVDimpute, LLSimpute, SLLSimpute and KNNimpute algorithms, and although we can't say it has significant difference with BPCAimpute and ILAW-LSimpute algorithm, it has a lower average rank than those two algorithms. To summarize, the proposed EELMimpute algorithm is a better choice than those popular imputation algorithms when there exists missing values in DNA microarray data.

4 Concluding remarks

In this paper, we presented EELMimpute, which is a flexible and robust ensemble regression model based on extreme learning machine for imputing the missing values in DNA microarray data. For a target gene, EELMimpute first constructs a relevant feature space for it by utilizing Pearson correlation analysis method, then randomly divides the space into multiple subspaces and trains ELM regression model on each subspace, finally integrates all models to calculate the imputation results for the missing values belonging to the target gene. The experimental results on eight different DNA microarray data sets have verified the effectiveness of the proposed EELMimpute algorithm. In comparison with several popular imputation algorithms, it has acquired significantly superior results.

References

1. S.D. Krämer, J. Wöhrle, P.A. Meyer, Sci. Rep., **9**, 13940 (2019).
2. A. Alonso, V. Larraga, P.J. Alcolea, Acta Trop., **187**, 129-139 (2018).
3. S. Draghici, P. Khatri, A.C. Eklund, Trends Genet., **22**, 101-109 (2006).
4. O. Troyanskayaet, M. Cantor, G. Sherlock, Bioinformatics, **17**, 520-525 (2001).
5. S. Oba, M.A. Sato, I. Takemasa, Bioinformatics, **19**, 2088-2096 (2003).
6. H. Kim, G.H. Golub, H. Park, Bioinformatics, **21**,187-198 (2005).
7. H. Wang, C.C. Chiu, Y.C. Wu, BMC Syst. Biol., **7**, S11 (2013).
8. Z. Yu, T. Li, S.J. Horng, IEEE T Nanobiosci., **16**, 21-33 (2017).
9. G.B. Huang, Q.Y. Zhu, C.K. Siew, Neurocomputing, **70**, 489-501 (2006).
10. G.B. Huang, H. Zhou, X. Ding, IEEE Trans. Syst. Man Cybern. B, **42**, 513-529 (2012).
11. G. Huang, G.B. Huang, S. Song, Neural Netw., **61**, 32-48 (2015).
12. J. Demsar, J Mach. Learn. Res., **7**, 1-30 (2006).

Research on the innovation of teaching mode of vocational and technical education

Fengchen Zhao, *Shuli* Liang, *Junpeng* Ma and *Ou* Qi*
Army Academy of Amored Forces, Changchun, China

Keywords: Vocational and technical education, Teaching mode, Innovation.

Abstract. Vocational and technical education group is the main training object of new high-quality talents in our school, and teaching is the basic link of Vocational and technical education. The current teaching mode of Vocational and technical education has the disadvantages of emphasizing theory and neglecting practice. Therefore, it is necessary to discuss the teaching mode of Vocational and technical education in our school. Based on the current situation of the teaching mode of Vocational and technical education in our school, this paper puts forward the teaching and assessment mode of "combining theory with practice" and "combining thinking cultivation with practice".

1 Introduction

For a long time, the theory teaching focusing on concepts, theorems and formulas and the examination mode focusing on problem solving have become the leading teaching mode of Vocational and technical education in most colleges and universities, including our university. The advantage of this teaching mode is that it pays attention to the cultivation of students' solid theoretical foundation, which helps to master the basic knowledge, but the disadvantage is that it ignores the Enlightenment of thinking, which is not conducive to the cultivation of students' practical ability to apply knowledge to solve practical problems. The transformation of talent training mode puts forward new and higher requirements for the teaching mode of College English.

As a specific term in modern teaching theory, teaching mode is a relatively stable implementation plan of organizing, designing and regulating teaching activities under the guidance of certain teaching ideas or teaching theories in order to achieve certain teaching objectives. Since the mid-1980s, in order to solve the problem of disconnection between teaching theory and practice, the research on teaching mode has become a hot topic in the domestic teaching theory research.

* Corresponding author: haikuotiankongru@163.com

The essence of human society is innovation. Innovation ability is not only a prerequisite for a nation and a society to be full of vigor and vitality, but also a symbol of the development level of a nation and a society's civilization. It is an important part of a country's comprehensive national strength. Innovation not only brings rich material output for the whole country and society, but also brings new impetus for the change of human civilization. It can improve the quality of life, open up the living space and realize the value of life. In this sense, the cultivation and development of innovation ability not only makes education become the promoter of economic and social development and change, but also the promoter of individual development.

2 Guiding ideology and teaching objectives

Following the guiding ideology of our school construction, through the reform of Vocational and technical education teaching mode, we can improve the modernization, scientificity and rationalization of curriculum teaching, and lay a solid foundation for the cultivation of new talents with high quality.

2.1 Students Are the Main Body of Teaching Activities

2.1.1 Students Are the Masters of Teaching Activities

Students' learning enthusiasm is the basis of successful teaching. Only students actively learn, actively recognize, actively acquire teaching content, and actively absorb the spiritual wealth accumulated by human beings, can they choose and receive knowledge and information, and promote their own development. In a certain sense, active learning is the basis of innovative education. Teachers' learning relative to students is external cause, external cause can only work through internal cause, and teachers' teaching can only take effect through students' absorption and digestion. In the process of teaching, the interaction between teachers and students aims to achieve students' creativity and personalization. Therefore, students are the masters of teaching activities, especially innovative education. Innovative education can only be realized in the process of students' active learning.

2.1.2 Students are active explorers of knowledge

In the innovative education activities, students are not only the receivers of the knowledge taught by teachers, but also the more important thing is to digest the knowledge, analyze the internal relationship between the new and old knowledge, dare to get rid of the old and bring forth the new, and dare to discover themselves. In this sense, students are explorers and knowledge seekers in the teaching process. For students, teaching is far from a simple increase in knowledge, but with the existing experience, knowledge and culture, and leads to the change of attitude, individual and their future choice direction. Therefore, only by giving full play to students' subjectivity can we make teaching more creative and make students develop better.

2.1.3 Students are the reflectors of learning activities

Learning has reflective nature, which is the metacognition emphasized by modern cognitive psychology. In innovation education, although there are also perceptual thinking that can be understood directly or directly, critical thinking is more important. With this kind of thinking, we can take into account the conditions available in learning, and can constantly verify the proposed hypothesis of problem solving, and obtain novel and unique problem-solving answers, so that learning activities can better achieve the functions of orientation, monitoring and adjustment. Therefore, reflective critical thinking is an important part of innovation ability.

2.1.4 Students have different personalities

Students have individual differences, which are related to heredity, environment, education and their own efforts. The individual differences of students are also the colorful embodiment of their subjectivity development. The development of students' individuality has both generality and individuality. While promoting the development of generality, school education should also promote the development of individuality. It is the traditional education that distorts the development of human beings and strangles the development of personality. Innovation education should respect and protect individual personality development, and provide loose space for students' personality development is also an important content of its implementation.

2.2 The innovation of classroom teaching should be mediated by problems

The transformation of knowledge to innovation is mediated by problems. In the view of innovation education, problem refers to the inherent contradiction of knowledge itself, that is, the limitation, relativity and deficiency of knowledge. Therefore, finding, raising, analyzing and solving problems are the process of knowledge development and innovation. The problems discussed in traditional teaching are superficial and repetitive, which lack the function of innovation.

2.2.1 The problem is the beginning of classroom teaching

This is because questions are the starting point and driving force of thinking. Only when students feel the need to ask "why", "what" and "how to do" can thinking really start. The primary task of innovative classroom teaching is to guide students to find all kinds of problems, and to learn knowledge with all kinds of problems.

2.2.2 Problem is the main line throughout the process of classroom teaching

The problem is the logical power of knowledge accumulation and development, and the seed of new ideas, new methods and new knowledge. Therefore, problems should not only be the beginning of classroom teaching, but also exist in the whole teaching process. Classroom teaching revolves around raising and solving problems. It goes up in a spiral way. Problems drive the display and learning of knowledge, so that students' understanding and mastery of knowledge reach a deeper level.

2.2.3 The problem is the end result of classroom teaching

The innovative classroom teaching should not only take the problem as the beginning and main line, but also take the problem as the end. The result of classroom teaching should not be to completely eliminate problems with knowledge, but to initiate more and more extensive new problems on the basis of initially solving existing problems. We regard the generation of new problems as one of the important results of innovative classroom teaching. This is because the significance of these new problems is not only that it can make teaching activities go on endlessly, but also that it can eventually lead students to the road of innovation and become innovators.

2.3 Classroom teaching should be characterized by innovation and openness

The openness of innovative classroom teaching corresponds to the closeness of traditional classroom teaching. The closeness makes "classroom teaching become mechanical, boring and stylized, lack of vitality and fun, lack of challenge to wisdom and stimulation to curiosity, so that the vitality of teachers and students can not be brought into full play in the classroom." Closure will inevitably lead to fossilization. Only by opening up can it be enlivened. Openness is a prominent feature of innovative classroom teaching.

2.3.1 The opening of teaching materials

Textbook knowledge is the unity of absolute truth and relative truth. As absolute truth, it has the characteristics of certainty, uniqueness and stillness; as relative truth, it has the characteristics of variability, diversity and development. Traditional teaching overemphasizes the absolute side of teaching materials, and regards teaching materials without omission as the fundamental and only purpose of teaching. Innovative teaching should face up to the opposite side of teaching materials, open teaching materials, enrich teaching materials, surpass teaching materials, make teaching materials become the real "springboard" of teaching activities, and become the powerful support of students' innovative activities. According to our experimental experience, the open teaching materials mainly include: 1. Reduction and activation. Restoring teaching materials is to restore the language of teaching materials to the actual things it reflects. By restoring, we can change the abstract into the image, the profound into the superficial, and the dull into the vivid, so that knowledge can "walk" out of the books, become vivid things, and enter the students' spiritual world. 2. Supplement and adaptation. Due to the limitation of written form, teaching materials are always concise and general. There are "gaps" and "short circuits" in teaching materials. Although the words are exhausted, the meaning is still. It leaves students free space for imagination and reasoning. This is a favorable factor for innovative teaching. Teachers should encourage students to expand, speculate, imagine, fill and describe. The purpose of the adaptation or reorganization of teaching materials is to change the existing way of teaching materials, which includes: "changing the genre", "text reorganization", "changing the angle", "changing the role", "changing one topic", "multiple solutions to one topic", etc. Through adaptation or reorganization, we can change the way of thinking and cultivate the flexibility and flexibility of thinking. 3. Question and surpass. Questioning includes criticizing the inadequacies or defects of the textbook, and also putting forward different opinions on the viewpoint of the textbook, which is not only the requirement of cultivating innovative quality, but also the requirement of improving the textbook itself. Transcendence is the ultimate goal of using textbooks, which means that students have risen to a higher level with the help of textbooks.

2.3.2 Process openness

The closed process is presupposition, and the open process is generative. Teaching should be planned, but not planned, or over rigorous (such as program teaching and target teaching). Regarding the relationship between plan and teaching, kraftky, a German educator, has made a brilliant argument: "to measure whether a teaching plan has the quality standard of pedagogy is not to see whether the actual teaching is as consistent as possible with the plan, but to see whether the plan can enable teachers to take flexible actions arguably in teaching theory, so as to make students carry out creative actions Learn by contributing to the development of their conscious abilities - even limited contributions. " Teaching plan and teaching plan should provide the pillar for creative teaching in class, instead of becoming the "tight hoop curse" of classroom teaching activities. Classroom teaching should not be a closed system, nor should it be restricted to the preset fixed and unchanging program. The pre-set teaching plan needs to be open to direct experience and flexible elements in the implementation process. Teaching objectives must potentially and openly accept the unexpected experience. We should encourage the improvisation of teachers and students' interaction and surpass the requirements of the target. The opening of the process may affect the teaching progress or the so-called teaching task of some classes, which is very prominent at the beginning of the experiment. However, we should have a developing vision. First, from traditional teaching to innovative teaching, this is a negative process, a process from order to disorder to order; secondly, the completion of teaching tasks in a certain class does not affect the overall development of students. The most important thing in classroom teaching is to cultivate students' independent learning ability and innovative quality. This is the process of students' independent learning Development is also the fundamental strength of teaching development.

In the actual teaching process, according to the different requirements of teaching objectives and teaching contents, while retaining the classroom teaching environment, we can create a diversified teaching environment of software and hardware, so that students can actively discover, explore and think, so as to cultivate students' creative and cognitive ability. To build a mature and relatively complete innovative classroom teaching system, we still need to study and experiment constantly.

3 Teaching mode reform plan

3.1 Reduce theoretical teaching hours and increase self-study links

Vocational and technical education group is the training object of high-level talents in our school. After the screening of entrance examination, they generally have a certain technical foundation and higher ability. The teaching task of Vocational and technical education stage should be located in the cultivation of thinking and the expansion of thinking. This provides the possibility for the compression of theoretical teaching hours. The compressed class hours can be used in the practice of teaching, so as to focus on cultivating students' ability to apply ideas to solve practical problems, so as to achieve the teaching purpose of "learning for use" and "learning for application".

3.2 Pay attention to the inspiration and guidance of ideas

For a long time, in the theoretical teaching, teachers pay attention to the explanation of specific theorems, formulas and problem-solving ideas. The existing problem is that they are divorced from specific practical cases, resulting in the abstract, boring and non targeted theoretical teaching. In the process of specific theory learning, students do not even know the role of formula, theorem and other knowledge points in solving practical engineering problems, which practical problems can be applied to which specific knowledge points, which makes the learning process full of blindness.

While paying attention to theoretical teaching, vocational and technical education should not ignore the guidance of ideological inspiration and ideas. Specifically speaking, when teachers explain specific knowledge points in the teaching process, they should focus on the idea of solving problems. At the same time, through the analysis of targeted engineering cases, they should explain the application fields of specific theories and the problems that can be solved, so as to lay a foundation for Vocational and technical education to participate in specific scientific research work.

3.3 Add Practice Link

At present, some practical courses have been set up in China, but they have not received enough attention. The purpose of practical teaching is to improve students' learning enthusiasm, improve their awareness of application, and cultivate their ability to understand and solve practical problems with their knowledge and computer technology. Different from the traditional way of learning, it emphasizes the students' hands-on and brain based learning. In practice, due to the introduction of computer and the application of software package, more and more extensive contents have been injected into the ideas and methods of mathematics, so that students can get rid of the tedious calculation and numerical calculation, and promote the combination with other disciplines, so that students have time to do more creative work. In fact, practice is to make full use of the advantages of fast computing speed of computer, combine knowledge with computer to promote traditional teaching, so as to use computer to help students solve practical problems with the knowledge they have learned. Therefore, the idea of practice should be integrated into the teaching, and the practice course should become an important technical basic course.

Schools should provide a good practice environment for Vocational and technical education students according to the actual situation. Teachers should combine the teaching content and vocational and technical education for scientific research, select some representative engineering and technical problems and abstract them into problems, teach students to use MATLAB and other common software for simple programming, data analysis and data processing, and improve students' ability to use ideas for abstract modeling and solve problems based on computer technology.

3.4 Improve the examination system

The traditional examination is mainly a closed book examination, which focuses on students' mastery of concepts, theorems and formulas and their ability to solve problems. For the vocational and technical education group, this way of examination is not conducive to the cultivation of students' thinking ability and hands-on ability. We should take a combination of closed book examination and practical examination. The weight of the two examination methods is 50% respectively. Students' mastery of basic knowledge points can be assessed through closed book examination, and their ability of innovative thinking and solving practical problems by using computer technology can be assessed through practice. On the one hand, it is conducive to enlightening thinking and encouraging "learning for application", on the other hand, it is conducive to all-round assessment of students' ability level.

4 Evaluation of teaching mode

The evaluation of teaching mode is a complex process of multi parameters. There are many evaluation parameters. The importance of each parameter reflecting the achievement of teaching purpose cannot be known exactly. Therefore, it is difficult to determine the weight coefficient of each parameter reasonably. This paper uses fuzzy clustering method to classify the parameters of state assessment from the teaching status data, and analyzes the influence of each attribute on the classification of state data samples to reflect the importance of teaching mode evaluation.

(1) Determine the matrix of teaching mode

The n decision parameters closely related to the change of teaching mode are $A=\{a_1,a_2,\cdots,a_n\}$ selected as the data samples of the m group $X=(X_1,X_2,\cdots,X_i,\cdots,X_m)$, and the decision matrix $X=\{x_{ij}\}_{m\times n}$ of the state information of teaching mode is obtained, which x_{ij} represents the attribute value X_i of the a_j parameters in the sample.

(2) Data normalization

Because the dimension of different parameters may be different, and the measured attribute value may not be in an order of magnitude, so the data should be normalized before fuzzy equivalence classification.

For the parameter with larger attribute value, the better, the normalization formula is

$$r_{ij}=\frac{(x_{ij}-x_j^{\min})}{(x_j^{\max}-x_j^{\min})}\cdot\alpha+(1-\alpha) \tag{1}$$

where i=1,2,…,m ; j=1,2,...,n. For the parameter whose attribute value is smaller, the better, the normalization formula is

$$r_{ij}=\frac{(x_j^{\max}-x_{ij})}{(x_j^{\max}-x_j^{\min})}\cdot\alpha+(1-\alpha) \tag{2}$$

where i=1,2,…,m ; j=1,2,...,n . α is the maximum $x_j^{\max}$ value of parameter j in all samples; $x_j^{\min}$ is the minimum value $x_j^{\min}$ of the j-th parameter in all samples; α is the equilibrium factor is usually taken as 0.9.

5 Conclusions

In view of the shortcomings of Vocational and technical education teaching mode, this paper aims at improving the modernization, scientificalness and rationalization of curriculum teaching through the reform of Vocational and technical education teaching mode, and laying a solid foundation for training high-quality new military talents, and probes into the new ideas of the reform of Vocational and technical education teaching mode, and puts forward the "combination of theory and practice" The teaching and evaluation mode of "combination of thinking training and practice" emphasizes the importance of practice in teaching, and provides suggestions for the transformation of school teaching mode.

References

1. Huang Jieru, Wang Tao,Saravanan Vijayalakshmi. Musical wisdom teaching strategy under the internet + background [J]. Journal of Intelligent & Fuzzy Systems, 2021, 40(2).
2. Guo Zheng, Jifeng Zhu,Saravanan Vijayalakshmi. Japanese translation teaching corpus based on bilingual non parallel data model [J]. Journal of Intelligent & Fuzzy Systems, 2021, 40 (2).

3. Wu Rong,Xu Jian,Qian Ping,Saravanan Vijayalakshmi. Situational inquiry method in the research teaching mode for ideological and political courses [J]. Journal of Intelligent & Fuzzy Systems, 2021, 40 (2).
4. Liang Xiufang, Haiping Lv, Liu Jie, Lin Lin, Saravanan Vijayalakshmi. Reform of English interactive teaching mode based on cloud computing artificial intelligence – a practice analysis [J]. Journal of Intelligent & Fuzzy Systems, 2021, 40 (2).
5. Lilingling,Saravanan Vijayalakshmi. Online mental health education teaching mode and empirical research based on Artificial intelligence [J]. Journal of Intelligent & Fuzzy Systems, 2021, 40 (2).
6. Yutuo Fei. Research and Practice on Multimedia Teaching Mode of Photography Fundamentals Course on SPOC [J]. International Journal of Social Science and Education Research, 2021, 4 (2).
7. Mengqi Zhou. Research on Interactive Teaching Mode of Basic Course of Spatial Art Design based on Digital Platform [J]. International Journal of Social Science and Education Research, 2021, 4 (2).
8. Li Long,Sun Miaomiao. Research on the Teaching Mode of the Interior Design Studio System in Universities Based on Computer [J]. Journal of Physics: Conference Series, 2021, 1744 (3).
9. Wang Linhan,Wang Ming. Application of MOOC in Physical Education Teaching Mode under the Background of Big Data [J]. Journal of Physics: Conference Series, 2021, 1744 (4).
10. Wei Wenting, Fang Wenxuan, Wei Jinrui. Research on the Innovation of College Basketball Information Teaching Mode under the Background of Internet [J]. Journal of Physics: Conference Series, 2021, 1744 (4).
11. Zhang Yan. Research on the Innovative Practice Teaching Mode of Applied Undergraduate Digital Electronic Technology Major Based on the Computer Aid [J]. Journal of Physics: Conference Series, 2021, 1744 (4).

AUTHOR INDEX

AUTHOR INDEX

EDP Sciences – Web of Conferences
17, Avenue du Hoggar
Parc d'Activité de Courtabouf
BP 112
F-91944 Les Ulis Cedex A
France

ISBN 978-1-7138-7345-7

CURRAN ASSOCIATES INC.
proceedings.com